THE PAPERS OF

Andrew Jackson

·

HAROLD D. MOSER, EDITOR-IN-CHIEF

THE PAPERS OF

VOLUME II, 1804–1813

HAROLD D. MOSER
SHARON MACPHERSON

EDITORS

•

CHARLES F. BRYAN, JR.
Assistant Editor

THE UNIVERSITY OF TENNESSEE PRESS
KNOXVILLE

Publication of
The Papers of Andrew Jackson
was assisted by grants from
THE LADIES' HERMITAGE ASSOCIATION
THE UNIVERSITY OF TENNESSEE
THE NATIONAL HISTORICAL PUBLICATIONS
AND RECORDS COMMISSION
THE TENNESSEE HISTORICAL COMMISSION
THE PROGRAM FOR EDITIONS OF THE
NATIONAL ENDOWMENT FOR THE HUMANITIES,
AN INDEPENDENT FEDERAL AGENCY

•

•

Clothbound editions of
University of Tennessee Press books
are printed on paper designed for
an effective life of at least 300
years, and binding materials
are chosen for strength
and durability.

•

Library of Congress Cataloging in Publication Data
(Revised for volume 2)

Jackson, Andrew, 1767–1845.
The papers of Andrew Jackson.

Vol. 2. edited by Harold D. Moser and Sharon Macpherson.
Includes bibliographical references and index.
CONTENTS: v. 2. 1804–1813.
1. Jackson, Andrew, 1767–1845.   2. United States—
Politics and government—1829–1837.   3. Presidents—United
States—Correspondence.   I. Smith, Sam B., 1929–
II. Owsley, Harriet Fason Chappell.   III. Moser, Harold D.
IV. Title.
E302.J35 1980   973.5'6'0924   79-15078
ISBN 0-87049-219-5
ISBN 0-87049-441-4 (v.2)

To L.D.K.

Contents

For the page number on which each document of the Papers begins, see the Calendar.

Illustrations

Embossed on front cover. Bas relief of Andrew Jackson. Courtesy of the Historic New Orleans Collection.

Frontispiece. Andrew Jackson, painting by unknown artist. Courtesy of The Camden District Heritage Foundation, Camden, South Carolina.

Following page 322.

Andrew Jackson, engraving by John Sartain after a painting by James Reid Lambdin. Courtesy of Colonel James S. Corbitt.

John Coffee, painting by unknown artist. Courtesy of the Ladies' Hermitage Association.

Charles Dickinson, miniature by unknown artist. Courtesy of the Howard-Tilton Memorial Library, Tulane University.

Thomas Overton, painting attributed to Gilbert Stuart. Courtesy of Mrs. Elbert C. Brazelton.

Aaron Burr, painting by John Vanderlyn. Courtesy of The New-York Historical Society, New York City.

Harman Blennerhassett, miniature by unknown artist. Courtesy of the Blennerhassett Historical Park Commission.

John A. Fort, drawing by Charles Balthazar Julien Fevret de Saint-Mémin. Courtesy of Mrs. Samuel G. Taylor III.

James Wilkinson, painting by unknown artist. Courtesy of the Francis Scott Key Memorial Foundation, Inc.

Rachel Jackson, painting by unknown artist. Courtesy of the Tennessee Historical Society.

Andrew Jackson, Jr., painting by Ralph Eleazer Whiteside Earl. Courtesy of the Ladies' Hermitage Association.

John Robertson Bedford, photograph of a painting by unknown artist. Courtesy of Kenneth C. Thomson, Jr.

James Jackson, photograph of a painting by unknown artist. Courtesy of the Tennessee Historical Society.

Silas Dinsmoor, engraving by unknown artist. Courtesy of the Baker Library, Dartmouth College.

George Washington Campbell, painting by unknown artist. Courtesy of the Tennessee State Museum.

Gideon Blackburn, painting by unknown artist. Courtesy of the Lumpkin Library, Blackburn College.

Willie Blount, painting by Washington Bogart Cooper. Courtesy of the Tennessee Historical Society.

Andrew Jackson, painting by John Vanderlyn. Courtesy of the City Council of the City of Charleston, South Carolina.

General Jackson's Campaign against the Creek Indians, 1813 & 1814, map by unknown cartographer. Courtesy of the National Archives.

Introduction

ANDREW JACKSON, 1804–1813

In 1804, at thirty-seven, Andrew Jackson retired from public office with a solid record of achievements and a sound reputation. Ten years later, he was again in public service and on the threshold of national fame. But the intervening years had brought setbacks and disasters, leaving a tarnish on his reputation that neither discourse nor future achievements could completely remove. The decade was one of the most troubled and controversial in Jackson's long life. His strong-willed nature and intensity embroiled him in almost constant turmoil. Yet, it was also the period when Jackson began to demonstrate those qualities of leadership that would win him the presidency in 1828. These contradictions, successes, and failures are the main subjects in this second volume of *The Papers*.

The Jackson who settled his accounts with the war department in early 1804 and resigned from the bench of the Tennessee Superior Court a few months later was in search of a solid income base. He turned to general merchandising and commercial agriculture, with high-stakes horseracing as a diversion. His business ventures, built upon credit from merchants in Nashville, New Orleans, and Philadelphia, and investments from friends and relatives, yielded only modest returns. To satisfy creditors he sold his profitable farm at Hunter's Hill and purchased the less-developed Hermitage. By 1807 he had abandoned storekeeping for farming and occasional trading ventures.

The documents of this volume catalog and illuminate a continuing series of quarrels, bullyings, canings, street fights, and duels, which many of Jackson's later critics called his "juvenile indiscretions." But it was Jackson's killing of Charles Dickinson in a duel that overshadowed all his other controversies. Jackson emerged from that affair only slightly grazed physically but severely wounded in reputation: it almost drove him from Tennessee, and haunted him forever. Similarly, the street brawl with the Benton brothers in 1813 confirmed for Jackson's detractors that forty-seven years had not matured him. The Dickinson and Benton affairs have long been part of the Jackson lore, but the documents here demonstrate the explosiveness of Jackson's quarrels and bring to light conflicts and aborted duels not previously known.

To a considerable extent, the decade from 1804 to 1814 was one of great personal unhappiness for Jackson. On at least two occasions, he found himself under suspicion and nearly ostracized from Nashville society. Several times he explored the idea of selling the Hermitage and moving to the new Southwest. But the counsel of friends and the ties of family held him. Jackson's commitments to Rachel's numerous siblings and their children were great and, after 1808, expanded with the "adoption" of Andrew Jackson, Jr.

Aside from his business and family affairs, Jackson remained devoted to public service, as evidenced in part by his pursuit of the governorship of Orleans Territory in 1804 and the judgeship of Madison County, Alabama, in 1809. His self-interest, his personal loyalty, and his concern for the welfare of the country also found expression in his defense of Thomas Butler, his denunciations of James Wilkinson and Silas Dinsmoor, and his involvement with Aaron Burr. The extant documents do not definitively establish what Burr intended for his western adventure or how much Jackson knew about Burr's plans. Nor do they prove the extent of Jackson's involvement in domestic slave trade. But there are many new documents that alter commonly held notions on both subjects as well as on Jackson's political activity.

Jackson found his greatest satisfaction and success during this decade in fulfilling his duties as major general of the West Tennessee militia. He devoted serious attention to the job, reacting—and occasionally overreacting—to skirmishes between settlers and Indians, to Spanish incursions in the Southwest, and to the growing threat of war with Great Britain. He lavished time and thought on militia organization and discipline and lobbied for reforms to improve efficiency. His success as a leader was confirmed in 1812 when, a few months after Congress declared war with Great Britain, the first quota of volunteers was quickly oversubscribed. Leading his troops to Natchez where the war department summarily dismissed them, Jackson defied authority and kept his army together for the return march to Tennessee. For this action, he earned a degree of national fame and the loyalty of his volunteers, who joined him again in the fall of 1813 for war against the Creek Indians. Swift incursions into the Creek country brought his forces two significant victories and, again, national praise. But a shortage of supplies, expiration of enlistments, and poor coordination of the war effort brought the campaign to a temporary halt.

The Jackson who emerges from the documents of this volume is a man of uncommon ability, strong-willed and determined, guided in his actions by a keen sense of honesty, uprightness, and integrity. He was an impetuous, violent man and, at the same time, warm and compassionate, intensely devoted to family and friends. He held the view that justice, honor, and loyalty best served all interests, personal and national; and that evil and corruption, the greatest threats to government and society, must be uprooted. With little thought of the consequences, he denounced those who violated his principles, whether a general of the army, a Choctaw agent, a Charles Dickinson, a Benton, or officials in Washington and Tennessee. To Jackson, authority had no sway if it conflicted with his definition of integrity and justice. As a result he found himself both admired and shunned, loved and hated.

ACKNOWLEDGMENTS

This volume of *The Papers of Andrew Jackson*, like the first, is the product of a major collaborative effort involving thousands of institutions and individuals. The list is too long to mention each separately, but to all of those who responded to our requests for documents, we are grateful, and especially to those furnishing manuscripts for this volume.

Several institutions deserve special mention, mainly for the magnitude of their contributions. Chief among these are the Library of Congress, the National Archives, and the Tennessee State Library and Archives. At the Library of Congress, John McDonough, Manuscript Historian, has assisted the project at every turn: he has made the Library's extensive Jackson collection readily available, he has answered innumerable research questions, and he continues to share with us his extensive knowledge. At the National Archives, the research staff of the National Historical Publications and Records Commission, and particularly Mary A. Giunta and Sara Dunlap Jackson, have been indefatigable in unearthing documents and answering difficult questions. Our demands at the Tennessee State Library and Archives have been incessant, but Kay Culbertson, former State Librarian, and Olivia Young, her successor; Jean Waggener, State Archivist, and her staff, Marylin Bell and John Thweatt; and Kendall Cram, Director of the Library, and Fran Schell, Reference Librarian, have always gone out of their way to make their collections available and to service our research requests. The staffs of the Vanderbilt University and the University of Tennessee libraries have been equally cooperative and helpful.

We are also deeply obligated to several individuals who have assisted us far beyond any normal expectations: to Debbie Cooney, in Washington; to Leland Johnson, freelance historian, Kenneth Thomson, a Donelson descendant, and Fletch Coke and Angie C.M. Donelson, members of the Board of the Ladies' Hermitage Association, in Nashville; to Daphne Gentry of the Virginia State Library and Archives, in Richmond; and to Patricia Schmit of the Historic New Orleans Collection. To each of them we offer our sincere thanks.

Among those to whom we are most indebted are Harriet Chappell Owsley and Sam B. Smith, former editors. They bequeathed to the project they had guided from its beginning a strong and firm base.

Our sponsors have seen to it that the work continued, and our indebtedness to them is great and our appreciation sincere: to John Cooney, former Resident Director of The Hermitage, to the regents, past and present, the Board, and the membership of the Ladies' Hermitage Association, and particularly to Ann Harwell Wells, who chairs the LHA's Jackson Papers Committee; to the National Historical Publications and Records Commission and its staff, Frank G. Burke, Executive Director, and his assistant, Richard N. Sheldon, and to Roger A. Bruns and George L. Vogt, Director and Assistant Director of the Publications Program; to the National Endowment for the Humanities, Research Programs Division, and especially Helen Aguera and Kathy Fuller; to the Tennessee Historical Commission, Herbert L. Harper, Executive Director, Walter Durham, Chairman, and Linda T. Wynn, Administrative Assistant; and finally, to our fiscal agent, the University of Tennessee-Knoxville. At the University, we are fortunate to receive the encouragement and support of Edward J. Boling, President, Jack E. Reese, Chancellor, and John W. Prados, Vice President for Academic Affairs; but we are particularly appreciative of the Office of the Dean, College of Liberal Arts—Deans Robert G. Landen and Charles O. Jackson, and Phyllis Cole, Administrative Services Assistant—for their patience, understanding, and guidance in the day-to-day administration of the project.

The supporting staff of the Jackson papers has made our work easier and, indeed, more pleasant. Volunteers Elizabeth King Folger, Mary Hathcock, and Maria Kieltyka helped us when there was no one else and they have continued to help us as the staff increased. John Reinbold, Assistant Editor, has saved us from many oversights and blunders by his critical reading of the manuscript of this volume; Daniel Feller, also Assistant Editor, and M. Philip Lucas, NHPRC Fellow, like Reinbold, have admirably and independently carried on the other activities of the project while this volume was in its final stages; and Rosemarie Stinemetz, Administrative Assistant, has relieved the editors of many of the duties which otherwise would have fallen to them. Our former administrative assistant, Linda Keeton, deserves our greatest appreciation, for at all times her performance and contributions have been above and beyond the call of duty. In 1979, she acquainted the new staff with the workings of Jackson; subsequently she typed the manuscript of this volume, assisted in copyediting it, and, in carrying out her duties conscientiously and effectively, supported us in more ways than we can ever detail.

Editorial Policies

PLAN OF WORK

The goal of the Papers of Andrew Jackson is to bring together the literary remains of Andrew Jackson and make them accessible to both the general reader and the serious scholar. An international search of almost 6,000 repositories, contacts with hundreds of private collectors, and an examination of newspapers, magazines, journals, and monographs has yielded a collection of some 60,000 documents. To make this material available, complementary letterpress and microfilm series will be published.

The microfilm publication will be a supplement to the existing collections—the seventy-eight reels in the Library of Congress Presidents' Papers Series and the various microfilmed records of the National Archives. Scheduled to appear following this volume, the film series will include approximately 20,000 items and will bring together for the first time all Jackson documents located by the project. To facilitate research, the project will issue a comprehensive guide and index to the Jackson documents on the three film series.

The letterpress series will be a selective edition of fifteen volumes, accompanied by a cumulative index. With its annotations, it will stand alone as a unit, but it will also facilitate access to the much larger body of material available on the microfilms. Each volume will include a calendar in which all unselected documents, except the most routine, will be described by their writer or recipient, subject matter, provenance, and location on the film collections. The letterpress series will thus serve as an indispensable guide to the entire body of papers.

EDITORIAL METHOD

In the interest of stylistic continuity in the letterpress series, the present editors have adopted generally the editorial practices established in Volume 1. The only major departure is in the inclusion of occasional introductory notes to letters and a calendar of the papers for the timespan of the volume.

The editors have broadly defined "papers" as outgoing and incoming correspondence, financial records, deeds, records of litigation, speeches and essays, memoranda, and military orders. In addition the editors have included all of Rachel Jackson's correspondence, whether or not with Jackson, and a small number of particularly significant third-party items essential to the understanding of an otherwise obscure event in Jackson's life. All documents are listed in the Calendar following the Papers, with page numbers indicated for those selected, and writer or recipient, provenance, and subject matter described for the others. Certain routine documents have been omitted from the calendar, notably ration returns, orders for payment of military accounts, passes, military furloughs, and muster rolls. With few exceptions, the routine military correspondence, signed by aides de camp on Jackson's orders, has also been omitted.

Documents in this volume are arranged in chronological sequence. The only exception is with enclosures, which may appear immediately following the document they accompanied. All letters are reproduced in full, except in those instances where the only surviving text is incomplete. If several copies of a document are available, the editors have relied upon the recipient's copy (whether AL, ALS, or LS) for the text. Where that is missing, they have then gone to the letterbook copy, the draft, or other manuscript copies, in that order. Generally, printed copies have been used only in the absence of manuscript versions, or when the manuscript copy has been mutilated or is a badly garbled copy. In several instances, variant manuscript copies of documents have been found containing additional text. If short, it has been incorporated into the document, with attention called to the source of that portion in footnotes. When lengthy or when some portion of the document may still be missing, the text source has been identified in an unnumbered provenance note immediately following that portion. Texts are taken from the first cited source.

The prime consideration in preparing the documents for publication has been fidelity to the original text. With the few exceptions noted below, the editors have made an effort to reproduce the papers exactly as written with all their peculiarities of spelling, capitalization, and punctuation. To aid readability dashes after commas, semicolons, colons, or periods have been omitted. Abbreviations, including the commonly-used ampersand and contractions, have been allowed to stand as written, with expansion in square brackets only when necessary for the understanding of the contemporary reader. Apostrophes below the line have been raised to their modern position above the line, and superscripts have been dropped to the line, retaining punctuation as in the original. Addressees' names, often written at the end of a document, have been omitted, as have words inadvertently repeated in the text. Dates written at the end of a document have been transferred to the beginning; interlineations and marginalia have been incorporated into the text as indicated by the writer.

Occasionally bracketed matter has been introduced into the text to clarify otherwise questionable or unrecognizable words, to supply characters in mutilated documents, to indicate with ellipses a missing portion of a document, and to insert the full name(s) of persons. Dates and names furnished by the editors for undated, misdated, unsigned, and unaddressed documents are also enclosed in brackets, with a question mark if conjectural. Significant cancellations have been incorporated in angle brackets.

Immediately following each document is an unnumbered note giving the provenance of that item and, if appropriate, identifying the writer or recipient. Significant postmarks, address instructions, endorsements, and dockets have also been included here. The symbols used in this note appear in the List of Abbreviations.

Introductory notes and footnotes are used to supply context and continuity and to identify persons, places, and events, usually at their first appearance in the text. Persons in the *Dictionary of American Biography* and the *Biographical Directory of the American Congress* have been identified only briefly, and symbols at their names in the index have been used to direct the reader to additional biographical information in those publications.

DOCUMENT SYMBOLS

AD	Autograph Document
ADS	Autograph Document Signed
AL	Autograph Letter
ALS	Autograph Letter Signed
AN	Autograph Note
ANS	Autograph Note Signed
DS	Document Signed
LC	Letterbook Copy
LS	Letter Signed

REPOSITORY SYMBOLS

A-Ar	Alabama Department of Archives and History, Montgomery
AH	Huntsville Public Library, Huntsville, Ala.
AHAB	First Alabama Bank of Huntsville, Huntsville, Ala.
CLCM	Los Angeles County Museum of Natural History, Los Angeles, Calif.
CSmH	Henry E. Huntington Library, San Marino, Calif.
CtY	Yale University, New Haven, Conn.
DLC	Library of Congress, Washington, D.C.
DNA	National Archives, Washington, D.C.
	RG 36, Records of the Bureau of Customs
	RG 46, Records of the United States Senate
	RG 59, General Records of the Department of State

RG 94, Records of the Adjutant General's Office
RG 107, Records of the Office of the Secretary of War
RG 153, Records of the Office of the Judge Advocate General (Army)
RG 217, Records of the United States General Accounting Office
RG 233, Records of the United States House of Representatives

G-Ar	Georgia State Department of Archives and History, Atlanta
ICHi	Chicago Historical Society, Chicago, Ill.
IHi	Illinois State Historical Library, Springfield
Ia-HA	Iowa State Department of History and Archives, Des Moines
InHi	Indiana Historical Society, Indianapolis
InU-Li	Indiana University, Lilly Library, Bloomington
KHi	Kansas State Historical Society, Topeka
KyCTa	Taylor County Archives, Taylor County Court, Campbellsville, Ky.
KyLoF	Filson Club, Louisville, Ky.
KyPBo	Bourbon County Archives, Bourbon County Court, Paris, Ky.
LNHiC	The Historic New Orleans Collection, New Orleans, La.
LNT	Tulane University, New Orleans, La.
MB	Boston Public Library, Boston, Mass.
MGrS	Groton School, Groton, Mass.
MH-H	Harvard University, Houghton Library, Cambridge, Mass.
MHi	Massachusetts Historical Society, Boston
MNS	Smith College, Northampton, Mass.
MeHi	Maine Historical Society, Portland
MiD	Detroit Public Library, Detroit, Mich.
MiU-H	University of Michigan, Michigan Historical Collection, Ann Arbor
MnHi	Minnesota Historical Society, St. Paul
MoSHi	Missouri Historical Society, St. Louis
MoSW	Washington University, St. Louis, Mo.
MoStgA	Ste. Genevieve Archives, Ste. Genevieve County Court, Ste. Genevieve, Mo.
Ms-Ar	Mississippi Department of Archives and History, Jackson
N	New York State Library, Albany
NHi	New-York Historical Society, New York City
NIC	Cornell University, Ithaca, N.Y.
NN	New York Public Library, New York City
NcU	University of North Carolina, Chapel Hill
NhD	Dartmouth College, Hanover, N.H.

NjMoHP	Morristown National Historical Park, Morristown, N.J.
NjP	Princeton University, Princeton, N.J.
OCX	Xavier University, Cincinnati, Ohio
OClWHi	Western Reserve Historical Society, Cleveland, Ohio
OFH	Rutherford B. Hayes Library, Fremont, Ohio
OHi	Ohio Historical Society, Columbus
OMC	Marietta College, Marietta, Ohio
OkChicW	Oklahoma College of Liberal Arts, Chickasha
OkTG	Thomas Gilcrease Institute of American History and Art, Tulsa, Okla.
PHC	Haverford College, Haverford, Pa.
PHi	Historical Society of Pennsylvania, Philadelphia
PPRF	Rosenbach Foundation, Philadelphia, Pa.
PPiU	University of Pittsburgh, Pittsburgh, Pa.
ScHi	South Carolina Historical Society, Charleston
T	Tennessee State Library and Archives, Nashville
TCMau	Maury County Archives, Maury County Court, Columbia, Tenn.
TDRh	Rhea County Archives, Rhea County Court, Dayton, Tenn.
TDSt	Stewart County Archives, Stewart County Court, Dover, Tenn.
TFLi	Lincoln County Archives, Lincoln County Court, Fayetteville, Tenn.
TFWi	Williamson County Archives, Williamson County Court, Franklin, Tenn.
TGSum	Sumner County Archives, Sumner County Court, Gallatin, Tenn.
THer	Ladies' Hermitage Association, Hermitage, Tenn.
THi	Tennessee Historical Society, Nashville
TKKn	Knox County Archives, Knox County Court, Knoxville, Tenn.
TKL	Public Library of Knoxville and Knox County, Knoxville, Tenn.
TLOv	Overton County Archives, Overton County Court, Livingston, Tenn.
TLWil	Wilson County Archives, Wilson County Court, Lebanon, Tenn.
TMM	Memphis State University, Memphis, Tenn.
TMRu	Rutherford County Archives, Rutherford County Court, Murfreesboro, Tenn.
TNJ	Joint University Libraries, Nashville, Tenn.
TSBe	Bedford County Archives, Bedford County Court, Shelbyville, Tenn.

TSRob   Robertson County Archives, Robertson County Court, Springfield, Tenn.
TU   University of Tennessee, Knoxville
TWFr   Franklin County Archives, Franklin County Court, Winchester, Tenn.
TxGR   Rosenberg Library, Galveston, Texas
TxHU   University of Houston, Houston, Texas
TxU   University of Texas, Austin
Vi   Virginia State Library, Richmond
ViHi   Virginia Historical Society, Richmond
ViU   University of Virginia, Charlottesville
WHi   State Historical Society of Wisconsin, Madison

SHORT TITLES

ABPC   *American Book Prices Current.*
AHM   *American Historical Magazine.*
ASP   *American State Papers.*
Bassett   John Spencer Bassett, ed., *Correspondence of Andrew Jackson*, 6 vols. (Washington, D.C., 1926–34).
Buell   Augustus C. Buell, *History of Andrew Jackson, Pioneer, Patriot, Soldier, Politician, President*, 2 vols. (New York, 1904).
Jackson   Sam B. Smith and Harriet Chappell Owsley, eds., *The Papers of Andrew Jackson*, vol. 1 (Knoxville, Tenn., 1980).
Parton   James Parton, *Life of Andrew Jackson*, 3 vols. (New York, 1860).
PMHB   *Pennsylvania Magazine of History and Biography.*
THM   *Tennessee Historical Magazine.*
THQ   *Tennessee Historical Quarterly.*
TPUS   Clarence E. Carter, ed., *The Territorial Papers of the United States*, 26 vols. (Washington, D.C., 1934–62).

TENNESSEE COURT ABBREVIATIONS

CC   Circuit Court
CPQS   Court of Pleas and Quarter Sessions
HDSC   Hamilton District Superior Court
MDSC   Mero District Superior Court
WDSC   Washington District Superior Court

Chronology

1804

February 13	Assaulted John C. Henderson.
March-April	Attended, for the last time as judge, the Washington and Hamilton districts sessions of the superior court.
April 19	Received license for the operation of a retail store, Andrew Jackson & Co.
April 28	Reached Washington en route to Philadelphia to purchase merchandise for stores.
April-August	Sought appointment as governor of Orleans Territory.
May 1	Reached Philadelphia; remained until May 13.
June 19	Arrived at his home, Hunter's Hill, from Philadelphia.
July 6	Sold Hunter's Hill to Edward Ward.
July 11	Aaron Burr killed Alexander Hamilton in duel in New Jersey.
cJuly 20	Resigned as judge of the Superior Court of Tennessee.
August 23	Purchased Hermitage property.
December 5	Thomas Jefferson elected president; George Clinton, vice president.

1805

May 11	Purchased the horse Truxton from John Verell.
May 29-June 3	Aaron Burr made first visit to Jackson at the Hermitage.
July 26	Thomas J. Overton and John Dickinson dueled; Jackson, Overton's second.
August 6–14	Burr made second visit to Nashville.
September 7	Thomas Butler died near New Orleans.
November 28	Scheduled race between Truxton and Ploughboy canceled.

1806

January 13	Caned Thomas Swann in Nashville.
January 27	Found guilty of assault and battery upon Timothy Baird.
cMarch 3	Arrangements for duel between Jackson and Nathaniel McNairy aborted.
April 3	Truxton won rescheduled match race against Ploughboy.
May 23	Challenged Charles Dickinson to duel.
May 30	Killed Dickinson in duel.
September 24–October 6	Burr made third visit to Nashville and the Hermitage; honored at public dinner on September 29.
October 4	Ordered militia to state of readiness in event of war with Spain.
November 10	Captain John A. Fort visited Jackson at Hermitage.
November 15	First non-importation act became effective.
November 27	Jefferson issued proclamation re conspiracy against Spanish possessions.
December 13	Burr arrived on fourth visit to Nashville; departed December 22.
December 30	Burr burned in effigy in Nashville.

1807

January 2	Placed militia on alert to counteract Burr conspiracy.
February 19	Burr captured near Fort Stoddert; sent to Richmond.
May 12	Departed for Richmond to testify before grand jury in Burr hearing.
May 22	Arrived in Richmond.
June 22	British ship *Leopard* fired upon the *Chesapeake*.
June 25	Gave testimony at Burr's grand jury hearing.
June 27	Left Richmond for Nashville.
August 3	Burr trial began in Richmond.
August 21	Steamboat *Clermont* completed roundtrip from New York to Albany.
September 1	Burr found not guilty of treason.
November 9	Found not guilty of assault and battery upon Samuel Jackson.
December	Sold Clover Bottom store to Samuel Pryor.

1808

December 4	Andrew Jackson, Jr., born.
December 7	James Madison elected president; George Clinton, vice president.

1809

January 16	Addressed citizens of Nashville on administration policy and relations with Great Britain.
September 20	Willie Blount succeeded John Sevier as governor of Tennessee.

1810

January	Sought judgeship in Mississippi Territory.
Autumn	Formed partnership with Joseph Coleman and Horace Green.
December	West Florida declared annexed to Orleans Territory.

1811

November 7–8	General William Henry Harrison engaged Indians at Tippecanoe.
November 29	Departed for Natchez to salvage investment of Coleman, Green & Jackson in slaves.
December 16	Severe earthquakes, centered about New Madrid, began along the Mississippi Valley; continued into 1812.

1812

January 10	The *New Orleans* completed first voyage of a steamboat from Pittsburgh down the Ohio and Mississippi rivers.
January 11	Madison signed bill to raise an additional military force.
cJanuary 15	Arrived in Nashville from Natchez with slaves.
February 6	President authorized to accept twelve-month volunteers to maximum of 50,000.
March 7	Issued call for volunteers.
April 10	Congress authorized the president to call up 100,000 detached militia for six months' service.

May 11	Departed for Georgia to settle land business with heirs of David Allison; returned June 4.
May 12	Creeks captured Martha Crawley in Humphreys County.
June 18	Congress declared war on Great Britain.
June 25	Tendered services of Tennessee volunteers to Governor Blount and the president.
August 16	General William Hull surrendered Detroit.
November 1	Governor Blount ordered Jackson to mobilize 1,500 men for a southern expedition.
December 2	James Madison reelected president; Elbridge Gerry elected vice president.
December 10	Second Division troops mustered in Nashville for expedition to New Orleans.

1813

January 10	Volunteers under Jackson's command departed for New Orleans.
January 22	Troops under James Winchester defeated and taken prisoner at River Raisin.
February 6	Secretary of war ordered Jackson's troops dismissed.
February 15	River-borne troops arrived at Natchez.
March 15	Received the secretary of war's order of dismissal.
March 24	Volunteers started on return march to Tennessee; arrived in Nashville April 22.
June 14	Jesse Benton and William Carroll dueled; Jackson, Carroll's second.
August 30	Creek Indians massacred settlers at Fort Mims.
September 4	Jackson and friends fought the Bentons in Nashville; Jackson wounded.
September 24	Second Division troops mustered in Nashville for departure to the Creek country.
October 5	Tecumseh killed in the Battle of the Thames.
October 7	Arrived at Fort Blount near Fayetteville.
October 12	Arrived at Camp Coffee near Huntsville.
October 24	Arrived at Fort Deposit.
November 3	Coffee destroyed Creek town of Tallushatchee; Lyncoya found.
cNovember 4	Arrived at Ten Islands (Fort Strother).
November 7	Major General Thomas Pinckney ordered to take command of Creek campaign.

November 9	Defeated Creeks at Talladega.
November 18	James White's brigade of East Tennessee Volunteers destroyed Hillabee towns.
November 29	Georgia militia under John Floyd attacked Creeks at Autosse.
December 4	Colonel William Martin informed Jackson that his regiment intended to return home on December 10.
December 12	John Cocke's East Tennessee Volunteers arrived at Fort Strother, Jackson's headquarters.
December 13	Ordered 1st Brigade, West Tennessee Volunteers, to return home for discharge.
December 15	Ordered John Cocke and 1st Division Volunteers to return to East Tennessee for supplies and recruits.
December 31	Garrisoned at Fort Strother, awaiting supplies and reinforcements.

The Papers, 1804–1813

1804

To John Coffee

Hunters Hill[1] January 7th. 1804

Dear Sir

To day there has been another quarrel between [John] Marlow and [Charles] Harryman—and McCallister waggon and waggoner gone—I have sent to engage Mr. Cloptons—it will never do, to have a waggoner, that we cannot depend on I need not detail the business, but one thing I have directed that the hands of each camp is not to disturb the other, I have only to say that I am apprehensive that Marlow and others have got a dislike to Harryman and wish him gone—Marlow went away immediately and I have not se[en] him [William] Searjeant talks of leaving the [camp] and if another hand that understands [boats] could be got, the injury would not be great it is certainly necessary to employ hands that will be Steady at their work, and a few days will put an end to the business which will be a gratefull thing to me—[2]

I enclose you a letter that perhaps will be of use provided you can make a purchase or lease of the Saline[3]—I forgot to name to you that Monday we will want Hemp—I have to go to Town on tomorrow or Monday and will be happy to see you before you set out—If you are not supplied with a horse I will endeavour to let you have my carriage bay, but as a saddle horse I cannot recommend him. Health & respect—

Andrew Jackson

ALS, THi. Coffee (1772–1833), a native of North Carolina, operated a general store in Haysboro (near Nashville) and ran flatboats in the river trade. When his business failed in 1804, he joined Jackson and John Hutchings in their mercantile operation at Clover Bottom, and in 1809, married Rachel Jackson's niece, Mary Donelson (1793–1871). A lifelong friend and adviser to Jackson, he served in the campaigns of the War of 1812 as Jackson's commander of cavalry and later managed his and Jackson's joint land interests in and near Lauderdale County, Ala., where he settled.

1. Jackson's farm on the Cumberland River, sold later in 1804.

2. Marlow, Harryman, McCallister, Clopton, and Searjeant have not been further identified. Most likely they were boatyard workers engaged by Jackson to carry out the contract the secretary of war had made with him in late 1803 for the construction of boats (see *Jackson*, 1:392, 395–96, 406, 410).

3. See below.

ENCLOSURE: TO JOHN COFFEE

Hunters Hill January 7th. 1803 [1804]

Sir

Should you find when you reach the Salines in the Illinois, that you can make a purchase, upon Terms advantageous to us you are hereby authorised to offer my signature to any instrument of writing for securing the payment to the vendors—[1]

I am not capable of Judging of their vallue, but suppose them a good purchase at Twenty five thousand dollars, payable in merchandize—If the payments can be stipulated at from three to five years in merchandize you may safely go as high as thirty five thousand dollars. If only three perhaps thirty thousand would be as much as could be safely given—I only give you these ideas for your reflection not to be strictly bound thereby—but forty thousand ought not to be exceeded—

If a purchase cannot be effected I wish you to Lease them for ten years, on such terms as you may think advisable—and this will authorise you to sign my name to an article for securing the payment to the Lessee—I wish at least to have one third of the purchase or lease, or one half if you wish us alone concerned—It will be well if we can meet to have some further conversation on this subject, and I will give you a full power to act in the premises—Health and respect—

Andrew Jackson

ALS, THi. Published in Bassett, 1:80–81.

1. Jackson had tried without success in 1802 to buy or lease salt lands (see *Jackson*, 1:306–13, 349, 361, 399). No evidence has been found that he and Coffee had any greater success at this time. The attraction of the venture, however, is confirmed by an undated estimate of expenses for entering salt production found in the Coffee Papers (THi), which projects a first-year profit of nearly $33,000 on a $60,000 capital investment.

To Henry Dearborn

Nashville January 13th. 1804

Sir

Inclosed I send you a statement of the amount paid by Messrs D. & T. for Twenty Eight Boats procured to be built by me[1] at your request for the convayence of the militia down the river,[2] a draft for the sum of $3566—I have this day drew on you in favour of Messhrs. Deaderick and Tatam at ten days sight, which I hope you will honor[3]

To prevent the necessity of drafting on you at an earlyer day, I applied to this house to make the necessary advances to carry on the work and to pay the hands and under takers as their wages became due, which they have done, their sum charged is as low as Boats of their description can be bought for at private purchase—and when we take in to view the number wanted, the shortness of time in which they were to be built, the high price of labour and waggonage, and the distance the plank had to be Halled, say from fifteen to three miles, they have cost less than I at first Expected the Twenty Eight are all finished except a few roofs to put on, and then to shove into the water they will be ready for sailing in two day—The other Two Boats are in such a situation, that I did not think myself authorised to direct payment to be made—one fifty by fourteen feet got injured when she was launched and is in a leakey condition, hands are at work on her, if she is made tight I am bound to receive her, and will draw on you for her amount—the other is forty five by twelve feet she is full of water, on a sudden fall of the river her bow lodged on the Bank and her stern sunk and she filled If she can be raised she is a good Boat, and when raised I will draw upon you for her amount—If they should be lost it rests with you to say whether their loss will be sustained by the united States or the builders, least these two should not be fit for service, and the whole number wanted by the united States, I have engaged two others in case ₎the united States has a call for them. If not they are not to be recd. I have engaged hands at each yard to take care of the Boats, to prevent them from being swept away by sudden swells or sunk by sudden falling of the water If directed to be sold, they will command untill the markett is supplied at least cost—should they be kept on hand untill the warm weather, they will season and loose their corking, they are made of Green timber from the saw and will only answer the present season—

I recd your favour of the 6th. ultimo[4] on the 8th. Instant and immediately attended to its contents, but as yet, has not had it in my power [to] engage a suitable person to build them, the place being far remove[d] from the settlements I fear it will be dificult to pr[o]cure workmen, however I will have it don[e] If Possible—and that at a short day

I am verry respectfully yr Hbl. Serv.

Andrew Jackson

ALS draft, AL draft fragments, DLC. According to the Register of Letters Received, Jackson's letter to the secretary of war arrived on January 24, but neither the ALS nor a copy has been found in DNA-RG 107.

1. Only a draft of the invoice for five fifty-foot boats at $150 each and twenty-three forty-five foot boats at $120 each has been found. George Michael Deaderick (c1756–1816) and Howell Tatum (1753–1822) operated a banking and mercantile partnership in Nashville, 1802–1805. Deaderick later served as president of the Nashville Bank and as a captain of Tennessee Volunteers during the War of 1812. Tatum was married to Rosannah Wendel, Deaderick's niece. A veteran of the Revolution, he held various offices for short periods: attorney general and treasurer of the Mero District, judge of the Superior Court, military storekeeper at Nashville. In the New Orleans campaign, he served as Jackson's topographical engineer.

2. See Dearborn to AJ, October 31, 1803, in *Jackson*, 1:392.

3. The war department made the payment on Jackson's account with Philadelphia merchants Thomas & John Clifford, February 17.
4. See Dearborn to AJ, December 6, 1803, in *Jackson*, 1:406.

Between 1795 and 1807 Jackson followed general-store merchandising at least as fully as farming, the law, or the military. His first store, in partnership with Rachel's brother Samuel (c1770–1804), lasted only about a year and was liquidated in 1796 to discharge debts Jackson contracted by endorsing David Allison's notes in Philadelphia. In February 1802 he entered a joint venture with a neighbor, Thomas Watson (b. c1768), and Rachel's nephew, John Hutchings (c1773–1817), embracing stores at Lebanon and at Watson's farm in Davidson County, a cotton gin with Hutchings, and a second gin and distillery with Watson. Watson left the partnership in July 1803, leaving Jackson and Hutchings with stores at Lebanon and on Jackson's farm at Hunter's Hill, presumably with the stock from the Watson location, and a store in Gallatin acquired during the previous year. For a period of time, at least from December 1803, Jackson also had an interest in a "stand" at the military cantonment on the Tennessee River, near present-day Tuscumbia, Ala., and when he sold Hunter's Hill later in 1804, the goods from that store were transferred to the cantonment. In late 1804 or early 1805, Jackson and Hutchings established their most ambitious enterprise—a store, tavern, racetrack, and boatlanding at Clover Bottom on Stone's River.

In the letter below, Jackson discusses an impending trip to Philadelphia to buy stock for the stores and offers, contingent upon Hutchings's agreement, to take Coffee into the partnership. The bargain appears to have been concluded, for Coffee was shortly participating in all the Clover Bottom ventures. The firm or firms under the names Jackson & Hutchings and Andrew Jackson & Company continued until the financial reverses of 1807 forced the sale of their business at Clover Bottom. At that time Jackson abandoned general merchandising.

To John Coffee

Gallatine February 28th 1804. 5 Oclock A.M.

Dear Sir.

I have Just recd. your letter of last night[1] at 5 Oclock P.M. am truly sorry that I had not the pleasure of meeting you at Colo. [Robert] Hays,[2] I was detained in the morning and truly lament the cause that compelled you to leave Collo. Hays before my arrival, but the last respects due to an affectionate and amiable mother,[3] from a much beloved and only son, required your presence, it was a duty you owed her, you have, and was right to perform it—She is gone to hapier climes than these, you have performed your duty by her—She is happy—you cannont help it (human nature is such) but you ought not to mourn—we will drop this subject and attend to the object of your letter—your company on to Holston would have been a gratefull thing to me, I saw your situation, your business requires your presence, and I forebore to name my wish—I expected Capt [William Preston] Andersons[4] company; business has prevented him—I fear not the Hellish crew, or any act they can do to me—some there are when I discover their names (if worthy of notice) I will punish.[5] a trusty friend on those occassions is important—but my dear sir whilst I unboosom myself thus, I know your happiness here below depends upon your attention to business to extricate yourself from surrounding dificulties, I therefore know the necessity of your stay in this country—at present—If arrangements can be made I would be happy you could meet me in Knoxville on the 23rd. of March—I would be still more so if you can make the arrangement, to bring on an assortment that would be advantageous to all—and that you could go on from Knoxville for them— If four hundred and fifty dollars or five hundred could be raised I have the ballance in my reach—but the cash I am able to will not bring on more than will be sufficient barely to assort the goods we have on hand; say $1000 clear of cash for expence I will leave this for you and Mr Jno Hutchings to converse on and if arrangements can be made in the cash way it will be gratefull to me if my credit can be servicable to you, and that you become one of our house—On the subject of a Boat Mr Hutchings bought three at the sale[6] one of which he intended and intends for you, and I directed Simon[7] thus to inform you; but expecting, to see you on sunday morning did not write you—Mr Hutchings did not obtain the first choice, he thought she went too high your choice you lost—he bought 2, 4, & 7, the 7th cost only 16 dols and is the one that got her bow plank sprung and that Searjeant repaired and pronounced a good Boat—She no doubt with a little trouble can be made tight, a better bottom never was put on a boat, no 2, is the one we made choice of, No. 4 a tolerable boat—I will Just conclude by saying to you that Watson did not accept your order on the ground that there were other receipts that were not produced you had better see Mr Watson shortly on this subject; cotton will be scarce with him I expect—Mr Hutchings will be down on friday, I wish you & him to meet—he is obliidged [to go] up to [William] Waltons[8]—as soon as he returns he will be at my house—I wish you to write me to Jonesborough as soon as you see Mr Hutchings If Possible by next Post—Accept my best wishes

Andrew Jackson

ALS, THi. Extract published in Bassett, 1:82–83.
   1. Not found.
   2. Hays (1758–1819), a Revolutionary veteran who had married Rachel's sister Jane,

served as marshal of the U.S. District Court of West Tennessee from 1797 to 1803. About 1807, after litigation had depleted his finances, he relocated to Rutherford County. Hays was muster master for the Tennessee Volunteers in the War of 1812.

3. Elizabeth Graves Coffee (1741–1804), widow of Joshua Coffee, accompanied her son to Davidson County when he moved from North Carolina in 1798.

4. Anderson (c1776–1831), lawyer and sometime U.S. attorney for the West Tennessee district court, occasionally joined Jackson as a partner in horseracing and cockfighting ventures. He was Jackson's aide de camp from 1803 to 1812, when he resigned to accept a commission as lieutenant colonel in the U.S. Army. The friendship ended sometime later, perhaps during Jackson's quarrel in 1817 with Anderson's father-in-law, John Adair.

5. Jackson was alluding generally to his longstanding quarrel with Governor John Sevier, which had reached a climax in October 1803, and specifically to the author of the essay signed "A citizen of Knox county," which accused Jackson of attempting to provoke Sevier into a duel (see *Jackson*, 1:492–96 and AJ to Coffee, March 4, below).

6. These were war department boats, sold on February 18 and 23 for $770.75, a loss of nearly $2,800 to the federal government.

7. Perhaps one of Jackson's slaves.

8. Walton (1760–1816), a Revolutionary War veteran and state legislator, operated a ferry on the Cumberland River in Smith County.

To John Coffee

Monday Morning—Knoxville 4 of March 1804—

My Dear friend

On last evening I reached this place has had an interview with Mr [George] Roulston,[1] on the subject of the author of the "citizen of Knox County" he informs me that Govr. [John] Sevier handed him the peace for Publication, but that he believes some other person will be avowed as such—he has promised me to cause the Governor to avow, the author or he will give him to the world as such—I will write you from Jonesborough, and will be under obligations to you if you can be here on the 23rd. Instant—and hope we can arrange matters in such a way as you can go on to Philadelphia—one thousand dollars can be raised—I am on the wing I expect to see you here at the time above mentioned—I am unfeignedly your friend—

Andrew Jackson

P.S. If you are of oppinion that the amount of cash, with my credit will be sufficient to bring on 12,000 dollars worth of goods[2]—I wish you to become a partner, less would not be an object, I suppose, let me Just say, that nothing that I can do to promote your welfare thru life, but it will give me pleasure to do—and if you can go on the full length of my credit shall go with you   A. J—

ALS, THi. Published in Bassett, 1:83.

1. Roulstone (1767–1804) was editor of the *Knoxville Gazette*.

2. See Jackson & Hutchings's invoice book, May 4, for lists of purchases totalling slightly more than $12,000, made during Jackson's Philadelphia trip.

To John Coffee

Jonesborough March 7th. 1804

Dear Sir

I reached this place today, after experiencing all the disagreable, sensations; that snow, rain, frost and disagreable roads—I wrote you from Knoxville hastily requesting you to come on to Knoxville, If you could with convenience agaist the 23rd. Instant[1]—I have not obtained the author of the peace signed the citizen of Knox county—Sevier handed for Publication and requested Mr Roulston to Publish it—When your peace[2] reached Mr. Roulston, he waited on Sevier, and at that time as Mr Roulston states neither expressed himself that he was not the author but the author would avow himself, when called on, whether old Jack will have to father this child of his own complection I know not—If he does the business must end there—Should another be avowed as the author, I will chastise him or <them> some how, in that case I may want a friend and if you can come in without making too great a sacrafice, I would be happy to see you there, the 23rd Instant—If matters could be arranged that you could go onto Philadelphia; It would be a pleasant thing to me, and I hope would be advantageous to all, let me Just add on this subject, that anything within my power to advance shall be done to promote your interest—I wish should you come on to Knoxville to bring with you, Mr Roulstons letter to you, and also a coopy of Governor Seviers circular[3] on the subject of his selecting the officers for the Louisiana campaign—a coopy you can get from [Benjamin J.] Bradford[4] the original is in his office—by a note to Wm. P Anderson, he will obtain it for me—It is late, I am fatigued and I bid you adieu

Andrew Jackson

P.S. If you cannot come with convenience I do not wish it—for I mean to punish the author myself if he is any other person but John Sevier—If you can with convenience I wish you to come—least I may have use for a friend   A.J—

ALS, THi. Published in Bassett, 1:84.
    1. See above.
    2. Coffee's piece for the newspaper has not been positively identified. Jackson may have been referring to "Veritas" (see *Jackson* 1:496–502).
    3. Jackson had accused Sevier of illegally appointing officers to command the 1803 expedition to New Orleans (see *Jackson*, 1:395–96). Sevier replied with a circular letter to the officers of the militia denying Jackson's allegation (Sevier Letterbook, T).
    4. Bradford (d. 1814) had published the *Kentucky Journal* in Frankfort before moving to Nashville and founding the *Tennessee Gazette* in 1800. He continued as publisher until 1806 when he turned the paper over to his brother, Thomas G. In 1808 he established the *Democratic Clarion*, again relinquished control to his brother, and founded the *Nashville Examiner* in 1812.

To John Hutchings

Knoxville March 17th 1804

Dear Jack

On yesterday I reached this place from Jonesborough and found your letter of the 13th. Instant[1] in the post office, enclosing the price current at New orleans of all kind of groceries—from which I am certain that we will find a great advantage and saving in laying in all our Groceries, nails, and steel at that place, and perhaps Nankeens—I wish you to make the arangement with Mr [Nathan] Davidson,[2] and I think the boat can reach Nashville from Neworleans against the first of July—this plan will enable us always to convert our cash to beneficial purposes in cumberland, and in case the Boat can reach Nashville against the 10th. or 20th of July it will be as early as our goods can reach there from Philadelphia, I therefore think that the better plan to adopt, is to bring our groceries, nails & steele from Neworleans—From the prices of Deer and Bear skins I think it will be well to sell at New orleans the small furs in Nashville, Bear skins sells well in Baltimore, but as our object is to get clear of Debt I think it best not to risque much, and to sell at any markett where we can sell to save ourselves I am sorry Mr [Elisha] Fisher[3] did not buy the Bearskins, but it may happen that we will receive a better price for them at New orleans—The iron is delivered at the north fork of Holston, I saw colo. [Francis] Preston,[4] and also Mr. [Endymion] Baker[5] who I had the contract with to carry it to Nashville he as soon as the iron was delivered declined taking Mr Kings[6] load, in short such was the situation of things I was obliged to agree to receive it—and from Mr Deaderick telling me he would not receive the half I have changed the contract in part. I have agreed to receive five ton of castings in lieu of that much iron, the castings at forty pounds pr ton, this in case the castings reaches the north fork before the water rises—Holston is now rising and I expect the Boat to descend the river in a few days—this expence will have to be met some how—I hope Mr Sewal has returned and has brought some cash and that Capt Campbell[7] has remitted the cash on hand, and that the Debt of Thos Mitchel[8] has been recovered, from this source I hope the amount of the freitage of the iron can be raised which will be \$375—if it cannot write me immediately and I will remit what I can to that use, it must be had, and be there at the arival of the Boat. I have stated to Mr Deaderick that he may still have half, and requested him to say to you whether he will receive it or not, if he does only half the above sum will be to be paid by us—write me on the receipt of this letter and inform me whether the sum can be raised or not there[9] and I will in case it cannot send on my certificates for two hundred dollars, and the Ballance in cash we can

make money out of the iron & castings we must sell for cash if Possible—
you will place the money in the hand of Tatam if you can raise it, to
whom I have directed Baker to apply—you will have to give [Vance]
Greer[10] a particular charge about the iron to have it all weighed, and get
Major Tatam to notify him on its arival—I shall expect you to send me a
statement of the amount of cotton shipped to New orleans by us—as
soon as sold send on the Bills to me in Philadelphia, directed to the care
of Meeker Denman & Co[11]—I stated to you in case Mr Coffee went on
to enclose them to me at Nashville but from your letter I expect he will
not, it would be gratefull to me if he could with advantage to all as it is a
long and tedious Journey—but I will encounter it—I am sorry I wrote
Mr Coffee to come to this place unless he comes on prepared to go on to
Philadelphia[12] The Severeites is all quiet, and the old rascal has to father
the Blackguard peace himself, altho he wishes to lay it on his son in law
[Joseph Hawkins] *Windel*[13] who can scarcely read english—They are too
base a set to speak about—My Dear Jack it is the last letter I will (I expect) write you before you set out—let me Just repeat, write me about the
cash to pay the freightage of the iron, whether it can be raised or not,
whether D & Tatam takes one half—send me the amount of our cotton,
and a memorandom of goods to be Bot. & lastly, send on the Bills as soon
as Possible to me at Philadelphia directed as before, and if Possible purchase they Groceries at Neworleans—you must state to me your determination on this subject and May heaven Preserve you farewell

Andrew Jackson

P.S. say to Mr Coffee if he is not started that he need not come on unless
he intends on to Philadelphia—
   would it not be well to sell as much of the iron at cost, say seven pence
pr. lb. as would pay the carriage, even at six pence if Mr Deaderick does
not receive half. I think some of the merchants would buy at this price—
the ballance we would then have to raise the original cost out of—if cash
can not be commanded in hand for it it will sell at one shilling for cotton
by retail and we will have to this time twelve months to make the cash
out of the produce we receive—if we can have a general assortment of
groceries iron salt &c we must make money the ensuing season—resolution and industry with oeconomy will remove mountains—will it not be
well to get the Boat to deliver the iron at my landing instruct Greer accordingly I wish a house prepared to receive the goods either the long
room of the new building or a house at the back as you & Mrs [Rachel]
Jackson[14] may conclude

ALS, DLC. Published in Bassett, 1:84–86.
   1. Not found.
   2. Davidson was the New Orleans representative of the Philadelphia merchant house,
Boggs & Davidson.

3. Fisher, a partner with Thomas & John Clifford until mid-1804, was a Philadelphia ironmonger in 1805. For additional information on the fur sale, see William Stothart to AJ, July 15, below.

4. In 1803 Jackson had contracted with Francis Preston, who manufactured iron and processed salt near his home at Abingdon, Va., for 12½ tons of assorted iron goods (*Jackson*, 1:328).

5. Not further identified.

6. Either James or William King of the Nashville firm of King, Carson & King.

7. Neither Sewal nor Campbell has been identified.

8. On January 26, Jackson secured a judgment against Mitchel, not further identified, for $159.75.

9. For Hutchings's reply, see Hutchings to AJ, March 30, below.

10. A clerk for Jackson & Hutchings, later a tavernkeeper in Fayetteville.

11. The Philadelphia mercantile partnership of William P. Meeker and Samuel Denman. Meeker later removed to New Orleans as a partner of Meeker, Williamson & Patton.

12. See above, AJ to Coffee, February 28.

13. Windle (1778–1840) married Joanna Goad Sevier in 1802.

14. Nee Donelson (1767–1828).

From John Hutchings

Nashville March 30th. 1804

Dear Sir

I this evening retched nashvill on my way to Orleans, after undergoing Some feteague, I had the misfortun of Sinking one of the Boates after being about half loaded, the Boate Sprung a leake in the Bow, and all we Could do She would go to Bottom, there was about Twenty or Twenty five Bales that got Wet, I gave them Two days Sune before I put them on Board, I also have plased them on Top of the Boates, I was under the necessaty of taking the publick Boate,[1] and was under the necessaty of Taking off Every plank all Round the gunnels—

The amount of Cotton is as follows

Cotton from Hunters Hill	25,567.
Cotton from Gallatin	16 364
from Lebanon	14,148
	56,079

I Recd your letter by the last mail,[2] I shew the letter to aunt Jackson, which has Served to gave her mi[n]d Greate ease, She had Taken up an Idia that mr. Coffee was going on Dueling Bisness—[3]

I have Seen Majr. Tatum and namd to him Respecting the Iron, he States that they will not Receive any part I am very much affraid that it will be very hard to Sell as the Season for Selling is past, for my part when every Cash is bought in Qustion, I feele feerful as noting will Command it—

I wish you to reeturn and let mr. Coffee go on, for god only knows how the mony is to be Raist for the Carriges for the Iron for my part I Cant See how this bisness to be Conducted in boath our absences

I have nothing more at present I will let you heare from me at Natchez. Health & Respect

J Hutchings

ALS, DLC. Published in Bassett, 1:86–87.
    1. The boat reserved for use of the war department in accordance with Henry Dearborn's order of January 11.
    2. Probably the letter above, AJ to Hutchings, March 17.
    3. For a discussion of Coffee's business in Knoxville, see AJ to Coffee, April 9, below.

To Rachel Jackson

Knoxville April 6th. 1804

My Love

I have this moment recd. your letter of the 24th of March,[1] and what sincere regret it gives me on the one hand to view your distress of mind, and what real pleasure it would afford me on the other to return to your arms dispel those clouds that hover around you and retire to some peacefull grove to spend our days in solitude and domestic quiet—Mr Coffee cannot go on, from this place he is obliged to return, was I to return from this place the question occurs, would it bring contentment to my love, or might it not involve us in all the calamity of poverty—an event that brings every horror to my mind—

The latest news from the city of Washington states that there is a probability of my appointment to the government of New orleans[2] Should this take place I will certainly return and Mr Coffee has promised me on that event he will arange his business and meet me on my return, at this place and proceed to Philadelphia—I hasten him from this place as he cannot go on, as I find from Mr John Hutchings letter[3] as well as your own that you are full of apprehension and doubt with respect to my safety, I have wrote you every post since I left you[4]—and will continue to do so untill I leave Philadelphia should I go that far, I am compelled to quit writing I am sent for to court.[5] I shall write you fully before I leave this place, and may the all ruling power give you health and Peace of Mind untill I am restored, to your arms is the sincere supplication of your unalterable

Andrew Jackson

ALS, PPRF. Published in Bassett, 1:87.
    1. Not found.
    2. For further discussion of Jackson's candidacy for governor of Orleans Territory, see AJ to George Washington Campbell, April 13, below.
    3. See above.
    4. No previous letters to Rachel written on this trip have been found.
    5. Jackson's last attendance as a superior court judge was on April 9, at the Hamilton District Court in Knoxville. His trip to Philadelphia absented him from the entire May session of the Mero District Court, and on July 24 the state legislature accepted his resignation, ending a judicial career that had begun in September 1798.

To John Coffee

Knoxville April 9th. 1804

Sir

I cannot think of leaving this place, without acknowledgeing the obligations that your friendship in coming on to Knoxville in the manner you did has laid me under, rest assured that I have treasured the act in my bosom, that neither length of time nor change of circumstances can eradicate or eface, and as long as my boosom beats with life, it will beat high with gratitude on viewing the event— [1]

The trouble that the malignant mind of that poltroon has given you, fills me with regret but rest assured that ample punishment will await him for the corrupt Deed—Heaven must have some choice curse in store for such Rascals.

I have enclosed to Mrs. Jackson my certifcates for my attendance as Judge at Jonesborough and Knoxville,[2] on which there is two hundred Dollars due, I wish you to be good anough to apply to her for them and Draw the money for her, If the iron goes on that sum will be ready to advance to Mr Baker in part of the carriages, I give him $30 pr Ton, I have directed him to call on Major Tatam—will thank you to name to the Major to notify you, pr boy, on the arival of the Boat—and state to him that, that sum is ready, I wish you to raise the Ballance from the sale of the iron, at any Price, rather than to disappoint or delay Baker, there is a Judgt. against Thomas Mitchel for $150—by Pushing that business that sum can be raised, and on the strength of this my letter perhaps you can borrow as much as will make up the ballance—untill you can, raise the sum on the sale of the iron and sell at six pence pr lb. to raise that sum rather than disappoint Baker—

I forgot to give you a memorandom of the money I recd. from you and the intention—I herewith enclose you a memorandom least some fatality should prevent me from returning—[3]

your expence to this place and back I will beg leave to bear and have Just named it, that in case death should meet me on my way that you, will shew this memorandom to Mrs. Jackson who will cheerfully pay it and should that happen have to request you will do it—

Should I progress to Philadelphia, will write you from there and name a place where I shall expect you will meet me—

If I should be appointed to the Government of Neworleans, will return immediately, the Rout named—and expect to meet you here or between this and home I will pass Waltons &c

I am on the wing my horse ready as S[oon] as I close this letter I am off—Make m[y] most affectionate respects to my friend Co[l.] Hays his lady and family—present them to Capt [Robert] Purdy[4]—& believe me to be with sincere Esteem friendship & respect yrs

Andrew Jackson

P.S. I must state, that on yesterday I was walking the street, the secratary happened to be out and at the turn of the street had like to have met me but as soon as he discovered me he wheeled to the left and stept into a house—he *appears verry wild*

ALS, THi. Published in Bassett, 1:87–88.
1. On March 28 in Knoxville, Coffee assaulted William Maclin (c1761-c1807), Sevier's close friend, secretary of state, and adjutant general. The Superior Court, with Jackson on the bench, was then sitting, and the grand jury promptly indicted Coffee. In September Maclin agreed to withdraw his prosecution if Coffee paid the court costs (John Williams to Coffee, September 6, AH).
2. See certificate of attendance at the Washington District Superior Court, March 13; Hamilton District certificate, April.
3. See below.
4. Purdy (d. 1831), a captain in the U.S. Army commanding the guards on the wilderness road between Southwest Point and the Cumberland settlements, met Jackson in 1800, and they immediately became friends. Resigning his military appointment in 1803, he served as Jackson's aide de camp from 1806 to 1809, when he again accepted an army commission, serving through the War of 1812. He was U.S. marshal for the West Tennessee district from 1820 to his death.

ENCLOSURE: MEMORANDUM FOR JOHN COFFEE

Knoxville [April] 6th. 1804

Recd of Mr John Coffee of Haysborough cumberland one hundred and forty Dollars, to pay part of the carriages on goods to be purchased by me in Philadelphia—The goods Bought, together with the goods on hand to make a stock in trade in which the said John is to become a partner— as soon as I return & the consent of John Hutchings obtained, the firm to be stiled Jackson & Hutchings & co,[1] and the Capital in trade to stand pledged for the payment of the goods and the sales to be converted to that use the Ballance after all expence is paid to be equally divided—Each Partner to bear an equal proportion of the expence and should one part-ner advance more than anot[her out o]f his private funds to be reim-bursed in [. . .]

AD fragment, THi.
1. On April 19, the Davidson County court issued a license to Jackson for a retail store to operate under the firm name of Andrew Jackson & Co.

To George Washington Campbell

Capt Craigs April 13th. 1804

Dear Sir

Having a direct opportunity for the convayence of a letter to Knoxville, I embrace it to adress a few lines to you—the oportunity is extremely gratefull to me, as I had not the pleasure of having that conversation that I wished yesterday when we met on the road—acts of disinterested friendship always leaves a lasting impression upon my mind and is always remembered with the liveist emotions of gratitude by me—your disinterested friendship towards me on a recent occasion merits and receives all those lively sensations that they ought to inspire in a susceptable breast—and should the choice fall upon me (of which I have not a sanguine hope) my endeavours shall be, that the feelings of those of my friends that recommended me[1] never shall be caroded or their minds filled with regret for the act—and let the choice fall on whom it may my gratitude toward my friends will be the same, and as long as my breast beats with life it will beat high with lively sensations for your friendship upon this occassion. I write in haste and in a crowd—I shall write you from the city—receive assurances of my warmest Esteem & respect

Andrew Jackson

ALS, NjP. Published in Bassett, 1:88–89.
1. Campbell, along with Tennessee's other congressmen and senators, plus Matthew Lyon of Kentucky, jointly wrote to Jefferson (n.d., received March 20), recommending Jackson for the governorship of Orleans Territory. Former senator Daniel Smith also endorsed his candidacy, February 5, but William Henderson of Sumner County in a letter of February 28, protested that Jackson was violent, disputatious, and arbitrary and "is now sued for an assault & Battery [upon John C. Henderson] & in a few days will be indicted for a breach of the peace." (All letters of recommendation from DNA-RG 59; for the Henderson-Jackson litigation, see CPQS Minutes, V:497, TGSum; MDSC, Record Book D:285–87, TNDa).

To John Coffee

Capt Craigs near Abingdon April 13th. 1804

Dear Sir

I reached here last evening and am now waiting for Doctor [Francis] May[1] who come by Jonesborough and was to have met me last evening at this place—as soon as he comes up we will proceed upon our Journey I am fearfull that my horse will perform badly he has taken the scratches,[2] and his back is getting sore with the heavy weight—I expect I will be able to get a fresh horse at the head of Holston—

I met Messhrs. Campbell and [William] Dickson yesterday,[3] having

company along had verry little conversation with them on the subject—
had Just a moment with Dickson who informed me, that the President
had not made the appointment, that he was authorised to make the appointment in the recess, that it was highly probable that the appointment
would be conferred upon me—thus the thing remains in doubt—and
should it ultimately fall on me—I will be so far on my Journey, that I
expect I shall not, hear of it before I reach the city should this be the case
I think I will progress to Philadelphia if Possible and lay in and send on
the goods to Pittsburgh, and write you from the city to meet me there and
I will proceed on to Nashville from Pittsburgh—this is the only certain
mode that at present presents itself to me—Should I meet the information by the next mail I shall deposit my cash and return without delay, so
that you can set out upon my arival at home—on this let the matter rest
untill you hear from or—see me—I forgot to name to you, or in my last
to mention it to you, that Mr John Hutchings under an impression that I
had returned home from Knoxville will enclose the Bills that he may receive on the sale of our cotton to me at Nashville—I have therefore to
request that you will attend every Post day at Nashville after you may
think that he has had time to reach Neworleans make sales and his letter
reach Nashvill—this you can easily conjecture taking into View the time
he left Nashville, the time that it will take him to reach Neworleans, and
then on enquiry of the post master of the time that letters are on their
passage to Nashville—the reason that I wish you there to attend is that
you may open them see whether they enclose the Bills, if they do to forward them on by the same mail to Philadelphia, address them to me in
Philadelphia to the care of Meeker Denman & Co—If they are not forwarded by the same mail it will delay them a week which I wish avoided
if Possible—I began this letter early this morning, was interrupted, by information that my horse was sick, on examining him found he had the
appearence of the scratches, and his back verry much swelled—I am of
oppinion it was some thing worse—and endeavoured to exchange him
which I have done—but like all those similarly situated to verry great disadvantage, I was compelled to give Eighty dollars in exchange—however
the horse I have got is a good one—but on the other you know that cash
is a necessary thing but it must be parted with on extreme cases The Doctor is this moment come up we will set out early in the morning, and pass
by Colo. Prestons with whom I will endeavour to cancel the contract
with respect to the iron If I can,[4] Should I do this I will inform you by
letter—

Be good anough to inform Mrs. Jackson that I am in good health—and
my Dear Sir attend to my letters from New orleans, least they should
be detained at Nashville, as I expect Mr Hutchings will write me there
under an idea that you have gone on and that I have returned—say to
Mrs. Jackson I would have wrote her from this place had I n[ot] have
wrote her from Knoxville—[5]

I shall write you again from the Federal city—and perhaps sooner—
Present my respects to Colo Hays and family and to my friend Colo.
William Donelson[6] & believe me to be sincerely yrs.

Andrew Jackson

ALS, THi. Extract published in Bassett, 1:89–90.
    1. May (d. 1817), a physician in Nashville from about 1790, was Jackson's surgeon at
the Jackson-Dickinson duel in 1806. Shortly before his death he alleged that Jackson had
not fought the duel according to agreement.
    2. Lameness caused by hard riding or stabling a horse without properly drying its legs.
    3. Campbell and Dickson, congressmen from Tennessee, 1803–1809 and 1801–1807
respectively, were en route to Tennessee from Washington.
    4. See AJ to Francis Preston, April 15. The contract was not cancelled.
    5. See above, AJ to Rachel Jackson, April 6.
    6. Donelson (1756–1820), Rachel's brother, owned a farm near Hunter's Hill.

To George Washington Campbell

City of Washington April 28th. 1804

Dear Sir

I reached this place on last evening—I have been detained on my Journey since I had the pleasure of meeting you four days by high waters and
an inflamation in my leg—which has in a great measure subsided but I
am not free from pain—

The President is at Monticello, he has lost his Daughter Mrs [Mary]
Epps[1]—not a hint who is to be appointed to the Government of New
Orleans—I did not call to see the President—my reasons I will concisely
state and leave you to Judge whether they are or not founded upon Just
premises—It was not known to me whether he had made the appointment—in case I had waited upon him and the office of Governor of New
orleans not filled it would have been perhaps construed as the call of a
courteor—and of all charectors on earth, my feelings despises a man capable of cringing to power for a benefit or office—and such charectors
that are capable of bending for the sake of an office is badly calculated for
a representative system, where merit alone should lead to preferment—
these being my sensations—And believing that a call upon him under
present existing circumstances might be construed as the act of a courteor I travelled on enjoying my own feelings—and let me declare to you
that before I would violate my own ideas of propriety, I would yield up
any office in the government was I in Possession of the most honourable
& lucrative—Who the choice is to fall on is not known here unless to the
Secratary of State—but I have reasons to conclude that Mr [William
Charles Cole] Claibourne will not fill that office,[2] I have also reasons to
believe that If a suitable charector can be found who is Master of the
French Language that he will be preferred—I think that a proper qualification for the Governor of that country to possess provided it is accom-

panied with other necessary ones—I never had any sanguine expectations of filling the office—If I should it will be more than I expect—But permit me here again to repeat, that the friendly attention of my friends, and those particularly that I am confident acted from motives of pure friendship towards me (among whom I rank you) never shall be forgotten gratitude is always the concomitant of a boosom susceptable of true friendship, and if I know myself my countenance never says to a man that I am his friend but my heart beats in unison with it—Permit me here with that candeur that you will always find me to possess, [to] state that I am truly gratified to find that your constituents alone are not the only part of the Union that think highly of your Legislative conduct, it extends as far as your speeches have been read and you are known as a member of the representative branch—May you continue to grow in popularity on the basis of your own merit—and as long as you are guided by your own Judgt. this will continue to be the case—This is in my oppinion the only road to a lasting Popularity for the moment, a man yields his Judgt to popular whim, he may be compared to a ship without its ruder in a gale—he is sure to be dashed against a rock—accept my Dear Sir my warmest wishes for your welfare—

Andrew Jackson

ALS, MNS. Extract published in Bassett, 1:90–91.

1. Mrs. Eppes (b. 1778), wife of Virginia Congressman John Wayles Eppes, had died at Monticello on April 17.

2. Jackson may have heard that Jefferson was considering Lafayette. Lafayette, however, did not receive the appointment, and, contrary to Jackson's prediction, Jefferson sent Claiborne his commission as governor on August 30 (*TPUS*, 9:281–82).

To John Coffee

City of Washington April 28th. 1804

Dear Sir

I reached this place last evening—after a detention of four days on my Journey with high waters and an inflamation in my leg—which has in a great measure subsided but not clear of pain—

Nothing on the subject of Governor of New orleans the President at Monticello—under present circumstances my feelings could not consent to pay my respects to him least it might be construed into the conduct of a courteor—and my vissit might have created such sensations in his mind—I therefore passed on without calling—of all ideas to me it is the most humiliating to be thought to cringe to power to obtain a favour or an appointment—feelings calculated to bend to those things are badly calculated for a representative Government—where merrit alone ought to be the road to preferment—

I have Just waited on the Secratary of war from him I learn that Two Boats will be wanted for the transportation of troops down the river—

you will without delay cause the one that is afloat at the mouth of the Spring branch to be reraised and repaired, and the other raised and repaired if Possible—If not possible a new one built which I mean to have done at my own expence—I expect if she cannot be raised perhaps she can be stripped of her plank which will answer same purpose I wish this done as early as possible the Boats may be wanted in six or Eight weeks— I would not for the price of three that the Publick should be disappointed or delayed—It is the wish of the secratary of war that chains for the Ferry Boats across Tennessee should be provided—I wish you to have them made on as low terms as possible—and forwarded on to the Tennessee by the first safe convayence you will be carefull in taking the Blacksmiths receipt for his work and an accpt of the weight of the iron that it takes—I cannot close this part of my letter without bringing again to your View the subject of the Boats which I hope you will pay immediate attention to—

I shall leave this tomorrow morning for Spuriers[1] to which place I hope my horse will carry me and there I expect his carcas will lie and manure that Poor soil he has been sick for some days with a distemper and looses about 50 lb of flesh pr day—as soon as I reach Philadelphia will write you when and where to meet me and should I hear any thing in the course of this evening will inform you thro my letter to Mrs Jackson—[2]

I hope you will attend to the forwarding my letters from Mr Hutchings least I may not be able to leave Philadelphia untill I receive the Bills—

May heaven bestow on you her choicest blessings

Andrew Jackson

P.S. I have since seen the Secratary of war—he says If the Boats can be got on land and repaired all but the corquing—that the had better remain in that situation, therefore the one that is sunk may be perhap got up so that she can be taken to peaces rebuilt, ready for turning except the corqing and thus remain the one full of water may be got in that situation also—I wish those Boats placed in that situation, or one new one built ready for turning—and the other timbers ready and thus to remain for further orders   A.J—

ALS, THi. Extract published in Bassett, 1:91–92.
  1. Not identified.
  2. Not found.

To John Coffee

Philadelphia May 3rd. 1804.

Dear Sir

On the first Instant I reached this place, find a number of our friends in great distress for cash amongst whom is S. Meeker[1]—& Meeker Denman & Co—I find those to appear more disatisfied with the short remittances than any other of our friends—but Mr Denman has that usual friendship that is always apparent in his countenance and acts—I am sorry as it respects him As well as all others of my Credittors that I am not able to make a larger payment—I find Mr [James] Boggs[2] quite accomodating and my namesake[3] quite the friend I am well anough pleased you did not come on you must exert yourself or your credit is gone and the Idea must not go forth that you are to be interested in the purchase I make for certain reasons that I will communicate to you which I know you will think right & proper—and if it has been hinted at you will say to your friends that the thing will not take place—that I have a wish to get you to attend to one store for me this season which you will do if your business will permit[4]

I will bring on a good assortment, but rest assured I have my dificultys from the situation I found Denman I have loaned him the money I have for my carriages which I hope, I will be able to command when I want it, I shall bring on no Brown sugar it is as high as 14/100 lb and carriage 6½/100 pr. lb. It is out of my power to say when I will be able to leave this—I fear I will be detained untill I get the amount of sales from New orleans I hope you have attended to my letters from the Natchez, and that they have been forwarded without delay at Nashville—If our Bear skins & Peltries had come on to this Port we would have done well Bear skins $5, pr peace and from that to $10—Deer @40/100 pr lb—furs in demand cotton from 18 to 20—I expect to start my waggons next week—and that I wil[l] be able to follow them in due time to overtake them [before] they reach Pittsburgh—I have contracted with Mr Wm Stothart[5] for a 60 feet Keel Boat ready at Redstone If not sold before his letter reaches that place—

I shall write you by next Tuesdays mail when I hope I will have it in my power to state to you when & where I shall wish you to meet me—If Mr Hutchings should not consent to the partnership proposed, I have a plan that will be equally beneficial for you and perhaps more profitable—I am determined to swim, If exertions will do it, If we can obtain a supply of salt, which we must do, If the iron has come to hand we will (I have no doubt) do well The Peltry business I find will be a profitable business, with a carefull hand at the Tennessee I think business can be done to advantage[6]—these I will further explain when I see you my wish at present is that you say to Major Tatam to write to the youn[g] man at the Tennessee to take in all the Peltry he can let them be smoked with sulpher they will keep through the summer—It is growing late with my sincere reguard and my Love to Colo. Hays & family and my respects to the Hasborough Batchellors[7] I bid you farewell

Andrew Jackson

The contents of this letter is for your own eye and none else—as soon as perused you will destroy it The embarassment of any charector I do not wish should be known to me—and the Peltry business I have no wish to make Publick—

ALS, TMM.

1. Meeker (d. 1832) was the principal owner of Samuel Meeker & Co. of High Street, Philadelphia.

2. Boggs was a partner in the Philadelphia merchant house of Boggs and Davidson.

3. Probably one of the Jackson brothers, John (1773–1832), James (1782–1840), or Washington (1784–1865), all Irish immigrants but with no verifiable relationship to Andrew. They started a mercantile business in Philadelphia, headed by John, while James and Washington moved to Nashville and founded their own company about 1801. Although Andrew Jackson continued to do business with John and Washington, who had established himself at Natchez by 1807, it was with James that he had the most enduring relationship. James Jackson's firm supplied merchandise to Andrew Jackson & Co. and more importantly served as a private banker for Andrew, extending large sums of money on promissory notes. They were later partners in numerous land ventures, including the Chickasaw Purchase speculation.

4. Jackson's warning to keep secret Coffee's investment in the purchases was probably a precaution against the claims of John Coffee & Company's creditors, many of whom were pressing for payment.

5. Stothart, postmaster at Nashville, 1797–1801, at this time appears to be the Philadelphia representative of the Nashville mercantile firm Stothart & Bell.

6. The store at the military cantonment on the Tennessee River engaged mainly in trading small goods for furs with Indians. The operation survived at least to the end of 1805.

7. Jackson was referring to Coffee, still a bachelor, to Patton Anderson, who datelined his letters "Bachelor's Hall," and perhaps to other friends in Haysboro.

To John Coffee

Philadelphia May 13th. 1804

Dear Sir

From some delay your letter of the 23rd of april[1] did not reach me before yesterday—and before I recd. it had compleated my purchases but I flatter myself, good assortments will & can be made out of the Purchase I have made at the three places—I have not Bot. largely of hardware or irish linen—the latter is verry high and the high price of carriage prevented me from buying much of the former—I have paid $7.25 pr C[w]t I have only laid in 3 crates queens ware—shoes I have laid in but from the scarcity of cash and the merchants being compelled to borrow from each other I found It would not be pallatable for any of them to Indorse a Bill for them at 90 days, I Bot from Wilson Hunt[2]—and you may expect a percent for lying out of the money—I started my last waggon last evening, and all my goods are on the way except one Box of Hats, that I could not get in, and I expect to reach the falls between the 15th. & 20th. of June at which place I shall expect you or Mr John Hutchings to meet me, I shall write from Redstone, at which time I can better Judge of the time I will reach the falls—but should you not hear from me again you may calculate that I will be at the falls about that time

before this reaches you I expect Mr Jno. Hutchings will be with you, and you and him can adjust the business between you—If he consents to the arangement that you and myself has made—It will be as well not to move the goods untill the new assortment arives, and carry them with the new goods I think it will give them a better sale but this for you & Mr Jno Hutchings to arange—I stated to you in my last if Mr Hutchings did not consent to our arrange[ment] that I had a plan in view that I think will prove advantageous—If Mr Hutchings comes into the measure would it not be well, to try if a stand at the Elinoise would not be profitable and whether a constant supply of salt could not be had for goods—If this could be done, it would sell a great deal of goods bring us in cash and at all times ensure good remittance, I name this to you for your and his reflection and consideration—I have laid in no brown sugar the high price of that article prevented me—nails I have not any—I think it might be well if the iron has reached you to make an exchange of a ton with Wn & Jas Jackson for nails—If you can this will give [us a] supply of that articles—I will conclude by observing that I leave the removal of your goods to your determination and Mr Hutchings—and I shall expect to see one of you at the falls which ever can be best spared—cash is scarcer here than it ever was since my acquaintance and one thing certain we can not expect longer indulgence than this year—Exertions must be made or the times will be bad—Accept of the good wishes of your sincere friend

Andrew Jackson

P.S. I have laid in a small supply for the stand on the Tennessee—

ALS, THi. Published in Bassett, 1:93–94.
   1. See Coffee to AJ, April 23.
   2. Philadelphia merchant, located on Front Street.

Account with Thomas Gassaway Watkins

Genl. Jackson   To Thos G Watkins   Dr.
1804

May 28.	To cash advanced Mr. [Joseph] Park[1] &	
	Messrs. Jackson for wine & loaf sugar (Mrs J)	$ 8.50
July 3.	Visit medicines &c. (Mrs. J)	8 —
8.	letter of advice medicines &c. (Mr. D.)	3.33
9	visit Express medicine &c. (Mr. Donl)[2]	9.16
		$28.99

ADS, OClWHi. Published in *South Atlantic Quarterly*, 21(1922):137. Endorsed in Watkins's hand: "Recd. paymt. for the within by Mr. Jno. Coffee in full. Oct. 28th. 1806. Thos. G Watkins." Endorsed in AJ's hand: "Thos. G. Watkins receipt in full of an extraordinary and unjust acpt. called to take dinner & a glass of grog on 3rd. of July 1804; bled Mrs J. & charg. $8 no medicine was given—" Watkins (d. 1830) was a physician, practicing in Nashville as early as 1803. He earned Jackson's enmity by prompting the mourning-border issues of the local newspapers in honor of Charles Dickinson after the Jackson-Dickinson duel in May 1806. Sometime later Watkins moved to East Tennessee where he married into the Samuel D. Jackson family (no verifiable relationship to Andrew). Early in the 1820s he lived in Albemarle County, Va., and served as a personal physician to Thomas Jefferson. He reconciled his differences with Jackson in 1822 and subsequently worked for his election to the presidency.

1. A Nashville merchant.
2. "Mr. D." and "Mr. Donl" probably refer to Rachel's brother Samuel Donelson, who died in the summer of 1804 at Jackson's home.

To John Coffee

Hunters Hill June 21st. 1804

Dear Sir

I reached home on the night of the 19th. instant, was sorry to hear that you had set out to meet me and that I had missed of you on the road but I suppose you reached the falls on Saturday evening and is now with the Boat as I had directed the young man whom I had hired to take charge of her to wait untill Sunday morning. I regret that I did not meet with you, upon more accounts than one—but particularly as the drafts are inclosed in a letter to me now in your Possession[1]—these Drafts ought to have been in Philadelphia ere this. I hope you will take the earliest opportunity to send on to me that letter—that I may forward them immediately to Philadelphia—I am truly sorry to learn that any of our cotton has taken its direction to Liverpool—I fear that the expence will destroy the profits—and what is still worse—the delay of having our money in the hands of our merchants—the cotton shipped in the B[r]igg Dean marked with our mark—has sold at /15d sterling—and I am Told that notwithstanding this that it will not neat more than 12/100 pr. lb. this is two exorbitant a charge to rest satisfied under, and ought to deter a future shipment to that Port—however it is done with 100 Bales this spring—& the conduct of my friend Davidson I have *noted*—

Expecting you with the Boat I have Just to observe—that I fear we will not be able to send down more than one Keel, she is large and perhaps will be able to bring up all the goods—if so you will take notice that there are four Packages, that is to say 3 hogheads & 1 Bale Blanketts for the united states severall Packages markett Wm. Taitte[2]—and 1 Keg marked King carson King[3] these goods are all to be left at Nashville those for the united states to be stored with Peter Johnston[4]—If the Boat will receive the whole, it will be well to have those packages placed in such a situation as they can be unloaded at Nashville—If the Boat will not receive the whole of the goods you will have those of the united states and Mr Taitte stored in safety and our flat Boat in which our goods are now—secured in such a manner as she will answer to carry our peltry from the mouth of the Tennessee &c—my chairs & settee I wish brought up. they can be lashed on Top the goods a cord for this purpose you will find in the Boat—you will find part of a piece of Blanketts open this will answer for coverring the goods should there be no tarpolin with the Boat—I wish you a safe and speedy Passage to Hunters Hill—with respect

Andrew Jackson

Memorandum—Viz—All the packages marked Jackson & Hutchings are to be brought in the first boat, and as many of the other Packages marked William Taite as she will hold. The goods marked the united States are to be brought up and stored at Mr Johnstons Nashville—one keg King carson & King is to be left at Nashville—

ALS, THi. Published in Bassett, 1:95–96.
1. Not found.
2. Tait (with numerous variant spellings), Nashville merchant, was one of the city's earliest settlers and its mayor, 1811–13.
3. Nashville mercantile partnership of James and William King and Charles S. Carson.
4. Johnson operated a ferry and keelboat landing on the Cumberland River south of the town square.

From William Stothart

Philadia 15th. July 1804

Dr Sir

Two mails ago I wrote you,[1] since which your cotton has arrived here from N. Orleans. the vessel had a good passage & arrived here a few hours before the advice of the shipment & thereby savd insurance—the cotton is in very bad order, nearly 120 Bales damaged 10 or 12 of these is good for nothing; this is owing to damage it has received upon the river as appears from the Bills of lading from N.O. Mr. Boggs has the management of it; who has just informd me that he has effected a sale of about 40 Bales at 17¼ Cents this is nearly all that is good of it. the Balce. must be sold for what it will bring

Mr. Boggs has just made me the advance upon that part Shipd. to England the money he has advand. is $2931.85 out of which there is cash payments to be made to the amt of 1074.10 the balance to be divided is 1857.75, which—being equally divided will not exceed ⅛ to each, or 12½ ₩ Ct. tomorrow I shall make that payment & by next mail forward You a Statement of it—no official acct. has been recd of Your Peltry. Mr Childress,[2] who is arrived, says he beleaves Mr Fisher had received it but Mr F. has been here for 5 weeks & made no mention of it; at present he is not in Town—the Messrs Cliffords[3] has applied to me to pay $124 over their proportion which they say is money advancd last year I have refused until I hear from you & also until Mr. Fisher give you credit for the payment in peltry

By Mr. [William?] Eastin[4] I have forwarded you 6¾ lb Turky Yarn at 13/ ₩ lb. amt. $11.70

Our latest foreign news is 23 may. the new ministry of England, with Mr [William] Pitt[5] at the *Helm*, & the creation of a new Emperor of the Gauls; seems to be the only topics worth notice nothing said of Moscow nor their intended invasion—You will have heard of the dueal between [Aaron] Burr & [Alexander] Hamilton at N. York Genl. H. died on Friday & was Burred Yesterday. this unfortunate affair has created much anxiety even in this place, & in New York much more

I have not heard from you Since you left Brownsville with much Esteem Yr Ob

Wm. Stothart

cotton	Ten. 17. or 17½
	Natchez 18. or 19
Kenty. Hemp	$225. ₩ T. in demand
Bear Skins	$2 or 4

PS. Mrs. S.[6] [sends] you repts.

ALS, DLC.
1. Letter not found.
2. Not identified.
3. Thomas (b. 1748) and John Clifford owned a general mercantile business and wharf on Water Street in Philadelphia.
4. Eastin (1784–1829), a merchant, married Rachel Donelson, daughter of Rachel Jackson's brother John, in 1809. He was one of the first directors of the Bank of Nashville, chartered in 1811.
5. Pitt, the Younger (1759–1806), prime minister of Great Britain, 1783–1801, 1804–1806.
6. Stothart's wife has not been further identified.

In late 1804 Jackson moved to the plantation that was his home for the rest of his life, the Hermitage. Although the property would eventually encompass about 2,000 acres, the move was clearly a step downward for the Jacksons at the time of the purchase. In order to pay outstanding debts, owed mainly to Philadelphia merchants, Jackson sold his well-developed 640-acre farm, Hunter's Hill, for $10,000, and in turn paid $3,400 for the adjacent 425-acre tract (see Deed to Edward Ward, July 6, and Deed from Nathaniel Hays, August 23). Jackson repurchased Hunter's Hill in 1833 but seven years later sold it to pay his adopted son's debts.

Edward Ward, the purchaser of Hunter's Hill, sold most of his sizable patrimony in Amelia County, Va., and moved his family and slaves to Davidson County, remaining until 1829 when he relocated in Shelby County. He served three terms in the General Assembly and unsuccessfully ran for governor in 1821. In 1837 he was murdered, allegedly by his nephews (AHM, 4[1899]:26).

Jackson's transfer of his 1794 stock mark and the registration of a new one, below, indicate that Ward received livestock as well as land and buildings in the Hunter's Hill transaction.

Registration of Stock Mark

July 23, 1804

The Stock mark of Andrew Jackson Esquire being a crop off each Ear, and Two Slits in each Ear, The said Andrew Jackson Comes now into court And Transfers the Right of said Mark to Capt. Edward Ward—And Records as his own Stock Mark in future, a crop and underbit in the Left Ear And a Slit in the Right Ear—

Copy, CPQS Minutes, D:291, TNDa.

To Thomas & John Clifford

Nashville July 24th. 1804

Gentlemen

your letter of the 27th. of June announcing the dissolution of the partnership of Elisha Fisher & Co and advising that the business will be carried on in future by your Thomas Clifford, has Just reached me,[1] the contents of which shall be duly attended to by me—The mail closes in one hour I have a number of letters to write, and at present shall confine my answer to that part of your letter that relates to the information given you by my friend Mr Stothart—

As you were advised our cotton reached Neworleans safe, and contrary to my express directions and wishes 100 Bales has been shipped to Liverpool—the Ballance to Philadelphia—in this transaction Mr Davidson has violated his plited pledge of friendship—and from our Mr Hutchings statement to me, every principle of Justice—I will sincerely State—that Mr Davidson was well advised by me of the offer you had made—and on the principles of Justice to my credittors in Philadelphia I Stated to him as my reason for declining your offer—I had also Stated to him that our Mr Hutchings was inexperienced, that I intended sending him with our cotton, that I wanted the aid of a friend to advise him & aid him in the sales of the cotton at Neworleans. If sales could not be effected there to advise him to what american port to ship the cotton, stating to him, that from the delay of sales last year and the vast expence, I would rather loose money on the cotton than to hazard another shipment—he very Politely tender his offer of friendship, Mr [Edward] Thursby[2] did the same (Mr Thursby unfortunately was not at Neworleans when Mr Hutchings arrived) When Mr H. arived at Neworleans cotton was selling at 12/100 pr lb. he applied to Mr Davidson for advice agreable to my instructions, who advised him to ship to Liverpool stating the price on the continent from the price at Neworleans must be low, and assuring him that in case he would ship he would draw for two thirds @14/100 pr. lb. Mr Massey agent of Green & Wainwright[3] was there and after inspecting the cotton gave assurances that the cotton would neat if shipped 18/100 pr. lb. Capt Jones[4] who recd the cotton on board agreed to freight @3½/100 pr. lb. these offers with the information th[at] cotton was low to the eastward induced our Mr. H—to consent to the shipment—as soon as it was on Board, our Mr H. called on Mr Davidson for a bill of laden & the Drafts agreable to promise to send with the next mornings mail but contrary to every promise, and all expectations, he detained Mr H untill the Post had left Neworleans, and then refused to invoice the cotton @ more than 13/100 notwithstanding his promise & the assurances of Mr Masey—and at last Mr H. was obliged to come away without the Drafts, barely supplied by Mr Davidson with a memorandom of the Bill of laden—I have wrote Mr Davidson on this subject, and I am certain he will not have pleasant feelings whilst reading the letter[5]—I have wrote Mr Stothart[6] advising him of the ballance of our cotton being shipped to Philadelphia of the time it sailed from Neworleans, and also enclosing him the amount of cotton shipped to Liverpool with directions as soon as the cotton arives to receive sell & apportion the amount of sales amongst our credittors and to demand of Mr Boggs to advance the 2/3 of the cotton shipped upon sight, and in case of delay or failure to pay to notify me thereof and I will sue Mr Davidson without fail—I have only to state to you that as far as I have it in my Power I will do Justice to you and all my creditors and rest assured it is the last transaction I will have with Mr Davidson or any house with whom he is concerned—I have wrote him to press the sale of our cotton at Liverpool and from Mr Maseys statement,

I hope in six months from the shipment, my Creditors will be possesed of the amount of sales—This transaction has filled me with deep regret, but *I have wrote Mr Davidson*, before I say more of his conduct I await his answer,[7] but one thing certain his conduct has injured my feelings, and his good conduct must restore them—or satisfaction I will have—Health & respect

Andrew Jackson

P.S. I write in haste without time to correct—   A.J—

ALS, PHi.
1. See Thomas & John Clifford to AJ, [June 27].
2. Thursby had a mercantile house on High Street, Philadelphia.
3. Green & Wainwright was a Liverpool mercantile house; their American agent Massey has not been further identified.
4. Not further identified.
5. Not found.
6. Not found. Stothart's reply, July 22, advised that Boggs & Davidson had advanced $2,250 of the sum owed to Jackson & Hutchings for 33,829 pounds of cotton at thirteen cents per pound.
7. See Nathan Davidson to AJ, July 14.

From John Smith T

Mountpisgah[1] July 30th. 1804.

Dr. Sir

I received my Deeds and your letter by Mr. [John] Overton[2]—The land you named to me of Mr. Waughs[3] he was anxious to sell when I saw him last should he not sell it previous to my seeing him, I have no doubt of getting it for you. He is expected here shortly from the Illinois and I suppose will come by the way of Nashville—I shall go to Loisiana this fall expect to call on you as I go but shall certainly as I return No exertion shall be wanting to meet your demand the fall of salt here will I expect affect the price in Cumberland and it will entirely depend on the price there what quantity I shall let you have—The amendment to the constitution has taken place what will now be done by the collected wisdom of Tennessee would require the foresight of George the third to predict Sevier, [Jenkin] Whitesides, McLin and Kennada[4] hold a caucus every night (as I am informed) and that Kennada influences the House—

My respects to Mrs. Jackson & believe me Dr. Genl. your obt. Servt.

Jno. Smith. T

ALS, DLC. Smith T (d. 1835) spent several years in Tennessee (which he honored with the "T" appended to his name), speculating in land and investigating opportunities in newly opened territories nearby. Early in 1805 he moved to Louisiana Territory, after he had purchased about $5,000 worth of store goods from Jackson & Hutchings on promissory notes that they later had to collect through legal action (see Bill of complaint in the case *Jackson & Hutchings* v. *John Smith T*, [June term], 1806). He settled in the Ste. Genevieve district, speculated in lead mines and salt lands, and secured appointments to militia and local civil offices, all of which he lost when implicated in the Burr conspiracy.

1. In Blount County near Knoxville.

2. Letter not found. Overton was in Knoxville to attend a special session of the legislature, convened July 23 to ratify the Twelfth Amendment to the U.S. Constitution and also to approve his report of North Carolina's action to confirm titles to Tennessee lands. Beginning late in 1803 and continuing through the first months of 1804, Overton and a clerk had copied from records in Raleigh all land grants made while Tennessee was still part of North Carolina in order to establish at last Tennessee's jurisdiction over the titles. In 1806 a tripartite compact, including the federal government, confirmed these actions by the legislatures of Tennessee and North Carolina.

3. Not further identified.

4. Either John Kennedy (1775–1845), who represented Washington County in this session of the legislature, or Andrew Kennedy (1751–1834), a resident of Blount County who had a decided interest in the third matter considered by the special session—appropriation of funds to build a road from Tennessee to Georgia. Andrew submitted an unusual bid for the contract of "One Dollar less than any other person"; nevertheless he was not the selected bidder (Robert H. White, *Messages of the Governors of Tennessee*, Nashville, 1952, 1:188). Whiteside was then attorney general and Maclin secretary of state for Tennessee.

To Boggs & Davidson from Jackson & Hutchings

Tenne. Hunters Hill 31st July 1804

Gentlemen

Your letter of the 23rd of June inclosing the acct. of sales of 130 Bales of cotton shipped in the brigg Maria the 16th June 1804 reached us the 24th Inst.[1] We observe from the receipt of your Mr. Davidson that there was recd. 133 Bales of cotton, one of which was injur'd, repacked with other Cotton and sent to philadelphia—two therefore remains unaccounted for—

We have with due attention viewed the amt. of expence as stated by Mr. Barber[2] which appears exorbitant—some of the Items we do not understand—and one of which we do not conceive cannot be consistent with the customs of Merchants and Justice apply to us—which shall be stated in order—The Items that we do not understand & wish to be explained are first "£1560 insured @3½ Guineas, &c. & carried out, £62.3.7"—What this insurance applies to we are at a loss, whether it is the Cotton, or the sum raised on the sales, therefore before we can say any thing on that subject we wish to know the real charge—second "Guarantee commissions on whole amt. 4 ℔ Ct. £.94.5"—we cannot well understand, whether this is a commission on sales or whether it is a charge for guarranteeing the payment of the purchase money—If the latter we would be happy to be advised how & by what law usage or custom, this is introduced & established—Just observing if it is an item customary amongst Merchants, & that others are in the habit of paying—we would not if in our power wish to be exonerated from it therefore wish your explanation on this Item—

The charge which we conceive cannot apply to us is the sum of £24.4. Interest on cash advanced: It will be recollected that the custom is well established in Shipments, that the shipper is entitled to draw for 2/3 of the amt. of the Shippment as soon as the Cotton is on board—last year this was done in every case except ours[3]—and the whole remained in your hands, Messrs. Stothart & Bell advises that they did not draw a cent on that cotton shipped—it follows that we were (or they, which is all one) entitled to receive from you on the shipment 2/3—therefore the expence paid by you were cash we was entitled to & there would be Justice in requiring interest on the Balance of the 2/3 in your hands, but cannot be a shaddow of claim upon us for that Interest as we understand the custom established—Your Mr Davidson well understood the advantage resulting to you by all this Cash remaining in your hands, & for this reason (as we suppose) did come into an express agreement & declaration that Stothart & Bell should receive a credit for the neet proceeds which should be entered as of the 16th June 1803, & that no Interest should be calculated on their debt to the Amt. of the neet proceeds from the above debt being the day of the shipment, these observations will apply to the charge of Interest that you have made in the acct. of Watson & Jackson, which we do not conceive we ought to pay for the reasons before stated & expect that the Interest in both cases will be struck out & a credit entered for the neet proceeds to Stothart & Bell as of the 16th of June 1803, agreeable to the promise of your Mr. Davidson—There is an item in your acct. against Watson & Jackson for "proportion of Postages & other small charges not included in the amt. of Sales." this is a small amt. but not being informed of the Justice of the demand, before we can say we are liable to pay, we wish the Justice of it to be explained—& rest assured as soon as we find it a charge that we are bound or ought to pay or allow it will give us pleasure to do it—but it being of date June 12th. 1804—long after the sales were made, the Cash in hand we are at a loss to know how it can apply to us as the Cotton was shipped for and on your acct. but still it may be Just & agreeable to custom if so as soon as it is shewn to us, we will with pleasure admit it—The statement of your Mr. Davidson of the time the credit should be entered has been the guide for the settlement between Stothart & Bell & us we therefore wish your answer as early as convenient that we may close those accts. Some few Posts ago I forwarded to Mr. William Stothart Philadelphia a Bill of Laden[4] of 100 Bales of our cotton shipped in Brig Felicity Capt. Jones, for Liverpool to be presented to you for payment of 2/3 the amt. shipped[5]— This shipment was contrary to expectation when our Andrew Jackson went on to Philadelphia his directions were different and did not expect it—some circumstances attending the shipment truly unpleasant—And tend to lessen that confidence in your Mr. Davidson that we flattered ourselves were so well placed—As advised by our Mr. Hutchings when he reached New orleans & found Cotton only @12/100—he applied to Mr. D. to whom he was referred for advise who advised a shipment to Liverpool and did expressly agree to Invoice the Cotton at 14/100 & draw bills for the amt. Mr. Massey agent for Green & Wainright being there and on examination of the Cotton stated that to a certainty it would neet from 17 to 18/100—as soon as the Cotton was on board our Mr. H. applied for the Bill of laden & the Bills—When your Mr. Davidson did refuse to Invoice the Cotton at more than 13/100 and would not draw any bills—but detained Mr. H. until the Mail had left the City and then only gave him the Memorandom which no doubt Mr. Stothart has handed you—This Sir is conduct that is unpleasant indeed—but as we have wrote your Mr. Davidson[6] on the subject expecting him to give directions for the payment of 2/3 @14/100 we shall refrain at present from remarking further on the subject; But we must observe that your Mr. David[s]on was well advised that we had been offered by the Mr. Clifford 14/100 for our Cotton to draw immediately for 2/3—Credit our acct. with part of the other third, & as soon as sales were effected the balance to be subject to our Order—this we refused to accede to from principals of Justice to our Creditors all of which your Mr Davidson was advised off and did applaud—& I cannot refrain from observing that the treatment to our Mr. Hutchings under the banners of promised friendship & services are such that require an explanation from your Mr. Davidson, & I hope he has ordered you to advance the 2/3 @14/100—

Sales are dull small quantities of Cotton planted—but at present look promising; our A. Jackson has made sale of his possessions[7] is to receive 2/3 of the amt. on Christmass day next—this we flatter ourselves will enable us to meet all our debts next spring—

With sentiments of Esteem & respect we are Gentlemen your mo. obt. servts.

Jackson & Hutchings

Copy, DLC. Published in Bassett, 1:99–101.
1. Not found.
2. William Barber & Co. of Liverpool.
3. Jackson had been dissatisfied with the way Boggs & Davidson handled cotton sales the previous year (see Jackson, 1:350, 357, 364, 370–71).
4. Not found.
5. Jackson had not yet received William Stothart's letter of July 22, stating that Boggs & Davidson had paid him $2,250 of the $4,397.77 owed on the cotton, which he divided among Jackson & Hutchings's creditors in Philadelphia.
6. Letter not found.
7. The property at Hunter's Hill.

In part Jackson's well-known hatred of James Wilkinson grew out of the determination of his friend Thomas Butler to march at the head of his regiment wearing his hair in an old-fashioned queue. Butler (1754–1805), a native of Pennsylvania and a veteran of the Revolution, arrived in Tennessee in 1797 as commander of U.S. Army forces at Fort Southwest Point. He established his family in Robertson County before he was ordered to take command of Fort Adams in Mississippi Territory, April 1802. Butler then attempted to resign his commission, and the secretary of war granted him a three-month furlough to attend to family business. When Butler did not report to his post until nearly a year later, a court martial convened in November 1803 at Fredericktown, Md., to try him on two charges: failure to report as ordered and refusal to obey the general order of April 30, 1801, requiring army personnel to wear their hair cut short. At the time of the order Butler had requested and received from General James Wilkinson, then the only general in the U.S. Army and commander of all its forces, an exemption, granted, according to Wilkinson, on account of Butler's age and health. Two years later, when they again met, Wilkinson was surprised to see that Butler still wore his queue and retracted the exemption. The court dismissed the more serious charge but found Butler guilty of refusal to cut his hair and sentenced him to be reprimanded in general orders. Wilkinson approved the mild sentence with reluctance, arguing that the court's compassion for an old soldier had defeated both justice and military discipline. In the meantime Butler had been waiting at his Tennessee farm for reassignment, and in the summer of 1804 he received orders to report to New Orleans. Still certain that he faced harassment by Wilkinson and another court martial for the queue he defiantly continued to wear, Butler nevertheless reported to his post (see Butler to AJ, August 4). As numerous letters below show, for the next year Jackson remained Butler's confidant and advisor in his struggle against Wilkinson.

To T[homas] J[efferson]

[August 3, 1804]

Sir

On the 7th. of August 1803, at the request of a number of the citizens of this District, I addressed a note to you, on the subject of Colo [Thomas] Butlers arrest,[1] which as then understood, was for not cutting of his hair agreable to an order of the General of the 30th of April 1801. your polite attention to that note was highly gratifying to the citizens who felt interested in the welfare of Colo. Butler, and truly pleasing to myself—and we rested well satisfied, from the information given to you by the secratary of war, and communicated to us by your note of the 19th. of September 1803 that, no "stress" would have been laid upon that specification for not cropping the hair[2]—and that the charges for disobedience of orders & neglect of duty "for not going to fort adams when ordered & absence from his command for near twelve months without leave" would have been the objects of enquiry by the court, and on this alone his peers would have pronounced his guilt, or innosency—

If guilty we knew that the rules and regulations for the government of the army required punishment But from our personal acquaintance with the Colo. attention to duty whilst within this State we were of oppinion that those charges would not be substantiated—The result, has shewn that in this good oppinion of the Colo. we were not mistaken <& find that contrary to the representation made to you by the Secratary> of war, the whole ground work of his conviction was for not conforming the cut of the hair to the order of the 30th. of april here sir I would stop without making another remark was I not well convinced from evidences that carries conviction to my mind that you are not informed truly of the sensibility of both officers of the army, and citizens excited on this occassion and that Colo. Butler is yet doom'd to persecution by the Genl [James Wilkinson] and if Possible to be made a victim to that order, to satiate the revenge of the Genl, by his oppression to be driven from the army and being conscious w[h]ere ever you see the buds of oppression you will lop them off. From the order of the Genl, of the 1st. of February last approving the sentence of the court, reprimanding the Colo. (in terms as novel as the order) and renewing the order of the 30th of april 1801, there is to say the least of it—sufficient evidence of ill will, and a disposition of oppression displayed—on the receipt of this order, the Colo. addressed a note of the 6th. of June to the Se[c]ratary of war among other things stating the receipt of the order—that the Genl must have been sensible that the first part of it (cutting of the hair) he would not conform to, as it would be a tame surrender of a natural right, over whi[ch] the laws of the country had given him no control—and if it was the intention of the Genl to arrest for d[is]obedience of the first part of the order, requesting that he might not be subjected to a vexatious Journey to new orleans, and back to Maryland there to stand a trial &c &c This letter has not been answered by the Secratary but sir you can easily Judge of our astonishment, when we found from the decission of the court, that the only charge that did authorise a conviction was the disobedience of the order of 30 of april 1801, on which by the sentence of the court he was subjected to a reprimand from the Genl, and this contrary to the information given you by the Secratary of war—

The order and the principles attempted to be established by the trial of Col Butler under it, has agitated the Publick mind—The citizens feelings are roused, and they think they see the buds of Tyranny, arising out of it, that may in a day of trial when the situation of their country calls them into the field, extend its baneful influence to them, hence resulted the pleasure we experienced from the information given by your note that stress would not be laid on this order and that it would necessarily sink into oblivion—had this been the case, we would have been silent, you would not have been troubled with this note, But sir this is not the case we see the order renewed in consequence of which we see the Colo addressing a note to the Secratary of war, of 6th. of June to which we refer and that unanswered, but submitted to the genl for inspection, and recognised by the Genl order of the 9th of July—by the order of the Secratary of war of June 22. and of the Genl 23 all avenue of communications that exc[e]pt thro the genl, whose oppression is complained of, under oppressions like these we cannot be silent, facts we wish to reach you [since] we rest assured that Justice will be done—

These facts under existing circumstances, will impress a belief upon the mind that the order of the 22 23 of June, was intended to fit the Colo case and shield the Genls conduct from investigation arising from complaints from this quarter—will not the order of the 22: & 23 of June place it in the power of the genl to oppress any officer under his command Tyranise over them and keep his conduct shielded from investigation and may it not be construed into a disobedience of these orders, if an officer does attempt to address a complaint to you, upon which the Genl may arrest the officer—from these same facts, we think an old and valuable officer [is] driven to be the Victim to satiate the spleen and revenge of the Genl, subjected to persecution and if Possible, by oppression to be driven out of the army, unless you do interpose—or continually harressed with arrest, for disobedience of orders that infringe his natural rights, which it is well understood he will not obay, and for obedience of which he would meet with the imprecations of every true republican in our country, and idea is taken up that the arest of Colo. Butler originated in Personal motives—from the avenues of communication to the heads of departments being closed except thro the Genl, ideas will be taken up that the aid of the Government is about to be lent to strengthen the hands of oppression, and to make a meritorious officer a sacrafice to private resentment an illegal order the instrument—and it matters not whether these ideas are correct or not the effect w[ill] be the same—If it is necessary that the Colo should be arrested again—that the legality of the order may be tested by a competant authority, I hope that this may be done without oppression and without vexatious Journeys, these are the objects of this letter, and that hope that under your administration the avenues of information will always be kept open and that you will not permit individuals by combination or otherwise to wall themselves around by orders that the injured cannot apply for redress but thro the organ of the oppressor—

It is unpleasant to think that such an order ever had an existance it is still more so to view how it has excited the Publick mind, and to see this order renewed at the present moment has roused the resentment of the citizens verry much, but in you sir both citizen and soldier has confidence, and we know, that it is only that you should be informed of facts and Justice will be done—I am sir with respect yr. mo. ob. serv.

Andrew Jackson

ALS draft, DLC. Published in Bassett, 1: 102–104. Date from endorsement. Jackson sent a draft or a copy of this letter to Thomas Butler, who returned it with some revisions in his letter of August 4 (Butler's revised copy not found). It is not known whether any form of this letter was actually sent to Jefferson.

1. See AJ to Jefferson, August 7, 1803, in *Jackson*, 1:353–54.
2. See Jefferson to AJ, September 19, 1803, in *Jackson*, 1:365, in response to Jackson's letter of August 7.

To Thomas Butler

August 25th 1804

Dear Colonel

I recd. your favour of the 23rd. instant,[1] and has given the subject every consideration, that my indisposition would permit—The conduct of the Genl is of that complection, that is always to be expected, from a base and vindictive mind, who thinks himself shielded from that punishment that ought to await him—and under coulour of authority, wishes to seek revenge, and inflict a wound in a way that a brave and virtuous mind would shudder at—But when the charector of the man is so well displayed, as his is, in his notes to you there is the less danger, and the shaft, that he aims at you, may be made to recoil upon himself—That firmness and fortitude that you are possessed of, will carry you out and the line of conduct for you to persue, is plain

I never can be brought to believe, that the Genl will arrest you—and if he does, the executive will be bound from his letter to interpose, and should he not, there is no doubt in my mind but the congress of the united states will—I would therefore recommend to you to address the president on the subject—(but not to await his answer) in that address I would state to him the orders recd. the duplicity of the Genl, and your firm determination not to crop the hair, and soon as you are on your march, I will have a remonstrance signed by all the respectable citizens of this District, forwarded to the president[2]—I recommend to you to march for this reason that should you be arrested it will place things beyond subterfuge that the specification must, be for not cropping the hair and should it stand alone on this, I will hazard an oppinion that the thing will end in the total disgrace of the Genl. It cannot be Possable that the President would hazard so much, as to countenance such an order—and should he deviate so much from that republican charector, that I think him so Justly entitled to—I have full confidence, that Congress will take it up and consign the order and the Genl to that merited contempt, & silent oblivion that they ought to meet under a Government like ours founded on a written constitution where implication is not tolerated—and where written rules are for our conduct both as citizens & soldiers—Such an order under any Governmt. is unprecedented—and could precedents be found under despotic governments amidst the rage of war where supplies could not be obtained, they could not bear upon this question—The circumstances attending the present order go to prove it a wanton act of Despotism—and be viewed as such both by the executive & congress &

against, such a precedent every welwisher to his country will struggle—from which consideration I think you have nothing ultimately to fear from this order—hence results the necessity, of obedience to every Legal order, in case you should be arrested it may stand alone on that specification and if any there should be wearing republican Coats that wishes to favour the Design of the Genl that they may appear in their true coulours—and if any does appear they shall be duly noticed—

Fatigue and expence you will have to encounter, but these are nothing to a brave and noble mind, when put in competition with his honor and feelings; to you sir I know they will be viewed as mere triffles, when compared with the main point—proceed then to your place of destination address the Executive, and leave the rest to your friends here—on whom you may rely, that every attention will be paid to the thing that is in their power—

I hope you will write frequently, and in particular as soon as you reach Neworleans—

As the Genl has threw the Gauntlet, would it not be well to collect all the charges against him, and lay them before the President—and If the thing should progress into Congress to lay them before the house—This for your own deliberation & conclusion—

My Dear Colo. I am sorry I could not see you at your own house—it was my intention—but I have sufferred much pain in my breast & bowels in these few days—Should I not have the pleasure of taking you by the hand, accept my best wishes for your health; May you ride triumphant over your enemies—and May the engines of Despotism be hurled from their offices with *disgrace*—is the fervent wishes of your sincere friend

Andrew Jackson

ALS copy, DLC. Extract published in Bassett, 1 : 105–106.
1. See Butler to AJ, August 23.
2. See AJ et al. to Jefferson, [cDecember], below.

To Nathan Davidson

Hunters Hill August 25th. 1804

Sir

Your letter dated New orleans the 14th. of July last,[1] addressed to me came duly to hand, and Should have recd. earlier attention had Mr. Hutchings been at home—from the tenor of that letter relative to circumstances that took place at New orleans, made it necessary that I Should See Mr. H. before I proceeded to answer—Mr. H. is now with me, and his letter herewith inclosed will be a Sufficient answer as to any misinformation Stated by you that I had recd. from him relative to those facts stated by me in mine of the 24th of June[2]—I must remark, that I never doubted of the correctness of Mr. H. Statement to me. I have always found him correct in his Statements. but Sir finding in your letter positive denials of your own declarations—of your agreement with me relative to the time Credit should be entered Stothart & Bell for the neat proceeds of our cotton Shipped last year, and a total perversion of my letter wrote you from Gallatine on my way to Philadelphia[3]—these Sir Strengthen my belief that Mr. H. is correct in his present statement, I am pleased with the mode you have adopted in addressing me alone, as it will afford an opportunity of closing the difference between us in our own names, without implicating the feelings of your partners, against whom I have no ground of complaint—you will recollect that the ground of Complaint stated in my letter against you, was, your declaritions of friendship that you would render Mr. H. when at New orleans, and in your conduct towards him whilst there a total deviation therefrom, nay worse a breach of contract, and overreaching him under the confidence of promised friendship—There is nothing contained in your letter that has removed those impressions but has added insult to injury, by telling me I am mistaken in facts which you know to be true, and which I had from your information, which Shall be duly notic'd—you State Sir "that I am mistaken as to the advantage accruing to the shipping Merchant from Shipments of this kind &c" you also State "as to interest being stopped on debts due by the shippers, it is more than ever you knew of" nor do you believe it to be the case &c. if Sir I am Mistaken it arises out of information recd. from you—and as you have hazarded a denial of this position in my letter I have thought proper to call on Major Tatom for his recollection of your Statement on this point as well as others, as you appear to be in the habit of denying information given by yourself, and denying your agreements, which must have been under the impression, that these things alone rested between us and not susceptable of proof, I inclose his letter to which I refer you to refresh your recollection on this point as well as others hereafter to be touched on, from which you will find that you have erred instead of me, and that from your own statement Shippers of cotton derive the benefit stated in my letter, and that he has understood you in the Same way I did. you go on to observe, "that if ever this was the case, this shipment of ours would be but a sorry assistance." sorry as it might be, it appears, it has had its influence with you, in causing you to deviate from your agreement with Mr. H. and added to this another Sorry advantage, has been a sufficient inducement, with all your boasted wealth and independence to make you deviate from truth deny your agreement, and violate your promise of friendship, to procure a sorry advantage that you could not have obtained, unless under the confidence that was reposed in you under your professions of friendship and offered Services, but Sir at this time we were not advised, that your profferred friendship was on commission. I have Now noted it in your letter and will hereafter View it in this way. I have said that another sorry advantage has been a sufficient inducement with you to deviate from truth, and deny your agreement. to shew this, it is only necessary, to quote your next sentence. read it. it stands thus "that I am also mistaken as to Interest charged on the shipment last year," you say "you recollect the enquiry I made of you when at Nashville, that you Stated that interest on 2/3 should cease on the shipment being made and 1/3 when the Sales were made, *on which you loose*, but choose to allow in Stothart & Bells Instance as the greater part was a payment to yourselves" (you ought to have said the whole of ours was a payment to yourselves) but to the point—I Stated in my letter, and repeat again Sir that you did expressly State to me and agree that the proceeds of our cotton Shipped by you last year and which was to be applied to the credit of Stothart & Bell should be entered to their credit, on the day the Shipment was made and on the amount of the Neat proceeds no interest Should be calculated, and I now state on this statement *thus* we made our settlement with Stothart & Bell at that time. this Sir you have denied which shews how regardless you are of truth, when your interest comes in competition with it. this delineates your charactor and proves that when interest is at stake you will hazard a denial of truth to avoid a compliance with your word or agreement, I must here Sir refer you to Major Tatoms letter and the inclosed certificate of Mr. Robert Stothart[4] (both men of respectability) to awaken in you a love for truth. what Sensations (after you telling me I mistake facts) must the reading of those inspire in a breast Susceptable of delicate feelings When the amount of the inducement is viewed, what confidence can or will be reposed in a man who boast of fortune and thus Violate his word for a mere pittance, *even worse than a sorry* assistance. It is not worth while to trace you farther, your whole letter displays you devoid of that candour that from your standing as a Merchant I had a right to calculate on, I Shall only make a few observations on *another* part of your letter and leave you for the present, *we Shall meet.* you are pleased to observe, that you always understood that our Cotton was to be sent to you untill you recei'd my letter of the 28th of February as I was on my way to Philidelphia, permit me here to ask a few simple questions. did I not State to you at my own house, and at Nashville that Mr. H. would proceed with our Cotton, did you not offer your polite and friendly aid to him when he reached New orleans, did I not consult with you on the subject of bringing groceries from there, and State to you, that Mr. H. would take funds with him to lay out in this way, and did you not offer your friendly aid to him on this point, you also state that in this letter I advised that Mr. H. had sufficient funds in his hands, to pay all our debts &c and requested you to receive your claim at New orleans &c. if it did it stated more than I ever thought, than I ever intended or what the copy says it states, and for this reason I hope you will forward it to me and keep a copy yourself That I may be convinced that my pen has expressed a thing that I had uniformly stated to you would not be the case, that the failure of Cotton crops had put it out of our power to make full payments. that letter from what appears in substance stated, that Mr. H. would be furnish'd with a Just account of our debts, that he would sell if possible at new orleans, and that I wished you (as I had before Stated to you in person) to receive your proportion of your debt at New orleans, that Mr. H. would carry on negroes to exchange for groceries, and Wishing you to make a sale of them before he came if you could, that a fellow answering the description you wanted was bought, but I was fearfull he would not suit you as he had once left his master &c. but as to stating that he had sufficient funds with him to pay all our debts cannot be correct. was not this the reason that I gave you for not acceding to the proposals of Messrs. Clifford because we would not be able to make full payments this Season & it would not be doing equal Justice to our credittors, but this in your letter you are also pleased to deny, but like the rest *Susceptable* of *proof.* I did Sir often State the offer of Mr. C. to you and my reasons for declining, but Sir I Shall leave you for the present, barely Stating that I expect you will order credit to be entered for the neat proceeds of our cotton shipped last year, to Stothart & Bell (if it is not done) at the time it was shipped, or I will be compelled from principle of Justice to the publick, & to ourselves, to publish your agreement, then your denial, and certificates to prove its existance as Stated by me. do this and retract your assertion that I have Mistaken facts mentioned in your letter, and I will try to harbour the charitable oppinion, that hereafter you will be carefull in making promises, but when made, Stedfast in performing them—I am sorry Sir that I have cause to alter that good opinion I once had of you, but Sir the testimony is strong, and candour has compelled me to State to you the sentiments of a mature reflection on the evidence before me. I have no doubt but we Shall have the pleasure of a meeting in the course of the present fall, when we can have a full investigation of all matters & things which has been the subject of this letter untill then I am Sir yr. &c &c.

Andrew Jackson

Copy, DLC. Published in Bassett, 1:106–109.
1. See Davidson to AJ, July 14.
2. Neither letter found.
3. Jackson's letter to Davidson, February 28, has not been found.
4. Stothart, postmaster in Nashville, 1802–11, was also a merchant in partnership with George Bell. Neither Stothart's certificate nor Howell Tatum's letter has been found.

Advertisement for Runaway Slave

[September 26, 1804]

Stop the Runaway.
Fifty Dollars Reward.

Eloped from the subscriber, living near Nashville, on the 25th of June last, a Mulatto Man Slave, about thirty years old, six feet and an inch high, stout made and active, talks sensible, stoops in his walk, and has a remarkable large foot, broad across the root of the toes—will pass for a free man, as i am informed he has obtained by some means, certificates as such—took with him a drab great-coat, dark mixed body coat, a ruffled shirt, cotton home-spun shirts and overalls. He will make for Detroit, through the states of Kentucky and Ohio, or the upper part of Louisiana. The above reward will be given any person that will take him, and deliver him to me, or secure him in jail, so that I can get him. If taken out of the state, the above reward, and all reasonable expences paid—and ten dollars extra, for every hundred lashes any person will give him, to the amount of three hundred.

> ANDREW JACKSON,
> Near Nashville, State
> of Tennessee.

Text from *Tennessee Gazette*, October 3, 1804. Original not found. The advertisement first appeared in the September 26 issue, but only a fragment of the text remains. It is also printed in the issues of October 24, November 7, and November 14 and probably appeared in the missing issues between September 26 and November 14. Thomas Terry Davis's letter to Jackson, February 20, 1805, below, is most likely a reply to this advertisement.

From Thomas Butler

Quarters eight miles from Orleans
October 21st. 1804—

Dear General,

The following I have extracted from a letter of General Wilkinsons to the officer in command at Orleans,[1] dated the 17th. of June "The General order respecting Colonel Butler has received the cordial approbation of our superiors, though some of his partizans equally ignorant and zealous, have made a feeble attempt to combat principles, which cannot be shaken. The destination of this officer seemes as yet undecided the Secretary of war had arrested his progress at Tennessee, but I shall I believe repeat the order for his descent of the Mississippi." also in a letter from the General to the Commandt. at orleans I find the following parragraph, which I also state for your perusal. "Augt. 31st. 1804. Colol. Butler has signified to me by letter dated the 8th. ultimo, his intention to proceed to New Orleans, to take the command agreeably to my orders, and to prevent trouble, perplexity and further injury to the service, I hope he will leave his tail behind him."

Unless the President & heads of departments have advocated the conduct of the General (which I can hardly suppose) the foregoing can be considered in no hig[h]er point of view, than the bombast of the General arising from chagrine.

I have assumed the command of the Troops in Lower Louisiana and shall proceed in the duties appertaining thereto, independant of any considerations except that of duty; until I receive the Generals answer to my letter of the 24th. Augt.[2] wherein I gave him to understand that I should not conform to the order of the 30th. April 1801. As soon as I receive his answer you may rely on receiving the whole in detail, if the General has received the countenance of the President of the United States, and of the heads of departments an arrest will be the consequence, if that should not be the case it will pass off in a puff and he will be convinced that I do not copy his example, in always leaving a *Tail behind me*.

The City of Orleans has been severely visited with the yellow fever, and is at present as dangerous to foreigners as at any other stage, and will remain so until frost comes—

Abstracted from the Town there is no danger. I have not time to give you an Idea of the situation of this country, be assured that it is not very pleasing, a leven has been left by the french that will (I am afraid) sour the whole mass.

My dear General, you shall frequently hear from me, you will please observe that the extracts are from official communications, your own good judgment will suggest the necessity of confining the contents to only those who you are sensible are interested in my welfare—

Do pray my Dr. Sir call frequently to see my family; incourage Mrs. Butler[3] to act like herself, in my absence.

Make my best respects to Mrs. Jackson, and except my best wishes yourself, and believe me Dear General yours Sincerely;

Thos. Butler Colonel 2nd. Regt.

LS, DLC. Published in *PMHB*, 17(1893):502–503.
1. Colonel Constant Freeman was left in command at New Orleans when Wilkinson went to Washington in April. Wilkinson did not return to the West until June 1805, having then been appointed governor of Louisiana Territory while retaining his army command.
2. A copy of Butler's letter to Wilkinson is included in Butler to AJ, December 31, below.
3. Sarah Semple (d. 1805) of Pittsburgh, whom Thomas Butler had married about 1782.

From Thomas Butler

City of orleans Novr. 20th. 1804

Dear Sir,

Last evening I was arrested by the general in the manner following,

Head quarters Frederick Town Maryland
Sir—   Octr. 10th. 1804

Your letter of the 24th. of august has come to hand like that of the 5th. of June which you addressed to the secretary of war, will receive all the consideration to which it is entitled: on the receipt of this you are to consider yourself in arrest, and will conform your conduct accordingly. (Signed) James Wilkinson—

Thus my worthy friend you see, that I am still persecuted. I have only a moment Just to state the case, by next mail probably he may deign to let me know the charge, which you shall be immediately furnished with, when I shall have to call on my friends for their assistance, to have the case stated to the President, as I presume the avenues to the President is shut against me, as the communication which I sent him before I left Tennessee, as you advised, has not been answered; surely the President will not tamely look on and see an officer boren down in this way, by oppressive Journey if so then have I faithfully served my country for nothing; in great haste I remain dear general your obedt. Humbl. Servt.

Thos. Butler

Do my dear friend see Mrs. Butler and impress on her mind the necessity of bearing up against these momentary evils.

ALS, DLC. Published in *PMHB*, 17(1893):503.

From George Washington Campbell

Washington City D. C. Decr. 6th 1804

Dear Sir,

You will long since have been informed, that Mr. Claiborne has been appointed Governor of Orleans Territory. Few with whom I have been acquainted, expected this event. Time will shew the propriety of the choice. The subject is scarcely mentioned here. You can determine how far on such an occasion, silence is to be construed into an approbation of an appointment. A letter was shewn to me this day, written by a gentleman of information in Orleans Territory, stating that the new Executive there had become very unpopular & that the people would not (if they had a choice) elect him to any office.

Our naval force in the Mediterranean, has bombarded the town of Tripoli with considerable success, having taken, or destroyed five of the Bey's gunboats and injured his town very much and it is expected before this, he has been compelled to accede to honorable terms.[1]

General [Louis-Marie] Turreau, Minister extraordinary from the Emperor of France to the United States,[2] has arrived and been received by our Government. Jerome Bonaparte attempted to leave the U. S. in the frigate that brought the Minister to this country,[3] but was prevented from clearing out of the bay by a british vessel that waited for him off the coast, he has therefore returned and will remain longer in this Country.

Your Most obedt. Svt.

G. W. Campbell

Typed copy, DLC.
1. Campbell was probably referring to the August 3 bombardment of Tripoli by gun-

boats under command of Edward Preble, in which several ships of Yusuf, the provincial governor, were captured or sunk.

2. Turreau de Linières (1756–1816) remained as French envoy until 1811.

3. Bonaparte (1784–1860), with his American bride, Elizabeth Patterson, was making his second attempt to slip through the British blockade and return to France.

From Thomas Butler

Orleans Decr. 31st. 1804—

Dear General,

You will observe by the enclosure,[1] the state of my case, and that the General is determined to harass and opress me until his malignant disposition is satiated; I should feel but little uneasiness under his persecution; had I not reason to suppose that he was countenanced in this persecution, by men in office; for the honor of our country; as well as of human nature, I hope I may be deceived in this idea, be that as it may General, I am sensible that power can only oppress for a time, principle must ultimately rise superior to tyranny.

I have frequently written to my friends at Washington, but have not had a line from that quarter since the meeting of Congress, and from the shortness of its session my enemy will gain his object by keeping back my trial until the session is over; if the General is countenanced in this persecution, it is with a design to force me out of service, a short time will develope the business.

As the mail is so uncertain in its arrival, I shall keep this letter open until the last moment of closing it, as probably I may receive something to communicate to you, and as the General means to raise his second charge on the sentiments expressed in my letter to him of the 24th. august last, I will transcribe that letter for your perusal, altho you must have seen a copy of that letter, but least you have not, it is as follows.

(*Letter quoted by the general*)[2]
Nashville August 24th. 1804—

Sir, By last mail I received a duplicate of your letter of the 9th. ulto., with an additional note, directing me to note an error in sd. letter "and read 1st. of February instead of 4th. of February in the second paragraph."

I cannot help expressing much surprise that such an error should have crept in to your letter of the 9th. ulto. when in the same letter you informed me, that my letter of the 5th. of June to the Honle. secretary of war, had been submited to you, on which you remark "and I note the contents."

The subject matter of that letter required an open and decisive answer; as I had therein announced my determination not to conform to the first part of the order of the 1st. Febry. 1804 (so far as related to cropping the hair) and had the order been correctly recited in your letter of the 9th. of July last, I should have reiterated in my letter of the 6th. inst. my determination not to conform to the first part of that order; having ever considered the order of the 30th. of Apl. 1801, as an arbitrary infraction of my natural rights, and a noncompliance on my part, not cognizable by the articles of war: A correct recitation of that order would have drawn forth my refusal to conform to the first part, and enabled you to have taken such measures to inforce obedience as you might have deemed expedient; and probably have saved me the fatigues of a journey, of which I complained to the Honble. secretary of war (in my letter to him of the 5th. of June) was vexatious.

Notwithstanding the obstacles which I perceive in my way, yet I flatter myself that I shall in due time surmount them all, therefore permit me to inform you Sir, that I shall commence my journey to the City of Orleans by land (the only alternative left me) on tuesday the 28th. inst., and in order that a decision may be obtained, as to the legality of that order, it becomes necessary for me to inform you, that I shall not conform the cut of my hair to the general order of the 30th. of Apl. 1801.

The above was my answer to the general which grew out of the nature of the case, and his communications, and cannot be tortured in to any other position. 'tis true I gave him to understand that I seen his object in the false quotation, which I presume he feels, but I am not affraid but that I shall defend myself on this, as well as on every other charge he may offer, provided I have an inteligent court, but he has in the inclosed letter observed that it must be *a proper one*, say of his chosing.

Make my respects to Mrs. Jackson and believe me your very Humbl. Servt.

Thos. Butler Col.

P.S I kept this letter open to the last moment. The mail has arrived, but none farther than Fort Adams   Butler

ALS, DLC. Published in *PMHB*, 17(1893):504–505.
  1. Not found.
  2. The parenthetical phrase is in Jackson's hand.

To Thomas Jefferson from AJ et al.

[cDecember, 1804]

Sir

Inclosed is a remonstrance signed by a number of the most respectable Citizens, and officers in this District, On the Subject of Colo. Thos. Butlers late, & present arrest—[1]

We hope the Shortness of time, added to the emergency of the Case, will in a measure account to you for the number of Subscribers, which are indeed inconsiderable, Compared to the Aggregate number Contained in the District and State; but we Solemnly pledge ourselves to you, that the Sentiments expressed in the remonstrance, are in perfect unison with those of the Community at large.

As we accord with the ideas and wishes of our State on this Subject and Occasion, and as we are impressed with a belief, that you, are not truly informed of the proceedings, now in being against Colo. Thomas Butler (as all avenues are closed, by a late general order, and no information can reach the Secretary at War but through the organ of the General, who is the arresting officer) it is most humbly hoped that you will pardon us for the trouble we have given, in a case & under circumstances which we conceive ought not to escapte your observation & attention

We have the honor to tender to you our highest consideration of respect

> Andrew Jackson
> J Winchester
> Edwd. Douglass
> Wm. Hall[2]

LS, DLC-Thomas Jefferson Papers. Endorsed, received January 25, 1805.

1. A copy of the remonstrance, [cDecember 1804], is in the Jefferson Papers, DLC. The Senate received the original, bearing seventy-five signatures, and referred it to committee on January 30, 1805. There was no further congressional action. The petition argues the illegality of the order for cropping the hair as ground for disobedience (DNA-RG 46).

2. Winchester, Douglass, and Hall were all Sumner County residents: Winchester was the commanding general of the 4th Brigade of militia; Hall, an officer of the county militia, was the commander of the 2nd Infantry Regiment on the Natchez expedition and general of the 1st Brigade of Tennessee Volunteers in the Creek War; Douglass (1745–1825), a Revolutionary War veteran and delegate to the Tennessee constitutional convention, was commissioned lieutenant colonel commandant of the Sumner County militia regiment in 1796. Later he served four terms in the state senate.

1805

From James Irwin

Cantonment Tenne. River 25th Jany. 1805

Dr. Sir

I inclose you a statement of the furrs & peltries recd. by me since my arrival[1] and am sorry to communicate the little encouragement I meet with in trade in consequence of several obstacles 1st from the high price the Blankets sells at not only that but they are entirely rotton which deters the Indians from trading for the cloths. When Mr. [James] Swanson left this there was two Bales of Blankets untouched,[2] after some time I opened one of them & found them so much damaged that they were entirely unsaleable in so much that the Indians would not buy them at all. I then opened the second Bale & if any difference they were worse than the first insomuch that when one would take them in their hands & give them a little girk they would break to pieces in sundry places & they are so verry narrow the Indians would not buy them if they were of a good quality.

2nd Double head & Tolon[3] two chiefs in the cherokee nation has recd. an assortment of Goods this season & sells verry large excellent Blankets at 3 dollar which cannot be but verry little more than prime cost in fact they sell many articles below prime cost. Mr. Colston & Mr. Milton[4] who keeps seperate stands in the nation sells verry low, they say they can afford it as they lay in their Goods at Charles Town at a verry reducd rate—The Cherokees will bring their Beaver & otter by here and ask money if they don't get it they carry it on to the shoals where they say they can get any thing they want for it—As for the chickesaws I have not recd. 10 dollars worth of peltry since I have been here, they have got disgusted at the store by some means or other previous to my coming; I have requested Majr. [George] Colbert[5] to tell them there was a new store keeper, as they & Mr. Swanson did not agree hoping that might be an inducement for them to come & deal again but all to no purpose Mr. Samuel Mitchel[6] agent for the chickesaws was here a few days ago on his way to the Federal City & told me the chickesaws carry their hunts to mobile where Goods sells at least 50 ℔ Cent cheaper than they do either at Bluffs or this place & peltry 50 ℔ cent higher than it does here which is a sufficient inducement for an Indian to travel 2 or 300 Miles for.

There is a number of articles I wrote to Messrs. Deaderick & Tatum for which are so esential in this place they could hardly be dispensed with, likewise Messrs. Deaderick & Tatum gave me instructions to purchase Beef Cattle & pork, but was I to offer six dollars ℔ hundred for either in Merchandise I could not buy a pound as they will not part with those articles for any thing but money—[7]

There is an Issuing commissary wanting at this place a[t] present & I would be glad [to] accept of it, as it would not interfere with my business or rather yours for it would not occupy more than half an hour once every four [da]ys; if you have no objections against my a[ccepting] as such I would be glad y[o]u would write my by [first] mail—Give my b[e]st respects to Mrs. Jackson accept of the same yourself—

I am Dr. Sir with every Mark of esteem yr. most Devoted Humbl. Servt.

Jas. Irwin

ALS, DLC. Irwin, manager of Jackson & Hutchings's Gallatin store, 1803–1804, assumed responsibility for the cantonment in November 1804 and remained in that position for almost a year. Sometime later he moved to Mississippi Territory near Port Gibson and took up cotton planting.

1. Not found.

2. Swanson was Irwin's predecessor at the cantonment. For his statement on the damaged blankets, see Swanson to AJ, September 7.

3. Doublehead (d. 1807), a chief of the militant faction of the Cherokees in the 1790s, accommodated to the system of annuities and bribes to the extent that he was assassinated by members of his tribe when he alienated land without consent of the tribal council. Tahlonteskee (Tolon) was a younger kinsman of Doublehead's.

4. Not further identified.

5. Colbert (c1764–1839), one of the sons of the Scots trader James Colbert who married a Chickasaw and remained as a leader of the nation, operated a store and a ferry across the Tennessee River near the present site of Florence, Ala. He was chief spokesman for his people in the treaty negotiations of 1805 but took a lesser part in the arrangements for the Chickasaw cessions of 1816–18 and the early 1830s. In 1837 he emigrated with the remaining Chickasaws to the reserved lands west of the Mississippi.

6. Mitchell was appointed agent for the Chickasaws and Choctaws in 1797 and the Chickasaws alone in 1801.

7. For further suggestion that Deaderick & Tatum were partners with Jackson in the cantonment store, see Deaderick & Tatum to AJ, December 11, 1803, in *Jackson*, 1:408.

From James Irwin

Cantonment Tennee. River 9th. February 1805

Dr. Sir

I have the honor to acknow[ledge] the receipt of your favor by Lieut. [John] Brahan[1] & hasten to comply with your request—I wrote you by last mail & enclosed you a memorandom of Furrs & Peltry[2] but have recd. none since & enclose you a second stating the agr. amt. of what I have recd. since my arrival—I omitted writing you relative to the purchase I made of Capt. John Smith T. I find from your letter he stated that the Tobacco weighed 550 lbs. Capt. Smith calculated on its weighing 600 lbs. but we could not weigh it in consequence of the River bottom being inundated, we could not get the carriage near to it & we had no steelards that would draw so heavy a draught; I then told Capt. Smith I would call on Lieut. [William] Simmons[3] to see it weighed which I did & it weighed 380 lbs. that at 31¼/100 ℔ lb. is $118.75 I also told Capt. Smith I would communicate the purchase to you in order that you might give his Acct. Credit for the Amt. thereof: I find no difficulty in retailing it 50 cents ℔ lb. & to the Cherokees I can sell it at 4 Shillings ℔ lb. in Furrs & Peltry— it is an article much in demand in this Place & there was none in the Store—

There was several remnants of muslin in the assortment that was on hand when I came in your employ that was quite unsalable in consequence of its being damaged (this is the muslin you allude to I suppose) but I am not able to inform you who you got it from or what quantity there was of it, as it was not Invoiced as such

I have met with but little encouragement in trade as yet though the Hunters begin to come in now but the misfortune of it is they want money for their Peltry & furrs in order that they may trade with Double head as they say he sells much cheaper than any of the other Traders which is Truly the case for he sells many articles under prime cost & the Indians is persuaded from that Circumstance that all the other Traders is extortioners & imposters but I hope Mr. Double heads store will not last long and particularly so to the grief of his Creditors I stated in my other letter every thing relative to the Trading business here, the advantages and disadvantages now attending—also relative to the Blankets on hand at this place which I find verry unsalable—

I here State the Memmorandom of Furrs & Peltry with their Amt. annexed, after deducting 20 ℔ Cent for Bates & Shanks—

A Memmorandom of Furrs & Peltry recd. by me since the 19th November 1804 until 6th February 1805—

No. Deerskins		No. Bear skins			No. Small Furrs			No. Otter's			Pr. 100 lbs. Beaver		Pr. 100 Panthers			
at 16⅔	$ Cts		at	$			$			$		$		37½	.75	Agt. Amt.
		2	100	2.	82	12½	10.						2			
		2	50	1.				9	200	18.	11½	11.50				
770	128.33⅓	2	25	.50	63	16⅔	10.50									$183.58⅓
		2	37½	.75												
	128.33⅓	8		4.25	145		20.50	9	"	18.	11½	11.50	2	"	.75	

Cash on hand is $194.⁵⁰/₁₀₀ those that Capt. [John] Campbell[4] & Mr. Swanson credited have no pretentions to paying their debts particularly the Indians, those that have Credit here carry their Hunts to the shoals and some to Mobile but never come this way except when they have nothing and want more credit—

I wish you to write by first Mail in answer to my last letter as I expect the Troops will be here shortly and the Commissary will be wanting then—[5]

I am Dr. Sir with every Sentiment of Esteem Your Mt. Hbl. Servt.

Jas. Irwin

ALS, DLC.
1. Letter not found. Brahan (1774–1834) arrived in Tennessee as a captain in the U.S. Army stationed at Fort Southwest Point. In 1809 he received appointment as receiver of monies for public lands in Madison County, Miss. Terr., resigned his army commission, and moved to Huntsville. During the Creek War he and his partner, Leroy Pope, were principal contractors for Jackson's army.
2. See above, Irwin to AJ, January 25; enclosure not found.
3. Simmons (d. August 1805) was a second lieutenant in the U.S. 2nd Infantry.
4. Campbell preceded Swanson as manager at the cantonment. In June 1805 he offered to buy the store (see Campbell to AJ, June 2).
5. It is not known if Irwin became commissary.

From Thomas Butler

orleans February 18th. 1805—

Dear General,

[I had] calculated upon receiving some info[rmat]ion from washington by this days mail, but as usual a blank. I have cause to complain of my friends in that quarter for their taciturnity.

I am now perfectly satisfied that the heads of departments are one and all my enemies, and have nothing to expect from that quarter but hard knocks. I shall prepare myself to fend off, so let them come on, I long to meet the tug of war.

I shall now inform you of a very unfortunate affair that took place a few days since. Young Mr. [Micajah Green] Lewis fell in a duel, he was shot through the breast, barely spoke, and then expired. the cause of quarel was the publications which have lately filled our papers, which you must have seen,[1] for any other news we have none. it would have given me pleasure to have received a line from you by this mail, but suppose that you have been too much hurried with business, of late. do my dear frien[d le]t me know if you have received [any inform]ation from the gentleman members f[rom th]e state, as I cannot conceive what is the cause of their silence.

Make my respects to Mrs. Jackson, and pray incourage my little wife as often as you can see her. Accept my best respects your self—and believe me Dear General Your Humbl. Servt.

Thos. Butler

ALS, DLC.
1. Lewis (1784–1805), only son of Jackson's neighbor William Terrel Lewis, was killed February 14 in New Orleans, where he was serving as secretary to his brother-in-law, Territorial Governor William Charles Cole Claiborne. The fundamental cause of the duel was the vicious newspaper campaign conducted by Claiborne's opponents. An article in the *Louisiana Gazette*, February 7, portrayed dancing and revelry at the governor's mansion, observed by the sorrowful ghost of Claiborne's wife, who had died the previous September. Lewis reacted to the newspaper account by challenging its author, Robert Sterrey.

From Thomas Terry Davis

Jeffersonville Indiana Territory Feby 20th. 1805

My Dear Sir.

I find one of your slaves has left you I firmly believe he is within six mile of this place at James Noble Woods Esquire[1] he answers your description as to Dress and time of coming here & freedom except you call your man a Mulatto this man is rather dark than Bright He has an excellent set of Teeth, is fond & Careful of Horses & Drives a waggon very well. This fellow calls himself *Tom Gid*[2] & passes for a Freeman tho he is supposed to be run away. My son of Ten years old red your advert[ise]-ment[3] & immediately fixed on Tom Gid for your runaway. I never red the advertisement till about one Hour ago. I have not said one word to any person on the subject. Please to write me, further descriptions & I will secure the fellow. When spoken to this Fellow answers with haste tho free from impediment. When siting this fellow leans forward puts his Knees wide apart & crosses his hands on his XXX. He effects humbleness tho. tis evident from the cast of his countenance that he is artful & impertinant when he dares. If he is your fellow rest assured on my activity & friendship in securing him for you. Your Friend

Tho. T. Davis

P.S. Tell Jno. overton God bless him

ALS, DLC. At this time Davis was territorial judge for Indiana. He and Jackson probably knew each other when both served in the Fifth Congress, Jackson in the Senate and Davis as a representative from Kentucky.
1. Woods (d. 1826) settled near Utica, Ind. Terr., in 1794 and established a store, tavern, and ferry service to the Kentucky shore. In 1798 he was appointed justice of the peace for Knox County, then comprising nearly all of southern Indiana.
2. Not further identified.
3. Probably Advertisement for Runaway Slave, [September 26, 1804], above.

From Thomas Butler

Orleans March 4th. 1805—

Dear General

I received your letter of the 7th. ulto.,[1] and you can readily conceive (my esteemed friend) what my feelings must have been on opening it; to find the death of a beloved wife announced, without having heard of her indisposition? but it shews the instability of earthly things, and I must continue to bear the lot of mortals; I say continue to bear, for I have had my share of trial, and I have not now to learn, that when the doors of misfortune are thrown open, that it is not an easy matter to close them again; nay I well know that no power but that of omnipotence can do it; I shall therefore endeavour to submit to the stroke, and recollect that it came from a hand, that cannot be resisted by mortals.

The friendship offered by you and your amiable wife, to my little orphan family,[2] is a solace to me in my distress, and merits my warmest thanks; to part with those we love and esteem is a severe trial, and requires the aid of philosophy; I assure you Sir, that I cannot say that I possess a sufficient stock at this moment, but I will endavour to summon as much as possible to my aid, as my life is still of some moment to those who have a Just claim to my protection; and I hope that I shall in this trying situation, acquit myself like a man of honor and principle.

In your letter of the 7th. ulto., you mentioned that you intended soliciting the secretary of war, for permission for me to return to Tennessee.[3] I also addressed a letter to him on the evening that your letter came to hand, requesting permission to return to Tennessee, as soon as the proceedings on my trial could be closed, and that the result, could be announced to me at Nashville; if this indulgence is granted, it will be much better than to have to return to this place, immediately after gaining Tennessee for trial, which I would certainly have to do, was I permitted to return before a trial took place, as I am determined that a court shall decide in that case, in order that a precedent may be established, that the army may know whether the powers of a general are circumscribed by the laws or not.

I sensibly feel, that the government has treated me ungraciously, but you may rest assured that I shall defend myself like an officer. Shall I tell you Sir, that I have not yet been furnished with the charge or charges to which I am to plead, notwithstanding that I had made an early demand, both of the general and secretary of war; but each have been deaf to the demands of Justice, nor have I as yet seen the order for convening the court martial, but expect (from indirect information) that it will be convened on the 10th. of April. Should that be the case, and the secretary grant my request, I shall be enabled to set out for Tennessee, in all the month of April.

I shall proceed on tomorrow for my nephews,[4] a small Journey will change the scene, and assist in diverting my mind, from brooding too much over my misfortune; if I find that the meeting of the court is delayed under any pretence whatever, I shall send my son[5] through to Tennessee; but if I find that the court is to assemble in a short time, I shall detain him, as I shall want his assistance on the Journey, but you shall be regularly advised of every movement.

I have written to Capn. Purdy to make some arrangements for carrying on the farm, and employing the hand until my return, which I am sensible he will do; pray general see my children as often as you can spare as much time. tell my Boys to act prudently until my return. I expect much from them and hope that they will not disappoint me.

Remember me respectfully to Mrs. Jackson, and accept my best respects yourself.

I am Dear General your obedt. servt.

Thos. Butler

ALS, DLC.
1. Not found.
2. Thomas and Sarah Butler had four children: Thomas, Jr., Robert, Lydia, and William Edward.
3. No letter to the secretary of war on this subject found.
4. Richard Butler (1777–1820), son of Thomas's brother William, resigned his lieutenant's commission in the U.S. Army in 1799 and married a New Orleans heiress. He settled on a sugar plantation near the city, managed his wife's property, and bought extensively of lands in Mississippi and Louisiana. Both Butler and his wife died of yellow fever in 1820.
5. Robert Butler (1786–1860) had joined his father in New Orleans, not returning to Tennessee until after Thomas Butler's court martial and sudden death. In 1808 he married a favorite niece of Andrew and Rachel's, Robert Hays's daughter Rachel (b. 1786). In 1812 he was commissioned captain in the U.S. Army and in 1814 became adjutant general for the Southern Division, serving as Jackson's most trusted aide through both the New Orleans and Seminole campaigns and until 1821 when he resigned in a dispute over reduction of rank. He was appointed surveyor general of Florida Territory in 1824, holding the office until his removal in 1842 and securing reappointment in 1845. Butler moved his family to Florida in 1825 and acquired extensive landholdings amid accusations of favoritism and mismanagement of the surveyor's office.

From Felix Robertson

Philadelphia March 25th. 1805

Dear Sir,

In writing to the different Gentlemen of my acquaintance in that Country, I should think it unpardonable were I to neglect shewing you that piece of respect—your unsullied private Character, and numerous public services to your Country, all conspire to make your friendship desired by every lover of virtue or Liberty, and when obtained to render no exertion for retaining it, too great to be performed—If I am not in possession of it, I cannot conceive it degrading, to own it is my anxious wish to gain it—If I already am favored with it, my greatest ambition is never to forfeit it—To the World perhaps, this might appear like Cycophancy, but to your better judgment I fear not to submit it—We have but very little political news and what we have you readily obtain through the medium of the public prints, therefore I need say nothing on that head—Your Friends in this place are generally well, some of whom I see almost daily—You have heard long since I expect that your Landlord Mr. [Joseph] Hardy[1] is dead—I saw on saturday last in the papers of this place an account of the Death of My Friend and schoolfellow Micajah G. Lewis[2] which has scarcely been out of my mind since for a minute. I sincerely lament the untimely fall of a young Man, whose acquirements and Talents gave rise to the most sanguine expectations of his usefulness in society—I dread even to reflect on the situation of his unhappy Parents—The Lectures have been over a considerable length of time, but I cannot leave this before some time in June—I have undergone the two first examinations for the Degree of M.D. so that I expect to return to Tennessee at least authorised if not prepared to practice Physic, but from accounts the Citizens of Tennessee have for some time past had but very little business with Physicians, I sincerely hope it may be always the case—Thinking that it might give you a momentary entertainment I have taken the liberty to send you a Copy of a letter from myself to Dr. [Benjamin Smith] Barton Professor of Natural History Materia Medica and Bottany in this University in answer to a piece which appeared in his periodical work (the Medical & Physical Journal,) on the Falls of Niagara;[3] His paper was an extract from his own journal through that Country, as I have since learned—I am sorry it is not in my power at present to send you also a copy of his paper the[re] having been not more struck off than was bound up. I will however bring the work out when I return at which time you can if you please have an opportunity of seeing it—I hope you will not consider my sending you this copy as the effect of Egotism, for I am very sensible it possesses not a single merit beside the principles it imbraces— It was wrote in great haste at a time I was very unwell and not expecting it would be published; The Dr. however done me the honor to think them worthy a place in his publication, and having to appear in a few days I consented to his inserting them with all their imperfections on their head I enjoy at present reasonable health—My respects to Mrs. Jackson— I remain Dear Sir yours &c.

Felix Robertson

ALS, DLC. Robertson (1781–1865; University of Pennsylvania Medical School 1805), son of Nashville founder James Robertson, established his medical practice in Nashville in 1805. He served two terms as mayor of Nashville but mainly devoted his time to the professional concerns of his practice, his membership in state and local medical societies, and his teaching responsibilities in the medical department of the University of Nashville. As a member of the Nashville Junto, Robertson helped plan and effect Jackson's election to the presidency.

1. Hardy, owner of Hardy's Hotel on High Street in Philadelphia, died February 15. Jackson probably resided at Hardy's during his congressional terms, 1796–98.

2. Most Philadelphia newspapers probably carried a report of the duel. For example, a reprint of the *Louisiana Gazette* account of Lewis's death appeared in the *United States' Gazette for the Country* on March 26.

3. Barton's article, "Description of the Falls of Niagara," in his *Philadelphia Medical and Physical Journal*, 1(1804): 39–46, was answered by Robertson's "Additional Observations on the Falls of Niagara," 1(1805): 61–68.

From Thomas Butler

Fort Adams[1] April 17th. 1805—

Dear General—

Last evening I had the pleasure of receiving your favor of the 13th. ulto.[2] expressing equal surprise at the silence of the members in congress from Tennessee. I certainly had reason to have expected answers to sundry letters addressed to them, but in that expectation I have been disappointed, and I have reason to presume that there is a fixed determination in the heads of departments to bear me down; but Sir, while I have one man of sense and worth to approbate my conduct, I shall meet the persecution undismayed.

Last evening I also received the charges as exhibited by the General, which I shall state for your information, they are as follows.

"Head Quarters Washington Febry. 11th. 1805.

Sir, The following are the transgressions for which you are arrested, and must hold yourself in readiness, to answer to a military Tribunal.

"Charge 1st.—Wilful, obstinate, and continued disobedience of the general order of the 30th. of April 1801, for regulating the cut of the hair, and also disobedience of the orders of the 1st. of February 1804. Specification, By refusing to conform the cut of your hair to the General order of the 30th. of April 1801, as directed in the order of the 1st. of February 1804, and contumaciously resisting the authority of the orders, after you had been tried by General Court martial, found guilty of the disobedience of the General order of the 30th. of Apr. 1801, and sentenced to be repremanded in general orders."

"Charge 2nd. *Mutinous conduct*—Specification—By appearing publickly in command of the Troops, at the City of New orleans with your hair cued, in direct and open violation of the general orders of the 30th. of April 1801, and of the 1st. of February 1804, thereby giving an example of disrespect and contempt to the orders and authority of the commanding General, tending to dissever the bonds of Military subordination, to impair the force of those obligations by which Military men are bound to obedience, and to excite a spirit of sedition and mutiny in the army of the united states."

These are the charges to which I am to plead to on the 10th. of May at the City of orleans; to which place I shall proceed in a few days; on the 25th. of last February I requested permission of the Honble. Secretary of War to return to Tennessee as soon as my trial should close, but from the treatment that I have received, I have little expectation to receive that privilege, as he has not answered a single letter addresse to him in my present case, therefore the presumption is strong that I shall be ordered to remain until the general may think proper to return the proceedings. the 10th. of October was the date of my arrest, and to say that the court will convene on the 10th. of May (which I doubt) will be a lapse of seven months, and if the secretary had been friendly towards me, he would not have suffered me to remain seven months in arrest without a trial; but do not be uneasy, I shall adhere to my old principles, *the laws of my country*, but should their protection be withheld by design, I shall then defend myself.

I have not had the pleasure of seeing Mr. Hutchings, he having passed to orleans[3] whilst I was on my way to Natchez to prepare my son to proceed to Tennessee, and I assure you my friend that I found it necessary to swap a way the Horse that your friendship furnished me with when leaving Tennessee, with another of my own, keeping became so expensive, that I put them both in one, for the manner in which I have been harassed has drained my pockets, but as soon as Mr. Hutchings returns from orleans, we will make such arrangements as will provide for his accomodation, and should I receive permission to visit my family, I shall lose no time after the close of my trial.

Make my respects acceptable to Mrs. Jackson, and accept my best respects yourself.

I am Dear General your Humbl. Servt.

Thos. Butler

ALS, DLC. Published in *PMHB*, 17(1893):506–507.
1. On the east bank of the Mississippi River, forty miles south of Natchez.
2. Not found.
3. Hutchings had apparently taken slaves to New Orleans to sell (see AJ to Edward Ward, June 10, below).

When Jackson bought Truxton (named for Commodore Thomas Truxtun, hero of the Barbary Wars), few American horses rivaled his breeding. Sired by the imported stud horse Diomede out of a thoroughbred mare belonging to John Verell, Truxton's only serious competitors were the get of another imported horse, Bedford.

Verell had brought Truxton to Tennessee for the races in 1804 and found that he could not leave the state with his property owing to an attachment levied against him by Parry Wayne Humphreys for payment of a debt outstanding since 1799. The memorandum below shows that Verell's financial difficulty was resolved by Jackson's assumption of this debt and another in exchange for the horse.

About Verell himself little is known other than that he resided in Dinwiddie County, Va. In January 1806 he sold Jackson the slave Dinwiddie

(Dunwoody, c1774-c1844—46), who became de facto chief of the stables and a trainer widely admired by horsebreeders in Middle Tennessee and Kentucky.

Truxton was five years old when Jackson bought him, and although he had earned a reputation as a long-distance racer, his turf days ended within a year of the purchase. Truxton had only two important races in that time, both against Joseph Erwin's stallion, Ploughboy. Erwin forfeited the first, scheduled for November 1805, and dispute over payment of the forfeit money provoked Jackson's duel with Charles Dickinson, Erwin's son-in-law. Truxton handily won the rematch in April 1806 but completed the race on two injured legs.

Starting in 1806 he stood at stud in Nashville, siring a prodigious number of successful runners. He spent his final days at Richard Butler's plantation in Mississippi where Jackson had sent him to retirement in 1817.

Memorandum of Agreement with John Verell for the Purchase of Truxton

Memorandom of an agreement made this 11th. day of May 1805 between Genl Andrew Jackson of the State of Tennessee, and John Verell of the State Virginia (VIZ) The said Verell; hath sold to Genl. Jackson his Diomed Stud horse (Truxton) for the sum of Fifteen hundred Dollars; that is to say Genl Jackson is to step, into the said Verells place and pay off & settle a debt due by said Verell (on which an attachment is levied) To [Parry Wayne] Humphries assinee of Caldwell;[1] which said debt is now estimated at nine hundred and seventy Dollars and to pay the further sum of two hundred Dollars towards the discharge of a Judgt. against the said Verrell obtained in behalf of Charles J[ones] Love[2] on which Judgment an Execution is Issued amounting in both sums to Eleven hundred and Seventy Dollars, and the said Jackson hath paid the further sum of one hundred & thirty Dollars in one gelding and doth agree to pay the remaining sum of two hundred Dollars in the ensuing fall in two good hundred dollar geldings—and it is further agreed and understood that the said Jackson is: in case the horse Truxton should win a purse or match in the fall ensuing, to pay the said Verrell the further sum of two hundred dollars in gueldings: in addition to the aforesaid sum of fifteen hundred Dollars—witness our hands & seals the day & date above

the words in the ninth line from the bottom. "The remaining sum of Two hundred dollars" interlined before signed

Test   D. Shelby[3]

Jn. Verell	Seal
Andrew Jackson	Seal

I John Verell do certify that the Diomed Stud horse sold by me to Genl Andrew Jackson is five years old the 4th. day of May 1805, that is to say the Stud horse known by the name of Truxton—

Test   D. Shelby   Jn. Verell

Recd. of Andrew Jackson the sum of Twelve hundred ninety nine dollars sixty five cents of the within, in the following manner Viz—one

horse as within expressed	$ 130
Paid to marshal on Charles J Loves Judgt.	200
To Humphries on acpt of Caldwell and Bond	
delivered Mr. Verrell	969.65
	1299.65

Leaving a ballance due of the cash paid by A Jackson to the marshal on acpt of Major Verrell two hundred twelve dollars ninety five cents with interest from 13th. of May 1805—and leaving a ballance due on the within contract to Major Verrell now due in horses two hundred Dollars & 35/100

Jn. Verell

ADS (in Jackson's hand), also signed by Verell and Shelby, DLC. Extract published in Bassett, 1:113–14.
  1. Caldwell has not been further identified. Humphreys appeared before the Mero District Superior Court, May 27, 1805, to withdraw his prosecution of Verell.
  2. Love (d. 1837), resident of Fairfax County, Va., had known Jackson since 1798 when he furnished information about the land frauds of James Glasgow, secretary of state of North Carolina (see *Jackson*, 1:168–71, 179–80). About 1820 he moved to Davidson County, and while Jackson was in the White House, Love regularly reported on the operations of the Hermitage. Nothing more is known concerning Love's judgment against Verell.
  3. David Shelby (c1763–1822) moved from Virginia to Sumner County in 1781 and served as clerk of the county court from its organization in 1787 to his death.

The following letter was written during the first of Aaron Burr's four visits to Nashville, 1805–1806. After a river trip to New Orleans in June 1805, he returned overland in August, probably retrieved his horses and coachman, and visited at the Hermitage for several days. On this occasion Jackson and other prominent men of the town feted Burr at a public dinner. Jackson was again his host at the Hermitage and at a subscription ball when he returned in September 1806, this time headed for Kentucky. But when Burr, again traveling toward New Orleans, arrived for his final visit in December 1806, preceded by accusations of treasonous designs, he lodged at the Clover Bottom tavern and a house in the town.

From Aaron Burr

Nashville, Sunday Evg. [June 2, 1805]

My faithful old coachman, Sam. Hutchins[1] takes the Black horses & will hand you this—He understands as well as any man living how to drive a carriage & manage horses and the care of horses, carriage & harness, and he knows nothing else and during thirteen years service his honesty has never incurred a suspicion—He will I hope in some way make himself useful to you; but if either he or the horses should for any cause become inconvenient, they must forth with seek other quarters—

If I can be of any use to you in Orleans, pray command me—Letters by the mail of next weeke will find me in that city—

Accept the assurance of the very great respect with which I am Yr Ob Svt

A. Burr

Monday Mong
our chamber not being weather proof, this got defaced by the rain last night

ALS, THi.
1. Not further identified.

To Edward Ward

June 10th. 1805—

Sir,

Imperious circumstances, compels me again to bring to your view, the subject of money, and to state that the amount due at present—would be a great convenience for me to receive from a view of the contract I cannot believe that you are seriously impressed with the belief, that you are now authorised to discharge a part thereof in negroes—had negroes been offered before Mr Hutchings descended the river with negroes for sale they would have been recd. notwithstanding the lapse of time of his departure, you were informed by me, with the express design If you thought proper that you might discharge part in negroes, which if you had I would have been in cash for them before this, as you did not name negroes, then and the time elapsed I did (and with propriety) conclude that you had provided other means, to meet your engagement—and negroes would not have been named after we had sent on to markett and the time so far elapsed—Looking over your letter of the 12th. ultimo[1] in which you seem to hold out the idea of the right still to pay part in negroes, induces me thus far to notice the subject & contents of that letter—

Should you still be of that oppinion I will thank you to explicitly declare it. If so, you know my oppinion, on that subject & we are at Issue—as to your offer of giving property at valluation, I have only to observe that If my Creditors would receive their debts thus, I would meet every demand in four hours, this not being the case, makes cash the object. I have to request your answer to this letter, and beg you to state whether you have found any Errors in the statement herewith forwarded, relation being had to the statement forwarded to you the 7th. ultimo[2]—and at what time you will be in cash to discharge your bond—next week I must have money, and should I not receive it from you will be compelled to bring your Bond into markett and raise what money on it I can to meet my pressing demands.[3] This will be truly disagreable to me and I have no doubt unpleasant to you, But my engagements I must meet, this was the object of my sale of my Possessions—and from that sale I must realise that object—on the first of May Ballance due me as pr statement rendered you

on the first of May Ballance due me as pr statement rendered you	$1721 88.½
Interest to the first of June next.	8.60 ¾
	$1730.49 ¼
deduct	278.68 ⅓
Ballance due 1st of June 1805—	$1451.80 ½
Contra credit May 20. 1805 By cash pr Mr Burton[4]	$ 278.22 [⅓]
Interest 10 days	.46
Deduct this from the above—	278.68 [⅓]

E. E.

I set out this evening for Robertson County—and will thank you for an answer pr bearer[5]—Should you not be at home, on the delivery of this at your house shall expect to meet an answer at home on Thursday evening—I am sir with due reguard yr mo ob Serv

Andrew Jackson

P.S. It of great importance for me to know early whether you will have it in your power to raise the present on Early part of the ensuing week—

A.J—

ALS copy, DLC.
1. Not found.
2. The original of AJ to Ward, May 7, has not been found. According to a published extract in the American Art Association catalog, April 8, 1926, Item 250, Jackson argued, "The Press for cash compels me to Inclose you the above Statement, and when you recollect that I turned myself out of house and home, by the sale of my possessions to you, purely to meet my engagements—that the anxiety must be great in my mind to meet them with the sacrafice of ease and comfort, that I made upon that occasion. I need only add that my creditors are growing clamorous and I must have money from some source. . . . "

3. Jackson held off on his threat temporarily, but on March 21, 1806, he delivered the bond for £1,000 Virginia currency to James & Washington Jackson with instructions to distribute the proceeds to his creditors.

4. Not further identified.

5. In his reply, Ward protested that he was trying to raise cash, but as a newcomer he had few sources (see Ward to AJ, June 10).

To John Jackson

Hermitage near Nashville June 18th. 1805—

Sir

A Mr Norton Prior of Arch Street Philadelphia[1] holds by marshals sale under a Decree of our court of Equity, for west Tennessee 40,000 acres of land, lying on the three forks of Duck river—This land I wish Bot. and If you will undertake the agency either as a partner in the purchase, or otherwise you will confer an obligation on me—This is a valuable tract; at present coverred by the Indian claim—but this encumbrance, likely will be removed, ere long by treaty—indeed there remains but little doubt, but at the ensuing treaty which is to be held next month the indian title north of the Tennessee will be Extinguished and Should this be the case, this will be a valluable property[2]

you will confer an obligation on me, on the Recpt. of this to see Mr Prior, and make him the following proposals, from, me—first If he will make a general Warrentee Deed I will give him fifteen thousand Dollars for 40,000 acres, lying on the three forks of Duck all in 5000 acre tracts the first beginning on a stone or rock in the mouth of the war trace fork, marked with a number of letters as named in the patton—in five anual payments, or if more pleasant will make him a payment, on the Execution of the Deeds, this as Small as can be Stipulated on and not to Exceed three thousand Dollars—the Ballance in five anual payments, without Interest, But rather than not close the Bargain, to bear Interest from the Date—Should Mr Prior be fearfull of the tittle, and prefer makeing a special warrenty—from him & his heirs only, in that case I will give him ten thousand Dollars; Two in hand on the Execution of the Tittles & the Ballance in four anual payments, without Interest—Notwithstanding I think the title a good one I would make one third difference for the risque and I have no doubt he as a prudent man and in great need of money would prefer the latter—his Debt to be well secured—If Either of these proposals suits him you are authorised hereby to close it on my part with him, so far as you can, so as to make the contract binding, on the money being paid and satisfactory security given to his agent here who he may appoint for the purpose of making the titles.

Should neither of these propositions meet his approbation draw from him a proposition in writing, what he will receive for the 40,000 acres as above described—the Bargain conclusive on his part—If I should exceed to it in a certain Period of time, allowing sufficient time for the passage of the letters by mail—Should you incline to be interested in the purchase, you may, as far as one fourth or one third—Should you not, will freely allow you a liberal commission, on the contract being closed—Will you on the receipt of this, be good anough to see Mr Prior, and sound him on the subject, and write me immediately on the subject—If he is inclined to sell close with him immediately; if he will exceed to either of the foregoing proposals—get it lower if you can—It is I repeat a valluable property—

Mr. Prior will recollect me, I was well acquainted with him whilst in congress, he often called upon me for information relative to this property, and is well advised of its quality, but I am informed he wishes to sell, should he not as soon as it is liable to taxation it will be sold for the taxes, unless great care and large funds, the tax will amount to from one to Two hundred dollars pr anum—

Our goods are not yet arived, we expect to hear from them daily—I have not recd. a line from you, since yours acknowledging the recpt. of the Bills—

I am sorry to find that any of my Phil. friends should be so contracted as to take offence at my entrusting my business to you[3]—I am attached to the name—have full confidence in you, and as long as you will forego the trouble will continue to entrust you with it—their offence notwithstanding—I am a free agent will do Justice to all—as far as exertion and honest endeavour will permit—and their smiles or frowns are equally indifferent to me—except, as a good citizen it is pleasant to have the smiles of all—Will you be good anough to ask Mr Boggs, to state to me whether he has heard any thing of our cotton shipd. to Green & Wainright by their Mr Ds[4] instruction spring 1804—and if Acpt. of sales has reached him to forward us a statement of acpt. &c—

I cannot conclude without calling your attention to the first object of this letter. If Bot. it is a handsome Estate, the purchase worth more than I dare name With best compliments to your lady & sincere wishes for your welfare & happiness believe me to be, you mo. ob. serv.

Andrew Jackson

A Copy Forwarded by me.   Jas S. Rawlings[5]

ALS copy, DLC. Published in Bassett, 1:114–16.
    1. Pryor was a broker, merchant, and dealer in hides.
    2. In 1802 Andrew Jackson had been instrumental in securing a marshal's sale of David Allison's lands on the Duck River (see *Jackson*, 1:283–84). For his part in the action he received 10,000 acres; Pryor got 40,000 and Joseph Anderson, 35,000. As the federal government moved to extinguish Indian claims and pass legislation accepting Tennessee's right to confirm titles to these Duck River lands formerly in Indian territory, Andrew sought John Jackson's assistance in effecting a purchase from Pryor. Pryor, however, sold his land to James Patton of North Carolina and Patton's partner and brother-in-law, Andrew Erwin (1773–1834) in August 1808. When the titles of all the holdings were jeopardized by the

finding that the federal marshal had lacked jurisdiction in the forced sale, Erwin and Jackson found themselves locked in litigation for more than a decade (see case file of *Jackson* v. *Erwin*, 1814–24, Middle Tennessee Supreme Court Records, T. A series of articles in the Nashville *Constitutional Advocate* August and September 1822, discussed the case). Erwin actively opposed Jackson's presidential candidacy in 1828.

3. Samuel Meeker complained that John Jackson had not given him a fair share of Jackson & Hutchings's custom (see Meeker to AJ, May 10, July 27).

4. Jackson was referring to Nathan Davidson's directing a cotton shipment to the Liverpool commission house, Green & Wainwright.

5. Rawlings, married to Rachel's niece Rachel Hutchings in 1806, owned a tavern in Lebanon and managed the Jackson & Hutchings store there for a time.

Delegated to serve as president of the dinner celebrating the Fourth of July in 1805, Jackson struggled with phraseology in preparing the following possible toasts, which he then numbered for order of delivery, skipping number sixteen. His volunteer toast at the gathering saluted "the rising greatness of the West—may it never be impeded by the jealousy of the East" (Tennessee Gazette, July 17).

Toasts for Independence Day Celebration

[cJuly 1, 1805]

1st The 4 of July 76. The glorious day, on which millions resolved to be free or die; May the present and future generations enjoy the blessings of a revolution achieved by the blood, virtue & courage of their ancestors, unimpaired and be ever ready to defend it—

2. The people of america, may they always view, the constitution our political bark, union the sheet anchor <(may the truth that we attempt to let the cable be)> and virtue the main pillar of our liberty and independance

3. Thomas Jefferson P.U. States, May the future like his past conduct, be founded on wisdom and virtue—procure for him the esteem of all good men, <and the admiration of his peers> and the admiration of his enemies. May he ever enjoy the affections of a gratefull country—

4 The patriots of 76. who preferred death rather than Submission to a Tyrant—a bright example to the oppressed, and a solemn warning <to a Tyrant despite the opposition> to tyrants

5 George Clinton, Vice President of the united States—the Sage, the Patriot and honest man

6 The memory of Genl G. Washington, and the band of heroes, who fought, bled and died to attain for the happy people of america their glorious Jubilee

7 The Militia of the United States—the sure Bulwark of freedom—May the always defend it

8 The State of Tennessee, <May She become a Key stone to our na-

tional arch.> May She always keep in View, that religion, morality, & virtue, combined with talents in her officers are the only sure pledge of internal happiness—national prosperity and future greatness—

9 The godess of liberty, may She range unconfined over the earthly globe, Spreading her benign influence from the Eastern to the western hemisphere, always finding <Voluneers ?> soldiers to put Tyrants down

10. Louisiana, May She be shortly <hailed> admitted as an independant member of the Union—and realise all the blessings attendant on a free and enlightened nation, under a government of laws of their own choice

11. The army of the united States—May the officer and Soldier that is willing to defend liberty ever enjoy freedom—may he never be doomd. to persecution and Tyranny under a goverment of laws to satiate the private spleen of a would be Despot—[1]

<The state>

17 The peoples Sovereign—the american fair, <may she be first and in comand and to the enemies of freedom [?]> May she only smile upon the lovers of freedom.

14 The tree of liberty, May <it be newly and constantly examined, that its Branches may not be defiled destroyed with caterpillers and or insects> its Branches ever be preserved from the ravages of catterpillers and insects

15 The Aurora[2]—may its Luster never be deminished by the rising suns of <apostasy> aristocracy and Federalism—

13 American manufactures may the soon be on a par with our agriculture & commerce and become equal to our wants—

12 May hypocrasy, faction and Strife be rooted from the Boosom of every true <american> republican, that the spirit of cordiallity love, and unanimity, may prevail <through> with every true american.

The American people The favoured of heaven reaping the golden harvest, peace and plenty whilst <the old world> urope is involved in misery and war—

The general and State governments—confined within their constitutional sphere—May the good and happiness of the people be their compass and square—

Colo. Thomas Butler—may private worth and virtue rise triumphant over persecution—

AD draft, DLC.
1. An allusion to Thomas Butler's stand against James Wilkinson's hair-cropping order.
2. *The Aurora and General Advertiser*, Philadelphia Republican organ.

Butler's court martial convened July 1 and adjourned July 10. James Brown, district attorney for Orleans Territory and counsel for the gov-

ernment in the case, reported to James Wilkinson, July 20 (DNA-RG 107), that Butler admitted his disobedience of the hair-cropping order, arguing its illegality, and accused Wilkinson of "inconsistency and persecution" in retracting Butler's exemption. According to Brown, the trial proceeded in great haste, owing to near panic over the virulence of yellow fever in New Orleans. Court member Richard Sparks heard most of the testimony from his bed, and two other members fell ill in the course of the trial. All departed the city for their posts as soon as the trial ended.

The court martial found Butler guilty on both specifications (refusal to obey the orders of April 30, 1801, and February 1, 1804, requiring cropping of the hair, and inciting mutinous conduct in appearing before his troops in New Orleans with his queue) and sentenced him to twelve months' suspension from duty, rank, and pay. James Wilkinson, then in St. Louis, confirmed the sentence September 21, not knowing that Butler had died September 7.

The Butler-Wilkinson quarrel was immortalized in Knickerbocker's History of New York by Washington Irving, who met Wilkinson in Richmond at the Burr trial in 1807, took an immediate and passionate dislike of him, and caricatured him as General Jacobus Von Poffenburgh, the martinet enemy of Old Keldermeester's queue.

From Thomas Butler

Orleans July 15th. 1805—

Sir,

I have now the honor to forward for your perusal a copy of my defence,[1] which I will thank you to confine to a few friends only, as it might be considered improper to let it pass to the world until the proceedings had passed to the proper department for approval or disapproval, the points on which I founded my defence are generally stated, and with an intelligent court might have secured a verdict in my favour—but this I have no hopes of receiving; for if I have any knowledge of countenances, I think I discovered a fixed determination in a bare majority of the Court to Legalize the order, in the face of a positive act of Congress, and a precedent set by an order as stated by the Marquis De-La Fayete, and a decision of the Secretary of the Navy in the Case of Doctor William Rogers,[2] proves incontestibly that an illegal order may be resisted.

I should not have consented to come to trial under the unfavourable circumstances that I was obliged to do, had I seen any possible mode of gaining a fair trial; but the general had nominated every member, and kept back those whom he doubted of, he even put two of my former court on the present, but I cannot express to you the base intrigue to gain a verdict against me, and altho I cannot speak positively as to the decision, yet I have no expectation that it is otherwise than as I have stated, I have not time to say half what I wish to say to you, nor would it be prudent, the court would not receive as testimoney the extract from the Presidents letter you were pleased to send me,[3] nor would I be permitted to prove the illegal orders as stated in my defence, but sir, as soon as the decision is known I shall advise with you on the proper steps to take to procure redress as I never will submit to so degrading an act where the laws should secure me.

in great haste Dear General I am your obedt. Humbl Servt.

Thos. Butler Col.

P.S. The secretary not having answered my letter requesting to return to Tennessee as soon as my trial would close I mean to leave the City in the morning for a farm lately purchased by my nephew about eight Legues up the coast where I shall remain until my case is known.   Butler

pray take care of the copy sent as I have none other but an incorrect one—

ALS, DLC. Published in *PMHB*, 17(1893):508–509.
1. Not found.
2. Navy surgeon William Rogers was arrested in 1803 for disobedience of orders and entered as defense that the orders were unnecessary and unauthorized. The secretary of the navy released him from arrest without calling a court martial. He invoked a similar defense on another charge in his court martial in 1807 but this time was found guilty and dismissed from the service. Lafayette's order has not been identified.
3. The only Jefferson to Jackson communication found on the Butler case is the letter of September 19, 1803, in *Jackson*, 1:365.

The duel described in Jackson's statement below was the second fought by Thomas Jefferson Overton in July 1805. On July 10 he had met Na-thaniel McNairy. Neither party was injured, and Overton declared that he was satisfied inasmuch as McNairy had fired before the word was given. No evidence has been found on the cause of that duel or the one fought with John Dickinson on July 26. Jackson states Overton's inten-tion to seek satisfaction (after his wounds healed) in another meeting with Dickinson, and although report of a rematch has not been found, Dickinson in a letter to Moses Fisk, August 12, said that the Overtons were still clamoring for a new contest (Nashville Tennessean, April 15, 1934). Jackson solicited a statement on the duel from John Childress, Jr., Dickinson's second, probably intending both for publication, but neither Childress's statement, which he enclosed in a letter to Jackson, August 6, nor a newspaper publication has been found.

Overton was the son of Waller Overton, who lived in Lexington, Ky., and a nephew of Jackson's friend John Overton. In 1804 he was admitted to the bar in Nashville but probably returned to Kentucky, as he received his commission as first lieutenant in the U.S. Army in 1812 with a Ken-tucky contingent. He was killed in action in Michigan in 1813.

Dickinson (1781–1815), a native of New Hampshire, followed his college tutor Moses Fisk to Knoxville upon his graduation from Dartmouth College in 1797. Two years later he moved to Nashville, studied law with John Overton, and commenced his lucrative practice of land and commercial law in 1800. During the few years he lived in Nashville, Dickinson won local public office and honors and accumulated a large fortune.

Memorandum of Duel between Thomas Jefferson Overton and John Dickinson

[cJuly 28, 1805]

On the 25 Instant I was notified by Mr Thos. Overton Junr. that he was called upon by Mr John Dickason, to meet him on the field of honour and render satisfaction, "in the mode which has hitherto been customary among Gentlemen"—and requesting me to attend him, being also advised from the coopy of Mr John Dickasons note to Mr John Childress,[1] of date the 16th. Instant, delivered on the 25th. that Mr J. C was to be the friend of Mr J. D. agreable to Mr T. O. request, I immediately repaired to Nashville, to see Mr J. C. on the subject of the note, and reached there on the evening of the 25th. waited upon Mr J. C. and informed him, agreable to the request of his friend J. D. I was the friend of Mr. T. O. was ready, to enter on arangements, to give the satisfaction required—after some conversation on the subject, I stated to Mr J. C. that agreable to custom and usage in these cases, being the friend of the Challenged, I had a right to name the distance—he observed that of this, he was not well advised, and asked me what distance I would name—I named seven feet, stand back to back, at the word prepare dress to the right—at the word fire—fire when they pleased—again stating to Mr J. C. that I as the friend of the challenged, agreable to every usage and custom on the subject, had the right to name the distance that this mode would place them upon an equal footing, and the best shot would have no advantage Mr. J. C. then observed he would see his friend, and give me an answer the ensuing morning—on the morning of the 26th. Mr J. C. met me agreable to appointment and stated to me, that his friend would not meet at less distance than twenty four feet I observed to Mr. J. C. that Mr. J. D. had no right to say any thing about distance; that he had called upon us to render satisfaction, in the mode usual & customary for Gentlemen in such cases—that agreable thereto we had named the distance and mode, which we would not abandon—Mr J. C. replied that his friend had instructed him to state, that his feelings was not wrought up to that Pitch as to throw away his life thus, that he would not meet at any less distance than Twenty four feet—

I was truly astonished to receive such a message from the challenger, and thus replied, If Mr. D. could put up, with the chastisement that he had received, if a caining had not roused his feelings to meet upon the grounds proposed, which were usual and customary, and from which we had the right to name it was with himself to descide—that If he did not come forward on this ground, he would be disgraced and that Mr T. O. would take the liberty to Kain him for some illiberal & unjustifiable expression in his note to Mr J. C. that Mr J. D. was a young man, we wished to treat him liberally—and notwithstanding we had the right, to retire and expose him—that we would wait for his further determination on this subject and requested Mr J. C. to return to his friend, and say to him—If he did not come forward, on these terms he would be exposed to the world and that Mr T. O. would Cain him for the expression used in the note aforesaid—we then Parted to meet at ten Oclock—A. M. of the same day—we met accordingly—when Mr J. C. informed me; that his friend J. D. said Possitively he would not meet, my friend at less distance than Twenty four feet, let the consequences be what the might—I then stated, twelve feet or fifteen, Mr J. C. stated his instructions were Possitive on the subject, and at no other distance would he meet—with astonishment—I observed he the challenger, and would not receive the satisfaction requested, and that too, to prevent him from disgrace or a Caining—Mr J. C. replied his instruction were Possitive—knowing we had a right, then to retire, proceed as we thought right, that we had offered the satisfaction required in the usual mode, but knowing that the wishes of my friend were to fight Mr J. D. even on his own terms, requested Mr J. C. to remain untill I could see my friend who was not far distant—to which he readily agreed—I repaired to my friend stated to him the answer received. my friend requested me to return, and say to Mr J. C. that, his anxiety was such to fight Mr J. D. that he would meet Mr J. D. on his own Terms, reserving to himself, all benefit from the ground he stood on, to make it known to the world, and seek redress for the language in Mr J. D. note such as he might deem proper—I returned to Mr J. C. communicated the same to him, with the reservations, and that it was not hereafter to be viewed as a precedent, or abandonment of our right to name the distance—but as a mere wish to fight Mr. J. D. reserving to Mr. T. O. the ground he then stood on—we then named the place and the time taking Mr J. D. own distance & Terms to wheel at the word, and after word fire, to advance or not, and fire when they pleased—at the time we met, all things duly prepared, the word given, with a pause of some time, with cool deliberation, the both fired without advancing and without effect—the Pistols being again charged—the word given—after a pause of some time with deliberation Mr Overton fired missing Mr Dickason—Mr. D. advanced with his Pistol in six or nine Inches of Mr. O. and fired—the Ball passing thro his arm & Breast—Mr Overton received the advance of Mr J. D. with more than usual firmness, of a youth of his age, under such circumstances—after Examining Mr T. O. wound I called upon the Gentlemen to know their wishes, Mr J. D. replied he was satisfied—I replied it was well, but that we were not—that satisfaction remained to be made Mr T. O. for the illiberal and unusual expression in the note of Mr J. D. and that he Mr J. D. must attone for them—Mr J. D. making no reply to me—but observed to Mr. J. C. he would not retract them—and Mr. O. communicating to me that he was becoming fainty—I observed to Mr. J. D. that the present situation of my friend, would not permit of a prosecution of the satisfaction then intended, but hereafter satisfaction must be made—Mr J. D. & Mr J. C. then left the ground, and I attended to my wounded friend—I certify that the foregoing is substantially the facts that attended the dispute between Mr J. D. & Mr T. O.

Andrew Jackson

ADS, DLC. Published in Bassett, 1:117–19.
1. Childress (d. 1819), a wealthy Nashvillian, was appointed marshal of the U.S. District Court for West Tennessee in 1803 and served successive four-year terms to his death.

From Thomas Jefferson Overton

Augt. 1st. 1805.

Dr. Genl.

I am induced to think the brush I got when you was with me is not likely to produce fatal effects. But I assure you General it would be almost a matter of indifference with me, if it were not for my wish to be with you once more; and oftener if necessary, for it seems as if my enemies as to numbers are something like the army of Xerxes combatting with the Grecians, who had to oppose them—Have confidence my dear friend—all that I ask, is that you may be along side of me in the hour of difficulty— when life ceases to be a blessing unless held on honorable terms—I have but one life to lose, and they shall have a chance for that, as long as it lasts; though I trust the God of heaven is just, and with your assistance will enable me, to give some account of the greatest monster of depravity, in the shape of a man, that ever disgraced the animal creation—I mean John Dickinson—the pupil, nay, I might almost say the child of Judge Overton;[1] and of certificate memory—This is the man with whom I cannot live on the same globe and I am sure our souls if he has one at all, are too uncongenial to be placed by providence in the same state of existance hereafter.

In justice I think he will be obliged to fight me the next time, upon my own terms; and if he does, I pledge myself (*accidents excepted*) that families when discharging the sacred duties of hospitality, shall no longer be affraid of finding a dagger in their breast or the poison of asps, and adders in their bowels, when least suspected.

I tell you Genl. I shall get well—you must come and see me if you can—I am too much fatigued to write any more

I am with sincere sents. of gratitude your friend

Th. J. Overton

ADS, DLC. Published in Bassett, 1:119–20.
1. John Overton had replaced Jackson as judge of the Tennessee Superior Court in 1804.

From Thomas Butler

Summer residence Eight Leagues from
Orleans Augt. 26th. 1805—

Dear General,

By last mail I had the pleasure of receiving your favor of the 2nd. inst.[1] but at too late an hour to be answered by the return mail. I was happy to hear of your health, and that you had received my letter of the 15th. ulto. with its enclosure.[2] you request me if possible, to give you a feature of the decision of the court on my trial; this I hinted at in my last, but it is impossible to give a correct idea as to what the sentence will be; and it will be some time yet before the decision is fully known; however Sir, I do not expect to be disappointed as to the results as I thought that I could discover, that the General had established a decided influence over a majority of the court, and my only object in puting myself on trial under such degrading and unfavourable circumstances was, to have it in my power (with the assistance of my friends) to lay a state of my case before Congress at their next session; as I well know, if I declined comeing to trial under every disadvantage imposed on me by the Genl., that he would procrastinate my trial and throw the blame on myself, and by that means defeat my object.

These were my reasons Sir, for puting myself on trial under every possible disadvantage, and if a majority of that court has decided against me, their decision is founded on the letter of the order, and consequently absurd! thence arises the necessity of laying the subject before Congress at their next session; who will no doubt, not only conceive it a duty to enquire in to the lawfulness of the Genl. order of the 30th. of April 1801, but also in to the arbitrary persecution with which I have been loaded for upwards of two years! but I have this pleasing reflection General, that I am certain, every independant and virtuous american, will spurn with contempt such base acts, and view these as calculated to destroy the principles, and cast asunder the sinews of our government.

Shall we never assume a national character! are we to be eternally goaded with the arbitrary customs of Europe, is it not evident that the principles on which our government is founded, the rules and regulations as established by law for the government of the army, as well as custom in the revolutionary war, are all with me on this occasion, nor do I doubt of haveing the approbation of every american who has the future welfare of his country at heart, as respects my conduct in this case.

I ask General, must not that cause be radically wrong, whose mover was reduced to the pitiful necessity, of artfully introducing long and laboured communications from the disciples of Marshal Sax,[3] in order to bewilder the Court, and prevent an investigation of the lawfulness of the Genl. order of the 30th. of April 1801, on which my charges were founded? has not one of them ([who]m the general stiles adjutant General to the last (*or lost*) army commanded by General Washington) told us in the language of despotism "His inferiors have nothing left to their discretion, *they must obey.*"[4] Yes, they must obey what the articles of war direct "*Lawful Commands*" and I will here venture to observe, that there never was, and I hope there never will be a Senate of the united States, that would by and with their advice and consent, place any man at the head of the american army avowing such principles. now Sir, let these gentlemen who were so alert in mounting their War Horses at the sound of the Generals Trumpet, lay their hands on their breasts and say, was it either lawful or honorable, to give an opinion whilst a trial was pending.

But do you believe, or even suppose Sir, that americans would submit to have their heads' shorn, and wear *Black* or *Grey* lambskin Caps as Marshal Sax recommended, let those who admire and subscribe to the vagaries of Sax, answer that question. they will doubtless tell us, that he has been considered as a great man, let them have it so, as they will have to acknowledge at the same time, that, (like many others who wish to be thought great men) he was visionary, fond of Change and little in many things. I would here ask the General and the imperist admirers of Sax; what would be the fate of a general in the Prussian service, who would have dared by an order to crop off the queues of the troops under his command, and substitute the Marshals lambskin caps in oposition to the established regulations of his King; I think old Frederick[5] would have spilled at least one pound of snuff on the faceings of his coat, to see his Prussians so treated; nor would it require the second sight of a North Britton to discover what the fate of that General would be? and shall a general in the american army, usurp with impunity such a power, in open violation, of the laws and established regulations; I shall never bring myself to believe that the legitimate authority of our country will suffer so dangerous a presedent to be established in the united States.

I shall close this letter with one other remark on the conduct of the General, in puting into action his plans, in order to gain his point. A few weeks previous to the commencement of my trial, he wrote to the commanding officer at New Orleans,[6] as follows, "You will be pleased to signify to the Gentlemen of the corps, that the President of the united States, without any public expression, has thought proper to adopt our fashion of the hair, by *Cropping*." Now Sir, I cannot believe, or even suppose, that the President of the united States, would stoop to such an expedient, in order to obtain a verdict against me! but if he has parted with his locks, and authorized the General to use his name for the purpose before mentioned, it would astonish me indeed, and for the honor of my country I hope and trust, that it is not the case, but if it should unfortunately be so, it would establish this position, that the President was sensible of the illegality of the order of the 30th. of April 1801, and that by cropping his hair, and adding his weight to that of the General's, it might probably reconcile the army, and prevent the national legislature from investigating the illegality of the order, and of the Generals conduct towards me.

I fear that I have tired your patience with this long letter, but as it may be of some importance to the interest of our country, to throw as much light as possible on a subject founded in tyranny, I shall from time to time take the liberty of stateing to you such matters as have occurred through the course of this unpresedented persecution.

Believe me Dear general, with sincere respect and esteem your Humbl. servt.

Thos. Butler

ALS, DLC. Published in *PMHB*, 17(1893):509–12.

1. Not found.

2. See above Thomas Butler to AJ, July 15; enclosure not found.

3. Hermann-Maurice, Comte de Saxe (d. 1750), marshal of France, instituted discipline and dress reform in the French army during the War of the Austrian Succession (1740–48). In a letter to Henry Dearborn, November 9, 1804 (DNA-RG 107), Wilkinson argued in support of his power to require the short hair style by citing the examples of most European armies, excepting the Prussian which wore queues and the British which left hair styles to the discretion of regimental commanders. Clearly Butler had received a copy of the letter.

4. Before Butler's 1803 court martial Wilkinson had solicited letters from the three surviving senior infantry officers of the Revolution: Major General Charles Cotesworth Pinckney, Brigadier and Adjutant General of the U.S. Army William North, and Colonel William Stephens Smith, adjutant and inspector general on the staffs of Lafayette and Washington. All three agreed on the primacy of subordination (letters included with Wilkinson to Dearborn, November 9, 1804, DNA-RG 107).

5. Frederick II (1712–86), King of Prussia, 1740–86.

6. Constant Freeman (d. 1824), lieutenant colonel of artillery, at this time in command at New Orleans, served in the U.S. Army from 1776 to 1815.

To Thomas Jefferson

Hermitage near Nashville Sept. 23rd. 1805

I have deemed it a duty which my respect for your public and private charactor could not dispense with, to make known to you an act of Gel. J. Wilkinson, which in a measure is supported and Sanctioned by your name. The following is a true extract of a letter written by Genl. J. Wilkinson to the commanding officer at New Orleans, dated the 31st. of March 1805 "you will be pleased to signify to the Gentlemen of the corps, that the President of the united States, without any publick expres-

sion, has thought proper to adopt our fashion of the hair by cropping"[1]
It is considered that means like these to obtain a verdict against Colo.
Butler (when you had refused to express a public sentiment) are improper
and unfair; When your charactor is thus draged in to support the order
and act aluded to, it appears like a prostitution thereof, which should not
be passed unnoticed—This attempt to corrupt the pure streams of Justice, is viewed by every citizen and officer of government within the circle
of my acquaintance with that Just indignation that the nature of the thing
is calculated to inspire.

you are at liberty to make any private or public use of this information
and my name that you may think the nature of the case requires. I hold
myself pledged for the correctness of the extract enclosed. With sentiments of due respect, I am Sir yr. mo. ob. serv.

Andrew Jackson

ALS, DLC-Thomas Jefferson Papers. Endorsed in Jefferson's hand: "recd. Oct 15."
  1. For the source of Jackson's extract, see above, Butler to AJ, August 26.

From Jesse Roach

West florida Baton Rouge 3d. Decemr. 1805

At the request of Dr [Daniel] Sayre[1] I Shall Give you All the information I Can At present recollect Respecting A Negrow taken on the Ohio
and Brout to N. Orleans—I was informd. By One of the hands that was
Along at the time Who lives at the falls of the Ohio that a Certan Koonrod[2] A Dutchman who had the Command of five or six Tobacco Boats
belonging to a frenchman[3] Of that place (the falls ohio) took in a Certan
Negrow who Came to them in a Canoe About 40 miles below the mouth
Of Cumberland and took him to Orleans, at ther Arival the Negrow was
taken and put in prison he also Said that he Advisd. Koonrod to have
Nothing to do with the Negro but the other said that the Negrow was
free he said that Koonrod and the Negrow was often talking privately to
Gether and he believd. Koonrod intended selling the Negrow for his
own—he also informed me the Negrow Said he belongd. to One Jackson
in C[um]berland. I had some thoughts It might be you having often seen
you at Knoxvill And knowing you livd. in that Cuntry And Mentiond. It
to Dr. Sayre the Dr. said he thought It was yours as you had a fellow of
that Description—he told Also that Sd. Koorod he Believd to be a rogue
for he was Constant drunk on ther Voyge and in Consequence of that the
had lost two of ther boats and he intended to Acquaint ther imployer
with his Conduct at his return Shortly after thare Came another of his
hands belo[w] and told the same Story which Confirmd. my belief

I am sr. yours &c

Jesse Roach

NB. I am the son of Jordan Roach[4] On holstun—
NB. the informers Name I Cannot recollect it he was an Elderly Man and
livd. At the falls of Ohio with a large family. I shall wrte to William &
Co[5] by next mail.

ALS, DLC. Roach has not been further identified.
1. Sayre was a physician who had lived briefly with Edward Ward at Hunter's Hill and
advertised his services in "Physic, Midwifery and Surgery" (*Tennessee Gazette*, October 3,
1804, and subsequent issues). He had written Jackson on November 30 concerning Roach's
information.
2. John Conrad (see John Williamson to AJ, December 12, below).
3. Identified by John Williamson in his letter of December 12 as James Berthoud, devel-
oper of Shippingport, a thriving transshipment town below the falls of the Ohio that retained its importance from 1804 to 1825 when the building of a canal around the falls made
Louisville the chief Ohio River port. With his son Nicholas and partners, the Tarascon
brothers, Berthoud owned a mercantile house, a shipyard, and a steamboat.
4. A resident of Jefferson County.
5. Probably Meeker, Williamson, & Patton of New Orleans.

To Norton Pryor

Nashville Decbr. 12th. 1805
Sir
Having been lately on Duck river to explore a tract of land I hold there
and the dificulty I experienced in finding the land marks, induces me to
wright you—The great length of time that has elapsed since your land
was survayed, will make it dificult to trace the lines and find the corners—a number of person apprehensive that it will be impossible to find
the old marks, and substantiate the Identity of the land, are making locations, and marking trees as far as the late purchase from the Cherokees
extends, to be in readiness to enter the land as soon a[s] congress ratifies
the treaty[1]—I would advise you at as early a day as Possible to have your
land resurvayed, and all the corners substantiated and marked. This will
be attended with considerable expence and trouble from the remote situation of your land from the inhabited part of the country, and a great
proportion of it being covered with cain—but perhaps it will be better to
encounter this expence at an early day than riske the loss of the land—
note sir that the locators & survayors may die remove or leave the country in which case it would be impossible to Identify or find the corners,
and should any person settle down on the land, before you could remove
them, this would have to be done—should you be of oppinion that my
Ideas are correct, and incline to have your land resurvayed, and direct
your agent whom you may send on to call on me, I will render him every
aid in my power—or should you have sufficient Confidence in me, I will
have it done should you think proper to direct it; I have no doubt but the
undertaker will take the amount of the expence of survaying and marking in land I have wrote Judge [Joseph] Anderson[2] on this subject, his is

in the same situation with yours, and I have no doubt but he will immediately order his to be resurvayed—rest assured that in writing you this letter I am actuated purely from motives to serve you, and advise you of the dificulty and danger that may result, from a delay in this business. Should you think proper to write me on this subject, address me at Nashville Tennessee—I am sir with due reguard yr mo. ob. serv.

Andrew Jackson

ALS, S. Howard Goldman.
1. Commissioners Daniel Smith and Return Jonathan Meigs concluded treaties of purchase with the Cherokees on October 25 and 27. The Senate ratified these and similar treaties with the Chickasaws and Creeks between December 13 and 19, 1805.
2. Anderson was currently in the Senate. His judicial title was by courtesy of his service as judge of the Territory South of the River Ohio. Jackson's letter to Anderson, December 12, not found. In his reply, January 5, 1806, and in letters of January 13 and March 24, Anderson agreed that the land should be resurveyed and said that he had written Pryor, who did not respond.

From John Williamson

New orleans 12th. Decem 1805

Sir,

Your favor of 22nd. Ulto.[1] came duly to hand, we are glad by it to find you had recovered one of your negros; respecting the other we have & shall continue to make every enquiry for him & should we be successful shall do the best with him for your interest.[2] We shall write Doctor Sayres on the subject. We have learned that three Tobacco boats arrived here in Septemr. and that two more of the same company were lost on the passage. These boats were from Louisville Ky & belonged to James Berthoud there, consigned to a Frenchman of this City, who has given us the names of the Boats which arrived here and the Patroons names viz. Boat Moses—John Conrad Pilot this Conrad had the Command of all—Boat Barbara, Peau[—]Boat Cesar[,] Patroons name not recollected, these three arrived[.] Boat Joseph, Avery[—]Boat Pompey[,] Cork these two lost[.] You will observe none of these names, answer even in sound to the one you mention (Frederick),[3] however it would be well for you to write Mr Berthoud as he could most likely give more correct information than can be obtained here of the boats. These were the only boats which arrived after august. The Insurance Co will not take the risk on rafts of staves as they but seldom would reach this place from the quantity of mud which would gather among & sink them. In Boats they will take the risk at 5 ℔ Cent from Tennessee but not from Kenty. Should you wish yours insured, you will please give us the names of the boats the Patroons the number of hands & the quantity of staves Cotton &c on board each with an order to insure the same which you may rest assured we shall have done for your account. There will be time enough for orders for insurance after you start the boats to arrive here before them or before any acct. of Loss may be received. You will also instruct the Patroon in case of Loss of his Boat to make the necessary protests at the first place he can and to send them on to us by safe conveyance that we may Recover from the Underwriters. It would also be well for you to send a Copy of your orders for Insurance to us—Your staves if here in March we shall be able to dispose of at $35 for Pipe $30 for Hogshead & $18 @ 24 for Barrel or nearly Perhaps more as the quantity in town may be at those prices. Groceries will be purchased on good terms if we have your order early—Sugars are now making & will be plenty & cheap. Other articles Can be had on quite as good terms as at Philada. Crockery also—Woolens & other Dry Goods will shortly be sold here as low as in Philad & on as good terms of Credit. We annex Prices Current & Remain with Respect Sir Your obed Servts.

> John Williamson
> For Meeker Williamson & Patton [4]

Cotton	20 @ 23 Cts.
Beef	$8 @ 9
B[acon?]	15 @ 18/100
Butter	37½/100
Lard	18/100
Pig lead	$10
Pork	14 @ 15
Tobacco	6 @ 6.50 first crop
Bees Wax	40/100
Coffee	35 @ 37/100
Sugar	8 @ 12 depends upon quality
Brandy	1.50
Gin	1 10/100
Spirits	$1
Whiskey	62½ @ 75 Cents

ALS, DLC. Williamson was a partner of the New Orleans dry goods and commission firm, Meeker, Williamson & Patton, that handled the bulk of Jackson & Hutchings's business at this time.

1. Not found.

2. The recovered slave has not been identified. The other was no doubt George, who was still being sought in April 1806 (see John Hutchings to AJ, April 7 and 24, 1806, below).

3. The boat captains have not been further identified. Jackson was misinformed on the name of the boatman who had taken up his runaway. He had told both Williamson and Daniel Sayre "Frederick" (see also Sayre to AJ, November 30).

4. The other members of the firm were William P. Meeker and Charles Patton, who was born in Ireland, moved to New Orleans from Pennsylvania, and held several offices under the territorial government between 1805 and 1809.

1806

Jackson's quarrel with Thomas Swann, a young lawyer, was the opening act in the series of events that ended in May with the death of Charles Henry Dickinson (1780–1806), also a lawyer, from Caroline County, Md. The remote cause was the settlement of a horserace that was never run. Jackson's horse Truxton and Joseph Erwin's Ploughboy were scheduled for a match race on November 28, 1805, but because Ploughboy was not in top condition, Erwin and his son-in-law and partner, Dickinson, elected to pay the forfeit of $800. The dispute began over the payment from lists of promissory notes that had been accepted as stake at the time of making the race. Jackson claimed the right to select notes, at least half of which should be due immediately in order to pay his two partners, John Verell and Samuel Pryor, who were leaving the state. In their statements, Jackson and Erwin (c1761–1829), whom Jackson may have known when they both lived in the Guilford County, N.C., area, substantially agreed that all misunderstanding about the payment had been quickly settled.

But rumors circulated that Jackson had claimed in public conversation that Erwin and Dickinson had attempted to pay the forfeit in notes different from those agreed upon. The story, allegedly first dispensed by Patton Anderson, brought into question the honor of all those involved in the dispute. Thomas Swann picked it up and checked with Jackson, who said, according to Swann, that Dickinson's notes were the same as those listed in the stake; Erwin's were different. Swann relayed the information to Erwin and Dickinson. They met with Jackson on December 28, and, Swann stated, at that time Jackson denied having made an accusation against Erwin and called the peddler of the tale a liar.

Swann considered his honor offended and wrote Jackson the letter below, plainly the first move toward a duel. In his reply (January 7, also below) Jackson warned Swann to stay out of business not his own. Subsequently Jackson declared that Swann, a newcomer to Nashville, lacked the credentials of a gentleman and therefore was not a fit candidate for duels, which occurred only between social equals, but that if he persisted in his harassment, Jackson would cane him. Without doubt Jackson's tactic was mere subterfuge, designed to avoid fighting a man with whom he had no real quarrel. Swann's status as a gentleman would have been well known to Jackson, as Swann arrived from Powhatan County, Va., with a letter of introduction to Jackson's neighbor Edward Ward.

From the outset it was clear that Jackson believed his disagreement was with Dickinson and that Swann was merely a puppet, but the exact cause of the enmity remains an intriguing mystery. Most Jackson biographers have claimed that the dispute was the result in part of insolent remarks Dickinson had made about Rachel. But, unlike Jackson's controversy with John Sevier in 1803, there is in the extant Jackson-Dickinson documents, published or unpublished, no reference to her. The story identifying Rachel Jackson's honor as the cause of the dispute first appeared in the 1860 biography of Jackson by James Parton, whose source for it was Sam Houston. Whatever the fundamental dispute, it was intense enough to keep Dickinson and Jackson at fighting heat for nearly six months, ending only when one lay dead, the other wounded and ostracized, and the Erwins departing for Louisiana. Jane Dickinson (1787–1821), Charles's widow, remained in Nashville and subsequently married John B. Craighead.

From Thomas Swann

NashVille Jany 3rd. 1806

Sir,

I was last evening informed by Mr Dickinson that when called on by Capt Irvin and himself at Mr. Winn's Tavern[1] on saturday last to say whether the notes offered by them, or either of them at the time the forfeit was paid in the Race between Truxton and Ploughboy were the same received at the time of making the Race; you acknowledged they were, and further asserted that whoever was the author of a Report that you had stated them to be different was a damn'd Lyar!

The harshness of this expression has deeply wounded my feelings; it is language to which I am a stranger, which no man acquainted with my character would venture to apply to me, and which should this information of Mr. Dickinson be correct I shall be under the necessity of taking proper notice of.

I shall probably be at Rutherford Court before this reaches you, from whence I shall not return to NashVille before thursday or friday, at which time I shall expect an answer

I am Sir yo: mo: ob: Servt.

Tho: Swann

ALS, THer. Published in *Impartial Review*, February 1; Bassett, 1:123 (text from *Impartial Review*).

1. Richard and B. B. Winn's inn was on the courthouse square.

Affidavit of Joseph Erwin re Forfeit in the Truxton-Ploughboy Race

[January 4, 1806]

Being requested By Genl. A Jackson to say in what way the forfet was paid By Mr. Dickinson & my self to him in the race Truckston against plowboy—the morning Genl. Jackson was to receve the forfet Mr. D. & my self was of the opinion that we had a right to pay the forfet in any of the Same Notes which he Gel. Jackson had agreed to receve in the stake—Mr. D took his List of Notes and Selected out of them such as he had rather part with & put them in to my hand to pay the forfet when I presented them togather with my own the Genl. objected saying he thought he ought to have Choise of the Notes & ask'd me for Mr. D's List of Notes. I put my hand in my pocket & Examied my papers & Could Not find the List, I told him I thought I had mislaid it But on a moments refliction recolected that I had gaven it to Mr. D. I stept to the Door and Cald on him for the List which he Emediately produced—the Gel. observed that he wanted as many Notes that ware Dew as would pay Two of his partenars that ware Not resdenters of this state I told him I had No objections if Mr. Dickinson had None Mr. D. answerd he had None—the List of Notes ware thrown on the Table for Genl. Jackson's Choise after the Genl. had taken from the List of Notes such as he was pleased with togather with two of my Notes there remaind a Ballence Dew to him of Ninety Nine Dollars & some Cents I wish'd the Genl. to take a Nother Note for it, he observed he had rather have my own paper for that sum which I gave to the house of king & kirson,[1] the Genl. appeared to Bee well plased & this has Been his uniform statement to me at all times since. Gaven under my hand this 4th January 1806

Jos Erwin

ADS, T. Published in *Tennessee Gazette*, June 28. Endorsed: "This Letter was handed me by Mr. J. Erwin open. I have took the liberty of folding it up—and putting on seal. from yr frend Chas. S. Carson."

1. King, Carson & King, the Nashville merchant house that included among its partners Charles S. Carson, the intermediary in the delivery of this affidavit.

To Thomas Swann

Hermitage January 7th. 1806

Sir

Late last evening was handed me amonghst my returns from Haysborough, a letter from you of the 3rd Instant stating information recd. from Mr Dickinson &c &c &c[1]

Was it not for the attention due to a stranger, taking into view its Tenor & stile I should not notice its Receipt

Had the information stated to have been recd from Mr D. stated a direct application of harsh language to you—had you not have known that the statement as stated in your letter was not correct had it not taken place in the same house where you then were, had not Mr. D. been applied to by me to bring you forward, when your name was mention and he declined, had I not the next morning had a conversation with you upon the same subject, and lastly did not your letter hold forth a threat of "proper notice" I should have given <all these things> your letter a direct answer—Let me sir, observe one thing; that I never wantonly sport with the feelings of innocence—nor am I ever awed into measures—If incautiously I inflict a wound, I always hasten to remove it. If offence is taken when non is offerred or intended, it gives me no pain—If a tale is listened to many days after the discourse should have taken place when all parties are under the same roof—I alway leave the person to Judge of the motives that induced the information, draw their own conclusions and act accordingly—there are certain traits that always accompanies the gentleman and man of truth—the moment he hears harsh expressions applied to a friend, he will immediately communicate it—that an <open> explanation may take place—*when the base, poltroon and cowardly <assassin> tale bearer, will always act in the <dark> back ground* you can apply the Two latter, to Mr Dickinson, and see which best fits him, <and> I write it for his eye—and the latter I *emphatically intend for him*—But sir it is for you to Judge for yourself, draw your own conclusions, and when your Judgt. is matured, to act accordingly—when the conversation dropt. between Mr D. & myself, I thought it was at an end. as he wishes to blow the coal I am ready to light to a blaze that it may be consumed at once, and finally extinguished—Mr. D. has given you the information, the subject of your letter—in return & in Justice to him I request you to shew him this. I set out this morning to S. W. Point[2] I will return at a short day—and at all times be assured I hold myself answerable for any of my conduct, and should any thing herein contained give Mr. D. the Spleen—I will furnish him with an anodine as soon as I return

The attention I have paid your note arises from your short acquaintance with me for I repeat again under existing circumstances, had it not have been for the respect due to the first note of a stranger it should have passed without notice

I am Sir yr. Ob. Serv.

Andrew Jackson

P.S. Note sir there was no notes delivered at the time of making the race as stated in your letter, neither was the meeting between me & Mr. D. at

Mr Wins on that subject—it was introduced by Mr. D. to change the subject I took him out to converse on—

ALS draft, THer. Published in *Impartial Review*, February 1; Bassett, 1:124 (text from *Impartial Review*).
1. See above.
2. Jackson's business at Fort Southwest Point, on the site of present-day Kingston, is not known, but it is possible he intended to visit Thomas Norris Clark, a longtime friend and occasional business associate who was also peripherally involved in the Burr affair.

From Charles Henry Dickinson

10th Jany 1806

Sir
  Last evening was shewn me by Mr Thomas Swann, a letter from you in Answer to a letter he had written you,[1] respecting a conversation that took place between you & myself at Mr Winn's tavern, (most of which was in the presence of Mr Samuel [Dorsey] Jackson[2] & Capt Joseph Erwin) on account of notes of hand exhibited by Capt Erwin & myself to stake on the race Truxton against Ploughboy & those notes that we brought forward to settle the forfeit with—I there informed you of a report Patton Anderson[3] had given publicity to; that a different list was produced when we were about paying the forfeit, from the one that we were to make our stake out of—& that he had it from you which you denied ever sanctioning; I then informed you I had another author, who said he did hear you say that a different list, was brought by Capt Erwin which as soon as I mentioned and before I could give my author, you declared the Author had told a Damned Lye that so far from saying so, you had never intimated such a thing to any one and immediately asked, who was the Author; to which I answered Mr Thomas Swann, you wished Mr Swann to be called forward; which I declined lest Mr Swann might think that I wished to throw the burden off my shoulders on his and the business then being entirely between Mr Swann & yourself—Mr. Swann asserting that you had told him that a different list was produced by Capt Erwin & you as possitively denying it—after the report was circulated by Patton Anderson; Mr. Swann (as he informed me), was anxious to know if Patton Anderson was your Herald and further as he had been introduced to Capt Erwin as a Gentleman, he was desirous of knowing if any improper conduct had been attempted and after he had mentioned the business to you, you answered concerning the stake & forfeit as stated above. Your letter is so replete with equivation that it is impossible for me to understand you; but in one part of your letter you say "had you not known that the statement of Mr D was not correct" which is denying, that you contradicted what Mr Swann had asserted. Should that be your meaning, I can prove it not Only by the assertions but oaths of Mr Saml Jackson & Capt Erwin whom I shall have sworn that the

world may know who can prove himself *the Gentleman* & *man of truth*. Why should you have wished to have Mr Swann called, had you have not denied what he had asserted? and Do you pretend to call a Man a *tale bearer* for telling that which is and can be proven to be the truth? Mr Swann after he understood an interview was to take place between you & myself; Gave me liberty to make use of his name and on our meeting which was a few days after; he asked me if I had made use of his name & what you had said, an impartial statement of which I detailed to him—As [to] the word *Coward, I think it as* [appli]cable to yourself as any one I [know] and I shall be very glad when an opportunity serves to know in what manner you give your Anodines and hope you will take in payment one of my most moderate Cathartics. Yours at Command

Charles Dickinson

ALS, DLC; Extract (mainly in AJ's hand), THi. Extract published in *Impartial Review*, February 15, and in Bassett, 1:128–29 (text from *Impartial Review*). Endorsed: "C. Dickeson letter recd. from the hand of Corbin Lee 24th January Nashville." Jackson apparently received Dickinson's letter when he returned from Southwest Point.
   1. See above, AJ to Swann, January 7, and Swann to AJ, January 3.
   2. Jackson (1755–1836) was a partner in the Philadelphia mercantile firm of John B. Evans & Co. before moving to Tennessee, probably about 1800. He bought Robert Hays's 1,500-acre home plantation when it was sold in 1806 to satisfy judgments against Hays. Although several sources identify Samuel as a cousin of Andrew's, the editors have been unable to confirm the relationship. For his affray with Andrew Jackson, see Court minutes in *State* v. *Andrew Jackson*, November [9], 1807, below.
   3. Anderson (d. 1810), was a brother of William Preston Anderson. He and Jackson shared an interest in horseracing, and from time to time Jackson entrusted him with tasks involving horses. Allegedly he recruited troops for Burr's expedition.

From Thomas Swann

Nashville, January 12th, 1806.

GEN. ANDREW JACKSON.

   Think not that I am to be intimidated by your threats. No power terrestial shall prevent the settled purpose of my soul. The statement I have made in respect to the notes is substantialy correct: The torrent of abusive language with which you have assailed me is such, as every gentleman should blush to hear; your menaces I set at defiance, and now demand of you that reparation which one gentleman is intitled to receive of another: My friend[1] the bearer of this is authorised to make compleat arrangments in the field of honor.[2]

Thomas Swann.

Text from *Impartial Review*, February 15. Original not found. Published in Bassett, 1:139.
   1. Nathaniel A. McNairy (1779–1857), a lawyer and brother of federal district court judge John McNairy.
   2. Jackson declined the challenge, threatening instead to cane Swann. The two met, at least partly by design, on January 13 at Winn's Tavern, where Jackson landed a few whacks

with his cane in a near comic-opera battle broken up by friends when guns were drawn. Each presented his side of the argument in the *Impartial Review*, Swann on February 1 and Jackson on February 15, after which Swann was nearly forgotten as the focus shifted to Dickinson. Determined not to accept his humiliation quietly, Swann published in the *Impartial Review*, May 24, half a dozen letters from prominent Virginians, testifying to his character as a gentleman.

From James Robertson

Nashville Febary 1st. 1806—

Sir

if I have wandred in aney maner from the true line of Frendship, will you pass it over as an Errore of one who wishes you well from the bottom of my hart, and beleave it my dutey to Render all service in my power, to my Country and Frends. I cannot Fail in my conjectual that you are in dispotion Eaquail or more the frend of the Human Race than myself and when I vew your superiour compacity I See thare is no Comparrison who is and may be most yousefull in Sociaty. this with other Reasons Compeld me to drop you these incorect scroals, hoping you will Reflect on there Contents, and not suffer pation to git the upper hand of your good Sence, and displese your Frends to gratify your Enimyes if any you have. disagreable as the subject is. I must tell you that this day I have seen a publication in [Thomas] Eastons paper[1] sined Tho: Swan. the sight of this may Erritate you so as in heat of pation, to do an act, that Sociaty may be deprived of a yousefull member, and on Reflection I am sertain your good senc will dictate to you that no Honer can be attached Ither to the conquered or Conquorer, and satainly the Consequances ought to be taken in vew. Should you fall, your tallance are lost to your County, besides the Erreperable loss your Famuley and frends must sustane and on the other hand, were you to Resque your life and in defening it take the life of your Fellow mortal, might this not make you misarable so long as you lived, instant Colo Burr. I sepose if dueling could be jestifiable, it must have bin in his case, and it is beleaved he has not had ease in mind sinc the fatal hour he killed Hambelton[2] will you pardon me my frend when I tell you that I have bin longer in the world than you have and ought to have heard the opinions of people more than you have, and do heare the fals honer of dueling Redeculed by most of thinking persons and I assure you that your frends do think a man of your standing ought to say but littel about duling and all I have spoake with think you ought to take no notice of the peice above mentioned. young hot heded persons to be in the fashon of the presant age, may talk of killing there fellow Creater, and do not Reflict that they are doing an act that will not be in thare power to Repare. I think you must have observe that persons killed in duel is sildom lemented and if ever so maney good trates are named in thare Charrectors, it will be aded at last that they were imprudant, and I cannot find whare aney honer is attached to dueling. if I had aney dout of being in your frendship, I should not have taken the liberty to trobel you with sentiments on this subject, but as I have from the Earleys acquaintance bin attached to you and the long acquaintanc and Frendship I have formed with the Famuley you are conected with makes it my dutey to give you my opinion. I should have said advice, if I had bin caperble of giving you such. and sir should I be so fortinate as to gain a Reflicting thought from you on my hasty and Complycated Centiments, it will give grate concilation that I have had the attention of so perticlar frend, or if your bravery was in the smallest manner doubted I should not have gon to such lenth. once for all let me tell you, that you will have more than ten to one which will applad your prudance in avoyeding a duel. your acquaintainces think your pation is such, that if you were to git into a duel I assure you it is my opinion you would have a full sheare of the blame attached to your self. I readely agree that in former days I might have suffered my pations to have over Ruled prudance and in hast have taken the life of my fel[low] mortal, but shour I am that I never after should hav[e had] one pleasant moment but on Refliction of the Cosa[quences] and in open vilation to the laws of my contry I have of late vewed Duelling with abhorance. Sir I feare I have all Ready truspased on your patiance and conclude with my best wishes for your heth and sucsess while I am your most Humb Sevt

Jas: Robertson

ALS, DLC. Published in *Cincinnati Commercial*, January 8, 1880.
1. Eastin (c1788–1865) established the *Impartial Review and Cumberland Repository* in December 1805 and continued as its editor until 1809. In 1810 he and James Walker founded the *Western Chronicle* in Columbia, but by 1812 Eastin had left the paper. He later published newspapers in Alabama and Florida. Apparently Robertson wrote this letter immediately upon seeing Swann's statement in the *Impartial Review* of February 1 (full text of Swann's statement published in Bassett, 1:122–26).
2. Alexander Hamilton.

To *Thomas Eastin*

February 10th. 1806—

Mr Eastin

The respect I owe to the world makes it necessary, that a publication under the signature of "Thomas Swann" in your "Impartial Review" of the 1st. instant,[1] should be noticed.

To impose upon the public attention, through the medium of your usefull paper is not my wish, but as Mr Swann has endeavoured to exhibit to the public eye, a statement of his case; and charector, an impartial public, will indulge such supplementary remarks, as may be necessary to compleat the caricature—In justice to Mr Swann, and least the figure when finished, may appear the work of differrent artists, the ground work, and even the various materials of which his drawing is composed, shall be carefully attended to. Not however in the new invented stile of support, adopted by his friends, Mr Nathl A McNairy and Samuel Jackson, one the accredited agent of Mr Swann, and the other invockd. in his support. To a perfect understanding of the case of the complainant, let it briefly be premised, that a course race was made between Capt. Erwin, and myself, for $2000, in cash notes payable at the day of the race—It was sugested, that all Capt. Erwins notes were not payable precisely at the day; an accomodation was proposed, and a *schedule of the notes*, and Charles S Carsons verbal assumpsit (being present) was offered for $440 or thereabouts, which was accepted—Mr Erwin was previously informed that I had not any power over one half of the bet, as Major Verrell and Capt [Samuel] Prior[2] who were interested in the other half were about to leave the country, that one half must be payable at the day of the race; the other which respected myself and Major W. P. Anderson was not material.

Mr Charles Dickason is the son in law to Capt. Erwin, and was interested in the race, as it is understood—This race was afterwards drawn, on account of the indisposition of Capt. Erwins horse, upon an agreement to pay $800, as a forfeit—The payment of this forfeit, is the circumstance, which gave rise to the conduct of Mr Swann, his publication, the following certificates, and subjoined remarks—The fact to be decided by the public, is, whether Mr Swann in his solicitude "to know the true statement," though unconcerned, has omitted in his assertion to Mr Dickason, and the public, some material fact, or in other words, whether I asserted that which was untrue—

Mr Hutchings has truly stated the assertion to which I have uniformly adhered, upon which Mr Swann and myself were at Issue; that issue has been decided; whether in a moral manner, casuists must determine, upon the following certificates, and analysis—

(here insert the Certificates No. 1. 2. 3. 4. 5. 6. 7. 8. 9.—10—11)[3]

Mr. Swann in his letter and publication in your paper of the 1st. instant, states "that the notes offered by Capt Joseph Erwin at the time of paying the forfeit &c were differrent from those Genl Jackson agreed to receive." What does Dickason his informant state? That Swann said *a differrent list was produced*. Mr Swann should have recollected, that the *list of notes*, and *notes offered*, were different—The first was produced, when an accomodation was proposed, respecting the commutation of notes not payable, for those that were—the second to the payment of the forfeit, a fact which took place sometime after the accomodation. By the accomodation one half was payable; when the notes offered: no list was produced—

How does Mr Swann prove the position he has taken, that differrent notes from the list were offered—

1st. By his own assertion, Mr Hutchings <and Mr Patton Anderson>[4] was present see his affidavit—

2nd Mr Charles Dickasons information is referred to. See an extract from Mr Dickasons letter.[5] he states no such thing, but refers to a *differ-rent list*. These two constative informants, speak, one of *differrent notes actually offered*, the other of a *differrent list of notes*. Happy concordance! These two gentlemen possess the key of consistancy.

3rd. Mr. Samuel Jackson is next refered to. Mr Swan has not been so obliging as to give in any certificate, nor even a quotation from Mr Jackson, of whom he was so polite, as to say in presence of Major Purdy, that he was a damd. Rascal! (an appropriate witness for Mr Swann) It is to be lamented that he did not, but it is to be hoped, that Colo. Hays and Mr Robert Butlers certificates, may ease Mr Swann of the labour of vindicating his friend Samuel, from any imputation. No doubt of their having well understood each other. Mr Jackson flatly calls Mr Swann a Rascal.[6] that they have confidence in each other, we have no doubt. Mr Jackson in his oppinion of Mr Swann—has disclosed the ground on which this good understanding rests. Upon principles of reason, and of law a man cannot discredit his own witness

4th. Mr Nathaniel A. McNairy is quoted by Mr Swann in support of his assertion of my inconsistancy—This young man has industriously acquired such a reputation, as to make it an arduous task, to add to it. But as the selected supporter of Mr Swann, in the cause of consistancy and bravery, it would being doing injustice to omit him—His certificate, which is only marked by a quotation, is introduced with Triumph. It is without date or signature.[7] This hopefull youth, who forgets today, what he has uttered yesterday, thinks himself secure: but read Messhrs. [John] Beards[8] & Purdys certificates and Mr Coffees affidavit, and see what credit can, or ought to be attached to the statement of such a charector.

Mr Coffee states in substance, that I would cane Mr Swann if he attempted to support the statement he had made: That he understood Mr Swann afterwards wrote me,[9] that the statement was substantially correct: That agreable to promise I did cane him: That Mr Swann said after this chastisement, that he had wishd to pave the way for an explanation: That he was present at a conversation immediately afterwards, between Mr. N. A. McNairy the friend of Mr Swann, and myself; when among other things Mr McNairy proposed a court of honour, note reader this champion of honour had once before endeavoured to evade a contest, by this singular device—saying at the same time, that his acquaintance with Mr Swann would not Justify his supporting him as a gentleman; and if Mr Swanns papers did not support that charector, he would withdraw himself. Note Messhrs. Beard & Major Purdy state in substance, that this young Squire of high renown, told them he observed to me, that if Swanns Charector as a gentleman was not known, he would meet me. Mr Coffee further states that this friend of Mr Swann, expressed much concern that the affair had terminated in so rash a manner; that Mr Swann had wished to see me, for the purpose of an explanation—that Mr Swann and himself had misconstrued the statement made; or in other words found out that they were in an error. How shamefull is it then to persist in it—

But Mr McNairy tells Mr Coffee that the *caning* was the only cause of complaint. Then, why bring the points of veracity and consistancy into view, in the publication? When Mr Coffee called on Mr McNairy to know what he thought of my proposition for redress, observing to him it was all he might expect, he declined taking any further part in the affair, and observed, he supposed it would end in a publication in Mr Swanns defence. The Squire had recourse to the same method on a former occasion and what effect it produced "the world might Judge."[10] Mr Coffee further tells us, that he was present when I called on Mr McNairy to know if he had made use of the language stated in Major Purdys & Mr. Beards certificates. Here the valiant squires memory failed him, he denied that he ever said it, nor "did he wish such an idea to go forth."[11] Major Purdy being convenient, was called on. He told the squire, what he had asserted, to which he answered, that Major Purdy must have misunderstood him. Modest youth! But the Major tells him he could not, for he gave his own words. *Misunderstood—How.* did Mr Beard misunderstand him also! This young man has either a vicious habit of deviating from the truth, or a natural weakness of memory, either of which is equally pernicious to society, and renders him a fit compeer for his friend. It is dificult to find an appropriate epithet, for a charector, who descends to state falshood in a situation, where the honour of a man is at stake; where truth and Justice ought to be the order of the day, with a person chosen to accompany another to the field of honour: and in many cases where integrity is the only shield of innocence. However, the Squires conduct is in perfect unison with a recent act on the field of honour. He fired before the word;[12] it was declared to be an accident; and this prevarication, or whatever you may please to call it, I suppose he will declare to be another. Combine these two acts, with the whole military fighting feats of this young Squire, and with his deviations from the path of candeur & truth in civil life, he is in my oppinion, (and I think the world will agree with me) deprived of that priviledge in society which the gentleman and man of honour ought in all cases in Justice to obtain.

Thus reader, I have endeavoured to finish the picture. The ground work only, appear to have been conceived by the author of the publication. The materials existing in the statements of his witnesses, may with propriety be said to have been selected by the author. They are however, the natural result of those chosen by himself. An application of such as were offered have only been made. It is true that the drapery sometime exhibits, black instead of white, but this the reader will excuse, when he considers that consistantly with the plan I adopted, no other materials could be had—A little more indulgence whilst a few other parts of the publication is noticed—

Mr Swann states in substance, he was attackd. in a defenceless sit-

uation, and off his guard; read the certificates of Messhrs. Coffee &
[Thomas Augustine] Claibourne[13] <and Patton Anderson, Judge>—
Judge for yourselves. His own declaration shews that he came into the
room, knowing I was there for the purpose (to make use of his own
words) "*to pave the way for an accomodation.*"[14] These Gentlemen state
that Mr Swann was about drawing a pistol. ¿Why did he not do it. Any
man can answer this question? Recollect reader his boast of "*certain
death in case I attempted to cane him.*"[15] He had previously every assurance that I would not treat him like the gentleman, but that a caning
would be given him in return for a challenge.

Here then the hero steps forward with all the ostensible bravery of a
duellist; the faithfull promise was executed and notwithstanding his gas-
gonading expressions "*that no power terrestial should prevent the settled
purpose of his soul*"[16] he shrunk at the sight of a pistol, and dropd. his
hands for quarters, although one of them was placed on, and in the act of
drawing his own. Is this like the man of courage who said "*that instant
death should be the consequence,*" or is it like the *coward* when his
settled purpose fail him. When true bravery is assailed or attacked in any
way, it will shew to the world its genuiness, yes, as much bravery is necessary in the act of self defence in all cases as in the act of duelling. See Mr
Coffees affidavit and Mr Claibourne's certificate

Mr Swann on this occasion has impertinantly and inconsistantly ob-
truded himself—he has acted the puppet and lying valet for a worthless,
drunken, blackguard scounderal, who now is at war, and flatly contra-
dicts and gives Mr Swann the lye. Here the reader can compare the extract from Charles Dickasons letter, with Mr Swanns publication—

Mr Swann states his desire to obtain satisfaction but "an ingenious
evasion had been discovered."[17] How does this agree with the evidence
of Mr Coffee and Major Purdy. He is told he can have satisfaction in any
manner, in any way or situation, but that I will not degrade myself by the
acceptance of a challenge from a stranger whose acts and conduct had
been inconsistant with that of the gentleman—from a man who was capable of acting and writing to me in the manner Mr Swann had done in
his letters of the 3rd and 12th of January, the former of which has been
published and the latter (*which* is *inserted for the edification*, as well as,
information of the public) reads as follows

(here insert Mr Swanns letter—No. 12)[18]

But Mr Swann complains I would not acknowledge him a gentleman,
and calls for prooff of the contrary. If therefore; I have not shewn suffi-
ciantly that he has no Just claim to the appellation of a gentleman, let
him bring forth his letters introductory or certificates so much talked
of—I was badly advised the day I chastised Mr Swann, If those Vouchers
were not given by men in Virginia of known immoral and disreputable
charector—

Is it worth while before I take my everlasting farewell of this group, to notice the last falshood asserted by Mr Swan in his publication—The fact is, I am only thirty nine years of age,[19] and if god should permit me to live thirty nine years more, I will never again be caught before the public, in competition with Mr Swann or any of his auxiliaries.

Andrew Jackson

ALS copy, T; AL draft (fragment), THer. Published in *Impartial Review*, February 15; Bassett, 1:127–39. Bassett took his text from the *Impartial Review*, which included the twelve extracts and affidavits omitted from Jackson's copy. Originals of the enclosures, including the extract of Dickinson's letter of January 10 in Jackson's hand, are in the Tennessee State Library and Archives.

1. See Thomas Swann to the Public, in *Impartial Review*, February 1, and Bassett, 1:122–26.

2. Kentucky sportsman Pryor (d. 1810) had a quarter-interest in Truxton's aborted November race. In December 1806 Pryor bought Jackson & Hutchings's Clover Bottom store and the next year moved to Davidson County.

3. The enclosures were: (1) affidavit of John Hutchings, February 5; (2) extract of Charles Dickinson to AJ, January 10; (3) affidavit of John Coffee, February 5; (4) statement of John Baird, [cFebruary 1]; (5) certificate of Robert Purdy, January 31; (6) certificate of Robert Hays, February 3; (7) Robert Butler to AJ, February 3, including certificate; (8) certificate of Thomas A. Claiborne, February 1; (9) William P. Anderson to AJ, February 8; (10) certificate of Charles S. Carson, February 8; (11) statement of Robert Purdy, February 8, all published in Bassett, 1:128–35.

4. Jackson's published letter did not include a statement from Patton Anderson.

5. Except for minor spelling differences and the insertion of italics, the extract is faithful to Dickinson's letter of January 10, above. Jackson omitted a brief passage near the beginning ("most of which was in the presence. . . to settle the forfeit with") and the remainder of the text following the words "Your letter is so replete with equivation. . . ."

6. The statements of Purdy, Hays, and Butler repeat remarks by Samuel Jackson to the effect that Swann was a liar and a rascal for having reneged on an offer to loan money.

7. Refers to Swann's quotation of McNairy in his publication in the February 1 *Impartial Review*.

8. Baird was a prosperous Nashville merchant.

9. See above, Swann to AJ, January 12.

10. Quoted from Swann's publication of February 1.

11. Quoted from Coffee's affidavit of February 5, paraphrasing McNairy.

12. Jackson was referring to McNairy's duel with Thomas J. Overton. Coffee's affidavit published in the *Impartial Review*, February 15, raised questions about McNairy's offer to fight Jackson in Swann's stead, prompting McNairy to publish an attack on Coffee's veracity (*Impartial Review*, February 22; Bassett, 1:140). On March 1 the two fought a duel in which McNairy again fired before the word, wounding Coffee in the thigh.

13. Claiborne (c1775–1815), W.C.C. Claiborne's physician brother, moved to Tennessee in 1801, represented Davidson County in the General Assembly for one term, and moved to Natchez in 1809.

14. Quoted from Coffee's affidavit.

15. Approximate quotation from Swann's statement of February 1.

16. See above, Swann to AJ, January 12.

17. Source of quotation and its significance have not been identified.

18. See above, Swann to AJ, January 12.

19. In the February 1 publication, Swann said Jackson was forty-five.

Despite the heated exchanges between Jackson and Swann, with the consequent involvement of Charles Dickinson, the rescheduled match be-

tween Truxton and Ploughboy took place as planned. Truxton won both heats easily although handicapped by two lame legs (see AJ to John Hutchings, April 7, below).

Announcement of Race between Truxton and Ploughboy

March 1st, 1806.

CLOVER BOTTOM RACE.

On Thursday the 3d of April next, will be run, the greatest and most interesting match race ever run in the Western country, between *Gen. Jackson's* horse TRUXTON 6 years old, carrying 124 lbs. and *Capt. Joseph Erwin's* horse PLOUGHBOY 8 years old, carrying 130 lbs. Those horses run the two mile heats, for the sum of 3000 dollars.

No stud horses can be admitted within the gates, but such as contend on the TURF—and all persons are requested not to bring their dogs to the field, as they will be shot without respect to the owners.

Text from *Impartial Review*, March 15. Original not found. Published in Bassett, 1:143. The announcement also appeared in the March 22 and 29 issues of the *Impartial Review*, and a shorter version, dated March 15, was published in the *Tennessee Gazette*, March 22.

In the letter below, John Brahan reported to John Overton, then in Jonesboro for the sitting of the Washington District Superior Court, on an aborted duel between Jackson and Nathaniel McNairy. No other documents or newspaper accounts of the event have been found.

John Brahan to John Overton

South West Point 8th March 1806

Dear Sir,

By a gentleman directly from Nashville I have received a letter from Mr. William Wright merchant of that place enclosing to me a news paper (one of Eastins) which details some of the military operations in that quarter. Mr. Wright states that Mr. N. A. McNairy challenged Genl Jackson & that Mr. [James?] Roney[1] was friend to Mr. McNairy & Majr. Wm. P Anderson to General Jackson, that the challenge was accepted, and the parties met, on the field, where a compromise was made on the Ground said to be honorable to both parties—Now Coffee comes on the ground; it is said that he attacked McNary at Winns Tavern with a loaded whip, that in the scuffle Mr McNairy got the whip from Mr. Coffee: at which time Mr. Coffee drew a Pistol. McN. then in the presence of the

Company called Coffee a pergured Villian & Cowardly rascal—Mr Coffee told him if if he repeated that again he would shoot him, McN repeated; I am told that this affray took place between Mr. Coffee & Mr McNairy, before Mr. McN challenged Genl Jackson—

Yesterday there was a Gentleman & Lady at Mr. [Thomas Norris] Clarks, who lives within five miles of Nashville, they told Mr. Clark that Mr. Coffee & McMcNairy had met & fought a day or two before they left Nashville, & that Mr. Coffee had recived a slight wound. I am told that before the fight between Coffee & McNairy, that Genl Robertson had interfered in order to put a Stop to the Business;[2] & had got the whole of the parties bound over, to Keep the peace—Capt Purdy is married[3] he has kept out of the action, and I am glad of it; I now enclose you Eastins paper, which contains all the publications on the existing wars now in the vicinity of Nashville.

I have taken the liberty to inclose you a few lines to Capt McCormack,[4] you have his note at home; if you see him please present this order to him & he will probably let you have the money; with great respect & esteem I am Dear sir yr. mo. ob Sevt

John Brahan

ALS, THi.

1. Neither Roney nor Wright has been further identified.

2. On February 28, Thomas Swann announced that the civil authorities had prohibited his replying to Jackson's recent article (*Impartial Review*, March 1). See also above, James Robertson to AJ, February 1.

3. Purdy married Elizabeth, daughter of Philip Philips, who had settled in Nashville about 1795.

4. Not identified.

From Aaron Burr

Washington City. 24 Mar. 1806

Dear Sir

Your letter of this 1st. Jan.[1] arrived here whilst I was in S. Carolina and was not received till about two months after it's date.

You have doubtless before this time been convinced that we are to have no war if it can be avoided with honor, or even without—The object of the administration appears to be to treat for the purchase of the Floridas, and the secret business which so long occupied Congress is believed to be an appropriation of two Millions of dollars for that purpose—This secret is a secret to those only who are best entitled to know it—our own citizens—[2]

But notwithstanding the pacific temper of our Govt. there is great reason to expect hostility, arising out of the expedition under General [Francisco de] Miranda[3]—This expedition was fitted out at New-York and the object is pretty well known to be an attempt to revolutionize the Caraccas, which is the native country of Miranda—Though our Government disavows all knowledge of this proceeding, which however is not justified to the entire satisfaction of the public, yet foreign courts will hold it responsible for the conduct of an armament composed of American citizens and openly fitted out in an American Port; and it would not surprize me if on a knowledge of these facts at Paris and Madrid our vessels in the ports of those kingdoms should be seized and measures taken for the reduction of Orleans—If these apprehensions should be justified by events, a military force on our part would be requisite and that force might come from your side of the mountains—It is presumed that West Tennessee could not spare more than two regiments—

I am glad to learn that you have had your division reviewed; but you ought not to confine your attention to those men, as officers, who accidentally bear commissions—your country is full of fine matterrials for an army and I have often said that a brigade could be raised in West Ten. which would drive double their number of frenchmen off the Earth—I take the liberty of recommending to you to make out a list of officers from Colonel down to Ensign for one or two regiments, composed of fellows fit for business & with whom you would trust your life and your honor—If you will transmit to me this list,[4] I will, in case Troops should be called for, recommend it to the department of war and I have reason to believe that, on such an occasion, my advice would be listened to—

But Mr [John] Randolph's denunciations of the President and the secretary of state engage at present more of public attention than all our collisions with foreign powers or than all the great events in the theatre of Europe—I did not hear Mr R—but am told that he charges the President with duplicity and imbecility—that he (the Prest.) used a bold language in his message to the two houses to amuse the public and secretly exercised his influence to prevent any vigorous measure, alluding to the business transacted with closed doors for the purchase of the Floridas. I will send you Mr. R's speeches as soon as published but presume that the acrimony which was manifested on the floor will not appear without some qualification in print[5]

You will herewith receive two documents respecting Barbary affairs[6]— It deserves to be remarked that though these facts were all known to the admn. long before the meeting of Congress, yet Col. [Tobias] Lear still holds his office and enjoys the Confidence and support of the executive— Nevertheless, it is thought that the treaty with Tripoli will not be ratified by the Senate—[7]

all these things, my dear sir, begin to make reflecting men to think— make many good patriots doubt and some to despond—

I am dear Sir faithfully & affectionately your friend & st.

A. Burr

ALS, NjMoHP. Published in Parton, 1:313–14.

1. Not found.

2. Both the House and Senate met in secret session in January and approved Jefferson's request for funds to purchase the Floridas from Spain through the French government. On March 13 Madison was able to offer $5 million for the Floridas and Texas.

3. About two hundred American recruits were aboard the boat dispatched by Miranda (1750–1816) from New York in February as part of his expedition to free Spain's American colonies from the mother country.

4. The list has not been found but was prepared, according to John Coffee, who stated in 1828 that James Robertson, Jackson, and "sundry others of the old respectable citizens" met in Nashville to make such a list "and as I supposed sent it on to him" (*United States Telegraph Extra*, October 11, 1828).

5. During the House debate on a proposal for non-importation of British goods, March 5 and 6, Randolph had accused Jefferson of duplicity in raging against Spain's encroachments in his December 2 message while secretly negotiating to avoid collision by paying France for Spain's territories on the American continent (*Annals of Congress*, 9 Cong., 1 sess., pp. 555–74, 592–605).

6. Enclosures not identified.

7. On April 12 the Senate ratified the treaty with Tripoli concluded by Consul General Lear in June 1805.

From Aaron Burr

Washn. 5 ap. 06

Dear Sir

Agreeably to my promise you will find here with enclosed a copy of Mr. Randolp's speech—it is accompanied by one of Mr. [James] Sloan a quaker-farmer from N. Jersey—Since these speeches have been published, the injunction of secrecy has been taken off and a Copy of the Journal of the proceedings with closed doors is also enclosed—[1]

Though you may not be immediately able to answer yet I beg that you will not delay to ackledge the receipt of my letter of the last month[2]—I am about to visit Philada. but you may continue to address me at this place—my letters will be carefully forwarded—

Your friend & st.

A. Burr

ALS, Ms-Ar. Published in Parton, 1:315.

1. Enclosures not found but were probably copies of Randolph's speech of March 5 and Sloan's reply on March 7. The resolution to publish the journal of the House in secret session was passed on March 31 (*Annals of Congress*, 9 Cong., 1 sess., 555–74, 605–23. The secret journal appears as an appendix to the proceedings, pp. 1117–44).

2. See above, Burr to AJ, March 24.

To John Hutchings

Hermitage April 7th. 1806

Sir

By last mail I wrote you enclosing Doctor [Benjamin] Rawlings Draft on Major [William] Bradford,[1] which was found in the Desk, some time after you left us which I hope has reached you in due time to present to the Major for payment—

On the third instant, the race between Truxton and ploughboy was run, in the presence of the largest concourse of people I ever saw assembled, unless in an army—Truxton had on Tuesday evening before got a serious hurt in his thigh, which occassioned it to swell verry much, and had it not have been for myself, would have occasioned, the forfeight to have been paid—but this I was determined not to permit—The appearance of Truxton induced his friends not to bet—This was unfortunate—or carthage would have been destroyed—All things prepared, the horses started, and Truxton under every disadvantage beat him with as much ease as the *Queen* beat, *Whistlejackett*[2]—But when he came out the last heat he was lame, in his hind leg and one of his four legs—upon his well leg the plate had sprung—and lay across the frog—under all these dificulties he could have distanced the ploughboy Either heat, he beat the last heat under a hard bearing rain, without whip or spur sixty yards, & run it in 3 m. 59. seconds. by Two watches, by another in 3 m 57½—by Blufords[3] pendulum—in 4 m. 1 second, by one other in 3 m. 57 seconds—There was about 10,000 Dollars won and if it had not been for the accident there would have been at lest 20,000—Thus ends the fate of ploughboy—Major W[illiam] T[errell] Lewis[4] lost considerably—at least 2000$

We have had no rain yet, it is now cloudy and cold the river verry low, and this day we mean to try to start our cotton Boat, but I am almost certain she cannot pass—Mr [Edward] Roberts has not yet returned from the Elinois,[5] therefore can give no direction as to the appropriation of the monies arising from the sales of the property gone to markett more than what I have heretofore given untill I hear from him—Capt [John] Crawly[6] has not got off yet—and Stones river has not Eighteen inches water—therefore no hope of our Boats up that river getting out—as soon as you can arrange your business at Neworleans It will be well for you to return—It is verry uncertain when the waters will permit the Boats to descend the river—we have wrote on to you on the subject of laying in our supply of goods at Neworleans, from Meeker, Williamson & Patton, we have been advised, that they can furnish us, the memorandom enclosed to you heretofore[7] will aid you in the situation—I have only to say that If any is laid in, we must have a supply of Blankets I have no doubt but you will push forward the Keel Boat as soon as possible—on the day of the race we Took in one hundred pounds cash on the field, and lost a great deal for the want of attendance—This will shew what could be made at that stand with a good supply and attention

Wishing you a speedy and safe return I am Dr Jack, your sincere friend

Andrew Jackson

P.S. Be sure to make Strict enquiry for George[8]—should he be gone to

Sea—By applying at the custom house office you can see the registration of the seamen—your friends will go with you who can make the necessary enquiry—

ALS, DLC. Published in Bassett, 1:111–12 (dated April 7, 1805).
1. Bradford was a veteran of the Revolution and resident of Sumner County; Rawlings practiced medicine in Sumner County. Letter not found; enclosure, order to William Bradford from Benjamin Rawlings, February 18. Hutchings acknowledged receipt of both (April 16).
2. Indian Queen was a mare that Jackson raced and bred for several years before selling her to Alexander Ewing. Nothing more is known of Whistlejacket or the race.
3. Probably Kentucky horseman Simeon Buford (b. 1756), sometime representative of Barren County in the Kentucky legislature and, starting in 1808, for several years a resident of Nashville and operator of the Sign of the Black Horse Inn.
4. Lewis (1757–1813) moved to Nashville in 1793 from North Carolina, where he had served in the legislature. A great landholder and sometime owner of the Nashville Inn, Lewis was the father-in-law of William C.C. Claiborne, Thomas A. Claiborne, John H. Eaton, and William B. Lewis.
5. Roberts (d. 1807) was the storekeeper for Jackson & Hutchings at Clover Bottom. The nature of the business he had transacted in Illinois is not known.
6. Crawley owned and operated boats on the western rivers. Creek Indians attacked his home on Duck River in 1812, killed some of his children, and captured his wife (see Thomas Johnson to AJ, May 27, 1812, below).
7. Not found.
8. Probably the same runaway slave discussed in Jesse Roach to AJ, December 3, 1805, and John Williamson to AJ, December 12, 1805, above.

From John Hutchings

New Oriel Apriel 24th 1806

Deare Sir

I this evening by mail receved your letter dated the 7th of apriel;[1] and feele more gratifyed to here the Success of Truxton Wining his race under all his dificulties, then I ever Can in Similar Curcomstances

I am truly sorry that mr. Dickerson and Capt Wright[2] left here befor this pleasing nuse reached me, so I might of had the pleasur of seeing them in their agganey.

I am sorry to say that our flats has not yet reach'd this port. Falkners Brage[3] only yesterday morning landed here and, [Hanson] Catlett[4] states that he past them neer the Buffts he set out from Nashvill on the same day I set out—

By this I flatter my self they will be here in the Course of this Weak—I have laid in our groceries, and Packed up some dry goods which think are laid in on good terms. I have nothing to do on the arvial of our flate Boates but unload, & starte the Barge Back—Cotton has fallen down to 20 Centes and some merchants 18 Cents[5]—But I am determined not sell at either prices, here is in this port about 60 large ships now weighing for freight and the expence of those Vessels to the owners amount about sixty Dollars ℔ day this will mak them purchase Cotton they are only weighting thinking that the market will be glutted with Cotton—here is a number of merchants offered to engage Cotton at 20 Cents. I will not tak it untill the last Hour—Staves still retain their former prices and in demand. I have been making all possable enquiery about gorge but Cant get the least inteligance about him I had the pleasure of meeting with our worthy friend Doctor Ciare,[6] who makes all possable enquiery about him, and apperes as much interested about him as you are. I shall wright you by the next mail, I hope when I shall be able to leave the City; and the Saf arival of our boats.

I am D Sir your Sin frend

J. Hutchings

ALS, DLC. Published in Bassett, 1:141–42.

1. See above.

2. Probably Henry Wright, who had sold Ploughboy to Joseph Erwin. Dickinson and Wright had left Nashville for Natchez and New Orleans to sell slaves during the interval between the writing and delivery of Dickinson's letter of January 10 to Jackson. Dickinson wrote his wife that he had sold eleven slaves in Natchez, "at good prices." From New Orleans he wrote that he had sold the remainder except for one man whom he hired out and one woman he hoped to place on his return trip through Natchez. He urged her to have his horse ready by his anticipated arrival, May 12 or 15, so that he could depart immediately for Maryland, presumably to join Joseph Erwin who was already there (Charles to Jane Dickinson, February 17 and April 17, LNT).

3. Possibly John Faulkner, owner of a barge and ropewalk in Nashville in partnership with Parry Wayne Humphreys.

4. Catlet (d. 1824) moved to Nashville about 1805 to practice medicine, for a time as the partner of Thomas G. Watkins. He had earlier served as a military surgeon, and in 1813 he rejoined the army, serving until 1821. He was Dickinson's second in the duel with Jackson.

5. Cotton had dropped from 24 to 22 cents just as Hutchings arrived in New Orleans. He finally sold the firm's shipment at 20 cents a pound (Hutchings to AJ, April 16 and May 23).

6. Sayre.

When Charles Dickinson returned from New Orleans, his quarrel with Jackson picked up where it had ended in January. Dickinson published the card below, Jackson responded on May 23 with a challenge, and immediately the seconds, Thomas Overton and Hanson Catlet, made the necessary arrangements.

The antagonists met in the morning of May 30 in Logan County, Ky. Attending Jackson were Overton and Francis May, Jackson's surgeon. Dickinson was attended by Catlet, who served as second and surgeon, and Corbin Lee, Ploughboy's trainer. At the word, Dickinson fired first, hitting Jackson in the chest. Jackson took aim and pressed the trigger; the pistol snapped but did not fire. He recocked and fired again. This time Dickinson fell with a mortal abdominal wound.

Charles Henry Dickinson to Thomas Eastin

21st May, 1806.

Mr. Eastin,

In looking over the tenth number of your Impartial Review, I discover, that *a certain Andrew Jackson* has endeavored to induce the public to believe, that some inconsistency had been attempted by me, relative to his dispute with Mr. Thomas Swann.[1] My letter to *Andrew Jackson* & published by Mr. John Erwin,[2] is, (I consider) a sufficient answer, with any impartial person.

I should never have condescended to have taken any notice of *Andrew Jackson*, or his scurrilous publication, had it not been promised by Mr. John Erwin, when he published my letter at length, which Mr. Jackson, for some cause, unknown, but to *himself*, had not the generosity to have published but in part.

I shall take notice, but of those parts of his publication, which are intended for myself. The first is, in his publication of the 8th of February,[3] which reads thus "Mr. Charles Dickinson's information is referred to—see Mr. Dickinson's letter. He states no such thing, but refers to a different list. These two correctative informants speak—one of different notes actually offered—the other of a different list of notes. Happy concordance! these two gentlemen possess the key of consistency."

I have no such accommodating disposition as to compare what I intend to offer to the public, with that of any witness whatever, and if it should differ, to correct it in such manner as to correspond. What any person offers for publication, if called on, I think it is his duty to swear to. Andrew Jackson has had several disputes, which have appeared in different prints of this state,[4] and if his mode of publishing his thoughts on his different quarrels, is such, as to alter his publications, to make them answer with those of his witnesses—I can only exclaim *O! tempore, O! mores.*

Another part of his publication of the same date, is as follows—"He (alluding to Mr. T. Swann) has acted the puppet and lying valit, for a worthless, drunken, blackguard, scoundrel," &c. &c. Should Andrew Jackson have intended these epithets for me, I declare him (notwithstanding he is a major general of the militia of Mero District)[5] to be a worthless scoundrel "a paltroon and a coward." A man who, by frivolous and evasive pretexts, avoided giving the satisfaction, which was due to a gentleman whom he had injured. This has prevented me from calling on him in the manner I should otherwise have done; for I am well convinced, that he is too great a coward to administer any of those Anodynes, he promised me in his letter to Mr. Swann.[6] His excuse I anticipate, that his anodynes have been in such demand, since I left Tennessee, that he is out of the necessary ingredients to mix them.[7] I expect to leave Nashville the first of next week for Maryland.

Yours &c.
Charles Dickinson.

Text from *Impartial Review*, May 24. Original not found. Published in Bassett, 1:142–43.

1. The issue of February 15, which carried the letter above, AJ to Eastin, February 10.

2. Erwin (1783–1828), Joseph Erwin's eldest son, had objected to Jackson's extract of Charles Dickinson's letter of January 10 published in the February 15 issue of the *Impartial Review*. He inserted the complete letter in the February 22 *Review* with a promise that Dickinson would answer fully when he returned from New Orleans. Erwin remained on a plantation near Nashville for many years after his parents' emigration to Louisiana, removing to Iberville Parish only shortly before his death.

3. Dickinson was mistaken on the date. Jackson's letter in the *Impartial Review* of February 15 was dated February 10 (see above). Jackson's publication on February 8 was only a notice that his reply to Swann would be delayed a week.

4. For Jackson's quarrel with John Sevier in 1803, see *Jackson*, 1:489–506.

5. In 1802 Jackson was elected major general, not of Mero District but of Tennessee. His command was subsequently divided so that after 1803 he was major general of the 2nd Division only.

6. See above, AJ to Thomas Swann, January 7.

7. Jackson offered anodynes to Dickinson in his letter to Thomas Swann (see above, January 7). Dickinson's gibes probably refer to Coffee's need for anodynes after the duel with McNairy and to the caning episode between Swann and Jackson.

To Charles Henry Dickinson

May 23rd. 1806.

Sir.

Your conduct and expressions relative to me of late have been of such a nature and so insulting that requires, and shall have, my notice—Insults may be given by men, of such a kind, that they must be noticed, and the author treated with the respects due a gentleman, altho (as in the present instance) he does not merit it—You have, to disturb my quiet, industriously excited Thomas Swann to quarrel with me, which involved the peace and harmony of society for a while—You on the tenth of January wrote me a very insulting letter,[1] left this country and caused this letter to be delivered after you had been gone some days; and securing yourself in safety from the contempt I held you in, have a piece now in the press,[2] more replete with blackguard abuse, than any of your other productions; and are pleased to state that you would have noticed me in a different way than through the press, but my cowardice would have found a pretext to evade that satisfaction, if it had been called for &c &c. I hope sir your courage will be an ample security to me, that I will obtain speedily that satisfaction due me for the insults offered—and in the way my friend, who hands you this, will point out—He waits upon you, for that purpose, and with your friend, will enter into immediate arrangements for this purpose—I am &c.

Andrew Jackson

Copy, T. Published in *Tennessee Gazette* and *Impartial Review*, June 14; Bassett, 1 : 143–44. Endorsed by Jackson: "& Dr. F. May Certificate."
    1. See above.
    2. See above, Dickinson to Thomas Eastin, May 21.

From Charles Henry Dickinson

23d. May 1806.

Sir,

Your note of this morning is received,[1] and your request shall be gratified—My friend who hands you this, will make the necessary arrangements—I am &c.

Charles Dickinson

Copy, T. Published in *Tennessee Gazette* and *Impartial Review*, June 14; Bassett, 1 : 144.
    1. See above.

Arrangements of Thomas Overton and Hanson Catlet for Duel

Nashville May 23rd. 1806

On friday the 30th Inst. we agree to meet at Harrisons mills on red river in Logan County State of Kentucky for the purpose of settling the affair of honor between Genl Jackson and Charles Dickinson esqr—Farther arrangments to be made—It is understood that the meeting will be at the hour of seven in the morning

Hanson Catlet
Tho. Overton

Sir,   23rd May 1806

The affair of honor to be settled between my friend Genl. Jackson & Charles Dickinson esqr. it is wished not to be posponed until the 30th Inst., (say friday) agreeable to your time appointed, if it can be done sooner, in order that no inconvenience on your part may accrue, if you can not obtaine pistols we pledge ourselves to give you choice of ours— Let me hear from you immediately—yrs

Tho. Overton

Sir,   24 May 1806

I press you in favor of my friend Genl. Jackson for immediate satisfaction, for the injury that his feelings had received from a publication of Charles Dickinson, your reply that it might not be in your power to obtain pistols, in my note of yesterday in order to remove every obstacle as it respected pistols, I agreed to give you choice of ours; the other we pledge ourselves to make use of. For gods sake let the business be brought to issue immediately, as I can not see after the publication why Mr. Dickinson should wish to put it off till friday—yrs.

Tho. Overton

Sir, May 24th. 1806.
I have received your notes of yesterday & this date, and can only answer, that it will not now be convenient to alter the day from that already agreed upon—I am Sir with respect your Obt. Servant.

Hanson Catlet

Nashville May 24th 1806.
It is agreed that the distance shall be 24 feet, the parties to stand facing each other with their pistols down purpindicularly—When they are ready, the single word fire, to be given, at which they are to fire as soon as they please—Should either fire before the word given, we pledge ourselves to shoot him down instantly—The person to give the word, to be deturmined by lot, as also the choice of position
We mutually agree that the above regulations shall be observed, in the affair of honor depending between Genl. Andrew Jackson and Charles Dickinson esqr—

Tho. Overton
Hanson Catlet

Copy, T. Published in *Tennessee Gazette* and *Impartial Review*, June 14; Bassett, 1:144–45. Overton (1753–1825), a veteran of the Revolution, moved from North Carolina to Davidson County in 1802 at the urging of his younger brother John and spent the remainder of his life working his plantation, "Soldier's Rest."

From John Overton

Nashville, June [1,] 1806.
Dear Genl:
Until yesterday evening, I must confess, my mind was not at ease. I was then relieved. To-day I have seen my brother[1] who tells me of a little circumstance I did not know, that you were a little touched, but not to do any great damage. Pope in his Essay on Man says: "Whatever is, is right." To this small inconvenience we must submit, which is not much more than the stumping of a toe, or the like.
It too frequently happens that the honest, unsuspecting part of society will be infested with reptiles, the heads of which must be sought after and bruised so as to be secure from their poison. God has so ordained it. You have been the instrument of doing so. Fear nothing. As soon as possible I will see you. Our mutual friend, Wm. P. Anderson, will come to see you, who makes my best wishes for you.

Apropos, aside, there is a few long faces in town, though but few, for it seems that this new-fangled Ajax had even went so far as to bet in town, before he went over, that he would kill Genl. Jackson.

Yr friend,

JNO. OVERTON

Text from Stanley F. Horn, *The Hermitage: Home of Old Hickory* (Richmond, Va., 1938), pp. 14–15. Original not found. Dated June 1 in sale announcement, American Art Association catalog, April 8, 1926, Item 299.
1. Thomas, Jackson's second.

In response to the petition of numerous citizens, the two Nashville newspaper editors ornamented their issues of June 7 with mourning borders in respect for Dickinson and in the same edition printed Jackson's letter below. There is no extant copy of the Tennessee Gazette *for June 7, but the June 13 issue contained a correction of two words in Jackson's letter published in the preceding issue. Only one page of the* Impartial Review *remains, bearing the penciled notation in an unidentified hand, "The portion of this paper torn off contained a request by many citizens that the Editor should dress the paper in mourning & Genl. Jackson's call on the editor for the names of the persons making such request." The reprinted version from* Truth's Advocate *appended a list of forty-six subscribers to the petition (including some of the wealthiest planters, merchants, and professional men in the community), with the statement that twenty-six others had erased their names when they heard of Jackson's demand.*

To Thomas Eastin

June 6, 1806.

Mr. EASTIN—I am informed that at the request of sundry citizens of Nashville, and its vicinity, you are about to dress your paper in MOURN-ING, as a "tribute of respect for the memory, and regret for the UNTIMELY death of Charles Dickinson."

Your paper is the public vehicle, and is always taken to be the public will, unless the contrary appears. Presuming that the PUBLIC IS NOT IN MOURNING at this event, in justice to that public, it is only fair and right to set forth THE NAMES OF THOSE CITIZENS, who have made the request. The thing is so novel, that the names ought to appear that the public might judge [whether] the true motives of the signers "were a tribute of respect for the deceased," or something else, that at first sight does not appear. Yours with esteem,

ANDREW JACKSON.

Text from Cincinnati *Truth's Advocate*, June, 1828, p. 234. Original not found. Published in William Joseph Snelling, *A Brief and Impartial History of the Life and Actions of Andrew Jackson, President of the United States* (Boston, 1831), pp. 203–204.

Jackson's letter to Watkins below enmeshed another of his friends in the events surrounding the Dickinson duel. Thomas A. Claiborne held a copy of the letter and, under Jackson's instructions, showed it upon request. When Watkins had not responded to its challenge after two weeks, Claiborne wrote him demanding a reply. Watkins refused to accept the note, and Claiborne posted it. On the evening of July 2, Watkins apprehended Claiborne at Winn's tavern and hit him with his stick. According to witnesses, both had drawn pistols by the time friends separated them. Claiborne opened the subsequent newspaper battle on July 12 with publication of a full-page extra of the Tennessee Gazette *including his letter to Watkins and the copy of Jackson's letter below. Watkins and Claiborne had exchanged a total of four extras by August 19, with one more reply promised for the no-longer extant August 26 regular issue. Watkins maintained that he had signed the mourning-border petition only out of sympathy for Dickinson's widow, not as an attack upon Jackson. But his chief argument was that, since dueling and its promotion were felonies, Claiborne should have refused to publicize Jackson's letter or become his spokesman. There is no record that either Jackson or Claiborne succeeded in bringing Watkins to the dueling ground.*

To Thomas Gassaway Watkins

[cJune 15, 1806]

SIR,

BEING well advised that you were the chief promoter of the address from a few individuals who assumed the name of the "Citizens of Nashville and its vicinity,["] to the Printers of Nashville, to clothe their papers in mourning as "A tribute of respect for the memory, and regret for the untimely death of Mr. Charles Dickinson." To dupe the citizens, you held out to them that the thing was only intended to console the widow's tears, when from your late conduct it plainly appears, that under the hypocritical garb of being moved by the widow's sorrow, you were preparing in the background to give my reputation a stab, with the hidden shaft that none but base minds and cowardly assassins use, and this too, under the smiles of friendship that on my part has never been departed from, and yours in return nothing but outward smiles and hidden enmity.

You in the present case have acted in perfect unison with your former conduct in other places, have intermedled in things that common delicacy ought to have prevented you from. Indeed sir, were you not an entire stranger to the feelings of a gentleman and humanity, you would not have wantonly interfered in this business, but devoid of both, your fertile genious invented this new mode of attack under the garb of mourning; had you possessed one grain of justice, you would not have hesitated to pronounced to the world your ostensible motives in promoting the address so fairly expressed by Mr. [George] Poyzer when it was presented to you.[1] But this sir, was not conginial with that dastardly disposition that governs your acts, you had some hidden enmity against me to revenge, this your nerve was not strong enough to seek in an open, brave and gentlemanly manner, there was more safety under the black garb of mourning for the widow's loss, and the still more base dissimulation of smiling friendship. This drapery you conceived would hide your treachery from the world, and if called out to account for your wicked design against me, you could reply, you had a right to mourn for whom and when you pleased. Notwithstanding I had so many proofs of your dark and hidden designs against me, not believing that any man, of any standing in life could do such base acts, and with such wicked views, who would not come forward and explain when an interview was asked; for this purpose and under this impression I got Mr. James Jackson to wait upon you— your own guilt stared you in the face, and your cowardice pointed out immediate punishment or atonement for your wicked and ungentlemanly conduct. You did not possess a sufficient share of honor and justice to comply with the latter, and your cowardice prevented you from the first. That I have unrobed you and your whole conduct in this business, shews you to be a hypocritical, cowardly assassin. I shall leave you for the present—I may in a short time pursue you to North Carolina and shew what effect female cries and tears have had upon your conduct there. I will conclude by telling you that I will receive no communications from you unless a call for satisfaction for the insult I now offer and intend for you, this must be made through my friend Dr. F. May, which shall be attended with promptitude. No communications thro' any other channel will be received.

Yours, &c. &c. &c.

Andrew Jackson.

Text from *Tennessee Gazette Extra*, July 12. Original not found.

1. Poyzer (d. 1818) first came to Nashville from Lexington, Ky., in 1804 as a collection agent for Thomas & John Clifford. He remained and became a merchant and owner of a cotton-thread factory. Shortly after he heard of the appearance of the mourning-border issues of the Nashville newspapers, Jackson dispatched Rachel's nephew, Donelson Caffery (1786–1835) to collect affidavits stating their reasons for signing the "address." Caffery secured a certificate from Poyzer, one of the signers of the request who subsequently asked that his name be removed. With Poyzer's statement, Caffery visited Watkins and "presented to him the note from Genl. Jackson to myself; he observed that he was not bound to explain his motives to any man, that they were sufficiently express'd in the paper, & were pure. After reading Mr. Poyzers note he again observ'd that he should nearly agree with Mr. Poyzer if he was to declare; but if Jesus Christ had call'd on him he should not consider himself bound to give his motives" (Donelson Caffery to AJ, August 25).

The main question in dispute after the duel was whether "a snap is a fire," in other words, whether Jackson was entitled, either by agreement or by the customary code of honor, to recock and fire his pistol when it failed to fire the first time. The agreement between the seconds (see above, May 23 and 24) said nothing specific about the circumstance, but a good share of public opinion held that Jackson had unethically taken advantage of this silence in the agreement to kill Dickinson. A letter to the Impartial Review (reprinted in the Tennessee Gazette of June 28) attempted to counteract such criticism with reports by Corbin Lee and Francis May, who were present at the duel, that everything was conducted fairly, and by the statements of the seconds, below. Because Jackson was "in a state of convalescence," the article appearing over Jackson's signature was actually written by John Overton (Overton to AJ, June 23, 1827, T).

In 1817 Francis May took John Adair's side in a dispute with Jackson and wrote Adair that after Catlet had delayed for eight or ten days in giving a statement, Thomas Overton bullied him with threats. May's statement, given in June 1806, was not printed in full, because, he said in a letter to Adair, Overton and Jackson had tried unsuccessfully to convince him to alter it in a way more favorable to Jackson. William P. Anderson, then Adair's son-in-law, published May's letters as part of his attack on Jackson in the 1828 campaign.

Whatever the truth of May's allegations, there are two Catlet-Overton statements, with significant differences, on the conduct of the duel.

Statements of Hanson Catlet and Thomas Overton re Duel

Nashville June 20th 1806

I do hereby certify that the affair of honour which lately took place between Genl Andrew Jackson & Mr Charles Dickenson was conducted agreeably to what was agreed upon, so far as any agreements were made.

Hanson Catlet
[Thomas Overton]

ANS in Catlet's hand, Mrs. Elbert C. Brazelton. The only portion of Overton's signature remaining is the top of the "Th" in Thomas and the crossing of the "t" in Overton. The formation of the portions of the letters present, however, is identical to those letters in Overton's signature in the June 25 statement, below.

Nashville, June 25th, 1806.

I do certify that every circumstance in the affair which lately took place between Genl Jackson & Mr Dickinson was agreeable to the impressions that Mr Dickinson & myself were under

Hanson Catlet

Nashville, June 25th, 1806.

I do hereby certify, that every circumstance in the affair which lately took place between Genl Jackson & Mr Dickinson, was agreeable to the impressions that Genl Jackson & myself were under.

Tho Overton

ANS in Catlet's hand; also signed by Overton, T. Published in *Tennessee Gazette*, June 28.

From William Harrison

Red river the 30th of June 1806

Sir.

I recved yours of the 19th. Int.[1] which was handed to me by a Mr. Holland[2] two Day ago. but my not being at home I Sopose might be reason of my not Giting your letter Sooner—however I have ancered as soon as oppertunity could promit—as to the reports that has Curculated from my house as to the Duel being fout on faire I Do Declear I Never heard any Shuch thing Mentioned by Mr Dickenson or any of his party but interly to the revirce—and that yourself and Mr Dickeson both acted like men of furmness and as to reports there has been Maney things Said by people who noes nothing a bout things of that kind, the loe Class of people will Say any thing and Many things which is not worthy of your notice—I Decleare I am Very Sory the thing Cannot be Settled and wish to God it Could if Satisfactory to your Self & others I Do declair that I Do not recolect to hear Mr. Dickeson Mention your Name Either befour or after the afair hapened there was Somthing of kindness I think I heard Mentioned by Doctr. Catlett on your Side to Mr. Dickeson prohaps by Genl. overton that a Bottle of Brand also one of wine which I think the wine was receved by Mr. Dickensons party but asto any thing being acted on fair or any thing of that kind there was not—

there has many people Said that had they ben in your place they would not have Shot Dickeson after the first pass but you must no them people Could not be a Judge of your fealings at that Time asto to my acquentenc with you it has ever ben my oppenion that you have acted the Gentelman and Man of honer—and asto Mr. Dickeson I never Saw untill the night befoure the Contest—and as a man I thought it my Duty to help the Distressed—pray if there is any way for the thing to Drop let it be So which would be a pleasing thing to your friend and Well wisher

Wm Harrison

P.S. asto any Statement mentioned yours I could not make any More then I have mintioned—the Grand Jury had me Sworne and very hard attemps made to have you indited—but all fell through—I sopose them attemps is all dun away.[3]   W. H.

ALS, T. Harrison owned a farm near the site of the duel in Logan County, Ky. Dickinson died at his house.

1. Not found.
2. Not identified.
3. The records of the Logan County Circuit Court show that the grand jury convened June 16 and heard seven presentments but brought in no true bills.

To Thomas Eastin

[cJune, 1806]

Mr. Eastin—

The late attempt, by a few individuals to interest the Publick feeling in a private dispute between Genl Jackson & Mr Charles Dickeson is truly Novel and in due time shall be placed in its proper light before the Publick[1]—It is truly unpleasant at all times to disturb the ashes of the dead— but when a few individuals will step forward under a pretext, of respect due to the deceased attempt to give tone to Publick opinion in a private dispute and thereby to impress upon that part of the Publick that is not personally acquainted with circumstances and charectors, that the loss of Charles Dickason is afflicting to Society—that his virtues are so rare, that he demanded this unusual respect from the Publick, the conclusions there from fairly to be deduced, is that it was impossible that so much virtue so much goodness could be capable of giving an insult that would Justify taking away his life—If anything should be observed relative to the deceased, in the investigation of this conduct of the five individuals[2] who gave rise & tone to this crocadile mourning (for the rest it is believed did not see the base design—but viewd. it as an innocent thing to console the grief of a widow—) it can only be ascribed to the unusual interference of those intermedling mourners of Nashvill and its viciny whose manner and motives in due time for the present it will only be observed that the deceased, could not be called a Citizen of this state—that he was engaged in the humane persuit of purchasing Negroes in Maryland and carrying them to Natchez & Louisa and thus making a fortune of speculating on human flesh—can it be that because he was engaged in this human trafic, he commands this unusual respect from his honour the Judge, the two Doctors, and the petyfoging lawyer—or is it because he had been commanded and instructed by his father in law on the night of the 24 Decbr last, to take away the life of the genl[3] & that he was persuing every method of insult to bring forth the Genl. and when he did step forward, is it Possible that these unusual marks of sorrow & regret is manifested, because he did not carry into effect the wishes of his father in law, and his own boasts—is it Possible, that Mr. Dickason, can be thus seriously regretted, who possponed the meeting for eight days to make himself more perfect in the art of Shooting—marked the genl, on a tree and boasted how often he had hit him—and when setting out to meet the genl left

300$ with Mr [Thomas E.] Wagaman[4] to bet he would kill the genl— This is impossible—some other motives must lurk beneath this thing that shall be endeavoured to be revealed—but it is a thing the owe the Publick to set forth the rare and unusual virtures that the Deceased possessed to intitle him to the unusual respect—had he ever rendered esential service to the Publick no—unless the introduction of two race horses, into the District, can be said to be a benefit, that has made, Debtor the Publick gratitude—

AL draft, T.
1. See above, AJ to Eastin, June 6.
2. Cf. below Jackson's reference to "the Judge, the two Doctors, and the petyfoging lawyer." The judge was John McNairy, and although several lawyers and doctors signed the petition for the mourning-border issue, Jackson probably meant Hanson Catlet, Thomas G. Watkins, and Thomas Swann since he later held them particularly blameworthy. The fifth individual may have been George Poyzer from whom Jackson later secured a certificate explaining his motives in promoting the petition (see Donelson Caffery to AJ, August 25).
3. Jackson secured from John Hoggatt a statement detailing a conversation between Erwin and Dickinson in which Erwin is alleged to have taunted Dickinson to duel Jackson and is quoted as saying, "by God Sir, I think you can kill him." Hoggatt said there were several witnesses to the conversation, which took place at Erwin's home on December 25 (see Hoggatt to AJ, June 24).
4. Waggaman was a Nashville merchant.

From Randal McGavock

Nashville Au. 23d. 1806

Sir

I will, a nearly as can now recollect, give the statement requested in your note of yesterday.[1] Some time in June last happening to meet with you in Nashville, after the usual salutation, our conversation turned upon the request made to the printers of Nashville to put their papers in mourning for the death of Mr. Charles Dickinson—You then observed that an application of such a nature appeared rather unprecedented; that you believed its object was to injure your reputation, and that you had some reasons to believe that Doctor Watkins was the promoter—You further observed that you wished to have a conversation with Doctor Watkins on the subject, in presence of two or three persons who were indifferent to, or friendly with the parties, and requested me to accompany you and Mr. John Childress to the store of Mr. James Jackson. After going into the back room of the store, you asked Mr. James Jackson to go to Doctor Watkins and request him to walk over to his store, that you wished to have some conversation with him in presence of Mr. Childress & myself—Mr. James Jackson left the room, and within a few minutes returned, said he had delivered the messuage to Doctor Watkins, that the Doctor refused to come, saying if Genl. Jackson had business of more importance with him than he had with Genl. Jackson, Genl. Jackson might come to him—Mr. James Jackson was again desired to wait on Doctor Watkins with the same request, on his return he said the answer of Doctor Watkins was, in substance, the same as before, with this addition, that if Genl. Jacksons request had been made previous to a certain letter being presented to him, by Mr. [Donelson] Caffery,[2] he would have met Genl. Jackson at any place. You immediately left the room apparently much irritated, saying you would call upon Doctor watkins in another way;[3] This I believe to be the substance of what passed in my presence or hearing that day.

I will further observe that from your conversation with me, I had no reason to believe that your intentions, in the requested interview with Doctor Watkins, were any other than peaceable—Indeed if I had thought your views were hostile I would have declined accompanying you.

I am, Sir, with esteem your most Obt. Servt.

Randal McGavock

ALS, T. McGavock (1766–1844) moved to Nashville with his brother David in the 1780s. Between 1802 and 1834 he served at various times as clerk of the Mero District Superior Court, the circuit court, and the Tennessee Supreme Court.
1. Not found.
2. See Caffery to AJ, August 25, for Caffery's report of the substance of his conversation with Thomas G. Watkins.
3. See above, AJ to Watkins, [cJune 15].

From John Overton

Jonesb. 12th Sepr. 1806

Dear Genl

This day week a report arrived here that you and Swann had faught,[1] that both fell, Swann shot through the heart, of which he died in six minutes and you through the head from which instant death, insued

Though I did not believe it, great uneasiness arose, knowing what the rascally conspiracy of which Swann is a part—You have several warm friends here, and if you knew the uneasiness they suffered, and their impressions, I am sure it would have some effect—Not only on this occasion, but before, the opinion of your sensible friends, of whom you have many was unanimous; *that nothing can justify your fighting Swan, or any of the pioneers of this dirty band*

I do not know that there is much danger of any of these flies infesting you, though fear tho. for their wile is good—and this you may in a measure know from the reports that are industriously circulated—I repeat it again general the respect you owe to the opinion of your friends, the duties you owe to your family, and to the world, forbids the idea of your putting yourself upon a footing with boys, especially when they are made the instruments of others—To use an irish bull, if it was me, I should to eternity, feel mean to be killed by one of these puppies—Your friends would have to lament your loss though not able to justify the act

On the other hand if you were to kill this Swann, or some such lad, what would be the consequence? why it would be said that you delighted in human blood—you had no business to notice a young man; poor hot headed young man, the populace would say; you had much better have reclaimed, than killed him—By the bye you are not to understand that these are my ideas but the same rascally conspiracy would use their best endeavours to impress these things, and would place you in a situation, that there would be but little choice between living, and being killed.

No man, even your worst enemies doubts your personal courage and you would gain much more, by not noticing any thing that these people may say, than otherwise—Be assured that their slander can do you no harm among your friends—

These observations, you know come from a friend who has not only thought maturely upon the subject, but from one who has consulted the feelings and opinions of many judicious men of honor—Should you be *assaulted* by any of the *younger*, or inferiour gang repel it with a stick &c—Those of stability & standing in society you will chastise should proper occasions occur, in a proper manner--But *never, never* my dear sir, hurt the feelings of your friends, by putting yourself on a level with *boys, instruments, mere tools of others*—doing yourself no honor, perhaps losing your life with one of them, and their enmity is bitter enough, to even *hire* if they could get hands—Beside the mortification to your friends—you might in this way deprive yourself of that life, which ought to be preserved for better purposes, among which is the chance (upon some proper occasion, which hereafter, by patience may occur) of chastising in a proper manner, the prompters behind the curtain

Should any difficulty occur may I ask you as a friend before you do any thing, to consult your friends—Patience, deli[b]eration and bravery will surmount all difficulties

I am yr. friend

Jno: Overton

ALS, THer. Published in *Cincinnati Commercial*, January 8, 1880.

1. No additional evidence of a renewed quarrel with Swann has been found. Overton, who was in East Tennessee for the sitting of the superior court, had probably heard a garbled report that substituted Swann's name for that of Watkins whom Jackson had attempted to challenge in June (see above, AJ to Watkins, cJune 15, and AJ to Eastin, cJune). In August that quarrel was being kept alive by Thomas A. Claiborne, and Jackson was continuing to gather information about Watkins's role in promoting the mourning-border newspapers (see McGavock to AJ, August 23, above, and Donelson Caffery to AJ, August 25).

To [William Preston Anderson]

Hermitage, Sept. 25, 1806.

Col Burr is with me, he arived last night—I would be happy you would call and see the Col. before you return—say to the Gen. O[verton] that I shall expect to see him here on tomorrow with you—Would it not be well for us to do something as a mark of attention to the Col. He has always and is still a true and trusty friend to Tennessee[1]—If Gen. Robertson is with you when you receive this Be good enough to say to him, that Col. Burr is in the country—I know the Gen. R. will be happy in joining in any thing—that will tend to shew a mark of respect to this worthy visitant. With due Esteem,

ANDREW JACKSON.

Text from *National Banner and Nashville Whig*, August 16, 1828. Original not found. Also published in *National Intelligencer*, August 25, 1828; Bassett, 1:149–50. Although the newspapers described the recipient of the letter only as "a Nashville friend," William Preston Anderson was almost certainly the addressee. In 1828, for example, Anderson identified an earlier letter, printed in *Jackson*, 1:397–98, as "Gen. Jackson's letter to me without date." Anderson's neighbor, Andrew Erwin, who had the letters in 1828, said that both were addressed to the same party. During August, September, and October 1828, the two Nashville newspapers disputed the name of the addressee and the correct year for the item in a series of exchanges widely reprinted in the national press.

1. Thomas Overton served as president and James Robertson as vice president of a public dinner at Talbot's Hotel on September 27, given in Burr's honor by "the most respectable citizens of this town and its vicinity" (*Tennessee Gazette*, October 4). Widespread appreciation for Burr originated in his extraordinary efforts in the Senate on behalf of Tennessee's application for statehood in 1796 (see James Robertson to Daniel Smith, February 2, 1807, DLC).

To James Winchester

Hermitage October 4th. 1806

Dear Genl,

It filled me with regret, that Colo. Burr and myself, was disappointed the pleasure of dining with you yesterday—I have not enjoyed a good state of health lately, and am subject to sudden attacks, this prevented me; and the Colo. not being acquainted with the way, and without company, was obliged to decline—The regret we feel upon this disappointment, is augmented owing to the Colo (arangements) not having it in his power to give you a call untill he returns to this country again—

The Hostile and menacing attitude of Spain in the neighbourhood of Natchitoches, has induced me to Issue the enclosed order[1] which I anticipated handing you myself—you, no doubt have seen from the late papers that the negociation for the purchase of the Floridas have failed—The certain consequence is war, and no doubt but less than 2 millions can conquer not only the Floridas, But all Spanish North america.[2]

I send home your mare I think Truxton has done her business—he had fine *fun* To comply strictly with your letter[3]—we gave two covers a day for three days, and ever after when we found her in the humour. She is certainly in foal, or entirely conquered

Since writing the above I have consulted Colo. Burr, who request me to say to you, that if in his power he will pass by your house on his return to the northward on Monday next.[4] he will be there on Monday night if nothing turns up to prevent him more than can be viewed or seen at present. on the event of his passing by your house I will (if healh permits) ride with him that far—

I have a hope (Should their be a call) that at least, two thousand Volunteers can be lead into the field at a short notice—That number commanded by firm officers and men of enterprise—I think could look into Santafee and Maxico—give freedom and commerce to those provinces and establish peace, and a permanent barier against the inroads and attacks of forreign powers on our interior—which will be the case so long as Spain holds that large country on our borders—Should there be a war this will be a handsome theatre for our enterprising young men, and a certain source of acquiring fame—I have a hope that you will partake in the campaign—if undertaken and ordered—With due respect I am Dr. Sir yr mo. ob. serv.

Andrew Jackson

P.S. I have seen an extract of a letter from a verry inteligent man dated 19th. Sept. Neworlean, which says "Wilkeson is at Natchitoch where it *inevitably* will come to blows immediately."[5]   A. J—

ALS, DLC. Extract published in *Old Folks' Record*, 1(1875):549.
1. See below.
2. Jackson was referring to the $2 million requested by Jefferson for purchase of the Floridas.
3. Not found.
4. According to the *Impartial Review* of October 11, Burr left for Kentucky on Monday, October 6.
5. Source of quotation not identified.

Order to Brigadier Generals of the 2nd Division

[October 4, 1806]

The late conduct of the Spanish Government, added to the Hostile appearance & menacing attitude of their armed forces already incamped within the limits of our government, make it necessary that the militia under my command, should be in complete order & at a moments warning ready to march.

This armed force under the sanction of their government, have imprisoned & transported five of the good citizens of the U. States to the dominnion of Spain—They have cut down & carried off the flag of the U. States, which was erected in the Cado nation of indians & within the limits of the U. States—They have compelled by force men in the employ of government when exploring the red river to desist & come home and they have taken an unjustifiable & insulting position on the East side of the river Sabine & within the Territory of New Orleans!!![1] Acts thus daring as well as degrading to our national Character & constituted rights demand prompt satisfaction & cannot fail to excite that resentment so becoming & so natural on the occasion.

In the first instance Gentlemen let it be recollected that our good *materials, our best of men*, must be properly deciplined & in this way the preparation cannot be too great to meet the wishes of the Genl. & the exegencies of our Country

Inspired with the laudable ambition of avenging our countries wrongs & impelled by the most cogant necessity of defending our national dignity & liberties, it is Calculated that but one voice will be heard among us & that, that will be for *preparation & decipline*.

You are, therefore ordered, without delay, to place yr. brigade on the most respectable footing & be in readyness to furnish the quota required of you at the shortest notice. All volunteer companies well equiped will be accepted of. If the full quota can be raised by voluntary enlistment it will answer government a better purpose than by pressing men from their families by draft; but if it be discovered that this cannot be done, you will direct that the effective men be classed & that the law in this respect be particularly attended to and when the government & constituted authorities of our Country require they must be in readiness to march.

Two regiments, it is expected, from my division (in the event of a call) will be required & no doubt if more are in readiness to march, a tender of their services will be accepted.

You will Gentlemen take the most speedy method of obtaining correct information of the number that can be raised by voluntary enlistment within your respective brigades thro Yr. Colonels or in such other manner as may to you be most proper & after this information shall have been acquired forward the same to the Genl. by mail

> Andw. Jackson
> Major Genl. 2 Division
> By W P Anderson
> aid de camp

Copy in Anderson's hand, DLC-Thomas Jefferson Papers; enclosed in AJ to Jefferson, [cNovember 5], below. Published in *Impartial Review*, October 4, from which the date is taken; Bassett, 1:68–69 (dated August 7, 1803), and 150–51. The commanders receiving the order were James Winchester (enclosed in AJ's letter above), Isaac Roberts, and Thomas Johnson.

1. These events were reported in the *Impartial Review*, September 27, quoting a letter from Natchitoches dated August 30. For several weeks the local newspapers had printed reports warning that war with Spain was imminent.

Account with Aaron Burr

A. B. in acct. with A. J.		Dr.
1806		
Oct 4	Expence of J. C.[1] & postage	$ 6.62½
	Spanish Horse	90.00
	W. P. Anderson	700.00[2]
	Cash p'd Yates[3]	60.00
	Donelson Caffery wages & expences[4]	29.00
	Boat of T. Dixon[5] & Cable	123.00
	Expence of do.	21.50
	Expence, at Sundrie times	8.00
	Keel Boat[6]	300.00
	Bill Stores Messrs F. & H.[7]	43.00
	Cash for do.	50.00
	J. & W. Jackson Bill do.	44.00[8]
	Cash to Mr. Adams[9]	5.00
	Boat of W. Crenshaw & C.[10]	123.00
	Expence for do.	18.75
	postage.	1.50
	3 Boats at $133.$\frac{33}{100}$,[11]	400.00
		2023.37½
	Cash on hand $1726 62½ [12]	
1806		Cr.
Oct 4	By draft on Buslard* & E.[13]	$ 250
Nov 3	By notes by W.[14]	3000
Dec 3	By do.	500
		3750

* The letters in the last syllable of this name are difficult to make out.

Text from Natchez *Ariel*, August 23, 1828. Original not found. Harman Blennerhassett introduced the account in his suit against Aaron Burr in Adams County Court, Miss. Terr., in which Jackson was called as garnishee (see statements to Adams County Superior Court re *Blennerhassett* v. *Burr*, March 25 and September 25, 1813, below). In 1828 an eleven-man committee of correspondence in Natchez stated that the account was in the same hand as a letter from Jackson to Peter Bruin, December 27, 1799 (not found).

1. Probably John Coffee who supervised the building of Burr's boats.

2. In 1828 Coffee said that he did not recall the purpose of this payment (*United States Telegraph Extra*, October 11, 1828). It was possibly related to Anderson's southern trip (see William P. Anderson to AJ, December 31, below).

3. Not identified.

4. Contemporary documents do not reveal Caffery's services. In 1828, then living in Mississippi, he said that Burr, whom he met in December 1806 when they were lodging at the same house, asked him to serve as a confidential messenger to Chillicothe, Ohio. Caffery said he insisted on consulting Jackson, who advised him to have nothing to do with Burr (*Port-Gibson Correspondent*, Miss., October 11, 1828).

5. Tilman Dixon (1750–1816), Revolutionary veteran from North Carolina, settled in Smith County in 1788, amassed a considerable fortune, and held numerous local offices.

6. The keel boat is entered on Jackson's account at the Clover Bottom store, December 9, below.

7. Probably John A. Fort and Anthony Hopkins (see Account with Clover Bottom Store, December 9, below).

8. This charge also appears on the Clover Bottom account, December 9, below.

9. Not identified.

10. John Coffee, acting for Jackson & Hutchings, paid William Crenshaw, a carpenter in Carthage, $123 for a boat and cable (Receipt to John Coffee, December 14).

11. Burr departed with two boats on December 22. According to Coffee's statement made in connection with *Blennerhassett v. Burr*, the remaining three boats were either delivered to Patton Anderson, who held a draft from Burr in his favor, or were sold and the proceeds given to Anderson.

12. In both 1813 and 1828 Coffee said this balance was paid to Burr before his departure in December. See, for example, AJ to the Adams County Superior Court, March 25, 1813, below.

13. Nashville mercantile firm Bustard & Eastin. In 1813 William Eastin testified that he had purchased a $500 bill of exchange from Burr, drawn on George M. Ogden and endorsed by Jackson (see enclosure in AJ to Adams County Superior Court, September 25, 1813, below).

14. Possibly Charles Willie, hired as a secretary by Burr in July 1806 in Pennsylvania. He testified in 1807 that he visited Nashville with Burr on his trips in September and December and made an additional trip from Lexington to deliver a letter to Jackson during Burr's "trial" in Kentucky, by which he could have meant either the dismissed hearing of November 8 and 12 or the grand jury hearing, December 2–5 (see Willie's testimony before the grand jury, June 16, 1807, ViU-Cabell Family Papers).

To Thomas Jefferson

[cNovember 5, 1806]

Sir

In the event of insult or aggression made on our Government and country from any quarter, I am so well convinced that the publick sentiment and feeling of the citizens within this state, and particularly within my Division, are such, of such a nature and of such a kind, that I take the liberty of tendering their services, that is, under my command; and at one moments warning after your signification that this tender is acceptable,[1] my orders shall be given conformably—

I beg leave to offer to your view the enclosed order some short time ago Issued by me;[2] since which time I have not been furnished with complete returns of the Volunteer companies; but from the information I possess, I have no doubt that three regiments of Volunteers (to be commanded by their own officers and such as may be recommended by their Genl) can be brought into the field and ready to march in twenty days from the receipt of orders.

Accept assurances of my high consideration and respect—

Andrew Jackson
M. G. 2 Division
Tennessee—

ALS, DLC-Thomas Jefferson Papers. Published in Bassett, 1:156. Endorsed in Jefferson's hand: "recd. Nov. 24. 06." Date determined by reference to AJ to Daniel Smith, November 12, below, in which Jackson says he had written Jefferson by last mail, probably a week earlier.

1. For Jefferson's reply, see December 3, below.
2. See above, [October 4]. Probably Jefferson had already seen the order, as it was published in the *National Intelligencer* on November 5.

While a hearing was underway in Frankfort, Ky., on Burr's activities, a young man heading for New Orleans stopped in Nashville, met Jackson, and disclosed to him a story about the former vice president's western objectives. In his letter to William C.C. Claiborne, Jackson did not reveal the source of his information, but to Daniel Smith, he identified his informant as "an entire stranger introduced to me by letter." Not until January 15, 1807, in a letter to George Washington Campbell, did Jackson mention the name "Capt. Fort" and the information John A. Fort (1778–1828) divulged. A native of New York who settled in business in New Orleans following the Burr trial in Richmond, Fort told Jackson what John Swartwout, brother of Burr's confederate Samuel, had told him about the enterprise.

In response to Fort's revelations, on November 12 Jackson wrote several warning letters: the one to Claiborne, below, which does not hint at Burr's complicity but clearly points to Wilkinson; to Senator Daniel Smith (also below), nearly accusing Burr; to Congressman William Dickson (not found); and, according to Jackson's grand jury testimony, to Burr, who responded promptly with a denial of illegal intentions (neither letter found).

John Shaw, commodore of the U.S. Navy stationed at New Orleans, testified at Burr's trial that Jackson's letter to Claiborne arrived by an irregular agency, tossed into Claiborne's office by an anonymous messenger. Its history thereafter was just as peculiar. James Wilkinson appeared at Burr's trial armed with a copy of it to justify his subsequent arbitrary actions in defending New Orleans. One of the extant copies, in an unknown hand, bears the endorsement, in a second unknown hand: "I contrived to put this into long[?] Jacks Hand to day—some delicacy ensued about reading it—I was turned out of the Room 20 minutes & when I returned he did not say whether it had been read or not" (PPiU). Whether this is the copy introduced by Wilkinson is not known, but Jackson's letter was incorporated in the trial record, ironically to the benefit of his bête noire Wilkinson.

Jackson's forces had some difficulty fitting the Claiborne letter into their defense of the candidate in the 1828 campaign. At first they argued that the warning to Claiborne was clear evidence that Jackson was not only loyal but was perhaps the first to sound the alarm against Burr. The opposition replied that if Jackson knew about the conspiracy as early as November 12, he had served as a willing accomplice when he delivered boats and supplies to Burr in December. In rebuttal Jackson's men contended that the collapse of the effort to prosecute Burr in Kentucky, added to Burr's unequivocal reassurance on the legitimacy of his project, restored Jackson's faith, leaving no impediment to his completing Burr's contract.

To William Charles Cole Claiborne

Private   Novr. 12th. 1806.
Govr. Claiborne.

Altho it is a long time since I sat down to write you, still that friendship that once existed, remains bright on my part, and altho since I had the pleasure of seeing you, I have waded thro dificult and disagreable scenes still, I have all that fondness for my old and former friends that I ever had, and their Memory has been more endeared to me, by the treachery I have experienced since I saw you by some newly acquired one—Indeed I fear treachery is become the order of the day—This induces me to write you—put your Town in a state of Defence organize your Militia, and defend your City as well against internal enemies as external: my knowledge does not extend so far as to authorise me to go into detail, but I fear you will meet with an attack from quarters you do not at present expect. Be upon the alert—keep, a watchful eye on our General—and beware of an attack, as well from your own Country as Spain, I fear there something rotten in the State of Denmark—you have enemies within your own City, that may try to subvert your Government, and try to separate it from the Union. You know I never hazard ideas without good grounds, you will keep these hints to yourself—but I say again be upon the alert— your Government I fear is in danger, I fear there are plans on foot—inimical to the Union—whether they will be attempted to be carried into effect or not I cannot say but rest assured, they are in operation or I calculate badly—beware of the month of December—I love my Country and Government, I hate the Dons—I would delight to see Mexico reduced, but I will die in the last ditch before I would yield a part to the Dons, or see the Union disunited—This I write for your own eye, & for your own safety, profit by it, and the Ides of March remember. with sincere respect I am as usual your sincere friend.

Signed   Andrew Jackson

Mrs. Jackson desires her best respects to you[1]

LC, Ms-Ar; Copies, DLC, PPiU. Published in *National Intelligencer*, October 21, 1807; *Annals of Congress*, 10 Cong., 1 sess., Appendix, pp. 571–72; James Wilkinson, *Memoirs of General Wilkinson* (Washington, 1811), pp. 107–108; Bassett, 1:152–53. Receipt acknowledged in Claiborne to AJ, December 5. At Jackson's request Claiborne sent him a copy of the letter (see Claiborne to AJ, December 3, 1807, below).

1. The postscript appears thus in the PPiU copy, and as "Mrs. Jackson desires her best wishes to you" in *National Intelligencer*, *Annals of Congress*, and *Memoirs of General Wilkinson*. It is absent in the other copies.

To Daniel Smith

Novbr. 12th. 1806—

Dear Genl

Impressed with a belief, that there are plans in operation in the west, innimical to our country and government induces me to write you, and whilst I write I would wish you to keep in view, that a mans mind may be perfectly convinced that a thing is so, and still not be in possession of Testimony, that would authorise names to be used or expressed. When great and sensible men form plans of operation, with deep design, the always keep out [of] view their real object, untill it is ripe for execution [a]nd unfold it to no one, unless the are certain that the person to whom the unboosom themselves will [go a]ll lengths into their measures—Men may hold out ideas of a patriotic nature which might flow from a love of country as the ostensible object, whilst they have in view some designs against that country that the profess to serve—others may hold out ideas, of large purchases & settling new countries,[1] when their designs may be by a conspiracy with a foreign foe, to make a stroke at their own government with those that they know love the government. under present circum[stances with?] spain the may hold out ideas of an attack on Mexico on the event of a failure of an accomodation with that nation of our differrences, either under the auspices of government, or under circumstances that government would wink at, and add Mexico either to the union, or alliance, with the government that might be there created, add to the growing greatness of am[erica,] give liberty and commerce to millions, and there[by] Snatch that country from the rapacious hands of Bonapart who might be a troublesome neighbour to the united States, when their plans might be, in common Concert with Spain to seize on Neworleans, and Louisiana, and attempt to divide the union—That some such plan is on foot, I have no doubt, and from a conversation with an entire stranger who came introduced to me by letter[2] I have no doubt but there is a plan on foot and that plan is to take possession of Neworleans,

the expression drop from him incautiously, and as soon as he dis[co]v-
ered that I had taken it up, he attempted to tak[e me] in, to explain &c
&c, but from circumstances I was in Possession off, it flashed upon my
mind that plans that had been named of settling new countries of Punish-
ing the Dons, and adding Mexico to the United States &c &c, were only
mere coverings to the real designs—Altho the expressions that fell taking
them abstractedly, from every thing else would not be sufficient to raise
alarm, or connected by [docume?]nt to absolute proof, still sir the are
strong anough to make me believe that a plan is in operation inimical to
the United States, that the Marqis de *Yrujo*,[3] is in the plan (if it does exist,) and that the army of the united States, as is hinted is to cooperate—
Let us suppose a case—That a plan for separating the Union is actually
on foot—how is it to be efected—permit me to bring to your view how it
might be jeopardize—and taking into view the attachment of [th]e western people collectively to the government. no other plan presents itself to
my view, that could furnish [hope] of success—first a difference exist between our government and Spain, their minister at open war with our
executive a designing man forms an intrigue with him to regain the purchased Territory—This designing man intrigues with the general of your
army, and he is fully into the measure. The Spanish forces under pretext of defending their frontier (where there has been no encrochment)
marches a formidable force, within two hundred miles of New-orleans,
your Governor of New orleans, organises the Militia [to] help to defend
your Territory, but your general orders him home at the verry moment
that he is advan[cing] to take possession of a position on the right ba[nk
of] the Sabine[4]—The two armies are near anough to make arangments
and to form plans of cooperation. at this moment a decent is made from
the ohio and uper Louisiana on Neworleans, which is in a defenceless
situation, two thirds of its inhabitants into the plan. The Town falls an
easy pray to its assailants and the two armies protect the conqu[erers]
with the aid of Spain Shut the Port against the exportation of the west,
and hold out alurements to all the western world to Join and they shall
enjoy free trade and profitable commerce—will not the precedent set, in
the case of Colo. [Thomas] B[utler] insure perfect obedience to the general orders, and do you not think the above plan all things ripe would
jeopardize the union, and be the most likely to insure success. it may be
asked how [the thing] could be carried into effect without coming to the
ears of the government, before the men could be assembled and reach
New orleans—The answer, suppose the contra[c]tor for carrying the mail
from the city to Neworleans into the measure with one of your Post masters. the dispatches could be taken out, or a better plan, all things ripe
your mail could be stopt[5]—untill the plan was caried into effect—I hope
I may be mistaken—but I as much belie[ve] that such a plan is in operation as I believe there is a god—and if I am not mistaken, there are in the
plan many high charectors from New york to Neworleans[—If] the plan

does exist the commander of th[e] army is much injured if he is not to be second in grade—and your own body is not clear of having some members within its walls, that are countenancing, and knowing to the thing[6]—that is to say They are concerned in the plan of purchases and settlements which I believe is only a cover to the true object as expressed to me by the person aluded to, who attempted to [cover] for the expressions—I must state I have no proof that would criminate any person in having designs against the government, but from what I do know of certain things my mind is convinced, that such things do exist and I am impressed with a full belief, that the approach of the Spanish troops is to aid in the project—and you may say to the president, that I am impressed with a firm belief that the have no time to loose—that the ought to keep out a good watch over their general, be carefull that their mail is not stopd. (this will be the plan to insure [s]ecrecy) and give orders, for the defence of New-orleans—I have written to the governor[7] [to b]e on the alert, be silent, and their plans may be dis[covered.] you will see the necessity of keeping this thing from all [but] the Executive—his wisdom will point out the best measures for the safety of the west, that can be adopted. he will find, that I have kept pace with my Jealousies—I have kept the militia in expectation of a call. he has my letter by last post[8]—unless interupted.

I endeavoured to see Doctor Dixson this morning before he started, when I got to Captain wards being detained in Nashville last night, he was gone—from some circumstances that was brought to my view today, I determined to send a servant after him with this letter, fearfull that it might not go safe by the mail—the servant and myself started, but finding that he intended [to] the cainey Fork to night, and I knew my servant [c]ould not over take him I therefore intrust it [to the] mail and wish it safe to hand—and let me imp[ress] strongly on your mind, that altho I am not in p[ossession] of positive proof, still my mind, is as clearly [convin]ced of the fact as tho I had—your own susp[icions] will immedeately bring to your view, the [person] I suspect to be at the head—I leave to your Judgt. and Doctor Dixsons how far it would be prudent to let my name as your informant be known to any person unless to the President, or those in [his com]pleat confidence—for you are to understand, that you may even in the departments, (*I do not mean the heads*) not be entirely in safety—This I only name as a caution for only a slight shade of suspicion rest there—I wish you to write me on the receipt of this, and by every mail I will write you by which you may Judge whether, any interference is in the mail untill christmas. I inclose, to Doctor Dixson, Judge [Seth] Lewis letter,[9] that you may see the situation of that country—

Health & respect,

Andrew Jackson

ALS, DLC. Published in Bassett, 1:153–55. Endorsed in Smith's hand: "I certify the within is an original letter addressed to me from Genl. Andrew Jackson and received in December

1806 Danl. Smith Washington Jany 27th 1808." Enclosed in Smith to AJ, January 27, 1808, below, in response to Jackson's request for its return (see AJ to Smith, November 28, 1807, below).

1. A reference to Burr's contention that the purpose of his expedition was settlement of the Bastrop grant on the Ouachita River.

2. John A. Fort. Letter not found.

3. Carlos Fernando Martínez de Irujo, Marqués de Casa-Irujo (1763–1824), Spanish minister to the U.S., 1795–1808.

4. Claiborne had accompanied the Orleans Territory militia to Natchitoches where they expected to aid the regular army in repelling a Spanish force encroaching on the Sabine River. Jackson could have read in the *Impartial Review* of November 8 that Wilkinson had discharged the militia.

5. Interruptions in the mail service raised Jefferson's suspicions sufficiently that in December he dispatched a special agent to investigate (see Henry Dearborn to AJ, December 19, below).

6. Of four senators eventually implicated in the Burr conspiracy, only John Smith of Ohio was sitting in this session. John Adair of Kentucky resigned November 18, 1806, when he failed of reelection; John Brown of Kentucky and Jonathan Dayton of New Jersey left office March 3, 1805.

7. See above, AJ to Claiborne, November 12.

8. See above, AJ to Thomas Jefferson, [cNovember 5].

9. Lewis (1764–1848) spent several years in Nashville during the 1790s studying and practicing law before receiving appointment as chief justice of the Mississippi Territory court. After resigning the office in 1803, he practiced law in Natchez and eventually settled in Louisiana where he served for about twenty-five years as parish and district judge. Letter not found.

To Daniel Smith

Hermitage, Nov 17, 1806.

Dear Sir:

By the last mail I wrote you lengthily upon a subject on which I have heard nothing since.[1] My mind is still as firmly fixed in the belief as it possibly can be in a thing of which it has not positive proof; however circumstances may arise that may bury the project in oblivion.

I have nothing new since I wrote you last. Report says Col Burr has been arrested at Frankfort, Kentucky, on a charge for raising men to invade Mexico;[2] whether this is the fact I cannot say, but from the channel through which the report has come,[3] I believe it true that he has been arrested.

Text from *National Banner and Nashville Whig*, September 16, 1828. Original not found. Also published in *Gallatin Journal*, September 20, 1828; Bassett, 1:156.

1. See above.

2. On November 5 Joseph Hamilton Daveiss, federal district attorney for Kentucky, appeared before District Court Judge Harry Innes and accused Burr of preparing to march on Mexico. On November 8 a grand jury was called but immediately dismissed until November 12, at which time it was dismissed again at Daveiss's request when he failed to secure an essential witness.

3. Jackson said in his testimony before the grand jury in Richmond that he learned these facts from Charles Lynch, a Kentuckian from Shelby County, who had sold Burr the Bastrop grant of 350,000 acres. Lynch had appeared as a witness at the dismissed grand jury hearing in Frankfort.

From Thomas Jefferson

Washington Dec. 3 06

Sir

I have duly received your letter, proffering the services of a very respectable corps of Volunteers, should the injuries offered our country render it necessary.[1] Always a friend to peace, & believing it to promote eminently the happiness & prosperity of mankind, I am ever unwilling that it should be disturbed, as long as the rights & interests of the nation can be preserved. but whensoever hostile aggressions on these require a resort to war, we must meet our duty, & convince the world that we are just friends & brave enemies. whether our difficulties with Spain will issue in Peace or War, is still uncertain; and what provisional measures shall be taken for the latter alternative, is now under consideration of the legislature. The offer of service which your patriotism has now made to your country, is a pledge that it will not be witheld in whatever form the National councils may authorise it's use. Accept my thanks on the public's behalf for the readiness with which you have made the honorable tender; with my respectful salutations and assurances of great consideration & esteem.

Th Jefferson

ALS copy, DLC-Thomas Jefferson Papers.
  1. See above, AJ to Thomas Jefferson, [cNovember 5].

The charges below were made to Jackson's personal account with the Jackson-Hutchings-Coffee store at Clover Bottom. They were almost certainly for supplies to outfit the keel boat mentioned and charged on Burr's account of October 4, above. Hopkins was probably the Anthony mentioned in the testimony of Daniel Bissell, Jacob Dunbaugh, and Thomas Hartley at Burr's trial in Richmond. According to Dunbaugh, Hopkins came from the main body of the boats at the mouth of Cumberland River to Fort Massac to determine whether the commander of the fort would allow Burr's flotilla to pass unmolested. All three witnesses said they saw Hopkins with Burr's boats and in frequent company with John A. Fort.

Calculated at six shillings to the dollar, the rate used in the December 17 account below, the bill totals $37.07, not $43 as shown in the charge for Fort & Hopkins's stores on the October 4 account, but the amounts and circumstances are coincidental enough to suggest that they are the same charge with the addition of some items recorded elsewhere.

Account with the Clover Bottom Store

Genl. And. Jackson pr. Mr. Hopkins   Dr   9th. Decr. [1806]

6 lbs. Coffee	@3/9
1 Coffee pot	@6/
3 Butcher knifes	@1/6 ea
2 soup plates	@1/4
2 glass Tumblers	@1/ ea
2 Shallow plates	@1/3 ea
2 knifes & 2 forks	4/6
1 Lanto[r]n	3/
1 quart Bottle	@1/6
1 yd. Country Cloth	@3/9
4 gallns. whs	@4/6
4 do. F. Brandy	@$4. pr. gallon
2 4 gallon Casks	@4/6 ea.
1 large kittle damaged	27/
1 poll axe	18/
1 keel Boat & rigging[1]	
1 60 foot Plank	12/

Bill with J. & W. Jackson $44.[2]

AD, THer-Clover Bottom Day Book, September 1806–April 1807.
    1. See above, Account with Aaron Burr, October 4, with a $300 charge for a keel boat.
    2. Also noted in the October 4 account with Burr.

From William Dickson

[December 15, 1806]

The President mentioned his intention to call on you and the Militia under your command to be prepared to intercept his descent of the Ohio[1]—the captain of his boats and provisions, the presidents proclamation,[2] & Burrs fallen credit will I presume so far prostrate his plans that no requisition will be made.

I believe few plans have been better laid or pursued thro all their different ramifications with more address than his. It is owing to the loyalty of the people of the United States that they have thus fallen. His calculations on the political divisions in the country were certainly illfounded—and the business has terminated in the disgrace of himself and his partizans.

Whatever may ocur relative to this or other public matters I will early

communicate to you. A line from you now and then will be very acceptable. accept Dear Sir; asurances of much regard from, your friend

Wm. Dickson

ALS fragment, NjP.
1. On calling into service the forces under Jackson, see Henry Dearborn to AJ, December
19, and AJ to Dearborn, [cJanuary 4, 1807], both below.
2. The proclamation of November 27, 1806, calling for apprehension of the conspirators, did not arrive in Nashville until about December 27, when a portion of it was published in the *Impartial Review.*

*Although Jackson & Hutchings frequently bought merchandise from
James & Washington Jackson for resale in their stores, this account is unquestionably for goods picked up by the Clover Bottom storekeeper Edward Roberts for outfitting the two boats that departed with Burr December 22. In the Clover Bottom day book under date December 18, this
charge is entered as "James & W Jackson Credit By bill rendered of articles furnished Colo. Burr $346.33." The entry is crossed out and en-
dorsed in Jackson's hand "pd. to them by Colo. Burr himself."*

Account of Jackson & Hutchings with James & Washington Jackson

Nashville Decr 17th 1806

Jackson & Hutchings Mr Roberts		D		
To 1 doz polished knives & forks			7	
" 1 Large pot 60 lbs	@	6d	5	
" 1 Small ditto			1	16⅔
" 1 Carpenters Hammer	3/		50	
" 3 pair fire Irons 106 lbs.		6d	8	83
" 1 Stock lock ea 7/6 & 6/9			2	37½
" 1 Gridiron 10 bars		10½d	1	46
" 1 Skillet and lid	12/		2	
4 Lanthorns	7/6		5	
2 large Camp Kettles	9/		3	
2 Small ditto ditto	4/6		1	50
1 large coffee pott	9/		1	50
1 Large trunk	36/		6	
1 Small ditto			4	
3 Boxes Mould Candles 139 lbs				
20				
20 lbs. wax candles 159	@20		31	80

	2 Barrels Superfine flour	$5	10	
	7 lb. 10 oz Feathers	3/6	4	45
	20 yards 5/10 Sheeting	8/3	27	50
	3 " fine linen for pillows	9/	4	50
	To 2 3/4 yards bed tick	9/	4	12½"
	Making 2 pair sheets	3/	1	
	ditto 4 Pillows	1/		66⅔
	ditto 4 Pillow Cases	1/		66⅔
	tape and thread	1/6		25
"	50 lbs. Muscavado Sugar	1/10½	15	62½
	Bag for ditto	4/6		75
"	1 Barrel flour		6	
"	6 Buffaloe rugs	@$6	36	
"	2 tea potts	11/3	1	87½
"	1 Salt Seller	1/6		25
"	1 Pepper Caster	1/1½		18¾
"	6 three poin[t] Blankets	21/	21	
"	2 Pair 10/4 rose ditto		12	
"	2 ditto 9/4 ditto	51/	17	
"	2 ditto 9/4 ditto	51/	17	
"	1 ditto 8/4 Rose ditto	45/	7	50
"	2 loaves Sugar 9 lb. 3 oz	3/6	5	18¾
"	1 Barrel Salt 244 lbs neate	4½ Cts	10	98
"	6 tin Cups	1/	1	
"	4 Augurs 14 Quarters	@ 1/	2	33⅓
"	4 Pair butt Hinges	2/3	1	50
"	½ doz Gimblets assorted	9d		75
"	1 Shaving Case each 12/ & 16/6		4	75
"	10 Gallons wine	$4	40	
"	1 Barrel to Contain ditto	6/	1	
"	91 lbs. Biscuit	10 Cts	9	10
"	1 Barrel to Contain ditto			25

[Total $346.32⅚]

AD, Mrs. Uhland O. Redd–Day Book of James & Washington Jackson.

While Burr, who had arrived in Nashville about December 13, made final preparations to leave for the southwest, officials in Washington continued their efforts to abort his enterprise. On November 27, President Jefferson had issued his proclamation denouncing the alleged conspiracy in the West; and on December 19, the secretary of war addressed the letter below to Jackson.

On December 30, 1806, eight days after Burr and his two boats left, a special agent, Seth Pease arrived from Washington, bearing these two documents on the Burr conspiracy and a letter, also of December 19, from Daniel Smith assuring Jackson of Pease's trustworthiness. In response to the proclamation, a group of citizens gathered in town on the evening of December 30, denounced Burr, and burned him in effigy. According to Jackson, however, the packet Pease brought did not reach him at the Hermitage, eleven miles from town, until late in the evening of January 1, 1807.

As revealed in the letters below, Jackson, major general of the Tennessee militia for the western part of the state, responded immediately to the alleged emergency once he received official communications from Washington: he placed the militia on alert; he conferred with local United States officials on the scope of his authority to order the state militia under his command beyond the borders of Tennessee; and he dispatched a special agent to the mouth of the Cumberland River to inquire into the extent of Burr's operations. At the same time, he made no attempt to conceal his disgust with the nature and tone of Dearborn's orders.

From Henry Dearborn

War Department Decr. 19. 1806.

Sir,

By your letter to one of the members of Congress from your State,[1] it appears that you have reason for suspecting that some unlawful enterprize is in contemplation on the western Waters. There can be no doubt, but many persons are engaged in some such enterprize; and, before this reaches you, it is not improbable, that a general movement will have commenced.

It is presumed that the Proclamation of the President of the United States, will have produced every necessary exertion in the Civil and Military Officers, for preventing the execution of the contemplated project. And it is confidently expected that, you will have been among the most Zealous opposers of any such unlawful expedition, as appears to be meditated, by a set of disappointed, unprincipled, ambitious or misguided individuals: and that you will continue to make every exertion in your power, as a General of the Militia, to counteract and render abortive, any such expedition or enterprize. The bearer Mr. [Seth] Pease,[2] is on business relating to the General Post Office, whose integrity and prudence may be fully confided in, and to whom you may, with safety, communicate any information you may possess. About Pittsburg it is industriously reported among the adventurers, that they are to be joined, at the mouth of the Cumberland, by two Regiments under the Command of Genl. Jackson—such a story might afford you an opportunity of giving an effectual check to the enterprize if not too late.[3] I am &c.

LC, DNA-RG 107.

1. Probably AJ to Daniel Smith, November 12, above.

2. Pease, originally from Suffield, Conn., was nominated by Jefferson as surveyor general of the territory south of Tennessee on February 23, 1807, and confirmed March 2. He served until June 1810 when he left Mississippi Territory to take up another office. In 1816 he was assistant postmaster general. Mail service from Orleans and Mississippi had become so irregular that the president and postmaster general suspected interference by the conspirators.

3. Rumors about Jackson's complicity with Burr were circulating in Washington. Captain James Read wrote Dearborn on December 4, identifying Jonathan Dayton, Jackson, and a third party not named, as Burr's chief officers, and on December 30 the *Virginia Argus* reported that suspicion had fallen on Wilkinson and "a militia General in Tennessee, who some time past, issued a thundering proclamation arousing the resentment of the people against the Spaniards" (Copied in the *Impartial Review*, January 17, 1807).

The unsigned letter below has been ascribed to Wilkinson on the basis of internal evidence and his testimony before the grand jury in Richmond that New Orleans merchants Chew & Relf had given him a letter from A. Tate, Nashville, intended for Burr's confederate Justus Erich Bollman, a German immigrant then living in New Orleans. It has not been established who Tate was, and no record of his arrest has been found. In his extant correspondence, Jackson never mentioned receiving the letter.

From [James Wilkinson]

Private   New Orleans Decemr. 19th. 1806—
Sir,

If you truly love your Country as I do, then Seize on the Body of A. Taite as a Traitor—I yesterday intercepted a letter from him to a Doctor Bollman Burrs Chief Agent here, whom I have seized and transmitted by the ocean to the Executive—which letter is evincive of his being a party to the Conspiracy which agitates your Country, and is intended to destroy the American Nation—I like you hate a Don[1] But would Steel through my father, to Defend the integrity of the Union—Great God what must be your Situation if you cannot find means to run Burr over the Mountains, Since he might be hid in a great coat Pocket—If He will give me four weeks more, I will promise him that He Shall "take a long leave of all his greatness"—for I Shall not value numbers—But if he comes as soon as Tate promises—this Country will be ruined, and I may have an opportunity of recording with my breath, the delusions & villainies by which I have been misrepresented, persecuted and defamed I have no Secrets except when necessary to the National Interests—This letter is Pro bono Publico—

<My situation here is dreadful but I will make the most of it—>

Copy, TxU. Endorsed "F," suggesting introduction of the letter as evidence, although not found in the records of Burr's trial or the House of Representatives' inquiry on Wilkinson in 1808.
1. Wilkinson's use of this phrase indicates that he had already seen Jackson's November 12 letter to Claiborne. Claiborne later said that he showed it to Wilkinson (see Claiborne to AJ, December 3, 1807, below).

From Daniel Smith

Washington Decr. 29th. 1806.

Dear Sir,

The machinations of Col. Burr have excited more uneasiness in the mind of the executive than any other matter has of late, but they now consider the danger as nearly passed over. By the energetic conduct of Governor [Edward] Tiffin of the State of Ohio, ten of his provision boats are arrested—two of his associates [Harman] Blannerhassett and Comfort Tyler[1] are fled. many young men who were on their march to join them have returned.

The intelligence respecting these matters you probably get before we do, being nearer the scene of action. The mails from the southward and westward arrive very irregularly if at all—especially from Orleans—That which is expected this evening (the stated time of its arrival) goes out so quickly there will be no time to answer any letter which may be conveyed to me by it.

There is a rumor here that a foreign power is to make an attack on Orleans by sea—I scarcely believe it. General Wilkinson is there—his army following him by the last accounts. The President confides in his fidelity.

No important business yet done by Congress—other than suspending the law passed last session prohibiting the importation of certain goods from Great Britain.

The same cause which at last session operated to prevent an appropriation to pay the indians for their land I fear will still prevail—I shall try one scheme to try to counteract it.

Judge Anderson not arrived yet.

I am Dear Sir with great esteem Your obedt. Serv.

Danl. Smith

Please communicate this to George.[2]

ALS, DLC. Extract published in Bassett, 1:157.
1. Tyler was recruited by Burr in New York City to raise men near his home in Herkimer and to deliver supplies to the Ohio River for the expedition. He was arrested in Mississippi and indicted for treason in Richmond.
2. Daniel Smith's son (1776–1849), a planter in Sumner County, who served in the state senate and in Coffee's cavalry in the War of 1812. He married Rachel's niece Tabitha Donelson.

Anderson's letter below raises more questions than it answers. The nature of Anderson's mission and Jackson's concern in it remain unclear. In the 1828 campaign Andrew Erwin claimed that Jackson had misrepresented the mission when he persuaded Anderson to act as Burr's messenger to his son-in-law, Joseph Alston, but that Anderson had learned while on this errand that Burr's objectives were not sanctioned by the government and abandoned the project (National Intelligencer, August 25, 1828). Anderson's statement, published somewhat later, made no charge of deception but said, "It was at the express instance and request of Burr I went to the south. Gen. Jackson knew all about the objects of my visit. They were all considered legitimate" (National Banner and Nashville Whig, October 4, 1828). In a statement probably prepared for the Nashville Jackson Committee but not published with the apologia on the Burr affair, John Sparks recalled that he left Nashville with Anderson in late November, accompanying him as far as Columbia, S.C., and that Anderson's object was to effect a large purchase of Negroes from a Mr. Alston, in which he was unsuccessful (John Sparks to John McGregor, September 4, 1828, T). Whether the $700 credited to Anderson on the October 4 account with Burr, above, was for use on this trip is unknown. Certainly the letter below confirms Erwin's judgment that the trip disillusioned Anderson but in what respect cannot be determined.

From William Preston Anderson

Federal Bottom Wednesday 31st Decr. 1806.

Not until Saturday evening last, did I reach this place and although, I have (in the broadest sense of the word) been on *"a fools errand"* and have been all thorough So. C. & Georgia Swiming rivers & *wading Swamps*, it was a pleasing circumstance to find myself at home in the *Cane* & amidst the *rocks* of Stones river. Indeed I would not under go the same route & under the same preexisting situation of my affairs, for any consideration—I found when in So. C. & after I wrote,[1] that all was *Stuff*, that all was but a *lullaby*—I then persued my own course & in a hidden part of Georgia found Genl. Houser & Major Conklin[2]—I got about 1200$ worth of property[3] from them & have it here with me.

I hope you have attended to what I wrote touching the *receipts*—I shall be down in all next week, if not sooner & whish then to close on the settlement—d___ Such fuss I would be in a hurry to see You, but depend upon it I have changed my setiments very much since I wrote or saw you, & have had the best cause for doing so—In truth what I wrote from Columbia was only Second handed—

Genl. how shall I pay you the amt. of my private acct.? whill you take a negro or will you take a land warra[nt] or both? Anything in that way I should be glad to do if Suitable to you. Mrs. A.[4] presents her best respts. to Mrs. J. & It is hoped you are both well by yr. friend

W. P. Anderson

If you have a safe oppty. of droping a line, do, in the mean time, give me the news of *Nashville*—I have seen no body nor heard nothing—I hear Patton is to be here to day—   WPA

ALS, THi. On address page in Anderson's hand: "As this is on private business, should Genl. J. not be at home Mr. Coffee will open it, but besides him no one WPA."

1. No letter written by Anderson on his trip has been found.
2. Not identified.
3. The nature of the property has not been determined.
4. Anderson's first wife, Nancy Bell (c1784–1809).

1807

To James Winchester

Hermitage January 1st. 1807. 11 oclock P.M.

Dear Genl

This moment by express, I have recd. a letter from the Secratary of War, (the enclosed is a coopy)[1] from which you will observe the necessity of prompt and eficient measures, to put a check to the illegal projects, contemplated, and aluded to by the letter of the secratary of War—By the bearer of this dispatch I am informed that rumor states, that a large number of Boats with armed men are collecting at the mouth of cumberland, and have there united with Colo. Burr, who left Nashville on the 22nd. ulto. with two Boats, two families Six horses and one cow—and Eight oarsmen—six of his oarsmen have returned and advise, that they left him at the mouth of cumberland, unable to proceed for the want of hands to work his crafts—Let these reports be true or false it behoves us to be in readiness to act, as soon as we can be in possession of the necessary information to act upon—for which purpose, I will on tomorrow, dispatch a messenger with necessary instruction to the mouth of cumberland & Massac[2] and you are required to have in readiness to march four companies of mounted infantry by the 5th. Instant from your Brigade if within the compass of your power; against that day, I may be in possession of information that May determin me in the rout and movement. The nature of the service requires a confidential officer to command, and you are selected for this purpose, and ordered to be in readiness to move with the troops that may be ordered for this service on the receipt of my orders for this purpose[3]—I have ordered four companies from Genl [Thomas] Johnstons Brigade, four companies from Genl [Isaac] Roberts Brigade to be furnished, and ready to Join you at whatever point, the information that may be recd. will sugest[4]—Should the force assembled at the mouth be considerable—It will require a larger force, than is ordered to be in readiness for this service—and should their force be considerable and they have descend the ohio & Missisippi—it will become necessary, that we should persue to a certain point where an effective check can be put to the illegal project and enterprise of the *adventurers* with all the *force in my power* This has induced me to Issue you the enclosed order requiring you to have in readiness all the Volunteer corps within your Brigade, &c &c—

From the Tender of services that I have made to the President of the United States and his acceptance thereof, government will expect us to act with promptness and effect, and your Patriotism is a sure pledge to me and to your country that nothing will be wanting on your part, to fulfill the object and wishes of the government and your Genl[5]—as soon as the messenger returns you will be advised of the point of rendezvous— I will appoint a muster master, in due time, to muster the troops. as soon as they are mustered, should you not be in possession of marching orders, you will permit them to return to their respective homes, untill further ordered—then to be in readiness to march at a moments warning—

I am Dear Genl, with high consideration and respect yr mo. ob. serv.

> Andrew Jackson
> M. Genl. 2d. Division Tennessee

ALS copy, DLC; ALS draft, CSmH. Facsimile in Cyrus Townsend Brady, *The True Andrew Jackson* (Philadelphia, 1906), after p. 216.

1. See above, Henry Dearborn to AJ, December 19, 1806.

2. See AJ to John Murrell, January 2, below.

3. In his draft AJ wrote: "Should, We be ordered to march, I shall expect you to take the command. perhaps it may be necessary, for me to accompany you—"

4. Johnson (1766–1825), delegate to the 1796 Tennessee constitutional convention, former state legislator, and officeholder in Tennessee and Robertson counties, had been elected general of the 6th Brigade in 1800. Roberts (1761–1816), a Revolutionary War veteran, also a former state legislator and officeholder in Davidson and Maury counties, had held various military posts before his election as general of the 5th Brigade. Jackson's orders to Johnson's and Roberts's brigades, not found, were probably identical to those issued to Winchester, January [2], below.

5. See above, AJ to Jefferson, [cNovember 5, 1806], and Jefferson to AJ, December 3, 1806. In his draft to Winchester, Jackson alluded to Jefferson's letter in a postscript: "P.S. these men must be ready—to amt of 240—I have recd. a letter from the President, and from the tender of service, this order must be compleat if required—from circumstances A.J."

ENCLOSURE: TO JAMES WINCHESTER

Division orders   Jany. [2,] 1807—
Sir

From circumstances made known to me, by letter from the Secretary at War dated the 19th. ulto. handed to me last evening by express as well as from circumstances ennumerated in the proclamation of the President of the United States of the 1st. Ulto.;[1] make it necessary that the militia that I have the honor to command should be in complete readiness to march all volunteer companies of mounted infantry in your brigade at a moments warning after the rect. of my orders for that purpose[2]—You will also have in readiness four full companies of Mounted Infantry to march On the fifth instant with provisions for 20 days & 15 rounds of powder [and bal]l—All volunteer companies will be held in readiness to march whenever the emergency of our country require it, and my orders are given to that effect. You will make known to me without delay the exact number of Volunteer companies ready to march in yr. brigade, and if there should not be yr sufficiant quota of Volunteers you will immediately make up such deficiancy by draft and hold them in readiness to march at a moments warning

You will also make known to me the precise Situation & State of the brigade under yr. command, the soonest possible.[3]

I am with considerations of the highest respect & Esteem Yr. friend

Andrew Jackson
M. Genl. 2d Divison

LS, DLC. Published in Bassett, 1:158.
1. Jackson was referring to Jefferson's proclamation of November 27, 1806, warning of a possible conspiracy to invade Spanish territory, which he had received on January 1.
2. For his orders, see AJ to the Brigadier Generals of the 2nd Division, January 5, below.
3. Reports not found.

To Thomas Stuart

January 2nd. 1807

Sir

Inclosed I send you a letter from the Secratary of war, of Date the 19th. ult. for your perusal, and wish your oppinion on the following points.

1st, whether, without proof, I would be authorised under the proclamation of the President and the enclosed letter, to order out a sufficient number of troops to search the ohio, for armed Boats & men, and if found to detain them untill an investigation could be had of their intentions, and destination—[1]

2nd. whether I would not be authorised under existing circumstances to hire an Express to go to the mouth of cumberland, and Massac; to bring the necessary information with respect to the assemblage, of armed forces & boats on the ohio—

3rd. if such a force is assembled and has proceded on to Natchez or Neworleans, would the enclosed, taken into view with the Presidents proclamation, authorise me to march such force as in a State of preparation through by land to intercept, them[2]—Health & respect

Andrew Jackson

ALS, THi. Published in Bassett, 1:157–58. Stuart (1762–1838) was United States attorney for the District of West Tennessee, having been appointed to that post in 1802 upon Jackson's recommendation. In 1809 he was elected judge of the Fourth Circuit Court in Tennessee, a position he held until 1836.
1. According to his letter to Winchester, January 1, above, Jackson had already placed the companies on alert, ordering their rendezvous on January 5.
2. Stuart's response has not been found.

To John Murrell

January 2nd. 1807—

you will proceed without delay to the mouth of cumberland, by the rout of Springfield, at Springfield deliver the letter addressed to Genl Thomas Johnston to Colo. [Archer] Cheatam,[1] with a request, that he without delay hand it to the Genl—Then proceed on to the mouth of cumberland, If there are an assemblage of Boats there, make your observations, with respect to the number of men how armed, and if any, what quantity of military stores on board, and as you make the observations commit them to writin[g.] Should there be no Boats, at the mouth—proceed on to Fort Massac, and if there are an assemblage of Boats there make the same observations as above—if Boats have been there, and have departed deliver the letter to Capt [Daniel] Bissle,[2] receive his answer and information and return without delay, and report your observations—to me—despatch is necessary and it is expected, you will with all possible speed return after performing the duty[3]—I am Sir with due respect

Andrew Jackson
M. Genl 2nd Div.

ALS copy, DLC; Copy, DNA-RG 107. Published in Bassett, 1:159. Murrell, a resident of Nashville, served with the Tennessee Volunteers as a private on the 1813 Natchez expedition.
1. Cheatham was a local political and militia leader in Robertson County. The letter to Johnson has not been found, but it was probably of the same tenor as Jackson's order to Winchester, January [2], above.
2. Bissell (d. 1833), a native of Connecticut, was a captain in the United States Army and commander at Fort Massac. In 1814 he was made brigadier general.
3. For Murrell's report, see Murrell to AJ, January 8, below.

To Daniel Bissell

[January 2, 1807]

Sir

Sundry reports which has reach'd me, State that there are a number of arm'd men with Boats loaded with arms and amunition; assembled on the Ohio at or near the mouth of Cumberland, with intentions hostile to the peace and interest of the United States. I have no doubt but you have received the Presidents proclamation, and orders from the Secretary of War, to interrcept and bring to Justice all men engag'd in any enterprise contrary the Laws or orders of our Government—If these you have not received, should it come to your Knowledge, that there is an assemblage of men and Boats, who have illegal enterprises in view—It is expected that you will exhort your force to take and bring to Justice all such—You will also be good enough to give me information of and concerning such assemblage of armd men and Boats loaded with warlike Stores, their number an point of rendezvous and dispatch the bearer back without delay, which such information as you may have in your power to communicate—[1]

With due regard I am yr. Mo. ob Serv

Andrew Jackson

Copy, DNA-RG 107. Published in *Impartial Review*, January 17; Bassett, 1:158.
    1. For Bissell's response, see Bissell to AJ, January 5, below.

To *[William Preston Anderson]*

[January 3, 1807]

I recd. your note:[1] its contents duly observed. the receipts as directed I have retained. the negro Girl named, if likely, at a fair price, I will receive. I have recd Some Communications from the President and Secratary of War,[2] and your presence is required, at My house to morrow Evening, or Early Monday Morning to consult on Means & Measure, and to determine the latitude of the authority. it is the merest[3] old woman letter from the Secratary that you ever Saw. your presence on Sunday Evening will be expected, and your presence on monday morning at 9 oclock cannot be dispensed with. you must attend. I have Sent an express to the mouth of Cumberland & to Massac to see and hear, and make observations.[4] I have wrote to Capt. Bissle:[5] but from information recd. at the moment the Messenger was Starting, Gives me reason to believe that Bissle is the Host of A. B. Wilkinson has denounced B. as a traitor after he found that he was implicated. this is Deep policy. he has obtained thereby the Command of New Orleans the Gun Boats armed and his plan can now be exicuted without resistance. But we must be there in due time, before fortifications can be erected, and restore to our Government New Orleans and the western Commerce. you must attend. Give to those officers that you see assurances that all Volunteer Companies will be Greatfully accepted off. we must have thirty, 35 or 40 Companies into the field, in fifteen or twenty days; ten or 12 in four, I have it from the President, I have it from Dixon[6] that all Volunteers will be gratefully accepted. To-morrow night Winchester will be with me, I wish you there, the Secratary of War is not fit for a Grany. I fear J. Randolphs Ideas were too Correct; but duberous as he has wrote there are sufficient authority to act. Act I will, and by next mail I will give him a letter that will instruct him in his duty, and convince him that I know mine.[7] If you Convenient bring the Girl with you and Health and respect

A. JACKSON.

Compliments to Mrs A. I must tell you that Bonepart has destroyed the prussian army. We ought to have a little of the Emporers energy.

Text from Cincinnati *Truth's Advocate*, October 1828, p. 390. Original not found. Copy, OHi. Published in Bassett, 1:160–61, as addressed to Patton Anderson, January 4. According to *Truth's Advocate* the letter was "without date but is endorsed as written the 4th and received the 6th of January, 1807, and was addressed to Maj. Wm. P. Anderson." Correct in naming the addressee of the letter, *Truth's Advocate* appears to have erred by at least one day in ascribing its date. The first Monday in January 1807 was January 5, and since Jackson requested his military aide's presence "to morrow Evening [Sunday, January 4], or Early Monday Morning [January 5]," the date January 3 seems more plausible.

1. See above, Anderson to AJ, December 31, 1806.
2. Jackson was referring to Jefferson's proclamation of November 27 and to Dearborn's letter of December 19, 1806, above.
3. "Merest" is rendered "worst" in the copy, OHi.
4. See above, AJ to Murrell, January 2.
5. See above, AJ to Bissell, [January 2].
6. See above, Dickson to AJ, [December 15, 1806].
7. See AJ to Henry Dearborn, [cJanuary 4], below.

From Daniel Smith

Jany. 3d. 1807.

Dear Sir,

By your letter of the 1st of last month it appears your mind is in suspence with respect to Mr. Burr's objects and intentions.[1] No doubt is entertained here that his designs are hostile to the peace of the United States. But in general this is to be inferred from a number of facts and circumstances all pointing that way rather than any positive and direct testimony.

He wrote to Mr. [Henry] Clay his Attorney in the Court of Kentucky where he was indicted. Mr. Clay is now a Senator at this place in the room of Mr. Adair. I have seen this letter. In it he says he does not own a single boat musket or bayonette and that the executive of the U. S. are acquainted with his object and view it with complaisance.[2] The executive say they never were made acquainted with his object. Of course no reliance is to be placed in his protestations—and of course you ought not to let your first faith be shaken.

I am Dear Sir Your obedt. Servt.

Danl Smith

ALS, DLC. Published in Bassett, 1:159.
1. Smith was probably referring to Jackson's letter of November 12, 1806 (above), which, according to his endorsement, he received "in December."
2. Burr to Clay, December 1, 1806, published in James F. Hopkins and Mary W. M. Hargreaves, eds., *The Papers of Henry Clay* (Lexington, Ky., 1959), 1:256–57.

To Henry Dearborn

[cJanuary 4, 1807]

Dear Sir

This will be handed you by Mr [Gerard W.] Hopkins, who is the bearer of Despatches from Governor Claiborne,[1] to the Secratary of State, in order to expedite his Journey I have furnished him, with a horse—

Mr Hopkins was the bearer of a letter from Governor Claiborne to me in answer to my letter to him mentioned to you in my last,[2] and I am happy to find, that it has had with the governor the effects intended by it—I hope a full disclosure of the traitorous designs against our government will be fully developed—I dispatched a messenger on the 2nd. to the mouth of Cumberland & to Massac from some hints I am fearfull that the influence of the Genl[3] has extended itself to that Post, and no aid to the government is to be expected there—This is merely a hint, as I hold it sacred to the reputation of every man that he never ought to be censured without proof but still hints under existing circumstances is sufficient to put people on their guard, and my instructions to the messenger is to be guarded—as soon as I am advised of the situation & strenth I shall be in motion—From looking into your letter of the 19th.[4] I am sorry to find that the orders are not more explicit—I am sorry to find that the individuals are not named the proof within your hands as stated to me, and which I was advised of by Doctor Dixson letter of the 15th. would certainly have authorised it[5]—Should they be moved on from the mouth of Cumberland, there is a doubt whether I am authorised to persue both by water and land to prevent the project.

I have given orders to have the militia ready 12 companies will be ready to act the 8th. if circumstances should require it—and should the real numbers be as stated viz. at 1,000 I shall conclude from your letter, and the situation of the country below that your meaning and intention was that I should with my force immediately proceed, to the spot where a certain check can be put to the enterprise—I have men but where is the supplies; where the magazine stores or the Bayonets to storm a fortress— and It is doubtfull from your letter whether I am authorised, to have the necessary means laid in for the use of the men necessary to carry into effect your order and wishes—however rest assured that nothing on my part shall be wanting to promote the interest of the government; & quell the conspiracy—resting confident that government will sanction my conduct and discharge all necessary expence as soon as the messenger returns I will be ready to act, in case they are in the ohio—four Boats belonging to merchants I have conditionaly engaged in case of emergency— amunition is verry scarce here—and I expect the lead at the mines near illinoise is secured by the conspirators—I shall await with impatience for your orders and instructions how these supplies is to be furnished, and what number of men it is expected for me to march and to what point unless as before stated I should find from the report of the messenger that they are in force superior to our strength below. in that case I shall send on a sufficient force to check them if the necessary supplies can be had— Mr Hopkins waits for this letter I have neither time to correct or to coopy it—Health & respect

A. Jackson

ALS, DNA-RG 107. Published in Bassett, 1:159–60.
1. Hopkins has not been further identified.
2. See William C. C. Claiborne to AJ, December 5, 1806; and above, AJ to Claiborne, November 12, 1806. Jackson's letter to Dearborn has not been found.
3. Wilkinson.
4. See above.
5. See above, William Dickson to AJ, [December 15, 1806].

To the Brigadier Generals of the 2nd Division

(Division Orders.) Hermitage January 5th. 1807.

you are required, to have the men directed to be furnished by my order of 2nd instant[1] Rendezvous & mustered into service, on the 8. 9th. & 10 Instant. Those from the 4th Brigade at gallatine those from the 5th. Brigade at Nashville and those from the 6th. at Springfield—and in case marching orders are not Issued—as soon as they men are mustered, you will direct them to retire to their respective homes, to be ready to march at a moments warning—I have appointed Capt James Deshea Muster Master,[2] and command all officers and soldiers to respect and obay him as such

Andrew Jackson
M. Genl. 2nd. Division

ALS copy, DLC. Published in Bassett, 1:161.
1. See above.
2. Desha, a merchant in Gallatin, had earlier resigned a commission in the United States Army. In 1808 he reenlisted and served another year.

From Daniel Bissell

Fort Massac Jan. 5th. 1807.

Sir,
This day per Express I had the honor to receive your very interesting letter of the 2d. instant,[1] & shall pay due respect to it's contents. As yet I have not received the Presidents Proclamation alluded to, nor have I received any Orders from the Department of War relative to the subject matter of your letter.

There has not to my knowledge been any assemblage of men or boats, at this or any other place, unauthorised by law or presidency, but should any thing of the kind make it's appearance, which carries with it the least mark of suspicion, as having illegal enterprises or projects in view hostile to the peace & good order of government, I shall with as much ardour & energy as the case will admit, endeavor to bring to justice all such Offenders.

For more than two weeks last past, I have made it a point to make myself acquainted with the loading & situation of all boats descending the river. As yet there has nothing the least alarming appeared. On, or about 31st. ultimo, Colo. Burr late Vice President of the United States passed this with about ten boats, of different descriptions, navigated with about six men each, having nothing on board that would even suffer a conjecture, more than a man bound to market, he has descended the rivers towards Orleans—should any thing to my knowledge transpire interesting to Government I will give the most early notice in my power, & have the honor to be respectfully sir yr. obdt. servt.

(signed)   Dan. Bissel
Commanding Capt

Copy, DNA-RG 46. Published in *Impartial Review*, January 17; Bassett, 1:162. On January 8, Jackson forwarded to Dearborn copies of his January 2 letters to Murrell and Bissell, Bissell's letter above, Murrell's letter of January 6, and Claiborne's letter of December 5. Dearborn in turn sent the letters to the President, and on January 28 Jefferson forwarded Bissell's and Murrell's letters of January 5 and 8 to Congress.

    1. See above.

From James Winchester

Cragfont 6th Jan 1807.

Dear Genl

Mr James Cage[1] has just arrived from the mouth of Cumberland He was there yesterday was a week past, and made particular inquiry concerning Col Burr &c. Was informed that he left that place the day before with Eleven Boats and between 110 and 120 men. this information Mr. Cage got from a Mr. Wood[2] a Gentleman of observation and information of that place. Thus 100 Boats is reduced to Eleven. I shall notwithstanding go on to raise the Volunteers as ordered. Because if Wilkeson is a Trator they will still be wanting at Orleans—

Yesterday evening at Gallatin I found Mr. Hopkins the carrier of the orleans dispatches. I sent for him and in strong terms reprobated his delay. He replied he was w[aiti]ng for a Servant he was about to hire; that he thought it necessary to protect him &c. I spurned the Idea of an express delaying for a Servant &c. He seemed hurt and said he would start this morning before day, but did not relinquish the Idea of a Servant. I thought he was a little intoxicated but I might be mistaken. I wish'd to bring him home with me but could not prevail on him to come.[3] Health & fraternity

J Winchester

ALS, DLC. Published in Bassett, 1:162.
  1. Cage was a native of Sumner County and former sheriff. His brother William was Winchester's business partner.
  2. Not identified.
  3. Hopkins's dawdling, delaying the delivery of Claiborne's letters to Jackson and to officials in Washington, also worried Claiborne. On March 6, 1807, Claiborne wrote to James Madison: "I fear I was greatly deceived in the character which was given me of a Mr. Hopkins, a young man who was the bearer of my dispatches of the 5. & 6. of December last—I have heard from good authority that he lost by gaming some money at Natchez and behaved otherwise imprudently—His indiscretions were renewed at Nashville; and I fear he is undeserving of confidence" (Dunbar Rowland, ed., *Official Letterbooks of W.C.C. Claiborne, 1801–16* [Jackson, Miss., 1917], 4:123–24). In his letter of January 8 below, Jackson informed Claiborne of Hopkins's "indiscretions" in Nashville.

From John Murrell

Nashville Jany. 8th. 1807.

Sir,

I received your instructions dated the 2d. instant[1] & agreeable thereto I delivered your letter addressed to Genl. Thomas Johnson to Colo. Cheatham,[2] & it was forwarded to him immediately. I arrived at Centerville on the 4th. instant, heard a report there that Colo. Burr had gone down the river with one thousand armed men, arrived at the mouth of Cumberland river that evening & made enquiry concerning Colo. Burr, & was informed that he left that place on the 28th. of December 1806 with ten Boats of Different descriptions, had Sixty men on board but no appearance of arms. I left there on the 5th. instant & arrived at fort Massac that evening, delivered your letter to Captain Bissle & received his answer,[3] made some enquiries of him & was informed that Colo. Burr had left that place on the 30 December 1806. with ten boats. He likewise informed me that he had been on board the boats & seen no appearance of arms or ammunition. On my return to the mouth of Cumberland River I was informed that three boats had been stoped at Louisville with a quantity of ammunition. There are about fifty men stationed at the mouth of Cumberland under command of Colo. Ramsey.[4]

I remain with the highest esteem yrs.

(Signed)   John Murrell

Copy, DNA-RG 46. Published in *Impartial Review*, January 17; Bassett, 1:166.
  1. See above.
  2. Letter not found, but it was probably similar to the letter above, AJ to Winchester, January 1.

3. See above, AJ to Daniel Bissell, [January 2], and Bissell to AJ, January 5.
4. Not identified.

To William Charles Cole Claiborne

Nashville January 8th. 1807

Dear friend,

On Sunday last I recd. your friendly letter, by Mr. Hopkins bearer of dispatches to the Secretary of State, of the united States, of date the 5th. of December last[1] acknowledging the rect. of mine of the 12th. of November[2]—and from the denunciation made by Genl. Wilkerson of Colo. Burr, as published in the Orleans Gazette of Decr. 11th. I find that my suspicions, and friendly warning, was in due time, and not without foundation—Mr. Hopkins produced to me your passport, stating him to be the bearer of dispatches, to the Secretary of State, and named to me he wanted a horse which I immediately furnished, on the faith of your passport, and the Idea of the exigency of the case—and he progressd. immediately—but from information, of his conduct, recd. before he reached me and of his conduct after he left me, I have Strong Suspicions that he is tainted, as to his conduct after he left me, I refer you to Genl. J. Winchester's letter a copy of which, is inclosed markd. No. 1.[3]

we have been in a bustle here for some days—owing to information recd. from the war department and his letter to me of the 19th. ultimo.[4] I cannot call it an order—It is of a doubtfull hue—a milk and Cider thing—displays a want of firmness that renders him unfit for the office he holds, or even for a scullion in a cook shop; but I knew my duty, and the appearance of our country required action—I ordered out 12. companies of the malitia—dispatched a messenger to Fort Massac, to be informed of the truth of a report, that was currently circulated, that Colo. Burr, was assembled at the mouth of Cumberland, with 100. Boats and 1000 armed men—the express has Just returned, and for the result of the enquiry I refer you to a copy of Capt. Bissell's letter to me and Mr. Murells report who was the messenger,[5] On which I have ordered that the Malitia return to their respective homes, and be ready to march at a Minutes warning[6]—Colo. Burr left Nashville on the 22nd. with two boats six horses and a Cow, and two families consisting of one man and three women—with eight Oarsmen, six of which, returned from the mouth of Cumberland—From the information on which my letter to you was written, altho it was asked by me whether Colo. Burr, was knowing to the plans, and answered in the negative, still my Suspicions were such, that I first wrote to him on the Subject and obtained an express pledge of honour, that he never had any Ideas hostile to the union or its interest, and that he had the authority of the united States, for any thing, or project he had in view,[7] after the Grand Jury had not only acquited him, in the District of Kentuckey but passd. an encomium, on his views, he returned here, and thus Shielded from Suspicion Still was entitled to respect, under these circumstances, he obtained, Stockley [Donelson] Hays, to accompany him,[8] with the consent of the Colo. under great promises of friendship, and Solemn pledges of no intention hostile or inimical to the united States, my letter by Stockley you will receive,[9] and I must confess I was not clear or free from Suspicion, and directed Stockley when he reached Orleans, to be subject to your advice and if he saw any act, or thing that wore hostility to our Government and laws, to burst the chains of friendship, and flee to the Standard of his country—this he has pledged himself to do. Since he left me, from Doctr. Dixons letter,[10] I have reasons to believe that testamony was filed, before the 15th. December of his hostile designs, against our Government, Still the Secretary at War's nerves is so weak, or his attachment so strong to his friend the Genl.[11] that his modesty is such he cannot give names but wishes to throw the responsibility off his Shoulders, on those of other individuals, O my friend you have a right to know my attachment to Republicanism, to the present administration but as to the War, department I am obliged to exclaim, O *Tempora, o Mores*—you I believe do know my attachment, to my Country— but Still I fear we want nerve, to purge the body politic of Treason and conspiracy, I shall write you more fully, when I have leisure, Should Stockley reach you keep him with you untill he can return, to his country and friends, I wish you to write me relative to Mr. Hopkins he stated to me that he was the bearer of the political death warrant of the Genls. military existance

you my dear Sir must be on the look out you must have confidence but in few, but apparantly in all, there is Genl. Adair that is gone to your country on some business whether of a public or private nature I know not,[12] but one thing is generally, believed that Wilkerson with Several others, will feel themselves, in despirate Situations, and make use of despirate means, to procure a Country and a home, and I am clearly of opinion the Seperation of the union is the first object, if in this they should be disappointed I know not neither can I conjecture what they will attempt, But my friend the patriotism of my Division has amply displayed itself— figure to yourself, Genl. Robertson at the head of a volunteer company, composed of old patriots, over fifty, such as Genl. Thos. Overton, Majr. Howell Tatum, Majr. Clem[ent] Hall, George Ridley, &c. &c. &c. tendering their services to their Genl. and Country[13]—what Sensations must this inspire, is more easily Conjectured than expressed, should danger threaten you—write me—and under your notification, on the wings of patriotism, I will hasten to the point of danger, to Support the union of our Country, the prop of freedom, with the arm of vengeance that shall burst, on treason and on treasoners heads if to be found—and on Spanish insolence and pride, should the constituted Authority order it, excuse the haste in which this letter is written and accept, assurances of a continuation of friendship—

Andrew Jackson

P.S. be good anough to give me the date the Genl divulged the treason to you—

A. J—

LS with postscript in AJ's hand, NhD; ALS copy, DLC. Published in Bassett, 1:163–66.
1. See Claiborne to AJ, December 5, 1806.
2. See above.
3. See above, Winchester to AJ, January 6.
4. See above, Dearborn to AJ, December 19, 1806.
5. See above, Bissell to AJ, January 5, and Murrell to AJ, January 8.
6. See AJ to the 2nd Division, January 10, below.
7. Neither Jackson's letter to Burr nor Burr's response has been found.
8. Hays (1788–1831), Rachel's nephew, served as quartermaster of the Tennessee Volunteers, 1812–14. When Hays arrived in Washington, Miss. Terr., Ferdinand Leigh Claiborne and Cowles Mead took him under their care. On April 20, 1807, he wrote John Coffee about his departure from Nashville with Burr: "Four months have now, with the setting of this days sun, elapsed since I parted with you at Clover Bottom. when you and all friends were doubtfull of my impending fate—when all was doubt, the question whether to go or not to go, you on whom I called as a friend and whose advise as such I received—" (DLC-Marquis James Papers). See also Hays to AJ, April 20, below.
9. Not found. During the 1828 presidential campaign, Hays discussed his association with Burr, reporting that he had taken with him a letter from Jackson to Claiborne.
10. See above, Dickson to AJ, [December 15, 1806].
11. Wilkinson.
12. Adair arrived in New Orleans on January 15 and was immediately arrested.
13. Hall (c1753–1824) and Ridley (1738–1836), like the others mentioned by Jackson, were Revolutionary veterans. For their tender of service, see James Robertson et al. to AJ and AJ to Robertson et al., [cJanuary 7–8].

To Daniel Bissell

Nashville January 9th. 07.

Sir

On last evening pr return of the express, I recd. your very interesting letter in answer to mine of the 2nd.[1] and for your promptness, in the fulfilment of my request, receive my thanks—

The publick mind has been much excited from numerous reports, in circulation, that I am happy to find are without foundation—These have reached the ear of goverment, and has induced a belief, that the western country are not attached to the union—This is a slander without foundation, and I have no doubt circulated by designing charactors—but I can say with truth we are firmly attached to our goverment and the union. There is but one voice—*united we stand, divided we fall*. This will be handed to you by Doctors [Thomas Augustine] Claiborne and [John Robertson] Bedford on their way to Neworleans, Gentlemen of respectability & information and to whom I refer you for the current news—[2]

Will you altho. unacquainted permit me to recommend those Gentlemen to your polite attention

I am sir with due respect yr mo. ob. serv.

Andrew Jackson

ALS draft, DLC. Published in Bassett, 1:166–67.
1. See above, AJ to Bissell, [January 2], and Bissell to AJ, January 5.
2. Bedford (1782–1827), a native of Mecklenburg County, Va., was a physician in Rutherford County. In later years he abandoned medicine for a mercantile business in Alabama and Louisiana. The journal of his trip with Claiborne is published in *THM*, 5(April, July 1919): 48–63, 109–22.

To *the 2nd Division*

[January 10, 1807]

Friends & Fellow Soldiers,

The President's *Proclamation*, as well as the Secretary of war's letter to me dated on the 19th of last month, has given rise to the preparatory steps taken, to have the militia under my command in complete readiness. Those communications sound the tocsin of alarm—They are sufficient evidences to us, that the repose of our country is about to be interrupted—That an illegal enterprise has been set on foot by *disappointed, unprincipled, ambitious* or *misguided individuals*, and that they are about to be carried on against the government of Spain, contrary to the faith of treaties—Other reports state that the adventurers in this enterprize, were numerous—that they had assembled at the mouth of Cumberland river, in considerable force and hostile array—that they had for their object, a separation of the Western from the Eastern part of the United States, & that an attack would, in the first place be made on New-Orleans.

These things, my Fellow Soldiers, gave rise to my orders of the 2d inst. to the end, that 12 companies of Volunteer corps, might be prepared to march on the 5th—I did at the same time order brigadier general James Winchester to take the command.[1] As a previous and necessary measure, to any order to march, I dispatched a confidential express to the mouth of Cumberland river and to Massac, with a letter to capt. Bissell, the commanding officer at that place. This express returned on the 8th inst. from whose report, together with the information given by capt. Bissell, we are furnished with the very pleasing news, that nothing in that quarter is the least alarming.[2] The alluded to address from the commanding officer has been read to you on parade.[3] Under all these circumstances, added to the limited point of view which the orders given me must be interpreted; I have deemed proper to dismiss the corps under my command, and direct them to return to their respective homes until their country shall require their services, and until further orders shall be given.

The appearances of unanimity, the ardour displayed on this occasion, and the promptness with which both the officers and men have attended to their duty and orders, are sure pledges to their country & to their general, that when emergency shall require, they will fly with the wings of Patriotism to support the United Government of their country, and the liberty it so bountifully affords—he also clearly sees the great Physical strength of our country displayed much to his satisfaction, in the promptness and alacrity with which Gen. Winchester, General Johnston, and the officers and men now in view, have shown in their attention to his orders. Here is the Bulwark of our country always sufficient to support and defend the constituted authorities of our government—When the insolence or vanity of the Spanish Government shall dare to repeat their insults on our flag, or shall dare to violate the sacred obligations of the good faith of our treaties with them; or should the disorganizing TRAITOR attempt the dismemberment of our country, or criminal breach of our laws; let me ask what will be the effects of the example given, by a tender of service made by such men, as compose the *Invincible Grays*, commanded too, by the father of our infant state Genl. James Robertson?[4]

It must and will produce effects like these, "the youthful patriot will be invigorated to a proper sense of duty and zeal, and the vengeance of an insulted country will burst upon the devoted heads of any foreign invaders, or the authors of such diabolical plans"—When we behold aged, deserving, and respectable men, whom the laws of their country exempt from common military duty, the very first to come forward in the event of danger, and whose situation is every how comfortable at home, thus to act, what must be the degree of feeling and sensibility excited? it is beyond expression, but merits the highest encomium.

Friends & Fellow Soldiers.

I can not dismiss you without making honorable mention of the Patriotism of capt. Thomas Williamson displayed on the present occasion, who, in twenty four hours after the receipt of my letter, notified me, he was ready to march at the head of a full company of Volunteers.[5] Such promptness as this, will be a fit example for the hardy sons of freedom—should the constituted authorities require our service.

Return fellow Soldiers to the bosom of your families, with the best wishes of your general, until your country calls, and then it is expected you will march on a moment's warning.

ANDREW JACKSON.

Text from *Impartial Review*, January 17. Original not found. Published in Parton, 1: 326–28.

1. See above, AJ to Winchester, January 1 and [2].
2. See above, AJ to Bissell, [January 2], and Bissell to AJ, January 5.
3. See above, enclosure in AJ to Winchester, January 1.
4. See Robertson et al. to AJ and AJ to Robertson et al., [cJanuary 7–8]. The Invincible Grays was a volunteer company of Revolution veterans and others over fifty years old.

5. Williamson (1767–1825), a resident of Nashville, was a saddler and state legislator. Most likely he had received a copy of Jackson's orders from Isaac Roberts, general of the 5th Brigade. Williamson's letter has not been found.

Despite Jackson's efforts to determine the nature and scope of the Burr enterprise, rumors persisted for months that he still supported the ex-vice president and his venture. On January 3, two days after he had called out the militia, an anonymous writer in the Impartial Review *called Burr and Wilkinson "traitors" and urged loyalty to the Union upon the citizens of the area. The writer justified his article by declaring that "these observations are necessary from the boldness with which Burr is defended and wished success." Two weeks later, on January 17, Thomas Eastin, editor of the* Review, *expressed the "hope [that] the late transactions in this country, will have a tendency to dispel the suspicions . . . relative to gen. Jackson."*

Suspicions nevertheless lingered, and on April 18, the editor of the Tennessee Gazette *asked: "Who will explain this? While Col. Burr was in this town, he told a gentleman of this place, that he had upon his honor, made a declaration of the intention and destination of his late expedition to a citizen of Davidson County and one only. Who is he? Will he be considered a Traitor? Will he be arrested by Wilkinson or will the civil authority take notice of him? His name will be announced in some future number, 'without regard to standing or station.' Traitors tremble."*

In the letters below Jackson discussed some of these reports. It has not been determined whether the Gazette *ever revealed the identity of the man to whom it alluded, but the suggestion is strong in Jackson's letter to Campbell, January 15, below, that the editor had Jackson in mind when he wrote his comments.*

To James Sanders

[cJanuary 13, 1807]

Sir

I had a hope whenever it was necessary for me to address you, that it would have been in the language of that true friendship which I thought existed between us and on subjects more agreable than the present—

I did flatter myself, that whatever might have been the conduct of base and unprincipled enemies, who have had me buried, and in tomb, who have, with all the ingenuity of falshood, been digging a pit for me, which they—themselves have fell into—That I never should have found you in the list, of those, under the cover falshood of the blackest dye—trying to infuse into the public mind, at a time when our country appears to be endangered, Jealousies respecting me well calculated, to abate that patriotism, that under present circumstances, ought to prevade, the mind of every true american—yes Sir I have heard, that you should have said "That I might be engaged in the treason of Colo. Burr." That you have expressed yourself, in this way I have no doubt off. As you have expressed yourself, that I am capable of *perjury*, it behoves you to give testimony to the world, that I am this base charector, or attone for the injury, thus done to my charector, by expressing publickly, that you have no grounds for the slander thus expressed off me—Or boldly find yourself answerable to me for the expression—I love my friend and situated as you & myself were, I tried to foster that friendship that ought to have existed between us—on my part it has never been departed from, but Sir when such declarations are made from you who the world believes to be my friend and capable of truth, the injuries resulting from them are such, that attonement must and shall be made—I have but one life to loose, that I have risqued in behalf of my reputation, I will again—and he that is of your standing that will attempt to deprive me of it, it is at their own peril—for by the gods I never will permit such an attempt to assassinate my reputation go unpunished—I did extend that hospitality to Colo. Burr that I would and ever will to man, that I think a man of honour who is banished from his Country and his home—and from the pledges he made (after my suspicions originated,) I did think, him a persecuted man—and when he returned under the acquittal of a respectable grand Jury, I thought him as innocent, as his declarations and pledges had made him—and as such I did treat him as an innocent and once deserving Citizen of the united States however Sir if I have done any thing contrary to the law of the united States, I am answerable to my goverment not to individuals, and I hold individuals answerable to me for any injury grounded on falshood that they may propogate—I shall suspend any decisive session on the information, I have recd. untill I receive your answer, but as it appears you took but little time to announce my guilt, I shall expect, a speedy answer—yrs &c.

A. Jackson

ALS draft, CtY. Sanders (1764–1836) was a Sumner County farmer and former delegate to the North Carolina General Assembly. In 1806, following the death of his first wife, he married Mary, the daughter of Daniel Smith and the widow of Samuel Donelson.

From James Sanders

Janry. 13th. 1807

Sir

I received yours By Mr. Bradford[1] and was much Surprised at the contents having as I conceive never given you cause to of produced Such a letter nor I hope never Shall no person, as to the buzz that has been raised by Colo. Burr I Suppose you have hearn that there was Some Suspitions that you knew that Burr Intended Some thing, which in Conversation I have taken a part and have assented to, but not that you was Knowing to his intending aney thing against this government. as to my endeavouring to influence the publick opinion gainst you is certainly Wrong, an expression may be cau[sed] to convey a differant Idea from the One intended; as to friendship it has always been my intention to act, particelarly so towards you, and towards all men, holding my Self Accountable for my Conduct, with the Same liberties of Other men. I am yours With Respect

Jas. Sanders

ALS, DLC.
1. See above. Bradford not identified.

To George Washington Campbell

(Confidential)   January 15th. 1807.

The late denunciation of Aron Burr as a traitor has excited great surprise, and general indignation against Burr—Still from the oppinion Possessed of the accuser[1] many there are who wait for the proof, before they will pronounce him guilty of the charge—one thing is generally believed, that if Burr is guilty, Wilkeson has participated in the treason—The public mind has been much agitated from various reports, of Burr having been met at the mouth of cumberland river with 100, boats and 1,000 armed men, & it was toled as a fact that the Capt at Massac & all the men were going with him, subsequent reports stated they had gone—an express which I started on the receipt of the S. of wars letter of the [1]9th. ulto has returned, and state that Burr left Massac on 30th. ulto, in company ten Boats, six men on board of each, with out arms or any thing that can afford suspicion—and that Capt Bissel has been doing his duty as a vigilant officer—I had ordered out 12 companies of Vollunteers on the receipt of the S. W. letter to check the adventurers which on return of express I dismised—I shall send you on a coopy of the S. W. letter to me[2] by next mail with the remarks I intend making on it.[3] It is couched in such offensive terms, that shews he is unfit to discharge the duties of his station, and that he is devoid of all knowledge on perilous occasions that ought compose the genl or commander—I hope I know my duty as a soldier and the first duty of a good citizen—when danger threatens to attend to the safety of his country—This being done I will pay my respects to the secratary of war and duly note his letter, which I will inclose you by next mail; & which I hope as a brother and a friend you will give that publicity to that I may direct—Will you permit me to bring to your view a subject that has been made known to me as a brother—I mean the dispute that is likely to arise between you and Genl Robertson respecting a peace of land, This dispute I would advise to be left to two or three

Brothers to decide—Should it get into court, it will be expensive, create passions that never ought to exist, between brothers—and I have no doubt, the dispute can be as well ended, and Justice be as much attained, by the verdict of three brethren as any other way—The land to Genl Robertson is a great thing, he has sold it, and made a general warrentee—and this he states I think before he knew of your claim—he also states that genl [Martin] armstrong[4] is willing to return you, your money with interest on your relinquishing to Genl Robertson Your claim to this tract—and there is five thousand acres on elk that can be had to satisfy the ballance of the Judgt. I hope sir you will view these Observations as from the heart of a friend, who wishes you both equally well, and who does not wish to see you in law, unless when the rules laid down by which we are united, cannot attain that Justice that each individual is entitled to—I have never heard from either how the right has been derived, neither do I know how Justice will decide but as the thing is between two brothers, and two that I highly esteem, and who I do know highly esteemed each other, I would be truly sorry to see any thing arise that would create a bitterness—and if you go to law I know it will have this effect—and have others also that would be painfull to me as a friend of both to see—The Genl appears much hurt at you making the purchase, after you knew (as he states) that he had purchased, from which, I am fearfull unless it is settled by two brothers or three, that it will lead t[o] statesments that may do neither of you any benefit. for these reason I have told him, as I now tell you the proper way will be to leave it to three brethren, such you can find legal charectors—This he states he is willing to do—and I hope it will meet your wishes—

I have no doubt but from the pains that have been taken to circulate reports, it will be rumored, that I am on full march to unite with Burr—This I know you never will believe untill you hear it from myself, or from such a source that you know cannot err—Should you ever hear that I am embarked in a cause innimical to my country believe it not—should you hear, that treasonable intentions have come to my knowledge, And that I have been silent believe them not—or that I would not put any man out of existance, that would name such a thing to me, without on the ground of discovering it to the proper authorities, believe them not—and if Burr has any treasonable intentions in view he is the bases of all human beings—I will tell you why—he always held out the idea of settling Washata—unless a war with Spain—in that event, he held out the idea, that from his intimacy with the S. of war, he would obtain an appointment, and if he did he would revolutionise Maxico—About the 10th. of Novbr. <a> Capt <Fort> called at my house and after a stay of a night and part of a day <he> introduced the subject, of the adventurers—and in part stated, that there intention was to divide the union—I sternly asked how they would effect it—he replied by seizing (Neworleans) & the bank shutting the port, conquering Maxico—and uniting the western part of the union to the conquored country—I perhaps with <a> warmth asked him how this was to be effected, he replied by the aid of the Federal troops, and the Genl at their head. I asked, if he had this from the Genl, he said he had not. I asked him if Colo. Burr was in<to> the scheme he answered he did not know nor was he informed that he was: that he barely knew Colo. Burr, but never had had any conversation—I asked him how he knew this and from whom he got his information, he said from Colo. [John] <Swarwout>, in New york—Knowing that Colo. Burr was well acquainted with Swartwout it rushed into my mind like lightning that Burr was at the head—and from the coulourings he had held out to me Genl Robertson & Overton, and the hospitality I had shewn him, I viewed it, as base conduct, to us all and hightened the baseness of his intended crimes if he really was about to become a traitor—I sat down I wrote to Genl Smith & Doctor Dixson[5]—I wrote to Gov. Claiborne to put his citadal in a state of defence, without naming names except genl Wilkason[6]—When this was done I wrote Colo. Burr in strong terms my suspicions of him, and untill the were cleared from my mind no further intimacy was to exist between us I made my suspicions known to Genl Robertson & Tatom with some others—not long I recd. his answer—with the most sacred pledges, that he had not nor never had any views innimical or hostile to the united States, and whenever he was charged with the intention of seperating the union, the idea of insanity must be ascribed to him[7]—after his acquittal in Kentuckey he returned to this country—and to all that named the subject made the same pledges, and said that he had no objects in view but was sanctioned by legal authority, and still said that, when necessary he would produce the Secratary of wars orders that he wanted but young men of talents to go with him—with such he wanted to make his settlement—and it would have a tendency to draw to it wealth & charactor—for these reasons—from the pledges made—if he is a traitor, he is the basest that ever did commit treason—and being tore to pieces and scattered with the four winds of heaven would be too good for him—but we will leave him for time and evidence, to verify his hue—I have given you the outlines—and a few weeks will give the proof—

I have no doubt tired your patience, but I must tresspass a little farther—and request your attention to a little private business—some posts ago I wrote to Judge [Joseph] Anderson[8] to send me on a Deed for 640 acres land, and enclosed the courses—by same mail I wrote Doctor Dixson and enclosed him also a coopy of the courses.[9] I am fearfull these letters have not went to hand, for which reason I take the liberty of send-[ing] you the courses, and request that you will obtain a Deed from Judge Anderson and send it on to me I have sold the land and the Deed was to have been made the first of this month, thus I wrote the Judge, and I know if he has recd. the letter he has sent it on, and it has been lost on the way—My Dr Sir your attention to this business will confer a lasting obligation—present my compliment to [Nathaniel] Macon [Thomas] Blount,[10] & any others that may enquire after me with friendly wishes for your welfare & happiness believe me to be with high Esteem yrs

Andrew Jackson

P.S. This letter for your own Eye[11]

ALS, NjMoHP. Extract published in *National Banner and Nashville Whig*, September 16, 1828; Bassett, 1:167–70. In preparing this letter for publication in 1828, the words and names in angle brackets were crossed out, indicating deletions probably to be made by the printer.

1. Jackson was probably alluding to Wilkinson or to William Eaton, who a few months earlier had disclosed his view of the Burr enterprise. The *Impartial Review*, January 3, 10, had carried the substance of Eaton's disclosure.

2. See above, Dearborn to AJ, December 19, 1806.

3. Jackson was probably referring to AJ to Henry Dearborn, [cJanuary 17], published in Bassett 1:175–78 (dated [March 17]). See also AJ to Henry Dearborn, March 17, below.

4. Armstrong (d. 1808), an associate with William Blount in land speculation, was former surveyor of military lands in Tennessee.

5. See above, AJ to Daniel Smith, November 12, 1806. Jackson's letter to Dickson has not been found.

6. See above, AJ to Claiborne, November 12, 1806.

7. Neither Jackson's letter to Burr nor Burr's response has been found. At least one other contemporary source suggests, however, that Burr did indeed respond to Jackson's inquiry. "It is reported," according to the *Richmond Enquirer*, December 30, 1806, "that Col. Burr addressed letters to Gov. Jackson of Tennessee, and Mr. Harrison, Gov. of the Indiana Territory, informing them, that there was every probability of a war taking place immediately with Spain; that he had received a high commission from the P.U.S. and requesting them to have the respective forces under their command, ready to join him on particular days. Jackson and Harrison are reported to have transmitted an account of these letters to the P.U.S who is said to have these letters or copies of them now in his possession." A copy of Burr's letter to Harrison, November 27, 1806, is in the Jefferson Papers, DLC.

8. Letter not found.

9. See AJ to William Dickson, November 17, 1806.

10. Macon and Blount had been Jackson's friends and colleagues during his service in Congress, 1796–98.

11. According to his note to William B. Lewis, April 3, 1828, Campbell referred Jackson's letter to "Mr. Jefferson, then President of the United States, immediately after it was recvd.; from which after perusing it, he desired permission to copy such parts as related to the affair of Burr, . . . which was freely given. . ." (NjMoHP).

From John Wilkes

New-York, 29th. January 1807—

Sir,

I AM desired to inform you, That a bill drawn by A. Burr on Geo. M. Ogden[1] & accepted by him Note for Five hundred Dollars endorsed by You[2] was protested Yesterday Evening, for non-payment, and that the Holder looks to you for payment of it.

I am, Sir, Your most obedient Servant,

John Wilkes Not. Pub.

Printed form with ms insertions, DLC. Addressed to Andrew Jackson, Lexington, Ky., where Burr had raised a portion of the funds to finance his enterprise; the protest notice had been forwarded to Nashville from Lexington. Wilkes, a notary since at least 1792, was affiliated with the Bank of New York and several commission merchants.

1. A native of New York, Ogden had partially financed some of Burr's activities. On the protested bill, see William Eastin's deposition, September 4, 1813, enclosed in AJ to the Adams County Superior Court, September 25, 1813, below.

2. Note not found, but it is most likely that of December 3, itemized in the Account with Aaron Burr, October 4, 1806, above. William P. Anderson had also endorsed a draft for $1,000 by Burr on George M. Ogden, which was also protested (see Thomas N. Clark to William Preston Anderson, June 30, THi).

From George Washington Campbell

Washington 6th. Feby. 1807

Dear Sir,

Your very much esteemed favour of the 15th. Ulto. was recd. by last mail[1]—Its contents have been perused and particularly attended to. The developement from time to time of Burr's treasonable project, excited much agitation in the public mind here, since the commencement of the session—But many of those who know Burr, were not so much surprised at the *turpitude* or *blackness* of heart, evidenced by the treasonable project, as they were at the extravagance of it, & the extreme improbability of its being attended with any success—Many persons, (of whom I was one) believed B. capable of committing any crime, however *base* & *detestable*, that can be conceived of by human nature, to agrandize himself, they believed his heart a composition of *base turpitude*, without a single atom of virtue or principle except personal ambition—and this imbittered by chagrine & disappointment—but they thought he possessed some talents that would have prevented him from makeing himself the *scoff* & *ridicule* of mankind, by attempting a *mad, extravagant project*, without the probable means of carrying it into effect. This it was that induced a number of the best informed to doubt for some time the reality of that part of his scheme, that contemplated a separation of the western States from the Union—But his views are now ascertained beyond a reasonable doubt. You have seen a developement of them before this time, inclosed in my last to you,[2] which will satisfy your mind on this subject. With regard to the suspicions you notice of your joining Burr &c. being in circulation here—It is true such suspicions were rumoured, for a short time—but the belief of them was confined to such only as did not know you, & who did not inquire of those who did know you, in order to be informed on this subject—Shortly after my arrival at the City & previous to my first letter to you,[3] I conversed with the President on the subject—he had heard of the suspicions alluded to—he declared his intire disbelief in them & his unshaken & unlimited confidence in your integrity—& on his mentioning the matter to me, my answer was that I would as soon suspect myself to be guilty of taking such a part, as I would you—that the thing was incredible—impossible—I saw him, & conversed with him frequently on the subject, since—and his declarations of confidence were uniformly the same—and his convictions of your integrity appeared as strong as mine, or, even *your own* could be[4]—We were at the same time apprehensive that Burr would find means, to lull you into security, until you should receive the dispatches from Government—& that he had probably found means to corrupt some post officer, which might prevent the dispatches being recd. by you in time—For these reasons with others which shall be stated I am strongly induced to believe, & indeed I may say, I am convinced, you have understood the orders of the Secty. of war, differently from what he intended you should understand them—or that you gave a meaning to the latter observations, he made in them, which he did not intend to communicate—Since receiving your last (of the 15. ulto.) I called on the President—the conversation turned on the affair of Burr—and he mentioned that he understood, (I presume from the S. of war) that you had taken offence at, or felt yourself injured by, the manner in which the orders of the S. were written—The Pr. said he had seen the letter, that he could not discover in it, any cause of offence—that the orders were written in direct & posi[ti]ve language, but that this was the usual & formal mode of issuing orders by the Secy. &c but he added that it was impossible that any improper insinuation or suspicion could have been-intended by the S. because he (the P.) had the highest confidence in you which was known by the S., & that on this acct. as well as for the sake of dispatch &c the orders were directed immediately to you without being transmitted through the executive of the State—who recd. dispatches at the same time—I immediately called on the Secty. of war, & he mentioned the subject to me himself—stating his surprise at some expressions in one of your letters, which shewed that you were disatisfied at the terms of his orders[5]—He then stated in substance the words of his orders—and added the observation he subjoined thereto, relative to the report of your intention to join Burr &c and that if such suspicion was *afloat*—(not if there was any ground for such suspicion) you might be inabled to strike a more effectual blow—or words to that effect—He declared unequivocally, that you must have intirely mistaken his meaning— That so far from entertaining any doubt of your integrity or any suspicion respecting it, his intire confidence in you induced him to send you, (to use his own words,) a *blank sheet*—or genl. orders & powers to take such measures as you tho't best to check the conspirators instead of specifying particular duties for you to perform—and that he added the observation respecting the report of your joining Burr on the same ground of entire confidence, & as he thought as a candid man he ought to do, that you might have the whole case, as report stated it here, before you, & act according to circumstances—not as you intimated to him, that you were to act the *smiling assassin*[6]—no such idea was intended, because it was not believed that you had given any ground for the report of your being concerned with Burr, but that if such report was *afloat*—the conspirators might on that acct. be less on their guard, & there by inable you to seiz or detect them—and certainly there would be no impropriety in this—you certainly were not bound to give them notice that you were about to arrest them—This statement in substance the S. of war made to me & authorised me to inform you thereof in case I wrote to you, which I promised him I would do—From the whole of this business that has come to my knowledge—I cannot believe the Secty meant anything in his orders different from what is above stated—but whatever may have been his meaning; his explanations of his own *order* or *letter*, I presume, in such a case as this, ought to be taken as compleatly satisfactory on that point. Hence I conclude at present you appear to have reasonable grounds to be satisfied—and perhaps in reality, the S. of war, may have some reason to consider himself the most injured of the two—This, however, I presume will satisfy you until I see you—I have dwelt at some length on this subject, because I do believe the offence taken arises from a misunderstanding, merely as such between the parties—and because I can not see any advantage that could arise from agravating the subject to either party—& the enemies of both would be disposed to take advantage of such a *collision* & use the circumstances that might transpire to the disadvantage of each—In regard to my opinion of your integrity, I surely need not add to what I have said—I never did, nor will I ever believe you *knowingly ingaged* in a dishonorable project—or in any project injurious to the Union until it is *impossible* to believe otherwise—

In regard to the claim of Genl. Robertson to a tract of land purchased by me, I need only observe at present, that I shall allways be willing to do whatever is *just, reasonable & honorable*—& consistant with *fair equity*—Genl. Robertson spoke to me on the subject at Knoxville, where I shewed him my deed—& gave him any & all the information he asked—He has since written me a letter on the same subject, some expressions of which, if I understood them right, I considered such as neither he nor any other man acquainted with me ought to have used—I have ansd. it at some length—and if he chooses to state the case to you, I wish you to see my letter to him—I will only observe further that when I purchased, I did not believe that he had any claim to that part of the tract in question, that I have purchased & for which I consider my claim good—and in fact if my claim was out of the question—I apprehend it would be found, his claim is intirely defective—& little better than a blank sheet of paper—However I will say no more on this subject until I see you—I recd. your memorandum relative to, & the courses of, a tract of land, Judge Anderson was to have convayed to you[7]—I would with pleasure comply with your request on this or any other subject, as far as it was in my power, but Judge Anderson has not yet arrived at this place during the present session—nor has any person here recd. a line from him—nor is he now expected during the session—of course it will be out of my power to obtain the deed here—This letter has already grown to an unusual length, I must therefore, refer you to the public prints for politicks—

I am requested to present you the compliments, & sentiments of esteem of Mr. Macon—Please present my respects to Mrs. Jackson and believe me with the highest consideration, & sentiments of real esteem, Your sincere friend and most obedt.

G. W. Campbell

ALS, DLC. Extract published in Bassett, 1:170–71.
1. See above.
2. Not found.
3. Not found.
4. In his letter to Wilkinson, January 3, Jefferson wrote: "Be assured that Tennessee, and particularly General Jackson, are faithful" (*ASP, Miscellaneous*, 1:567).
5. See above, AJ to Henry Dearborn, [cJanuary 4]; and AJ to Dearborn, January 8.
6. Dearborn sent similar orders to Wilkinson on November 27, 1806: "There can be no doubt but Col. Burr is generally considered as the head; but his real object has been so covered, as to prevent any conclusive evidence of his ultimate views. Your name has very frequently been associated with Burr, Dayton & others: and the new edition of the old Stories, lately published in Kentucky, serve to increase the suspicion now in circulation" (DNA-RG 107). Jackson had used the term "smiling assassin" in his letter to Dearborn, January 8.
7. Memorandum not found.

To Daniel Smith

Nashville February 11th. 1807

Dear Genl

I hasten to announce to you, the pleasing information, that Colo. A. Burr on the 16th. ulto. surrendered himself, to the civil authority at Washington five mile from Natchez that on the second instant his trial was to commence he is now under an investigation, ordained by our constitution, to protect innocence and punish guilt—Wilkingson is summoned as a witness against him—says a letter to me of the 26th. ulto.[1] and adds "but it is thought he will not attend" the publick will soon know, whether the confidence of the goverment in Wilkingson is well placed or not—The enclosed paper[2] will give you a full detail of the conduct and surrender of Burr his force &c—Tranquility is now restored in Natchez—but in Orleans, report states there is nothing but distrust, disquietude, and comotion a serious quarrel has arisen between Govr. Claibourne and Wilkingson[3]—it is stated, that this dispute took place in the court house & that the Govr. slapt him in the face—the last part of this is not well authenticated, but that they have had a violent dispute I believe is true as it comes from Mr. [George Michael] Deadedridge of Nashville who was in Orleans at the time—

It is repeated in every letter from the City that Genl. Wilkinson stands high in the confidence of the executive—rest assured, that that confidence is not well placed—The western people since the investigation of the Spanish associates in Kentuckey—all in one voice deprecate the man & view him as a Spanish hireling—and in a few days, the Reverend Thos. B[rown] Craigheads deposition will be taken[4]—he will positively prove that Wilkingson, the last time he returned from Neworleans, say in 1790 or 1791—wore suspended from his neck a Major's commission which he said himself was given him by the then Spanish Governor add this to the other prooffs, and what ideas will the bring to the mind—view his Robertsperian conduct in Neworleans—denouncing Bollman as a traitor—and snatching him from the Jaws of the civil authority the only power competant to punish—and at a time that 48 hours could have proved his guilt and suspended him in the streets of Neworleans as a fit example for the moment—This stride of military despotism it is expected will be duly noticed by the legislature of the union—Should it not, it will have effects injurious to our goverment and will destroy that confidence that at present exists in the administration—What; a military charector trample under foot all civil authority—when no insurrection or impediment existed to the due execution of the law—and this pass unnoticed under a republican administration—This is not believed, but if It should happen, it will have a banefull effect—and you may rest assured, that the western people have no confidence in Wilkingson—[5]

I am sir yours with Esteem

Andrew Jackson

ALS, NjP. Published in Bassett, 6:426–27.
1. Not found.
2. Not found.
3. No further evidence, beyond a brief mention in the *Impartial Review*, February 7, has been found on the Claiborne-Wilkinson quarrel.
4. Craighead (c1750–1824; Nassau Hall 1775), a native of North Carolina and a Presbyterian minister, had settled in Davidson County in 1785. He had variously served as teacher and director of the Davidson Academy and Cumberland College. For a time he lived in Kentucky, where he may have seen evidence confirming the persistent rumor of Wilkinson's Spanish pension. His deposition has not been found.
5. In an open letter in the *Impartial Review*, February 21, "A Citizen" (perhaps Jackson) expressed sentiments on Wilkinson almost identical to Jackson's.

To Henry Dearborn

17th. March 1807

Sir,

Since the mighty sound of internal war, and conspiracy has completely subsided, since I have made use of every measure in my power as a "*Genl. of the militia to counter act and render abortive*" any plans hostile to the interest of the Union or to the peace and harmony of our country, and since then I have done these things from principle, from duty and from motives quite different from such as you were pleased to insinuate, (in your letter of the 19th. of December last)[1] me capable of, I cannot longer smother the indignation excited on the Occasion. It is a subject that shall have further explanation, and in the mean time, it is my determination that this correspondence be handed out to the world.[2]

I will, in the first instance, take the liberty sir of asking you, whether you did or did not, from this *Story in circulation*, believe me concerned, with any citizens of the U. States, in a *criminal attempt contrary to law, to carry on, a military expedition against the Government of Spain*? And if you did, Was it your belief at the time you honored me with your address of the 19th. Decr., that you could, by inviting me to the Commission of a treacherous act alter such views, and effect the purposes intended?

You say sir that ["]it is industriously reported amongst the adventurers that they are to be joined at the mouth of Cumberland by two regiments under the Command of Genl. Jackson—Such a *Story* might afford him an opportunity of giving an effectual check to the enterprise, if not too late." After I have given, the most deliberate consideration to your expressions, thus, in a degree, ambiguously made, I cannot draw from them any other conclution than this: that you believed me conserned in the conspiracy, that I was an fit subject to act the traitor of traitors, as others have done, and that it was only necessary for the Secretary at war of the United States, to buy me up without, honour, money or price. Under these ideas and impressions of this subject, I shall view it and treat it, *for the present*, in my own stile and in such way as I am confident the world will approbate.

If sir *stories* are to be attended to, recd. and acknowledged as evidence of a mans' innocence or guilt, you stand, convicted at the bar of justice, of the most notorious & criminal acts, of dishonor, dishonesty, want of Candour & justice. Aside with *stories* & I am well satisfyed in my own mind, that you are (altho yr. guilt is not so publickly known) more unprincipled and worthy of punishment, than the nine tenths of those who have suffered under Robesphere, Marat & Wilkinsons despotism.

The late Colo. Thos. Butler of the U. States army, who had spent more years in the service of his Country, than did the ever memorable Washington, under the Combined influence and villanous treatment of yrself and yr. much loved Genl. Winkinson, died the death of persicution. But it was necessary, it was indispenscably so, that Colo. Butler should by fair or foul means, be driven out of the army. He was a man of Worth, of honest principle & incorruptable hart, and Consiquently always in the way and in Collision with his Superior officer, & so was Genl. [Anthony] Wayne equally obstructive. By commiting murder on the object who would dare to be thus presumptive, there remained little or no difficulty to encounter—*Spanish associations*, conspiricies & treasonable purposes might then have their freest exercise. Under the sanction and auspices of the government the Secretary at War and Genl. Wilkinson might from *stories or suspicion* arrest any citizen in it, make all civil authority subservient to the military, suppress the liberty of the press, transport at pleasure, to Washington or Botney bay, every suspicious charecter in it and let such part of the Constitution of the United States, as secures the benefit of the writ of *Habe. Corpus* pass for a mere blank.

It is a well known fact that you have been uniformly the intimate friend and supporter of Genl. Wilkinson, that you were partial & hypocritically mean to him in the Case of Colo. Butler, and in consequence of the part which I took in favor of the Colo. your spleen your hatred to me became settled & fixed.

In the present instance, the first opportunity of gratifying yourself, was afforded and under the garb of official security & importance, you have sought yr. revenge.

It has been not only *storied* in this part of the western country, but has been asserted on the most respectable authority, that Colo. Burr and his adventures held your order, as Secretary at war, purporting a furtherance & governmental support of the enterprise. A worthy and respectable member of congress wrote me on the 15th. of Decr. last that complete and formal proof was then lodged against Colo. Burr in your office[3]— Why then Sir were you so modest on the 19th. day of the same month as to talk about *stories* as it respected myself, and others, who you stiled *disappointed unprincipled ambitious or misguided individuals*, and whose names you had not the manly firmness to give up? This kind of duplicity and temerity Calculated alone to throw the responsibility that a government of laws ought to take upon its own shoulders, upon those of an individual, is an additional proof of your original knowledge & privity of those unlawful designs. Those orders to me founded upon *stories* & purporting your wish, that I should descend from the command of my division and act the part of an deceptive assassin, as did all the rest of yr. orders (if they may be so called) reach here immediately after Colo. Burrs departure—In this the design of fatality was evidantly marked—But let it be granted that such orders (pretty ones indeed for a military man to write) had been recd. before Colo. Burr descended the river, let me ask the world, if there was any thing in them, that would have authorised his arrest? I presume they will readily say there was not—This then goes still further to prove your good wishes in the enterprise.

In as much as I have enemies as well as friends to encounter in this charge of conspiracy, I shall in justice to myself and my friends, whilst on this subject close it with a few general remarks

It is sir only *base* minds that are capable of recommending the commission of a base act. The government must indeed be tottering with its own imbicility, when the principal supporters of it, shall be thus insulted, thus assailed, by an officer of government, devoid of talents, integrity and altogether ignorant of the duties attached to his elevated Station. The nominal dignity that the Secretary at war acquires at the first entrance upon the duties of his office, will always give to his assertions a degree of credit—I know what he has done is unworthy the character of a genl. or a man of honor. I care not, where, when nor how he shall be met on this emergency—I am equally regardless of His own defence to the world—I know it cannot be predicated on principles either tenable or true.

I have no idea that power shall or ought to secure any man, from the resentment, the punishment proper and such as the injury merits.

Colo. Burr when in Tennessee was from time to time at my house, say about 12 days, in the course of said period nor at no other, did he ever utter to me one, single syllable of treasonable matter—He on the contrary stated in strong terms his love of country, and after his arrest in the State of Kentucky discounted largely on his uniform obedience to the Laws of his country and of his intention to continue such obedience. He was an old acquaintance and a Gentleman that I highly respected & was by me treated as such—He purchased two boats from me & could have had ten more on the same terms & under the same impressions which I then entertained of him.

It betrays great ignorance in the character of any man who may suppose, that two men can be found in the western country willing to form a seperation of the western from the atlantick States. The influence of no man or set of men in the united States at this time or any other previously, could ever have effected any thing like this.

I have sir transmitted a copy of this letter to the president of the U. States,[4] & the primary object in so doing, is to assertain through him whether yr. orders of the 19th. of Decr. last was given, with his knowledge or with his approbation.

I am yrs. &c.

A. J.

Copy in William Preston Anderson's hand, DLC. Published in Bassett, 1:172–75. It is highly likely that Jackson never sent this letter to Dearborn: a thorough search of DNA-RG 107, Records of the Secretary of War, has failed to turn up any mention of it.

1. See above.
2. No contemporary publication of the Dearborn-Jackson correspondence has been found.
3. Jackson was probably referring to Dickson's letter, [December 15, 1806] above, of which only a fragment survives.
4. Copy not found.

A few days before Burr's arrest in Mississippi, the legislature of Orleans Territory initiated an investigation into General James Wilkinson's actions in New Orleans. As the debate on the presentation of a memorial to Congress progressed, the Orleans House of Representatives called upon Governor Claiborne for an accounting of his role, since neither he nor Wilkinson had explained the reasons for their "extraordinary measures."

In response to this call in late January, Claiborne submitted to the legis-

lature, along with other documents, a copy of Jackson's letter of November 12, 1806 (see above). As the legislators were quick to point out, Claiborne and Wilkinson had used parts of Jackson's letter before a group of merchants in early December to justify the imposition of an embargo; but on that occasion they had not identified the author—he was merely "a gentleman of high respectability in Tennessee"—and they had suppressed Jackson's allusions to General Wilkinson.

Although the Orleans legislature failed to adopt the memorial on Wilkinson, Claiborne, aware that Jackson would see the debates in newspapers, addressed him in the letter below, attempting to explain his use of Jackson's letter before the merchants in December.

From William Charles Cole Claiborne

(Confidential)   New Orleans March 27th. 1807.
My Dear Sir,

I inclose you a paper, containing addresses from a number of respectable Citizens approbatory of the Conduct of General Wilkinson and myself.[1]

I will not undertake to say, how far the political character of the General may be justly subjected to exceptions; but I do verily believe, that he opposed Burr from principle, and that his late acts here, were done with the best intentions.

I must again pray you not to credit all the Reports and publications which reach you from this quarter; Believe me many are erronious. You may perhaps see a Copy of a Memorial to Congress which was reported by a Committee of the Legislature, and which has been rejected by a great majority in the House of Representatives.[2] The Committee was greatly imposed upon, and have given the sanction of their names to many misrepresentations; The conduct of the public' agents is not justly stated; The embargo was resorted to on the unanimous recommendation of the Merchants, and the measure was not previously advised either by the General or myself. I did not declare (as is stated in the Memorial) the letter to which I alluded to be "Anonimous." I did (it is true) avoid naming the writer, but stated it to be from a highly esteemed friend of mine; a Gentleman of the greatest respectability in Tennessee, and who held, and deservedly so, a great share of public' confidence; I added "that there was no deception; the letter was from my friend, for I knew his hand writing."[3] In the discharge of my duty I lately communicated in confidence (among other Letters) to the Legislature, a Copy of your friendly and patriotic' communication to me, and in this way they became acquainted with the name of the writer. I have been thus particular, in order that the perusal of the Memorial may make no unjust impressions upon your mind.

I shall write you fully on the return of my Brother.[4] You will have seen [James] Workman's letters and Oath; this man is not worthy of public' confidence; he was justly suspected to be concerned with Burr;[5] My Conduct has been correct. It is approved by my judg'ment and will I am persuaded be satisfactory to the President.

My Situation has been embarrassing; but I acted with deliberation and with the best intentions; I consulted also from time to time the opinions of Men in whom both the Government and myself could confide; These Men were the Members of the Legislative Council Messrs. [Julien de Lalande] Poydras, [James A.] Mather, [Joseph Deville Degoutin] Bellchasse, [John Baptist] Macarty & [Pierre] Fauchet,[6] & I have the satisfaction to add, that by them, my general conduct during the late interesting Crisis was approved; These Gentlemen knew of Workman's Communications to me, & deprecated the Idea of my introducing a Civil War by arraying the Militia against the regular Troops.

May God bless you! your friend sincerely

William C. C. Claiborne

P.S. The paper containing the addresses is not printed & as the mail is about closing, I am obliged to close my Letter   W. C. C.

LS with postscript in Claiborne's hand, DLC. Published in Bassett, 1:179.

1. For the addresses, see *Louisiana Gazette*, March 27.

2. Most of the debate on the memorial of the Orleans legislature occurred in mid-March, but the Nashville newspapers did not report it until a month later. For the memorial and the debate, see *Impartial Review*, April 18, 25, May 9, 16, 30, June 6.

3. The *Impartial Review*, April 18, carried the portion of the memorial to which Claiborne was referring.

4. Claiborne was probably referring to Dr. Thomas A., who had made a trip down the river in early January.

5. Workman, an English immigrant and judge of the Orleans Parish court, was a prominent member of the Mexican Association in New Orleans. Charged as an associate of Burr and arrested by Wilkinson, he was expelled from the bar but acquitted before the court. Workman's letter and oath had been sent to the legislature in late January or early February.

6. Mather, an Englishman by birth, became mayor of New Orleans in 1807 following his resignation from the legislative council. Bellechasse, a Creole, had served as commandant of the New Orleans militia under the Spanish and as colonel of the 1st Brigade, Louisiana militia, following the area's transfer to the United States. Macarty (d. 1808), a resident of New Orleans, had also been a militia colonel and had served in the territorial House of Representatives before his nomination to the legislative council in 1806. Fouchet, a Creole and militia officer, had been nominated to the legislative council in 1806.

From Stockley Donelson Hays

Greenville Aprile 20th. 1807.

Dear Uncle, Sir,

I feel myself at a loss, how to adress you, at this time, feeling a conscious remiss, in not writing more frequently: but as nothing has occured which might claim your attention I hope this will be a sufficient apology.

The day is drawing near when I shall feel myself once more relieved from my present embaresed situation, when I shall be at liberty to act as my friends may advise. when it will be in my power to remove myself from a country, which has been rendered tiresom, in the extreem, from the uninged and idle situation in which I have been placed, which from experience, I have found to be the most intolerable of all lives, less desirable than the most abject toil; the most entertaining and improving books, serve only as a temporary relief to the discontent, brought on me by this almost insupportable condition. in company, the most agreeable, I find myself, absent, and unamused.[1] I have lately been to Mr. A[braham] Greens, where I saw Uncle [John] Calfrey[2] who has given me the History in detail of my friends since I left home; he mentioned the settlement of several of my fathers most unwise most distressing debts, which would in my fathers unhappy situations, have been inevitable distruction, had it not have been for your most friendly nay parental aid, which is ever ready in impending danger to ward off the theatning blow, from the inocent and ungarded; and for which you deservedly merit the esteem of every good citizen; (and as a party relieved permit me Sir to offer you my unfeigned thanks, and ever gratefull services, too inconsiderable.)

I have heard of an affray, which took place a few days since between Sam Jackson and yourself, in which you wounded him,[3] happy I am, to hear his life was alone spared, not for his sake, for he is too much of a smiling too much of a calculating villian to live in a civilized world if he could be misplaced without indangering the life the feelings, or property of some worthy member of society; but he is a man not to be avoided and yet not to be bos[o]m with. May you ever keep at an awefull distance your enemies, when your friends, the honorable the virtuous, may be your associates in mirth and enjoyment, your comforters in adversity.

I have not as yet been to New Orleans, seeing no probability of selling my horses here. I deemed it advisable to defer my trip, untill I could recruit them so as to render them salable at that place, but if I can sell them here to any advantage I shall not go there this summer. your pleasure shall direct me which I hope you will forward on the receipt of this, to Natches, where I shall be to receive it. I write you this from Mr. Henry Greens,[4] who has been very friendly to me and wishes me to present his best respects to you and Lady; and I expect it will be handed you by Dr. Claibourn, who I have not seen, but will pass this, to day on his return, be pleased to present my compliments to Aunt Jackson and all friends, and receive sir, with reverence due the well wishes of your ever gratefull and obedient nephew

Sto. D. Hays

ALS, DLC.
   1. Hays had gone down the Mississippi River with Aaron Burr in late December 1806 and he remained in Mississippi Territory until mid-June 1807 (see above, AJ to W.C.C. Claiborne, January 8).

2. Green, son of Thomas Marston, had married Rachel's niece, Eliza (d. 1823), the daughter of John Caffery (1756–1811) and Mary Donelson Caffery (d. 1823). The Cafferys had settled in Mississippi Territory.

3. For a discussion of the affray between the two Jacksons see Court Minutes in *State* v. *Andrew Jackson*, November [9], below.

4. Green, also a son of Thomas Marston, was a justice of the peace in Jefferson County, Miss. Terr.

To his friends Jackson stood ready to offer assistance when it was requested, whether they sought help in the resolution of some business dispute, in the payment of debts, in the guardianship of orphaned children, or in the settlement of marital disputes. Sometime in early 1807, George Michael Deaderick had asked Jackson to help reconcile disagreements between him and his wife Mary ("Polly," d. 1833), whose parents (unidentified) lived in the Nashville area. Jackson complied, went with Deaderick to talk to his estranged wife, and drafted a reconciliation agreement for them (see below). The agreement was short-lived, for on March 5, 1809 (see also below), Deaderick again approached Jackson with the same problems. George and Mary did not come to a final reconciliation, however, and in 1812 the Tennessee legislature granted him a divorce (Laws of Tennessee, 9th General Assembly, 2nd sess., Ch. 19).

From George Michael Deaderick

Nashville 25th. April 1807

Sir,

It is a painfull consideration to me when I bring into view the task impos'd on you, nothing less than a consciousness of your uniform friendship could have inducd me to be thus troublesome. The anxiety, the sincerity, added to many other motives all combined in inducing me to make the effort, of which you are a witness, of eternal reconciliation between Mrs. D. & myself;[1] the manner in which she is fetterd to the will of her Father & relative mother induces me to think, that however humiliating my conduct may be, the object that I have most sincerely at heart will not easily be brought about No sooner had you opend the object of your wish, than I became the object of reflection, had I utterd one word in defence of myself, their rage, malignant rage would have lighted into a flame, & peals of abuse heapd on me, to evade what I knew was certain to come, I preferr'd withdrawing. As to any reflection made by me on Mrs. D. relative to the use of her eyes, neither her Father, nor relative mother knows more than what has been handed them by her. Nothing is too improbable for them to believe, when the assertion is accompanied with tears, to me they are not in all cases evidence of <guilt> innocence. I did not ride out with you to learn that it was Mrs. Ds. determination to ahere to her former principals & manner of life. All that I shall observe on this subject at present is: that if they advocate the going to private dances, in and out of Town, Assemblys, Inviting Gentlemen & Ladies to my house all without my knowledge or consent, I must beg leave to differ with them as to the propriety of the thing, the principal shall never be approvd of by me. By the expression of the eye, as much levity, & Viciousness can be expressd as the tongue is capable of uttering, and as strong declarations made, and as easily understood. I have never debarr'd Mrs. D. the exercise of priviledges proper for a Woman to enjoy. And do most solemnly declare to you that my heart is transported with joy when I see her engagd in innocent Amusements and reputable society. I need not tell you Genl. that my character has been aspersd, and that the invention of Mrs. Blake[2] togather with others have been put to the rack fabricating illibiral and base tales to impair my standing in society. I know, & have always known it that perfection belongs not to me. One of the great wishes of my heart is to receive that justice from others that I am fairly entitled to, more I desire not. Should Mrs. D. be determin'd on remaining where she now is, out of my protection, it shall not debar me from offering her a competency, as occasion may require. You will pardon me for those things that I have stated, that to you may appear improper and assure yourself that in every thing you may recommend not derogatory to my feelings shall be implicitly complied with. In the mean time believe me to be with Real Sincerity yr. friend

George. M. Deaderick

ALS, DLC.
 1. See Reconciliation Agreement, [April 1807–1809], below.
 2. Not identified.

Reconciliation Agreement between George Michael and Mary Deaderick

[April 1807–1809]

Conditions of reconciliation, Between Mr George M. Deaderick, and his lady Mrs. Mary Deaderick Viz—

Mrs. Mary Deaderick, do solemnly agree and promise: that she will live a chaste and upright life, and that in no instance will she deviate from virtue prudence and discretion She further promises to be a dutifull and obedient wife to George M. Deaderick—and that she will not invite to the house of him the said George M. Deaderick, any person or persons whatever, without first knowing, whether such invitation will be agreable to him the said George—and lastly doth agree and promise, that she will not resort, or visit any assemblies p[r]ivate dance or entertainment, without first obtaining his approbation and consent—and the said George M.

Deaderick on his part, do most solemnly promise and agree, that his conduct towards his lady Mrs. Mary Deaderick, shall be Strictly, and uniformly upright—and further does engage, that he will not debar her from privileges that are proper for a virtuous, prudent and obedient wife to possess and enjoy—To all of which things we promise and agree—and have hereunto set our hands in the presence of our Mutual friend—

Test   George M Deaderick
 Andrew Jackson   Mary Deaderick
 John Marr

AD in AJ's hand, signed by George M. and Mary Deaderick, AJ, and John Marr, DLC.

After leaving Nashville on December 22, 1806, Aaron Burr traveled by boat down the Cumberland River to Fort Massac and down the Mississippi River to Bayou Pierre, in Mississippi Territory, where he arrived on January 10. A week later he surrendered himself to the civil authorities, posted bail, and awaited an inquiry into his activities. Although he was arraigned before the Supreme Court of Mississippi Territory in Washington, Adams County, the grand jury refused to indict him, and the court dismissed charges on February 4. Burr forfeited his bail and left Washington, only to be arrested some two weeks later at Fort Stoddert. By March 5, Burr was en route to Richmond for arraignment before the United States Circuit Court of Virginia, with John Marshall, Chief Justice of the United States, presiding. Following his arrival in Richmond on March 26 and a preliminary appearance before Marshall, the court bound him over to a hearing before a grand jury at its next scheduled term on May 22.

In preparation for the grand jury hearing, the United States subpoenaed forty-six witnesses who were thought to have some knowledge of or involvement in Burr's enterprise. From Tennessee two—Jackson and William Preston Anderson—were called. Only Jackson honored his subpoena, and on May 12, he set out on his ten-day trip to Richmond. Before he left, however, Anderson coached him on his testimony before the grand jury (see Anderson's letter, below).

While in Richmond waiting to give his testimony, Jackson developed a reputation for outspokenness. On May 30, John Randolph, foreman of the jury, wrote James Monroe that "there are I am told upwards of forty witnesses in town, one of whom (Genl Jackson of Tennessee) does not scruple to say that W[ilkinson] is a pensioner of Spain, to his knowledge, & that he will not dare to show his face here" (DLC-Monroe Papers). Two weeks later, on June 14, George Hay made a similar report to President Jefferson. "Gen: Jackson, of Tennessee," he wrote, "has been here ever since the 22d. denouncing Wilkinson in the coarsest terms in every company. The latter shewed me a paper which at once explained the motive of this incessant hostility. His own character depends on the prostration of Wilkinsons" (DLC-Jefferson Papers). James Parton, one of Jackson's earliest biographers, contended that Jackson "harangued the crowd in the Capitol Square, defending Burr, and angrily denouncing Jefferson as a persecutor" (Parton, 1:333). A later writer, Augustus C. Buell, noted for his inaccuracies and fabrication of letters and documents, reported in his History of Andrew Jackson *(New York, 1904, 1:204–206) the only text found of a speech that Jackson allegedly delivered.*

On June 25, the day after Burr's and Blennerhassett's indictments, Jackson appeared before the grand jury to give his testimony (see below), and on June 27 he left to return to Nashville. In western Virginia, he encountered a rumor that he had greeted Wilkinson when Wilkinson arrived in Richmond. This story Jackson denied in his correspondence with Andrew Hamilton and William P. Tebbs, also below.

As with Jackson's alleged speech, there has been no agreement among scholars as to whether Jackson returned to Richmond for the Burr-Blennerhassett trial, which commenced on August 3. In the absence of direct evidence, most have concluded that Jackson did not.

There is, however, strong circumstantial evidence that he did return to Richmond in August. He had been subpoenaed to appear in Burr's behalf—he was the only Tennessean on Burr's list of witnesses (List of Witnesses for A. Burr Sworn in Court August 21, 1807, U. S. Circuit Court, Virginia District, Ended Cases: 1807: U.S. v. Aaron Burr, Vi). Also, en route home, Jackson wrote Hamilton on July 2 (see below) that he would return to Richmond later that month. Jackson was apparently away from Nashville for a good portion of August and September, and the only evidence found suggests that he had returned to Richmond. George Poyzer, a businessman looking after accounts in Nashville for the Philadelphia firm of Thomas and John Clifford, wrote the Cliffords on August 17 that "Campbell & Boils promise to pay very shortly; of the others whose accounts you are pleased to forward me I can give no account until their return from Philad[elphi]a. & Richmond." Five weeks later, on September 25, after Jackson's return to Davidson County, Poyzer reported that "Genl. Jackson has assured me he is doing all he can to close his accounts. of Stump, & Allen I can give you no acct. untill their return home! You will be good enough to inform me if they, or any others who may have been in Philaa. this Summer have paid you any part of their accounts" (PHi). Moreover, on August 30, Harman Blennerhassett confided to his diary that he had "heard this morning fr[om Matthew] Ellis," a native of Natchez and also a witness subpoenaed on Burr's behalf, "that Genl. Jackson is hourly expected in town" (DLC-Blennerhassett Papers). While Jackson likely reached Richmond before September 14, when Burr and Blennerhassett were acquitted of the alleged treason and misdemeanor at Blennerhassett Island, he was not called upon to give testimony.

The final phase of the Burr trial in Richmond began on September 16

to determine if there were grounds for remanding Burr and Blennerhas-
sett to the Ohio or Kentucky courts. In this hearing Burr's counsel made a
subtle shift in their defense, directing attention from Burr to Wilkinson
and his Spanish connections. Jackson, Thomas B. Craighead, Thomas A.
Claiborne, James Robertson, and Howell Tatum—the first three known
to be among Wilkinson's enemies—were called as witnesses from Ten-
nessee, but no evidence has been found that they honored their subpoe-
nas. Furthermore, the Ohio court, to which the questions of misdemea-
nor and treason were relegated, found no cause to indict Burr and
Blennerhassett.

From William Preston Anderson

Federal Bottom. 10th may 1807

Nothing but a combination of the most untoward circumstances, could prevent me from an obedience of the supa. issued by the S. court of the U. States in the case of Colo Burr[1]

Without enumerating these circumstances it will be with you I know sufficient to say, that from them it is impossible for me to visit Richmond at this time or at anytime before the 1st. monday in August next.[2] Besides my family cannot be left alone at this period.

It would be to me not only a party of pleasure; but it would be perfectly agreeable to my inclination, to proceed on & attend this trial, if the same was within the compass of my power.

Your correspondence with Colo. B. shews completely his objects at that period—You are certainly a material witness & so would I be.[3]

I could swear this among other things of no great consequence, as coming from the Colo—I told him that you would not coopperate in the enterprize unless you had the order of government before you—He replied that he had or would have the P. order's & until they were produced he did not expect your assistance & that war was inevitable &c. &c.

Situated as you and myself are you particulary (who by the rascally world that you care nothing about, has been termed one of his Colo. Burrs friends) it would seem more than requisit to obey the summons. The testimoney given in would be published & after that nothing dare to be said even indulgent of suspicion—You can do as you plea[se] but, if you could attend, as it strikes me at present, I think it would be right & proper to do so—yr real friend

W. P. Anderson

ALS, DLC. Published in Bassett, 1:181.
    1. Anderson's suggestion that his and Jackson's subpoenas came from the "S. court of the U. States" is somewhat puzzling. Neither Anderson's nor Jackson's subpoena, issuing from the United States Circuit Court of the District of Virginia, has been found.

2. No evidence has been found that Anderson was later subpoenaed or that he went to Richmond for the Burr trial.

3. Anderson's comment implies that he not only was very familiar with the Burr-Jackson correspondence but that he also perhaps had some of the letters or copies in his possession. In 1828 he furnished some of his materials to Boyd McNairy to use against Jackson in the presidential campaign.

From Robert Gamble

Wednesday 3rd. June 1807

Ro Gamble's best respects await Genl. Jackson—& requests the favor of his Company to dinner—on Friday—4 oClock—

(Ro G intended personally paying his respects to Genl. Jackson. but on calling at his Lodgings[1] was told the General had walked out—)

AL, TNJ. Gamble (1754–1810), a veteran of the Revolution, was a prominent merchant in Richmond. One of his daughters, Elizabeth, was the wife of William Wirt, one of the prosecuting attorneys in the Burr trial; another, Agnes, was the wife of Governor William H. Cabell of Virginia.

1. According to the address on the cover of the letter, Jackson was staying at the Washington Tavern.

To [William Preston Anderson]

Richmond, June 16th. 1807

I am still detained in this place, and at what time I shall be able to leave it is altogether uncertain.

General Wilkinson, after detaining the court twenty days, has made his appearance, and the bills prefered against colonel Burr are sent up to the grand jury. Whether the testimony will be sufficient to convince the minds of the grand jury that guilt exists, either as it respects the charge of treason or that of high crimes and misdemeanors, is quite problematical. I am more convinced than I ever was before, that *treason* was never intended by Burr; but if ever it was, you know my wish is, and always has been, that he be hung. I also feel more satisfied in the opinion, that whatever may have been the projects of Burr, general Wilkinson has and did go hand in hand with him, until *Eaton like*,[1] he found such was the integrity and virtue of the western citizens, that sufficient force could not be obtained; and then, became the *patriot*, to save himself from the frowns and indignation of an insulted people. This was the means projected by him to effect that lawless tyranny which he found could not be done by force.

There are a variety of opinions on this subject, and but a few days when we shall be furnished with light more satisfactory for the impartial mind to act upon.

My wish is, wheresover guilt ever did exist, as well as all concerned therein, that the same may be ascertained, and the culprit brought to punishment, and that the innocent may be acquitted. I never deemed it just, nor never shall, to make sacrifice of any individual as a *peace offering* to policy, and especially when others are permitted of equal guilt to pass with impunity. You will see more particularly the shape this political prosecution has assumed from an examination of the papers of this place, which I am informed you take.

A subpoena has been sent on for the president of the United States, with a *duces tecum*—whatever may be the return I know not.

It appears Mr. Hay, by a charge, is placed in the opposite situation that he acted in when Callender was tried, and his own doctrine used against him.[2]

As soon as the grand jury shall have acted in this business I will advise you [thereof. At the race I hope you will see Mrs. Jackson tell her not to be uneasy].

I will be at home when my obedience to the authority of my country shall permit. [I have only to add as to the race that the mare of Williams[3] is thought here to be a firstrate animal of her size. But if she can be put up she will fail in one heat it will be then proper to put her up to all she knows at once.

Adieu   (Signed)   A. Jackson]

Text from *Impartial Review*, July 11, with bracketed additions from Copy, OHi. Original not found. Published in Cincinnati *Truth's Advocate*, October 1828, p. 391; *National Intelligencer*, October 20, 1828; Parton, 1:334–35; and Bassett, 1:181–82.

1. In the fall of 1806, William Eaton, a Burr confidant, had disclosed what he purportedly knew of Burr's ambitions and plans in the West.

2. George Hay, son-in-law of James Monroe and a prosecutor in the Burr trial, had been one of the defense counsel in the Sedition Law case brought against James Thomson Callender in 1800.

3. Not identified.

Testimony before the Grand Jury in the Case of Aaron Burr

25th. June [1807]

In may or June 1805 came to w[itness]'s neighbourhood. Enquired for lands in a large body. He went down the river & returned in Augt. Spoke of his wish to buy the Washita lands. Went thence to St. Louis. Decr. 1805. 6. w. heard of Colo. Burr at Washington, & got a letter from him saying war was thought inevitable with spain.[1] Burr returned to w.s house in Octr. 1806. Then spoke of his <visit> purchase of the Washita, his intention to attack the Spaniards in case of war, of emancipating millions. w. said he wd. only march by orders of govt. Burr said surely, he wd. produce the orders of the secretary of war. Burr's trial in Kentuckey, reports of Burr & Wilkinson. Fort told w. that wilkinson and Burr in conjunction with the Spaniards were to take new Orleans &c. Mere report. First idea of it came from Colo. Swartwout <Lynch brough> of New York, & from N. Orleans. His letter to Burr abt. 12th. Nov. reproaching him; B.s answer denying the charges,[2] brought by one Lynch, & not by Willie. He told B. of Fort's remarks when B. came again to Nashville. In autumn of 1805. wilkinson <was> settled the plan of attack on Mexico, with B. at St. Louis. This B. said <was com> to Jackson.

AD by Joseph C. Cabell, Cabell Foundation, Inc. Cabell, the brother of Governor William H., was a member of the grand jury in the Burr hearing.
  1. See above, Burr to AJ, March 24, 1806.
  2. Neither letter found.

To Thomas Monteagle Bayly

Richmond June 27th 1807.

Dear Sir.

Agreable to promise I set down to give you a detail of the proceedings vs Burr as far as the trial has progressed.[1]

On yesterday the grand Jury finished their Session and after returning true bills for Treason, against Aron Burr, Blanerhaset, Jonathan Dayton Genl. [John] Smith Senator in Congress from the State of Ohio, a Mr [Israel] Smith from New. York[2]—Tyler, and Daveis Floyd from Indiana Territory, they were discharged. It is stated that the grand Jury divided on the question whether they should present Genl Wilkingson for treason, Eight for and Eight against.[3] It is no longer doubted now, but he is as guilty as any—and it is stated that one of the grand Jury did state in the course of their deliberations within their chamber, that he thought Wilkingson, more base and more guilty, than any of those presented to the court. The trial is posponed untill some day in august by the attorney of the United States, the day is to be named to day, I do suppose that as Burr cannot have it Brought on immediately he will pospone it to a day that will give his witnesses time to return home and regulate their domestic business, and return to Richmond—I do expect that it will be placed about the 20th. of August[4]—I am certain, from what I heard from two of the grand Jury versed in law, that the indictment for treason will not be Sustained before a Pettit Jury—on principles of law <as well as fact>—there is no doubt but there has been strong and bold Swearing before the grand Jury, by three persons, whose credit it is said will be impeached on the trial in chief—Burr was committed to close gaol in the Common Prison on the 25th. instant, yesterday on motion it was directed, that the room he formerly occupied should be so secured with iron bars, that a guard should be furnished, and he confined therein which place he is now confined under a strong guard—It is astonishing but true, that under these circumstances he appears cheerfull and no alteration visable in his countenance—

The degradation offerred to our goverment by the British, in the attack, of our armed vessel, the chesepeak, by the British ship Leopard within our waters, which no doubt you have seen, has roused every feeling of the american heart, and war with that nation is inevitable[5]—I refer you to the prints for a detail of this humiliating blow against our independence & sovereignty—

Accept Dear Sir my best wishes for your welfare & hapeiness and that of your family and believe me to be with Sentiments of great respect yr. mo. ob. servt.

Andrew Jackson

P.S. it is said that there were three of the Jury disenting. I write in haste I set out for home in one hour

Copy, CSmH. Bayly was at this time a Virginia senator.
 1. Bayly, leaving Richmond for Ohio, had requested that AJ write him (see Bayly to AJ, [cJune 20]).
 2. Smith, a resident of Cayuga County, N.Y., was a relative of Burr's confederate, Samuel Swartwout.
 3. According to Albert J. Beveridge, *The Life of John Marshall* (Boston, 1919), 3:464, the division of the grand jury on indicting Wilkinson was seven for, nine against.
 4. The trial actually began on August 3, but Jackson probably did not arrive until late August.
 5. On July 29, a group of citizens met in Nashville to discuss the attack of the *Leopard* upon the *Chesapeake*. In a daylong meeting in which Jackson played a prominent role, the group adopted resolutions denouncing the attack, approving, after considerable discussion on phraseology, the course adopted by the president, and appointing Jackson and others a committee of correspondence to communicate with similar committees elsewhere in the state (*Impartial Review*, July 30).

To Andrew Hamilton

Mair Maid[1] July 2nd. 1807

Sir

From the good oppinion I formed of you on the first introduction, and which continued to increase, upon an acquaintance I flattered myself, that when I wrote you it would be in the language of unfeigned friendship, for permit me to remark that I never wear two appearences, where I profess friendship, in that I am sincere where I profess enmity, in that I am equally sincere—From those preliminary remarks, you may easily Judge of my feelings, when I reached Mr [Peter] Franciscoes,[2] and was there informed by him, "that you had stated that I was loud in my expressions relative to Genl. Wilkingsons' business and connection in the plans of burr—and the first man that Took him by the hand when he (Wilkingson) reached Richmond, and that I was silent ever afterwards—"[3]

The declarations of Mr Francisco that thus you had expressed yourself—and this too in the presence of Mr [Daniel] Sheffee,[4] compelled me to answer, that I was truly astonished at you thus expressing yourself, that if you had done so you had sinned both against light and knowledge, by stating a thing to be true which you knew to be false and which you, did know, being present (as you have stated yourself) when Wilkingson reached the Eagle tavern—we called at Major [Henry?] Floods[5] being advised you had made similar statements there—The Major stated that he did not recollect, you had made any such statement there

The object therefore of this letter is to be informed from yourself, whether you have or have not made such a statement—If you have not that you may correct the misconception of Mr Francisco and others, if you have that you may avow it to me by letter to Nashville, Tennessee, so that it may reach me before I leave there for Richmond—which will be between the 25th. & 30th. instant health permitting—Never having a wish to condemn any unheard, I shall subscribe myself for the present yr. Hbl. St.

Andrew Jackson

ALS, ViU. Hamilton (d. 1823) was a lawyer in Fincastle, Va. From 1817 to 1818, he represented Botetourt County in the Virginia House of Delegates; from 1818 to 1822 he sat in the state senate. Jackson had met Hamilton in Richmond.
  1. Probably the Mermaid Tavern in Salem, where Jackson's letter was postmarked.
  2. Francisco (c1765–1831) maintained a tavern at New Store in Buckingham County, Va. At the time of his death, he was serving as sergeant-at-arms of the Virginia House of Delegates. Apparently Francisco's tavern was a popular stopping-place, for Blennerhassett, en route to Richmond for the trial, spent the night of August 2 there (Entry of August 2, DLC-Blennerhassett's Journal).
  3. Wilkinson did not reach Richmond until June 13.
  4. Sheffey was a Virginia congressman.
  5. Flood (c1755–1827) was a veteran of the Revolution from Buckingham County, Va.

From William P. Tebbs

Fincastle 10 July 1807

Dear Sir,

Majr. A. Hamilton has this day sh[owed] me yr. letter of the 2 Int.[1] the contents of which astonished me beyond description—

I dare say you know that Gentlm. & myself were almost constantly together while in Richd. & we left that city & traveled together to this county. I of course had an opportunity of knowing his centiments relative to yrself & Genl. Wilkinson & I do positively pronounce the declarations made by Francisco false & without the semblence of truth—for Majr. H. often in my presence while in Richd. made declarations as unfavble. to Wilkinson as Honble. to yrself & I well recollect that at Francisco's as well as at other places he gave *the Lye* to this report which had been made on that Road as well as in Richd. before we left that—my abhorance of falsehood has impelled me thus to do Justice to innocence

& truth.[2] with the most profound respect I am with every good wish yr. Mo. Obt. Humb. Servt.

W. P. Tebbs

ALS draft, ViU-Albemarle Historical Society Collections. Tebbs (d. c1826), a native of Prince William County, Va., had large financial investments in Botetourt County, Va., mainly in iron furnaces.
1. See above.
2. On August 1, Jackson responded to Andrew Hamilton "that the information now before me is satisfactory to my mind that his [Francisco's] statement, was a misrepresentation either *wilfull* or otherwise, and it gives me pleasure, to renew to you those friendly sentiments, that I poss'd when I parted with you."

On May 15, 1807, three days after Jackson left for Richmond, a Davidson County grand jury presented to the Mero District Superior Court an indictment against Jackson for "assault with intent to kill" Samuel Dorsey Jackson. The two Jacksons had enjoyed a business and social relationship since 1799, but on March 6, they had fought each other on the street in downtown Nashville. The fight apparently grew out of some misunderstanding about debts, or at least so Samuel Jackson suggested three days after the scuffle. "I will not pay any of those notes to Andrew Jackson," he informed Robert Hays, "and if they remain in his hands I will not pay them until compeld by due course of law for his late attempt to assassinate me will authorize this determination, it wont be in my power to meet you tomorrow nor for a month to come owing to the wound through my booddy I received last fryday from A. Jackson" (Jackson to Hays, March 9, ICHi).

The details of their confrontation remain unclear. Two conflicting versions of the episode appeared during the campaign of 1828. According to the anti-Jackson account, Andrew assaulted Samuel "and the latter not being disposed to stand still and be beaten, stooped down for a stone to defend himself—While in the act of doing so, Gen. Jackson drew the sword from his cane and run it thro' Sam'l Jackson's body, the sword entering his back and coming out of his breast" (Coffin Handbill). The pro-Jackson version, drafted by John Overton, claimed that "General Jackson, in the ordinary pursuit of his business, was passing Samuel Jackson's door, walking with a cane, which had a sword in it, . . . without having any cause to suspect that Sam Jackson had any intention of making an attack on him. So it was, that as the General passed the door, Sam who was unseen and without any previous intimation, threw a large ro[ck at th]e head of the General, which, if it had struck him, as intended; from its size and form, must have put an end to his existance. Upon this large stone or rock being discharged without effect, Sam Jackson instantly stooped down to pick up another, . . . and in the attitude of throwing the second stone, the General made a thrust at or towards him, with his drawn sword. . . . *The cane pierced a loose-coat that Sam Jackson had on, but not his flesh, which caused him to drop his rock, and close in with the General, who threw away the sword and cane; and a violent scuffle ensued, which however, was soon put an end to by the bystanders . . ."* (John Overton to Moses Dawson, June 7, 1828, OCX).

When the case came before the court at its November session the jury acquitted Andrew of the charges. The court minutes reproduced below, however, do not shed additional light on the details of the episode or the defense at the trial.

Court Minutes in State *v.* Andrew Jackson

November [9,] 1807

Pleas at the Court house in Nashville before &c Nov Term 1807.
The State vs Andrew Jackson   Indictment
Be it remembered that heretofore to wit, on Friday the fifteenth day of May 1807 at Nashville in the State of Tennessee and District of Mero, by the oath of twelve Jurors honest & Lawful men of the state and District aforesaid, then and there being empannelled Sworn & charged to enquire for the District aforesaid. It is presented that Andrew Jackson late of the County of Davidson in the District aforesaid Esquire on the sixth day of March one thousand eight hundred & seven, with force and arms at Nashville in said county of Davidson within the District aforesaid an assault did make in & upon one Samuel Jackson, in the peace of the State then and there being, and that the said Andrew Jackson, with a certain drawn Sword which he said Andrew Jackson in his right hand then & there had & held in and upon the Left side of him the said Samuel Jackson above the Short ribs of him the said Samuel did Strike & thrust, giving to the Said Samuel Jackson then & there with the Sword aforesaid in & upon the aforesaid left side of him the said Samuel above the short ribs of him the said Samuel a wound of the breadth of half an Inch and of the depth of four inches with an Intent him the said Samuel Jackson then & there feloniously wilfully and of his malice aforethought, to kill & murder, and other wrongs & enormities to Said Samuel Jackson then and there did to the great damage of the said Samuel Jackson and against the peace & dignity of the State.
Jenkin Whiteside Attorney Genl.
    And the trial of the premises aforesaid is continued until the next Court at which day, to wit, the first above mentioned, the said Andrew Jackson appeared in court according to his recognizance, and thereupon pleaded not guilty to the Indictment & for his trial put himself upon his country whereupon came a Jury of good & Lawful men, to wit, Silvanus Castleman John Buchanon, Edward Gwin, Scion Hunt, James J Kinnard James Dickson, Ewen Cameron, Laurence Whitsett, Arthur Harris, Henry Rieff

David Edmiston & Archibald Cheatham who being elected tried and Sworn the truth of & upon the premises to speak & having tried the evidence on their oath do say that the said Andrew Jackson is not guilty of the Trespass assault & battery charged upon him in the Indictment as in pleading he hath alledged. Therefore it is considered by the court that the said Andrew Jackson be acquitted & discharged

Copy, TNDa-MDSC Law Minute Book, 1805–1807, pp. 479–80. Extract published in Bassett, 1:182.

To Daniel Smith

Hermitage Novr. 28th. 07—

Sir

I am solicited by Doctor Thomas A. Claibourne to name young Mr. [Benjamin Franklin] Harney[1] as an applicant for surgeons mate in the army of the united States—

This young gentleman I have been acquainted with since his childhood, he has always demeaned himself with propriety, and I have the assurance of Doctor Claibourne (with whom he has studied) that he is clever in his profession—I have no doubt but if he should obtain the appointment, he will do Justice to it—by being servicable to the united States, and agreable to the command to which he is attached—will you be good anough to name this young man favourably, to the president of the united States— the reduced state of his fathers property puts it out of his power to do more for him than he has done—and young Mr Harney appears to possess both brains and enterprise—he *will do well* I have no doubt—provided he meets with friends to push him forward—otherwise his talents may be lost, both to society and himself—

Some time ago I made a return to the Secratary of war of the volunteers who had tendered their service to the united States, under the law, and who were ready for service at the call of the goverment, and that at a minutes warning[2]—I stated at that time that it was only a partial return, and as soon as I obtained compleat returns under my orders for that purpose I would forward them—requesting of him in th[e meantime] to advise me how they were to be organized, and whether any particular form was to be observed in making out the returns, other than, the one I had adopted—I have lately recd. returns compleat from the differrent Brigades and was about to forward them by this mail but casting my eyes over the Presidents message on the subject of the Volunteers, I observe this sentence—"They are ordered to be organized, and ready at a moments warning &c. &c. &c." Not having recd any such orders, I have posponed any further returns—least his honour thro the influence of his virtuous, immaculate, unspotted, and patriotic Genl Wilkingson, from whom perhaps he has recd. another Bulletin, that may still hold me out as a conspirator—to hide his own guilt[3]—his excellency the secratary at war may think it dangerous to trust me[4]—for these reasons I have not sent on my full returns, nor will I untill I receive an answer to my other letter to him on this subject—I forwarded to him returns, of 22 companies compleat—since which I have recd. returns of Eight more mounted infantry and cavalry—and from Genl Roberts I have recd. no additional return—notwithstanding I have been informed from his regimental officers—that there are several companies, made up since his return to me— The object of this part of this letter is that you may name it to the President, that there is ready at a minutes warning, and subject [to his authori]ty Eight full companies, with officers at their head that will give a good account of any equal number, that dare insult freemen—

From certain inteligence, that I am in possession of—that not only from Genl Wilkingson, but from two other channels that are and may obtain higher respect,[5] than any thing that could come from the genl, particularly from the heavy clouds of guilt that now hang over him; that certain communications have been made to the President, relative to me (from one I have recd. acknowledgements of the injury he had done me,[6] by the communications and this too at the time I was informed that such communications were made) I say from this circumstance, it may become a duty I owe my own feelings (for Publick oppinion I am reguardless of), to make a statement, to the publick, accompanied with such proofs as I am in possession of, to shew my [friends] that the confidence once reposed in my patriotism and republican principles, have never been violated on my part[7]—and if I have been suspected by the administrators of the Goverment—that I am still pure, and those perhaps (I mean the Secratary at w[ar who gave] credence to it[)]) from proof presumtive,[8] has been acting the same game with Jamy wilkingson—raising suspicions against others—to hide his own guilt—for this purpose then; I must request you to forward me a coopy of my letter to you & Doctor Dickson, of date about this time twelve months with your certificate thereon that it is a true coopy.[9] I observe from the proof that [Albert] gallatine is hinted at[10]—believe not this, if any of the Secrataries were knowing to the thing, the proof if ever reached, will bring it home to the *war* department—but I hope, for the honour of republicanism for the honour of our nation, and the sake of virtue that none of them were knowing to the plan, I mean of an *attack* on the *integrity* of the *union*—I have no doubt nor have I had of the guilt of Wilkingson from the proofs I see exhibitted against him at Richmond—these are light as air compared to those that will be exhibitted if I am rightly informed;[11] and say to the President, for his own sake, for the sake of the honour of the nation—and the republican cause to shake off this viper—It is reported that the President has said that he will support him—This is why the prooffs positive of his guilt is kept back— in order to damn, the Prest. by the production of them when the thing can be Established that he has tried to shelter him from that indignation, that from an indignant publick awaits him—would Joseph H. Davies have hazarded the Publication that he has,[12] if he [had not possessed] the proof positive—Rest assured that John Adair whenever he let loose his port folio—it will produce testimony, as he himself has said, "that scepticism itself cannot doubt["][13]—I have seen lately, both Davies and Adair, I have conversed with the travelling companion of Adair from Neworleans here, a man of strict verracity—who does tell me that the prooffs of wilkingson guilt, both as a pensioner of Spain and a colleague of Burrs, will be made manifest—

I name this to you knowing you to be the real friend of Mr Jefferson and the republican cause and let me once more and for the last time repeat that, if Mr Jefferson hugs this man to his boosoom they will both fail—this has been long my oppinion I am now certain of it—the Publick mind now plainly evinces it—and notwithstanding I have loved Mr Jefferson as a man, and adored him as a president, could I see him attempt to support such a base man with his present knowledge of his corruption and infamy, I would withdraw that confidence I once reposed in him and regret that I had been deceived in his virtue—

Whether my ideas may meet yours or not, you will at least ascribe to them pure motives—for you certainly do know, that I am [not clamoring for] patronage or in persuit of office—it is well known, that neither the state or general goverment has an office in its gift, that I would accept of—My only pride, is, if our country is involved in war, in the Station I fill; I will do my duty. My pride is that my soldiers has confidence in me, and on the event of a war I will lead them on to victory & conquest—Should we be blest, with peace—I will resign, my military office, and spend my days, in the sweet calm of rural retirement—May you have a pleasant session, and a safe return to your family, friends & country

Andrew Jackson

P.S. your friends enjoy health—your little grandsons[14] are learning well, and, often speak of you—

ALS, DLC. Extract published in Bassett, 1:183–84.
1. Harney (d. 1858) was the son of Thomas Harney, former business partner of Robert Hays and John Coffee. He was appointed surgeon of the U.S. 3rd Infantry in 1814 and served to 1821.
2. See AJ to Henry Dearborn, August 1.
3. It has not been determined what specifically Jackson meant by Wilkinson's "Bulletin." He may have been referring to letters Wilkinson had written to Dearborn and Jefferson or to "A Plain Tale," by A Kentuckian, published in late October 1807 and attributed, perhaps erroneously, to Wilkinson by Daniel Clark.
4. Jackson was alluding to Dearborn's orders of December 19, 1806, above.
5. Not identified.
6. Jackson may have been referring to the letter above, William C. C. Claiborne to AJ, March 27.
7. No public statement by Jackson on the Wilkinson matter has been found.
8. See above, AJ to Dearborn, March 17.

9. See above, AJ to Smith, November 12, 1806; and AJ to William Dickson, November 17, 1806.

10. Jackson was referring to suggestions made in Joseph Hamilton Daveiss's *View of the President's Conduct Concerning the Conspiracy of 1806* (Frankfort, 1807).

11. Jackson's comment suggests that he was already aware that Congress, which had been in session for almost a month, would undertake an investigation into the affairs of Wilkinson.

12. The publication of Daveiss's pamphlet, *View of the President's Conduct*, had been announced in the *Impartial Review*, November 12.

13. Adair had already begun to make public his knowledge of the affairs of Wilkinson. He had called Wilkinson a pensioner of Spain in his letter to the *New Orleans Gazette* in mid-June (copied in the *Impartial Review*, August 6), and he had initiated a lawsuit against Wilkinson in the federal court at Natchez. Jackson may have been referring to Adair's letter or to anticipated testimony before the court.

14. John Samuel (1797–1817), Andrew Jackson (1799–1871), and Daniel Smith (1801–63), children of Smith's daughter, Mary, and Rachel's brother, Samuel Donelson.

From William Charles Cole Claiborne

New Orleans Decr. 3d. 1807.

Dear Sir,

Your letter of the 17 of October[1] was handed to me by Mr. [Thomas Bolling] Robertson; the Secretary for this Territory, whose appointment is to me the more satisfactory since so many of my old friends unite in representing him "as a Gentleman of worth and a true Republican."

In compliance with your request, you have inclosed a copy of your letter of the 12th. of November, giving me informa[tion] of plans (either formed or forming) "inimical to the Union, and advising the organization of the Militia and preparations for the defence of New-Orleans," as well against "internal as external enemies."[2]

This letter was esteemed of such importance to our Country that I immediately transmitted a copy to the Executive of the United States; It was also seen by General Wilkinson (being convinced from my knowledge of your character that you would have no objections) and was for a short time in his possession, but he did not receive a *copy* from me, nor did I know that the General had *one*, until I saw it referred to on the trial of Burr.[3]

No man can be more desirous than myself that the conspiracy should be thoroughly developed, and the agency of every individual concerned, explained and exposed; of the innocence or guilt of *General Wilkinson*, there seems to be a diversity of opinion; but for myself, I am free to declare that my impressions *are greatly in his favour*.

I feel no hesitation in informing you the time when and the manner in which General W. advised me of the Conspiracy; it was by letter bearing date at Natchez the 12 of Nov. 1806, and which I received per Express in four days hereafter.[4] Your communication did not reach me until the morning of the 5th. of Decr. and tended to confirm the statements which

General Wilkinson had previously made me, as well verbally as in writing.

I am persuaded you will not suppose that I did, either unnecessarily or improperly expose the contents of your communication; It reached me at an interesting crisis, and was only resorted to with a view to serve our Country and Gouvernment, to which I always believed you to be ardently attached—

Present me most affectionately to your amiable Lady—and believe me to be, with great esteem and respect—Your mo: obt. Servt.

William C. C. Claiborne

LS, DLC. Published in Bassett, 1:184–85.
1. Not found.
2. See above, AJ to Claiborne, November 12, 1806. Claiborne's quotation is inexact.
3. On October 2, before the court in Richmond, General Wilkinson had remarked: "Here is a paper, a letter of advice from General Jackson to Governor Claiborne, warning him of the approach of a large body of men to New Orleans, combined and engaged for unlawful purposes" (*ASP, Miscellaneous,* 1:554).
4. Wilkinson's letter to Claiborne, November 12, 1806, and Claiborne's response, November 17, are printed in Dunbar Rowland, ed., *Official Letterbooks of W. C. C. Claiborne, 1801–1816,* 4:44, 55–56. In his letter above of January 8, and perhaps again in his letter of October 17, Jackson had asked Claiborne when Wilkinson informed him of the "treason" contemplated by Burr.

One month after the Mero District Superior Court acquitted Andrew of assault upon Samuel Jackson, the two Jacksons were again meeting, as evidenced in the letter below, to settle their complicated debts, some of which probably arose out of Robert Hays and Thomas Harney's joint business ventures and Hays's recent bankruptcy.

To Robert Hays

Sunday Morning Decbr. 7th. 07—

Sir

I had an interview with Mr Whitesides yesterday. I have agreed to meet him on wednesday next in Nashville. It is highly probable, the thing will be adjusted—I wish you to be there, and for god sake be Cool—I recd Mr S. Jacksons letter last evening in which he inclines to settle,[1] but will make an attempt to keep the Duck river land or have $1000 dollars profit thereon—this will not do—It must be put beyond his reach, and his five hundred dollars will pay the expence—however before I recd his letter I met with him in Nashville; I am to see him again there on wednesday next. If the thing can be accomodated with Whitesides, all will be well I hope If Mr Porter[2] could be with you I would be glad to see him yr &c

A Jackson

Mr S. Jackson states in his letter that Major Harney will pay $500 in part of the $1000, Major Harney in his to me denies this,[3] but says to bring about an accomodation he is willing to loose one third, altho not able to loose any thing, in case the land is not secure from Jackson This does not appear to be unfriendly.

ALS, Edward N. Bomsey.
   1. Not found.
   2. Not identified.
   3. Not found.

From Francis Preston

Abingdon Dec 17h. 1807

Dear Sir

The bearer hereof Mr [William?] Trigg[1] a Young gentleman of my acquaintance has been so kind as to take charge of this letter and promises me any return you shall confide with him, he will safely bring on—This is so safe and so favourable an Opportunity for you to remit me the ballance of our Iron Contract that I trust you will not omit to forward it on by him[2]—I am at present from home and cannot have referrence to the Contract so as to make out a correct statement of the ballance, but will confide that to you as you have a copy of the Contract.

The length of time this transaction has remained unsettled will I trust be an apology for my pressing Payment, besides I am extremely anxious to have all my affairs completely settled, Particularely those at a distant as in the event of War, the various vicissitudes attending such a state of things may produce difficulties which cannot be controuled.

The Alarms on this Point in this Part of the Country are viewed with great seriousness, but I believe the People here will manifest the same spirit in defending our Country and our rights as our forefathers did on a former occasion. Should there be an appeal to arms (which from present appearances is more than probable but which I most solemnly pray Heaven will avert) I expect to be in the active scenes of Warfare, where I also expect to meet you which I assure you will afford no little satisfaction to your Friend & Hble Ser

Frans. Preston

ALS, DLC; Copy, ViHi.
   1. Trigg (1784–1813), was a partner in the King Salt Works, a trustee of Abingdon and of the Abingdon Academy.
   2. For the iron contract with Preston, April 11, 1803, see *Jackson*, 1:328.

1808

On December 28, 1807, shortly after Congress reconvened, John Randolph, who had served as foreman of the grand jury during the Burr hearing in Richmond, introduced a resolution in the House of Representatives to inquire into the conduct of General James Wilkinson. Several witnesses had suggested at the trial that Wilkinson had been and remained a pensioner of Spain, indeed perhaps the leader in those schemes to separate the West from the East which had been attributed to Burr. Randolph's proposal had Jackson's backing. Even before Burr's trial, Jackson had begun to collect documents to prove the charges.

Randolph's and other investigations into Wilkinson's affairs, continuing off and on for several years, were a key topic in Jackson's correspondence, even as late as 1810. The inquiries never proved Wilkinson's involvement with Spain to the satisfaction of either Congress or Presidents Jefferson and Madison, but they did not change Jackson's opinion, either. As he prepared to lead his Tennessee troops against the Creek Indians in 1812, he and some of his officers yet contended that Wilkinson, still in command of the United States Army, had earlier betrayed the nation's interests and was unworthy of the confidence of the war department and the executive.

From Joseph Anderson

Washington 12th of January 1808

Dear Sir

About two weeks Since I wrote you—requesting you wou'd pay my taxes on the Duck River lands I own in my own right—about three thousand acres of the Tract—out of which you got the 640[1]—there is also on the middle fork—2500 acres belonging to Major [Pierce] Butler—and him and myself hold Jointly ten thousand acres on the South fork—I have to request you will have the goodness to pay the whole and transmit me—if you please the amount so that I can Settle with Major Butler—Shou'd I live to return home—I intend Visiting Cumberland in the Spring, or early in the Summer—and we will then make a Settlement of our concerns—I have no other chance to pay those taxes but through you—and your Compliance will much oblige your friend—

I have before inclosed you Several papers—containg Wilkinsons Letters to Mr. Randolf[2]—also—Some charges exhibited by Mr R. to the House of Representatives agt. Wilkinson—I now inclose you—a Scrap—I cut out of a New York Paper which came here last night—*this* decent publication has not yet appeared—in the National intelligencer—I expect *they* begin to think—Such language from The Military Chief—to a member of the House of Representatives—is carrying the matter—rather too far—for the dignity of the nation[3]—Randolph however—as a member—does not take notice of these abusive and insulting publications—But he has taken that kind of Ground—that must Sustain him—in the Opinion of Every Unbias'd Citizen—

In Consequence of a Resolution of the House of Representatives—Mr Daniel Clark—Delegate from Orleans—yesterday proved incontestably before the House—as I have been inform'd by some of the members—That General Wilkinson—had for many years been a Spanish pensioner —The particulars of this Testimony—I will Send you by another mail[4]—Mr [George Henry] Rose the British Extra minister is still at Norfolk[5]—his reason for remaining there no one can tell—Our Country will be Singularly fortunate—if we can avoid a war—with either England or France—our Political Hemisphere is not chang'd since my last—passing Events, I will let you know—Shou'd be glad to hear from you—please present me respectfully to your Lady—and accept assurance of my sincere respect and Esteem—

Jos: Anderson

ALS, THi.

1. Letter not found.
2. Wilkinson's letter to John Randolph, December 24, 1807, challenging Randolph for comments on his character; Randolph's response, December 25, declining to "descend" to Wilkinson's libel; and Wilkinson's final response, again urging Randolph to accept his challenge, were reprinted in the *Impartial Review*, February 11, 18.
3. Anderson was probably referring to Wilkinson's posting Randolph as a "prevaricating, base, calumniating scoundrel, poltroon and coward" (*Impartial Review*, February 4).
4. Clark's statement on Wilkinson, January 11, appears in *ASP, Miscellaneous*, 1: 704–705.
5. Rose (1771–1855), British diplomat, had arrived in the United States in late 1807 on a special mission to discuss the *Chesapeake* affair and impressment.

Between 1805 and 1809 Jackson was involved, as plaintiff or defendant in numerous civil suits. These were hard times for many West Tennesseans, who, suffering the effects of the embargo, poor crops, and low prices, used cash, drafts, notes, crops, and even land to meet their obligations. Most of the cases concerned Jackson and Hutchings's efforts to collect debts owed to their firm or Jackson's deep involvement in the financial transactions of Rachel's relatives. The litigation was exceedingly complicated, involving overlapping mortgages and innumerable draft and promissory note transfers, some peculiar to early nineteenth-century America.

The exchanges of letters between Jackson and John McNairy below focus upon their disagreements over the settlement of a debt John Caffery, Jackson's brother-in-law, owed McNairy. Jackson and McNairy tried to reach a settlement out of court, but they were unable to agree, and McNairy took the case to arbitrators and the court. The issues in the case are typical of much of the litigation involving Jackson in debt collection.

In November 1805 Caffery had borrowed some $2,240 from McNairy at 6 percent interest, payable in a year. Caffery mortgaged his farm to McNairy as security for the loan. Unknown to McNairy, another person already held a lien on Caffery's property, also due in November 1806, for approximately $610. When Caffery defaulted on the loan, Jackson, the highest bidder, purchased the property at a sheriff's sale.

In his complaint McNairy charged, first, that Jackson and other Donelson relatives had conspired to deprive him of the property by borrowing funds and raising the bid; and second, that Caffery had failed to make any payments on his debt. Jackson denied these charges. He contended that McNairy refused to bid the value of the property at the sheriff's sale, and that he and others had raised the necessary money. Also, Caffery and Robert Hays had made payments against the debt. Hays, in debt to Jackson, had arranged with Jackson and McNairy to ship cotton to New Orleans with the proceeds of the sale credited to McNairy. Hays had shipped the cotton, and, in payment, McNairy had accepted a draft which was later protested.

In June 1809, several years after Caffery and his family had moved to Mississippi Territory, the Superior Court rendered its decision in John McNairy v. John Caffery and Andrew Jackson. *The court directed Jackson and Caffery to pay McNairy the balance of $999 on the debt, allowing them credit for previous payments and for the draft on the sale of Hays's cotton.*

To John McNairy

a Copy   January 20th. 08
Sir,

I have postponed answering your bill, to which I am made defendant[1] (the object of which is to foreclose the mortgage, given as you state by John Caffery) expecting that you would have made enquiry relative to the cotton being sold for cash, and bills purchased therewith, and notified me of the result, as you had stated if that was the fact you would give the credit on the mortgage for the proceeds of cotton say $995 or thereabouts I do hate law—this being done which in justice ought to be & which in point of law, from the Statement of Mr. [William] Taite[2] to me I have but little doubt a court of equity will compel to be done, this business can be accommodated without much farther trouble. The land near Jefferson that you conveyed to [Ethelred?] Williams[3] for and on behalf of Colo. [Robert] Hays, and which deed Williams Did or would not accept, in all probability might satisfy the balance if this was thought insufficient the difference between that land and the bond assigned to you by the Colo. for one third of 5000 acres on Mr. John Nelson[4] might be considered, and as there appears to be a difference in point of fact between you and Colo. Hays, the thing may be adjusted by reference to honest upright and honourable men, and let the facts controverted be ascertained by disinterested proof.[5] This will at once shew that transaction in its true colours and prevent a lengthy disagreeable and expinsive investigation in a court of Chancery—You may believe me for I am candid if this equitable honest upright and just method is refused, it will compel the thing into a court of chancery to prevent a worthy and meritorious family from injury and unjust want as it is believed by many. let me farther State and that with candour, I will be egregiously mistaken, if on an investigation it is not established by proof of high respectability, that the statement made by Colo. Hays is correct as to the bond being transferred to you, and the land and the bond valued and the difference paid by you to him—recollect sir that you did request me to apply to Major [William Preston] Anderson on the subject of this tract of land on elk you stating it to be of little value. I did sir, and have for answer that you held on the entry on 2000 acres of that tract that is worth $6000 cash, the balance of the warrant removed and laid on land said to be valuable now sir, this 2000 acres would produce (one third to the bond nothing of this for locating) $2000 to the bond The balance of the Warrant, valued at the time removed, would have produced (say 1000 acres) from 75 cents to a dollar; is it possible under these circumstances, that you in your exalted Station will refuse a reference as above, and that you will endeavour to deprive a numerous and worthy family of a habitation or sustenance. impossible— the whole world (when the thing would be known) would execrate the act—and the gods would frown on it with indignation, a reference as before will do justice to you your character and the family of Colo. Hays. I place this in the hands of Mr. Stuart to be handed to you & shall want your answer and determination before I proceed—If compelled into law, it will be with regret, but still justice to the family of Colo. Hays will compel the measure—A refusal to submit it as before stated will compel me into court—A refusal on your side will indicate, a something that cannot comport with equity or justice, or a want of confidence in men, that, no doubt you may be permitted to name yourself (provided they are of respectability information and disinterested) I can only add that if the propositions herein alluded to are not on the broad basis of honesty honour & Justice its only necessary to point them out and they will be acceded to—For the present Adieu Yrs. &c.

Andrew Jackson

Copy, DLC. McNairy (1762–1837), superior court judge for Mero District when he moved west with Jackson and later a judge for the Territory South of the River Ohio, had with Jackson and three others represented Davidson County in the Constitutional Convention of 1796. From 1797 to 1833, he was federal district judge for Tennessee.

1. McNairy's bill of complaint, dated September 10, 1807, appears in *John McNairy* v. *John Caffery and Andrew Jackson*, Minutes of the Superior Court of Mero District, 1807–1809, pp. 286–94. Jackson's answer to the complaint (pp. 294–97) came on May 18, 1808.

2. The Hays cotton had been shipped to New Orleans on Tait's boat. For his statement on the protested bills, see Tait to AJ, November 23, 1807.

3. Williams, a resident of Grainger County, was former federal tax collector under John Overton. He, Hays, Samuel D. Jackson, and Andrew Jackson had already engaged in litigation to settle disagreements over land and debts growing out of Hays's declaration of bankruptcy a few years earlier.

4. Nelson (d. c1838), a native of Mecklenburg County, N.C., and former North Carolina state legislator, was at this time a resident of Washington County. In the mid-1820s and early 1830s he served in the Tennessee legislature.

5. McNairy and Jackson at one point did submit their disagreements to arbitrators.

From John McNairy

Bellview 23d. of January 1808.

Sir

You mention that you hate law. I assure you I do. And would not have engaged in it, if I had not conceived that I was compelled or loose my just right. If the proposition which is named hereafter will finally close & settle the law suit and secure to me, what is justly due on Cafferys Mortgage at any reasonable given time it will do. With regard to the cotton which was sent by Mr. Tait to New Orleans and sold for Colo. Hays, you have enclosed a letter from the commission Merchants who sold it, I presume it will be conclusive on this point[1]

With respect to the bond on John Nelson which was sold & transferred to me unconditionally, but since the Indian title has been extinguished & the lands in that country become valuable unreasonable & unjust requisitions have been made & I believe if that country was still Indian land I never would have heard a word on that subject. To be done with this bussiness, however, I propose that Colo. Hays [bond] to be cancelled the Deed for 200 acres of land near Jefferson which was given for this bond and I will do the same as to the endorsement of the bond to me. It was at Colo. Hays' request this contract was made & he has told me since that the land I let him have, did not answer the purpose intended, that being the case, I would suppose that each reconvey back their own thus could be no injury done to either.

You State that you applied to Majr. Anderson for information and that you have for answer that I "*held on the entry on 2000 acres of that tract that is worth $6000, the ballance of the Warrant removed and laid on land said to be valuable*"[2] As to the Value of the land I cannot say as I have not seen it, but it has been represented to me that the Warrant was more valuable than the land and I still think it must be so or Mr. Nelson who surveyed & explored the land would not have removed it. But the other part of the Answer I know to be incorrect. I do not hold 2000 acres (if I do some one must have made entries for me that I know nothing of) what I do hold is on entries made after Robert Nelson[3] removed this 5000 acres W[arran]t. and the Warrants which covers those entries, I borrowed from Majr. Anderson & Capt. [John] Strother[4] or chief part of them.

It must be that after the Wt. was removed any person had a right to enter the land. The whole of the Wt. was removed by Nelson & by him apporiated to his own use. I do not hold any entry by Virtue of that Wt. you must have misunderstood Majr. Anderson. However all this makes no difference, provided the present mode is adopted. Colo. Hays can give security that the title which I made to the 200 acres is not injoined & I will do the like to him for the transfer of the bond each to be answerable according to the injury sustained. if this does not do equal justice I know not what will

Your Obt. &c.

John McNairy

P.S. The foregoing has been proposed with a design to put an end to law, you may rest assured that I do not dread any investigation of this bussiness either in law or equity, but by the accommodation we avoid trouble expense. I presume any thing transacted with you is the same as if done with Colo. Hays.   J. McN.

ALS, DLC.
    1. Letter not found.
    2. Letter not found.
    3. Nelson (1760–1808), was deputy surveyor for North Carolina in Tennessee and variously justice of the peace and clerk of the county court in Montgomery and Stewart counties. From 1803 to 1806 he sat in the Tennessee legislature, representing first Montgomery County and subsequently Stewart.
    4. Strother (d. 1815), from Orange County, N.C., was a surveyor and lawyer in the Nashville area and a speculator in West Tennessee lands. A captain in the Robertson County militia, he served as Jackson's topographical engineer in the Creek War.

From Daniel Smith

Washington Jany. 27th. [1808]

Dr Sir,

I have at length procured your original letter and herewith enclose it to you. I never got it till la[st] night.[1]

We understand that Mr. Madison and Mr. Rose t[he] British envoy extraordinary are engaged in a [negotia]tion on the subject of our differences with that [govern]ment. What progress they make is unknown, their [whole] proceedings being kept secret—indeed they oug[ht to] be till it is over. I should hope for a favourable [result] were it not for the late proclamation from the B[ritish] King published about the time Mr. Rose left England. If Mr. Rose is bound to adhere to the princi[ples therein] contained, the attempt to make a treaty I str[ongly feel] would be useless and vain. You will see this proclamation, probably have, in the papers.[2]

A meeting or cacus was held here on saturda[y] evening for the purpose of recommending to the p[eople] of the United States suitable characters to fill t[he offi]ces of President and vice President of the U. S. next after 3d March 1809. The [result] was that James Madison and George Clinton the p[resent] vice president, were recommended by an almost un[ani]-mous vote—The former as President the latter to con[ti]nue in his present office. It ought to be understo[od] that in this meeting the members acted in their p[ri]vate characters. I refer you to the public papers [for] the news.

Your obedt. Serv.

Danl. Smith

ALS fragment, DLC.
1. On November 28, 1807 (see above), Jackson had asked Smith to return copies of his letters to Smith, November 12, 1806 (see above), and Dickson, November 17, 1806.
2. Smith was referring to George III's proclamation of October 17, 1807, calling for more vigorous impressment of British subjects serving on neutral vessels. The proclamation had been printed in the *Impartial Review*, January 21, 1808.

To John McNairy from AJ and Robert Hays

A Copy.   Hermitage, February 13th. 1808
Sir,
Your letter of the 23d. of January last[1] was handed to me by Mr. Stuart in Nashville some days ago and the pressures of business at the time and being called from home has prevented an answer until now.

I have carefully perused your letter, and am happy to find that you as well as myself hate law There is hopes that law will be avoided. where justice can be obtained without it and where we differ on points of law and Justice for myself, and when I say myself I mean to include Colo. Hays thro out this business [(]the present subject). I am always willing to leave it to disinterested legal characters to decide. You observe that you would not have Engaged (in law) had you not conceived that you were compelled or lose your Just right. how? did you not know that Hays was bound to discharge the mortgage by special contract? did you not receive thro him the cash as per your receipt paid you by the Marshal, and was there not cotton to the amount of one thousand dollars or thereabouts placed in the hands of William Tait by Samuel Jackson, the proceeds of which for your use &c &c. did any of them wear the appearance of depriving you of Justice? it certainly did not—But this cotton or its appropriation by your agents has given rise to the only thing of difference now between you (for your proposition relating to the other cause of dispute will be acceded to, this you know was offered some time ago) I say your agents for it is not contended on any side but that you were to have the neat proceeds, and that any directions was given by Hays relative to the sale of the cotton after it was on board the boat, except Colo. Hays and yourself (as Mr. Tait states[)] requesting Mr. Tait after the cotton reached New Orleans to attend to it. Now Sir what is the case Mr. Taite states thus "I wrote Gray & Taylor[2] and enclosed one of [W.] Mullins receipts desiring them to send the cotton to the best advantage and nearest one. the proceeds of the sale after deducting their Coms. in Branch Bank notes of the United States or drafts drawn by a good man payable here or in Philadelphia this letter or a copy of I shewed to Judge McNairy and he approved of it before I sent it off as I was acting as his Colo. hays agent in this business["][3]—He writes and you approve of the letter directing this cotton to be sold for bills, the cotton is sold for bills agreeable to your direction. (having approved makes them yours). these bills drew not in the name of Colo. Hays but in the name of Mr. Taitte and all this by your direction and without the direction of Hays, and still you wish to throw the responsibility of the bills or their loss on Colo. Hays. This sir in my opinion is neither law Justice equity or Gospel, but sir this can easily be determined by disinterested legal characters to whom I am Willing that it should be submitted and who can decide whether the bills are yours Hays or who is to bear the loss of them. It is certain Saml. Jackson has received with Hays a credit for that Cotton it is as certain you were to have the proceeds of that cotton and that it was to be to the credit of the Mortgage. This question being Settled you will find, that you have no need of applying to law to obtain your just right. It is and has been my opinion that law equity and Justice will apply the amount of sales of that cotton to part discharge of the Mortgage—however you think different I suppose; but Mr [John] Haywood and Judge Overton can easily determine that point and if they disagree they can choose a third character.[4] I am by no means tenacious of these characters, but willing to any who have correct Ideas of the doctrine of bills and transactions similar to the one aluded to. if you are willing to submit this point to disinterested legal characters this is my agreement there to & there is No need of bills cross bills &c &c in equity.[5]

Relative to Nelsons bond Colo. Hays wrote you on the terms proposed by you. the deed made by you will be given up and cancelled and security given which would be satisfactory that the title remains unimpaired and without injury by any act of his or any person for him or under him, or by Williams or Under him since the date of your conveyance & you re-convey the bond to him with security that the bond is not impaired and is without injury by any act of yours, or the acts of any person acting under you or your directions each to be answerable according to the injury sustained. This sir I believe meets your ideas and is compleat Justice to all. To shew you the assent & consent of Robert Hays he places his signature hereunto

I am Sir yr. ob[t. Svt.] &c.

Andrew Jackson
Robert Hays

Copy, DLC.
1. See above.
2. J.F. Gray and John Taylor were partners in a New Orleans mercantile firm.
3. See William Tait to AJ, November 23, 1807. Mullins has not been further identified.
4. Haywood was at this time practicing law in Nashville.
5. Efforts at arbitration in the case fell to Hugh Lawson White and John Dickinson rather than Overton and Haywood.

From Robert Barr

Locust Grove near Lexington 28 feb 1808
Sir

Long since I had the pleasure of seeing you at french broade springs,[1] I have often Heard that you have sported it on the turf, and that you have frequently been a fortuanate adventurer—And as I have a verry fine Mare I wish to sell, is one reason that I forward you this note. This mare is a whip Colt,[2] out of Col John Vanrells of Petersburg Virga Mare Nancey, and I am informd by young Mr Garret[3] who showd me a letter from Vanrell that your famous Horse Truckson was out of the same Mare—of this you can be well informd, as I met Co Vanrell at Mr Richd Mitchels at Hawkins Courthouse[4] and took the Mare with this foal in her, and Richd Mitchel brought her out to Kentucky—I was to give 150 Dolls if the colt was dropd alive and put the Mare to the Horse. she stands me 200 dolls besides risk of life and raising, and I would be glad to get 500 Dolls. She is large, lofty Carriage Heavey made a fine bay upwards of 15 hands last spring. she now must be one or two higher. Col Abram Beauford[5] traind her on the turff last fall. he says she performd well amongsd his tryal Horses, but by some accident she was not in order when our races came on to Start—As for her aperance and caracter I can refer you to Mr [William T.?] Banton and John Wagnon Lexon.[6] and Col Abram Beauford near this, she may be said still a untryd Animal, but from apearance a verry fine one, and as she is large, and I took more pains to keep her in order not to force her when young with corn.

The principle reason I want to make sale of her is I have chaingd my stock into Mule raising. I put last season 53 Mares to my Jack—I have sent of two crops to Market, last season I sent 56 mules. as I am geting too old to Give Attention to fine Horses, shall give it up as every person here is pursuing it—Note if you are raising Colts perhaps this Mare may suit you and her like Hard to come at—And should any of your acquaintances be in want and likely to purchase will thank you to inform them— As Buzzard and Dragon, Sterling &c all stand in Lexon. any purchaser choosing to breed out of Her, I could have her carefully put without any expense of corn or passtuarage, to the horse the choose.

you and Mrs Jackson must have heard of the Misforten that I and family met with eighteen Months past, of loosing Mrs Barr.[7] all my trouble and fateague of taking and keeping her, near two years with the famd Doctr Tate[8] at Philada who sent her home supposed Curd., but about ten Month after broke out and Hurryd her out of existance, to the great loss of self and family—youl on recipt of this, not to forget to deliver my best and Kindest respects Joind with my female familys to Mrs Jackson, for her Civilities shown Mrs B. at the springs, as my Girls have often heard their Mother speak of Mrs J. with gratitude. please let me hear from you by post.[9] I am &c. with sentiments of great Esteem

Robt Barr

ALS, DLC. Barr (c1749–1821) was a merchant in Lexington, Ky., having moved there from Philadelphia about 1784. At the time of his death he was living in Franklin, Mo.

1. A therapeutic warm springs resort on the French Broad River about five miles over the Tennessee-North Carolina line in present-day Madison County, N.C.

2. Whip, the English-bred son of the 1783 Epsom Derby winner Saltram, had been imported into Virginia by William Lightfoot sometime between 1800 and 1805.

3. Probably John Mountjoy Garrard (1778–1836), of Bourbon County, Ky., the son of former governor James Garrard. Garrard had briefly lived in Nashville and worked with Jackson in training horses.

4. Mitchell was clerk of the county court in Hawkins County, 1787–1812.

5. Abraham Buford was at this time living in Scott County, Ky.

6. Banton was a Lexington innkeeper and manager of the stables of the Kentucky Hotel; Wagnon was also a Lexington innkeeper.

7. Rebecca Barr had died on July 19, 1806.

8. Not identified.

9. Jackson's response has not been found.

From John McNairy

Nashville 11th. of March 1808.

Sir.

I have received yours dated the 23d. Ulto.[1] and have delayed thus long answering, expecting to see you, so much time having elapsed it becomes necessary to write you.

In my second to you I state thus "If the proposition which is named hereafter will finally close and settle the law suit, and secure to me what is justly due on Cafferys Mortgage, at any reasonable given time it will do."[2] The objection then made to the liability of Colo. Hays for the amount of [E.] Browns Draft,[3] was that the others was sold for cash & the cash given for Browns Draft. This point I endeavored to elucidate by the letter of the commission Merchant transmitted to you with my last. None other objections are made. If I have done any thing which make me sustain the loss of Browns Draft, it was done to serve Colo. Hays who said to me that he did not wish to be seen in it. for that the Marshall (as he had heard[)] designed levying an execution on the cotton, that this was his situation is self evident from this circumstance Colo. Hays without my consent or knowledge took a bond in my name from Samuel Jackson for this very cotton which I refused to take. However from your letter, you seize on with avidity one part of my proposition and leave the other totally uncomplyed with, except it may be done by arbitration or proceeding at law; no conclusion of my law suit for the foreclosure of Cafferys Mortgage, but leave that part of the bussiness to be settled by future investigation. This will not do, I cannot acceed to it, and am therefore done corresponding on the subject.

I am sir your Obt &c &c.

John McNairy

ALS, DLC.
1. McNairy probably meant Jackson's letter of February 13, above.
2. See above, McNairy to AJ, January 23.
3. E. Brown, a cotton merchant in New Orleans, had issued a bill of exchange on James Brown of Philadelphia, for $995.97, the net return on the cotton Hays had shipped to New Orleans for McNairy. Brown's bill, however, had been protested. For a discussion of the bill, see William Tait to AJ, November 23, 1807.

As major general of the 2nd Division of the Tennessee militia, Jackson maintained that he always stood ready to march the troops under his command wherever needed to protect the frontier settlements. In April 1808, William Meadows hastened to Nashville with the news that a band of Creeks had massacred white settlers near the mouth of Duck River. Jackson immediately placed his forces on alert, only to learn a few weeks later that Meadows had lied.

To the Officers of the 2nd Division

Division Order   Hermitage April 20th 1808

From General Thomas Johnstons advice of the 3rd. instant,[1] and William Meadows statement under his hand of the 18th. instant[2] it appears that 25 of our inocent Citizens have fell victims, to the ruthless hands of Savage barbarity, and from strong circumstances it appears that the Creeks who have perpetrated this horrid massacree has been excited to this hellish act, by the instigation of whitemen agents under foreign influence, who have stimulated those barbarians to lift the scalping knife and Tomhawk against our defenceless women and Children. it is stated by Mr. Meadows that a hostile band of Creeks to the amount of four hundred and forty with twelve whitemen are encamped on the south ba[n]k of Tennessee—There on the 3rd. instant they attack Colberts boat, having five men on board killed two and wounded three, one of which was since dead—and on the 5th. massacreed three whole families twentyone in number three miles below the mouth of Duck—this brings to our recollection the horrid barbarity committed on our frontier in 1777. under the influence of, and by the orders of Great Britain, and it is presumeable that the same influence has excited those barbarians to the late and recent acts of butchery and murder, but the blood of our innocent Citizens must not be shed with impunity—prepare then for retaliation, the relation of this horrid scene will rouse our countrymen, they will pant for the Orders of our goverment to punish the ruthless foe, who has deprived us of our fellow Citizens of our Brothers our wifes & our children and the influence that gave it birth—you will therefore without delay place your Brigade in compleat readiness to march at a minutes warning. you will have the voluntiers within your Brigade in readiness to march at a very short notice, provided the defence of our frontier and imperious necessity should from information to be recd. make it a measure of defence to dislodge this hostile marauding band from the present position they now Occupy—you will hold your Brigade in compleat readiness untill further information is recd. from the mouth of Duck River and untill further orders from me and from the goverment. heath & respect.

A. Jackson Major G. 2nd. Division—

DS copy (with revisions in AJ's hand), DLC. Published in Bassett, 1:188–89.
1. Johnson's communication has not been found.
2. See Report of William Meadows, enclosed in AJ to Jefferson, April 20, below. Meadows has not been further identified.

To Thomas Jefferson

April 20th. 1808—

Sir

I hasten to transmit to you the inclosed statement of William Meadows[1] (which if true) connected with the information transmitted to the Secratary of War, by Brigadier Genl. Thomas Johnston commanding the Sixth Brigade under date of the third instant, to which I refer you, will shew the alarming and hostile attitude of the creek indians, on our frontier—alarming, because there can remain no doubt but the twelve whites, with them must be agents of a foreign nation; exciting the creeks, to hostilities against the united States—These horrid scenes bring fresh to our recollection, the influence, during the revolutionary war, that raised the scalping knife and Tomhawk, against our defenceless weomen and children—I have but little doubt but the present savage cruelty is excited from the same source—The blood of our innocent citizens must not flow, with impunity—Justice forbids it, and the present relative situation of our country with foreign nations require speedy redress, and a final check to these hostile murdering creeks—I am not personally acquainted with Mr Meadows, am informed that he is a man of truth—but as he lived last year in the neighbourhood of Genl D. Smith our Senator, I refer you to him for his charector—On the recpt of Mr Meadows statement, I hastened to Issue a general order to the Brigadiers of my Division,[2] to place their respective Brigades in a state of preparation to march at the shortest notice—I have directed Genl Johnston to be upon the alert, and to act on the Defensive only untill farther orders—and by confidential spies to find out the position, numbers, and situation of these marauding creeks, and communicate the same to me without delay[3]—and by no means to persue beyond the Tennessee river, unless the protection of our frontier, and imperious necessity require that the should be dislodged from the position they now occupy, and upon such an event that this is to be done with a sufficient force to insure success—Should the information recd. from the spies render this step necessary (which nothing can do unless that should appear the point to which their whole strength is to collect) I will with a small but well chosen band march for that purpose—and should I, I pledge myself to my goverment, that I will destroy the coalition—Would it not be proper, that some mode should be pointed out by government, how and in what manner expresses should be paid. Under present circumstances, serious inconveniences may arise and many parts of our frontier, fall a sacrafice to savage cruelty, for the want of some arangements on this subject—few there are who is able out of their private purse to hire and pay expresses—and none can be got to perform this duty without compensation, another deplorable event—It is well known that there is a great deficiency of arms, not only on our frontier, but throughout the interior of our country—and on the eve of war and no provisions Either by our State Legislature or congress to remedy this evil—Without arms, altho brave we cannot fight—no love of country, or bravery can supply the want of arms—The certainty of war and our defencless situation in this respect—and the subject being overlooked by our State Legislature, and as yet by congress, I have thought it my duty to bring this subject to your view, that the evill may be remedied before the rise of congress—I am Sir with due consideration & respect yr mo. ob. serv.

Andrew Jackson

ALS, DNA-RG 107; Copy, DLC. Published in Bassett, 1:186–87.
   1. See below.
   2. See above.

3. Jackson's instructions to Johnson have not been found. For Johnson's report, see Johnson to AJ, May 7.

ENCLOSURE: REPORT OF WILLIAM MEADOWS

Clover Bottom 18th Aprail 1808

Account of Savage cruelty by William Meadows (viz) myself and Brother with two other young men have been setled near three months on the north bank of Duck River, about four miles above the mouth, the nearest white settlements we knew of was fourteen miles from us. about the middle of March there came ninety Creek Indians among which were Seven squaws, and encamped on the South bank of Duck, one mile below our improvement, they visited us frequently, and appeared friendly, though often spoke of an intention to attack the whites, when the leaves were pretty well grown, and said the whites were intruding on their Territory—there was also another Camp of Creek Indians, on the south bank of Tennessee River, three quarters of a mile above the mouth of Duck, that we were informed by the former Indians, had been there near three months, and that when first there, they were 40. in number, but had increased now to 350, among which were 14 Squaws and 12 white men, we went in our Canoe up the north side of the River, opposite this Camp, and saw the Indians and white men, and from the appearance, we thought the account of their number, was correct. they spoke to us, and invited us over, which we declined and returned to our Settlement. On Sunday the third Instant we visited the camp on Duck near us, when we were surprised finding, the camp evacuated, not knowing, why or wherefore this precipitate move, this we thought a bad Omen, and gave us much alarm; so that we thought it dangerous to remain at our house where we had cleared and fenced 14 Acres of ground. we had lost some horses, and took this moment as a favourable one to hunt them, we accordingly hid out our plunder, and all went into the woods, in search of our horses, we would usually be out two or three days at a time, when we would return to our goods, and finding all safe would return again without going in public, to our improvement, untill friday the 15 instant, we could not find Six of our horses, which we now concluded were stolen, by the Indians, we then all set out to the Settlements, of Yellow creek, for supplys of meal and Bacon, to return and plant our Crop. as we travelled into the settlement we found all improvements uninhabited, for upwards of thirty miles, untill we reached Sterling May's on Yellow creek,[1] we there learned that on sunday the 3rd. instant, a keel boat the property of Colbert, loaded with whiskey, flour, powder, and lead, had touched at the large camp of Indians above the mouth of Duck, the Indians wanted whiskey, flour, powder, &c. but the Capt.[2] refused to supply them, and pushed of up the River, when he had gone about one quarter of a mile, the Indians in a large body, fired from the bank into the boat, who contained five men only, two of which was killed and three were wounded one of which is since dead and another expected to die of his wounds, we were further informed, that on tuesday the fifth instant, three families, about four or five miles below the mouth of Duck were all killed by Indians, the families were in numbers, One of Nine, One of Seven, and one of five, these accounts appear well authenticated. On Yellow creek we met One hundred men marching out to guard the frontier untill further advices. I am now come in after arms and amunition, for myself and Comrades, who intend to return (under the protection of the guard) and pla[n]t our Crop.

a Copy Test   William Meadows
Jno. Coffee

Copy, DNA-RG 107.
1. May, nephew of George Michael Deaderick and a resident of Stewart County, operated a cotton gin on Yellow Creek.
2. John Gordon (1763–1819). Gordon operated a hotel and mercantile firm in Nashville and, in partnership with George Colbert, a ferry and inn on the Duck River. He commanded a company of spies in the Creek and Seminole wars.

In the 1808 presidential campaign Tennessee's Jeffersonian Republicans, like those in most other states of the Union, divided into two camps: supporters of the congressional caucus nominees, James Madison and George Clinton; and adherents of James Monroe, the candidate supported by John Randolph and others in Virginia disillusioned with the administration's continuing support of James Wilkinson and its mild policy toward the British. Monroe, as American minister to England, had firmly denounced British impressment of American citizens and the attack of the Leopard *on the* Chesapeake.

The earliest evidence of a break with the administration in Tennessee came on July 29, 1807, when a group of citizens gathered in Nashville to voice their outrage against the British. A heated debate arose over the wording of a preamble to proposed resolutions. "The citizens of West Tennessee . . .," ran the contested clause, "have beheld with indignation the pacific conduct of our government returned by acts of concealed or open warfare, and the friendly and forebearing disposition of the nation ascribed to cowardice & fear." James Robertson opposed the statement as a censure of the president, but Jackson disagreed. Their two factions eventually worked out a compromise, accepting the preamble with an appended statement approving the "measures adopted by the president" (Impartial Review, *July 29, 1807).*

As the presidential race moved forward, Jackson and Robertson once again found themselves on different sides within the same party, with Jackson supporting Monroe, as suggested in the letter below from Sampson Williams, and Robertson supporting Madison. The extent of Jack-

son's canvassing for Monroe has not been established, but its lack of success is clear. Tennessee's five electoral votes went to Madison for president and Clinton for vice president.

From Sampson Williams

Carthage April 25th 1808

Dear Sir

Since you left here politicks have ceased and the greatest harmony immaginable pervads all ranks—the only two Converts you made while here have retrograded—or in other words they say that they only Suppported Munroe out of politeness to you, because that you were a Stranger—and I can assure you Sir without you or Some other friend of Munroes return to this quarter he will have but few friends—at present I know of none nor do I Suspect but one.

I know that you have been at considerable trouble and expence in Electioneering for him and I thought it a duty that I owe you from our long and friendly acquaintance to inform you that any further Exertion in his favor will be lost for your friend cannot come in this heat

your friend [Leonard] Fite[1] says that he cannot Stand alone and at present he does not know who he shall support for Elector and without James Lyon[2] declares unequivocally in favor of Madison he shall not vote for him but let the presedential Election terminate as it may—my friendship for you is the same it ever was and will not cease untill I have reasons to change my present opinion—you know caucasing is necessary on Extraordinary Occasions—at all events my Sincere wish is that the best man may be Elected and if I should be mistaken in my Choice and hereafter be convinced as I heretofore have been I shall acknowledge my error and repent for the injury done my Country and try to repair it on some future occasion which is all I think that is required of Sinners—but I hope that we Shall get all right after a while—

Accept Sir the assurances of my Esteem and believe to be a true Republican of 76

S. Williams

ALS, DLC. Published in Bassett, 1:189. Williams (1762–1841), a native of South Carolina and former sheriff of Davidson County, was at this time a farmer in Smith County. He served in the Tennessee senate, 1799–1801, 1805–1807, and 1811–13.

1. Fite (1761–1842) was a Revolutionary War veteran in Smith County.

2. Lyon (1776–1824), the son of Matthew, was a farmer, land speculator, newspaper editor, and entrepreneur in Smith County. In 1807, he failed in his bid for election to Congress. Instead of Lyon, William Martin, a Madison supporter, was chosen as presidential elector for the district.

To Thomas Jefferson

Nashville May 14th. 1808

Sir,

On the 20th. ultimo, I wrote you, enclosing a statement made by William Meadows relative to the depredations lately committed by the indians on our frontier[1]—and a large party of the Creeks apparently hostile, who occupied the South bank of the Tennessee—I then stated the substance of my orders to the several Brigadier generals, Issued on that occasion, and my special order to Genl Johnston through some confidential person in whom he could rely, to find out their numbers, position and hostile attitude—and report the same to me without delay &c the enclosures will shew you how that duty has been performed,[2] and in all probability, William Meadows is a base, man, and devoid of truth—But I am still apprehensive, that part of the Creeks, are not friendly disposed towards the united states—and it is still probable that there are agents, from some foreign power, instigating them to mischief—This may not be the case—but still I must confess I am not free from some suspicions of this kind—In my last I took the liberty to sugest the propriety, of some mode being Pointed out by law, through which, expressed [expresses] employed to distribute military orders, should be remunerated, a letter recd. yesterday from Genl T. Johnston, has brought this subject before me, and compels me again to renew that subject. I inclose you a coopy of his letter[3]—and without any comment of mine it will forcibly strike you, what sensations it will raise in the minds of the militia—Sir at a time when it was thought necessary, for the safety of our country, that every exertion should be made to crush this conspiracy that the goverment, had ordered this exertion, and that the expence of difusing these orders through the Brigade should be thrown upon the Pocket of an individual by the goverment—is calculated (at a time like the present) to damp the ardour of the militia when it is certainly the duty of the goverment to promote it—This is taxing patriotism in a way that will not be agreable—and no man will be got to perform this duty—even in cases of great emergency should the arise—But it is stated "that This is the exoficia duty of a militia officer"[4]—This is a new idea—where is the power in a superior to command an officer to make use of his horse in the Publick service, without compensation—and where the power to punish for disobedience of such order—neither will it be conceded—that in time of peace or at the order for war, a militia officer is exoficia bound to distribute orders any farther, than throughout his company Batalion or Regiment to which he belongs—Where then is the officer near the Brigadier or Major genl of militia, that he has a right to command to convay his orders—in many instances, sixty or seventy miles at his own expence—when in the field it is and would be verry differrent—I must confess that I cannot see the officer in the list of my Division, that I have the power to order to perform such duty at their own expence—and certain I am, I will never attempt to exercise such an inniquitous arbitary order—The publick good has and ever will be a sufficient inducement for me to have this duty performed when the safety of my country requires it, but Just compensation shall be always made by me out of my own Pockett if goverment refuse to compensate the individual, for his own service and that of his horse—few militia officers but what have large families to support, and few there are that can conveniently spare from their own Pocketts with Justice to their families, either the sum necessary for the expence of travelling, or the hire of a horse (and it is not always the wealthy that is the most brave or patriotic) in the day of danger the wealthy enjoy too much ease to court danger—the poor always make the best Soldiers—permit me to ask—you are commander in chief of the united states Where is the officer that you have a right to claim exoficia, his services to convay your orders to any part of the union—If you as president of the united states has this right I will give up the question and admit, that I have or ought to have some officer that I can order to distribute my orders throughout my Division—This duty was performed from my order—Justice requires compensation to be made, whether you have the power or any officer under you to order or make the payment I cannot say—but if no power exists it will shew the necessity of providing for such cases by law—From the spirit of Genl Johnstons letter it is easy to discover the temper of his feelings on this occasion—and I well know there is no officer in the union more attentive to his duty, nor more attached to his country than he is—This claim having been once before the accountant—rejected—presented to me—I have thought it proper to bring it to your view and the consequences, that will ensue—from the refusal to allow and pay the account—It will give me pleasure to have it in my power—to remove from the mind of genl Johnston, the sensations that this has occasioned—The vallue to him is nothing—it is the evil that will grow out of the thing in the moment of necessity—I am with due reguard yr mo ob Serv.

A. Jackson

ALS, PHi.
1. See above.
2. Johnson acknowledged Jackson's order (not found) on May 7, when he sent the report of Thomas Swann's patrol, forwarded by Jackson to Jefferson.
3. See Thomas Johnson to AJ, May 13. Johnson had asked to be reimbursed for sending expresses with Jackson's orders in January 1807.
4. Source of quotation not found.

For several years after the sale of Jackson & Hutchings's store in late 1806, the partners continued to face problems in closing out the business

of the firm, as indicated in the correspondence below with George Bullitt,
lawyer in Missouri, and Henry Clay, lawyer in Kentucky.

From George Bullitt to Jackson & Hutchings

St. Genevieve, 13th. July 1808.

Gentlemen,

Mr. [William C.] Carr this day favoured me with a view of your letter
to him bearing date 12th of June last, in which you seem disposed to allow *him only* fifty dollars as a full compensation for his services as an
assistant attorney in your suit against John Smith T.[1] The practice in Louisiana is quite different from that in Tensee. as stated by you, therefore it is
expected that you will pay to myself and Mr. Carr five pr. centum upon
the amount of the judgment obtained by us for you against Smith. By
your letter it appears you are willing that Mr. Carr should retain fifty dollars for *himself*; I claim a commission of five pr. centum on the amount of
the judgment, and unless I receive that, I take nothing for my trouble.
The unnecessary expences of Mr. Hutchings to this Country on the subject of your claim agt. Smith, cannot have any influence in regulating my
Commission.[2] The money has been obtained as soon as the regular
course of law would admit of which will appear by a reference to the
records. You hold my receipt for the note,[3] and untill that is returned, I
Consider myself right, in retaining the Bal due you on the Judgt.

I am Gentlemen with respect yours &c.

Geo. Bullitt

ALS, DLC. Bullitt was sometime speaker of the Louisiana Territory House of Delegates,
territorial judge, 1814–20, and register of the land office at Cape Girardeau starting in
1820.

1. Carr (1783–1851), assistant counsel in the case *Jackson & Hutchings* v. *John Smith
T*, served as agent of the Louisiana Territory board of land commissioners, 1805–1809,
and later as circuit court judge at St. Louis. The case arose out of Smith T's defaulting on a
promissory note made to Jackson & Hutchings in February 1805 for merchandise advanced, probably for Smith T to open a store in either Illinois or Missouri. Jackson's letter
to Carr has not been found.

2. At its June 1806 term, the court assessed Smith T with the debt and damages, roughly
$5,000; but it was not until 1808, when John Hutchings, partner in the defunct firm, went
to Ste. Genevieve, that Jackson & Hutchings finally collected.

3. Not found.

To George Bullitt from Jackson & Hutchings

Nashville Agust 6th. 1808—

Sir

your letter of the 13th. of July[1] under cover of Mr Carrs,[2] is Just recd.
and it fills us with astonishment, that at this late Period we should be

favoured with a line from you when during the whole period of time that the suit was Pending (and before you abandoned it) could we receive a line from you advising us of the state of the suit, and when our letter was handed you by Mr. Stothart the reply to him, that you had abandoned the cause and referred us to Mr Carr[3]—but behold a Judgt has been recovered by Mr Carr, and you now want five pr cent commissions—This Sir is a verry modest request indeed—you abandoned the cause after filing the declaration, Mr Carr prosecuted the suit to Judgt. and now sir you want to take it up again and claim commissions—upon what Principles of Justice, honesty, or custom is this claim founded—for what services is a lawyer entitled to commission, is it for prosecuting a suit to the filing of a declaration or is it even for prosecuting a suit to Judgt.[4] it is neither—It is for collecting the money, running the risque of safe keeping and remitting it to his client—have you performed either of these—you have not—but still your modesty is equal to the task of demanding commissions on a Judgt. you never recovered, and which was recovered after you had voluntary abandoned the cause—This unjust, unprecedented demand will not be gratified—you are pleased to state that the practice in Louisiana is quite differrent from that in Tennessee—if sir such a practice prevails with you as you state of Taxing five pr cent on the Judgt. (whether you collect it or not, or whether the Judgt. is ever collected) it is such a practice as prevails no where else, and never ought to prevail anywhere—it is buying Justice at two high a premium—it is Taxing the honest creditor too dear—you are pleased to state, that the uncessary expences of Mr Hutchings to that country, can have no influence on the subject of your claim—Could it be called uncessary, when we were unadvised when from the losses of time we had a right to expect a Judgt.? it was necessary; from your omission of advising us that we should attend to the subject; we found it was well—from experience—and from the moment we were advised you had abandoned the cause, we never viewed you as having any thing to do in the suit, and when it is over we are determined you shall have nothing to do in it; and have instructed Mr Carr to pay you whatever is a legal fee in your country for a lawyer Issuing a writ and filing a declaration on a plain note of hand, here your labour and attention ended and of course your claim for compensation; and we have only to add, if you attempt to detain any of our Judgt. we will find means of instructing you, that since your abandonment of the suit you have no power to act in our business—to Mr. Carr and the Clerk we look and will look for our money no commissions shall be paid you, and should you not receive the fee that we have directed to be paid you, you will receive nothing—in fact a lawyer that is entrusted with a suit and abandons it before Judgt. ought not to be paid unless he employs another to prosecute it, this you did not do—as to returning you the receipt, spoken of, it is uncessary. this letter together with the record of the cause, will be a sufficient voucher to shew, that we have no claim on you in consequence of having had the note in your possession and instituting the suit—The only claim we will have against you will be, in case you attempt to inter-meddle with our money arising from the Judgt. over which you have no control, or agency, nor had not since you abandoned the suit, nor we suppose never would have been thought of by you; had it not been for the commissions.

we are Sir with respect yrs. &c

Jackson & Hutchings

ALS copy in AJ's hand, DLC.
1. See above.
2. Carr's letter not found.
3. Letters conveyed by William or Robert Stothart, not found.
4. As Jackson pointed out, the bill of complaint in the case, *Jackson & Hutchings* v. *John Smith T*, June Term 1806, had been drafted and filed by Bullitt.

Receipt for Fifty Shares of Bank Stock

Nashville 24th October 1808

Then receiv'd from Andrew Jackson his due bill payable on demand for Five hundred Dollars—which when paid will be in full for his first instalment on fifty Shares by him this day subscrib'd to the Nashville Bank[1] in the book of subscription deposited in my hands

George. M. Deaderick

ADS, DLC.
1. The Nashville Bank, incorporated with a capital of $200,000 and shares at $50 each, had been established by the Tennessee legislature on November 26, 1807.

To Henry Clay from Jackson & Hutchings

Nashville October 27th. 1808

Sir

By advice Just recd. from Mr. J[ohn] W[esley] Hunt we are informed that you are attorney for us in the suit Jackson & Hutchings vs. John. M. Garrard[1]—Mr Hunt also advises, that Mr. Garrard has put in a plea relative to the Justness of our claim against him and concludes, "we had better confer with you upon the subject," we therefore take the liberty, altho unacquainted, to write you—And beg leave to observe—that the claim on which Mr Garrard is sued, originated, in merchandize sold to him, in cash loaned, and in orders drew on and accepted by us—in the fall 1805—in 1806—(we believe in may) a final settlement took place, between us, and he closed his acpt. by his note with assurances that the money should be paid before he left this country—but contrary to our expectations and the good oppinion we had entertained of him, he went off without taking up his note, altho he carried with him at least one-thousand dollars in cash—and on the day of settlement he drew an order on Major Verrell, in part of the debt due us which Verrell did not accept—This is over and above the amount of his note and for which he stands Justly indebted—We have no doubt, from the conduct of John M. Garrard he is capable of doing any thing—or sugesting any thing that is either dishonest or dishonourable but it is strange to us, that such sugestions should way any thing, in a court of Justice against his own note which was given on a final settlement since which no kind of intercourse or dealings has taken place between us—you will therefore be good anough to advise us, the state and situation of that suit—the nature of the plea he has put in and what kind (if any) proof may be necessary for us to forward you and send on commissions for that purpose—and be good anough to draw on us for your fee, which shall be honoured on sight.[2]

your attention to this will much oblige yr Hmble servts

Jackson & Hutchings

ALS draft in AJ's hand, DLC. Published in Bassett, 1:151, and in James F. Hopkins and Mary W. M. Hargreaves, eds., *The Papers of Henry Clay*, (Lexington, Ky., 1959), 1:250 (both under date of October 27, 1806).

1. See Hunt to AJ, October 6. Hunt (1772–1849) was a Lexington, Ky., merchant and manufacturer.

2. According to Hopkins and Hargreaves (1:250), Clay filed a bill of complaint in the case, *Andrew Jackson* v. *John M. Garrard*, "asking payment of a note for $193.74 and damages of $100. Judgment favoring the plaintiff was rendered in August, 1809." That case file has not been found.

From Stockley Donelson Hays

Lexington November 6th. 1808.

Dear Uncle,

Immediately after my arrival I delivered your letter to Mr. Hunt,[1] who stated that he had given your papers into the hands of Mr. Clay for collection & refer'd me to Mr. Clay for further information, who was then attending Court at Frankford & I had not an opportunity of seeing him—I understood he had returned & road out to see him to day—he was not at home; but I again fell in with Mr. Hunt & from him learned that suit had long since been commenced against Mr. Garrart that he had awarded [avoided] Judgement by putting in a plea, the nature of which he could or would not tell me further than he believed it related to a horse you should have sold Mr. Garrart said to be unsound. I find Sir, that your business has been intirely neglected by Mr. Hunt, which is owing to an exception that Mr. Hunt should have taken to your conduct towards him, when he was last in Nashville—He states that you were in Town while he was there—That you would not take the trouble to walk from

Mr. [Thomas] Tolbots to Mr. Winns[2] to see him; & I assure you Sir, that this neglect (wonderfull to be sure in its nature) has been the sole cause of your business remaining thus long in Court undetermined. This Gentleman has really acted the part of friend towards you & like a man too!! Became offended with you—declined doing any thing in your business, and strangely neglected too to inform you, that you might look out for another agent.

He says that as the business was not of importance enough to yourself to take the trouble to walk from Mr. Tolbots to Mr. Winns to see him, he did not think it of importance enough for him to take the trouble of riding to Burbon to attend to it for you. This is the way he argues. I find it will not be possible to get a Judgement this court, since you cannot have it in your power to answer to the plea put in by the defendant in time; But I will endeavour to procure from the Clerk of the court a copy of the plea & all other information relative to the case as it now stands and forward to you by the next mail or so soon as I can procure such information. School commences this day[3] and as I have not seen the professors, who have been absent since my arrival, & I cannot say any thing relative to them—I commence study with a determination (I think not to be overcome) to prosecute it to the utmost of my abilities & to refrain from all kind of dysipation which shall be esteemed prejudicial to a young man in the pursuit of usefull knowledge. You'll be pleased to present my compliments to aunt Jackson & all inquiring friends & except sir, the gratefull esteem of your affectionate nephew & Obt. Sert.

Sto. D. Hays.

ALS, DLC.
1. Not found.
2. Talbot and Winn were innkeepers in Nashville.
3. Hays was matriculating at Transylvania University.

From mid-1807 on, West Tennessee echoed with demands for retribution against Great Britain for her impressment of American seamen, interference with American commerce, and incitement of Indian raids on white settlements. Though President Jefferson had imposed economic sanctions, many frontiersmen condemned the government's policy and called for war in defense of American honor and security. As revealed in the orders below, issued three weeks before he received the directive from Governor Sevier, Jackson shared this frontier militancy.

To the Brigadier Generals of the 2nd Division

DIVISION ORDERS   Hermitage, December 19, 1808.

Having seen in the publick papers, as early as the 1st day of November last, a requisition from the president of the United States, through the secretary of the department of war, on the respective states,[1] for their quotas of militia, under the act of Congress passed on the 30th day of March 1808, entitled "An act authorising a Detachment of the militia of the United States, &c," requiring the governor of each state without delay to take proper measures to perfect the organization of the respective quotas required, into companies, battalions, regiments, brigades and divisions, completely equiped with arms and accoutrements fit for service, including blankets and knapsacks, and to hold them in readiness to march at a moment's warning. In the above alluded to orders, it also states, that if any corps of volunteers, who, previous to the orders for taking the field, may tender their services to the commander in chief of the state, conformably to the second section of the above alluded to act, they will be accepted as part of the detachment, and also any company or companies of volunteers, either artillery, cavalry or infantry, who will associate and offer their services, will be accepted as part of the quota of the militia required by the president of the United States.[2]

Having waited with anxious expectation for many weeks, the orders of the commander in chief of the state[3] requiring of me without delay, to carry into effect the orders of the secratary of the department of war, and not as yet having received any; but viewing it as my duty from the delicate situation of our common country, with the great belligerent powers of Europe, to have the division under my command placed in the best possible state of readiness to meet the wishes of the president of the United States, as soon as his orders shall be officially made known to me. You are therefore requested, without delay, to place your brigades, in the best possible state, to perfect the quota that may be requested from you, as soon as you receive orders for that purpose. You will not fail in appealing to the patriotism of the citizens that compose your brigade, that the full quota required may be made up by voluntary enlistments. From the military ardor displayed on a former occasion, I am confident it still exists, that it is not abated, has increased and will still increase, with the dangers that threaten our country—And when there is a call to arms, there will be but one voice, defend the liberties and independence of our country, or die nobly in the cause.[4]

ANDREW JACKSON.
MAJ. GEN. 2d division of
Tennessee

The General commanding the 2d Division of the militia of Tennessee, requires the attendance of all his field officers, on the 3d Monday of january next, at Talbot's Hotel, in Nashville at 11 o'clock A.M. on business of importance—he also requires the attendance of all those patriotic Captains, who on a former occasion, tendered their services in defence of their country—and also the Captains of each volunteer corps that may be associated together to defend their country's rights, and independence, before that day.

Andrew Jackson.
Major general 2d division of
Tennessee

Text from *Democratic Clarion*, January 3, 1809. Original not found. ADS draft (fragment), DLC. Text in Bassett, 1:192, from the draft.

1. Secretary of War Henry Dearborn had sent his orders to the governors of the states on October 28.
2. Tennessee's portion of the requisition was 2,612.
3. For Sevier's orders, January 12, 1809, see below.
4. In the draft of the orders, Jackson wrote "in the last ditch" for "in the cause."

1809

From John Sevier

Knoxville 12th day of January 1809

Sir

The president of the United States by virtue of an act of Congress passed on the 30th day of March 1808. entitled "an act, authorising a detachment from the Militia of the United States," have requested the executive of the State of Tennessee, to take effectual measures to organize arm and equip according to law, and hold in readiness to march at a moments warning, our respective proportion of one hundred thousand Militia—This therefore is to require of you, to take early and effectual Measures within the shortest period that circumstances will permit, for having the Quota ready to march on the shortest notice, which have already been called for in a former order from the Executive as the proportion of your Division,[1] and as nearly as practicable in the following proportions of Artillery, cavalry, Riflemen and infantry. (Viz) one twelfth artillery, one sixteenth Cavalry, and from one sixteenth, to one twelfth riflemen, and the residue Infantry; to be compleatly equiped with arms and accoutrements, fit for actual service, including blankets & Knapsacks—

Any corps of volunteers who previous to orders for taking the field, who may tender their services according to the second section of the aforesaid act, will be considered as part of the Quota of said division, according to their numbers—And you are also authorised to accept as a part thereof, any company, or companies, of volunteers, either of artillery, cavalry, or Infantry, who may associate and offer themselves for the service, agreeably to an act of Congress (a copy of which is enclosed) passed "on the 24th of February 1807."[2] And I have to request you will endeavor to encourage as general a disposition as possible, for volunteer offers of service, especially under the last mentioned act.

Permit me to suggest the propriety and importance, of having such field officers, Captains, and subalterns selected, as can in all respects be relied upon, in case the detachment should be called into actual service. When the Detachment and Organization shall have been compleated, the respective corps will be exercised under the officers set over them, but will not remain embodied, or considered in actual service, until by subsequent orders they shall be directed to take the field.

You will please direct correct returns to be made of the corps to be raised in your Division, and that Copies thereof, be immiadeatily transmitted to this department. Seperate returns should be made of those who have heretofore volunteered, and of those who may volunteer under the last mentioned act.

Permit me to observe that Brigadier General James Winchester, is appointed to take command of the whole troops to be raised for the service aforesaid, and you will please correspond with that officer, on any incidal occurrences that may be necessary on the Occasion—

When the Executive takes into view the constant and invariable conduct of the General Government of friendship, honest neutrality, and the accommodating measures manifested towards the Bellegerant powers since they have been engaged in War, seemingly for the designed purpose of desolation and distruction of each other; he is inspired with full confidence, that his fellow Citizens will on the present Occasion demonstrate to the world that they will not tamely submit to the insults and aggressions unmeretted by the Government of their Country, to no tyranical Nation of people whatever: That they will recollect that the Americans have not trespassed upon, or violated the rights of any neighboring, or foreign Nation; that in all cases, the United States, have been unoffending towards those Waring powers, who have been for a length of time, wantonly sporting with the lives, liberties, and properties of the American people. The Governor flatters himself, that his fellow Citizens will on the present occasion, exhibit to the world a spirit of patriotism and Military Ardor, that cannot be exceeded, and evince to the nations of the earth, that if invaded by any of the Marauding despots of Europe, that the infamous feet of their inslaved Armies, shall not dare to tread the ground of our peaceful shores—It is regretted that a number of reasons have induced the Executive to postpone so long issuing the present orders. Among those reasons are, that some hundreds of families have lately settled, in our State, and I need not remark they are in want of almost every substantial necessary for their subsistance, and will require all the time they can be indulged with, to provide for their families to support upon, in their absence—The extreme intensity of the Winter has been another formadable impediment, and many other precarious circumstances could be named were it necessary—

It would have been extremely difficult under those embarrasments, to have Organized completely the troops, before a more Moderate season approached.

It is also to be observed, that there is no appropriation for supplying with blankets, Knapsacks, tents, or any contigency whatever—some of those articles are indispensable in the time of such an inclement season, and soldiers cannot take the field without them: The infancy of our state will sufficiently apologize, as it cannot be presumed our troops can so immediately be provided for a Campaign, as those in the Original states— Also our local situation is such, as will occasion our troops a long march, let the scene of action be where it may—The foregoing considerations have had much weight with the Executive, who have considered the present as the most fit and favorable time, for carrying the same into prompt and complete success relying with unbounded confidence, in the patriotism and unshaken fidelity of his fellow Citizens, that they will as usually heretofore, rally round the standard of their Country, with all that active alertness, that is becoming a brave and independent people, and be in perfect readiness to obey any request they may receive from the Government of their Country

I have the honor to be Sir, with all due consideration, Your ob. Hbl Servt.

John Sevier

LS, DLC. Published in *Knoxville Gazette*, February 8; Bassett, 1:193–94. Governor Sevier issued identical orders to John Cocke, Major General of the East Tennessee militia. Jackson endorsed the letter, "Recd. 10 February 09—"

1. Not found.

2. Sevier was referring to the act authorizing the president to accept the services of up to thirty thousand volunteers (2 *U.S. Statutes at Large* 419–20).

Jefferson's embargo, adopted in December 1807, became increasingly unpopular in 1808. The disruption of trans-Atlantic commerce had little impact on the attitudes or policies of the European belligerents but it brought severe economic distress upon New England and New York merchants and southern and western farmers. By late 1808, many New Englanders openly denounced the policy in town meetings, and state legislatures challenged its constitutionality. Some southerners and westerners clamored for the passage of stay laws, postponing debt foreclosures.

The debate over a stay law in Tennessee was at its height when Jackson's brigade and field officers met in Nashville on January 16. Numerous appeals, all ignored, had already been made to Governor Sevier to convene the legislature to consider some relief measures; and a few days after Jackson issued his orders on December 19 (see above), an anonymous request for delegations from Davidson and other middle Tennessee counties to meet in Nashville, also on January 16, appeared in the newspapers. This second call led to speculation in the Democratic Clarion *over the nature and purpose of this meeting. "By what authority or who is it that has invited the delegation from each county in the last Review to meet at Talbot's," the* Clarion *asked on December 27, 1808. "Are some so anxiously alive for the debtors as to take advantage of the unwary by first exciting their patriotism and then endeavor to force down an infamous petition long since consigned to oblivion? Or why the mysterious invitation?"*

Jackson attended both meetings in Nashville on January 16, serving as president of one and chairman of the resolutions committee of the other. Before the courthouse gathering, he delivered a strong appeal for unity and support of the administration in Washington (see address, below). Harmony prevailed on January 16. The committee's resolutions in support of Jefferson were adopted and the anticipated debate over a stay law did not erupt. But the stay law was not dead: militia officers held several additional meetings calling for stay-law legislation. No evidence has been found to link Jackson with these subsequent meetings, which the Clarion *on February 7 labeled as unfriendly to the administration. Although the* Clarion *reported that there was little support for a relief measure in Nashville and Davidson County, the legislature in its special session in April passed a law staying executions on judgments for a limited period.*

Resolutions of 2nd Division Officers

[January 16, 1809]

At a general meeting of the Officers composing the 2nd Division of the militia of the State of Tennessee convened by publick notice[1] in the Town of Nashville on monday the 16th day of January 1809, for the purpose of taking into consideration the critical situation of the United States with those beligerent powers of Europe who have, by the most unprecidented Edicts and orders of Council violated the laws of Nations and committed infractions upon the commerce of the Nutrals, Majr. General Andrew Jackson was appointed President and Capt Thomas Swann Secretary.

It appearing from the patriotism of the Field officers (they having all tendered their services to their Country, which services cannot be accepted under the present requisition of the United States[)]; It is the opinion of this meeting, that under the present emergency as well as in all others, the best rule to call on those officers whose duty it is to perform the first Tour of Service

Therefore Resolved, That the present meeting deem it assential to that spirit of emulation which ought to pervade the militia, that a roster should be Kept of all their Services, and that the senior officers of each grade for duty shall be first ordered into Service, even on organising Volunteer Corps, except so far as relates to officers who have, or may raise such company of Volunteers.

And whereas, the success of an Army depends much upon the confidence the officers and Soldiers repose in the *patriotism*, honor, fidelty and talents of the commander in chief, Resolved therefore unanimously, that the officers composing the 2nd Division of Militia of the State of Tennessee have not confidence in James Wilkinson the present commander in

Chief, in the event of War between the United States and any foreign power.

Capt. Frederick Stump[2] presented a Copy of a Roll of Volunteer mounted Infantry with a tender of their Service to the president of the United States, consisting of 1 Captain 1 Lieutenant 1 Ensign 4 Sergeants 55 Rank & file Total 62

Capt. Thornton[3] presented a Copy of a Roll of Volunteer Mounted Infantry with a tender of their Services to the President of the United States, consisting of 1 Captain 1 Lieutenant 1 Ensign 2 Sergeants 1 Fifer 55 Rank & file Total 61

Capt. James Henderson[4] presented a Copy of a Roll of Volunteer Cavalry with a tender of their Services to the President of the United States consisting of 1 Captain 1 Lieutenant 1 Ensign 1 Sergeant 1 Trumpetter 35 Privates. Total 40

Capt. Obediah Bounds[5] presented a Copy of a Roll of Mounted Infantry with a tender of their Services to the president of the United States consisting of 1 Captain 1 Lieutenant 1 Ensign 2 Sergeants 52 Rank & file [Total] 57

Capt Swann made a tender of the Service of his company of Volunteer Cavalry.

High waters and bad roads having prevented the attendance of the Volunteer officers from the distant Counties; It is believed if they could have attended the full Quota of West Tennessee would have tendered their Services[6]

Resolved that Copies of the foregoing Resolutions be transmitted to the Editor of the Impartial Review the Editor of Knoxville Gazette, & the Editor of the Clarion for publication

> Andrew Jackson President
> Thos Swann Secy.

ADS (in Thomas Swann's hand), signed by AJ, DLC. Published in *Democratic Clarion*, January 24; *Knoxville Gazette*, February 15.

1. See above, AJ to the Brigadier Generals, December 19, 1808.

2. Hans Friedrich (Frederick) Stump (1723–1820), a native of Pennsylvania and an early settler of Nashville, operated a mill, store, tavern, and distillery. Despite his advanced age, he led a company on the 1803 expedition to Natchez, volunteered to lead men against Burr in 1807, and took his company to the Creek Nation in 1813. In 1816 he married his second wife, the twenty-five-year-old barmaid in his tavern.

3. Not identified.

4. Henderson (d.1814), colonel commandant of a Rutherford County regiment in 1812, served as brigade quartermaster on the Natchez expedition.

5. Not identified.

6. On January 24, 1809, after several weeks of carrying notices of heavy snow and rain, the *Democratic Clarion* reported that "two such freshes in the same time as have been in the Cumberland river this winter were never known before."

Address to Citizens of Nashville

[January 16, 1809]

MR. CHAIRMAN,[1]

The awful crisis to which the affairs of this country is rapidly hastening, and the all importance of an unanimity of sentiment at such a time, is the cause of the present meeting being convened, and precludes the necessity of any apology for my addressing you. The people of this portion of the union, Sir, burning with indignation and resentment of the tyrannic decrees of the French government and British orders in council, which at once prostrates the rights and sovereignty of our common country—are assembled here to-day to give vent to their feelings, and pledge their lives and fortunes in defence of their own and the nation's rights. The measures which the administration have taken, in the new and dificult situation in which they have been placed, are such as entitle them to the support of the union. As that conduct has been assailed, it may not be unnecessary for us to come forward and assure them of our undeminished esteem & warm & energetic support. Our enemies have long calculated on our divisions, and the conduct of some of our citizens have furnished grounds for the opinion. Let the event of this day's meeting prove to the world, that no matter what privations we suffer, or inconveniences we feel, we are willing to expend the last cent of our treasure, and the last drop of our blood, in giving effect to any measures that may be taken in support of our liberty and independence.

There is no man who hears me that will not acknowledge that our acquiescence and submission to the wishes of either of the belligerent powers, would reduce the nation to a standard unworthy her reputation and resources.

The means of resistance then, is the only subject on which there can exist any difference of opinion.

Viewing as I do (said general Jackson) the peculiar situation in which this part of the union is placed, I cannot but think such an expression of public sentiment extremely proper. Attempts have been made to divide the union, such attempts may be made again. Attempts have been made to divide us in sentiment, without which such a measure never can be carried into effect; and though our attachment to the federal compact ought not to be doubted, yet our conduct this day may furnish ANOTHER EVIDENCE that we are deeply impressed with the truth & importance of the maxim—United we stand—divided we perish. I conceive there can be but one sentiment, on the subject, all must feel the injuries we have received, all must be determined to resist them, let us then, sir, with one heart and hand declare to the world, that firm determination, united in sentiment & undismayed by the storm that's approaching, we solemnly pledge ourselves to go any length with the government of our country, in defence and support of the nation's rights and independence.[2]

Text from *Carthage Gazette*, February 6. Original not found.
1. James Robertson.
2. See resolutions adopted by a meeting of citizens of West Tennessee, January 16.

From Stockley Donelson Hays

Lexington, January 28th, 1809.

DEAR UNCLE—

Your affectionate letter of date the 15th December[1] I have not had an opportunity of answering 'till the present moment. And now on the subject of your business: I can only observe that it is in the same situation as stated in my last letter, and as to the fee which Mr. Clay may claim, it is presumable that it will be proportionate to service rendered, and it will be the proper time when such service is rendered, to make out a charge. However, as Mr. Clay has been absent ever since the receipt of your letter, I have not had it in my power to make the inquiry, and it is probable I shall not for some time, as Mr. Clay has been unfortunate enough to receive a wound in a duel with Mr. H[umphrey] Marshall, which will delay his return to this place.[2] The dispute originated in the Legislature, from whence the combatants repaired to the scene of action, which was on the other side of the Ohio. They fired three rounds, and at the third Mr. Clay was shot through the thigh—a flesh wound. It was, perhaps, one of the most singular and interesting duels that ever was fought, and one which appears to have excited in the highest degree the feelings of the grand (political) divisions of the State, Mr. Marshall being at the head of the Federalist party. It is stated that there was on the banks of the river three thousand spectators, thirty of whom crossed the river as guards. Should this be a fact that will merit the attention of the Historian, and will no doubt be handed down to posterity as a circumstance Pregnant with Curiosity.

Text from *Cincinnati Commercial*, January 8, 1881. Original not found.
1. Not found.
2. On the Clay-Marshall duel, see James F. Hopkins and Mary W. M. Hargreaves, eds., *The Papers of Henry Clay*, (Lexington, Ky., 1959), 1:397–400.

From George Michael Deaderick

Browns Creek 5th March 1809—

Dear Sir,

The dissentions that have for years existed in my family[1] proceeding from an alledg'd cause the means pursued to excite animosity between you and myself, togather with an effort made to effect a misunderstand-ing between Mr. Donalson Caffery and Stephen Cantrell Junr.[2] all com-bine, and urge the propriety of making the following candid statement of facts accompanied with the Solemnity of an Oath. this is done to convict your mind that my Varacity is not to be doubted. and if ever I become base enough to make a communication to you, not founded on fact, as I conceive, may I be instantly hurld out of existance. I do solemnly declare to you that I never have conveyd an Idea to Mrs. Deaderick or to any other individual that I was impress'd with a belief, or even suspected that you had any carnal knowledge of her. My knowledge of you for many years, the high Idea ever entertaind of your rectitude forbad the impres-sion. your friendship for me I have long known and have held it dear to my heart; and do at this moment; to avow a truth is only doing justice to our feelings. My esteem for you has been uniform and remains unabated. Your recent exertions to restore harmony between Mrs. Deaderick and myself call for my warmest acknowledgements,[3] the desire of my heart has been that you should be instrumental to effect the first object of my wish, peace with a companion whose friendly converse has often been balm to my Soul. The extreme agitation evincd on friday last, when en-quiry was made whether Mr. Stephen Cantrell Junr. had ever communi-cated certain facts relative to Mrs. Deaderick and Mr. Donaldson Caf-fery, really excited astonishment. the charge alledg'd against Mr. Cantrell is, utterly untrue and without foundation. I hear declare to you by all that is dear & sacred to my Soul, that Mr. Cantrell Junr. never did make com-munication to me that Mr. Caffery had presented a Ticket to Mrs. Dead-erick either for a play or Ball, and further declare on the Veracity of a Man that I never did hear Mr. Cantrell make use of one expression de-rogatory to the reputation of Mrs. Deaderick or Mr. Donaldson Caffery, on the contrary I ever have believd that Mr. Cantrell & Mr. Caffery were highly pleasd with each other, and know of nothing to the contrary at present. Your discretion in my view stands high, but let me here advise you not to put implicit faith in reports coming from the source you have deriv'd your information relative to the facts which Mr. Cantrell & my-self have been chargd with. you will not, I know Abandon a Man who you have once acknowledgd to be a friend, unless substantial reasons are producd, that he no longer merits your good opinion. Mrs. Deaderick & Mrs. [Mary McConnell White] May[4] have for many months evinc'd a disposition, the former by abuse, by tears by threats, to stir up animosity between Mr. Cantrell & myself, and can only account for it in one way. that is, Mrs. Cantrell has nam'd her Son, George. M. Deaderick[5] this was a circumstance entirely unknown to me untill Mrs. May at her house communicated the information so soon as it was nam'd I candidly de-clard, & in truth, that I had never before heard of it. Mrs. Dk. imme-diately replied with much apparent illnature that it was all a scheme, a plott, and signified that the child was nam'd after me with a view that it might inherit my property. if my relatives all have the same motive in view, ascribd to Mrs. Cantrell in naming her infant, some of them certainly will be disappointed; for I am informd by a Nephew & Brotherin-law, that each have nam'd a Son after me.[6] for this high offence Mrs. Cantrell has become, as I am impressd the object of unmerited abuse, from Mrs. Dk. Mr. Hinchey Pettway[7] several months ago inform'd me that a serious dispute was likely to take place between Doctor May & Mr. Cantrell & stated the cause that gave rise to it. Shortly after I namd the subject to Mr. Cantrell he observd that Doctor May could not take exceptions, or become displeas'd with him from any offence he had given him. but that it must proceed from his requesting Mrs. Cantrell not to Visit Mrs. May, that the many tales put in circulation between the family connection, might involve her in the feuds, and become unpleasant to his feelings consequently recommended the course of not Visiting, the source from which you have receivd your information relative to Mr. Cantrell, Mr. Caffery & myself, is to be guarded against. the whole is unfounded & shamefully untrue. They are both young Men who I once esteemed & do still for strict integrity, Veracity & worth. the latter, from an impression that he Violated my rights has lost the high regard fondly and proudly entertain'd for him. If an improper opinion has been entertaind and cherishd by me, of his Virtue, No Man on earth would more cheerfully acknowledge the error than I would do, and embrace the first opportunity of doing him that justice the injury requir'd. No Man can assert that I ever utterd a sentence of Mr. Caffery in derogation of his Character. Altho I have frequently passd without noticing him. I sincerely wish that my Soul could have been so moulded as to have been the grave of human frailty, but unhappily it has not. You have reason to infer that I behold grievances with the eye of youthfull inexperience, & would rather indulge in emaginary evil than enjoy the sweets of friendly converse with a companion. Do not Genl. give into this belief. The God of my creation knows how ardently I have desird domestic peace & what sacrifices, I would even at this day make to obtain it. I am Sir with much sincerity yr. Obt. Servt.

George. M. Deaderick

ALS, DLC.
1. For a discussion of Deaderick's earlier marital problems, see above, Deaderick to AJ, April 25, 1807.
2. Cantrell (1783–1854), merchant and later contractor during the Creek War, mayor of Nashville, and president of the Bank of Nashville, was married to Deaderick's niece, Juliet Ann Deaderick Wendel.
3. See above, Reconciliation Agreement, [April 1807–1809].
4. Mrs. May (1782–1862), the sister of Hugh Lawson White, was the wife of Dr. Francis May, George Michael's stepbrother. Following May's death she married John Overton.
5. Cantrell (1807–86).
6. Samuel M. Perry, son of one of George Michael's sisters, had named his son George Michael, as had John and Elizabeth Deaderick Murrell of Lynchburg, Va.
7. Pettway, a business associate of Deaderick's, was a merchant in Franklin.

To James Winchester

March 15th. 1809—

Dear Genl.

I have Just recd. your letter of the 4th instant inclosing the Detail of your Brigade—[1]

On the 20th ultimo I wrote the Governor[2] and stated to him the absolute necessity of Directing the adjutant Genl[3] to forward to me without delay, the quota required of my Division under the present requisition, fearfull that the former order alluded to in his late order of the 12th. of January[4] had not reached, you nor the other Brigadiers of my Division—knowing none such had ever reached me—not having recd. any answer from him as yet I dispair of his noticing my request—I am therefore the more pleased, with the plan you have adopted. If *war* there cannot be too many in readiness if peace it will do honour to the patriotism of the Division that such ardor was displayed on the signal of our government that our country and our Liberties were endangered—It is certainly true that the regular channel & mode would have been as you have stated, and it is much to be regretted, that the governor did not persue it, on the present urgent occasion, but you know as well as I do that if he knows his duty as a military man he never performs it—Therefore to remedy this defect as far as possible, I have this day wrote to Generals; Johnston & Roberts, To furnish from their respective Brigades 500 men including Volunteers and to be completely officered as pr your detail[5]—and as soon as their quota is made up to inform you thereof, and transmit to me, a compleat return, of the officers & men ready for the field—as soon as this is done I will furnish you with a duplicate return—and forward one to the executive—the governor has directed me to corrispond with you "upon any incidental occurrence that may be necessary on the occasion."[6] This will give me pleasure, and I hope by the next mail after this reaches you to receive advice, that the quoto in your Brigade is ready for the field

I am Sir with due reguard yr mo. ob. servt.

Andrew Jackson
Major Genl. 2. D. Tennessee—

ALS copy, DLC. Published in Bassett, 1:196.
1. See Winchester to AJ, March 4.
2. Letter not found.
3. George Wilson (1778–1848) was adjutant general of Tennessee from 1807 to 1811, when he left that post to represent Knox County in the state senate. From 1804 to 1818 he published *Wilson's Knoxville Gazette* and from 1819 to 1827, the *Nashville Gazette*.
4. For Sevier's order of January 12, see above.
5. Letters not found.
6. See above, Sevier to AJ, January 12.

From James Sanders

March 26th. 1809

Sir

a few Days ago I received a letter from you[1] in Which you have given a Statement made by Jackeye[2] as you Say, which you have made the grounds of an a busive letter. I think it proper to State what Did pass, he had been for Several Weaks from home contrary to his mothers Orders She had frequently Sent for him and he had as Often Disobeyed, at hur request I went to the School house for him and brought him home his mother Scholded him for Disobeying hur he replied that it was your Orders he Should not, I told him you had no wright to give Such Orders and that if I had to bring him from the School house again I should bring my Cowskin withe me was what passed, and Suppose you had the wright was it prudent to Order a Child to Disobey its mother, there mothers Orders was that they Should go to no place with Ought her leave, and with it they might go aney where, I have given them no Orders except that they Should Obey there mother, I Dont wish you to under Stand me to mean that I had not a wright to Do so, the mother is the Only legal Guardian and the Only person that has a wright to controle them, I admit that if that power is a bused the court may interfer and controle it and if the court should require me to give Security I Shall not Object to it, you talk very freeley a bought your cow hide I tell you I fear not your threats nor cow hide, and in your weay of giving advice, I causion you to be a ware how you youse you[r] cow hide, or it may fall never to rise, I tell you I shall act as I think proper takeing no notice of your a buse, but [a]lweays accountab[l]e to the laws of my Country.

Jas. Sanders

ALS, THer.
   1. Not found.
   2. John Samuel Donelson, Sanders's stepson.

From Thomas Swann

Springfield May 26th. 1809

Sir.

Inclosed I send you a copy of Brigadier Genl. Thomas Johnson's order to me bearing date 20th. April 1808: in pursuance of which a secret expedition was performed on the Western frontier, to ascertain the Strength, position &c of a hostile party of Savages then reported to be stationed on the West bank of the Tennessee: Of the discoveries made in that Tour I have before informed you, by a report dated 7th May 1808:[1] which I presume unnecessary for me to subjoin, as a certificate from you [to] the Secretary at War stating that the services as [list]ed in my a/c. were performed will be sufficient:[2] It will also be needless to state the perils, hardships and fatigues encountered and endured in the execution of the Trust then confied in me But I think I may with safety affirm that the result of my mission was a saving to the UStates of several thousand Dollars, the Militia who were then stationed at the mouth of Panther Creek being discharged in consequence of my letter to Lieut. Colo. Thomas Clinton[3] dated, Duck River May 5th. 1808. which is contained in my report—To conclude, the annexed a/c. against the UStates is in my opinion extremely moderate, at least the Items for monies actually expended and services performed is far less objectionable than Jimmy Wilkinson's a/c for Segars &c &c &c. Confiding in your Judgement I commit the management of this business entirely to your discretion.

And am with Respect Yr: Mo: ob: Servt.

Tho Swann

United States

1808.		To Thomas Swann	Dr.
May 7th	To Expenses incured on a mission to ascertain the strength, position &c of a hostile party of Creek Indians by order of the Brig. Genl. of 6th Brigade		$ 13
	To Ten days absence from professional duties during sessions of the Court of pleas and Quarter Sessions for Davidson Cty @$10		100
			$113

ALS, DLC.

1. Copies of Thomas Johnson's orders to Swann, April 20, 1808, and Swann's report, May 7, 1808, are in the Daniel Parker Papers, PHi. For a discussion of the Meadows report of the Indian massacre which resulted in Johnson's orders, see above, AJ to the Officers of the 2nd Division, April 20, 1808; AJ to Thomas Jefferson, April 20 and May 14, 1808.

2. Jackson's letter to the secretary of war requesting reimbursement has not been found.

3. Clinton, a resident of Stewart County, had formerly been a justice of the peace and county court clerk.

On July 7, 1809, the Democratic Clarion lamented that "Nashville presented nothing worthy of the day to designate the late anniversary of American independence from any other day." Perhaps the reason was that most people were attending a cocking main staged by Jackson and his friends near Nashville on July 4.

From William Preston Anderson

At Mr. McCullochs. 25th. June 1809—

Mr. Coffee has this moment communicated to us the contents of yr. letter to him,[1] so far as it respects the main of Cocks to be fought on the 4th. of next month.

We think Mr. Parruns[2] idea of the number of cocks necessary to make a good shew of 20 is a very correct one indeed if you could Raise 50 it would be so much the better

I find many of my cocks badly feathered & not fit for battle & what's worse than all such as are in this situation are of the Very best kind.

I shall however be able to Raise 13 or 14 fine two year old Cocks & 6 stags of the largest & best *blood of the country*. You may depend upon every care & attention On our part—we shall not have our cocks at nashville until saturday next & we shall travel them after night in bags

I will command the Fed. Bottom forces in person & shall continue with them night & day until the battle Commences—I know you and Gnl. Overton & Capt. [John?] Hoggatt[3] will not be half as attentive as I will—Gnl. Overton has promised to be up here tomorrow or next day & by his return You will again hear more particularly from yr. friend

W P Anderson

P.S. please send my mare
Mr. [Alexander] McCulloch[4] will go down with me
Please send Francis[5] back to night   WPA

ALS matched fragments, DLC.
    1. Not found.
    2. Not identified. Anderson may have been referring to some member of the Perrin family in Tennessee or Kentucky.
    3. Hoggatt (d. 1824), a Revolutionary War veteran, resided near the Hermitage.
    4. McCulloch (1777–1846), a wealthy farmer and neighbor of Anderson's in Rutherford County, served as aide to John Coffee in the War of 1812.
    5. Probably one of Anderson's slaves.

Agreement of Thomas Claiborne et al. re Cocking Main

[June 1809]

We and each of us bind ourselves jointly and severally to become partners and also to abide by and pay or receive any sum or sums that may be won or lost on our part in a main to be fought on the 4th day of July next at

McNairy's spring near Nashville between Genl. Andrew Jackson of the one part, on whose side we are and Will. B. Vinson[1] of the other part Witness our hands & seals

Thos Claiborne	(seal)
Wm P. Anderson	(seal)
J[ohn] G[ray] Blount[2]	(seal)
Wm T Lewis	(seal)
Saml Hogg	(seal)

Copy, TNJ. Endorsed by AJ: "Memorandom of the Gentlemen engaged in the main 4th of July 1809—"

1. Vinson, probably a native of Pennsylvania, had recently married Isabella Fowler Butler, the widow of Edward.

2. Blount, Jr. (University of North Carolina) was the son of John Gray Blount of North Carolina and the nephew of Willie Blount.

In 1808, Jackson's aide, Robert Purdy, wrote Jackson about the birth of his daughter Martha, for whom he was sure that Jackson "would wish to have a son." Purdy chided Jackson that he thought his "chance" was "bad" (Purdy to AJ, June-November? 1808). The Jacksons did have a love for children, but it was not until 1809 that they had a child they could call their own, the son of Rachel's brother Severn (1773–1818) and his wife Elizabeth Rucker Donelson (1783–1828).

The account below reveals that Andrew, Jr., the twin brother of Thomas Jefferson Donelson (1808–95), had become a part of the Jackson household by October 1809 and also illustrates the medical treatment available to the family, their slaves, and farm animals. Jackson recorded that this child, Andrew Jackson (d. 1865), as he was called by his natural parents, was born on December 4, 1808 (undated memorandum, DLC). According to Jackson, he and Rachel adopted Andrew, but whether through an agreement with the parents or in some other way, Jackson never specified. The descendants of Andrew, Jr., however, later contended that the Jacksons received the child when he was three days old and that a few weeks later Jackson appeared before the Tennessee legislature to formalize the adoption.

The record of a petition to adopt Andrew, Jr., has not been found in Tennessee's legislative proceedings, nor are there legislative adoptions for any other children. There was at that time no provision in Tennessee for judicial adoption. Moreover, the Tennessee legislature was not in session when the adoption was supposed to have been considered; and a careful search of records for subsequent years has failed to turn up any reference to the matter. Whether officially sanctioned or not, Jackson always contended that Andrew, Jr., was his adopted son (AJ to Francis Saunders and John Donelson, Sr., January 31, 1823, Stanley F. Horn; Memorandum for AJ, Jr., December 1, 1844, DLC; Will of AJ, June 7, 1843, DLC).

Account with John Robertson Bedford

Genl. Andrew Jackson Dr.	To J. R. Bedford Cr.

1809

Octr.	26	Visit Medicine & for Andrew [1]	6.00
Nov	19	Visit at night through rain to Mrs. J.	8.00
		Catharsis 25, ℨiii Laud[anu]m. (vial 9d)	
		162½	1.87½
		ℨiii Tinct. Cantharides [2] (vial 9d) 25	.87½
		℥ii Ol. Ricini [3] (vial 9d)—25	.62½
		Venesection	1.00
		1 vial pectoral drops [4] for Andrew	1.50
			18.87½
Decr	8	8 ozs Soap Linament for Mrs. J. 25	2.00
		24 Crataceous powders for Andrew	1.00
		24 Pills Extract. of Bark [5] Ditto	.50
	30th	Hi Camomile Flowers	3.00
		4 oz. Peruvian Bark 50	2.00
		4 oz. Creamor Tarter [6] 9d Per order	.50
		1 Dose Calomel & Jalap Doctr. Butler [7]	.25
		1 dose Manna & Senna [8]	.37½
		1 Box Merc. Unguent [9]	.37½
			10.00

1810

March	5	℥ii Anise Seed 50— ℥ii Caraway Seed 50 [10]	1.00
		℥ii Cardamon Seed 150— ℥iv Flor. Sulpher	
		50	2.00
		℥ii Tumerick Pulv. 75—Hi Sugar Candy 1.	1.75
		℥iv Liquorice Ball 50— ℥ss Saffron 150	2.00
		℥i Oil of anise 300 vial 9d.— ℥iss Liquorice	
		Powd. 75	3.87½
		Hss. Flor. Sulpher 75— ℥iv Anti. Levig [11]	
		75	1.50
		℥ii Aloes 50 ℥ss Diapente [12] 50	1.00
		℥i Powder of Senna 75— ℥ss Sal Tartar	
		9d.—vial 9d	1.00
		8 oz. Castile soap	.50
			14.62½

		Sundry medicine for horses, first entered on Petty Ledger from 28th. Aug. to 1st. of Octobr. 1809	13.62½
March	22d	℥ii Astringent mixt. for Andrew	1.50
		℥iii Laudanum 50	1.50
		℥i Olive Oil	.25
		2 Horse Purges—125	2.50
	25	2 oz. Crude Sal ammon [13] ℔ Jas. Jackson	.50
			19.62½
March	30	Hi Flor. Sulph. 100—Hss. Levigated Antimon 125	2.25
April	21	Visit to Andrew, cutting Gums & medicine	6.00
	24	2# Glauber's Salt 50	1.00
May	1	Hss. Red Bark	5.00
		Hi Sago 100—1# Tapioca 150	2.50
		2 Clyster Pipes	.25
	13	℥ii Spanish Indigo F lot. No. 1 Mrs. J. 50	1.00
		Sundry medicine for Andrew	2.00
	20	℥ss. Cantharides 50—℥i Fly Stone 25	.75
	25	Hi Leviated Antimony	2.00
			24.75
June	7	Visit, Cutting Gums & medicine to Andrew	6.00
	12	Ditto—Ditto—Ditto	6.00
July	12	Hss. Spanish Indigo F lot No. 1 Mrs. J.	3.00
		Sundry medicine for 4 horse purges	6.00
		2# Flor Sulpher 100	2.00
			23.00
	18	℥i anise seed 25—℥i Caraway 25	.50
		℥i Cardamon seed. 75—℥ii Flor. Sulpher. 25	1.00
		℥i Tumerick Pulv. 37½—℥ii Saffron 75	1.12½
		℥iv Sugar Candy 50—℥ii Liquorice 25	.75
		℥i Ol. Anise &c. 162½—℥iv Antimon Pul. 50	2.12½
		℥i Liquorice Powder 50—℥iv Antimon lev. 75	1.25
			6.75
		three other parcels of the same at 6.75	20.25
		Hi Castile Soap	1.00
Aug	21	Visit medicine &c. to Andrew	6.00
	27	1 oz Verdegris [14]	.25
Sept	1	1 Quart Linseed Oil	.50

	15	4 ozs. Sal Ammon. 25	1.00
	17	1½ Quart Wine Vinegar 100	1.50
	29	2 oz Crude Sal Ammon.—25	.50
		1 Box Basilicon Ointment¹⁵	.50
Octobr	4	1 Quart Wine Vinegar	1.00
		4 oz Nitr. 25—Hi Castil Soap 100	1.25
1811			
Jany	4	2# Spanish Whiting e Mrs. Ja. 25	.50
			34.25

1 Box Basilicon Ointment [15]

1810			
Decr.	13	1 Vial Calomel 62½—1 do. Jalap 62½—	
		ʒss Rhellent 25	1.50
1811			
May	8	ʒi Anise Seed 25—1 do. Caraway Seed 25	.50
		1 oz Cardamon seed 75—ʒii Flor Sulpher	
		25	1.00
		4 oz Sugar Candy 50—ʒii Saffron 100	1.50
		2 oz Liquorice 25—½ Gal. Wine Vinegar	
		150	1.75
	18	4 ozs. Sulpher 50	.50
	31	Hss Spanish Indigo 300—1 Vial Laud. a/c	
		Mrs. J.	3.37½
July	1	Medicine & prescript for Andrew	1.50
	10	1 Box Citron Ointment	.50
Aug	22	4 horse purges 125	5.00
		1# Castile soap	1.00
			18.12½

Sept	11	ʒi Caraway Seed 25—1 oz anise seed 25	.50
		ʒi Cardamon seed 75—1 oz Tumerick	
		37½	1.12½
		ʒii English Saffron 75—ʒiv Sugar Candy	
		50	1.25
		ʒii Liquorice 25—ʒss. Ol. anise &c 1.62½	1.87½
		ʒii Liquorice Powder 37½	.75
			5.50

		To two other parcels as above @550	11.00
		Hi Pulv. Antimon 150—Hi Flor. Sulph.	
		100	2.50
Octobr	23	3 oz. Cloves 112½—ʒi ⎫ Per	
		mace 125 ⎪ Mrs.	3.37½
		ʒss. Oil Orange 75— ⎬ Jackson	
		ʒii Ol. Cinnamon 2.00 ⎪	2.75
		2 Vials containing ⎭	.25

Nov.	23	Visit at night & medicine for Andrew	8.00
	27	ʒss. Tonic drops & vial	.50
		1 Vial Eye water	.37½
Decr	20	ʒi Jalap 50—ʒi Calomel 50	1.00
			28.75

½ Gal. Wine Vinegar omitd. in posting
  29th. Septr. 1810   1.50
2 oz. Crude Sal Amoniac omitted 12 Oct.
  1810   .50
1 Quart Wine Vinegar—Ditto   1.00
2 oz Crude Sal Ammon. 17th Octobr.   .50
Error in adding in 3d line from bottom
  first page   .25
                                                           3.75

                                                        $208.00
                                                            Cr.

<u>1810</u>

Feby	28	By 66½ Gals. Whiskey		
		@50	33.25	
		Bbll. containing Whiskey	2.00	
May	17	2 Gals. double distilled first shot	6.00	
		Cash	20.00	
Augst	1	By Season of Grey mare to Truxton	30.00	
	20	By Cash	30.00	
			$121.25	
Sept	17	" Cash on a/c	10.00	
Octbr	30	" Ditto on a/c	23.75	
			$155.00	
		Ballance up to Jany 1st. 1812		
				$ 53.00

1812

May	13	ʒi Aloes .25—ʒii diapente 25	.50
		ʒss. Powder of Senna 37½—ʒij Sal Lot. 25	.62½
		ʒi Anise Seed 25—1 oz Caraway Seed 25	.50
		ʒi Cardamon Seed 75—ʒij Flor Sulpher 25	1.00
This		ʒi Tumerick 37½—ʒij Saffron 75	1.12½
medicine		ʒij Liquorice Ball 25—ʒss Oil of anise 150	1.75
for		ʒiv antimony Pulv. 75—ʒvi Castile soap	
		75	1.50
Horses—		ʒiss Liquorice Powder	.50
			7.50

To 5 other parcels of the same at 7.50   37.50

		2# Antimony Powdered 150	3.00
		2# Flor. Sulpher—100	2.00
	15	1 Bottle Castor Oil opt.	2.50
		written prescript for Negro woman	1.00
	22	2 ozs. Unguent Basilic for negro man's lege	.50
			45.50
June	10	2 Visits & medicine to negro same	10.00
Sept	1	℥ij Volatile Linament 25 (vial 9d)	.62
		℥i Chamomile Flowers	.25
		℥i Pectoral mixture 2/3—(vial 9d)	.50
		1 dose salts	.25
		written prescript for Mrs. Jackson	1.00
			2.62½
		Ballance E. E.	$119.62½
		2½ ozs Crude Sal Amoniac 25	" .62½
			$120.25
		4 oz Crude Sal Ammoniac—25	1.00
			$121.25
Sept	29th	Cr. By check on the Nashville Bank of this date	120.00
1812		Ballance due J. R. Bedford this day	1.25

AD by Bedford, endorsed by AJ, DLC.

1. Andrew Jackson, Jr.
2. Used as a skin irritant in plasters.
3. Castor oil.
4. Generic term for mixture to correct bronchial mucus.
5. Cinchona (appears below also as Peruvian bark, red bark). Not immediately recognized as a treatment for malaria only, cinchona was used in treatment of all types of fever.
6. Alkaline laxative similar to magnesias.
7. Not identified.
8. Calomel and jalap were powerful purgatives. Jalap also has diuretic effect. Manna and senna, aloes, and sal tartar are also purgatives of various strengths.
9. Usually rubbed on the thighs to stimulate expectoration.
10. Bedford supplied the household spices and dyes and carried books and paints in his shop (see numerous advertisements in *Democratic Clarion* and *Tennessee Gazette*, 1811).
11. Levigated antimony, used as a stimulant and emetic.
12. A horse remedy comprising gentian, bayberries, honey, juniper, and a fifth ingredient.
13. Often used in combination with chamomile flowers to promote sweating in treatment of fever and as a gargle for sore throat.
14. Forms of copper had many medical applications—as stimulant, emetic, and laxative, as treatment for epilepsy, and in small doses as pain reliever.
15. Basilicum Unguent Flavium, an ointment of yellow rosin, useful in treatment of wounds and ulcers.

Horseracing in frontier Tennessee often involved high stakes of money, notes, land, and slaves, and frequently led to disputes. In 1809 and 1810, as in 1806, Jackson was entangled in controversies growing out of horse-racing events, both times with Dr. William Purnell, a signer of the Cumberland Compact and John Donelson's brother-in-law. These misunderstandings stemmed from rumors implicating Jackson, in the first instance, in the death of a horse and slave, and in the second, in the death of Purnell's horse Dean Swift (see James W. Camp to Purnell, November 18, 1809; AJ to Edward Ward, October 26, 1810; and Purnell to AJ, December 14, 1810, all below). Jackson's papers fail to shed additional light on these disputes, but, in contrast to the sequence of events in the Jackson-Dickinson affair in 1806, Jackson and Purnell apparently reached an early understanding.

James W. Camp to William Purnell

Novbr. 18th. 1809—

Sir

The unjust and unprovockd. attack you made on my feelings and reputation, publickly on the race field clover Bottom, on the 9th Instant is not forgotten by me—The death that happenned in our family the next day, and the particular engagements of my friend Genl Jackson has occasioned it to Sleep so long—But my feelings no longer can Brook silence—no act of my life, can warrent the epathet of Rascal or Scounderal—The information I gave my friend Genl Jackson, from the rules of hospitality and friendship, was correct & what both the rules of Justice friendship & hospitality cogently required—He was defamed & traduced at your house & to many others, under the race & notwithstanding Mr Irwin[1] did deny in your hearing that he never had said that he had made a race with Genl Jackson and that he never had said that he had lost a horse & boy in consequence thereof[2]—and that he never had; had any mistrust or allusion to Genl Jackson in such conversation, you know to the contrary, and your stepping forward at the time and declaring that such conversation did pass at your house proves the contrary of his assertion—is it then thus because I would not, permit the reputation of Genl Jackson, with whom I was in the habits of intimacy & friendship, to be a silent sacrafice to the Slander and calumniating tongue of Irwin, silently circulated amongst almost strangers to Genl Jackson, that I am Thus denounced by you—forbidden your house and pronounced to be a *damd. Rascal* & scounderal—These are epithets, I never merited, that I never will merit, and when uttered against me shall always be attoned for some way or other—you are advanced in life, I Just coming into life—you know from experience how to apreciate a good charector, and having a rising family ought to know how to despise a liar and a defamer of reputation I can only Judge from my feelings, what I ought to do, Just entering into life, that is to act consistant with truth, honour & honesty—and when my reputation is wantonly assailed, to screen a liar & calumniator, from detection it is my duty to protect my reputation & feelings—and as it appears you have threw the gantlett—and pronounced me a Rascal & Scounderal for unveiling to Genl Jackson, the calumny used against him by Irwin which he has denied, in your hearing, I have no doubt but you have reasons for your conduct, and stand ready at all times to do me Justice by a retraction of your expressions or rendering satisfaction to me agreable to rule & right—This will be handed by Genl J. who will receive a written answer[3] and will communicate the same to me I am Sir yrs &c

James Camp

Draft (in AJ's hand), THi. Camp (1789–1845) was a native of Virginia and probably the son of James Camp, a Nashville merchant. Within a few years after his encounter with Purnell, he settled in Huntsville, Ala., where he was a member of the North Alabama Jockey Club and one-term legislator.
1. It is not known which of the local Erwins-Irwins was meant.
2. The race to which Camp and Jackson were alluding has not been identified.
3. For Purnell's answer to Jackson, see below.

From William Purnell

Haysborough 19t. Novr. 1809

Sir,
I have just recd. by Mr. Stockly D. Hays your Letter enclosing one from Jas. W Camp,[1] And have only to inform you that from the conduct of said Camp, I have determined to take no further Notice of him—

I am perfectly willing that the Public shall be acquainted with the whole affair, and let infamy be attached to him who merit it.[2]

I am respectfully yrs.

Wm. Purnell

ALS, THi.
1. For the draft of Camp's letter, see above. Jackson's letter to Purnell has not been found.
2. No 1809 publication on the dispute has been found. For Purnell's discussion of the rumor that Jackson's trainer had poisoned his horse, see Purnell to AJ, December 14, 1810, below.

From Washington Jackson

Natchez Decr. 20th. 1809

Dear Sir
I have at length made Sale of your Wench & Child, to a free French Negro Woman, with whom they have been since they came into my pos-

session, for $325 say three hundred & twenty five Dollars, which sum Mr. D[anie]l D Elliott[1] is to pay me in a few days, & which when rec'd shall advise my Brother thereof so that he may pay you the money as you may require. I think it a fortunate Sale as there are but few would take them as a gift, (altho the Wench is a very valuable one,) owing to her having the fits & the Child being sickly.

I have no charges against them, having got my Washing my done by her, it about amounts to what Cloathing I furnish her with,[2] please make my best Respects to Mrs. J—& am Sir, very Respectfully, Your obt. servt.

Washn. Jackson

ALS, DLC. Published in Bassett, 1:196.
    1. Not further identified.
    2. For Jackson's later use of this information, see AJ to an Arbitrator, February 29, 1812, below.

From Willie Blount

Knoxville Decr. 28th. 1809

Dear Sir,

It would be to the interest of the United States to accede to the proposal of this State respecting an exchange of territory with the Cherokees and Chickasaws agreeably to the plan proposed by me to the legislature on the 15th. & 30th. Octr. last,[1] that is, to give them lands west of the Mississippi in exchange for their claim—the time seems to be fast approaching when it will be indispensably necessary for the general government to have Nations of friends settled on that their frontier—I mean by it, that the conduct of the european nations is such, that neutral rights are now and have been long disregarded, and if the United States should in support of their rights have to contend with those nations, it would be sound policy in us to gain strength in that quarter of our territory, for it is not unreasonable to suppose that a part of foreign policy would be to get possession of that part of the territory of the United States—

The State of Tennessee having an undivided interest in the vacant lands west of the Mississippi held in common with the other States has an undoubted right to propose an exchange of territory situate there for such part of our territory as the Cherokees and Chickasaws claim near us; it would be better for her now to surrender her right to a certain portion of that territory for the accomplishment of so great a good to this State, than hereafter to use it in any other way—we really do own the lands claimed by those nations within our limits, the uncontrouled jurisdiction over it we must sooner or later have and exercise, to exchange with them is an act of liberality on our part—Tennessee in aid of the policy of the United States towards Indians has as yet acquiesced in considering them as tenants at will, but for this state to think of raising a sufficient sum of money by tax on the people to purchase their claim, say at an expence of hundreds of thousands of dollars would be but an idle thought—those nations of Indians are now friendly to the United States and the liberal policy of the latter towards the former will, and I wish it may preserve the friendship and secure the attachment of those nations for the United States for ever—but for our benefit and accomodation as a State, I wish them led away from us—I am willing to act justly towards them—it would be promotive of their interest as Nations to settle over the mississippi—game is there very abundant, the climate friendly to their constitutions, and much of the country is inhabited by people (Indians) whose manners and customs are more assimilated to their's than those of the people where they now live—at present they are surrounded by States thickly populated by people who have different interests—their friendship for the United States being firm (bottomed on their interest) they could assist in protecting the citizens of the general government over them, could longer preserve their national character, more easily and conveniently supply their individual wants, and by their intercourse with the neighbouring Indians could by precept and example civilize them faster and make more favorable impressions on them of the friendship of the United States towards Indians in general than could be effected in any other way with ten fold the expence to the United States who have for many years thought it good policy to cultivate the friendship of Indian tribes & they have done it at very great expence to the government attended with much individual sacrifice—

The best exertions of every citizen of the State should be used in endeavoring to accomplish the views of the State in relation to this exchange of territory—I am convinced yours will not be withheld[2]—this letter contains the outlines of what would probably be a conversation between us if together—should be glad to hear from you occasionally and am your friend

Willie Blount

ALS, DLC. Blount had succeeded Sevier as governor on September 20.

1. For Blount's recommendations to the legislature, see Robert H. White, *Messages of the Governors of Tennessee*, (Nashville, 1952), 1:285–88.

2. Jackson's response has not been found.

1810

From William Oliver Allen

St. Louis upper Louisiana 10th Jay 1810

Dear Genl.,

I received, your complimentary and friendly letter yesterday;[1] and hasten to write by the return of the mail.

The papers, you mention'd, are in my possession, but, as to their production, before the public, &c. I feel much doubt, perplexity, and great solicitude.

You Know, my [Dear][2] Genl., that I am *poor*—that, I am a stranger *in this Country*—that my profession is my only means of support: And that the success of my practise, is to depend on the *Good opinion of the World*.

If then, I should leave this, my residence, and go on to the City, there to mix in the scenes of the contemplicated investigation—to enc[ounter] the machinations, of *Genl. W.*, and his powerful [friend]s—*Cut myself loose from my increasing* busin[ess; ex]haust my *money*, and spend twelve months of my *time*—What, I demand, would be the difficulties, the loses, and privations, that I must necessarily forego? It is impossible for me to enumirate—most of them will occur[r, to you]r strength of mind.

But Sir, if it sh[oul]d be asked, what is it that you would not do, for the [benefi]t of your Country? I would unhesitatingly answer, *e[ver]ything*, that is within the *reach* of my *physical or mental powers*! No Sir! for so long as my nerves or mind would act, so long, would I *attempt* to surch for the interest of this beloved Union! Yet Sir, this question arrises, is this the *time*, and *that*, the *subject*, for which my prosperity is to be put afloat; and is it indispensible, that I should give my aid in that investigation? If it is, I will *obay the call of my Country*, when made by a constituted authority.

Your information relative to the letters &c in my possession is not circumstancially correct. but it is thus,

There, once lived in Louisvill Ky., a French Gentlm. by the name of Michael Laca[ssange], a mercht.[3] Mr. L. and my Brother-in-Law, were ([I believ]e) connected in trade. I presume that Mr. L. is the person alouded to, by Mr. Clark of Oleans, in his communications to congress—Mr. C.

states that, "he was, late postmaster at Louisville"—Mr. L. was postmaster at that place.[4]

Mr. Lacassange died, some years since, and left my Brother-in-Law, Ro: K. Moore Esqr.[5] one of his executors. Mr. M. transacted most of the b[usines]s of Mr. L's Estate, In consequence whereof Mr. L.['s papers] came to the possion of Mr. M.

Mr. Moore died in 1807, and [my] sister[6] invited me to come out, and superintend the business of her decd. husbands Estate—I did so: And thus Mr. L's papers, were placed in my hands.

As to the tendancy of those pa[pers, I] will not give an Opinion *Now*— But surely, a [*part* o]f Genl W's history *&c* may be collected from their per[usal.]

If any impression has been made on your mind averse to the Honor of my Brother-in-Law's memory, it should be instantly removed, for from all of L's. and his own papers it does appear, t[hat *h*]*e* was *always an excellent patriot.*

Be careful, in your use of this letter, but, at the same time, consult the *interest of my* Country.

Take, and Keep a copy.

Receive, Dr. Genl., my thanks for your hospitable and friendly letter to Govr Clabourn[7]—I have not as yet, been down the river, therefore, it is uncertain whether, I shall ev[er re]ap the benifit that would flow from your friends attention in Oleans—But General, I have now, the pleasure of declaring myself, much honored by your confidence[,] and that I hope, always to be ranked with your Best Friends.

Wm. O Allen

ALS fragment, DLC; Copy in AJ's hand, DNA-RG 107. Extract published in Bassett, 1: 197–98. Allen, a native of Virginia, practiced law in St. Louis for a time and served as a captain in the U. S. Army, 1812–18. He made several unsuccessful attempts to secure civil office in Arkansas Territory, where in 1820 he was killed in a duel.

1. Not found.
2. The bracketed portions of the letter are taken from the copy in Jackson's hand.
3. Lacassange (d. 1797), a French refugee, was a member of the Kentucky Convention in 1787 and the first postmaster of Louisville.
4. For Daniel Clark's comments on Wilkinson before Congress, see *ASP, Miscellaneous*, 1: 704–705. Clark also discussed the Lacassange connection in *Proofs of the Corruption of Gen. James Wilkinson* (Philadelphia, 1809).
5. Not further identified.
6. Anna Moore. See Anna Moore to AJ, July 22, 180[9], for her effort to settle some of her deceased husband's business with Samuel Donelson through Jackson.
7. Letter not found.

From Jenkin Whiteside

Washington 26th. Janry 1810

Dear Sir

I received your favour of last December,[1] in which you mention that you would accept of the appointment of a Judge of the Mississippi territory for the County of Madison if an additional Judge should be appointed for that purpose. A Committee of the house of representatives for that purpose have made a report a Copy of which I have Just received and you have inclosed.[2] I have no doubt that a bill will be passed making provision for the appointment of a Judge as recommended in the report, such Judge will be obliged to reside in Madison County.[3] From your Letter it does not appear to me that you contemplated removing to that County, if appointed, please to inform me soon as possible whether I may take the liberty of naming you for that appointment, should the Law require the Judge to reside in that County.[4] I am convinced that a great majority of the most respectable persons who intend to settle in that County would be pleased with your appointment as Judge there and I assure that it will afford me pleasure to be instrumental in obtaining the place for you, if you accept of it under the Terms of the Law. Genl. Wilkinson has not yet arived and I believe is not expected before April.[5] Very little is said here respecting him. I can say no more at present as the mail will close in a few minutes.

I remain your friend & most obt

J. Whiteside

ALS, DLC. Whiteside served as U.S. Senator from Tennessee, 1809–11.

1. Not found.

2. George Poindexter's report, not found with Whiteside's letter, appears in *TPUS*, 6:41–42. The appointment went to Obadiah Jones (see Whiteside to AJ, March 11).

3. On March 2, 1810, President Madison signed the bill extending the franchise to Madison County citizens and authorizing the appointment of an additional judge, who was required to reside in the county.

4. For Jackson's response, see AJ to Whiteside, February 10, below.

5. Wilkinson's Spanish connections were again under investigation by the House of Representatives. The inquiry can be followed in *Annals of Congress*, 11th Cong., 2nd sess., pp. 1606–2288 passim.

To [Jenkin Whiteside]

Hermitage February 10th. 1810

Dear Sir

Last Thursdays mail brought me an answer to my letter[1]—I informed you I had written to a gentleman of my acquaintance,[2] in whose hands and possession I was advised, were a serious of letters which contained the communication between Genl. Wilkeson and his deceased brotherin-law—which went plainly to prove, the receipt of large sums of money by Wilkeson from Spain—and compleatly to shew the nature complection and tendency of that conspiracy—from which I find my information was correct as to the letters being in his hands but incorrect as to his brother-inlaw being the individual with whom Wilkeson had and held the corre-spondence but that it was with a Michael Lacasange, the person named by Danl. Clark in his affidavit and aluded to in his pamphlet—

My Dear Sir I think it a duty I owe to my self & country to enclose you a coopy of this letter—that you may shew it to the President of the U. N. States that you & he may see the effects of over grown treason treachery and corruption when cloathed with power and supported by the smiles of goverment however Virtuous poverty in private station—yes Sir I know the writer to be a patriott—and possessing virtue such as every citizen ought to possess, who the god of nature has intended to live in a land of freedom and to enjoy the blessings of a goverment like ours and which alone can perpetuate to the nation of america its freedom and indepen-dance and yet with all his firmness & virtue, he dreads to meet the influ-ence of W & his powerful friends—yes Sir I know he is a man of firmness, and I once knew him before he obtained possession of these papers at Richmond in 1807, the open and avowed supporter of the Genl—View now his feelings from facts & events—at that day any virtuous patriot who had honesty & firmness to come forward and disclose facts was im-mediately branded with the apethet of *Traitor Burritt* &c and let his rep-utation or standing be what it might, he fell a ruthless victim at the shrine of the lords anointed to sheald this hidden but well known villain from that Just Punishment, that a fair and impartial enquiry into his conduct would have lead to—My god is it possible, that the influence of a great & publick villain and his friends in this infant republick are such as to over-awe the poor but virtuous from disclosing evidence that would when lincked with that before the public, go to shew compleatly that our gov-ernment has been heaping all their favours upon a wretch who was medi-tating this destruction and the greater the strength of evidence against him, the more favours and encomiums, by goverment bestowed upon him which at once gave the lie to his accusers, and as I observed before the vir-tuous patriot who had courage anough to step forward to warn the coun-try to unmask Treason & Treachery fell a ruthless victum before the im-pious and thundering accusations of Wilkeson untill *virtue itself* stood *apalled* and *amased* at the sight of this hardy villain who spurns the power of truth and enquiry and riding triumphant over virtue and his ac-cusers. These are the effects that has been produced in society—and a sufficient proof is contained in the letter a coopy of which I inclose (and the mock trial by the court of enquiry and the executive approbation so loudly proclaimed was the engine that has lead to it)[3]—But I hope the energy and firmness of the present chief-magistrate will compell an enquiry—and I am well convinced, if ever an enquiry is had and that before a tribunal that can enforce the production of those letters which are in the handwriting of the Genl it will with other proofs before the publick *compleatly unmask* him—What my Dear Sir Just on the eve of war, and a Treator at the head of the army—a commander in chief in whom the citizens that is to fight your Battles have no confidence[4]—that they know is every thing but a honest man & virtuous patriot—and still with all the prooffs that is before the public and in the hands of individuals still enjoying the confidence of goverment. What impressions is this calculated to make upon the publick mind—I can tell you what it is making—That the people begin to think there are some favorites who have been high in office in the united States whose complection would be scorched by the enquiry—I have just to add that I enclose you a coopy of the letter with a request that you shew it to the president with the injunction that the name of writer is only to be made publick when the good of the publick requires it—as to this letter of mine you are at liberty to do with it as you please—I am reguardless of the smiles or frowns of the Genl or his friends altho he may be supported by the favours and smiles of Govt when I obtain information of Treason treachery or vilainy Either in publick or private walks in church or state—regardless of smiles or frowns I will do my duty, I will make them known to the publick, and if possible bring them to meritted punishment—I shall await on this occasion—an enquiry by goverment. Should that not take place I shall make known to the publick, the corrispondance between the Genl & Mr. L. if I can obtain[5] For villainy has too long escaped punishment—and virtue in the united States appears to groan under oppression, whilst treason and treachery is idolised, and hailed as the savior of our country yrs &c

A. J—

ALS draft, DLC. Published in Bassett, 1:198–99.

1. See above, Allen to AJ, January 10.

2. Neither Jackson's letter to Allen nor to Whiteside has been found.

3. Jackson was probably alluding to Jefferson's comment in his letter to the House of Representatives, February 4, 1808. In transmitting extracts of letters requested by the House, Jefferson wrote that "in no part of the papers communicated by Mr. [Daniel] Clark . . . have we found any intimation of the corrupt receipt of money by any officer of the United States from any foreign agent" (*ASP, Miscellaneous*, 1:712).

4. For the attitude of West Tennessee militia officers toward Wilkinson, see above, Resolutions of 2nd Division Officers, [January 16, 1809].

5. No evidence has been found that Jackson got copies of the Lacassagne-Wilkinson papers or that he issued any publication on the matter.

To Jenkin Whiteside

Hermitage February 10th. 1810

Dear Sir

I have Just recd. your friendly and polite letter of the 26th. last month[1] to which I hasten to reply—When I was solicited by those respectable citizens and particular friends of mine who are about to remove to the county of Madison to accept of the appointment of Judge in that county <of Madison> in case such arangement was made, I had it not in contemplation of becomeing a citizen of that county[2]—from my persuits for several years past—from many unpleasant occurrencies that took place during that time it has given to my mind such a turn of thought, that I have laboured to get clear off—I have found this impossable, and unless some new persuit to employ my mind and thoughts <upon>—I find it impossible to divest myself of those habits of gloomy and pevish reflections that the wanton and flagatious conduct—and unmeritted refletions of base calumny, heaped upon me <through dark and hidden communications> has given rise to—in order to try the experiment how far new scenes might relieve me from this unpleasant tone of thought—I did conclude to accept that appointment in case it was offered me—and I was careless about the compensation attached to the appointment—since the arival of last mail which brought your letter two of my friends—fearfull from <of> the provisions of the law, that it would prevent me from accepting in case it was offerred to me has visited me whose arguments and wishes has brought me to the following conclusion That in case the office should be offerred to me I will accept thereof if the compensation is such that will meet necessary annual expences—it is stated to me that the salary of the Judge of washington county is $1000—1200, or 1500—Either of these sums is fully adequate to my expence lower than either would not—and for a less than the lowest I would not accept, and notwithstanding I am not needy, and have a wish to gratify my friends—still it is a duty I owe my self & family, not to impair my little copetency which I possess from my <hard> Own industry to the gratification of my friends or the service of my country when that service can be performed as well by others—you may think it curious that I have been so unatentive to the civil list of late years, as not to know the compensation of the differrent officers of government—but it is really the fact—and I do not know the salary that Judge [Harry] Tollman receives—I therefore state to you if the salary is $1000 or upwards under the condition of the law I will accept and if permanent residence is not required, for any salary for the before mentioned reasons I would accept—far from the Temporising disposition displayed by congress, I am well aware that no act of insult, degradation or contumely offerred to our goverment will arouse them from their

present lethargy and temporiseing conduct, untill my name sake[3] sets fire
to some of our seaport Towns and puts his foot aboard a British man of
war—Then perhaps, the spirit of 76. may again arise—I was in hopes,
that the energy of the executive would have been followed up by congress—but the arguments made use of and the opposition to their resolution from the Senate[4] has convinced me that the present congress will not
act with energy, that some of our old republican friends, have either lost
their usual good Judgt. or their political principle—from all which I conclude that as a military man I shall have no amusement or business—and
indolence and inaction would shortly destroy me—for these reasons and
under the provisions of this letter I authorise you to say that if appointed
I will accept—(The length of the other letter which accompanies this to
you[5]—prevents me from coopying this—you will therefore receive it
with its obliterations and interlineations)—accept of assurances of my
Esteem & respect—& believe me to be yr mo. ob serv.

Andrew Jackson

ALS, DLC. Extract published in Bassett, 1:199–201.
  1. See above.
  2. No memorials in support of Jackson's appointment as judge in Madison County have
been found.
  3. Francis James Jackson (1770–1814), minister from Great Britain, had arrived in
Washington on September 8, 1809, and was recalled in April 1810.
  4. Jackson was referring to the resolution of the Senate approving the conduct of the
president in refusing to hold any further communication with the British minister to the
United States. Introduced on December 5, 1809, the resolution had passed the Senate on
December 11; in the House of Representatives, however, a lengthy debate had ensued with
concurrence delayed until January 4. Jackson had not yet received news of the resolution's
passage through both houses (*Annals of Congress*, 11th Cong., 1st and 2nd sess., pp.
480–81, 511, 706-1152 passim, 2590).
  5. See above.

To John Randolph

[cFebruary 10, 1810]

Sir

I should have adressed you some weeks ago, had I heard, that your
health had permitted you to take your seat in congress—I now hope this
will find you in your seat.[1] It is highly probable from what is stated in the
public prints, that an enquiry may be had into the conduct of Genl Don
James Wilkison[2]—should this be the case I think it a duty I owe myself
and country, that it may be known; where testimony exist, in the hand
writing of the genl, that may throw some light upon the enquiry—This
(as I am advised) is a lenthy corespondence had and held between the
Genl and Mr Lacasang formerly Postmaster at the fall of the ohio—The
letter from Obediah B. Hays Esqr which you will receive by this mail—
will give you the channel through which I obtained my information[3]—

The publick I think will be much indebted to him—The enclosed coopy of a letter,[4] will shew you in whose hands the corespondence are—and when you are informed, that my letter to which the inclosed is an answer[5] stated, that as I was "informed; the corespondence would establish the genls being a pensioner of Spain—who were concerned & the object of the conspiracy; the severance of the western from the Eastern states &c &c" you will perceive from the answer that these papers prove *much* I have no doubt from the information I have recd. from Mr Hays that they will prove more than I anticipated—

It is to be regretted that the arm of Govt. has been stretched forth to shield this publick villain, from that Just *publick* punishment that he merits—It has appeared to me that the closer the clouds of testimony of his guilt thickened around him—the more the respectability of his accusers the more the favours of goverment was heaped upon him—and by this means enquiry crushed—and truth intimidated—and from the enclosed you will see, that this object has been attained—for I believe Capt OAllen a man of firmness, and a patriot—and with what solicitude he writes, and expresses himself on the occasion The publick mind is now calm, This villain of corruption & iniquity must be draged from his lurking place, and unmasked to the world—The stain that the government of our country has recd by having such a charector at the head of our army must be washed out by a Just and publick punishment—and I fear that there is not a man on the floor of congress that has firmness and independance anough, to bring forward to the bar of Justice this *once favorite* of *presidential* favor but yourself—I therefore write you, and in close the information in whose hands this previous corespondance between the Genl & Mr Lacasang can be found—I have to request that the enclosed will not be made publick untill It is necessary—you will see with what caution he confines me to the use of his letter—as to my letter you may use it as you please—where villainy is concerned I have no secrete & I neither fear the frowns, nor court the smiles of *Genl Wilkeson and his friends—however influential the may be*—I have sent a coopy of the inclosed letter to Mr Jenkin Whiteside of the Senate with a request that he shews it to the President—That he may take early measures for the preservation of this correspondanc—should he *not act* so as to procure them; I write this to you, that measures may be adopted; that this corespondance may be obtained, and laid before the publick.

The subject of this letter I hope will be a sufficient apology for my intruding it upon you The matter it contains induces me to write you—our verry slight acquaintanc I know would not warrent me in opening a corespondance—but the subject requires a man of talents & firmness on the floor of congress—and for this reason I intrust the subject to your hands—I am sir with high reguard for your charector yr. mo. ob. serv.

Andrew Jackson

P.S. Capt. Oallen was raised in or near Petersburgh has been well recommended to me—It is likely you are personally acquainted with him, when I first knew him it was in Richmond in 1807 he was then the open supporter of Wilkeson & I believe from a sincere belief of his merit—he came to the western country in the fall of that year—these papers fell into his hands which has verified to him that the Genl was Just such a compositon of corruption as I had assured him he would find him to be upon inquiry and investigation—from the small acquaintance I have with Capt. Oallen, I have I high confidence in his integrity & probity—and he is thus considered by all his new acquaintances in the west that I have heard speak of him—

ALS draft, DLC. Published in Bassett, 1:203–204 (dated February 20).
 1. Randolph did not take his seat in Congress until March 12.
 2. The House of Representatives inquiry in 1810, like previous investigations, failed to prove that Wilkinson had been a Spanish pensioner. For the committee report, see *Annals of Congress*, 11th Cong., 1st and 2nd sess., Appendix, pp. 2288–381.
 3. Letter not found; Hays has not been identified.
 4. See above, Allen to AJ, January 10.
 5. Jackson's letter to Allen has not been found.

To Willie Blount

[February 15, 1810]

Dear Sir

your letter of the first of this instant is before me[1]—and it will aford me pleasure to comply with the request, I would herewith enclose to you the returns from the differrent Brigades composing my Division in 1809 which at one glance would shew you the state & condition thereof and from which you would discover that there is a great deficiency of arms and acoutrements But presuming, that these returns you will find at the seat of Goverment in the office of the adjutant Genl. of the state,[2] or amonghst the archives which were handed over to you by your predesossor—I omit enclosing them It is certainly true that at a time like the present great attention ought to be paid to the dicipline of the militia—they ought to be in readiness to act—But sir under the laws of our state the militia never will be diciplined, the never can and it appears, that as danger approaches the less attention is paid to this all important subject to the Defence of our country by Congress who alone can pass eficient laws to difuse dicipline amonghst us and which will give us a uniform militia throughout the union before the militia under our state regulations can be diciplined—the mode pointed out by the consti[tution] for the election of officers must be changed[3]—without this; proper subbordination never will be maintained amonghst the militia hence no dicipline—This is the first change—that must be effected—next to this the must be classed (and as you have asked my oppinion on the most proper plan of clasification I will here give it) first I would class the militia into two classes only the first class should be from the age of 18 to 28 inclusive the second from 28 to 40—The first class should be the first for duty—This class would form an army too numerous for any one requisition from the genl Goverment upon the state—I would then divide this first class, into as many divisions as it would admit of—to meet the demands of the general goverment on any case of emergency that might occur, this could be easily Known from the number of militia required by the laws of the union to be held in readiness to act at the call of the President—when this was done at the expence of the publick compleat camp equipage should be furnished for the number in the first class for duty, which first class should be held in readiness for service for one year in case during that time there should be a call after such clasification this first class should be ordered into the field and there cantooned at given points, placed under the directions of officers appointed by goverment competant to dicipline both officers and men for the space of two months from the date of their arival at the place of rendezvous at which period the should be dismissed (unless their service should be required against an enemy) and would carry with them amongst their fellow citizens the knowledge of the discipline they had acquired—and when dismissed the second class should be called on and undergo the same rotine of dicipline under the same drill officers as the first class—&c &c untill the whole of the first class shall be Thus diciplined and anured to the duties of the field—when they are dismissed and intermix with their fellow citizens again the will carry with them a knowledge of Tactics that they can difuse throughout our fellow citizens, will raise a military ardor, throughout the country—and stimulate others to vie with them in the knowledge and art of war—But this I know will be objected to because it will occasion expence—To which I answer—our independence and Liberty was not obtained without expence—it was dearly Bought—both with Blood and Treasure, It must be preserved—the pence on this subject never should be counted—and its only real and substantial defence is a well organized militia—and we cannot we find from experience have this without expence—From the scenes of corruption, that has lately been discovered in the genl of our regular army, the ideas contained in the constitution is verified, that the sure defence and Bulwark of our Liberty is in a well organized militia I would also advise that every three years, the militia should be classed and thus diciplined—this will always keep ready for duty, the young & healthy part of our citizens who will be able to undergo any hardship or fatigue and keep our militia in a proper state of discipline, laws well calculated to enforce a subordination when thus introduced by the dicipline of the first class for duty it can be kept up—and every three years being classed the rising youths, will become diciplined on cases of emergency, our state in a verry few years could furnish an army sufficient to face any enemy that could be introduced by an invading foe—If this plan or any similar should be adopted—it will at once present to your view the necessity of our state or the general goverment supplying the militia with arms and accoutrements our state possesses fine raw materials for an army it only requires a little manufactory, to be able if necessary to oppose with success Boneparts invincibles, but to do this with success, it will require two, things: first *dicipline* second arms, to carry into execution, all the benefits of dicipline—But to shew you, the military ador that prevades my Division I enclose you Genl. James Winchesters Report[4] to me under my last order under the requisition of the genl Goverment the Detachment was filled on short notice by voluntary enlistment—But sir the frequent calls for the militia by the Genl Goverment, without action is well calculated to destroy the military ardor that has prevailed and which I still hope exists—It has frequently Brought to my mind the fable of the wolf & the Shepard—and the Temporising spirit that appears to prevade Congress under passing insulting and degrading scenes, convince me, that let the pulse of the nation be what it may congress will try to paralise it—the nation is possessing a proper dignity of feeling for the many degredations and insults our goverment has recd the are ripe for war but congress is Temporising—But I will do my duty and aid you in maturing any plan to dicipline the militia[5]—which when well organized, may emphatically be stiled the sure Bullwark, and defence of the nation—I am yours with respect

A. J—

ALS copy, DLC. Published in Bassett, 1: 201–203.
1. Not found.
2. George Wilson.
3. According to the Tennessee constitution (Sect. 7), field officers, captains, subalterns, and non-commissioned officers of the militia were to be elected by citizens subject to military duty; brigadier generals, by the field officers; and major generals, by the brigadiers and field officers.
4. Not found.
5. Insignificant revisions of the laws regulating the Tennessee militia were made in 1811 and 1812, but no changes were made in the election of officers (*Laws of Tennessee*, 9th General Assembly, 1st sess., ch. 93; 9th General Assembly, 2nd sess., chs. 28, 46, 78).

From Willie Blount

Knoxville March 15th. 1810

Dear Sir,

Knowing as you do that I have much writing to do as matter of duty I make no apology for the nonobservance of punctuality as respects answering such letters as I occasionally have the pleasure to receive from you particularly your last on the classification of the militia[1]—your plan is a most excellent one if it could be carried into effect—it wants nothing to do it but a little of the exercise of liberality in those who hold the purse-strings—liberality did I say no nothing but an exercise of duty toward men who are necessitated to perform service in duty to themselves and country—surely if the general government duly appreciate the blessing of liberty they will not count the pence which may be proper to be expended in support of it—The United States cannot think of supporting an army of regular troops & I hope they will never think of it to any considerable extent—The militia well organized & regularly & strictly disciplined will make an army of the proprietors of the soil & could & would drive Napoleon or any other power back into the seas—It would be acceptable, to receive from you the returns from the different Brigades composing your division in 1809 as I would like to have at one glance the state and condition of those Brigades—The returns in the Adjutant General's office are not as regular as might be expected to be found in a regularly kept office of Rolls—it would afford me great satisfaction to under stand the present state of the Militia of Tennessee and as much or more if any thing I can do will assist in well ordering of it in future—I think you & the officers under your command could by correspondence with each other on the subject of the condition and disciplining the men &c. promote a military ardor—I of the same date of my last to you[2] addressed a letter to each Brigadier in the State requesting information of the state of their Brigades respectively but have received answers from none except Genl. Winchester who answered promptly—By this day's mail I have forwarded to Col. [Robert] Weakly who is a member of the committee to whom the Militia business is refered an extract of yours to me so far as relates to the classification—I wish it might be adopted[3]—your further ideas will be thankfully received by me at any time on that important head—I believe if the people at home do not start some plan by which the militia of the Union can be well ordered &c. that we never shall have a respectable force in readiness to take the field—we may have the strongest army in the world, and certainly we Americans have more at stake because we boast of the enjoyment of freedom—If the congressional law makers [(]who I am willing to believe would do for the best in their judgments[)] have to sketch a plan of operation & defence I have not the charity or liberality to suppose that it will be very perfect in its outline—I take it the knowledge of a majority combined don't amount to much on the scale of military tacticks—the principal object of all men should be to substantially serve or benefit the community & I have thought that if success attended attempts in that way that all would be pleased, if not all, all whose good opinion is worth having—I wish Tennessee could exercise jurisdiction over her chartered limits and have an outlet for redundant produce, if this could be effected it would vastly meliorate the condition of Tennesseans—the fertility of our soil ought to produce many comforts—I believe Congress have not done much & not much of the little they have done is of any substantial consequence—I suppose you have seen the squabble between the two great Virginia men Mucius & Camil-

lus[4]—what a squabble they have about their half handed consequence—
as Bob King[5] says leaden men ought to be about something more than
indulging in personal abuse—I have hoped for a long time to be able to
see you at home that hope was bottomed on the belief that I should soon
hear from our members in Congress on the subject of exchange of Territory with our neighbours, but their conduct seems to be a verification
of the old addage that great bodies move slowly—I am yet without any
information on that head—I wish they would communicate so that I
might get time to go home a while—to be a State prisoner is not agreeable to me I would rather be a hewer of wood and a drawer of water near
the Barrens and be at liberty—the priviledge of being employed in a way
partaking of the likeness of private life is the greatest priviledge I ever
enjoyed or wish to enjoy—I wish I could hire a substitute here until Septr.
twelve month, what a long time it seemeth to be, to be absent from domestic concerns which alone affords substantial comforts to your sincere
friend

Willie Blount

Tell Genl. Overton how de, don't forget it, I think very highly of that
good man and gentleman—one evening's chat with you & him would
rub a good deal of rust off my clouded ideas these bright moonlight
nights—

[The Se]cy. of War has sent to me for the use of the militia the set of
B[ooks] entitled "martial Law"[6] one I would wish to be in your [hands
and the] other have delivered to Genl. [John] Cocke—[7]

ALS, DLC.
1. See above.
2. Not found.
3. Weakley was at this time serving his only term in Congress. No evidence has been
found that he introduced any measures embodying Jackson's recommendations.
4. Not identified.
5. Not identified.
6. Alexander MaComb, *A Treatise on Martial Law and Courts-Martial* . . . (Charleston,
1809).
7. Cocke was major general of the 1st Division, East Tennessee militia.

From Bennett Smith

Oa[k F]orest May 1st. 1810

Dear Genl.

I recd. your polite & friendly letter,[1] by the hand of my little son lately
under your care, and I do most gratefully acknowledge the favour done
me in the case of William[2] by yourself & Mrs. Jackson to whom through
you I present my most sincere Respects.

Genl. the real friendly intention of your letter, and the friendship therein
contained is as pure as the heart from which it flowed; and I solemnly

declare that a remembrance of our long and well Established friendship, and equally now for your Lady is one of the comforts of my declining days; and as well may the Rivers revert their courses, and the stag feed upon the op[en] air as to erase from my mind an early and well [esta]blished friendship as now exists between you and my[self].[3]

Dear Sir the information on which the public opinion has been founded is not intirely correct, therefore I must enter into an explanation which to no other man on Earth would I attempt to make; there is a fault somewhere and I much rather that the World should impute it to me than to any of my Children, hence I give them no explanation as they see proper to center the blame on me; I agree Sir with you precisely that public opinion is the standard by which a man's respectability in Society is to be measured, but that opinion must be founded on Just & true premises, and not on conjecture & Error, as I well know the present case to be; But I am willing to bear whatever a rash & uninformed public may chuse to utter rather than throw one sparke of blame on my Daughter Matilda,[4] who always has been and always will remain my best & dearest friend; and if any Difference between her & myself had ever taken place (But none has) an Empty minded public never should know it, who are always more willing to Condemn than to acquit, when they lack good breeding & good sense to keep up conversation they then turn to their inexhaustable store of slander; General Jackson a public opinion made up on Just & true grounds is to me heavier than a Mountain & sharper than a two edged Sword, but Sir when it is made up from untrue grounds & augmented by evil Hearts & empty heads it is lighter to me than the chaff and pitching of straws;

Docr. Bedford for causes yet unknown to me saw it to be his interest to spurn at & refuse every friendly offer made to him & Matilda; I never have done one Single act by word or deed (designedly) by which they or either of them are injured in feelings or reputation nor never will while my life lasts; However Dor. Bedford might see pleasure & gratify ambition in treating with contempt my offers of property to him & Matilda; It by no means alienated that affection which I had for my Daughter, or prompted me to do him any injury, but on the contrary I vented my soul in Silent sorrows unknown to all the world, comforting myself that I had the means, & had the will, to aid Matilda in time of want; yet Sir an Idle public has thought proper to say that I have treated Matilda ill & refused her my house; true it is when I was at Nashville I did not visit Matilda and the reason was I did not want to mortify her feelings, and add fuel to my own grief, by seeing her have a small attendance by hired servants when there was plenty in her Fathers house[5] & he more than willing to give her part, and she was not allowed to receive them; but she always has been and always shall be welcome to my house & paternal protection, and when she thinks proper to come she shall not go empty.

As to the case of Thos. being married[6] he never in his life named the business to me only through his Mother, I made no objection to it, this was Twelve months past, when he made an attemp to purchase a remnant of goods in Nashville for a very large sum he never let me know any thing of the business at all, even when he was Two days at my house on his way to Huntsville; after he was gone his Brother Jos.[7] made it known to me which was the first time I heard it yet the public *chit-chat* was that I had refused to be his security, when I never heard it spoken of by himself or any other but his Brother Joseph as stated, he came no more to my house untill on last of March past he stayed several days in complete friendship never mentioned to me his intentions & I was Ignorant of the same only from his mother, his Marriage met my full approbation but I was so sick with a cold that I could not go from home, it was agreed that Pollie[8] and Mrs. Smith[9] should go & myself stay at home & send out for a party to meet them at my house on the next day after his marriage, accordingly Pollie & Mrs. Smith with several servants proceeded to make preparations in the best stile we could reach that on the next day after his marriage we might recive & make welcome to our house our new friend, on the day of his marriage Mrs. Smith & Pollie were ready & waited for him very patiently who came about three or four O'clock in the evening, they then had Eight Miles to ride, I was in the house when Mrs. Smith & Pollie were siting in the riding chais waiting for him, he came into the house and I said it was very surprising to me that he would keep company with the old Woman Lytle[10] or any of her crue when he knew their mean standing & false Toungues, I went out of the house to the place where Mrs. Smith and Pollie were siting in the Chais ready to start, the first I knew or they he went to a different place mounted his horse rode off in a gallop saying he never would come on my plantation any more, leaving his Mother & sister and going a different way from what they intended so that a Chais could not pass, of course they could not follow him & did not go, this is the whole that past, he went on give no reason why the family was not there, left the world to conjecture & of course they laid the blame on me & made what additions seemed most proper for the occasion—

Sir as to my property you know already what I offered Bedford, and Two grown Negroes on my plantation I give Thos. a Bill of Sale for, which he may have any time he will come or send, but he has before his eyes the late & generous example of Dr. Bedford not to take any without he gits all, this letter contains nothing as to my statements but what is Justly true but I feel my pride above giving a slanderous public any satisfaction or information; therefore I request that nobody may know the contents except Mrs. Jackson; Mrs. Smith tells me that you and Mrs. Jackson expect to give us a call on your way to Duck River about the middle of May Instant. On the 21st. day by long appointment I start to North Carolina and must infallible go if life & health lasts, a word of friendship and advice from you has its full weight with me, if you will be so good, as to send for Matilda bring her up with you & Mrs. Jackson on Thursday the 17th. of this Instant I will have some respectable company send for Mr. Bass's Daughter wife of my son Thos. and in the presents of Mrs. Jackson give them three Negroes each and give such Bill of sale as you shall direct but at that time I neither want Docr. Bedford present nor my son Thos. but those two women shall have what I promise neither do I want Bedford or Thos to know my intentions as I think I have not been in the wrong; now sir I send my son William to convey this letter to you, by whom I expect to know if you will trouble yourself so far as I have requested & what you & Mrs. Jackson does shall govern me, I am yours with the greatest Respect &c

Ben. Smith

PS. Bring with you Two or three of your friends be at my house for Dinner, I shall invite Capt. Coffee & Lady come there on Wednesday, There will be plenty of Lamb & peas at the White house &c &c &c—

B. Smith

ALS, DLC. Smith, a lawyer, the son-in-law of former congressman Joseph Dickson of North Carolina, was the brother of William Smith, later senator from South Carolina, whom Jackson twice nominated for associate justice of the Supreme Court. Bennett Smith had moved from Lincolnton, N.C., to Rutherford County with his and his wife's families in 1803 or 1804. He was cotton inspector for Rutherford County, 1807–1808.
1. Not found.
2. William Hunter Smith (1797–1871), Bennett's son, and a lifelong resident of Rutherford County.
3. It has not been established with certainty when Smith and Jackson formed their friendship. Various reports state that Jackson and William had been classmates in childhood. It is possible that Bennett and Andrew had also known each other in North Carolina.
4. Isabella Matilda (b. c1787) married Dr. John Robertson Bedford on December 6, 1809.
5. According to the census of 1810, Smith owned thirty-nine slaves.
6. The marriage bond for Thomas, Bennett's son, and Temperance W. Bass had been issued on March 26, 1810.
7. Joseph Smith married Irene Bradley.
8. Mary, nicknamed "Polly" (d. 1813), Bennett Smith's daughter, who married John Hutchings in 1810. Jackson served as guardian for their son, Andrew Jackson Hutchings (1811–41), after John's death.
9. Isabella Dickson Smith (1762–1845), the daughter of Joseph Dickson.
10. Not identified.

To Francis Preston

Nashville May 3rd. 1810—

Dear Sir
your letter of the 19th. ultimo is recd. and now before me [1]—and I am sorry that I cannot make out a statement of our Iron & Casting transaction for want of the original contract It being locked up and Mr Jno Hutchings now at Natchez having the Key—I find from our Books that agreable to the acpt stated by Mr John Armstrong your agent of date the

22nd. of October 1804,[2] the amount of Iron & Castings recd. amounted to $1998.33⅓ It appears, from Mr. Bakers recpt,[3] that the castings & iron never came to hand untill the 20th. of May 1804 and then only a part[4]—and you recollect the situation in which I was placed in by Deaderick & Tatom by your not delivering the Iron & castings at the time stipulated, *that they were threw on my hands, their proportion of the contract.* The first payment from the Books was 1000 dollars and that before any Interest is *calculated*[5]—it is presumed before any was thought to accrue—It appears you are charged with $20 paid your order to Doctor May June 10th. 1807—there is interest calculated on the Ballance of the principle of $998.33⅓ untill that date from the 1st. of January 1806— & the $20 deducted from the Interest—and Interest calculated to the 5th of october 1808—this date there is a credit by $800 paid by Major [James B.] Risque[6]—& deducted from the principle, and interest calculated on the Ballance to the 17 of Novbr. 1808—when there is a credit of $200 by Major Risque which leaves a ballance of principle & interest due you of $130.44½ If my recollection is correct the date of the first of January 1806 from which the interest appears to be calculated is not from the date of the article, but from an assumed date arising from the Hardship of the case, that is to say, from the circumstance of D & T not receiving their part because you had not delivered them agreable to contract, by which they were thrown on my hands—of course I had no benefit from them untill that date, and from the delay of delivery—the delay of their arival here and the above circumstances it was supposed that Justice would give the above date for the calculation of interest on the $998.33⅓. agreable to your request I have forwarded by Mr. L[illburne] L. Henderson[7] a horse—whose strength is equal to 270, and whose gentleness is well calculated for the age of forty five he is a good draft horse, and gentle in geer—and not a bad riding horse—I got him from Capt. H[enry?] Thompson,[8] at a pretty round price—and as things is as they are—Send me a pair of Boots of the manufactory of abington, when such things are manufactured there and close the acpts—This is not perhaps a settlement agreable to Bookkeeping but as *Judge* [David] *Campbell*[9] *says agreable* to the equity of the case—I always have t[he] Blue devils about me when old a[ccounts] are mentioned, and I would not run over an old acpt for a nice sum there fore cannot settle our account unless in the above way of round numbers—Make my respects to your amiable lady[10] & believe me to be with sincere Esteem yr mo ob. servt

                                                                    Andrew Jackson

ALS, N.
    1. Not found.
    2. See Armstrong to AJ, October 22, 1804. Armstrong has not been further identified.
    3. Not found.
    4. Jackson had requested Preston to cancel his order unless the goods were shipped before May 20, 1804 (see AJ to Preston, April 15, 1804).

5. For the transmittal of that payment, see AJ to Preston, January 23, 1805; for additional discussion of this account, see above, Preston to AJ, December 17, 1807.

6. Risque, a resident of Fincastle, Va., was frequently in the Nashville area, particularly during the racing season. He was either part-owner or sometime manager of the Clover Bottom race track. In 1808, Jackson had made him a loan. Risque discussed that loan and Jackson's indebtedness to Preston in his letter to AJ, October 9, 1808.

7. Henderson was a resident of Abingdon, formerly engaged in the salt trade with William King.

8. Probably a neighbor who on occasion delivered cotton to Jackson's gin.

9. Campbell (1750–1812), a native of Virginia, was a colleague of Jackson's on the bench of the Tennessee Superior Court, serving until 1807.

10. Sarah Buchanan Preston.

From John Coffee

Sugar Forest 14th. May 1810

I reced your line by Jim[1] covering the letter to Doctor [Charles] Kavanaugh,[2] and least some accident might happen, I went to the Doctors myself, who was from home and will not return untill tomorrow evening, however Mrs. Kavanaugh[3] appeared perfectly to understand the complaint and how to treat it, in the same manner the Doctor would have done was he here, or even with you—You'll receive her medicine and instructions, I wrote them by her directions, she says, there is not the smallest doubt but a continuance of the medicine will in a short time perfectly restore the Child.[4] She also and further asked me to say to you that the Doctor had learnt his daughter, (Henry [Tate] Ruckers wife)[5] how to make the preparation, and who will at all times prepare it for you when required, as well as her father could do. I told Mrs. Kavanugh to request the Doctor to meet the appointment of yourself and Doctr. Bedford should he come home on time.

I shall expect to see you and Mrs. Jackson here (if Andrews health will permit) on tomorrow or next day on your way up the Country. Polley and Betsey Harris,[6] is gone a straberrying to the barrens, or she would be very glad to send her respects to her aunt.

I must trouble you with an enquiry for my horse, before you come up. on this day week I loaned my horse saddle & bridle & great coat to Stockley Hays, to enable him the more conveniently to carry down Robert Butlers Negroes, and under a promise that I should have him the next day or the day after, which is the last of him, and being ever since on foot or the borrow, I would be extremely glad know if I am to get him again— will you be so good as make the enquiry for me and let me know when you come up

with respect and esteem dear Sir yours

Jno. Coffee

the sun is not one hour high have directed Jim not to stop untill he gets home—

ALS, DLC.
1. One of Jackson's slaves.
2. Neither letter found. Kavanaugh, formerly of Bedford County, Va., and at this time a physician in Rutherford and Williamson counties, later served with Jackson as a cavalry captain in the Natchez and Creek campaigns and at New Orleans. Following the war, he remained in Mississippi as a sutler and eventually settled in DeSoto County.
3. Not further identified.
4. Andrew Jackson, Jr. See Robert Purdy to AJ, May 24, 1810, below.
5. Nancy Kavanaugh, who had married Rucker (1786–1866) in 1807.
6. Harris, Coffee's niece, was the daughter of his sister Mary and her husband, Simpson Harris, a Nashville merchant.

From Donelson Caffery

Mouth Bayou Sarah May 20th. 1810.

Dear Uncle

I have delay'd writing to you thus long that I might be enabled to give you some information respecting the prospects of business in this place— Times were at first so discouraging, I thought I would not give you the first unfavorable account; but I am sorry to inform you that I fear from the situation of this Country business cannot be done to advantage It is true Goods may be sold on credit, but contrary to the opinion I had form'd from the accounts of people; There is no such thing as making collections; The Spanish Authority is here suspended by a feeble thread, there is only the mere shadow of a Government; The Commandant at this place may be bribed to any thing, he will grant a decree for the recovery of money and by the Debtor's slipping a few Dollars in his hand will suspend that decree during his pleasure. From what I can learn the Rapides of red river would have been a much better place, but moving the goods would be attended with considerable expence and trouble—As soon as I can make sale of some Negroes, I will go to New orleans to buy Groceries its the only business that can be done here for Cash—There is no business in this Country like farming An industrious man, with a few negroes may soon make a fortune—I shall not remain in this business longer than I can help—Cotton is now $14 25/100 French weight at New Orleans provision of every kind comes low—Bacon at N. O. from 2 to 3 cents at this place 5 cts. Flour $6 to $6½ ℔ bl.—Corn 3½ cts ℔ bushel—

My father Mother & family were in good health I am very much pleas'd with the part of the Country he lives in—As soon as this reaches you I wish you to write—tender to aunt Jackson all the affection that a nephew or a son can feel—and for yourself accept all that Gratitude, love, and respect, should inspire—Yr affectionate nephew

Donelson Caffery

P.S. I have as yet seen no girl that I would be willing to tie myself for life to—perhaps I shall have yet to seek a wife in Tennessee   D. C.

ALS, DLC.

From Robert Purdy

High Wassee May 24th. 1810

Dear Sir,

Your letter of the 12th. Instant, I had the pleasure to receive by last mail[1]—on the subject of that wretch Judge Campbell.[2] I only wish the general opinion of all those that were acquainted with the business, as he insists, he done Justice—what our great people will do with Genl. Wilkinson, *god* and themselves can only tell—what has become of Genl. [Wade] Hampton.[3] I heard of his crossing Tennessee river on his way to this Country, and nothing since. I am anxious to see him at this post—I am realy sorry to hear of the indisposition of yourself and *Son*, but I am fearfull he will be hard to raise, at all events soon enough for Martha[4]

Captain [Thomas John] Vandykes Court of inquiry has been sitting for some time, the court has ajourned untill the first day of next month, for the purpose of giving him time to procure his witnesses. I am at a loss to form an opinion on the subject, but I have every reason to think he has acted improperly.[5] Congress has given us leave to remain in service some time longer, but next session will disband the greater part of the new Corps—By last mail, I received the promotions of the Army from the war office, that *holy Pet* Gilbert C[hristian] Russell is a Major[6]—I think it more than probable we will be sent per plan to the Shoales there to erect a garrison all setlers are to be moved of the Doubleheads reserve &c—Mrs. Purdy has not been well for some weeks, Polly Philips not returned from Knoxville.[7] Please Present our best wishes to Mrs. Jackson, Colo. Hays, & family, Ro Butler, & family and am happy to hear you are all doing well—Martha says she is anxious to see her friends in Cumberland, with real respect your friend

Rob. Purdy

ALS, DLC.
1. Not found.
2. The reason for referring to David Campbell as a "wretch" has not been firmly established. Purdy and Jackson may have been responding to Campbell's recent and somewhat satirical comments as a trustee of the Tennessee Academy in Rhea County. Campbell, in calling the other trustees together, had written that "My motto is '*without religion, learning and a well instructed militia, no republic can be permanent.*' I intend amongst other regulations to propose a military school; we will be in the neighbourhood of the Garrison at Hiwassee, and can get occasionally military music and instructors. This will be a fine exercise and amusement for the boys at play time" (*Knoxville Gazette*, April 7).
3. Hampton was made brigadier general in February 1809.
4. Purdy's daughter, approximately two years old.
5. Vandyke (d. 1814) entered the U.S. Army in 1794 and served at various ranks until his appointment as captain of the 7th Infantry in May 1808; he resigned December 3, 1810. From 1813 to 1814 he served as surgeon with the Tennessee Volunteers. The subject of the inquiry has not been determined.

6. Russell, a native of Tennessee, was appointed ensign in the U.S. Army in 1803, and periodically promoted. The Senate confirmed his promotion to major on May 1.

7. Elizabeth Purdy's sister Mary ("Polly"), who later married Elisha Williams. Purdy had written Jackson on April 20 that she had gone to Knoxville with Charles McClung.

From Wade Hampton

South Wt. Point 3d. June 1810

Dear Sir.

I had this afternoon the pleasure of receiving your favor of the 25th. Ulto.[1] My *Light corps* had passed this, before I reached it, but not so far, but by express, I was able to have them halted at some distance. [Electus] *Bacahas* their leader,[2] returned to me, and among other things, I suggested my wish of sending back to you one of the Boys—they are family Negroes, & his impression was, the sale I had made & the *distance*, would create great affliction amongst their relations, were Either of the Boys left—And when I found that neither of them could ride at less than 100 ls. I gave over the idea. I met, between NashVille & this place, a gentleman who was present at the Charleston races—an excellent judge, & one in whom the utmost confidence can be placed.

He assures me that the sorrel I sold Mr. [Robert?] Bell,[3] was opposed by several who had been winners during the season, & that he ran the first heat two miles, in 3.50—one second quicker than it had been done by gallitin, & that the second he did, or could evidently have placed the few that remained on the wrong side of the distance pole.

In a word, that he was considered, as well by that run, as the ease with which he after wards beat Peggy, to be the best colt that ever started upon that ground—

Had these particulars been as well detailed to me, I would certainly not have taken any such sum for him; sick, & disgusted as I was with the subject. I mention these particulars to your self alone—for really I think you ought to get hold on this Horse. He will be *a shield* to you for years, & then remain *a standard* in your stable—for he is as hardy as a lightwood knot, and is capable of sustaining more work, & tryals, than any colt I ever trained. Be patient, until you can get him wholy into your hands—and if it is your choice to have a partner in him, I would join you myself rather than you should have any other.

I do not think he cost Bell more than $800 for, in conscience, the other two are worth $700—

Upon a retrospect; I regret your absence, when I called upon you, more than ever! Should you get hold on this Horse, and will be *patient*, and exercise your usual judgment, you may levy upon your competitors any *contributions* you may chuse. The motive must appologize for the freedom of this letter, to which I beg leave to add my best wishes.

W. Hampton

P.S. I pray you to excuse the paper, & the hurry in which the scrawl is written. I have spent a week here with Col. Purdy, & am preparing to proceed as far as Knoxville tomorrow. You may stipulate for any paper of Bell's in my hands, or any discount on it. I am in no hurry to know the fate of the two colts—and recommend *time* to you.   W H.

If I can procure you such a rider as discribe, I Will do so, & find some safe conveyence so soon as possible.

ALS, DLC.
   1. Not found.
   2. Backus (d. 1813), from New York, was promoted to lieutenant colonel of the light dragoons in 1809.
   3. Bell, soon to settle in Louisiana as a sugar planter, frequently raced horses in the Nashville area. He married Caroline, the daughter of Edward Butler.

From Donelson Caffery

Bayou Sarah June 10th. 1810

Dear Uncle

Since I wrote by Mr. [J. F.] Gray[1] Wn. Jackson and myself have concluded to, remove the Goods to Natchez; in a few days I shall start them up—I think we will do better there than remaining in this place—The people in this Country appear to be on the eve of shaking off the Spanish Authority, a few popular men, with spirit and sense enough to conduct an enterprize of the kind could at any moment revolutionize the province. Any Act of oppression committed by an officer on any respectable American, would immediately put the thing in operation—I have just heard the Govonor at Batton rouge, has orderd all the French, out of the province, whether this extends to old French Settlers, I do not know, but expect will only be put in force against straglers of that Nation—What a pity the Goverment of the U. States had not taken possession, when the Spaniards were prepar'd to give it up[2]—This I suppose must be ask'd Genl. Wilkinson The Country is now an assylum for rogues, profligates— & Deserters, and what is worse than all, Americans who have renounced the principles of their Country & Government. I have had much reason to be discourag'd, in consequence of the dullness of business here, but hope will be able to sell our goods at Natchez; I expect Mr. [James] Baxter[3] on he[re] the latter part of the summer; if we make sufficient sales perhaps one of us may go in the winter or Spring; I must confess, my der Sir, I feel as yet somewhat like a lost child, altho my Father & mother live nearer to me; yet the recollection of the friendship & attention I have experienc'd in Tennessee, draws my affections, & no man need blush to own the sentiment of Gratitude—give my best respects to aunt Jackson when I get a little more knowledge of the Country I will give you a description as far as my information extends, please give my respects to uncle & aunt Hays & Family—Mr. & Mrs. [Robert] Buttler. Thos. Buttler[4] lives at Pinckneyville about 20 miles from this. I am told much esteem'd as a lawyer. Yr. affectionate Nephew

Donelson Caffery

P.S. I wrote to Cousin Sandy[5] by this mail. D.C

ALS, DLC.
1. See above, Caffery to AJ, May 20.
2. By order of the Madison administration, William C.C. Claiborne led occupation troops into the district of Baton Rouge in December 1810 and declared the area annexed to Orleans Territory.
3. Baxter (d. 1819), probably from York County, S.C., had long been an acquaintance of Jackson's. Commissioned a captain in the 24th Regiment, Tennessee militia, from Montgomery County in 1807, he served as assistant deputy quartermaster general for the East Tennessee troops in 1813.
4. Thomas Butler (1785–1847), the son of Thomas, later a judge in Louisiana.
5. Alexander Donelson (1784–1814), son of Rachel's brother John and Mary Purnell Donelson. He was killed in action at Emuckfau.

From Donelson Caffery

Natchez July 20th. 1810

Dear Uncle,

I recd your esteem'd favor of the 4th Instant.[1] Your advice my dear Sir shall be my constant companion, it shall ever be present to my memory & stimulate me to perseverance and Industry in business—I must own I have sometimes desponded since I came to this Country. I have either an acquired or constitunal melancholy, perhaps it may be acquired from an early habit of reflection, on my own situation and that of my family. I am almost asham'd to own this many times weighs me down—but it's a fault! I see its a fault, and I will try to get rid of it. our vexations are enough in reality without the help of imagination to increase them—

I am truely sorry to hear that our friend R[obert] B[utler] will be too apt to be doom'd to deplore the melancholy effects of passion and imprudence in a wife[2] Good God! what a mortifying disappointment to a man who has fondly dreamt of enjoying the utmost happiness in the possession of a woman for whom he would have sacrificd almost any thing— But just Heaven that you should experience ingratitude from that family. I know Sir, with many, that friendship shewn most disinterestedly and obligigations conferd with no other motive than the relief of the objects on whom they were conferd—would excite no sentiment but ingratitude and no other return than calumny—but I trust they of whom I am speaking have been warp'd from their duty and principles by passion, or something which may admit palliation—and that they will see and acknowledge their *error* not to speak of it with a harsher name—What a reward to aunt J.—! for her care, and affection for that family—Instead of such a return she had a right to expect the most endearing attentions, & had reason to rejoice in the society of these friends—[3]

It would give me great pleasure to see you in this Country. I hope your business will permit you to visit it this fall; I canot pretend to advise you to move to it, that you would make more money is certain, but you are comfortably situated, and notwithstanding the unpleasant feeling you and Aunt must experience for this ungrateful requital to all your kindnessess, still I see no reason why you should not rather feel a virtuous triumph from having fulfill'd more than even generosity should expect— & lament the degeneracy of human nature—Since my removal from Bayou sarah the people of W. Florida have had a meeting & framed a kind of constitution, but have not declared themselves independent unless Bounaparte should succeed in Spain—Jas. Baxter is now at this place & will start up in a few days—he came down with Goods for W. J. & Co. I expected we would have got a supply, but W. J. is not willing to make up the amt. which J & W. J. was to do for obvious reasons The goods brought are new & laid in for Cash, I find, Sir, there is not much generosity to be expected here Considering the number of Stores & the badness of our assortment we have done tolerably well here & hope we will increase our business—please give my love to aunt Jackson—

I am dear uncle yrs. affectionately

Donelson Caffery

P.S. You will hear by Cousin John [Hutchings], from my father—DC

ALS, DLC.
1. Not found.
2. On August 30, 1808, Robert Butler had married Rachel Hays. The meaning of Caffery's statement has not been established. Rachel Hays had, however, been the subject of gossip in the community at least since early 1808, when a rumor circulated that she had been seen nursing a child. Jackson traced the tale to Samuel Jackson's wife, Elizabeth, and demanded from him and others denials (see AJ to Samuel Jackson, March 10, 1808; affidavits of Robert Purdy, February 15, [John?] Boyd, March 12, Shadrack Nye, March 20, George Blakemore, Benjamin Rawlings, and Robert Williamson, March 22, 1808).
3. On this family gossip and misunderstanding, see also Isabella Vinson to AJ, below.

From Isabella Vinson

Bell Ville, Septer. 10. 1810—

Sir,

I received by mail yours of the 5. Septer[1] the subject matter of which boath surprised & astonished me as being of a much more serious nature than any thing Mrs [Caroline] Bell had communicated to me *would warant*, & indeed did I believe you had taken up a wrong Idea I should not have writen you on the subject, as I think your language entirely too harsh without your information had been more correct. Mr. [William]

Easton either misunderstood me, for I cannot think he would inten-
tionaly misrepresent the thing—This was my statement to him exactly—
in a conversation with him at my table on family disagreeaments in your
neighbourhood (no person present but my husband) Mr. Easton observed Mrs Bell had been brought in, that it had been stated Mrs Tate[2] &
Mrs Bell had had a very serious quarrel when at the springs together. I
observed it was not so that I had understood Caroline had call'd at your
house for the purpose of having some misunderstanding among the
Ladies rectifide, Say Mrs. Jackson[3] Mrs. [Mary] Deadrick Mrs. Tate &
Mrs. Bell, but that I had understood it respected Mrs. R. Butler, & not
Mrs. T. & B. that Mrs Bell had tould me she had taken a memorandom or
certificate in writing which Mrs. Jackson assented to & that Peggy
Watkins[4] I think was present, but I plege myself to you, Mrs Bell did not
either directly, or indirectly, say aney thing tending to injure the reputation of Mrs Jackson, but as I understood the thing it was not contradict-
ing what she Mrs Jackson had said but what Mrs. Deadrick *said she had
said*—be this as it may, it was in no wise injurious to the reputation of
Mrs. Jackson nor did Mrs. Bell tell me, Mrs. J had given it from under her
hand—I have writen Mrs Bell on the subject & I am confident she will
not shrink from aney inquiry you may deem it proper to make, if you
consider it worthey farther attention; I assure you I thought it of so little
importance & mearly a little feamale controversy that I did not charge
my memory as I might have done—I regret Mr. Easton has involved me
in this affair as it places me in a delicate situation where my child is in
question, but as you deem it of importance I have given you all the information I am in possession of—I am sir with Real respect Your most obet

Isabella Vinson

N.B. Will you have the goodness to give me *Parson* [Robert] *Donnol's*[5]
address—Mr. Vinson tenders you his best wishes—   I.V.

ALS, DLC. Mrs. Vinson, the widow of Edward Butler (1762–1803), had married William B. Vinson of Maryland in 1809.
   1. Not found.
   2. Not identified.
   3. Mrs. Vinson may have been referring either to Rachel Jackson or Elizabeth Catherine
Woodrow Jackson (1764–1844), wife of Samuel.
   4. Possibly Margaret Watkins, the daughter of Jacob and Sally Williams Lloyd Watkins,
who had moved from Virginia to Tennessee about 1806.
   5. Donnell was a Presbyterian revivalist, living and preaching in Tennessee at this time.

From Walter Hampden Overton

Cantonment Washington Sepr 26th 1810

Sir.
   My long absence from your part of the country & my remote situation
heretofore which debarred me from all communications, together with

that respect which I have always had for you & your good lady induces me to drop you a line. you no doubt have heard ere this of the internal commotion of East florida on the 23d the Americans declared themselves independent & on that day two hundred & fifty of them, marched & that night took possession of Baton Rouge. Killed the commanding officer a mr [Louis de] Grandpre[1] & a few Spanish Soldiers, without losing a man they are headed by a Genl [Philemon] Thomas formerly of Kentucky they also have the governor [Carlos de Hault de] Lasuse[2] in Irons. Governor [Juan Vicente] Folk[3] is now marching to meet them. In a few days we shall have the particulars of that battle it is said Folk has five hundred men you have no idea of the anxiety of the army to assist their brave countrymen in taking possesion of that Elegant part of this country, which our non energetic government long since purchased. the Governor of this territory has ordered out a part of the militia to be stationed on the line to prevent any intercourse & to obstruct the negroes from passing to the assistance of Either a part of our troops I think will be requested also, & there is but little doubt of the request being granted, as we are panting for Exercise. If you have never visited this country I think Sir it would be well worth your while as it is much the finest I have ever seen. this Sir is the place for making fortunes, I have persuaded my father much to remove here but he pays no attention to my entreaties I think were you to see this country you would move the whole neighborhood. pray Sir favor me with a scroll, present my best respects to Mrs Jackson & Believe to be with the highest Esteem, your friend & Ob Serv

W H. Overton

ALS, DLC. Published in Bassett, 1:204–205. Overton (1788–1846), a son of Thomas and a nephew of John Overton, was at this time a first lieutenant in the 7th U.S. Infantry in Mississippi Territory. Shortly before his resignation from the army in 1815, he was made brevet lieutenant colonel for his gallantry in the Battle of New Orleans.

1. Grand Pré was the son of Carlos de Grand Pré, the former commandant at Baton Rouge, 1798–1808.

2. Delasuss (1767–1842), a native of France, succeeded Grand Pré as commandant at Baton Rouge. After the fall of the fort, he left Spanish service and spent the remainder of his life as a private citizen of New Orleans.

3. Folch, a nephew of Estevan Miró, was governor of West Florida, 1796–1811.

To Edward Ward

Octbr. 26th. 1810—

Sir

I did intend on yesterday to have addressed you on the following subject, but hearing you had company declined it, the object of this letter being to make enquiry of and concerning the death of Doctor Purnells horse[1]—the causes of Suspicion of his being Poisoned—&c &c; I have therefore to request, that you will be good anough to State—at what time of the day the horse took Sick—whether before or after his mornings exercise—and whether before or after his mornings feed—had his stable a lock or how fastened, if any what appearance of any person known of visiting his stable what were the different remedies applied—and which of them and how many by and with the directions of Doctor Purnell—at what time did the Doctor first state his oppinion of his being Poisoned—whether before or after the horse was oppened—did the horse swell much, and if he did, how long after he was first taken before he did swell whether he appeared to be convulsed & at what time what was the appearance of his stomach when oppened—and the distance of time from the date of the horses being taken ill, as nigh as can be recollected, untill the time he was disected—and how long after his death—I have had a statement from Mr William Sanders and Eli Hammonds[2]—but these Gentlemen not being there when the horse was first taken nor at his death I wish to have a full statement from you—If the horse was poisoned, the villain that did it ought to & must be punished, if not that man who has been malignant anough to give rise to the idea of his being poisoned, that suspicion should light somwhere or innocence that even on a slave—deserves punishment

I was compelled to Bedford court,[3] or I should have called on you for the before information—I hope you will have the goodness to furnish me with it today[4]

I am sir yr mo. ob. serv.

Andrew Jackson

ALS copy, DLC. Published in Bassett, 2:262–63 (dated October 26, 1816).
1. For the report on the Nashville races, held on October 18 and at which Purnell's horse died, see *Democratic Clarion*, November 16. For the discussion of an earlier dispute with Purnell over horseracing, see above, James W. Camp to William Purnell, November 18, and Purnell to AJ, November 19, 1809.
2. Sanders (c1776–1846) was a lawyer in Davidson County, having been admitted to the bar in 1807. Jackson's neighbor, he later owned and operated the Fountain of Health Mineral Springs, created by the earthquakes in 1811 and 1812. Hammond, a Davidson County farmer and occasional officeholder, commanded a company of rangers in the Creek War. Neither Sanders's nor Hammond's statement has been found.
3. Jackson may have gone to the Bedford County court to appear as a witness in the Anderson-Magness civil case over land or he may have been referring to a call to appear before a grand jury hearing on the October 24 murder of Anderson.
4. Ward's response has not been found.

On October 24, 1810, on the courthouse square in Shelbyville, David Magness shot Patton Anderson, brother of Jackson's aide de camp William P., and one of Jackson's longtime business and sporting associates. With the Bedford County Circuit Court in session, a grand jury immediately indicted the three Magnesses for murder and, at the request of the defense, the court granted a change of venue to Williamson County for the trial in late November.

The trial in Franklin attracted considerable attention. A distinguished

defense and prosecution panel, including Felix Grundy, Jenkin Whiteside, John Haywood, Stockley Donelson Hays, and Thomas Hart Benton, appeared to argue the case before Judge Thomas Stuart. Numerous witnesses—more than a hundred as William Preston Anderson suggests below—were to be called. According to John Reid, who attended the trial, Jackson "deposed generally to A's character. A heart humane, honest and generous; the natural enemy of villains and scoundrels" (DLC-Reid Papers). The court found David Magness guilty of manslaughter instead of murder and sentenced him to eleven months in prison and the branding of M on the hand, but the court postponed the trials of Jonathan and Perry Green until the following May. At that time they were found innocent of the murder charges, but unable to pay court costs and attorneys' fees, they were remanded to prison where they remained for two years (Democratic Clarion, November 2, 23, 30, 1810; May 21, 1811).

Several scholars have suggested that Jackson did his utmost—in his testimony, in haranguing the crowd at a tavern in Franklin, and in assisting the prosecution—to secure the conviction of the Magnesses for murder, but documents to sustain this contention have not been found.

From William Preston Anderson

Franklin 17th. Novmr. 1810

I am more determined upon & anxious to close my business of every Nature & discription in this Country, than ever man was, under the same circumstances, before.

Besides this & my great wish always to see you, you may depend upon it that the order I shall take in the progression of this desireable object, will be first, to give Crosthwait & Keeble[1] possession of the property sold them, receive the payments & close with them—This I hope I shall be able to do next week, & but for the absolute necessity there is, that my attention & presence be given, at the trial of those villians, I should have now been with Crosthwait & Keeble. My next & 2 Second step will be to see & close all things with you—The Caldwell[2] debt shall then be paid & I have only to lament that my situation has been such heretofore as to involve you my friend, in *Duns* so disagreable—With [John F.] Clay & About Truxton[3] w'll then do every thing & I dont think it shall exceed two weeks from this day before I will make it a point to call upon & see you

I don't think I can git off from here before wednesday next—

If the trumpet of hell had been sounded & a general Jubalee pervaded the whole infurnal regions, such a lot of murderes, thieves & scoundrels, could not have appeared, as the Magness have to sware for them—

I believe there is about 40 or 50 witness on the part of the defts. & about 90 on the part of the State. They have this morning just commenced on the testimony on the part of the State—I don't altogether like the jury—Grundy & Hays was guilty of a most ungentlemanlike & in fact rascally act in packing some of them. Mr H. Can tell you how things appear to move on.

Give not only my best respts. to Mrs Jackson & the little son but my love to them also. yr friend

W P Anderson

ALS, DLC.
1. Not identified.
2. Not identified.
3. Truxton occasionally stood at stud on Clay's farm.

From Donelson Caffery

Natchez Decembr. 5. 1810

Dear Uncle:

In my last I inform'd you I should be up by the middle of January,[1] but am apprehensive will not be able so soon to see you Altho nothing would give me more pleasure, yet when my Country calls I feel bound to obey— A detachment of the U. States Troops, under Command of Colo. [Leonard] Covington,[2] saild from this on 3rd. Inst—The remainder, now at Camp Washington, I believe the 3rd. Regiment under Command of Colo. [Zebulon Montgomery] Pike will leave this in a day or two[3]—No doubt their destination is to take possession of West Florida—It is said Govonor Claiborne, who left this a few days ago, has orderd out the Militia of the Orleans Territory And, it is expected a Detachment from this Territory will receive orders to march in a few days—In which case, I shall go, If my health will possibly permit. If reports are true there will be some difficulty in taking the Forts of Mobile & Pensacola, Tis said they are in a good state of defence & all fill'd with Troops—that Governor Folch is at Mobile, expecting to receive a reinforcement from the Havannah—A Detachment, from Bayou Sarah said to be 1500 men march'd on 24th. ult. for Pensacola—

By last mail I rec'd letters from Cousin Sandy & Mr. Eastin, in which they mention'd, Mr. Jno. Hutchings was to be married to Miss Polly Smith; I guess from the time mention'd, 'twill not be far from the Date of my letter, I wish them much happiness—Cousin Sandy informs me you are determin'd to move to this Country,[4] I will not pretend to advise you, but persist in the opinion I have before express'd, that were I, in your situation would not move—You have nearly got through all your embarrassments, you have a delightful farm, from the produce of which you will at least be able to live comfortably; by the respectable & well inform'd part of the Country you are highly esteem'd; you are able to select a good society from yr. neighborhood. You have been able there to read the Characters of men & In their actions; here another volume will be presented to your view in which human baseness will take up a considerable part—I have lately turnd a leaf, altho the characters were a little wrrap'd in mystery, yet they wore a dark, and doubtful aspect—I cannot as yet form an opinion—Please give my most dutiful respects to Aunt— & believe me dear Uncle Yr. most affectionate Nephew

Donelson Caffery

ALS, DLC. Extract published in Bassett, 1:201.
1. Letter not found.
2. Covington (d. 1813), from Maryland, was colonel of the U.S. Light Dragoons.
3. Pike was at this time a lieutenant colonel with the 4th Infantry instead of the 3rd.
4. On Jackson's consideration of moving from Tennessee, see also Wade Hampton to AJ, December 9, below.

From Wade Hampton

Mouth of Elk 9th. Dec. 1810

Dear Sir

As I am fearful my Horses in your hands may not arrive in time to go down with my own, I will beg the favor of you to make the most of them. I am sure you will with them as you would with your own, and be pleased to request Capt. Brahan to do the same with the Dragon. I am vastly partial to your eligant seat & fine tract of land, but my face is turned the wrong course for purchases. In truth my thoughts are very much occupied with the objects of my journey, altho perhaps to much less account—

I see I must come and give you all a *lesson* or I shall loose my credit as a sportsman—

very truly & respectfully yrs.

W. Hampton

I am off in half an hour.

ALS, DLC. Published in Bassett, 1:205

From William Purnell

Haysborough, Dec. 14th, 1810

Sir,

Believing as I do that no gentleman will injure the feelings & reputation of another without remunerating him to the injury sustained on being convinced of the error into which he from precipitancy, has been led; and being willing to believe you, sir not divested of the finer feelings of a gentleman, I hisitate not to appeal to your honor to retract the anathemas that you on the 10th ult. in the race field near Nashville pronounced against me for having said that which I positively declare I never had uttered to any person living—namely that your man Dinwiddie poisoned my stud horse Dean-Swift,[1] nor can any person have the hardihood to assert any such thing in my presence—If I am correctly informed your author was Col. William Donelson, his informant was his carpenter and that Mr. James Mitchell, (carpenter)[2] informed him that I had said that your man Dinwiddie poisoned my stud horse Dean Swift—I do now positively assert that I never have interchanged a word or words with said Mitchell on the subject of the death of my stud until Monday the 10th inst and then only to know whether or not he had asserted that I had informed him any thing relative to the death of my stud and he positively declared that he never had informed any person that he ever heard me say any thing on the above subject as will appear from the annexed certificate.

I feel such confidence that you will do that justice to my character that it so imperiously demands and in so doing you will be entitled to the respect of yours,

Wm. Purnell.

Text from *Tennessee Gazette*, December 21, 1810. Original not found.
 1. On the death of Purnell's horse, see also above, AJ to Edward Ward, October 26.
 2. Not further identified.

ENCLOSURE: AFFIDAVIT OF JAMES MITCHELL

Being called on, on Monday the 10th inst by Doctor William Purnell to know whether or not I had ever heard him say that General Andrew Jacksons man Dinwiddie poisoned his stud horse Dean-Swift.

I do hereby certify that I never did hear Doctor Purnell say or that he should have said any thing directly or indirectly tending to accuse any person whatsoever of having poisoned his stud horse Dean-Swift.

James Mitchell.

Text from *Tennessee Gazette*, December 21. Original not found.

1811

From Willie Blount

Knoxville Feby 26th. 1811

Dear Sir,

I have this winter urged the necessity, expediency &c. of the United States inviting the Southern Indians to settle west of the Mississippi & have endeavored to shew that the doing so will promote the interest of the Government & better the condition of the Indians[1]—it is as clear to my mind as that two and two make four—I hope we shall have a free communication with Mobile—the government have undertaken to represent to the Creeks the propriety of our having the use of such ways thro' their country—the hope is entertained that Mobile will be given up without any difficulty—Col. [Charles] McClung[2] has just returned from that country and says its a good one—I see that a new Bill has been introduced in Senate for returning the charter to the United States Bank notwithstanding the other House had just before rejected a Bill for the same purpose[3]—money matters have many laborers in their train. A new French Minister has arrived at Washington[4] & its probable we shall soon see a number of dear Sir letters passed between him & our Secy of State the one expressing very great sincerity of attachment for the American people & the other doubting the fact—we should mind our own business & be no longer amused by France & England—let them get to heaven their own way—have heard nothing of Genl. Wilkinson's trial of late except that he is writing a book with the hope of washing away his sins[5]— he will have hard work to effect his purpose—I am with regard, yours

Willie Blount

McKee is in the employ of the United States at Mobile & I understand that he stands well with the heads of department. God never made a better man than John McKee[6]—I don't know who will offer here for Congress when [Pleasant Moorman] Miller's time expires[7]—Judge [Hugh Lawson] White[8] & W[illiam] G[rainger] Blount are well—

ALS, TNJ.
1. In his address to the legislature on October 15, 1809, Blount had suggested that "if the United States will extinguish the Indian claim at the expense of the general government, and

give the Cherokees in exchange for their claims; lands on the western side of the Mississippi, happy consequences would result to the United States, to Tennessee, and to the Indians—and if so they could afford this state a reasonable time of indulgence to reimburse to them the expenditures." Between the time of adjournment of the 8th General Assembly and the convening of the 9th in September 1811, Blount continued to explore the matter of Indian removal (Robert H. White, *Messages of the Governors of Tennessee*, Nashville, 1952, 1:286, 316).

2. McClung (1761–1835), a native of Philadelphia, had settled in Knoxville, where he was a merchant, lawyer, and land speculator. Clerk of the Knox County Court, 1792–1834, he had also been a delegate to the Tennessee constitutional convention in 1796.

3. The bill for rechartering the first Bank of the United States, the original charter of which was to expire on March 4, failed to pass.

4. Comte Louis Barbe Charles Serurier (b. 1775), French envoy to the United States, 1811–16, 1831–35.

5. James Wilkinson, *Memoirs of General Wilkinson* (Washington, 1811).

6. McKee was agent to the Choctaws in eastern Mississippi, 1802–16.

7. John Sevier succeeded Miller.

8. White, Jackson's colleague on the bench from 1801, continued to serve as a judge of the superior court and its successor, the Tennessee supreme court, until 1815.

To William Eustis

Hermitage near Nashville May 10th. 1811—

Sir

I have Just recd. the enclosed from the officers of the Volunteer corps of infantry of the Town of Nashville soliciting me to write you on the subject of arms[1]

This is a corps of respectable Merchants and Mecanicks, whose military Pride will prompt them on to acquire a knowledge of tactics and discipline[2]—and I have no doubt but in a short space of time, they will be able to vie in the field with the oldest veterans—provided they can obtain arms *proper* for field exercise

In this state we have no such thing as musketts indeed the Legislature of this state has shamefully neglected their duty in this respect—and in every other respect as it relates to a well organised militia—There are a number of stand of arms at High wasie—and I am told in a bad state— Would it not then be well to make a deposit of sixty stand of Musketts in the hands of Capt. [William] Carrol—Lt. [Joshua] Paxton and Ensign [Wilkins] Tannehill,[3] these officers are gentlemen of Property and standing in society, and in whom confidence may be placed that the arms will be well taken care of, and faithfully delivered to any agent of the united States on demand—and from Nashville the arms can find a speedy and safe convayence to any point southwestward; should the united States have a call for them in that quarter—and I will vouch for this corps (should their country call) that they will make as good a use of those arms as any other corps belonging to the army of the united States—and that they may be counted on with certainty in case of any emergency— and *in the hour* of *danger.* Wishing to augment the military ardor of the

militia of this quarter, (which appears to Slumber) I would be much gratified, in this corps being furnished with the musketts—their appearencee
in the field would act as a stimulent to others and in a short time we
might have several well trained corps ready for the field—If therefore it is
consistant with your powers—I have no doubt from your military charactor that the request of the Volunteer corps of infantry of Nashville will
be granted, and that you will enclose me an order to the proper officers to
deliver to capt. Carrol &c &c—the sixty stand of Musketts &c &c the
Gentlemen applying for them giving security that the shall be kept in
good order & safely returned to the order of the united States when demanded—on these terms they arms will be thankfully received—

Altho not personally known to you—the subject of this letter will in
itself be a sufficient apology for the intrusion—particularly, when the
clouds of war appear to be hovering around us—[4]

I am Sir with due respect yr mo. ob. Serv.

Andrew Jackson

ALS, DNA-RG 107. Published in Bassett, 1:205–206. Eustis served as secretary of war, 1809–13.

1. See William Carroll, Joshua Paxton, and Wilkins Tannehill to AJ, May 8.

2. Jackson was seeking arms for the Republican Blues, the independent company authorized by the General Assembly in 1807 who became Jackson's guards on the Natchez
expedition.

3. Tannehill (1787–1858; College of Pittsburgh), a native of Pennsylvania, had served an
apprenticeship at the Saline Salt Works in southern Illinois before he settled in Nashville in
1810, where he first managed a salt warehouse. Shortly, he opened grocery stores, served as
cashier and president of the Bank of Nashville, and held office as mayor. By 1820, he turned
more and more to writing and the publishing of newspapers, books, and journals. Paxton
has not been further identified.

4. For Eustis's pledge of muskets, see Eustis to AJ, May 29.

*In the fall of 1810 Jackson, Joseph Coleman (d. 1819), former mayor of
Nashville, 1806–1808, and Horace Green, probably a native of Natchez,
formed a partnership to market Tennessee cotton and tobacco in New
Orleans. Green successfully managed one shipment in the spring of 1811
and returned to Nashville in May. Shortly, Green left with another shipment for the firm, a group of slaves which had been recently purchased
from Richard Apperson, a tavern operator from Mecklenburg County,
Va. Finding the Natchez market glutted, he subsequently abandoned the
slaves and the partnership, and John Hutchings, Jackson's former business partner then living in Port Gibson, took the slaves to his plantation.*

*In December Jackson went to Natchez and Port Gibson to salvage the
investment. He bought out Green's interest in the business but, realizing
only token success in his effort to sell the slaves, he decided to return them
to his farm in Davidson County. En route through the Indian country*

with twenty-six slaves, he ran afoul of the Choctaw agent, Silas Dinsmoor (1766–1847; Dartmouth College 1791), who demanded strict obedience to the Indian intercourse acts which required passports for all
travelers. Jackson defied Dinsmoor's authority, proceeded without passport, and, upon reaching the Hermitage, began immediately to demand
Dinsmoor's removal.

The Dinsmoor affair and, to an even greater extent, Jackson's involvement in Coleman, Green & Jackson became issues in the 1828 presidential campaign. Shortly before the election, Andrew Erwin, a resident
of Bedford County with whom Jackson was locked in litigation over land
deals from 1814 to 1824, publicized Jackson as one who had been "traf-
ficking in human flesh." Erwin claimed to have seen one of Jackson's account books in the offices of the Nashville Bank which confirmed his involvement in "negro trading" and established beyond doubt that Jackson
was a full partner in the firm.

Jackson denied the charge, and Jacksonian newspapers immediately
published the document below, suggesting that he was a silent and inactive partner in the firm, who merely provided security for Coleman and
Green. But Jackson's letter to an unidentified arbitrator involved in settling his account with Green (see February 29, 1812, below), suggests
otherwise. From the extant documents, it is difficult to determine whether
Erwin's allegations or the Jacksonian rebuttal more accurately reflected
the true nature and extent of Jackson's role in the firm (Andrew Erwin,
Gen. Jackson's Negro Speculations, and his traffic in Human Flesh, Examined and Established by Positive Proof, [n.p., 1828]; A Brief Account
of General Jackson's Dealing in Negroes . . . , New York, 1828).

Memorandum re Purchase of Slaves
from Richard Apperson
and Cotton and Tobacco from Bennett Smith

May 18th, 1811.

Note—The said Andrew Jackson has no interest in the purchase from
R. Apperson of the negroes, or cotton and Tobacco from Bennet Smith,
he only holds a lien on them for the payment of the purchase money, for
which he is bound as security, for Jos. Coleman.[1] Signed,

ANDREW JACKSON.

Text from *Nashville Republican*, July 11, 1828. Original not found. The agreement, on
which the above was said to be an endorsement, has not been found.

1. An endorsement in Jackson's hand on his account book with the Bank of Nashville
suggests that Jackson's involvement in the purchases of Negroes, cotton, and tobacco may
have been more than simply that of providing security. The endorsement reads: "A Jackson
amount of proportion of cash for negroes Bott of Richd Epperrson $929[.]45 J Coleman is

to pay the note in bank for interest on purchase of Cotton from B Smith for $613.39 and the sum of $191 1/3 which he is to pay & the sum of 125 makes up his proportion—A. Jackson has paid for keel Boat—$50. To Capt Witherall discount this 20th. of Novbr. 1811 on the Bill remitted W. Jackson & Co on Jas. Jackson & Co. $14.51 & also $16 on note endorsed by J. H. Smith—Note provisions furnished cotton Boat 500 lb pork & flower and meal in all $17.50." See also promissory notes to Richard Apperson, May 18.

From Robert Purdy

Fort Hampton May 28th. 1811

Dear Genl.

On the 22d Instant Col. [Alexander] Smythe[1] arrived at this place, and remained untill the 24th. during his stay here, he issued sundry orders, in one of which he orders me to proceed as soon as possible to Cantonment Washington, with the Infantry at this post—I have reason to think he has a great deal of power given him by Genl. Hampton, and am of the opinion he may possibly dictate a letter to the Genl.

In two weeks from this time, I hope to be able, to set sail, being now imployed in repairing boats &c. This arrangment is not a pleasant one to me, as the warm weather is about to commence. however we thats bound, must obey, *even the whims of others*—Genl. Hampton in a memorandom resquests that you send his colts to Mr. [James] Lyons near South West Point, and observes that Capt. Brahan will pay all expences, who will also send a horse that he has in his possession to the same place. I shall write Capt. Brahan on the subject—Lieut. Colo. [Richard] Sparks is honorably acquitted by the court. Colo. [Thomas Humphrey] Cushing was *put to his plea, guilty* or not *guilty*. He answered not *guilty*, and hope not *suspected by any honest men*.[2] Colo. Cushing made oath that he could not have Justice done without the depositions of Majr. [John] Fuller and Capt. [Mossman] Houston.[3] The court then adjourned untill the first of December then to convene again at Baton Rouge—I think it more than probable I shall have the command at Washington Cantonment, from which place I shall write you, and give you a correct statement of the Situation of the troops &c at that place. god send that I may have the pleasure of seeing General Andrew Jackson in that nation. We would finish a bottle or two of clarrett, before we parted. Mrs. Purdy Joines me in best wishes for the health and happiness of Mrs. Jackson, and yourself, please tender our best respects to Colo. Hays, and family, Robt. Butler, and family John Hutchings and Lady, as well as all friends farewell

Rob. Purdy

The pen is bad

ALS, DLC.
1. Smyth was colonel commandant of the regiment of riflemen in the U.S. Army, 1808–12.
2. Both cases grew out of the movement into Mobile and West Florida. Sparks (c1760–

1815), a native of Pennsylvania and the son-in-law of John Sevier, was a career army officer, serving largely on the southwest frontier after 1792. A court martial in April acquitted Sparks of "unofficerlike and disgraceful conduct." He remained under arrest, however, until December 5 when the secretary of war ordered his release. Cushing (d. 1822), from Massachusetts, had served in the Continental Army and as inspector of the army, 1797–98. He was under arrest by April 4 and charges (not determined) had been preferred against him in early May. The outcome of his case has not been determined. Promoted to brigadier general in 1812, he was discharged three years later.

3. Fuller (d. 1839), from Vermont and a major in the rifle corps, resigned from the army in 1812. Houston, from Georgia, was a captain in the 3rd U.S. Infantry. He resigned from service in 1810, was recommissioned as major in 1812, and left the army again as lieutenant colonel in mid-1813.

From Thomas Augustine Claiborne

Natchez June 26th. 1811

My dear Sir,

The intimate acquaintance which I had the satisfaction to maintain with you during my residence in Tennessee renders it unnecessary for [me to] offer an apology for obtruding on your notice, the particulars of a recent affair of honor, in which I officiated as Surgeon to one of the gentlemen engaged. Indeed it so frequently happens on such occasions that facts are mistated, either with, or without, an intention of producing an improper impression, that I feel particularly anxious, that you should know the circumstances from one who witnessed them precisely as they occured—[During the] late election contest; the most violent struggle was made to prevent the reelection of George Poindexter Esquire, as our representative in the Congress of the United States. The means imployed by the federalists, were deemed by Mr. Poindexter to be of a personal nature highly indecorous & insulting to his feelings—Among those who were most active & vigilant in the circulation of hand bills, to promote the views of the federal party & the election of Robert Williams, was Abijah Hunt Esquire merchant of Natchez.[1] The Election resulted in favour of Mr. Poindexter by a majority of 1346 Votes—This part of the drama, was followed by an immediate demand, of Mr Hunt, to come to an eclaircissement on the field of honor, with Mr Poindexter, for the personal injuries & insults which he believed he had sustained from Mr Hunt, during the canvass. The invitation was accepted; & the parties met on the western margin of the Mississippi, on Friday the 7th. Instant. Wm. C Mead Esq. late an officer in the army of the United States & Lieutenant James [R.] Peyton[2] were the friends of Mr. Poindexter & I at his particular request attended him as Surgeon. E[benezer] Bradish & Elijah Smith Esquires[3] were the friends of Mr Hunt, and Doctor [Stephen] Duncan[4] attended him in the character of Surgeon—At four oclock the parties took their posts, at the distance of ten paces, and at the first exchange of fire; Mr Hunt received the Ball of his Antagonist through the Abdomen of which wound he expired, on the Sunday Evening following. It is due to

Mr. Poindexter to remark, that from the commencement, to the close of this unfortunate affair, he behaved with the greatest coolness and composure, and observed the strictest attention to etiquette and the principles of honor—[5]

It will afford me much pleasure to hear from you, when your leisure will permit, and I shall take equal pleasure, in communicating to you, the interesting events which may occur in this Country—Make if you please my best respects acceptable to Your amiable Lady—and accept Sir for yourself the assurances of my perfect esteem & consideration

Thos. A. Claiborne

ALS, DLC. Extract published in Bassett, 1:207–208 (dated November 26).

1. Hunt, a native of New Jersey, had first gone to Ohio and later moved to Mississippi Territory, where he was a merchant with establishments in Natchez, Washington, Greenville, Port Gibson, and Big Black.

2. Mead, a native of Georgia, had resigned his commission as first lieutenant on January 1, 1810. In September 1811, Ferdinand L. Claiborne, recently named brigadier general of the Mississippi Territory militia, appointed Mead as his aide. He served as Poindexter's second in the duel. Peyton (d. 1812), a native of Virginia, was at this time a lieutenant with the 1st Infantry.

3. Bradish was a native of Massachusetts and a former infantry lieutenant. Smith was a resident of Natchez and later a judge in Mississippi.

4. Duncan was later president of the Bank of Mississippi.

5. For documents recounting the duel, see J.F.H. Claiborne, *Mississippi as a Province, Territory, and State* (Spartanburg, S.C., 1978 reprint), pp. 371–73.

From Anthony Butler

Russelville Sep. 28. 1811

My dear General,

Our neighbourhood is crowded with race horses, and all circumstances concur in promising us handsome sport on the first Wednesday in October: You must not fail to visit on that occasion, and bring with you all the Turf nags that you have; Stables are provided for you at my house, and as I live in Russelville at present, we can attend the Turf with more convenience than on last Year.

The Gentleman who will hand you this Letter is Mr [James] Ogilvie[1] of Virginia, a Gentleman of Taste, Talents, and great literary reputation. He is on a visit at present in the Western Country and takes Nashville in the Route. You have no doubt seen his name frequently mentioned in our Newspapers to the Eastward during the last 12 months with great eclat as the author of certain Orations on various subjects which he has been delivering throughout the U. States; You cannot but be pleased with him; I therefore give him this letter to you with the more pleasure, and bespeak for him, all your civility and attention which you so well know how to make acceptable, to a stranger. It is very probable he may desire to deliver some orations at Nashville, but may wish at the same time to do so, at the request of some of yourselves, in this case I know you will assist him to make the commencement. Introduce him to such of our friends as you think he ought to know. Mrs. Butler[2] begs to be presented to Mrs. Jackson, and to say that she will expect her with you on or before the first Wednesday in October. At that time we shall expect to see you without question, and till then assure yourself of my perfect Esteem.

A: Butler

ALS, TNJ. Butler (1787–1849), a lawyer from South Carolina whom Thomas Sumter had introduced to Jackson in March 1807, settled in Russellville, Ky., later that year. Following service as a colonel in the War of 1812, he sat in the Kentucky legislature, 1818–19, and ran an unsuccessful campaign for governor in 1820, whereupon he moved to Mississippi. In 1829 Jackson appointed him U.S. minister to Mexico and authorized him to purchase Texas. Failing in this, he attempted bribery, which resulted in a demand for his recall. At that time, he settled in Texas, taking an active part in Texas politics.
  1. Ogilvie, born in Scotland, was a public lecturer.
  2. Not identified.

From Alexander Donelson

Twickenham October 9th. 1811

Dear Uncle

Your favor, by Colo. [William?] Ward of the 6th. of August[1] I received previous to my going to the Tombigbee: and should have wrote you then, only for the very short notice, I had, to get, in readiness, to set out with the Colo. and his Company, as I was not apprised of their going untill they had arrived in Twickenham.[2] I had designed going a different rout, (that is) to have crossed the Tennessee river opposite this; and to have pursued nearly a South course to the waters of the Tombigbee, and to have continued down, on the East side of sd. river to St. Stephens. But being dissuaded from this by all my friends here, I concluded probably it was safest to keep the Beaten tract, and with about 18 or 20 in company we set out from Twickenham on the 13th. of August in all appearance for a 6 months Campaign, which had like to have been realised, for it was 15 or 16 days before we arrived at the first settlements, when our provisions were nearly exhausted, & the whiskey quite out—some of our thirsty souls began to be much alarmed, least that dreary looking country might not afford this forced necessary of life, in such abundance as they could wish. I am much pleased with a great proportion of that country. The present settlements I think much the least desireable. But immediately above commences the richest country of lands I see, which continues almost to the source of the Tombigbee, and in many parts finely watered, which combined with a most salubrious and healthful atmosphere, and a climate that is so congenial to the culture of every article that can give Luxury and Wealth to any Country, and a river of the easiest navigation of any other in the world—makes this (I have no hesitation in saying) the most desireable country I have ever seen, if settled by civilized people.

I left in that country your old friend Colo. McClung, his Brother Hugh & Mr. Williams[3] industriously exploring every part of the Country. The Colo. was some what disappointed at this sale, owing to the country on the East side of the river, not being prepared for sale, in which he designs settling. This part it is supposed will be offered for sale in the course of 10 or 12 months, and by such time there will be a road opened the nearest rout to the upper end of the Shoals—and perhaps you can then make it convenient to visit that country—if you continue in the notion of moving, I think you would be pleased with it.[4] Society is in a most miserable condition in that country—nothing but Jealousy, slander, & envy—the most of the inhabitants having lately emigrated there for the purpose of becoming polititians, each is endevouring to aggrandise himself on the rouins of the other. The Town of mobile was daily expected to be delivered to the United States. My love to aunt, I am Yours Sincerely

Alex. Donelson

ALS, DLC.
1. Letter not found. Ward (d. 1836), a Kentuckian and a brother-in-law of Richard Mentor Johnson was traveling around Mississippi Territory at this time, acquiring land for speculation.
2. The early name for Huntsville, Ala. President Madison had recently directed the transfer of the land office for northern Alabama from Nashville to Huntsville.
3. Neither further identified.
4. On Jackson's earlier consideration of a move to Madison County, see above, Jenkin Whiteside to AJ, January 26, and AJ to Whiteside, February 10, 1810.

From Anthony Butler

Russelville. 12 Oct. 1811

My dear General
By the last mail I had the pleasure of receiving your favor of the 2d instt.[1] and shall hope to hear from you again in a day or two by Mr. Ogilvie whose furlough from this place will by that time have expired, and we are all very anxious to have him at his post. I hope Nashville has profited of his visit [since] such characters visit us, but seldom; I shall endeavour to detain him here till your arrival at our races, which commence on the first Wednesday, in November and not October as you say my last letter expressed,[2] it was my mistake.

If I can possibly get over to your purse & sweepstake I shall certainly do so but my situation is at this time so peculiar that it is impossible to say when I shall be at leisure for a week at a time—I have stables ready for you, and shall expect you to bring us some good Nags; let them be the best you can lay your hands upon. I have three training but suspect I shall do but badly in the business.

All our members of Congress are off and I presume Mr. Madison's first bulletin will be the most important state paper since the Declarati[on] of Independence: much will depend n[o] doubt upon whether old George[3] is alive or dea[d] at the last period of our information, for if he lives Mr. *Jean Bull* will shake his horns & perhaps attempt to run a muck at us— for this we are not completely prepared to be sure but I trust in God that we shall notwithstanding make a respectable stand. I like the election of Geo. W. Campbell because I think he is good Game, and will take the pit freely. The first word that is said will let me into what is intended, for we have no alternative between War, submission & perpetual embargo—and as no American *can or dare submit*; War or Embargo is the question. I think a little blood-letting would relieve the system and therefore at present I should prefer hearing that the *Guerrier* & *President* had been along-side;[4] but whatever our private opinions we must still hear what is said by the Wise men in the East. By the time we meet it is likely something may transpire to give a clue to the ultimatum.

Present Mrs. Butler & myself to Mrs. Jackson most respectfully, we have a snug little room ready for you. I must see you at Russelville on the first Wednesday in November. In the mean time and at all times believe me your very sincere friend

A: Butler

ALS, DLC.
1. Not found.
2. See above, Butler to AJ, September 28.
3. George III (1738–1820).
4. The *Guerrière* was a British frigate; the *President* a U.S. frigate. Action involving the two had taken place in May. The *Guerrière* had impressed an American sailor from a coasting vessel; in retaliation, the *President* a few days later fired on what was believed to be the *Guerrière*, but was instead a British sloop-of-war, *Little Belt*. The naval skirmish resulted in nine British seamen killed and twenty-three wounded.

From Donelson Caffery

Carlin Settlement. Parish St. mary's
Attakapas October 23rd 1811

Dear Uncle

I had the pleasure of receiving yours of Septr. 1st.[1] It gives me the most heart felt satisfaction my dear Sir to hear that you, Aunt and our friends enjoy good health, for my part I have the greatest reason to be thankful, for I have better health than I have enjoyed at this season for several years, although it has been sickly in the neighborhood, but very few deaths and the Country generally cannot be said to be sickly by any means—As to a probability of your having health in this Country you can be the better Judge when you visit it. I am in hopes your business will permit that this fall. If Cousin S. Hays & Mr. Wm. [Edward] Butler[2] have still a thought of moving to the lower Country I would advise them to come with you; I really think there is a good opening at present for both professions—I have not yet been to the Bay As soon as I do, will give you as good a description of it as I will be able—I intend to go to the Attakapas Church in a few days, when there, will make enquiry respecting Doctor Jno. Sappington from what I can learn here there is not much prospect of geting any thing out of him[3]—Cousin Jno. Hutchings inclosed an a/c to me agst. Reevs.[4]—I have spoken to him respecting it when I had not the a/c with me and have since been to see him but he was absent, as soon as I see him again will present the a/c he acknowledged he owed something, he is very much embarrassed but tis said he does not refuse paying his old debts as far as he is able—The boy of Mr. K[inchen T.] Wilkinsons[5] has had the ague & fever for some time so that I could not offer him for sale, but will take him to the Church with me—Our Crop of Cotton is as good as could be expected, we will make I suppose about fifty bales—the price I fear will be very low. I intend geting into the seed of Sugar Cane this fall. Cane planted this fall if good will produce six to one next year, I will plant about three acres this fall, in the second fall will have a full crop—I am told only midling cane will produce 1500 lbs. Sugar to the acre and in forty days some say only 25. Sixty Hogsheads of Sugar can be manufactured by twenty five hands the Culture is attended with about as much labor as the Culture of Corn and much less than Cotton—a profit of 50/ ℔ Ct may be calculated on the Capital employed—for besides the 1500 lbs. Sugar there is the Taffia and molasses—Land could be got here now on pretty good terms—I intend going over to my mothers as soon as possible—I recd. the paper inclosed in your letter but fear nothing can be done—I have employed an overseer to set in at January; cannot leave this untill that time, but have written to my mother to buy what property she will be obliged to Keep and that I will assist her in paying for it.[6] Whenever your leisure will permit, I will be much gratified my dear Uncle you would write—and direct to Carlin Settlement St. Mary's Parish—You will please give my sincere love and respects to Aunt Jackson: and other friends and relations who may enquire [for] me—

I remain dear Sir yr. affectionate nephew

Donelson Caffery

ALS, DLC.
1. Not found.
2. Butler (1789–1882; Transylvania University 1812), son of Thomas, studied medicine and served as surgeon with Jackson in the New Orleans campaign. In 1811, he married Martha Thompson (Patsy) Hays, sister of Stockley Donelson Hays, and on the same day Stockley Donelson Hays married Butler's sister, Lydia. Following the War of 1812, William Edward and Patsy settled in Jackson.

3. The source of Sappington's indebtedness to Jackson has not been determined.

4. Not identified.

5. Wilkinson (d. 1817) was a physician practicing in Haysboro, a settlement north of Nashville on the Gallatin Pike. The slave mentioned may have been among those taken to Natchez by Horace Green.

6. Apparently, he was urging his mother to purchase necessities from the estate sale of his father, John Caffery, who had recently died.

To William Henry Harrison

Hermitage 28th. November 1811—

With deep and heart felt regret, I received the information of the loss you sustained, on the morning of the seventh instant, by the attack of the Indians upon your encampment[1]—upon the receipt of this information, and hearing that you were slowly retreating I issued orders to my respective Brigades; to hold themselves in readiness to march to your support, in case the safety of your frontier, and your request, might make it necessary and proper.[2]

Should the aid of part of my division, be necessary to enable you, to revenge the blood of our brave heroes, who fell by the deceitfull hands, of those unrelenting barbarians—I will with pleasure march with five hundred or one thousand brave Tennesseeans. The *blood* of *our murdered Countrymen must be revenged*—That banditti, ought to be swept from the face of the earth—I do hope that government will see that it is necessary to act efficiently, and that this hostile band, which must be excited to war, by the secret agents of great Britain, must be destroyed. Should my services, be necessary to your safety; and that of your Country, by notifying me thereof, and at what point I can meet with supplies, I will have the number required at a short day at the appointed place—

Being called by imperious business from home for a short time, I have directed my aids Major Anderson and Major Coffee,[3] to attend at Nashville, receive letters to my address, and should you require men; to have them ready and prepared to march at my return[4]—you will please address me at Nashville—[5]

Accept assurances of my esteem & respect,

Andrew Jackson
Major General 2 Division
Tennessee

LS, DNA-RG 107; ALS copy, DLC. Published in Bassett, 1:210 (dated November 30).

1. Jackson was referring to the Battle of Tippecanoe. Although his men sustained heavy losses in the battle on November 7, Harrison and his forces drove back the Indians and destroyed their village, whereupon they withdrew to Fort Harrison.

2. See AJ to the Brigadier Generals of the 2nd Division, November 28.

3. In his orders to the brigadier generals of the 2nd Division, November 28, Jackson announced the appointment of John Coffee in place of Robert Purdy, resigned. Coffee served as Jackson's aide until late 1812.

4. Jackson was about to depart for Natchez to reclaim the slaves taken down by Horace Green. For his instructions to Coffee, see AJ to Coffee, [November 29].

5. On December 11, Harrison forwarded to Secretary of War Eustis Jackson's letter "to shew you to what a pitch the Spirit of the Western Country has risen . . . General Jackson (the writer)," Harrison concluded, "bears a high Character as a Soldier & a Patriot" (DNA-RG 107).

From Felix Grundy

Washington City, Nover 28th 1811

Dear Genrl,

It is now late at night and I have Just returned from a meeting of the Committee on our Foreign Relations, of which I am a member. If the opinion of that Committee is to prevail I may say, The Ruebicon is pass'd—With a full determination to report in favor of actual War at a given period, we for the present, shall recommend, filling up the ranks of the present military establishment, which will make ten thousand; in addition we recommend, the raising ten thousand more regulars, also the acceptance of 50,000 Volunteers, detachments of the Militia &c arming the Merchantmen &c The above, I am authorised to say meets fully the approbation of the Executive, and indeed the cooperation of that department in ulterior measures was promised, before a Majority of the Committee could be brought to so mild a Course, and, sir, I must say that I as one member wanted a pledge as to the application of the force before I could heartily Join in raising it—and still, I could not think of War untill I saw something like the means provided—Rely on one thing; we have War or Honorable peace before we adjourn or certain great personages have produced a state of things which will bring them down from their high places, If there be honest men enough to tell the truth loudly.

On the business named in Yr. letter[1] you shall hear from me next week—at present my account would not be satisfactory—The contents of this may be no secret—but it is not written for publication—I am yrs

F Grundy

PS. As to young men in my District who ought to be applied for as proper persons for appointments in the Regular service, you know I am at a loss—Young B[e]d[ford] lives with Elihu S Hall, I have forgotten the christian name of,[2] let me know it. I believe, John is the name of the Mr. Reed who acts as clerk in the Bank.[3] If wrong put this right—An[d] give me any further informed in yr power— F. Gr

ALS, DLC. Published in Bassett, 1:208. Grundy entered upon his first term in the House of Representatives in March 1811.

1. Not found.

2. Hall (d. 1830) was a justice of the peace in Davidson County and prominent supporter of Nashville's educational institutions. Bedford was probably one of the sons of Thomas Bedford.

3. Reid (1784–1816), a lawyer from Virginia, had moved to Rutherford County in 1807 and two years later established a practice in Williamson County. He served Jackson as aide, companion, and confidant in the Creek War and on the New Orleans campaign. In 1815, he began a biography of Jackson, which John Henry Eaton completed.

From Willie Blount

KNOXVILLE Dec. 4. 1811.

DEAR SIR,

YOURS of the 28th, Nov.[1] I did not receive until the return mail had gone out, otherwise you, would have been answered by that mail.

Your tender of individual service, and offer of aid from your division of militia to Gov. Harrison, meets my entire and most hearty approbation[2]—such tender is highly honorable and patriotic in you, and in those, who propose to accompany you—If Gov. Harrison, accepts your tender of service, and of support, he will doubtless point out to you how you may be supplied with provisions on your march.

A voluntary offer of service in time of need and danger bespeaks love of country, and shews patriotism in highest terms, and it affords me satisfaction to receive from you information of the readiness of yourself, and of part of your division, to volunteer your services in defence of our common country against the attack of a savage foe.

If you march, you have my best wishes for success, & I entertain no doubt, but you, and your men, will act in a manner becoming yourselves, much to the credit of Tennessee, and for the benefit and glory of our country.

I much regret the death of our worthy friend Col. [Joseph Hamilton] Daviess,[3] but he will live in the memory of his countrymen, for whom he has died, in a manner becoming the soldier.

If you march I hope you will purge the camps of the Indians of every Englishmen to be found there in opposition to the forces of the U.S. and also bring the Indians to their proper senses.

The invincible Greys, and Captain Carrols company of Infantry, will I have no doubt, act like themselves, and shew to the world, that they deserve well of their country—with best hopes for you success, I have the honor to be with highest respect and esteem.

Your Obt. Servant,

WILLIE BLOUNT.

Text from *Knoxville Gazette*, December 30. Original not found.
1. Jackson had forwarded to Blount copies of his letter to Harrison and orders to the brigadier generals of the 2nd Division, November 28. His covering letter has not been found.
2. See above, AJ to Harrison, November 28.
3. Wounded at Tippecanoe, Daveiss died on November 8.

To Rachel Jackson

Natchez Decbr 17th. 1811.

My Love—
on last evening I reached this place after a detention of two days at
Mr A[braham] Greens near Gibson Port by the loss of my horses—on
tomorrow I shall set out from here homewards, on the Biopierre I expect
to be detained Some days preparing the negroes for the wilderness My
trusty friend John Hutchings, on the recpt of my letter[1] had come down
to this place recd. all the negroes on hand and had carried them up to his
farm—I have Just seen Mr. [Horace] Green last evening this morning he
was to have Seen me, but as yet, he has not appeared as to the State of the
business I can give you no account—untill I have a Settlement with him—
or have an account of the appropriation of the amount of sales from him I
shall bring home with me from twelve to Twenty—I hope to be able to
sell some of them on the way at good prices—but many of them I Shall be
obliged to bring home and as most of that number will be females I leave
you to point out to Mr [John] Fields[2] where to have the house built for
them—I shall be home as early as business will permit—your sister[3] and
her family are well—the mail closing I can say no more only to kiss our
little son for me and tell him I shall see him shortly if life and health permits—believe me to be your affectionate Husband.

Andrew Jackson

ALS, InU-Li.
1. Not found.
2. Fields was an overseer at the Hermitage from about 1811 to at least 1815, with a brief
interruption in 1813.
3. Mary Caffery.

From George Washington Campbell

Washington City 24. Decr. 1811

Dear Sir,
Your favour of the 30 ult. was duly recd.[1] The cases of Capt. [William]
Rickard and Mr. [John] Crawford,[2] therein noticed, shall be duly attended to, when brought forward, and their respective claims supported,
so far as justice, and the nature of the demands, will render the same
proper—
The public prints will give you the ordinary proceedings of both
houses—By these you will see we are raising *large regular* armies—and
making preparations for *war*—and talking a great deal about *taking*

Canada &c—Some are in earnest in all this—& others, it is believed are not—The Government, no doubt, mean what the message of the Executive Stated to the nation—That it is high time to take a firm position & maintain it—though war should be the consequence—From present appearances it is extremely difficult to perceive, how war can be avoided, without degrading the national character, still lower, than it now is—which certainly cannot be desireable—For there is no ground to expect G. Britain will abandon her system of depredation on our commerce—or her habitual violations of the personal rights of our citizens in the impressment of our seamen—It is understood & believed here, that Mr. [Augustus John] Foster[3] has no powers, whatever to negotiate respecting those great subjects of complaint on our part—unless it be to receive propositions, & forward them to his Court—and it is probable, our Government will make no further propositions to that nation unless she changes her course of measures towards us by revoking her orders &c. violating our neutral rights—under these circumstances the prospect is very gloomy, and a rupture between the two countries seems more than probable. To prepare for such event is certainly the duty of Congress. There is no doubt, at present, but the regular military force, will be increased to, 25,000, men, or more—authority will also be given to raise volunteers—call out the militia &c—probably merchant vessels will be permitted to arm—and our present naval force fitted out & prepared for service—but what will be the final result of all this cannot, at present, be determined—Many, who vote for armies—a navy, & all other expenditures that are proposed will vote against war with England!! time alone will develope *their views*—

Please present my compliments to Mrs. Jackson, & our friends generally—in that quarter, and believe me with due consideration, Sir, Your most obedt.

G. W. Campbell

ALS, DLC. Extract published in Bassett, 1:211–12.
1. Not found.
2. Rickard (c1762–1812), a native of Massachusetts, and Crawford (1756–1818), a native of Virginia and member of the Tennessee state legislature, 1807–13, were both Revolutionary War veterans. Jackson had probably written Campbell urging that they be allowed pensions.
3. Foster (1780–1848) was British minister plenipotentiary to the United States, 1811–12.

From Felix Grundy

December 24th 1811—
Dear Genrl,

I know you must be extremely solicitous to be informed of the proceedings of Congress; and nothing would give me more satisfaction, than to be able not only to inform you of what we are doing, but what will be the result of our deliberations—At this time the House of representatives are engaged on common and trivial subjects; waiting for the report & Bill of the Committee on our Foreign relations, on four subjects—One for an increase of the regular military Establishment, another for a Volunteer Corps, a third authorising the president to call out detatchments of militia &c a fourth authorising our merchantmen to arm &c[1]—Being a member of that Committee, I believe I can venture to say that Bills on the two subjects first named will be reported on the 26th instant, the principles have been settled in Committee and on Tomorrow the Bills will be drawn. In that way we have agreed to spend our Christmas—The first Bill will provide for the raising of 15,000 regular troops in addition to the present military establishment, which will when the enlistments for the present establishment are filled up amount to twenty five thousand regular forces—To encourage enlistments a bounty in land, from 100 to 160 acres will be offered, a bounty in money of $16 besides the usual pay & rations—term of enlistment five years—I have no doubt, but great exertions will be used in the house to destroy or diminish the land bounty, but I hope it will be without effect—It requires, but little reflection to shew, that the Western Country at least will be benefited by it, and I believe the whole United States. The Volunteer Bill, will authorise the acceptance by the president of 50,000 men, in companies not less than 60 nor more than 80 men in number—they are to nominate their Captain & subalterns to the president—The Majrs. Cols. & Generals to be appointed & commissioned by the president, no higher officer than a Brigadier Genrl will be attatched to the Volunteers—In addition to the pay heretofore offered to Volunteers, some Honorable marks of distinction will be conferrd. on officers & soldiers after their discharge, such as a set of arms used by them in service, with *suitable inscriptions*—I name these things to you, believing that you can turn them to your Countrys service—As a majority of the Committee above named are opposed to the appointment of officers for the Volunteer corps by the different states, you will readily see the propriety of your communicating with me or some other member from our State freely on this subject—and rest assured, that in no instance shall private feelings influence my conduct and on all occasions I shall pay that regard to your opinions which is due to superior military information—

I have with great pleasure, receivd. a newspaper, containing Genrl. Jackson's Division orders,[2] they breath no doubt the sentiments of my District and what added much to my gratification was the circumstance of their arrival a few days after I had in a speech stated what I believed the sentiments of my Constituents were[3]—while others were speaking doubtingly about the sentiments of their Districts, I had only to pull out, my Genrls orders—as I often said to shew, what my Constituents thought & felt for he had confirmed every thing I had said on the subject—I took the liberty of transmitting the paper containing those orders to the president—I firmly believe, that G Britain must recede or this Congress will declare war—If the latter takes place the Canadas & Floridas will be the Theatres of our offensive operations—If War is not resorted to, one thing is certain to my mind, this nation or rather their representatives will be disgraced—

You may use this letter in the most public manner (newspapers excepted)—I wish the people of my district to have as early an opportunity as others of knowing what is doing here & If from my peculiar situation as a member of a Committee I can get a little a head in point of information, it may in some degree remedy inconveniences growing out of the remoteness of their situation—

permit me, to remark, that this Country is now in a situation which requires not only the best exertions of our National Councils, but every citizen should now step forward & in some shape promote his Countrys cause—Our Fathers fought for and bequeathed liberty & Independence to *us* their children—shall they perish in our hands? No, a firm & manly effort now, will enable us to transmit to *our children* the rich inheritance unimpaired—

I am yr humble servt.

Felix Grundy

I have forwarded a copy of the above to each Brigadier Genrl. under your Command   Gr

ALS, DLC. Extract published in Bassett, 1:210.

1. The bill to raise an additional military force became law on January 11, 1812; the bill authorizing the President to accept and organize certain volunteer and military corps, on February 6; and the bill to authorize a detachment from the militia of the United States, on April 10.

2. See AJ to the Brigadier Generals of the 2nd Division, November 28.

3. For Grundy's speech, see *Annals of Congress*, 12th Cong., 1st sess., pp. 422–27.

1812

To Willie Blount

Hermitage Jany. 25th. 1812

Dear Sir,

When I left this Country for the Natchez, it was on business that would not admit of delay—I had a hope, that Silas Dinsmoore had ceased to violate the rights of the honest American Citizen, and that after the letter of Mr. Monroe to Governor [Charles] Scott, the Secy War's letter to him, together with yours,[1] he would have ceased to seize on the Servants of Gentlemen, the property of honest emigrants to that Territory—in this I found I was mistaken—when I reached the Agency[2] I found three families from Georgia, who had passed a wilderness of 700 miles stoped for the want of a passport, having three waggons and twenty two negroes along—their wives and children exposed to all the inclemency of the Season (Decr. 10th.)—I expostulated with the Deputy Agent Mr. Smith[3] (for Silas assumes the power of appointing a Deputy) against the illegality of the measure, and the impolicy thereof; stating as we were on the eve of War, it must be the wish of Government to strengthen that frontier with good Citizens, and instead of treating our Citizens emigrating to that Country in this way which was well calculated to sour their minds with the Government, every facility ought to be adopted by the Agent to hasten them to their place of destination; but all in vain this Deputy Agent could not be moved; and there they were obliged to remain until they sent & obtained a passport from the Governor of the Mississippi Territory, who knew as much about them as the Pope of Rome—these families being within forty miles of their place of destination by passing down Pearl river, created a wish in them to travel a new road, opened by the Indians, or I should have marched them into the Territory—Silas and his Deputy notwithstanding—The Deputy observed to me, that from my observations in behalf of those families, and on the rights of the Citizens to pass this road, ceded by solemn Treaty, he supposed he need not ask me for a passport—I replied, being a citizen of the United States the only passport I carried was, an honest face and a good reputation—that I might have been a subject of Spain had it not have been for such despotism—and bid him farewel—this was communicated to his high mightiness, Silas, who issued his Bull against me—It was well known that my business to that Country was to bring away a number of negroes which had been sent to that Country for sale, and from the fall of the market and scarcity of cash remained unsold—finding as I passed thro' the Choctaw Country that I could sell several of them, I applied for a Permit to the acting Governor, to sell in the Nation—this was denied under an idea of the want of legal power—I was prepared to give any security—as soon as I heard this declaration I suspected there was a combination to compel me to take a passport; for Mr. [Henry] Dangerfield Secy. M. T., acting as Governor[4] politely offered me a passport, which I as politely declined accepting of—I set out with twenty six negroes, and my servant, every step I advanced I was met with the threats of the Agent of *destruction, death* and *confinement in chains* if I attempted to pass the Agency without a passport—Knowing my rights as an American Citizen, I was determined not to yield them unless with my life—every threat I received, I answered, that I acted only on the defensive, and if I was attacked on the public highway I should treat the assailant as a highway robber, and I should be careful to be able to give a good account of the Agent to my Country—when I reached the confines of the Agency I was well advised that there were at least twenty men summoned, and attending, with four Choctaws, to arrest my progress, this being confirmed to me by Mr. Crozier[5] from Kentuckey, and Mr. [George B.] McCluskey,[6] I armed in my own defence with two cases of Pistols, one Rifle gun, two axes and six Clubs (the axes and Clubs in the hands of my negroe fellows)[7] I approached the Agency in such an attitude as I conceived best calculated for defence—I lead on the van armed enflute—I saw a large assemblage of people; some the Possee of the Agent, and some led there to witness the scene; for the reports had lead to a belief that I would be attacked—when I got opposite to the agency in solid column, I ordered a halt in the public road to give the Agent an opportunity to display his columns and to make the threatened attack; but whether from my attitude of defence, or from a dread of his own person, or from a doubt of his powers, I know not, but much to my gratification and disappointment I was very politely treated by Mr. Smith Deputy Agent, and passed on without interruption—But from the conduct of Silas in this as well as in other cases he must be removed, or our citizens will rise and burn his Tavern and Store with Silas in the midst of them—He is concerned in a Store and Tavern at the Agency—He is opening a large Farm, and building a large House—it is therefore a profitable thing to Silas to stop all the negroes he can—He makes them labor on his Farm and House, and then charges the owner at Tavern rates for their board—And if a gentleman's servant is detained, and he will delay for a passport for him, he obtains a guest for a week or two, whose pockets sweat in paying the Tavern Bill—this is making money in true Yankee stile—the proof of his being a partner in the Store (which is expressly contrary to law) can easily be had, Mr. John H.

Smith[8] of Nashville, and Major [Alexander] Montgomery, President of the Council of the Mississippi Territory,[9] can prove the fact—nay more, his own receipt in the hand of Capt. Thomas Hardeman[10] will prove that Silas has demanded and actually extorted from the citizen twelve dollars for his Servant being found travelling this road without a passport—It is more than probable Capt. Hardeman has made known to you since his return this fact, together with the treatment he received from Silas— there are hundreds of cases of equal despotism, and certainly our Government cannot suppose when we are about to declare war against great Britain for her infringement of our maritime rights, that we will tamely submit to the infringement of our Territorial rights; and I speak truth when I say to you, that the western citizens are so disgusted with the despotism of Silas, that if Government should not remove him, he will be buried in the ruins of his Tavern &c. &c.—That citizens are to be threatened with chains and confinement for peaceably travelling a road ceded by solemn Treaty—that the savages and Indian-countrymen should be assembled to carry these threats into execution is too intolerable to bear— that a man's family should be kept in terror from such reports, shews that the Agent is a barbarian, and delights in alarming women by threats that he dare not himself to carry into execution—I hate to become a public prosecutor, but if he is not removed I will have him indicted under the Statute for being concerned in trade with the Indians—The character of a public informer under Statutes that give part of the penalty to the informant, I do dispise—but should it become necessary for his removal, it shall be done—His own Partner Stophel Stump,[11] says he is a partner in the Store—Accept my best wishes for your health and happiness, and believe me to be, your M. Obt. Servant

signed   Andrew Jackson

Copy, DNA-RG 107. Enclosed in Willie Blount to William Eustis, March 22; also enclosing George McCluskey to AJ, January 2, and John Miller to AJ, March 15.

1. Letters of Monroe and Blount not found; for an extract of William Eustis to Silas Dinsmoor, October 15, 1811, see Parton, 1:351. Scott (c1739–1813) was governor of Kentucky.

2. On the Natchez Trace, several miles northeast of present-day Jackson, Miss.

3. Not further identified.

4. Daingerfield (d. 1815) was acting governor during the absence of David Holmes, October 1811–June 1812.

5. Not further identified.

6. McCluskey wrote on January 2 of having heard Smith threaten to detain Jackson if he attempted to cross the Choctaw country without a passport. From 1814 to 1815 and from 1816 to 1818 McCluskey served as an infantry officer in the U.S. Army.

7. For Robert Weakley's recollection, dated June 14, 1828, of Jackson's encounter at the Choctaw agency, see Parton, 1:354–55; see also James A. McLaughlin to Amos Kendall, January 30, 1843, DLC.

8. Smith (d. 1834) was a Nashville merchant.

9. Montgomery (d. 1812) served on the legislative council of Mississippi Territory, 1800–1809, and was an incorporator of the Bank of Mississippi, 1809.

10. Hardeman (1750–1833), a veteran of the Battle of King's Mountain, settled in

Davidson County in 1783 and in 1803 moved to a 2,000-acre plantation in Williamson County. In 1816 he emigrated to Missouri Territory, returning to Tennessee shortly before his death.

11. Possibly "C. Stump, a linseed trader in the Choctaw Country," whose letter warning Dinsmoor of Jackson's intention to secure his removal is published in Parton, 1:355—56.

From Thomas Hart Benton

Nashville, Jany. 30th. 1812.

Dr. sir,

I had expected to have seen you at this place; not having the pleasure to do so, I have taken the liberty to trouble you with this letter.

In the event that a volunteer force should be raised, there is no question, I fancy, but that you will command the division which goes from this state; and as I have always been resolved to quit the gown for the sword, whenever the sword was to be used, I mean, on some terms or other, to be in that corps. I can and will raise a company from my own county; but a more eligible situation would be that of Aid to the General.[1] Now the truth is, I know of nothing that could recommend me to such a place; but the natural inclination which all young men feel, or ought to feel, to advance themselves in the world, has induced me to say to you, that if you should lack an officer of this kind; and should be able to find none better than myself, that I should deem myself honored by your approbation. I beg you not to answer this application, or to take any other notice of it than merely to remember that if you should think proper to use me, I am entirely at your service.

As soon as the bill for raising volunteers has passed, and we have learnt its details, I shall do myself the pleasure to come and see you, that I may get your advice and instructions about raising and organizing as many as possible of them. For I do not content myself with raising a single company: I wish to bring out the largest possible force from this state: and for that purpose I mean to exert myself throughout the sphere of my influence. I have a strong hope that a regiment may be raised from the southern counties in which I have practised; and if it is not done, it shall not be for the want of my exertions.

If there should be an expedition to the Canda's I shall make an experiment of my capacity to use the pen as well as the sword. I mean to preserve a journal of the operations of the army; and to give a history of such transactions as are worthy of being remembered.[2] You Sir, who feel a generous wish to see young men come forward by their own intrinsic strength, will not smile at this presumption. You recognize the principle that to mount the eminence of distinction, the votary for fame must chance every thing. I deem it more honorable to fail in honorable efforts than to make no attempt at all to drag myself from obscurity. I think with

Tacitus, that every man should aim at doing something worthy of being written, or of writing something worthy of being done.

Respectfully &c.

Thomas H. Benton

ALS, DLC. Published in Bassett, 1:213–14.

1. Jackson appointed Benton as one of his aides, probably in June upon William Preston Anderson's resignation. He served until December, part of the time simultaneously as colonel of the 2nd Regiment of Volunteers.

2. On the Natchez expedition in 1813, Benton did keep a journal, parts of which he sent to the *Democratic Clarion* for publication.

To Mary Caffery

Hermitage near Nashville February 8th. 1812

Dr Madam

your letter of the 11th. of January is now before me,[1] I have duly observed its contents, and am sorry indeed that an illiberal world has prevented you from buying in Jacob—[2]

The negro fellows that I brought thro with me owing to their exposure in the wilderness have all been sick and were the *well* neither of them is such that I could recommend to you—nor could I think of selling such to you—I have delayed one week answering your letter to see whether I could meet with a fellow to buy that would suit you; as yet I can hear of none for sale that I could buy—and had I such a negro, I am fearfull, it would (from the convulsed state of the Earth and water from the frequent shocks of Earthquake)[3] be dificult to obtain a passage for him down the river—few Boats will venture the passage of the Missisippi this spring— and from the last shocks here, being so violent it is to be feared that a vast many of the Boats that are on the river is lost—I am therefore fearfull, that it will not be in my power shortly to send you one down—but I have a fellow, that ranaway from the Natchez—in last Novbr called Jessee[4]— he is a valluable fellow, at least such he ought to be he cost $500 here—he is in the neighbourhood of the Natchez—Capt [Henry?] Hunter, Mr Trigg, or Mr Hardin who live in the Natchez, know him—also Mr Fleming[5]—if Jackey[6] will go down it is highly probable he can be got, and if so take him and keep him—if he should prove to be such a negro as you want you can buy him if not you can keep him untill another can be got—Mr Fleming of Natchez (Tavern keeper,) Told Mr Hutchings that he had heard that such a negro had been taken up by a boat, on the bank of the Missisippi—some where above Natchez—he promised to go and see the negro, if it was him that he would take him into Possession for me—If Jackey goes down for him and can find him this letter will be full authority for taking him into possession—Capt Hunter Mr Trigg or Mr Fleming will give him any aid in their power in regaining him—and I have no doubt but he can be got if Jackey will make search for him, and I will freely pay any expence that may accrue in getting him—your daughter Kitty[7] is well. she is a fine traveller—she passed the wilderness without a complaint or murmer—she is now at school in good health and spirits—from a letter I have recd from Donelson [Caffery][8] since I reached home I expect he is with you—if so tell him to write me—I wish much to see him—and say to him when there he can easily ride here, and I shall expect him to come up—at any rate to write me that I may know where to write him—

your sister and all your friends are well, but verry much alarmed, with the frequent shocks of Earthquakes, some of which have been so severe as to throw down chimneys, and to crack brick walls—but I hope these alarms will subside, and the shocks cease here but I am fearfull, that the inhabitants on the west side of the Missisippi, in the neighbourhood of New Madrid and the little prararie have sufferred—

Miss Catharine writes you by this mail and your sister Joins me in good wishes for the health and happiness of you and your family to whom we beg you to make our best compliments and with sincere Esteem believe me to be your Friend

Andrew Jackson

P.S. I flatter myself, that your Brothers William and John [Donelson] and myself, will settle you in this country[9]—I have had some conversation with them on this subject, as soon as my business will permit I shall see them fix upon something permanent and write you—say to Jackey as soon as I get his horses back well I shall send him down by the first opportunity—present our compliments to Mr Knox and lady to Mr Green Betsy and family, and to Mr Vandoren and Sophia—[10]

ALS, DLC. Extract published in Bassett, 1:214–15.

1. Not found.

2. Probably a slave that Mary Caffery had been unable to buy at the sale of her husband's estate.

3. Jackson was referring to the severe earthquakes centered in New Madrid, La. Terr., that began December 16, 1811, and continued into 1812.

4. Jesse, one of the slaves taken to Natchez by Horace Green, was shortly captured and a bill submitted to Jackson for the reward and expenses (see bill from Benjamin Foy, May 8, and Robert Sprigg to AJ, November 3).

5. Hunter was holder of a 2,000-acre Spanish grant on Bayou Sarah and sometime speaker of the territorial legislature. Trigg, Hardin, and Fleming not further identified.

6. John Caffery, Jr., who appears to have been living with his mother in Claiborne County, Miss. Terr.

7. Catherine Caffery, who in 1814 married George Walker, her sister's widower.

8. Letter not found.

9. William and John (1755–1830) were planters in Davidson County near the Hermitage. It does not appear that they succeeded in relocating Mary to Tennessee.

10. Mary Caffery's three married daughters and their husbands: Mary (Polly), married to John Knox in 1805; Eliza (Betsy), married to Abraham Green in 1801; and Sophia (b. 1792), married in 1811 to Peter Aaron Van Dorn (College of New Jersey 1795), a lawyer and clerk of the Claiborne County Superior Court.

From Felix Grundy

Washington, February 12th. 1812

Dear Genrl,

On this day, I receivd. yr friendly communication[1] & could I be with you, I could talk over many matters & things to much advantage, perhaps, to the Community but prudence forbids to commit to paper, fears, doubts conjectures, suspicions &c &c The Bill for raising 25,000. men has been a Law of the Land for about six weeks, and wonderfull, not a single officer except the Commander in chief is appointed—This is Henry Dearborne—Is there nothing rotten in Denmark? The Cabinet are in daily Council—Are they not examining the papers in Wilkinsons Case to see whether he shall not be second in Command[2]—and of course the Commander of the Southern & Western Armies? Should this be the case, It will damp the spirit of the nation much—This is mere conjecture, and untill I saw the Intelligencer of Today I inclined to a belief that, the British Minister & the Cabinet were negociating[3]—The Volunteer Bill for accepting the service of 50,000 men has become a law, & the states are to officer these troops; of course, that is a matter, not to be acted on here, as soon as I can get a Copy of this law I will send it to you—In West, Tennessee—we are only entituled to the Following officers in the 25,000— One Lieut Colo, 5 Capts. 4 first Lieuts. 4 Second ditto—3 ensigns— From all the applications made a selection has been made in the manner practised on such occasions and the following will no doubt be the appointments—Wm P Anderson Colo. Thomas Claiborne Robert Butler, Robert Desha Junior, of Sumner, Alexander Gray of Carthage, Francis Armstrong of Franklin County—Captains—Mr Reed of Nashville, Tilden Taylor of Sumner Don Carolus Dixon of Smith, Isaac Walton of Smith, first Lieuts. James H. Gamble of Davidson, Avery Clark of Robertson, Mr Smith of rutherford, (Bennetts son I understand) and some other not now recollected second Lieuts. Mr Harmon Hays could not be appointed more than an Ensign[4]—There is a vacancy for a Surgeon's Mate, in my District. To whom can this be given? write to me, I shall keep it vacant untill I am advised—[5]

Poor Crawfords claim has been rejected at the War office[6]—It is however to be brought before the Committee of Claims I shall appear before them in propria persona & endeavor to force it thro, of which I have strong hopes If I fail there, I will rally in the house & If I fail there, I shall warp the patriotism of men, who talks of War while they suffer the old Soldier to starve for bread. For my part, I should think as well of the unnatural son, who should suffer his own Father to die for food, which he had the power of furnishing as I can of men who will refuse to support the Revolutionary Invalids to whose exertions, they owe their present elevation & prosperity—

This Congress will do more *harm* or *good* than any that has preceeded for some years—how things will end God only knows, for I am sure no man here can tell how this Session will end—For my part, I shall endeavor to pursue a consistent course, and one which shall in my opinion promote the prosperity of the Country. A Seat in Congress at present, is too responsible a Station to be even tolerably pleasant—A Bill for Classing & arming the whole body of the Militia has failed in the house of Representatives, it was by three votes only A Bill is now before us, which will probably pass for arming them only—I was in favor of the first & of course shall vote for the latter, altho it is only half doing what ought to be done—[7]

Silas Dinnsmore Esquire, has been the subject of one Conversation between the Secretary at War, Mr Poindexter & myself—In that Mr Poindexter gave him a severe dressing, & shall in a day or two repeat it—

I am much gratified at the disposition shewn by the Citizens of my District in Volunteering their services in behalf of their Country. It does them much honor, and I confess I feel my own pride increased in consequence of it—No man in Congress can say, that his Constituents have stepped forward in half so magnanimous a manner—To represent such a District would be an Honor to any man and you may rest assured, that my every exertion has been & shall be used to demonstrate to them, that however unqualified I am to be usefull, I am not deficient in a disposition to be so—

Shall we have War? That is the question you want answered—*So do I*—I thought some time ago, there was no doubt—But, If in six weeks only one man out of 25,000 is furnished, how long will it take to furnish 25,000—See Mr Gallatin's Budgett, it talks, of Stamp duties, Excises, Direct Taxes &c &c &c. Did it not make its appearance at an unfortunate moment?

Mr [Ezekiel] Bacon the Chairman of the Committee of Ways & Means has Just left my room and I now see a dreadfull strom a little ahead. He says he will push his Tax Bills as hard & as fast as possible—I say to him, the questions of War plainly & distinctly put shall go in front—In what a situation would this Country be, should a heavy system of Internal taxes be imposed and payment enforced; when the people of the United States were not compelled to have recourse to them for the purpose of avenging injuries inflicted by Foreign Nations—or in other words, in case we do not go to War—Would there not be danger of such a system becoming permanent? There is great intriguing for the presidency going on. It seems to me, that Mr. Madison's situation is a very delicate one, but more of this by & by—

You have heard, of the Newyork Mammoth Canal which the Legislature of Tenessee requested their members in Congress to support[8]—

Good Easy men, did they know that Dewitt Clinton lived in Newyork? that this was a mere electioneering hobby & in itself impracticable I presume had they known these things, they would hardly have wished us to support a project which would cost the U. States ten millions of dollars and by which no other purpose could be answered, except to increase the power of the northern Section of the Union—I shall at all times respect the opinion of the Legislature of Tenessee, but in this instance they are no doubt mistaken—and as I am the representative of the people of [Tenn]essee I shall look to their interests and act upon my own responsibility, for I am very far from thinking that my Constituents would be satisfied, were I to do wrong & have no other apology than that the Assembly told me or requested me to do so—

You will readily discover that this letter [is] not designed for Newspaper publication—hoping for the best & fearing the worst that can befall our Country, I remain your humble sert

Felix Grundy

PS—Make a low bow and present my best respects to the Invincible Grays conjointly & seperately   F Gr

ALS, DLC. Extract published in Bassett, 1:215–16.

1. Not found.

2. Wilkinson's court martial, meeting in Fredericktown, Md., September 2-December 25, 1811, acquitted him on all charges. Madison approved the court's decision on February 14 and recommended Wilkinson's promotion to major general on February 27. He was returned to his command at New Orleans.

3. On both February 11 and February 13 the editor of the *National Intelligencer* commented that prospects were dim for an accommodation with Great Britain.

4. Secretary of War Eustis submitted for Senate approval his list of nominees for commissions on February 24; most were confirmed on March 12. Claiborne was not nominated; no Read, Reed, or Reid was appointed at this time, although Eustis mentioned a Thomas Read of Tennessee for 1st Lieutenant in his March 7 amendment to the list; two Smiths were nominated and approved—John M., 1st lieutenant (resigned May 1812) and Joseph D., 2nd lieutenant (resigned September 1812); Hays was appointed cornet, resigning July 1814; Taylor resigned in August 1812; Clark, Dixon, and Walton resigned in 1813; Anderson, Armstrong, Butler, Desha, Gamble, and Gray served until discharged in June 1815. All but Desha and Gamble (artillery) and Hays (dragoons) were appointed to the 24th Infantry Regiment.

5. Jackson's response has not been found.

6. On Crawford's claim, see above, George Washington Campbell to AJ, December 24, 1811.

7. The bill for arming and classing the militia by age was defeated on February 4. The substitute bill, for arming only, was voted down on February 20.

8. A proposal to use federal funds to build a canal from the Great Lakes to the Hudson River, first passed by the New York state legislature on April 8, 1811. On November 14 and 15, 1811, the Tennessee House and Senate concurred in a resolution that the senators and representatives of Tennessee "are respectfully requested to support any laudable attempt of said company . . . soliciting the aid of the general government in relation to the aforesaid canal navigation" (*Tennessee Senate Journal*, 9th General Assembly, 1st sess., pp. 182–83).

To an Arbitrator

February 29th. 1812—

Mr Jno. Coffee communicated to me the other day some information relative to the acpt. of Mr. H. Green, before you from which I am fearfull there has been something in that letter I wrote you & Messhrs. Hall and Smith, that has given offence[1]—not having a coopy of that letter, and having written it in a hurry, if any expression or idea is contained therein calculated to Touch the feelings of Either you or the other gentlemen I do not recollect it and I can assure you that if there is any such, it has incautiously been introduced without any intention, far be it from me, in any situation to make use of any expressions calculated to injure the feelings of gentlemen acting as arbitrators, and particularly those for whom I have the highest veneration and respect, as is the case in the present instance—for this reason I trouble you with this letter at the present moment—to state to you what give rise to the letter I wrote the other day—

I did find from looking over all the accounts of the shipment of cotton from here to Neworleans and the expence of Negroes, that Mr Greens account exceeded them greatly—the highest Expence of any that did accrue during the time we were engaged in the Mercantile transactions was (including provissions hands and return expence) two hundred and fifty dollars, that Mr Greens acpt provissions and hands furnished except a steersman (for he had on board a number of Negroes) amounts to three hundred and Eighteen dollars and 75/100 twenty five being deducted for differrence of vallue for a horse leaves the amount still greater than any sum that any Boat load of Cotton ever costs us, I also found from examining the acpts of Negroes sent to Markett that the expence never averaged more from here than fifteen dollars a head except one wench and three children, who had been subject to the fits remained better than six months in the Natchez,[2] she cost with her children twenty five dollars, finding his acpt so exorbitant, and in lumping charges without any specification, I did not think that Justice to myself would permit of me admitting his account without vouchers or specifications such as would in your oppinions when specifically stated, the sum paid & the object to which applied, that it was Just and reasonable that it should be admitted, and that I by the terms contained in the proposition to buy was bound to pay it.[3] I did think and still do think—that where a special copartnership is formed for a particular purpose—particular agreement entered into as in the present instance, that the property is to be taken to a certain Markett, and the partner deviates from his agreement and instructions as in the present instance and thereby encurs heavy and unexpected expence—that unless he is able to shew, that this was owing to some unavoidable occurrence, and the expence incurred thereby such as could not be avoided under existing circumstances that the partner is not by the rules of law Justice or reason liable for such expence, and particularly that the acting partner in the above case ought to shew that he has actually and for the benefit of the firm laid out and expend the sums exhibited in his acpt, for this reason when it was submitted I did remark, that I should require vouchers on particular specifications, such as would enable you to Judge under existing circumstances, that the specified sum had been properly applied to the use of the firm, I did see that you were about to take a differrent view of the subject, and would leave the thing inconclusively settled as it respected the hire of the negroes, and was about to conclude the subject without any specifications, that would put it out of my power even where I had proof to correct the account, when by specifications made to amount to the sum claimed by him, Justice to myself and family and creditors, forbade me to yield to such a course, and I am sure you must have mistaken me if ever it was understood to consent to such a rule by which the settlement was to be concluded—I claimed the right of having either vouchers shewing the payments of particular sums, or such specifications as is usual and necessary in all cases of accounts, and particularly in such an account as this, leaving you to be the Judge of its Justness and propriety—I had farther made a statement of what sum would be necessary to have laid in a sufficient supply of provissions and covered all necessary expence and when this is done, taking no notice of the time the negroes have been hired out, or the reduction of their expence by sales, and one having run away, from which statement, there is a ballance of three hundred and forty dollars—and from every inquiry I have made on the subject, that fifteen dollars pr head is about the usual expence, and finding this to amount including the amount of the price of the Boat, and not taking into view the children at the breast, it makes the cost on each negro $44.66.⅔—this as I am advised is more than double what is usual, therefore necessary to be particularly set forth how it has accrued, and whether (if it has accrued at all), it has arisen in such a way as the situation in which I stand as a purchaser is bound for. These reasons induced me to write the Gentlemen—arbitrating the acpt the other day[4]—I will here state the view of expence I took—three months provision was talked of as necessary to be laid in as an outfit—I have thus stated the subject you can see how far it wears the appearance of being Just—and here I will remark, that finding there would be a great loss on the cotton Bot of [Bennett] Smith those negroes were bought, to indemnify us from the loss thereby sustained & agreed on by all concerned that industry and oeconomy must be used to obtain the object—now sir I take the charges for the outfit and see from the prices of provisions in this country then whether it would not lay in a sufficient supply for three months—let us take the soldiers ration for the Basis—there was 25 grown negroes with two sucking children they always count with the mother—then say 25 for three months will take 1125 lb Beacon this at the then selling price say

16th of May 6/100	$ 67.50
50 Bushels of corn meal will be more than sufficient we will say however to have enough for this	25
add 57.50, to make up and lay in Mr Greens supply	57.50

This 3 months will take us up to the 16th. of august—another three months will take us up to the time or nearly so, that Mr [John] H[utchings] recd the negroes at Natchez—they are now there and let us take his letter [5] for the price of Beacon which is 12½ cents—

then say 1125 lb beacon at 12½ cents	140.62½
50 bushels of meal at 75 cents	37.50
Mr Greens Board for four months in the Town after he left his Boat at $5 pr week	80
let us add fifty dollars more for his expence	50
let us give $60 for cloathing (there was 13 wenches one habit each the fellows recd naked)	60
let us add $160 for steersmens Doctors bill and any extra provisions coming down the river	160
this makes an agregate of this sum	678.12½

leaving a ballance of his account unaccounted for of $340.6.¼—now I cannot see for my soul how he has properly, and agreable to the intention of the partners oeconomically, for the necessary support expended this ballance of 340$—hence resulted to my view from my first objections to Mr Greens account the propriety of specifications or vouchers particularly as I do believe I am in the reach of proof to shew that sum of this money whenever the specifications are made, are such as the concern or partners except Mr Green ought not to pay—I will ask if Mr. Green chose to give ten dollars pr month to a dray man to Hall water for his negroes unemployed would such an item be thought reasonable, or Just—or suppose Mr Green had given a mantua maker—say two dollars for each habit when he had three negroes with him that could make their own cloaths and that of the others would the arbitrators say that it was reasonable or Just that I should pay it standing as I do as a purchaser—or even as a partner—I put these cases for example—suppose he had expended in fine muslin and silk for the negro one hundred dollars would you say that it was reasonable or right that I should pay it—hence results the reason and Justice to my mind for a particular specification—and as I thought would have been called on for, as well as for the time of the hire of the negroes, and to whom hired—I will make one simily as to the acting partner in a special partnership as ours and for a special purpose, deviating from his instructions and agreement and incurring expence thereby, for your consideration and reflection—let us recollect that by special agreement these negroes were to go to a certain markett and there was to have been sold for cash—instead of selling them for cash Mr Green had sold them for horses, and kept the horses in a livery stable in the Natchez I ask would I without any knowledge thereof have been bound to receive the horses under my proposition to buy, and pay the expence of the horses—I trust not—but law Justice and reason would say that he should keep the horses pay the expence and account in money for the price of the negroes—apply the case—it was agreed on all hand that the Natchez was glutted with negroes, and at that place the negroes was not to be stopped unless for a supply of provisions a keel Boat is therefore Bot that he may go every where below, first to Biosarah, next the coast, next the rapids of red river &c contrary to this he stops at Natchez sells some of the negroes for an old horse foundered—encounters as his account states in the lump unusual expences, am I by the rules of law Justice and reason bound to pay for the expence of horse believing as I did when I made the proposition to buy that no expence except Mr Greens would have been on the negroes, believing as I did at that time that he had so managed the negroes that at least they would have cleared there own expence, if not neated some thing to the owners, I believe this was not ideas uncommon—for every person but Mr Green that I know of whose negroes have been there four or six months has made a great deal of money by the hire—has Mr Greens conduct been such to me or the firm that I should have confidence in him or has not his indolence and going counter to his agreement been the cause, that a sacrafice will be upon the negroes of at least $1500 if not 2000—then certainly I hope that none of the Gentlemen on the arbitration will think, that I infringe on them or their feelings by insisting on Mr Greens, producing vouchers or specifications—if he has actually expended that sum for the use and support of the negroes he can shew it—and the mail will afford a speedy channel through which he can obtain vouchers, and he can certainly shew by a regular acpt and statement how he fed the negroes or how the were fed—But sir after all I have said, if there is any thing improper in me or the demand I have made please to say to me as a friend in what, and was it to reduce me with all the Rheumatic pains about me to plow for my bread, I will immediately abandon it, I wish to pay him every cent that he has advanced necessarily for the support of the negroes, but I do not wish to be first injured by his *inatention* and *gambling* and then pay his gambling debts—I beg you to say to the other gentlemen if there is any thing in my letter improper (which I hope there is not[)], that it would give me pain the longest day I live to be informed that I had done any thing to injure their feelings—and accept assurances of my high respect and Esteem—

Andrew Jackson

P.S. I fear you cannot read this scroll I write it in the night and with the Rheumatick in my right rist so that I can scarcely wield the pen—you may shew this to the other gentlemen or not as you think proper—

ALS, DLC. Published in Bassett, 1:217–20.

1. Letter not found. Hall and Smith were possibly Elihu S. Hall and John H. Smith, merchant, who stated in 1828 his knowledge of the Coleman-Green-Jackson transaction, mentioning that he had many dealings with Jackson at this time but not identifying himself as an arbitrator in the dispute (*National Banner and Nashville Whig*, August 23, 1828). For a discussion of the Coleman, Green & Jackson business, see above, Memorandum re purchase of slaves, May 18, 1811.

2. Probably the slave sold for Andrew Jackson by Washington Jackson in Natchez (see above, Washington Jackson to AJ, December 20, 1809).

3. Green, when solicited in 1828 for his account of the venture, stated that he sold his interest in the slaves to Jackson. "In May, 1811," he wrote, "*we* purchased a number of negroes from a Mr. Epperson, for which *we* were to pay part in hand—I paid *one third*, and understood *the balance was paid* by capt. Coleman and *Gen. Jackson*. The negroes were taken by me to Natchez *for sale*, and a part of them sold. In the month of December (I think) of the same year, I received letters from General Jackson, (which letters are at this time mislaid) advising me *he had purchased out* capt. Coleman in *both* these transactions, and offering to *sell out* to me at cost by securing him, or *to buy me out*, and refund to me all the advances I had made. I thought proper to sell. In relation to the purchase of the negroes, although I had no understanding to the effect from either captain Coleman or gen. Jackson, I thought it probable he stood in the *same situation* as in the purchase of the cotton and tobacco, from the circumstances as I then believed, *it was his credit which enabled us to make the purchase*" (*A Brief Account of General Jackson's Dealings in Negroes*, New York, 1828?, p. 12). In his letter to Samuel Carswell, May 19, 1813, Jackson confirmed that he bought out Green's and Colemans's interests.

4. Letter not found.

5. John Hutchings's letter has not been found.

On learning of the passage of the act authorizing President Madison to organize and accept volunteer corps, Jackson issued the following order.

To the 2nd Division

Division orders.   March 7th, 1812—
Volunteers to arms!
Citizens! Your goverment has at last yielded to the impulse of the nation. Your impatience is no longer restrained. The hour of national vengeance is now at hand. The eternal enemies of american prosperity are again to be taught to respect your rights, after having been compelled to feel, once more, the power of your arms.

War is on the point of breaking out between the united states and the King of Great Britain! and the martial hosts of america are summoned to the Tented Fields!

Citizens! an honourable confidence in your courage and your patriotism has been displayed by the general goverment. To raise a force for the protection of your rights she has not deemed it necessary to recur to the common mode of filling the ranks of an army.

No drafts or compulsory levies are now to be made.

A simple invitation is given to the young men of the country to arm for their own and their countries rights. On this invitation 50,000 volunteers, full of martial ardor, indignant of their Countries wrongs and burning with impatience to illustrate their names by some signal exploit, are expected to repair to the national standard.

Could it be otherwise? Could the general goverment deem it necessary to force *us* to take the field? We, who for so many years have demanded a war with such clamorous importunity—who, in so many resolutions of town meetings and legislative assemblies, have offerred our lives and fortunes for the defence of our country—who, so often and so publickly have charged this verry goverment with a pusillanimous deference to foreign nations, because she had resolved to exhaust the arts of negociation before she made her last appea[l] to the force of arms. No, under such circumstance it was impossible for the goverment to conceive that compulsion would be wanting to bring us into the field. and shall we now disappoint the expectations which we ourselves have excited? shall we give the lie to the professions which we have so often and so publickly made? Shall we, who have clamoured for war, now skulk into a corner the moment war is about to be declared? Shall we, who for so many years have been tendering our lives and fortunes to the general goverment, now come out with evasions and pitifull excuses the moment tender is accepted?

But another and a nobler feeling should impell us to action. *Who are we? and for what are we going to fight?* are we the titled Slaves of George the third? the military conscripts of Napolon the great? or the frozen peasants of the Rusian Czar? No, we are the free born sons of america; the citizens of the only republick now existing in the world; and the only people on Earth who possess rights, liberties, and property which the dare call their own.

For what are we going to fight? To satisfy the revenge or ambition of a corrupt and infatuated Ministry? to place another and another diadem on the head of an apostate republican general? to settle the ballance of power among an assasin tribe of Kings and Emperors? "or to preserve to the prince of Blood, and the grand dignitaries of the empire" their overgrown wealth and exclusive privileges? No: such splendid atchievements as these can form no part of the objects of an american war. But we are going to fight for the reestablishment of our national charector, misunderstood and vilified at home and abroad; for the protection of our maritime citizens, impressed on board British ships of war and compelled to fight the battles of our enemies against ourselves; to vindicate our right to a free trade, and open a market for the productions of our soil, now perishing on our hands, because the *mistress of the ocean* has forbid us to carry them to any foreign nation; in fine, to seek some indemnity for past injuries, some security against future aggressions, by the conquest of all the British dominions upon the continent of North america.

Here then is the true and noble principle on which the energies of the nation should be brought into action: *a free people compelled to reclaim by the power of their arms the rights which god has bestowed upon them, and which an infatuated King has said they shall not enjoy.*

In such a contest will the people shrink from the support of their goverment; or rather will the shrink from the support of themselves? will the abandon their great imprescriptible rights, and tamely surrender that illustrious national charector which was purchased with so much blood in the war of the Revolution? No: such infamy shall not fall upon us. The advocates of Kingly power shall not enjoy the triumph of seeing a free people desert themselves, and crouch before the slaves of a foreign tyrant. The patriotic tender of voluntary service of the invincible grays Capt. F. Stumps independent company[1] and a correspondent display of patriotism by the voluntary tender of service from the counties of Davidson Sumner Smith and Rutherford, is a sure pledge that the free sons of the west will never *submit to such degradation*

But the period of youth is the season for martial exploits; and accordingly it is upon the young men of america that the eye of the nation is now fixed. They in a peculiar degree are the proper subjects of a volunteer expedition. To say nothing of the generous courage which distinguishes that period of life, they, from their particular situation, can quit their homes at the shortest notice with the least inconvenience to themselves. Unencumbered with families and free from the embarrassment of domestic concerns they are ready at a moments warning to march to any extremity of the republick.

Should the occupation of the Canadas be resolved upon by the general goverment, how pleasing the prospect that would open to the young volunteer while performing a military *promenade* into a distant country, a succession of new and interesting objects would perpetually fill and delight his imagination the effect of which would be heightened by the war like appearence, the martial music, and the grand evolutions of an army of fifty thousand men.

To view the stupendous works of nature, exemplified in the falls of Niagara and the cataract of Montmorence; to tread the consecrated spot on which Wolf and Montgomery[2] fell, would of themselves repay the young soldier for a march across the continent. But why should these inducements be held out to the young men of america? They need them not. animated as they are by an ambition to rival the exploits of Rome, they will never prefer an inglorious sloth, a supine inactivity to the honorable toil of carrying the republican standard to the heights of abraham.

In consideration of all which and to carry into effect the object of the general goverment in demanding a voluntary force, to give the valiant young men of the Second Military Division of the state of Tennessee an opportunity to evince their devoted affection to the service of the republic; the Major General of the said division has thereupon ordered

1 That the militia of the second military division of the state of Tennessee be forthwith be mustered by the proper officers.

2 That the act of Congress for raising a volunteer corps of 50,000 men be read at the head of each company.

3 That all persons willing to volunteer under the said act be immediately *enrolled* formed into companies, officered, and reported to the Major Genl

4 The Generals of Brigade, attached to the Second division are charged with the prompt execution of these orders.

Andrew Jackson,
Major Genl. 2 Division

ADS copy, DLC. Published in *Democratic Clarion Extra*, March 10; Bassett, 1:220–23.

1. The Tennessee General Assembly authorized Frederick Stump to raise an independent cavalry company in 1807 (*Laws of Tennessee*, 7th General Assembly, Ch. 101).

2. James Wolfe (b. 1727) was in command of British forces when he was killed at the Battle of Quebec, September 13, 1759. Richard Montgomery fell while leading an American assault on Quebec in 1775.

The extract below, used by anti-Jacksonians as part of their proof that Jackson engaged in the domestic slave trade, has been found only in the campaign literature of 1828. In 1828, Andrew Erwin stated that he had the original of the letter, in Jackson's hand and signed. Jackson was an interested party in a case on the docket of the March 23–26 session of the Wilson Circuit Court (see Edward Williams v. *William Edwards,* September 7, 1813), *and Jackson's supporters accepted the other fact in the letter, identifying the slaves as those he recovered in Natchez (*Nashville Republican, *August 8, 1828). There is no evidence, however, that Jackson made a trip at this time to sell the slaves. He did go to Georgia in May on other business but said nothing about selling slaves there (see AJ to John Strother, May 1, below).*

To ?

Hermitage, March 20th, 1812

Having to attend Wilson circuit court, it will not be in my power to be in Nashville next week. I am very much engaged to arrange my business, so that I can leave home on the trip *with my negroes for sale.*

Text from *National Banner and Nashville Whig*, August 2, 1828. Original not found. Also published in *Nashville Republican*, August 8, 1828.

To John Coffee

Lebanon 25th. of March 1812—9 oclock at night

Dr. Sir

This momoment Mr John Childress gave me the information inclosed—I have Issued my Division order to Genl Winchester (who is now with me) to immediately march with his Volunteers, to Rendezvous at Philips horse mill,[1] with Eight days provision for man & horse, and forty rounds of amunition—and to proceed on to the Fishing ford[2] on Duck river, unless otherwise orderd I wish you immediately to Issue orders to Colo. [William W.] Searcy[3] and [James] Henderson, to march their Volunteers immediately to the relief of the frontier—I shall expect to meet you and their Volunteers on friday next at Philips horse mill but if you find that they can be raised sooner, and information reaches you confirming the Carnage and the danger of that frontier you will proceed immediately to the spot where the mischief is doing and done, and render relief as far as you can to the sufferring families—but not to attempt to persue the indians beyond the frontier without sufficient force to ensure success untill the main body gets up, you will coopy the enclosed and give Each Colo. a coopy of the order, with such other aditon as you may deam necessary from any other information you may have recd. in haste your friend

A. Jackson

ALS, DLC. Published in Bassett, 1:224.
1. Probably in Williamson County. Jackson's order to Winchester has not been found.
2. About twenty miles downriver from Shelbyville.
3. Searcy (1769–1846) was lieutenant colonel commandant for the 22nd regiment of the Rutherford County militia. Before his removal to Rutherford County in 1804, he had been in mercantile business in Nashville with his brother Robert. He served in the state senate, 1821–23.

ENCLOSURE: FROM JOHN CHILDRESS

on the morning of Wednesday the 25th. March 1812 I saw in the Town of Nashville a leter in the hand wrighting of Doctr. Charles Mcallister[1] addressed to Majr. T. G Bradford of Nash. as well as I can recollect be[ing] to this Effect

Sir

The Indians have commited a horrid Carnage on Bradshaws Creek[2] of Elk River. I have not time to give you particulars: you as an officer I presume will know your duty. the express states they Killd 25 familys and are Creek Indians

I am Respectfully Sir your &c

J. Childress

ALS, DLC.
1. A resident of Williamson County, appointed justice of the peace in 1811.
2. Enters Elk River about fifteen miles below Fayetteville.

To John Coffee

Hermitage March 26 1812. 1 Oclock P.M.

Sir

I this moment met an express on my arival home anouncing that the alarm of yesterday, which was brought by express, is groundless—that it originated by some villians who was encamped on the Indian land who had a wish to get possession of some houses possessed by others, who painted themselves, raised the indian yell and fired, those in possession immediately ran and gave the alarm—and as it spread it magnified, when it got to Nashville it had increased to what you will see in the enclosed[1] you will therefore countermand the orders of yesterday for assembling the Vollunteers and if any should be assembled order that they be immediately discharged—I am in haste yrs. &c &c &c

Andrew Jackson

ALS, DLC. Published in Bassett, 1:224–25.
1. The enclosure was probably a copy of the flier headed "Horrid News!" and repeating substantially what Childress had written to Jackson the day before (DLC).

From George Washington Campbell

Washington City 10 April 1812

Dear Sir,

Since my last to you[1] an order has issued from the War department to Mr. Dinnsmoore agent &c. of which the inclosed is an extract—and appears sufficiently explicit to produce the desired effect—[2]

our preparations for war continue to progress—we have laid an Embargo for 90 days.[3] It is considered by those who supported it as the precursor of war—There is not the slightest ground to hope that G. Britain will revoke her orders in council—We must look to & depend on *ourselves*. our people ought to prepare for war—It appears unavoidable— unless indeed there shall be found among us too many whose *fears*, & *apprehensions* will overcome their *resolution* & *judgment*; and make them shrink from the contest, when the last *step* is to be taken, & the *important question* of *war*, to be decided—Whether this will be the case or not, time alone can decide—For the honor of our Country—& of human nature, I should hope it would not! But the conduct of some men is so extraordinary, that there is no calculating, with any certainty on events, which depend on their vote. Some appear anxious to adjourn for

40 or 50 days—This measure, if adopted, will, it is believed by many, damp the public spirit, & paralize the energies of the nation.

Please make my compliments acceptable to Mrs. Jackson, & our friends in general, and believe me with much respect Sir, Your most Obedt.

G: W: Campbell

ALS, DLC.
1. Letter not found.
2. On the Dinsmoor issue, see also above, Felix Grundy to AJ, February 12.
3. On April 4, President Madison signed into law the embargo act.

ENCLOSURE: WILLIAM EUSTIS TO SILAS DINSMOOR

War Dep. 23 March 1812

The laws regulating trade & intercourse with the Indians provide against all trespasses, and encroachments on the Indian Territory, but are not construed to authorise the stopping of any person travelling through the country in a peaceable manner on the public road or high way; *you will therefore refrain from the exercise of any such authority hereafter.*

The above is an extract of a letter from the Secretary of war to Silas Dinsmoore Esqr. agent to the Choctaw Indians—

Copy in Campbell's hand, DLC.

Jackson's trip to Georgia in mid-1812 was for the purpose of securing a release of claim to David Allison's lands in Tennessee from Allison's surviving heirs. In 1802 Allison's 85,000 acres on Duck River had been auctioned at a U.S. marshal's sale to satisfy Norton Pryor's claim of $21,000 on Allison's estate. As Pryor's agent, Jackson had been awarded 10,000 acres, most of which he sold in small parcels. According to George W. Campbell's recollection in 1821, he had told Jackson in May or June of 1809 that the federal court lacked jurisdiction in the Allison foreclosure, and, since he had heard that Thomas and John Gray Blount, the original grantees, were planning to institute proceedings to recover the land by paying off the mortgage, he advised Jackson to act to protect his titles and those of his buyers. There is no evidence that Jackson took action at this time.

Meanwhile Pryor had transferred title to his remaining 40,000 acres (35,000 acres had gone to Joseph Anderson) to Andrew Erwin and James Patton, who first appeared in Middle Tennessee as Pryor's agents about 1808. At that time Jenkin Whiteside warned Erwin about the imperfection in the title, or so he testified in 1820. Like Jackson, Erwin sold the land piecemeal.

Why neither Erwin nor Jackson made any effort in 1808 or 1809 to *clear title is not known. Why Jackson chose to confront the problem in 1812 may be explained by the 1822 testimony of William B. Lewis, who said that the Blounts had determined to proceed, as Campbell had earlier warned, and were sending John Strother to Georgia as their agent to get a settlement with Allison's heirs. Whatever the reason, Jackson walked away from the meeting with Allison's surviving brothers in Georgia holding a deed to all of Allison's lands in Tennessee for the consideration of $500 and cancellation of Allison's indebtedness to him (see Deed, August 3).*

At this point Jackson had ground for a claim to the entire 85,000 acres, not just his original 10,000. According to Whiteside, shortly after his return from Georgia Jackson offered Erwin an amicable settlement, rejected by Erwin. Litigation between Erwin and Jackson commenced in 1814, but the final decree did not come until 1824 (Case File, Jackson v. Erwin, Middle Tennessee Supreme Court Records, Box 25, T).

To John Strother

May 1st. 1812. 10 oclock at night

Sir

I am this moment honored with your notification, that you will leave Mr Caldwells[1] on Elk for Georgia, on next Monday week; can I ask the favour of you to tarry there untill, thursday week—I shall set out from home on Sunday week, and I am fearfull I cannot get up before Thursday, I have a great desire to travel with you and I know I can make it to your advantage, I send a boy with this, and beg you to write me, whether you will wait for me at caldwells on Elk, untill Thursday week should I not reach you sooner;[2] money matters will detain me untill Sunday—I am sir with Esteem, yrs &c.

Andrew Jackson

ALS, DLC.
1. Not identified.
2. Strother's response has not been found, but he did accompany Jackson to Georgia (see AJ to Willie Blount, June 17, below).

On May 12 a party of Creeks attacked settlers in Humphreys County, killing six and carrying into captivity Martha Crawley, wife of riverboatman John Crawley. Jackson was en route to Georgia, and the militia response to the incident was organized by Thomas Johnson, who led a detachment to the site, and William P. Anderson, who as Jackson's aide de camp, ordered out reconnoitering parties.

From Thomas Johnson

3 Springs May 27th. 1812

Dear Genl.

Last evening I returned from my expedition to the head of Sandy river; when I arrived at Humphreys Court House I recd. certain intelligence of the Murder of Six Persons[1] on the frontiers, depositions respecting it I will send you by Next Mail;[2] from that I immediately sent a small detachment to the House of Mr. Crawley on Duck river where the Murders was Committed, with spies to cross Duck river, and make discoveries if any Indians was incamped in that quarter, they returned to me at the Camp on Tennessee River, with the information of only the tracts of two at Crawleys since the Murders was Committed, and one Indian in a canoe on the oppisite shore of Tennessee—

Owing to the scarcity of provisions, after crossing the Tennessee I discharged all the troops on foot, and such As had not good Horses, and proceeded with 270 Veterans well mounted, with Mr. Harman my pilote,[3] who was at the Creek incampments on the waters of Sandy & Blood rivers, last fall, we came to Sandy river supposed 20 Miles above the Mouth, followed up the river as near as the situation of the country would admit, the quantity of fissures in the earth & sand thrown up occasioned by the earthquake made it dificult traveling & impracticable near the river, at proper distance I had the swamps & low growns recournitred by detachments on foot. at one place a large incampment was found which appeared to have been some time evacuated, in tracing that river about Thirty Miles & exploring the most of the heads of the Eastern branches, we discovered no fresh sign except of two, whos tracts was in the Swamps of Sandy—when falling on the Head of blood river (being the Name our pilote says it bears) which heads with the waters of Sandy we came to a large incampment where our pilote saw them last fall, but not a tract of recent date to be seen, from the appearance of those camps I think they have not visited them (with a force) since the shakes—Notwithstanding the high Waters and other dificulties in traveling through that country I am confident from the extent of the Rout we took, there is no large town or incampment near that place, because the force represented to be there must live by hunting, and the Country we passed through is favourable for that Object, and no late sign discovered except as above mentioned—

When I returned to the Tennessee I met a small detachment from Williamson County Commanded by Captain [John] Crawford;[4] I ordered a pilote to accompany him into the fork between Duck & Tennessee, where I think it probable the small parties of Indians who infest the frontier have their camps—On my return I conversed with Mrs. Manley[5] who is wounded but still living she says there was only 5 Indians who done the Mischief. I think it probable they are the five remaining after [James] Barfield shot one, a copy of his deposition I sent you—[6]

I shall have prepared by next Mail a particular account of the expedition, with an acct. of the White suspected persons that I apprehended &c—[7]

Had there been a body incamped, and we fortunate enough to find them, I am sure the materials of which my little Army was composed, was such as would have successfully contended with a superior force—the frontier in that quarter is gaurded by the Militia of Humphreys & Dickson; rangers certainly would answer a better purpose: Health & respect

> Thos. Johnson B. G.
> 6th. Brigade of the
> Militia of Ten.

ALS, PHi.

1. According to Martha Crawley's deposition of August 11 (DLC), the six victims were two of her children, a Mr. Hays who lived at the Crawley home, and three of Mrs. Manley's children.

2. The only deposition found is Martha Crawley's.

3. Not further identified.

4. Crawford (Crafford) was commissioned captain in the 21st Regiment of Williamson County in 1809 and served as captain of a volunteer rifle company in the Creek War.

5. Not further identified.

6. Barefield was commissioned ensign in a Rutherford County regiment in 1808. Deposition not found.

7. See Johnson to AJ, June 8.

From Kinchen T. Wilkinson

Nashville may 28th. 1812

My Dear sir,

Tomorrow I start for Giles County, and in consequence of your absence I am induced to trouble you with this—

Every exertion has been made by myself to obtain cash for my Philadelphia friend; I have failed; I am not able to get hardly any thing for my negro men; [(]the only article I calculated on;) suffer me here, again to solicit your goodness. as my place of abode is far remote from nashville; and its being greatly inconvenient for me to attend this place often; I must request of you; in case Mr. Hutching should receive any thing for my negro boy; that you would send it on to Samuel Carswell Philadelphia;[1] I am indebted to him Two hundred and ninety Eight Dollars and 50 Cents with interest from the first of march—

I have partially sold my land; a short time will descide; I will again shortly visit nashville; when I will call and see you.

Present my best respects to mrs Jackson.

I am sir respectfully you &c

K. T Wilkinson

ALS, DLC.

1. Jackson frequently dealt with Samuel Carswell & Co., merchants at 52 Chestnut Street, Philadelphia. He discharged Wilkinson's debt the following year (see AJ to Samuel Carswell, May 19, 1813). It seems probable that the slave mentioned was among those sent to Natchez with Horace Green and perhaps left with John Hutchings at Port Gibson for sale.

The letter below is published in two versions, the copy in Jackson's hand and the polished product in the hand of his aide William P. Anderson. From this point in his career, Jackson entrusted increasing quantities of correspondence to aides and secretaries, either for complete composition or for revision.

To Willie Blount

Hermitage June 4th. 1812—

I have this evening reached home, from my trip to Georgia and my heart bleeds within me on the recept of the news of the horrid cruelty and murders committed by a party of Creeks, on our innocent, wifes and little babes, since I left home—It is with regret I find that Genl Johnston at the head of 500 men was near this place where this horrid scene was acted, and did not either send a detachment in pursuit or follow the trail of these marauders, with his whole force even to their towns—as far as I have yet heard they have Escaped with impunity—*But they must be punished*—and our frontier protected—and as I have no doubt but the are urged on by British agents and tools, the sooner the can be attacked, the less will be their resistance, and the fewer will be the nations or tribes that we will have to war with It is therefore necessary for the protection of the frontier that we march into the creek nation demand the perpetrators, at the Point of the Bayonet—if refused—that we make reprisals—and lay their Towns in ashes—I think I can in three weeks, raise a sufficient force—for this purpose and in six weeks lay their Towns in ashes—I only *want your orders*, the fire of the malitia is up, they burn for revenge, and now is the time to give the creeks the fatal blow, before the expect it—as far as I can learn from the Cherokees, the Creeks are making every preparation for war—the Cherokees will Join us, if we shew an immediate spirit of revenge, and it may deter the bad men of the Choctaws and Chekesaws, from aiding the Creeks—give me the power to procure provisions and munitions of war, by your orders and I will pledge myself for the ballance—powder is scarce but I believe, a sufficient quantity could be obtained for this Expedition in Nashville—lead can be had—I think 2500 men (Volunteers) could quell the Creeks, and bring them to terms without presents or anuities—This number I think I can raise on a short notice—I intend Issuing an order to prepare the minds of the militia for such an event and await your orders or the orders of the Genl Govrt. In the mean time I shall give orders, that a sufficient protection be afforded to the frontier[1]—I shall be impatient for your answer.[2] I am sir with high consideration & respect yr mo. ob. serv.

Andrew Jackson

ALS draft, DLC. Published in Bassett, 1:225–26. Endorsed by William P. Anderson: "A Copy of Letter to Governor Blount," to which Jackson prefixed "Substance of—"
   1. See AJ to the 2nd Division, [June 5].
   2. For Blount's response, see Blount to AJ, June 12, below.

To Willie Blount

Hermitage June 5th. 1812

Dear sir,

I have this moment returned from the State of Georgia. My heart bleeds within me at hearing of the wanton massacre of our women and children by a party of Creeks since I left home.

With infinite regret I learned that Genl. Johnson at the head of 500 men was in the neighborhood of this massacre, at the time of its perpetration, and yet omitted to send a detachment against these marauders or to follow them himself, with his whole force. Thus far they have escaped with impunity carrying off an unfortunate woman along with them. But this cruel outrage must not go unrevengd. The assassins of Women and Children must be punishd.

Now Sir the object of *Tecumpsies* visit to the creek nation is unfolding to us. That incendiary, the emissary of the *Prophet*, who is himself the tool of England, has caused our frontier to be stained with blood, and our peacefull citizens to fly in terror from their once happy abodes.

The sooner we strike, the less resistance we shall have to overcome; and a terrible vengeance inflicted at once upon one tribe may have its effect upon all others.

Even the wretches upon the wabash might take some warning from such a lesson. We must therefore march to the heart of the Creek Nation: a competent force can be raised at the shortest notice; for the spirit of the whole people is on fire. They burn to carry fire and sword to the heart of the Creek Nation, and to learn these wretches in their own Towns and villages what it is to massacre Women and Children at a moment of profound peace. I wait therefore for your Orders! Give me permission to procure provisions and munitions of war, and I pledge myself for the ballance. Twenty five hundred brave men from the 2nd Division will be ready on the first signal to visit the Creek towns, and bring them to terms without the aid of presents and annuities.

In the mean time I have issued an order to prepare the Militia for this Event:[1] and I only wait your orders or those of the general government to carry it into effect. Other orders shall be issued for placing an immediate force upon the frontier, under cover of which the citizens may resume the labours of their fields. I wait with impatience for your answer. I have the honour to be with great consideration yours Respectfully

Andrew Jackson

LS copy, DLC. Published in *Knoxville Gazette*, June 15. Blount probably received a copy of the version dated June 5. He refers to "yours of the 5th. . . ." in his second letter of June 12.
  1. See AJ to the 2nd Division, [June 5].

To George Colbert

Nashville June 5th. 1812.

Friend & Brother!

I learn from the talk which you have sent to Genl Roberts[1] that the Creeks who have been killing our women & children, have passed through your nation carrying along with them stolen horses, scalps, and a white woman prisoner. You tell us that you took two horses from them. Brother, could you not also have taken the woman?

Friend & Brother!

You know I am your friend, and the friend of your nation. The United States is also the friend of the Chickasaws; but this friendship will stop if the Creeks are suffered to march through your nation to attack our frontiers.

You say your nation is a Small nation and the Creeks are numerous. But what have the Chickasaws to fear from the Creeks when the white people are their friends? Do you not remember when the whole Creek Nation came to destroy your Towns that a few hundred chickasaws aided by a few whites chased them back to their nation, Killing the best of their warriors, and covering the rest with Shame?[2] Brother we will do so again if the Creeks dare to touch you for your friendship to us.

Friend & Brother!

If you suffer the Creeks to pass through your nation our people in pursuit of them may kill the Chickasaws through mistake.

If your nation suffers any more scalps or stolen horses to be carried through your nation, your Father the President will have reason to think that the chickasaws are about to let go the treaty they have made with him, and take his enemies by the hand.[3]

Friend & Brother!

Mark what I tell you! The white people will do no wrong to the Indians, and they will suffer the Indians to do no wrong to them—The creeks have killed our women and children: we have sent to demand the murderers, if they are not given up, the whole creek nation shall be covered with blood. fire shall consume their Towns and villages: and their lands shall be divided among the whites—Friend & Brother! You tell us you are the friend of the whites. now prove it to me.

Send me the names of the creeks who have killed our women and children: tell me the towns they belong to; and the place where they have carried the woman.[4]

I am your friend & Brother.

Andrew Jackson

LS copy, DLC. Published in *Knoxville Gazette*, June 15; Bassett, 1:226–27.

1. For Colbert's letters to Isaac Roberts, May 22 and 24, see *Democratic Clarion*, June 2.
2. Jackson was referring to a skirmish in 1793 when several white men joined the Chickasaws against the Creeks, using arms supplied by Southwest Territory Governor William Blount (*ASP, Indian Affairs*, 1:403, 441).
3. Jackson was probably referring to the treaty with the Chickasaws of October 24, 1801 (*ASP, Indian Affairs*, 1:649).
4. A reply from Colbert has not been found. The Creeks, however, did apprehend and execute those involved in the massacre.

From Willie Blount

Knoxville June 12th. 1812

Dear sir,

In reply to your observations respecting the policy of the United States engaging the Cherokees to act against the Creeks[1] I feel myself bound to use with you the utmost candor—I have no confidence in the assurances of any Indians whatever—[John] Lowry and [John] Walker[2] are both said by those who know them to be clever men but they are Indians in part and live amongst Indians and they will play into each others hands—I have no reason to believe that they the Cherokees have at any time been in council with the leaders of the disaffected partisans of the Prophet's party but should not be surprised to learn that they are as far as they dare be secretly influenced in a greater or less degree by these malcontents—and it may be that they have been taught to hold out false colours for special purposes—about 18 months ago there was a very shrewd Indian from the Northern tribes a man of much learning educated in England where he then had correspondents—He staid among those Southern tribes for upwards of one year spending part of his time with one Nation part with another & so on pretending that his Nation and theirs were related & that he was desirous to learn their languages & to unite them in league with each other & with their northern relations and so on[3]—Lowry made strong assurances to you no doubt & he individually ought have thought himself sincere but he don't live among us but with the Indians who could ruin or kill him any hour or day they might find him working in their opinion wrong—There is moreover a strong british party in the Cherokee Nation tho' rather on the back ground in point of strength for some years back—many old tories among them who have been there since the revolution—there is a small british party among the Chickasaws too and among the Creeks that party is very strong—among the Choctaws many and I have no doubt but they all have their lesson & know the part they are expected to act—indeed the American party as I suppose are to be found only just around the Agency houses in the nations respectively—they are in a common way the only part of the Nations who derive benefits from the liberality of the United States—the Agents you know are quite stationary they go but little about in the nations & the Indians know & care but little about them or the United States either—The british Agents no doubt are very busy. why do the Indians in general seem to be in such commotion now we are on the eve of a war with England? it is not long since when they were quiet no way restless—in my letter of this date you see that there is a report that the Cherokees have killed a woman and child[4]—the report came from Mr. [Joseph Hawkins] Windle to Luke Lea[5]—it is true it has not been confirmed by any account of it rendered to me but nevertheless I credit the report—Windle says the report no doubt is correct—He would give no currency to it if he did not believe it—yet another part of the Nation are making friendly assurances nay willing to make a tender of service to Government—I really have no confidence in them as a people and do believe their talks are all fudge—

There should be in each regiment of militia one or two companies of volunteer mounted infantry well equiped holding themselves in readiness to march in a moment—to be willing young men with good aged and experienced officers do you not think so? they could be much relied on—I am told that a number are associating themselves in this end of the State & getting ready as fast as they can—frontier counties should have such in readiness at all events & you should have a list of them—If you would just write to certain men in whom you have full confidence suggesting the thing as proper making no fuss about it, it would soon be done—if troublesome times do come every man should be prepared to do something—each should believe that he could render some important service to his country—one such company in each regiment could be of well picked men, well equiped—John Williams says he will raise such a Company here[6]—It will fall to the lot of Tennessee to defend this frontier—Congress will have enough to do elsewhere & they know nothing of the extent of this frontier—let us be prepared as above stated—I am your friend

Willie Blount

I wrote Major Coffee by last mail the extent of my powers—see it.[7] the

Genl. Government should give the Counties of the states instructions to act according to circumstances.

ALS, DLC.
    1. In the draft letter above to Blount, June 4, Jackson mentioned the idea of Cherokee-white cooperation against the Creeks, but Anderson omitted the reference in the letter forwarded to Blount. Most likely Jackson again referred to the matter in either or both of his letters of June 8 and 9 (not found), acknowledged by Blount in Blount to AJ, June 12.
    2. Lowry, a half-Cherokee chief, owned a ferry across the Tennessee River near the mouth of the Sequatchie River. Contrary to Blount's expectation, Lowry raised nearly 400 Cherokee warriors to fight under Jackson and provided invaluable intelligence information during the Creek War. Walker, also half Cherokee, aided the Americans during the Creek War and during later treaty negotiations was accused of taking bribes for bargaining away Cherokee interests.
    3. This may have been Seekaboo (c1771-c1818), a Shawnee prophet who served as Tecumseh's interpreter. Fluent in several Indian languages and English, he came south with Tecumseh in 1811 and attempted to arouse support for an Indian confederacy. After the Creek War, he escaped into Florida and remained with the Seminoles until his death.
    4. See Blount to AJ, June 12, in which he identifed those attacked as the Williams family in Cocke County. In his letter of June 14, Blount informed Jackson that Williams's neighbors had perpetrated a hoax by feigning an Indian attack.
    5. Lea, from Hawkins County and former clerk of the state House, later represented Tennessee in the U.S. House of Representatives.
    6. Williams, adjutant general of the state of Tennessee, commanded the 39th Regiment, U.S. Infantry, 1813–15.
    7. Letter not found.

To Willie Blount

Nashville June 17th. 1812

Dear Sir
    I have the honor to acknowledge the recpt of your two letters of date 12th. instant, which is Just to hand[1]—and I am favoured with the perusal of your letter to Major John Coffee of the 6th instant[2] all of which I have carefully perused—and their contents duly noted—I heartily concur with you in your ideas with respect, to the little confidence that ought to be placed in the aid or friendship of Indians—but I do think that policy will dictate the propriety of inlisting one nation against another—if they will go to war, those that are not for us must be against us—if the will attempt to deceive by part of a nation holding out the olive branch whilst the others are scalping us let us make the aparent friends, Join in punishing the hostile part—If we get the Cherokees, engaged with the Creeks, they will be obliged to be friendly with us to preserve themselfs—I believe self interest and self preservation the most predominant passion— fear is better than love with an indian—Therefore the policy to enlist Lowry, Walker & the Ridge[3] in our service, and make them furnish a sufficient number for pilots, to the Creek towns, and manage the ballance so as to deceive the Creeks, by giving them orders to march always at a distant period, when troops would at that time be actually in the creek

towns for I am of the oppinion that either the Cherokees or chickasaws would advise the Creeks of any campaign against them if the knew it—

I am happy to find that a supply of arms & equipments can be had, and immediately on the recpt of your orders for the arms and equipments, I shall send Mr Eli Hammond for them across by land, to get them put into some of our merchants Boats who are loaded for this place three are shortly expected from Pittsburg to pass Newport—on their way thither— Mr. Hammond is a man in whom the utmost confidence can be placed and well acquainted with boating.

Rest assured I have the militia in a state of readiness that I could in three days move with 2500 volunteers against the creeks—& I shall have (where there is not already) one company of mounted infantry as you recommend in each Regiment—Should the report of Mrs Williams and her child being murdered be true, it proves fully the combination of all the nations to the south with the phrophet[4]—as soon as I can get the arms from Newport I will be ready—and the spirit of the times here says speedy vengeance will await the friends of the phrophet—for let Col. [Benjamin] Hawkins say what he will the truth is the great body of the creeks are for war—and it is almost impossible that he Colo. Hawkins could have wrote on the 18th of May, and that reached North Carolina, & there published in the Raleigh paper and in Nashville on the 12th of June[5]—Mr. Luster[6] did state to Capt. Strothert and my self on the night of the 24th. of May, that on the 22nd. he saw the Colo. and his family in milledgeville and that he had moved his family owing to the hostile attitude of the creek nation we had the same report from other channels—I see and note from your letter to Major Coffee, the extent of your power— Indeed I knew, that by the laws of the state you had no other power but to order out men to repell invasion &c &c—that you could only make defencive war but I did expect that the President seeing the situation of the north western frontier would have given you full and ample power, to have defended your frontier in every way necessary & proper, and not to have waited untill a blow was struct, and then give you orders to apply a remedy—This is sending for a Phician after the patient is dead—rest assured that my malitia are ready and will act promptly and eficiently when ordered—

I hope to be able to have compleat returns to you, under your two last orders[7] in a verry short time I wrote for some explanation to the adjutant genl. by last fridays mail[8]—which I hope to receive by next friday; the differrent Genls, are acting in anticipation of my order having seen yours and will have their respective quotas in ten days from the time they receive my order, I can only make the apportionment by Brigades—The law does not require the Brigade Major to make a return to me of the strength & condition of their Brigades, I have no data to Judge of their respective strength, and can only divide the men wanted equally between the five Brigades—

I am advised that Capt [David] Masons Company[9] is not yet in the field but will march on saturday—with assurances of respect and Esteem I am yr mo. ob. serv.

Andrew Jackson

ALS draft, DLC. Published in Bassett, 1:227–29.
1. For the two letters, see above, and Blount to AJ, June 12.
2. Not found.
3. Major Ridge, leader of the Cherokee party that cooperated with Jackson's army.
4. For Blount's account of Mrs. Williams, see Blount to AJ, June 12 and 14.
5. In his letter of May 18 (published in the *Raleigh Register*, May 29, and extracted in the *Democratic Clarion*, June 16), Hawkins, Creek agent, wrote that "our Chiefs are unanimously opposed to having any thing to do in the wars of the white people; some of our wild young people are for mischief, & will act as the impression of the moment impels them: But such is the state of the Indian preparation for peace, that they cannot do mischief with impunity."
6. Not identified.
7. Blount to AJ, April 17, is the only order found relating to returns.
8. Letter not found.
9. Mason was commissioned lieutenant in the Williamson County militia in 1811. In June 1812 he organized a company of volunteer rangers to patrol West Tennessee and later took a company to the Creek War.

To Willie Blount

Nashville July 3rd. 1812

Dr. Sir

On the 29th ultimo, Mr E. Hammond set out for Newport Kentuckey, with instructions, and determination to be here at as Early a day as possible, I hope he will be at Nashville on the 20th Instant—with the arms and Equipments, doubts has been sugested here, of there being the quantity of arms at Newport, and it has been stated, that what are there, is not fit for use—this has reached me since Mr H Started—let this be as it may, I have directed Mr Hammond to receive good arms, and I have requested the agent to send none but such as are fit for immediate use—I am really fearfull that we will be disappointed, in the receipt of them—

I have had my eye to the recpt. of those arms, to commence my movements against the Creek nation—on the event that the captive, together with the captors are not delivered to the United States, which I do not expect—The safety of our whole frontier requires, a speedy stroke against the Creeks, and with or without orders, the present spirit of the Citizens require, an immediate movement to be made—Nay I may say the safety of our Frontier, and that a speedy end may be put to indian hostity imperiously demand it. I shall wait no longer than the 20th. or 25th. instant— with such arms and supplies as I can obtain I shall penetrate the creek Towns, untill the Captive, with her Captors are delivered up, and think myself Justifiable, in laying waste their villiages, burning their houses, killing their warriors and leading into Captivity their wives and Children—untill I do obtain a surrender of the Captive, and the Captors—I find a great scarcity of amunition here it will be dificult to obtain a supply—Should I be disappointed in the musquetts from Newport, it will be a serious, injury and inconvenience in the contemplated scurging of the creeks—I am Just (verbally) advised that Capt Masons Spies five in Number, fell in with four indians believed to be Shaonese, and killed one and wounded two, so soon as I receive Capt Masons report, will advise you thereof— [1]

I shall thank you for any advice you have recd. from the war department on the subject of the Depredation of the Creeks—

By next mail I shall write Colo. Thos. P[etters] Carnes of Georgia[2] asking his cooperation with me, with a body of men from Georgia to make an attack upon the South Eastern tribes of the Creeks at the same time I make the stroke on the north western a combined movement and sudden blow will give us eternal peace with the Southern tribes—

I am Sir with due respect & Esteem yr mo. ob. serv.

Andrew Jackson

ALS copy, DLC. Published in Bassett, 1:229–30.
1. Mason reported on July 22 that his patrol had mistakenly fired on a Choctaw hunting party.
2. Carnes was a former state legislator, congressman, and judge of the western circuit court of Georgia. Letter not found.

Though acquitted of treason in 1807, Aaron Burr remained entangled in the aftermath of his ill-fated western venture. So did Jackson. When Burr journeyed south from Nashville in December 1806 (according to newspaper reports in 1828), he had carried with him the October 4, 1806, account with Jackson (see above). Burr left this and other papers in Mississippi Territory at the time of his arrest. These documents eventually fell into the hands of Harman Blennerhassett, who had settled near Natchez as a cotton planter after the Richmond trial. Blennerhassett had financed much of Burr's abortive enterprise. He tried to recover his losses from Burr and some of Burr's other associates but, by 1808, when Burr left for Europe, he had secured only a partial repayment from Burr's son-in-law, Joseph Alston. Under financial distress in 1811, Blennerhassett attempted to extort the funds Burr and Alston allegedly owed him by threatening to publish documents in his hands which he claimed would reveal the "truth" about the western conspiracy. Among those documents was Burr's account with Jackson. In the letter below, Jonathan Thompson, acting for Blennerhassett in Natchez, implicitly threatened Jackson with blackmail.

Neither Jackson nor Burr succumbed to Blennerhassett's threat. Never-

theless, Blennerhassett did not publish his documents. Instead, he took his case before the Adams County, Miss. Terr., Superior Court in 1813. Based on the Burr account with Jackson, which suggested that Jackson still owed Burr money, the court subpoenaed Jackson as a garnishee in Blennerhassett v. Burr. While in Mississippi on the Natchez expedition, both Jackson and John Coffee filed depositions with the court on March 25, 1813 (see below). The case was continued from the April to the October session, 1813, with Jackson again summoned. Then preparing to leave with his troops for the Creek country and unable to attend, Jackson filed another deposition, supported by a statement from William Eastin (see AJ to the Adams County Superior Court, September 25, 1813, below). In April 1815, the court rendered its verdict, setting aside any claims upon Jackson.

From Jonathan Thompson

Natchez July 3d. 1812

Sir

There has been lately put in my hands by a person to whom Col. A. Burr is indebted among other papers an account Current apparntly in your hand writing and between you and him on which appears a balance due to Col B. of $1726.62½.[1] The person who put these papers in my hands wishes to have his debt, and has instructed me to write you on the subject. My object now is to learn from you whether the said balance is yet due from you and if not wheʀt and how it has been paid.

No person is acquainted with these circumstances except the one who gave me the papers and myself & it would be with reluctance that he would be the cause of their being further made known.

I should be glad to hear from you on the subject of this letter as soon as may meet your convenience. I am Respectfully your obdt. Sevt

J. Thompson

ALS, DLC. Thompson had accompanied Burr on the expedition down the river in 1807. He remained in Natchez, where he died of yellow fever in 1823.
1. For the account, see above, October 4, 1806.

The following article appeared in the Democratic Clarion *in response to Blount's letter of July 4, relaying the news from the secretary of war that negotiations, not punitive action by the Tennessee militia, would be undertaken to free Martha Crawley from her Creek captors. The style and tone of the article and its treatment of matters which Jackson and Blount had discussed in correspondence that had not been published in the newspapers, are persuasive evidence that Jackson was the author.*

The Massacre at the Mouth of Duck River

[cJuly 7, 1812]

It is now nearly two months since this cruel outrage, this act of war against the peaceful inhabitants of our country, has been perpetrated. No vengeance has yet been taken: no atonement has yet been made: The Creek nation has taken no step to absolve themselves from the guilt of this offence; in fact they have made the crime their own by the reception which they have given to the assassins, & by refusing to send home the prisoner who has been carried to one of their principal towns.[1] But the remembrance of this bloody deed is not to pass away: its actors and their patrons are not to escape with impunity. An urgent application has been made to the general government for permission to lead an expedition to the heart of the Creek nation;[2] an answer is expected in a very few days; and it is evidently hoped that the only measure which can secure to the frontiers safety and tranquility will not be prohibited.

Preparations in the mean while are not delayed. A thousand stand of arms had been destined by the general government to the state of Tennessee; they had been sent to Newport on the Ohio, opposite Cincinnati; but the legislature had omitted to make any appropriation to cover their transportation to this state. To get the arms to this place was now an object of the first magnitude; but there was no money to defray the expense of bringing them. The zeal of the Major general of the second division has not been stopped by this obstacle. In conjunction with the governor he has caused the necessary sums to be advanced. A messenger has been dispatched to Newport, and it is now expected that one thousand muskets with their bayonets and equipments, and 18 thousand cartridges, are on their way to Nashville.[3] Provisional contracts for powder and lead, and supplies for the troops, have also been contemplated.

But we are fearful to rely with an implicit confidence on the disposition of the general government. Facts present themselves to our remembrance, the evidence of which cannot be rejected. In the settlement of Kentucky and Cumberland, in the wars between the whites and the Indians, every expedition by the former into the country of the latter, was made not only without the consent of the general government, but in defiance of its prohibition. The celebrated expedition against Nick-a-Jack, which put an end to the Cherokee war, was a secret movement on the part of the people, as carefully concealed from the constituted authorities as from the Indians whom they were going to attack.[4] Even at the present moment, when the blood hounds of the prophet are traversing the Indiana Territory; when governor Harrison is bound up in Vincennes; when the peaceful cultivators are flying from their farms, or killed at their firesides; it is a fact that the governor is not permitted to march out and disperse the wretches who are laying waste his country and threatening to storm his capital!

With these evidences before their eyes the people of Tennessee cannot but reflect upon the possibility of seeing the application rejected which they have made for leave to march to the Creek nation. We earnestly hope, trust, and pray that this may not be the case: but as it is possible, and as we have been the sufferers, and must be so again, it behoves us to be prepared at all points and for all events.

If then the expedition to the Creeks is not permitted by the general government the people of Tennessee will have to consider for themselves what ought to be done. It is impossible for them to permit the assassins of women and children to escape with impunity and with triumph. They cannot submit to the prospect of an Indian war, protracted through several years, and kept alive by the murder of peaceful families in the dead hour of the night. They know that the exertions of the rangers cannot terminate the war: they are a sort of defence only calculated for exposed points: in fact their utmost vigilance can easily be eluded, and the frontiers continually harrassed in defiance of their care. What then can we do, but to imitate the conduct of those who marched to Nick-a-Jack and terminated by one blow the war which had so long depopulated the infant settlements of Tennessee.

Citizens! hold yourselves in readiness: it may be but a short time before the question is put to you: *Are you ready to follow your general to the heart of the Creek nation.*

Text from *Democratic Clarion*, July 8. Original not found.
1. In a statement which preceded the essay above, the *Democratic Clarion* reported that Mrs. Crawley was held at Tuckabatchee.
2. See above, AJ to Willie Blount, July 3.
3. See Blount to AJ, June 12 and 23; see above, AJ to Blount, June 17, July 3.
4. On the Nickajack campaign, see *Jackson*, 1:102–95 passim.

To Willie Blount

Nashville July 8th 1812

Dear Sir

I have to acknowledge the recpt of your letter of the 25th of June enclosing a coopy of yours to the Secratary of war of the same date,[1] making a tender agreable to my request of the services of the Volunteers of my Division to the President of the united—The sentiments you have been pleased to express to the Secratary of war of me, is truly gratefull to my feelings, and in return I can only observe, I will endeavour to merrit them[2]—your letter of the 30th of June announcing a declaration of *war* with great Britain has been recd. and duly *noted*;[3] and for the event we are ready, and if the arms had arived; I could say perfectly prepared—The return of the muster rolls of the Volunteers shall be made to you at as early a day, as the can be obtained from the respective corps in the dif. ferrent Brigades. some of the returns have been made to me by Genl Winchester whilst commanding the 4th Brigade, stating the number of officers and men—Through Genl [William] Hall[4] I expect to recive a compleat Roll as early as he can obtain it from the differrent captains all of which shall be forwarded as soon as obtained—I have the pleasure to acknowledge the receipt of your favour of the 4th instant[5] covering a coopy of the Secratarys letter of the 22nd. of June acknowledging the receipt of your letter to him on the subject of Mrs. crawly captive with the creeks, and the murders committed on our frontier by a party of that nation—It would have afforded me much pleasure to have seen the Secratary of war treating that subject with that serious attention that its importance deserved, and the magnitude of the offence required and meritted—But to pass over it with a bare acknowledgement of the receipt of your letter, that he has transmitted it to B[enjamin] H[awkins] Esqr with directions to procure the release of Mrs. Crawley, and to demand a surrender of the Indians to the authority of the united States, is as little, as he could have said on the receipt of a communication from you as chief executive of the state, stating that a party of Creeks had Killed an old sow with her litter of pigs, and drove one off to the nation—This is not such a notice as I expected from the crisis and the extent of the murders, (with the unusual barbarity even among savages) would have been paid to this subject—The time, and circumstances, together with the influence under which government think the indians are excited to hostility on our frontier ought to have induced the Secratary, to have said to you a little more, and at least, to have given you authority, on the answer of Hawkins to you, that the captive with the captors was not surrendered, to have marched a campaign against the creeks—This would have been noticing the subject as its importance required, and calculated to give the frontier full confidence that the goverment of the united States would aid the state goverment in protecting them—and put an end to their breaking up on the frontier—I would barely ask; was it not as violent attack and marked with as much indignity towards our goverment as any ever committed. was not the murder of our weomen and children in a state of profound peace more aggravating, than any act of great Britain and does the government with their long experience still think that this too is a subject for negociation—and that the feelings of a country possessing humanity can wait the slow opperations of a tedious negotiation for a redress of their wrongs of such a bloody hue, and at a time that nothing but energy and dispatch will prevent their frontier from breaking up, this cannot be seriously calculated on by rulers that reflect—I anticipated that you would receive an answer from the Secratary of war about the time you did, and on the 8th. instant requested a council of officers from my Division, in Nashville—which will determine the date of our movements against the creeks—the result of our deliberations shall be made known to you in due time The war begun must not linger on our part—and as Mr. Grundy has made an appeal to our patriotism, in my division he will not be disappointed[6]—and we hope we will not be disappointed in his support and that of the goverment of the united States—

with Sincere Esteem and due respect I am Sir yr Mo. ob. Serv.

Andrew Jackson

P.M. I enclose you a paper that contains Capt Masons report[7] to me of the indians Killed alluded to in my last—[8]   A. J.

ALS copy, DLC.
1. See Blount to AJ, June 25.
2. In his letter to Eustis, Blount described Jackson as "a brave and patriotic Genl. . . . He loves his country, and his countrymen have full confidence in him—He delights in peace; but does not fear war—" (Blount to Eustis, June 25, DLC).
3. See Blount to AJ, June 30. Congress declared war on June 18.
4. Hall commanded the 1st Infantry regiment on the Creek expedition.
5. See Blount to AJ, July 4.
6. For Grundy's July 7 circular letter to the citizens of West Tennessee, appealing for volunteers, see *Democratic Clarion*, July 7.
7. Probably the July 7 *Democratic Clarion*, containing David Mason to AJ, July 1.
8. See above, AJ to Willie Blount, July 3.

To the 2nd Division

July 9th, 1812.

CITIZENS! SOLDIERS OF THE SECOND MILITARY DIVISION!

IT is now more than a month since you were ordered to prepare for a march to the Creek nation.[1] At the moment of issuing that order, a report of the cruel massacre at the mouth of Duck river, was forwarded to the executive of this State, and by him to the Government of the United States.[2] It was expected that the official account of the invasion of our Territory, the capture of one of our people, and the massacre of so many others, would have drawn from the General Government permission for the brave men of West-Tennessee to have demanded at the point of the bayonet, immediate and ample atonement for an outrage so atrocious and so unprovoked. In the belief that an order to this effect would have been received by the mail of the 7th inst. such of the officers of the Second Division as were at hand had been convened on this day at Nashville, for the purpose of fixing on the moment when your march should commence. But the expected order has not arrived. In place of it, the Executive of the State has been informed by the War Department that a formal application is at this moment making at the instance of the U. States through Col. HAWKINS to effect the liberation of Mrs. CRAWLEY, and the surrender of the Creeks who committed the murders at the mouth of Duck river.[3] Your just vengeance, your impatience to appease the manes of so many women and children inhumanly massacred, must therefore be deferred for one month longer. In the course of that time the result of the application through Col. Hawkins will be known. If the assassins are delivered up and the unfortunate woman restored to her friends, then the Creek nation will have absolved themselves from the guilt of a great crime. But if this is not done, then will the Creek nation have adopted the crime of some of her individual members & the nation must be held responsible for it. The brave men of the second Military Division will then have to march; and woe to the man who is unwilling to do so! He that can see the infant babe of nine days old torn from the arms of its mother and beat to pieces upon the walls of the house—he that can see children of six years of age stabbed with knives, their heads split open with *Tomahawks*, and others torn to pieces, and devoured alive by dogs—he that can view in the midst of this scene a distracted mother crying in vain for pity, and receiving from the hands of savage monsters stab after stab, and arrow after arrow, into her body: He that beholds all this, and yet say no vengeance ought to be taken for such enormities, may indeed be a happy man, but I envy him not his feelings. No! The wretch who can view the massacre at the mouth of Duck river, and feel not his spirit kindle within him and burn for revenge, deserves not the name of a *man*; and the mother who bore him should point with the finger of scorn, and say "*He is not my son.*"

Tho' suspended for a moment, the idea of a march to the Creeks is not, cannot be abandoned. The military preparations will not be relaxed, but will go forward with the same activity as if no demand was making. Measures have been taken to transport to our state A THOUSAND STAND OF ARMS, destined to our use by the General Government. Provisional contracts for Powder and Lead have been entered into. Supplies of provisions will be attended to with the most anxious solicitude on the part of your General. The Officers and Soldiers of the second Division commanded by the order of June 5th,[4] to place themselves in readiness for a march to the Creek towns, are accordingly again commanded to hold themselves completely prepared to move at the shortest notice.

Citizens! Soldiers of the Second Military Division!

War has been declared by the United States against the King of Great Britain. As a constituent part of the American nation we are ready, at any moment, to march to any point, to meet the enemies of the Republic. But, before we march, we must have an assurance that our wives and children are to be safe in our absence: and that assurance can only be derived from the surrender and punishment of the assassins who have taken refuge with the Creeks, or by marching an army into their country and laying it waste with fire and sword.

The Generals of Brigade attached to the second division, are charged with the execution of this order.

ANDREW JACKSON, *Major General*
of the Second Division

Text from *Democratic Clarion*, July 14. Original not found.
1. See AJ to the 2nd Division, [June 5].
2. See above, AJ to Willie Blount, June 5; see also Blount to AJ, June 25.
3. See Blount to AJ, July 4.
4. See AJ to the 2nd Division, [June 5].

From Willie Blount

Knoxville July 21st. 1812

Dear Sir,

I have the pleasure to transmit to you, and thro' you to the volunteers of your Division, the copy of a letter this day recd. from the Secy War[1] in answer to mine of the 25th. of June, in which, I communicated to him, their, and your patriotic tender of service to the President of the United States, in conformity with the provisions of the act of Congress, passed Feby 6th. 1812, authorizing him to accept the services of fifty thousand volunteers—

The high terms of satisfaction he expresses in his acceptance of the tender, evinces his pleasure at your conduct; and is also expressive of the very high opinion he entertains of the genuine patriotism and zeal felt and manifested by such brave defenders of their country's rights—Such an evidence of the readiness and desire to be useful, as this, and your tender affords, reflects the highest honor on them, on you, and on the State; whilst, at the same time, it teaches the enemies to American liberty and Independence to know, that they shall not only cease to violate, but shall respect our rights.

For the honor done to the State, by making this tender of service, permit me to offer my thanks to you, and to the volunteers of your Division; & to say, that I believe the most perfect reliance may be placed in your, and in their exertions, on all trying occasions—

I have reason to believe that a considerable number of volunteers raised under the act, are about to make a tender of service to the President, from the first Division—what can be more pleasing or interesting than to see citizen soldiers, animated with the love of country, vieing in a laudable manner with each other who shall be foremost in taking the field in defence of their common country? nothing can be more to the credit of any people—I am respectfully, your Obt. Servant

Willie Blount

Of this date I have written a letter to Capt. Eli Hammond, directed to him at Nashville & have informed him that in his absence you would be requested to open it and attend to the contents—it is directed to your care—and hope you will not find it too troublesome to comply[2]—send a copy of the Secy. War's letter to each of them as they otherwise may be at a loss to know what that letter will inform them of—

you observe that the Secy. War in his answer to mine of the 25th. Instant has observed entire silence as to that part of my letter which recommended that the Creeks should by order of the General Government be soundly drubed[3]—I cannot account for silence on that head—Col. Hawkins has not yet acknowledged the receipt of my letter making the demand—I have no doubt but he has recd. it and also the Secy. War's letter to him on the same subject, but I have not been so informed—flying report says that the Creeks have sent the unfortunate Mrs. Crawley home but it has not been communicated to me thro' any authentic source[4]—I am willing to hope it is so but I don't know that I believe it is—I shall not believe without full evidence—A Cherokee is here who says the murderers have gone off to the Prophett—fudge—

ALS, DLC.
1. See below.
2. Letter not found.
3. See above, AJ to Blount, July 8.
4. Mrs. Crawley escaped from her Creek captors in late July.

ENCLOSURE: WILLIAM EUSTIS TO WILLIE BLOUNT

Copy   War Department July 11th. 1812
Sir,
   I have the honor to acknowledge the receipt of your Excellency's letter of the 25th. of June—The tender of service by General Jackson and the Volunteers under his command, is received by the President with peculiar satisfaction, and in accepting their services He cannot withhold an expression of His admiration of the zeal and ardor by which they are animated.

   The addition to the volunteer act authorising the President, in the recess of the Senate, to commission the officers, passed on the last days of the late Session, will be transmitted as soon as it can be published.[1]

   Very respectfully Your Excellency's obt. Servant

                                        Signed   W. Eustis

Copy, DLC.
1. Under the act of February 6, authorizing the president to accept the services of 50,000 volunteers, the officers of units already organized were to remain in their posts, and officers for newly organized units were to be selected in accordance with state and territorial laws governing the militia. Their service was to be for twelve months after the date of rendezvous unless earlier discharged. The July 6 amendment to the act empowered the president to appoint and commission officers of previously organized volunteer units as well as of those which would in the future be organized. This change in the law, passed after the Tennessee

Volunteers had tendered their services, became a matter of considerable concern to Jackson and some of his officers as they prepared to leave for the Natchez expedition (*Annals of Congress*, 12th Cong., 1st sess., Appendix, pp. 2235–37, 2362; see also, AJ to John Williams, August 25, below).

To the Tennessee Volunteers

Division Orders!   July 31st 1812.

Patriotic Volunteers of the Second Division!

At the signal of your Country's danger you have repaired to the national Standard with the ardor which characterizes freemen. The tender of service which you have made to the President of the United States, has been accepted by him;[1] and your names are now enrolled among the defenders of the rights and liberties of the only free people remaining on earth.

The sacred charge which you have taken into your hands will not be abandoned by you; nor will the sword which you have drawn be returned to its scabbard untill the proud Mistress of the Ocean has been taught to respect the rights of a great and rising Republic. But at the moment that you are entering on a new profession, remember that military ardor and Civil virtues will be inefficient in the hour of Battle unless accompanied by other qualifications. Discipline, a knowledge of the art of War, a strict subordination, are the pride of the Soldier's character: they lay the foundation of success against the enemy, and make a conquering army the blessing and the ornament of its Country.

Brave Soldiers!

A slight alteration has taken place in your organization. The commissions of your officers will be derived from the President, instead of the State Executive. Hence the necessity of compleat and correct Muster rolls being immediately made out, and forwarded to the Major General.

Brave Men!

The War has now begun. Your Brothers in arms from the Northern States are passing into the country of your enemies; & (I know your impatience) you burn with anxiety to learn on what theatre your arms will find employment. Then turn your eyes to the South! Behold in the province of West Florida, a territory whose rivers and harbors, are indispensable to the prosperity of the Western, and still more so, to the eastern Division of our State. Behold there likewise the asylum from which an insidious hand incites to rapine and bloodshed, the ferocious savages, who have just stained our frontiers with blood, and who will renew their outrages the moment an English force shall appear in the Bay of Pensacola. It is here that an employment adapted to your situation awaits your courage and your zeal: and while extending in this quarter the boundaries of the Republic to the Gulf of Mexico, you will experience a peculiar satisfaction in having confered a signal benefit on that section of the Union to which you yourselves immediately belong. The Generals of Brigade attached to the Second Division will cause muster rolls to be made out, and forwarded to the Major General in conformity with the intention of this order.

(Signed)　Andrew Jackson
Majr Genl Second Division

Typed copy and copy fragment, DLC.
1. See above, Willie Blount to AJ, July 21.

To John Williams

Nashville August 25th. 1812

Sir

I have the honor herewith to inclose to you muster rolls and inspection returns of the Detachment from my Division in conformity with the orders of his Excellency Willie Blount Esqr Governor of the state, through you of Date the seventh of June 1812.[1]

you will observe from the returns that I have caused this Detachment to be organized into five Batalions, which makes one Batalion from each Brigade—which I have organized into one regiment and ordered Colo. John K[nibb] Winn Lt Colo. commandant of Wilson County to Take the command thereof and hold himself in readiness to march at the first signal from the President of the united States.[2]

I have recd no return from the Seventh Brigade—I have taken the necessary steps to enforce a return from the Brigadier General commanding said Brigade at an Early day—I am advised that his quota is ready for the field—but not officially from him, therefore cannot notice it—as soon as I receive his return shall forwarded it without delay—[3]

The returns forwarded, only reached me this morning by mail—Therefore my return inclosed, is made in a hurry before the mail closes that no time may be lost in forwarding them on to the Department of war—

My Volunteers are ready for the field, and their rolls nearly compleat—I am instructed by the Governor to make return of them to him here or I Should have forwarded them to you by this mail—some of the boisterous patriotts of the day, on the promulgation of the suplementary act to the act of Congress of the 6th. of February 1812 have like valient heroes shrunk from their tender under the pitifull evasion that the Volunteers will not be commanded by the officers of their own choice—This conduct I have viewed with regret, whilst on the other hand I have the pleasure to see others—who have not been so clamourous, but with that calm deliberate firmness that always characterise the good citizen and brave soldier stepping forward to supply their places—and rallying around the eagles of their country determined to protect them or die in the last ditch—

accept assurances of my Esteem & respect

Andrew Jackson Majr.
Genl 2 Division Tennessee.

ALS, PHi; ALS draft, DLC.

1. Neither Blount's orders through Williams nor the muster rolls and inspection returns have been found.

2. Wynne (1765–1847), a Wilson County planter, served periodically in county government and the state legislature. From the fall of 1813 until his discharge in January 1814, he commanded the 1st Regiment of the West Tennessee detached militia. For Jackson's orders, see AJ to Wynne, August 25.

3. See AJ to Bird Smith, August 13 and September 8. Smith (1761–1815), an early settler of White County, served in the Tennessee General Assembly, 1809–13, and was commissioned general of the 7th Brigade in 1810. He commanded a brigade of volunteers in William Carroll's division during the New Orleans campaign.

By September 1812, Jackson's volunteers were ready to be mustered into service, but the war department did not call for Tennessee troops until the end of October, and Jackson did not officially enroll his army until December 10.

To Willie Blount

NASHVILLE, SEPTEMBER 8th [1812]

Sir

I have received roll from the volunteers, of my division, tendered thro' you to the President of the United States and which I have the honor to command, to the amount of two thousand.[1]

I have ready for the field, under my order of the 19th of June,[2] eleven hundred and eleven men, officers inclusive, being part of 100,00[0] militia which the President is authorised to call into the field.[3]

I have also standing in readiness the class of the Militia of my division all which or any part thereof I am ready to march at the head of to any point your Excellency may please to command.

The unpleasent news of Gen. [William] Hull's surrender to the British and their savage allies, received this day may make aid in that quarter desirable,[4] it will give me pleasure, with your approbation, to march to the relief of that quarter without delay. The General Assembly being in session can easily afford the means of supply, until provided, by the General Government. I have the honor to be with high consideration & respect your Excellency's most obt. servant.

ANDREW JACKSON.

Text from *Democratic Clarion*, September 11. Original not found.

1. For the tender of service of the Volunteers of the 2nd Division under the act of Congress of February 6, see Blount to William Eustis, June 25, DLC; for the acceptance, see above, Eustis to Blount, July 11, enclosed in Blount to AJ, July 21.

2. See AJ to the 2nd Division, June 19.

3. Jackson was here referring to the act of April 10, authorizing the detachment, organization, and arming of 100,000 militiamen, apportioned among the states, to be called when needed into service for six months from the time of rendezvous (2 *U.S. Statutes at Large* 705).

4. On August 16, William Hull surrendered his army at Detroit.

To the 2nd Division

September 8th, 1812.

Citizens! Soldiers of the second Division!

Your division has already produced a greater number of volunteers than any other section of the Union of the same population. But because you have done much, you are not to stop short in your exertions, and to think of doing no more.

The disaster of the north western army should rouse from his apathy every man who has yet slumbered over the public welfare: it should induce a universal determination to reject and to despise the allurements of repose until the memory of that misfortune shall be effaced from the public mind, and lost in the triumph of numerous victories.

Citizens! The war into which you have been forced by the crimes of England has received your entire, your warmest approbation: your determination to support it with your lives and fortunes has been repeatedly avowed: judge then of the regret with which it must be learnt that, at a moment so eventful, there should be found one American citizen who comes forward with excuses and pitiful evasions to screen himself from the honors and the dangers in the field. That there are some such, cannot be denied; that there are many, cannot be pretended: The crowd of volunteers who have already enrolled their names, evinces the patriotic ardor of the great body of the people.

Citizens! These are the times which distinguish the real friend of his country from the town-meeting-bawler, and the sunshine patriot. While *these* are covering their conduct with the thinnest disguises, and multiplying excuses to keep them at home, the former steps forth, and proclaims his readiness to march. But it is not every individual that is required to quit his occupation and march to the frontier. Our State contains more than 40,000 men able to bear arms; cannot one out of eight be spared for the service of his country: may not the State of Tennessee have the honor of sending 5000 volunteers to the field of battle?

Brave Citizens! Do not stand to stipulate for the theatre on which you are to fight. It is enough for a brave man to know that his country needs his services; no matter whether against the *Creeks* in the south, or the

Showaneese in the north; whether against the blacks at *Pensacola*, or the *British* in Detroit. He that tells you one place is too cold, will say that another is too hot; nor any climate be found that will suit his temperament.[1]

Young men who are anxious to share in the perils of their country, and who have omitted to raise companies under the division orders of March 7th.[2] are now invited to come forward; the crisis demands their services; and their tender will be thankfully received. Those who have already raised companies are requested to augment their numbers to 66 rank & file, and to add a second lieutenant to each Company.

Citizens! The soldiers of your Ancient tyrant profane with their invasion the soil of the U. States. Michilimackinack, Detroit, and Brownstown, are in their possession, and crowds of ferocious savages are carrying death and terror before them. The State of Tennessee will be called upon soon, a greater number may be required than the volunteers enrolled, and the quota of the hundred thousand militia.[3] By the division orders of June 5th[4] the first class of the militia of the second division, or the second where the first had performed a tour of duty, were ordered to be held in readiness to move at the shortest notice. The same order is now reiterated. It is also ordered that the rolls of volunteers which have not been returned be forthwith forwarded, without further delay.

The Major-General remarks that if the first class held ready for duty join themselves to the volunteers, they will participate in the honors and emoluments of that *corps*, if they are forced out as militia they will serve under all the disadvantages of that species of troops.

Citizens! Let not the rumored armistice relax your exertion. It will be an armistice on one side alone. For while the American army shall sheathe its sword, the tomahawk and the scalping knife will redouble their activity, and mingle together the blood of grayheaded age, of the tender mother, and the infant babe.

Disastrous intelligence is received from *New Orleans* the hand of Providence has smote that city;[5] the approach of the enemy adds to the horror of its situation. The *Balize* is already occupied by the English, and they march to the attack of *Plaquemine*! *Citizens*! Be ready! you must and will be employed and how scandalous to be found unprepared, when you are ordered to march to the assistance of your brethren.

The Generals of Brigade attached to the second division will attend to the execution of this order.

ANDREW JACKSON,
Majr. Genl. 2nd Division of Ten

Text from *Democratic Clarion Extra*, September 8. Original not found.

1. On August 22, Secretary of War Eustis informed Blount that Tennessee's militia might be called into service on the northwestern frontier under General William Henry Harrison (DLC).

2. See above.

3. On October 21, Eustis directed Blount to call out and place in readiness 1,500 Ten-

nessee militiamen in conformity with the detached militia act of April 10 (Eustis to Blount, October 21, DLC).

4. See AJ to the 2nd Division, [June 5].

5. A violent hurricane, destroying naval vessels and defensive positions, had hit New Orleans on August 18.

From Jonathan Thompson

Natchez Sept. 30. 1812

Sir

I had the honor some time since to address you a letter, which I fear may not have come to hand.[1] In that letter I informed you that a Friend of mine (Mr. Blen[ne]rhassett) had some years ago advanced considerable sums of money to Col. Burr and on his account which still remained due to him. I also stated that Mr. B. had put into my hands an a/c current apparently in your own hand-writing and on which appeared a balance due from you to Col. B. of something more than $[1]700.[2] If this sum be due to Col. B from you, Mr. B. thinks it might as well be paid to him, and thus save a small part of his otherwise great & probably total losses as to be otherwise disposed of. I also repeat to you that not knowing the motives under which the transactions between you and Col. B. took place, or the inducements that might operate with you to wish to prevent their being disclosed; you might rely on inviolable secresy on my part and that of Mr. B. while any hope remained of bringing the matter to an amiable arrangement. With your answer to this letter, which I shall expect in three or at farthest in four weeks all our hopes of that nature must cease or must be realised.

You will excuse the trouble this letter will give you; when I assure you, that the belief, that my former letter had not come to hand, was the only motive, that could have induced me to have troubled you again in this manner, on this subject.

In expectation of hearing from you as soon as meets your convenience I remain Sir Most Respectfully Your Obdt Servt

J. Thompson

ALS, THi.

1. See above, Thompson to AJ, July 3.
2. For the account, see above, October 4, 1806.

ANDREW JACKSON

John Coffee

Charles Henry Dickinson

Thomas Overton

Aaron Burr

Harman Blennerhassett

JOHN A. FORT

JAMES WILKINSON

RACHEL JACKSON

ANDREW JACKSON, JR.

JOHN ROBERTSON BEDFORD

JAMES JACKSON

Silas Dinsmoor

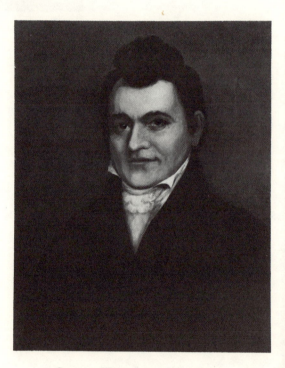

George Washington Campbell

GIDEON BLACKBURN

WILLIE BLOUNT

Andrew Jackson

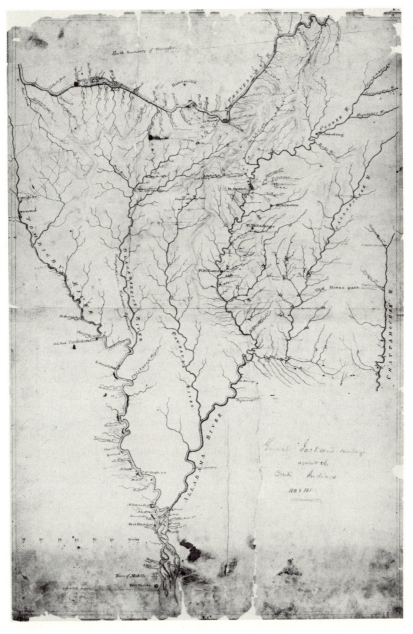

GENERAL JACKSON'S CAMPAIGN AGAINST THE CREEK INDIANS, 1813 & 1814

To George Washington Campbell

Hermitage near Nashville October 15th. 1812.

Sir

You will receive herewith inclosed, the certificate of John Gordon and Major Thomas G Bradford editor of the Clarion on the Subject of the card bearing date Sept. 11th. 1812 published in the Clarion on the 26th. of Sept. 1812 from Silas Dinsmore united States agent to the Choctaw nation being in the proper hand writing of the said Silas Dinsmore you will also receive enclosed, the paper of the 26th. Sept. containing the Card of Mr Dinsmore, which I beg you to lay before the Secretary of War, as soon as the reach you,[1] and I beg of you to communicate to me without delay his determination as it respect the removal of Mr. Dinsmore. When I recd your letter of the 10th. of april last inclosing me an extract of the Secretary of Wars letter to Silas Dinsmore agent to the Choctaw Nation,[2] I, nor the Citizens of west Tennessee, hesitated not, to believe that Silas Dinsmore would cease to exercise over our Citizens such lawless tyranny as he had been in the habit of, and that our peacefull and honest citizens would be left to enjoy the free and unmolested use of that road as Secured to them by treaty—you can easily Judge and so can the Secretary of War, our surprise and indignation, at the wanton insult offerred to the whole citizens of west Tennessee by the publication of his card in the Clarion—in which he boasts—that he has set at defiance the solem treaty that secures to our citizens and those of the united States the free and unmolested use of that road as well as the express instructions of the Secratary of War of the 23rd. of March last, and boast his detention of a defenceless woman & her property—*and for what*! the want of a passport ¿and *my god*; is it come to this—are we *free men or are we slaves is this real or is it* a *dream*—for what are we involved in a war with great Britain—is it not for the support of our rights as an independant people and a nation, secured to us by nature and by natures god as well as solem treaties and the law of nations—and can the Secratary of War, for one moment retain the idea, that we will permit this petty Tyrant to sport with our rights secured to us by treaty and which by the law of nature we do possess—and sport with our feelings by publishing his *lawless tyranny exercised over* a *helpless* and *unprotected female*[3]—if he does he thinks too meanly of our Patriotism and galantry—were we base anough to surrender our independant rights secured to us by the bravery and blood of our forefathers, we are unworthy the name of *freemen*—and we view all rights secured to us by solem treaty, under the constituted authority, *rights* secured to us by the blood of our fathers and which we will never yield but with our lives—The indignation of our citizens are only restrained by assurances that goverment so soon as they are notified of this unwarrantable insult, added to the many injuries that Silas Dinsmore has heaped upon our honest and unofending citizens, that he will be removed—Should we be deceived in this, be *frank* with the Secratary of War, that we are freemen, and that we will suport the supremacy of the laws, and that the wrath and indignation of our citizens will sweepe from the earth the invader of their legal rights and involve Silas Dinsmore in the flames of his agency house—we love order, and nothing but a suport of our legal and inalienable rights, would or could prompt us to do an act, that could be construed as wearing the appearance of rashness—but should not the source of the evil be removed, our rights secured by treaty restored to our Citizens—the agent, and his houses will be demolished—and when government is applied to, and so often notified of the injuries heaped upon our Citizens and they will adhere to the agent who delights in treading under foot the rights of the Citizens, and exults in their distresses—the evil be upon the goverment not upon the people who have so often complained without redress—we really hope that the evil will be cut off by the root, by a removal of the agent, should this not be done we will have a right fairly to conclude that the administration winks at the agents conduct under the rose, notwithstanding the instructions of the Secratary in his letter to Mr Dinsmore of the 23rd. of march—the right of nature occurs—and if redress is not afforded, I would despise the wretch that would slumber in qu[i]et one night before he cutt up by the roots the invader of his solem rights, reguardless of consequences—let not the Secratary of war believe that we want more *than Justice*, but both from idians and indian agents, we will enjoy the rights secured to us by solem treaty or we will die nobly in their support, we want but a bare fulfilment of the treaty—we neither under stand the Tyranny of the agent in open violation of our rights secured to us by treaty— or the Creek law, that takes from the united States the right guranteed by treaty that the indians who commit murders on our citizens, shall be delivered up when demanded, to be tried by the laws of the united States & punished—the *Creek law says the Creeks will punish them, themselves*— These innovation without the consent of the constituted power of the goverment being first had our citizens do not understand, the information of Colo Hawkins U. S. agent for the Creeks and the information of Genl James Robertson agent of the Chickasaw nation, to the contrary notwithstanding neither can we the citizens of Tennessee believe without better prooff that the hair of the head of one of the murderers of Manleys family and Crawleys at the mouth of Duck river are disturbed by the Creeks, when we have proof that they have lately passed near to Caskaskia fifteen in number to Join the Prophet—In this particular we want and do expect the murderers delivered up agreable to treaty—this is only *Justice* this we ask of Goverment—this we are entitled to, and this we must (sooner or later) and will have—This may be thought strong language—but it is the language that freemen when the are only claiming a fulfilment of their rights ought to use—it is a language that the ought to be taught to lisp from their cradles—and never when they are claiming rights from any nation ever to abandon—

Pardon the trouble I have given you in this long letter—it relates to the two subjects that has for sometime iritated the publick mind, and is now ready to burst forth in Vengeance—I am Dr sir with due reguard yr mo ob Servt.

Andrew Jackson

ALS, NjP; Copy and AL draft fragment, DLC; Copy, MHi. Published in *National Intelligencer*, April 9, 1828; Bassett, 1:236–38.

1. In his certificate of September 26, Gordon stated that Dinsmoor had demanded a passport from him in August; on October 8, Bradford wrote Jackson that the card published in the *Democratic Clarion* of September 26 had been written by Dinsmoor.
2. See above.
3. In his letter to Bradford, Dinsmoor wrote that he had arrested "ten negroes and people of colour, in possession of Mrs. Silbey."

The question of who should command the Volunteers on their expedition to the lower Mississippi, discussed in the letter below, was only the first in a long series of problems resulting from the vagueness of federal statutes governing the new military force and the failure of the war department to provide adequate regulations interpreting the laws. By far the most vexing question was the matter of enlistment terms. Under the law of February 6, 1812, the term for volunteers was twelve months, unless earlier discharged. The law of April 10 required six months' service from the detached militia. By November 1813 Jackson was being joined in the Creek Nation by East and West Tennessee troops enrolled for three months. Finally at the end of 1813, volunteers for sixty days appeared in the field, and while reluctantly accepting their services, Jackson confessed he knew of no law authorizing enlistments for so short a time. The so-called mutinies of December 1813 resulted from differing interpretations of the laws governing enlistment terms, almost wholly attributable to the federal government's failure to coordinate its efforts governing personnel.

To Willie Blount

Nashvill Novbr. 11th. 1812—

Sir

At a period like the present when the din of war revebrates from shore to shore, it is the duty of every citizen to do something for his country— with these impressions at an early period of the symtoms of approaching war, I excercised my influence with citizens composing the soldiary of the second Division of Tennessee which I have the honor to command—to Excite them to assume a proper attitude as *americans, as soldiers*, who had important rights to protect and defend, and which had been invaded by the unhallowed and sacraligious hand of great Britain and her emisaries. Twenty seven hundred and fifty brave Tennesseans under my order, stepped forward and enlisted under the banners of their country, resolved to protect their own and their countrys right or nobly die in the glorious struggle—These brave men had chosen me to lead them to the field, and required me thro your excellency to make a tender of their & my own services to the President of the united States.[1] This Tender was made, and the terms of its acceptance too flattering for me now to repeat[2]—suffice it to say—that it made us feel like americans anxiously waiting the call of our country, that we might mingle with the heroes of the day and measure our strength and courage with the enemies of our country—we did expect when called on, it would be agreable to the tender as made—permit me to remark when the tender was made, compensation was out of view, and I pledge myself it is not now taken into the account—But I feel that military Pride that I hope will go down with me to the grave when the Tender was made the Secratary of war well knew, that I had the honor to command a Division in the State of Tennessee, and as such the Tender was made and accepted—I have read the orders of the Secratary of war to you which you had the goodness to shew me with care and calm attention—The orders and instructions do not relate to any Volunteers already tendered—The words are "should Volunteers offer &c &c," and I am clear in the oppinion, if the Secratary did intend to embrace the Volunteers tendered by me that the order recd. by yesterdays mail, was either to exclude me from the command—or if I did command by an apparent willingness and condesension on my part to place me under the command of Genl Wilkinson[3]—I cannot disguise my feelings—had the Secratary of war directed you to call me and my Volunteers into the field, and had confined my compensation to that of seargeant or private soldier I should have been content, but he has not even daigned to name me or the brave fellows who long since have tendered their service, and enrolled themselves under the act of Congress—There appears something in this thing that carries with it a sting to my feelings that I will for the present suppress—The place of destination, and the officer under which they are to be placed when the reach that destination, cannot be mistaken—But sir viewing the situation of our beloved country at present, should your Excellency believe that my personal service can promote its interest in the least degree, I will sacrafice my own feelings, and lead my brave Volunteers to any point your excellency may please to order all I ask is that we may be ordered to a stage where we may pertake of active service, and share the dangers and laurels of the field—

I have the honor to be with high consideration and Esteem yr excellencies, mo. ob. serv.

Andrew Jackson Major Genl
2 Division Tennessee

P.S. I await your orders & instructions[4]

A. Jackson Major
Genl 2d. Division

ALS, DLC. Published in Bassett, 1:238–39.
1. See Blount to AJ, June 25.
2. See above, Blount to AJ, July 21; and enclosure, Eustis to Blount, July 11.
3. On October 21, Secretary of War Eustis had written Blount "to call out, organize arm and equip fifteen hundred of the militia of Tennessee. . . . Should volunteers offer under the acts of February 6th & July 6th 1812 your Excellency is authorized to organize them for the whole, or such part of the detachment as you may deem expedient." Eustis concluded his letter by requesting Blount "to order these troops to move for New Orleans by land or water" and "to communicate with General Wilkinson at New Orleans, keep him advised of your arrangements, the number of troops in each detachment, and the time of their rendezvous and march from the several points" (DLC).
4. For Blount's response, see below.

From Willie Blount

Nashville Novr. 11th. 1812

Sir,

I am required by Brigadier Genl. Harrison who acts under the authority of the President of the United States to hold two regiments of the militia of the 2d. Division detached conformably to the act of the 10th. of April 1812, in readiness to march as soon as they may be called for, either by Governor [Benjamin] Howard or Governor [Ninian] Edwards, for the protection of their Territories, or for an expedition against the hostile Tribes of the Illinois river—[1]

You will give the necessary orders in your Division to cause two regiments of said detached militia to hold themselves in readiness for that service to move at a moments warning when required by either Governor Edwards or Governor Howard;[2] and you will without delay transmit to me a Roster of the officers selected to command in said regiments, and state the number of men detached and held in readiness for said service—

I am required by the President of the United States thro' the Secy War to call out, organize, arm and equip fifteen hundred of the militia of Tennessee detached conformably to the act of April the 10th. 1812; or of Volunteers who have tendered their services to the President of the United States under the acts of Feby 6th. & July 6th. 1812, for the whole or such part of the required detachment as may be deemed expedient, to be rendezvoused at such parts of the State as may be judged most convenient for their march to New Orleans for the defence of the lower Country—to be organized as far as practicable according to the laws of the United

States, under the command of a Brigadier General. I am authorized to assure the Volunteers that they will not be continued in service in the lower Country during the next Summer—commissions are forwarded for officers to command the volunteers as selected—when said volunteer Corps may be commissioned and organized the fifteen hundred will be ordered to move to New Orleans either by land or water as shall be most convenient—to go on all together, or by detachments of four or five hundred accordingly the necessary arrangements therefore can be made[3]— They are the volunteers under your command who are to perform this service whose services with yours have been tendered to and accepted by the President—you will command them—[4]

you will please notify the Officers of said Volunteer Companies who have made a tender of Service under said acts and who have forwarded rolls that I am authorized to commission them as selected by their Companies; and also to request the said officers to meet at Nashville on the twenty first day of November Instant. for the purpose of nominating and selecting the field officers to command—[5]

you will please procure the necessary Boats for the transportation of the Troops to New Orleans, together with the necessary Camp equipage; tho', it is to be understood that for supplies of the latter description including Tents the General Government rely principally on the patriotism of the Citizens of Tennessee—hence with such each man will be expected to furnish himself as fully as it may be in his own power to do—this reliance on the patriotism of our fellow citizens in part is owing to the great and extensive calls for tents & other Camp equipage, and the time required for transportation—

The Troops will also be expected to take with them their own arms and equipments such as may be fit for service including rifles—those who have not arms will as far as practicable be furnished by Government meaning both detached militia and Volunteers—

For the necessary expenditures under this order I am authorized to draw Bills on the War Department—

The well known attachment of yourself and the volunteers for your country is a sure pledge for the prompt execution of this order—respectfully your obt. Servant

Willie Blount

ALS and LC, DLC; Copy (extract), DNA-RG 107. Published in *Democratic Clarion*, November 17; Bassett, 1:239–41.

1. On August 22, Secretary of War Eustis had written Blount that William Henry Harrison, since September 17 the supreme commander of the Army of the Northwest with the rank of brigadier general, would be communicating with him on reinforcements from the Tennessee militia (DLC). Howard and Edwards were the governors of Missouri and Illinois territories, respectively.

2. For Jackson's compliance with Blount's orders, see AJ to the detached militia companies, November 11.

3. Blount's orders to Jackson were based on the directives in William Eustis to Blount, October 21, 23 (DLC).

4. On the question of who should command the Tennessee Volunteers, see also Memorandum, [cDecember 27].

5. See AJ to the Tennessee Volunteers, [November 14], below.

To Robert West Alston

Nashville Novbr. 12th. 18[12]

Sir

I expected to have had the pleasure of seeing you at Franklin last Tuesday, but I was arrested on my way by an order from Governor Blount to march my Volunteers to New orleans, for the defence of the lower country.[1] This has engaged me here until now. I shall set out home in about an hour, and send on your horse on tomorrow—I expected to have had the pleasure of sending herewith the paper that contains the Jockey club fall running here[2] but owing to the press of publick matter the printer [informs me] he cannot have it out before tuesday next, I [will send] it by mail to you at Sparta Georgia—I wish you to write me when you reach home informing how you got on, and the health of your family. I shall [be] off in about three weeks in that time I expect to be able to sail—let the Storms of war waft me wheresoever they may, rest assured you will occupy the most lively recollection and esteem in my brest—as I am pressed for time I have only to add, my best wishes for your happiness and welfare and that of your family thro life to whom present me respectfully

Andrew Jackson

ALS, Samuel Alston Wragg. Alston (1781–1859) was born in Halifax County, N.C., and lived for several years in Sparta, Ga., before moving to a plantation near Tallahassee, Fla., sometime after 1829. He maintained an active interest in horse breeding and racing. On his trip to Georgia in May 1812, Jackson may have visited Alston.

1. See above, Blount to AJ, November 11.

2. In the fall races of the Nashville Jockey Club, Jackson entered Alston's four-year-old colt Stump the Dealer in two three-mile heats. The colt won both (*Democratic Clarion*, November 17).

To the Tennessee Volunteers

[November 14, 1812]

In publishing the letter of Gov. Blount,[1] the Major Genl. makes known to the valiant Volunteers who have tendered their services every thing which is necessary for them now to know. In requesting the Officers of the respective companies to meet in Nashville on the 21 Inst. the Governor expects to have the benefit of their advice in recommending the field officers who are to be selected from the officers who have already volunteered; also to fix on the time when the expedition shall move; to deliver the definitive instructions, & to commission the Officers in the name of the President of the United States. Companies which do not contain 66 rank and file are required to complete their compliment to that number— A second Lieutenant should be added where the company contains but one

The Major General has now arrived at a Crisis when he can address the Volunteers with the feelings of a soldier. The State to which he belongs is now to act a part in the honorable contest of securing the rights and liberties of a great and rising Republic. In placing before the volunteers the illustrious actions of their fathers, in the war of the revolution, he presumes to hope that they will not prove themselves a degenerate race, nor suffer it to be said, they are unworthy of the blessings which the blood of so many thousand heroes has purchased for them The Theatre on which they are required to act is interesting to them in every point of view. Every Man of the western Country turns his eyes intuitively upon the mouth of the Mississippi. He there beholds the only outlet by which his produce can reach the markets of foreign Nations or the atlantic States: Blocked up, all the fruits of his industry rots upon his hand—open and he carries on a trade with all the nations of the earth. To the people of the western Country is then peculiarly committed by nature herself the defence of the lower Mississippi and the city of New-Orleans. At the approach of an enemy in that quarter, the whole western world should pour forth its sons to meet the Invader, and drive him back into the sea. Brave Volunteers! its to the defence of this place, so interesting to you, that you are now ordered to repair. Let us show ourselves conscious of the honor & importance of the charge which has been committed to us. By the alacrity by which we obey the orders of the President, let us demonstrate to our brethren in all parts of the union, that the people of Tennessee are worthy of being called to the defence of the Republic.

The Generals of Brigade attached to the second Division will communicate these orders to the Officers commanding volunteer Companies with all possible dispatch using expresses, and forwarding a statement of the expense to the Major General.

> Signed   Andrew Jackson
> Majr. Gen. 2nd. Division T.

LC, DLC. Published in *Democratic Clarion*, November 17; Bassett, 1:241–42.
  1. See above, Blount to AJ, November 11.

To the Tennessee Volunteers

[November 24, 1812]

General Order!

The major Gen. of the 2nd. Division is commanded by his Excellency governor Blount to call into service the organised volunteers who are destined for the defence of New Orleans and the lower Mississippi.[1] The whole of the volunteers from the second Division are included in this order. They will accordingly rendezvous in Nashville on Saturday the tenth of December, prepared to descend the river without delay. The Cavalry will provide themselves with Pistols & Sabres; the Infantry with rifles as far as it may be convenient; for which they will be allowed a fair compensation. Such of the non-commissioned officers and privates as bring with them a blanket for their own use will be paid for it a full price. They are particularly requested to furnish themselves with this article.

On their arrival at the place of rendezvous, the officers, non-commissioned officers & privates will receive two months pay in advance, and the non-commissioned officers & privates will receive seventeen dollars for the half pay of one year's clothing.

The Major Gen. informs the volunteers that upon a consultation with the field officers, it has been resolved that the respective companies which form the detachment will appear in uniforms dark blue, or brown has been prescribed for service, of homspun or not, at the election of the wearer—hunting shirts or coats at the option of the different companies, with pantaloons and dark colored socks, white pantaloons, vests &c. may be worn upon parade. As the expedition will not terminate under five or six months and will include the winter and the spring, the volunteers will see the propriety of adapting their clothing, in quantity and quality to both seasons.

The field officers will wear the uniform which is prescribed for officers of the same grade in the army of the U. States. Company officers will conform to the same regulations, if convenient otherwise they will conform to the uniform of their companies.

The constant and honorable zeal which the volunteers have evinced, excludes the idea that any one of them will voluntary absent themselves, now that they have received the final summons to repair to the field of honor and of danger. If sickness, inevitable necessity, or real absence from the state, should detain any one, he will make known his situation to the commanding officer of the company. In all cases where this is not done to the satisfaction of the Major Gen. the absentee will be put upon the list of Deserters, exposed to the scorn of his fellow-citizens and the severest penalties which the laws will inflict upon him.

Capt. William Carroll of the Nashville volunteers is appointed brigade inspector to the organised volunteers and [Thomas H.] Fletcher[2]—is appointed second aid to the Major General in the place of Major John Coffee promoted; the officers and privates of the volunteer detachment are commanded to honor and obey them as such.

The colonels commanding regiments will distribute their orders by express; the expense of which will be reimbursed by the assistant Deputy Quarter Master[3]

Signed   Andrew Jackson
Majr. Gen. 2nd. Division Ten.

LC and printed broadside, DLC; LC, AHAB. Published in Bassett, 1:242–43 (dated November 23, 1813).
1. See Blount to AJ, November 23.
2. Fletcher (1792–1845) was a clerk in Andrew Hynes's store. After resigning as Jackson's second aide, Fletcher served in the artillery during the Creek War. He then studied law and established a practice in Franklin County, later serving as attorney general of the Eighth Circuit Court and of the federal district court for West Tennessee, and as secretary of state in the 1830s.
3. William B. Lewis.

To George Washington Campbell

[November 29, 1812]

Sir

I had the pleasure of receiving from you by mail the Presidents communication to Congress, from which I plainly see, that war must rage untill the pride of England, Humbled[1]—If ever a nation, did refuse such fair and honourable, (which includes Just) propositions as has been made by our goverment lately to england, I have never come across it in print—and those propositions made too at a time when england must know, that in six months with our presen[t] preparations, we can conquor all her north am[er]ican possessions—There cannot after a rejection of the terms offerred by our goverment to england, be one single decenting voice in america, that our war is not only Just, but necessary, and must continue untill our national and individual rights are permanantly Secured—*This is the Voice here*—and we have set to work in good earnest—I have been engaged for about ten days organizing the Volunteers—The Governor on the 21st. Instant commissioned by order of the President 41 forty one captains—we have organized three regiments; there will be a fourth—one of the finest Regiments of Cavalry I ever saw, they have chosen Coffee to command them—they are not quite equipt—Pistols cannot be had here—Colo. Coffee has equip with swords [Eighty], They are in uniform of homespun, blue, with caps complete—The regiment is full—and the only thing wanting is arms, I wish about 500 swords and 250 cases of pistols could be forward—The two regiments of infantry in a short time with the General and regimental staff that is selected will be in a good state to render service to their country, and with the officers selected, I have no doubt could be marched any where that the Goverment requires service—on the 10th. next month we rendezvous at Nashville by the 15th. I hope to send on the Cavalry and one Regiment of Infantry for the defence of the lower country and by the 20th. or 25th. I expect [to] be able to follow with the ballance of the detachment. In the organization of the Staff, we were obliged from necessity to depart from the law—The acts of congress say that the staff must be taken from the line—in the line we could not get proper materials—in the line of a regular army proper materials for the Staff can always be had—I had to invite from higher grades fit persons for adjutants &c—their compensation—(they not being taken from the line) is not adequate and I do hope you will have provisions made by law in all such cases—say that they shall receive a Lieutenants or Captains pay in the line—and then the extra pay now allowed by law—The late retrograde movements of the ohio and Kentuckey Volunteers, has tarnished the reputation of their States[2]—with this before my eyes when I view the materials of my Detachment, I feel confident they will "quit themselves like men and fight." and they have too much pride ever to leave their duty without orders—There is but one thing I fear, Should we be ordered to Join Genl. Wilkeson, he is so universaly disliked by our citizens, that something unplesant may arise—It was whispered that he was to command—It raged like wild fire—and it was only laid by the governor stating positively in his order that I was to command them[3]—as to myself, you know my sentiments—it is a bitter pill to have to act wit[h] him, but for my countries good I will swallow [it.] I go with the true Spirit of a Soldier—to defend m[y coun]try and to fight her battles—and should any thing [come] between him and myself to put a speedy end t[o it with]out injuring the service or disturbing the Publi[c. It is] much to be wished that he would be moved from the South and west—I have Just seen a letter from an officer from Washington M. T. saying the militia in west florida has refused to be commanded by him—Why then not let us have an officer in whom we have confidence, why corode the feelings of an extensive & rising country in these trying times, by keeping him in command in a quarter where the people have no confidence in him at all—advise goverment of the fact, and then let them act—It required some adress & some exertion to prevent a unanimous remonstrance from all the officers to the President on this Subject—and the only thing that prevented it was, that it was stated to them that it was an improper time, and it would be said it was only a pretext to avoid the service—to this the yielded[4]—receive my best wishes,

Andrew Jackson

ALS, DNA-RG 107. Published in Bassett, 1:244–45. Endorsed: "Gen And. Jackson Nashville 29 Novr. & 1 Decr. 1812 Recd. 18 Decr. 12 ansd. 27th Decr. 1812 To be attended to particularly as to appointment of Staff & as to Wilkinson Inquire of Secty of war as to the above."

1. See Madison's annual message to Congress, November 4, in *Annals of Congress*, 12th Cong., 2nd sess., pp. 11–16.

2. In the fall of 1812, William Henry Harrison launched a campaign against the Delaware and Miami Indians, but bad weather and poor discipline of the Ohio and Kentucky militias forced him to abandon the effort.

3. See above, Blount to AJ, November 11.

4. In addition to Campbell's endorsement, the presence of the original of Jackson's letter in the records of the department of war suggests that Campbell did take up the question of staff and Wilkinson with the secretary of war. Campbell's response of December 27 (see endorsement above) has not been found, but the Memorandum re commander of the Tennessee Volunteers, [cDecember 27] most likely came from the war department and may have been forwarded to Jackson by Campbell in his letter of that date. According to that memorandum, "if it shall be considered, that Volunteers are preferable to the Militia, and that it will not be possible to procure them, and insure their services, under any other commander than Major Genl. A. Jackson, especially as a constitutional question may arise with the Militia officers, as has already arisen with the Militia of New york which cost an army a defeat, perhaps it would be expedient, to appoint a Major Genl.—raise the Volunteers, organize them, and await the confirmation of such appointment from the Genl. Government.

"The antipathies, which are certainly entertained, by the citizens of the western country, to being put under the command of Genl. Wilkinson, may furnish sufficient ground for the apprehension, that the constitution will be resorted to by the Militia as a pretext for preventing their being put under the disposition of Genl. Wilkinson."

In Nashville on December 10, Jackson mustered into service his volunteers, exceeding the quota requested by the Secretary of War by some 500. He divided his troops into three regiments: two infantry, commanded by Thomas Hart Benton and William Hall, and one cavalry, under John Coffee, each consisting of approximately 700 men.

Almost a month elapsed before the Tennessee Volunteers began their move southward. Cold weather, an inadequate supply of arms and equipment, and a shortage of bank funds to convert the soldiers' pay in government notes into specie occasioned the delay. Jackson convinced the Nashville bank to issue to Alpha Kingsley (c1779–1846), district paymaster in Nashville, one-third of the funds needed in specie and the remainder in post notes, and, once paid, the troops began their movement toward New Orleans on January 10, 1813.

To Alpha Kingsley

Headquarters Nashville Decbr 23rd. 1812—

Sir

The whole detachment under my command for the Defence of the lower Country, are ready to march, nothing now detains them but the receipt of their two months pay, and the supplies of munitions of war, which is expected daily—If this detachment was paid I would move them on immediately and charter a Keel Boat to follow with their arms and equipments, and the magazine stores—I have to request that you will loose no time in sending them off, as delay may not only prove injurious to the service but bring reflections on the officers and men for their tardiness in movement—let it be recollected that the success of military men depend on celerity of movement & ought to be like lightening—they never ought to consume their supplies, in slothfull indolence in camp— these reflections and the good of the service I have no doubt will have its due weight with you in expediting the payment of the detachment—The Boats are all ready, and as the infantry are paid I wish to embark them for Neworleans I am sir with due reguard & respect yr mo. ob. serv.

Andrew Jackson
Major Genl Commanding

ALS copy and LC, DLC.

From John Reid

30th. Decr. 1812.

Sir

As you have now, two Aids, I conceive it of importance to know whether I am to be considered as the first or the second.[1]

I make this inquiry with considerable diffidence; but I am sure you will readily excuse me for wishing to understand *clearly*, in what capacity I am hereafter to appear with you.

Altho I was, probably, appointed in consequence of the resignation of Mr. Fletcher—who seems to have been your second Aid, it was never my belief that I was to stand precisely in his situation. Under a different impression, I accepted with great satisfaction, the appointment which you tendered me;[2] & my first persuasion was subsequently confirmed by assurances from yourself. Has it been found expedient to make any arrangement, different from that originally intended?

In the late general order, publishing the organization of the Army, I have observed myself announced as the second Aid.[3] I was surprised at this: & should, before now, have expressed to your Excellency my feelings upon the occassion had I not considered it a temporary arrangement which would, in a short time, be superseded by new regulations.

I am very Respectfully yr. Obt. St.

John Reid

ALS and ALS copy, DLC. Published in Bassett, 1:251.
  1. For Jackson's appointment of Reid, see AJ to Reid, December 11.
  2. See Reid to AJ, [December 11].
  3. See order informing troops of the organization of the army, December 13.

To John Reid

30th. Decr. 1812

Sir

Your note by Mr Thomas Eastin, was this moment handed me, bearing date the 30th. instant.[1] From the recommendation of my bosom friends as well as from the small acquaintance I had with you, I felt truly gratified, on the information that you would become one of my family during the present campaign, as soon as your consent was known to me I made it known in a general order issued for the purpose to make known that the organization of the detachment was completed, and that you were appointed my second Aid in the room of Mr. Fletcher resigned[2]—how any distinction between aids crept into the order—at present I cannot say— Col. Benton was still acting as aid and as far as his time and duty from his regiment would permit render all the aid in his power. This is the only general order that has been published, therefore the only one you alude to—and I am really astonished that this should be even noted in your letter, as at that time it was well known to you that Col. Benton still continued to act as one of my aids, and had acted in that capacity for a long time—being advised by our mutual friend Col. Coffee, that he was fearfull, that there was something that corroded your feelings, to prevent which, and that harmony might prevail, I requested him to explain to you fully which I am confident he must have done, in that explanation I have no doubt he brought to your view, that there was no difference in the rank, pay, or emoluments, of aids, and which I did hope would be fully satisfactory, and restore your feelings, for I beg you to believe, that nothing would give me more pain, than that any act of mine should tend to injure the feelings of any individual—I did expect the greatest harmony; this was my sole object, added to talent, and respectability; which I was certain of in the choice I had made. Sir, If there is any thing that has arisen that has given you an idea of the contrary it is without my knowledge and altho, it would fill me with the greatest regret that I should be deprived of your aid and service, still a duty I owe to you compels me to say that if any circumstances has arisen since the explanation by Col. Coffee that makes your situation unpleasant or disagreeable, I have only to add that I sincerely regret it—and that I would not (let the inconvenience to me, be what it might) hold you one moment longer than, your pleasure dictated to you to remain—

accept assurances of my respect and esteem.

Andrew Jackson
Major Genl

LS and Copy fragment, THi; ALS copy, DLC. Published in Bassett, 1:252.
  1. See above. On the aide issue, see also Willie Blount to AJ, December 31.
  2. See order informing troops of the organization of the army, December 13.

To *the* Tennessee Volunteers

Headquarters Nashville, Decr. 31, 1812

General Orders

It is with extreme regret that the Major Genl. witnessed to-day the seeds of mutiny in the Volunteer Camps;[1] but 'tis with pride your General recollects with what alacrity the great mass of the Volunteers flew to his aid to suppress it. He cannot refrain from tendering to Capt. [James] McEwen[2] his thanks for the promptness with which he obeyed his orders—indeed, he most cheerfully gives his thanks to all the officers present, except those few who appeared to countenance mutiny and disorder.

The Major General thinks it important that all officers and Soldiers should know the penalty which the Martial Law inflicts for disobedience of orders—*for mutiny, mutinous conduct or exciting others to mutiny*; therefore, orders that the Major of Brigade read to the first and second Regiments of Infantry, the sixth, seventh, eighth, and ninth articles of War[3] to-morrow at twelve O'clock; and all officers and soldiers are commanded to conform thereto, under the pains and penalties which said articles inflict.

The major General flattered himself there was not an officer, or soldier, in the detachment of volunteers, who would have tarnished that fame, which, from their patience and forbearance, under the most trying circumstances, they had so justly merited; but, with pain and mortification he witnessed a disposition in *some*, not only to cast a shade over their own conduct, but anxious to involve in shame and disgrace, the whole detachment under his command. This cannot, nay, shall not be. The Major General feels well assured that a large majority of the Volunteers have too much sense, not to know that every exertion have been made to accelerate their payment; and that the delays of which they complain have been occasioned from circumstances over which their general has no control. He also feels assured that they have too much confidence in their officers to believe, for a moment, that they could be actuated from motives of partiality. None but disorganizers, and those, who are mutinously disposed, would attempt to plant the seeds of discontent in the bosom of those, who, when too late, will repent of their timerity. The boast and the pride of the Major General was, that the brave Volunteers whom he has the honor to command, had tendered their services to their country from the most patriotic motives—that, to a man, they were anxious to see her elevated to the highest pinnacle of national prosperity, renowned among the nations of the earth, and crowned with ever shining emeralds of Liberty. But he fears these pleasing expectations in *some in-*

stances, will prove delusive—that there are some who are not impelled to the defense of their country, from patriotic, but pecuniary motives. Why, if the love of Country has drawn you from the bosom of your families, such anxiety about who shall be first paid? do you not know that all cannot be first? Can you not exercise a little patience? Take care how you indulge this restless disposition, least the world should say that you are *ostensible* patriots, but *real mercenaries.*

The Major General hopes that the mutinous and disorderly conduct of this day was more the effect of imprudence and incaution than the result of pre-determination to disobey. He flatters himself that no one during the whole campaign will be found so far lost to a sense of duty—so regardless of their fame and their reputation as to be guilty of the like conduct again; but should he be disappointed in this expectation, he pledges himself that the Law Martial shall be fully and completely executed on every individual concerned. Every expression either of officers or soldiers having a tendency to excite disobedience of orders are forbidden, and, if used, shall be punished agreeably to Law. Let it be remembered that the duty of a parent is to chastise and bring to obedience an undutiful child. The Major General has pledged himself to act towards you as a father, and now exhorts you to obedience.

Capt. [John] Kennedy's[4] company Infantry of the second Regiment, will march to Nashville, and be at the Paymaster's office precisely at 2 O'clock p.m. tomorrow.

The brigade major being absent with leave, the reading of this order is entrusted to Major [George] West,[5] quarter master of the Second Regiment

> By order of the Major Genl.
> Andrew Hynes[6]
> aide-de-camp

LC, DLC. Extract published in Bassett, 1:253–54.

1. Jackson was referring to unrest occasioned by the delay in pay.

2. McEwen (1752–1821) commanded a company of Williamson County volunteers until December 1813.

3. These articles prescribed punishment for disrespect to superior officers, inciting mutiny, failure of officers to suppress mutiny, and striking a superior.

4. Not further identified.

5. West (d. 1824), from Montgomery County, was a lawyer.

6. Hynes (1785–1845), a Nashville merchant and manufacturer, served as one of Jackson's aides until the army's return from Natchez in the spring of 1813. From April 1814 to the end of the war he served as state adjutant general.

From Willie Blount

Nashville Decr 31st. 1812

Dr Sir

You will as soon as practicable after the Troops are paid, move with the detachment of Tennessee volunteers under your command, consisting of one thousand four hundred Infantry and Riflemen, and six hundred and seventy mounted Infantry and Cavalry, in all, two thousand and seventy, men and officers included, to New Orleans for the defence of the lower Country—transporting the Infantry and Riflemen by water, and ordering the mounted Infantry and Cavalry to proceed by land, on the main road leading from this to New Orleans, via, Natchez, Mississippi Territory—

You will in giving your instructions to the commander of the mounted Infantry and Cavalry, order, that the greatest caution and care shall be observed and used by him, and the whole Detachment under his command, not to molest, or in any way to injure the peaceable tribes of Indians inhabiting the Country thro' which they may march on said road.[1]

On your arrival at New Orleans, you will await, the order of the President of the United States—

The Detachment under your command is several hundred more than is required by the Secy War's order of the 21st. & 22d. Octr last, to me—the excess is to the credit of the State, and the good of the service, at this all important crisis in American Affairs, is unquestionably consulted, and will most certainly be promoted, by permitting the excess to enter into the service of the United States, as the patriotic ardor of the volunteers would otherwise be chilled, since they have been at such vast expense to equip themselves, in order to attend most promptly, to the call of their Government, which it is their delight to support, from a thorough confidence in the regularly constituted authorities of the Nation—

It is due to you sir, here to say, that you deserve well of your country for the active part you have taken, and uniformly pursued, to encourage, prepare, and bring into the field, in the hour of danger, such a patriotic band of invincible citizen soldiers. May the God of Battles and the supreme ruler of the Universe aid and protect you and each of your valiant volunteers acting in support of the righteous cause of the best of Governments, which you have volunteered your service to defend—I have the honor to be very respectfully & most sincerely your Obt. Servant

Willie Blount

ALS, LC, and Copy, DLC; ALS copy and Copy, DNA-RG 107. Extract published in Bassett, 1:252–53.

1. In his letter of January 7, 1813, Jackson ordered Coffee's cavalry to Natchez to rendezvous with the infantry and instructed Coffee concerning his march through Indian lands.

1813

To James Monroe

Nashville, Jan. 4, 1813

Sir,

I have received the orders of his excellency Gov. Blount, to march with the detachment under my command to New-Orleans as soon as the troops are paid off, and the arms and equipments arrive, and there await the orders of the Government.[1] The payment of the Troops has detained me for some days; the scarcity of circulating medium, put it out of the power of the Paymaster to procure sufficient funds from the sale of bills on Government. application was made to the Nashville Bank, whose directors has made every exertion to procure the funds necessary and the indefatigable attention and industry of the Cashier, and clerk, has furnished as many post notes as will complete the payment of the Troops in a few days. I hope on the 7th. inst to be able to strike my tents and march for New-Orleans—the arms and munitions of War ordered for this detachment has not yet arrived—Should they not come on in due time I shall charter a barge, leave a detachment to bring them after me with orders to overtake me before I reach New-Orleans—Would it not promote the service by establishing magazine stores in every frontier state, and keeping them well supplied? Would not Nashville and the mouth of Cumberland be proper scites for this purpose, and would not government find a great convenience in placing funds in the State banks, to enable the banks at all times to accommodate them in times of war—all delays in the movement of troops are injurious to the service—Military operations to be successful, ought to be well planned and executed with the rapidity of lightning.

I have the pleasure to inform you that I am now at the head of 2070 Volunteers the choicest of our citizens, and who go at the call of their country to execute the will of the Government; who have no constitutional scruples; and if the Government orders, will rejoice at the opportunity of placing the American Eagle on the ramparts of mobile, Pensacola, and Fort St. Augustine. And effectually banishing from the southern coasts all British influence. At New-Orleans I shall anxiously await the orders of the Government.

I am, with high consideration & respect Your mo: obt. servt.

Andrew Jackson
Majr. Genl.

LC, DLC. Extract published in Arthur St. Clair Colyar, *Life and Times of Andrew Jackson: Soldier-Statesman-President*, 2 vols. (Nashville, 1904), 1 : 85. Monroe served ad interim as secretary of war, between Eustis and John Armstrong.
1. See above, Blount to AJ, December 31, 1812.

To William Charles Cole Claiborne

Nashville, January 5, 1813.

Sir:

It is a long time since I have done myself the pleasure to write you, the distress of our country, and the war we are involved in by the injustice of England, will cause us to meet once more. I am ordered with the volunteers of Tennessee to the defense of the lower country, New Orleans, my first point of destination, there to await the orders of the government.[1] I have been detained for the want of arms and munitions of war for some time. These are expected to reach me in two days. The want of funds in the hands of the paymaster has occasioned considerable delay in the payment of the troops owing to the scarcity of the circulating medium, the bills on government could not be sold to procure sufficient funds for the payment of the detachment, and nothing could have afforded relief in this respect but the great exertions of the bank in Nashville. The directors exerted every nerve and deserved the thanks of the government.

The payment of the troops will be completed in a few days and I shall strike my tents in all probability the present week. I march with fourteen hundred infantry and six hundred and seventy cavalry and mounted infantry, the choice citizens of our country. I hope the government will permit us to traverse the Southern coast and aid in planting the American eagles on the ramparts of Mobile, Pensacola and Fort St. Augustine. This alone will give us security in that quarter and peace on our frontiers. British influence in East Florida must be destroyed, or we have the whole Southern tribe of Indians to fight and insurrections to quell in all the Southern States. Enclosed I take the liberty to send you a letter to the contractor at New Orleans, and the assistant Deputy Quartermaster, which I beg you to address to them, presuming that you are acquainted with them. I am sorry to trouble you, but being unadvised, who the gentlemen are that fill these offices at New Orleans, and it being necessary that they should be notified of the movement of the detachment under my command, that they may have the necessary supplies in readiness, I have taken the liberty to enclose them to you, that the notifications may certainly reach them.[2]

With a tender of my best wishes, believe me to be with sentiments of respect and esteem, your most obedient servant,

ANDREW JACKSON.

Text from *Nashville Banner*, January 5, 1914. Original not found.
1. See above, Blount to AJ, December 31, 1812.
2. See AJ to Benjamin Morgan, and AJ to Bartholomew Schaumburgh, January 5, respectively the contractor and assistant deputy quartermaster. On the same day, Jackson also asked David Holmes and Washington Jackson to forward copies to Robert Andrews, the assistant deputy quartermaster, and to the contractor in Natchez.

From James Wilkinson

Head quarters, N. orleans Jany. 6th. 1813

Sir

This Letter will be delivered to you by Capt. D[aniel] Hughes of the 1st Regt. of Infantry, Brigade Inspector,[1] who is Instructed to muster & Inspect the Corps under your Command, and to afford to your Captains every aid & advice they may require, in the formation of their Rolls & Returns.

As soon after the arrival of your Corps at Natchez as may comport with the accommodation of the men, I will thank you to transmit me a General Return of your force, agreeably to the form which will be furnished by Capt. Hughes.[2]

With consideration & respect I am sir your obedt. servt

Jas. Wilkinson

ALS and LC, DLC. Published in Bassett, 1:255.
1. Hughes, from Maryland, served in the U.S. Army from 1799 until his discharge in 1815.
2. For Jackson's response, see AJ to Wilkinson, February 16 and 20, below.

To Rachel Jackson

Nashville January 8th. 1813

My love

I have this evening since dark received, your affectionate letter by Dunwodie,[1] I was down at the Boat receiving the arms Just arived, and did not get up untill dark, when I found the old man waiting for me, he has carefully handed me your miniature[2]—I shall wear it near my boosom, but this was useless, for without your miniature, my recollection, never fails me of your likeness The sensibility of our beloved son, has charmed me, I have no doubt, from the sweetness of his disposition, from his good sense as evidenced, for his age, that he will take care of us both in our declining years—from our fondness towards him, his return of affection to us, I have every hope if he should be spared to manhood, that he will with a carefull education reallise all our wishes—Kiss him for his papa, and give him the nutts and ginger cake sent him by Dunwodie

I thank you for your prayers—I thank you for your determined resolution, to bear our separation with fortitude, we part but for a few days, for a few fleeting weeks, when the protecting hand of providence if it is his will, will restore us to each others arms, In storms, in battles, amidst the raging billows recollect, his protecting hand can save, in the peaceful shade, in cabins, in pallaces, his avenging hand can destroy—Then let us not repine, his will be done, our country calls, its rights are invaded, the innocent babe, and helpless mother, masacred by the ruthless savages, ecited to these horrid deeds, by the infernal engines of British policy, and British depravity recollect then, that the god of Battle cries aloud for vengeance, we are the means in the hands to punish the impious Britains, for their sacraligious Deeds, we trust in the righteousness of our cause, and the god of Battle and of Justice will protect us, hence then dispel any gloomy ideas that our seperation may occasion, bear it with Christian cheerfulness—and resignation, I shall write you often, and shall be always happy to hear from you

If I can get the arms on board tomorrow, I shall sail, Early on Sunday morning—My fatigue has been great, but when I get afloat, they will be measurably over, compared to what the have been My expense has been great, surpassing any thing I had any idea of—I have sent my horses & Stephen[3] on to Judge Overtons, I am fear full I cannot send you any money enclosed I send you a ten dollar note for Colo. William Donelson, when this is paid I do not ow a relation I have a cent Every individual that I owed one cent to except Josiah Nichol, and Mr. [Joseph Thorp] Eliston[4] has called on me for the amount, these two have treated me with liberallity—James Jackson has treated me with the liberallity of a true friend, John H Smith has also acted like himself—

I enclose you a paper[5] which I wish you to keep, I thought it proper to enclose it, least accident might happen for the safety of yourself and our darling son, keep it safe—I enclose you a letter recd. from Mr. [William] Trigg[6]—you will see that on next Tuesday my waggon must go on to Mr Looneys[7] for a waggon load of Pork, you will send the overseer with the waggon, and he can by enquiry find the road, he lives as near as to gallatine—I shall send my papers up by some safe hand—I would send them by Dunwodie but I have to keep them for settlement with sundry persons—say to Mr. [John] Fields I have sent him all the money I could raise and that I shall not leave, Nashville with more than thirty dollars

It now one Oclock in the morning the candle nearly out, and I must go to bed, May the angelic hosts that rewards & protects virtue and innocence, and preserves the good, be with you untill I return—is the sincere supplications of your affectionate Husband

Andrew Jackson

ALS, CtY. Extract published in Bassett, 1:271–72 (dated January 18).
1. Letter not found.
2. The miniature has not been identified.
3. Probably a slave.
4. Nichol (1772–1833) was a Nashville merchant and banker. Elliston (1779–1856), a silversmith, served periodically as alderman and mayor of Nashville, 1806–16.
5. Not identified.
6. Letter not found. Trigg (d. 1831) was a Gallatin merchant and lawyer.
7. Not identified.

From Thomas Hart Benton

Robertsons landing, six miles below
Nashville, January 9th, 1813.

Sir,

Twenty minutes after ten in the morning of the 8th instant I received the orders of your Excellency to superintend the embarkation of the first and the march of the second regiment Tennessee volunteers, destined for the defence of New-Orleans and the Lower Mississippi.[1] I repaired immediately to the camp, and found on my arrival there the tents already struck, the boats nearly loaded, and all the necessary preparations going forward with the most cheerful activity. Major Carrol, who had preceded me with the orders of your excellency, had conducted every thing with the ability and diligence for which he is distinguished.

Capt [Brice] Martin,[2] on account of his knowledge of the river, was directed to take charge of the boats until he should arrive at Robertsons landing. I committed to him the order of your excellency to impress for the public service the private boats which he might find upon the river.[3]

At half after twelve the signal was given for slipping the cables. In an instant the boats were wheeled into the currant. It is impossible to describe to you the enthusiasm with which the men committed themselves to the stream. I looked in vain for a single countenance which was not animated with joy.

At one o'clock the second regiment took up the line of march. The swamp which lay in the rear of the camp compelled us to make a circuit of nine miles to reach Robertsons landing. I marched on foot at the head of this regiment. In two hours thirty minutes we reached the point of destination. Never did men go forward with greater alacrity; it was necessary continually to repress their ardor, and direct them to march slower.

The boats, which had made a circuit of fourteen miles by water, arrived at the same instant; and the two regiments encamped together for the night. Capt. Martin found a very excellent new boat on the river which he brought off; but he was not so fortunate as to see the owner, so that no certificate for its value has been delivered. Another boat was procured at Robertsons landing, built for the public service, and complete, except the chimneys.

Friday the 9th instant, the regiments again moved for the mouth of the Harpeth, 30 miles below Nashville; upwards of two hundred of the second continuing their march over land, at the mouth of the Harpeth th[ey] will find five boats; when the transportation for the whole will be complete.

The very excellent officers Captain [William] Reynolds & [George W.] Gibbs,[4] marched on foot at the head of their companies. Health and respect.

THOMAS H. BENTON
Col. 2d Regt. Ten. Volunteers.

Text from *Democratic Clarion*, January 19. Original not found.

1. For Jackson's general order, see AJ to the Volunteer Brigade, January 6. His specific order to Benton has not been found.

2. A Smith County resident, Martin (1770–1856), brother of Col. William Martin, commanded a company in Hall's 1st Regiment on the Natchez expedition and served in the Creek War and New Orleans campaign.

3. Order not found.

4. Reynolds (1763–1834) served as a company commander during the Natchez expedition and the Creek War until the end of December 1813. Gibbs (1785–1870) resigned his commission in the fall of 1814 to serve in the General Assembly but rejoined the army as a captain of volunteers in William Carroll's division in November 1814. After the war he practiced law with Felix Grundy in Nashville.

To William Berkeley Lewis

Clarksville January 13th. 1813 on Board my Boat

Dr. Sir

I reached here this evening after seven oclock, being detained at the mouth of Harpeth one day delivering out the arms, at which place I was obliged to leave five companies for the want of the Boats that [Eldridge?] Nusom had engaged to deliver, they are fast ashore about 20 miles up the river says the information recd.[1] I have sent up a detachment under the command of Major [William] Martin[2] after them—and in case he cannot get them down I have left four Boats to bring their baggage to Clarksville—with Nusoms Boats, is part of the supplies intended for the detachment under my command whether the deficiency can be supplied here I cannot say, as I have sent Colo. Hall to make the enquiry; and he has not returned—as soon as I get the supplies ordered by the contractor at this place; and for which the officers has due bills and given receipts I shall proceed on, leaving orders for the four companies behind in Boats—to immediately to follow, and those without to press them where ever they can be had, and follow after—The receipts for the arms returned given by Mr [Joseph] Wood,³ shall be forwarded to you as soon as Colo. [Edward] Bradley⁴ comes up he was left behind this morning to see the arms safely deposited on Board Mr Woods Boat—amongst the arms are eleven riffles, given up by part of Capt. [Travis Coleman] Nashs Company,⁵ inspected and pronounced unfit for service—I have to ask the favour of you, to see these arms depositted safe, oiled, and placed in such a place that they will not be injured by the rust—these men are poor, and altho the guns are not fit for service still they think them valluable—I have said they should be taken care of—I wish you as soon as you are informed that the Boats cannot be had, agreed for by Nusom, that you have him send on his agreement—he had plenty of water to have brought them down—the failure is insufferrable and ought to be punished—I have caught cold, and has such a pain in my shoulder and neck, I cannot wield my pen without great pain—I must close this with presenting you my best wishes

Andrew Jackson
Major Genl

PS. I oppen this letter at 2 oclock pm, 14th. to say to you we have had the necessity for the want of supplies to detain thus long, and furnish the troops here with such supplies as we could get from the contractors agent and from the citizens—I do not wish you, to fill up the abstracts untill you are advised that the second regiment is supplied—I proceed with twelve companies in one hour adieu—

ALS, NHi.

1. Newsome (d. 1831), a boatbuilder and merchant in Davidson County, later served as justice of the peace. According to the January 12 entry in "A Journal of the Trip Down the Mississippi," an anonymous account of the Natchez expedition surviving in the Jackson Papers, DLC, Newsome's "religious prejudices prevented him from starting with the Boats on sunday, altho' the public exigency required all possible dispatch."

2. Martin (1765–1846), a Smith county farmer, was major of the 2nd Regiment of Volunteers in the Natchez expedition. He was lieutenant colonel of the same regiment and second in command to William Pillow early in the Creek campaign; when Pillow was wounded at the Battle of Talladega, Martin assumed command.

3. Woods was a Nashville merchant and boatbuilder.

4. Bradley (d. 1829), from Sumner County, was lieutenant colonel of the 1st Regiment under Hall's command on the Natchez expedition and was on the early Creek campaigns, commanding the 1st Regiment, Volunteer Infantry. He served in the September 1813 session of the state legislature.

5. Nash (1783–1844) commanded a company of Rutherford County volunteers in the Natchez expedition and the early Creek campaigns.

To *Cantrell & Read*

Clarksville January 14th. 1813

Gentlemen

We have been much pestered here for the want of the supplies expected to compleat the ration for sixty days, we found but sixty Barrels of flower, hearing of about seventy more I have directed Colo. Benton to secure for the Second Regiment when it arives, we found the pork, part barrelled & half salted, and part Just cutting up—this has detained us to have pork drawn and resalted—not more salt than will secure as much of the pork as will supply the Boats that are here—We could find no person here who would acknowledge themselves the contractors agent, not being able to purchase any flower I have taken a barrel of flower which I would have paid for if I could have found any person to have paid it to, you will have to charge it to my acpt—I am Just Slipping Cable leaving Colo. Benton to bring up the rear—adieu

Andrew Jackson
Major Genl.

ALS, MeHi. Cantrell & Read was the Nashville mercantile firm of Stephen Cantrell and Thomas J. Read. The partnership was dissolved June 7, 1813.

From James Wilkinson

Head Quarters New Orleans Jany. 22nd. 1813.

Sir,

Understanding casually that you are approaching Natchez with a body of Dragoons, Infantry and mounted Gun Men, destined to this city, it becomes my duty to request you to halt in that vicinity; to report to me your instructions and your force, and, in concert with Colonel [Leonard] Covington, the officer in command at Washington,[1] to provide the most comfortable accommodation, for the citizen soldiers of your command, which the country can afford and the regulations of the government may permit.

The only advice I have received from the War Department, or elsewhere, respecting the auxiliary force under your command, excepting your letter of the 5th. instant to the Assistant Deputy Quarter Master,[2] bears date the 21st. and 23d. October, and is now transmitted to Colonel Covington to be submitted to you.[3]

There are several reasons which will prevent my calling you lower down the river than Baton Rouge, if the enemy should not invade the country. Vizt. the impracticability of providing for your horses, for any length of time; the monstrous expense of such provision, if to be had; the health of the troops and the stipulation of the government not to keep them in this low country during the warm season: To these may be added the policy of holding your corps on the alert at a suitable point, for giving succor to the feeble and exposed settlements on the Mobile, should the enemy make their first landing there, or at Pensacola, which is very probable.

Although I had received no certain advice of the levy of your corps, I sometime since took the precaution, to warn the Contractor to be prepared with a competent supply of provisions, and the Brigade Inspector, Captain Hughes, and the District Paymaster, Lieut. [Simeon] Knight,[4] were ordered to Natchez, the first to muster and inspect, and the last to pay the Volunteers and militia which the Government had required from the state of Tennessee. You will find those officers at their posts, ready to give every aid and facility to your subordinates, in the formation of their Returns, Musters and Abstracts; and if it is in my power to add to the comfort and accommodation of the band of patriots under your orders, it is only necessary to point out the mode to me.

I expect you may find quarters for a great part of your corps, in the late cantonment built by the Second Regiment near Washington, and at that place: Any defect must be supplied by billeting your men, or by encamping or huting. Should you, however, be pressed for quarters, and have only 4 or 500 Infantry, you may order them on at once to Baton Rouge; and to make room for them, the troops there will be ordered lower down. I shall be anxious to hear from you,[5] and, in the mean time, have the honor to be, respectfully, Sir, Your obedt Servant

Jas. Wilkinson

ALS and LC, DLC; Copy, PHi. Published in Bassett, 1:273–74.

1. Covington (d. 1813) was commander of the U.S. Light Dragoon Regiment at the Mississippi Territory capital, five miles east of Natchez. He was promoted to brigadier general in August 1813.

2. See AJ to Bartholomew Schaumburgh, January 5.

3. Wilkinson was referring to William Eustis's letters of October 21 and 23, 1812, to Willie Blount, copies of which probably had been forwarded to Wilkinson. In his first letter, Eustis had exhorted Blount "to communicate with General Wilkinson at New Orleans, keep him advised of your arrangements, the number of troops in each detachment, and the time of their rendezvous and march from the several points." In his October 23 letter, Eustis had written Blount that the troops from Tennessee would be "under the Command of a Brigadier General" (DLC).

4. Knight served in the regular army as an infantry officer, quartermaster, and paymaster until he resigned in 1820.

5. For Jackson's response, see AJ to Wilkinson, February 16, below.

From James Wilkinson

Head Quarters New Orleans January 25th. 1813.

Sir,

I have received a letter from his Excellency Governor Blount of Tennessee, under date of the 5th. inst. wherein he informs me you were about to move from Nashville, with one thousand four hundred Infantry and Riflemen, and six hundred and seventy Dragoons and mounted Infantry, destined to this City: and the requisitions, which you have made, through Governor Claiborne, to the Assistant Deputy Quarter Master and the Contractor's Agent here, have been put into my hands. Without knowing what may be your orders, instructions or the extent of your command, I must regret, that you have not done me the honor to communicate with me; because, being placed in the command of this department by the national executive, I could have better forwarded your views than any other person, and you can find no man more zealously disposed to cherish the band of patriots, whom you lead, than myself. But, under the orders which direct my conduct, my personal honor, my public obligations and the national interests forbid that I should yield my command to any person, until regularly relieved by superior authority.

I beg leave to refer you to my letter of the 22nd. Inst.,[1] and must repeat my desire, that you should halt in the vicinity of Natchez, until I may receive the communications required in that letter, and furnish you an answer.[2]

At present, Sir, the corps of your command could not find quarters, forage or provisions, but for a few days in this city.

Your letter to the Assistant Deputy Quarter Master, at Natchez, notified him of the approach of four hundred Infantry, instead of fourteen hundred, which led to the proposition, contained in my letter respecting the movement of that Corps.[3]

At the same time that the troops of your command should be held in readiness to traverse the country for prompt operations on the side of Mobile and Pensacola, it is important your boats should be carefully preserved for the descent of the river, should the enemy make his attack directly against this city; and, for this purpose, it is adviseable they should be secured on the side of the river opposite to Natchez, in charge of a vigilant officer and a suitable detachment.

With consideration and respect, I have the honor to be, Sir, Your obedt. Servt.

Jas. Wilkinson

ALS and LC, DLC; Copy, PHi. Published in Bassett, 1:274–75.
1. See above.
2. For Jackson and Wilkinson's exchanges, see AJ to James Wilkinson, February 16 and 20, and Wilkinson to AJ, February 22, below.
3. See AJ to [Robert Andrews] and contractor, January 5. The copies at PHi and TxU report the detachment under Jackson as "four hundred Infantry, six hundred and seventy cavalry and mounted Infantry."

A month after Jackson and his volunteers left Nashville for Natchez, John Armstrong, who assumed the duties of the secretary of war on February 5, ordered Jackson, in the letter below, to dismiss his troops. Several copies of Armstrong's letter, sent by various routes, were inadvertently dated January 5, an oversight which Jackson seized upon to express his frustration that the Tennessee volunteers did not see battle on the Natchez expedition.

From John Armstrong

Duplicate   War Department February 6th. 1813.
Sir,

The causes for embodying & marching to New Orleans the Corps under your command having ceased to exist, you will on receipt of this Letter, consider it as dismissed from public service, & take measures to have delivered over to Major General Wilkinson, all articles of public property which may have been put into its possession.

You will accept for yourself & the Corps the thanks of the President of the United States.

Very Respectfully I am Sir your most obt. Humble Servant.

John Armstrong.

LS copy, DNA-RG 107. Published in Bassett, 1:275–76 (dated February 5). LS, LC (two, dated January 5), Copies (dated January 5), DLC; LC, DNA-RG 107 (dated February 6); LC, PHi (dated January 5); Copy, MoSHi (dated January 5).

From Rachel Jackson

Feby 8th [1813]

My dear Husband.

Your Letter of the 18th January from the mouth of Cumberland river Came Safe to hand,[1] it was Every thing to me I rejoiced I was happy To heare you war in health it was my nightly prayers to the Almighty God my thoughts forever on the whar er I go whar er I turn my thoughts my fears my doubts Distress me, then a Little my hope revives again. that Keeps me a live was it not for that I must sink I should Die in my present situation. But my blessed redeemer Is making intersesion with the Father for us to meet again restore you to my bosom wher Every vein Every puls beets high For your helth you[r] safety all your wishes Crownd, Do not My beloved Husband let the love of Country fame and honour make you forgit you have me Without you I would think them all empty shadows You will say this is not the Language of a patriot but it is the Language of a faithfull Wife, one I know you Esteem & Love sinceerly, but how many pangs how many heart rendings Sighs has your absence Cost me My time passes heavily not in good health but I hope to see you once more on this globe and after this frail life Ends be with you in happyer Climes wer I shall Experience no more painfull seporation and then I'll be at rest I feel a foretast of the Joys that is to the virtuous souls Gracious God help me to pray for your happiness I was delighted to hear you war pleased with Mr [Learner] Blackman and the other two Clergymen[2] & the society in jeneral our Little Andrew is well the most affectionate Little Darling on Earth often dos he ask me in bed not to cry. Sweet pappa will Come home to you again feel my Cheeks to know if I am sheding Tears. One of them Extreem Cold nights he got a little vext and said he wondered his pappa did not Come home & sleep with him in his big bed on sunday last Mamma said he lets go to Nashville & See if he is ther. I told him wher you wer gone he said dont Cry Sweet Mama, you cant think how that has supported me in my trials. I wish I was with you, vain wish pray my Dear write to me often Its a cordial its balm to my mind lonesome hours I treasure Them up as [a] miser does his gold. I could write more to your satisfaction Could I refrain from tears But you know how to make allowances for me.

Catharine Caffery returned in a few Days after you set out the stock wants ther Masters Eye all your household regrets your absence all wishing & praying your Return. I paid Fields every Cent that I Did not send you In my Letter, he was not satisfied then borrowed thirty Dollars and paid him he was going aboute trying to sell your Note I have made nearly Enough to pay him off.

Sister [Jane] Hays Mrs. [Maria] McKeane Mrs [Sarah] Jackson Mr. [Daniel] Small[3] Catharine sends their best wishes to you please to present mine to Mr. Blackman A. Hines Carroll, and may the Almighty God of heaven Shower down his blessings his mercy on you assist you in the ways of life in the ways of righteousness be your Shield in the time of dainger support you in all things, keep you in the paths of wisdom the way thereof is peace. Farwell think on me your Dearest friend on Earth.

Rachel Jackson

Typed copy, DLC. Published in *Cincinnati Commercial*, January 8, 1880; Bassett, 1: 272–73 (dated January 1813). Original not found.
    1. Not found.
    2. Blackman (1781–1815), a Methodist missionary and presiding elder of the Cumberland District, was Jackson's staff chaplain on the Natchez expedition. Samuel John Mills (1783–1818) and John Freeman Schermerhorn (1786–1851), sent by the Connecticut and Massachusetts missionary societies on a tour of the West, accompanied Jackson's army to Natchez.
    3. Maria McKean, a frequent correspondent of Rachel's, was the widow of Gallatin merchant Joseph McKean. Sarah Moore McCullough was also a widow when she married James Jackson in 1810. Small (1772–1830) married Rachel's niece, Mary Hutchings.

From William Berkeley Lewis

Nashville Feby. 8th. 1813

My dear Sir

Your letters written from different points on the Cumberland have been recd.[1] and the requests contained therein, shall, as soon as practicable, be complied with; the arms have but just arrived, some in good order, and others very rusty. I have not yet made an estimate of such things as were brought back by Woods, owing to my not having been in town when they were deposited in the ware house—I have been waiting until S. Cantrell shall finish a ware house that is nearly compleated, into which I mean to deposit all the public property, at which time I will make out a correct invoice of the whole. I am not able to give you any information about the horsemens tents; further than, the three waggons which I met on the Sunday evening that you took your departure, just at the river whilst you were yet in sight. I was very much astonished that they should have been sent to the place of your embarkation, when I knew you had ordered them to Robertson's landing: they said that they had been ordered there by the quarter master! Rest assured, my dear Genl., all things shall be attended to.

Govr. Blount left here the tuesday after you did, for Knoxville, where he has since married Mrs. Mary White.[2] he has not yet returned. Genl. Armstrong is appointed Secretary of War. [William] Jones of Philladelphia, Secretary of Navy. Maj. William T Lewis died on thursday morning last about 4 O'clock. I am told he has left you, with Mrs. [Mary Hipkins] Lewis, Mr. [Thomas] Crutcher and Mr. [Alfred] Balch[3] Executors of his will. One of the Volunteers left in the hospital, by the name of Gist,[4] died since your departure. If there is no impropriety, I wish to keep another of the volunteers left in the hospital, now nearly recovered, for the purpose of putting the arms in good order, and to keep them so: please signify your approbation or disapprobation of such a measure. The mail is just closing—please write frequently. Receive the best wishes of your best unfeigned friend

W. B. Lewis

P.S. I had like to forgotten in the hurry of writing to inform you that a report has been softly whispered here since you left W[est] T[ennessee] that may if generally accredited may have a tendency to injure you; I keep a close look out, and if it becomes necessary, I shall contradict it in that manner which it deserves, with the insertion of piece in the papers with my name affixed. It has been stated to me that you declared previously to your leaving this Country that the same County should not contain both you and Genl. Wilkinson. Knowing a statement of that kind to be so contrary to what you always assured me was your intentions, I shall feel myself perfectly authorised to contradict it in the most positive manner.[5]

I hold your reputation as dear to me as my own, and you may rest assured that injustice shall not be done to my absent friend. I will write you more fully on this subject when I have more leasure, in the mean ti[me] accept the best wishes for your health a[nd] success—yours &c.

W B Lewis

ALS, DLC. Extract published in Bassett, 1:276.
    1. See AJ to Lewis, January 13 (above), 16, and 17.
    2. Mary (1782–1824) was the widow of Hugh White of Knoxville.

3. Mrs. Lewis was William T.'s widow. Crutcher (1759–1844), an early settler of David-son County, served as treasurer for the state of Tennessee from 1803 to 1823 and as mayor of Nashville, 1819–20. Balch (d. 1853), a Nashville lawyer and judge, was married to Wil-liam T. Lewis's daughter Mary. A member of the Nashville Junto during Jackson's cam-paign for the presidency, he later moved to Florida.

4. Not identified.

5. For Jackson's comments on serving under Wilkinson, see above, AJ to Willie Blount, November 11, 1812; AJ to George Washington Campbell, [November 29, 1812]; AJ to Lewis, February 21, below. Although Jackson authorized Lewis to contradict the rumor, it has not been established that Lewis published anything.

To Rachel Jackson

On board my Boat 2 miles above Natchez
February 15th. 1813. 8 oclock at night—

I reached Shore at this Point this moment with my detachment, all in good health, after experiencing all the inclemency of the coldest weather ever felt in the same Latitude, and sundry delays from the floating of the ice in the ohio and Mississippi—experiencing no other accident but the wreck of one Boat which sunk to her roof in three minutes after she recd. the Shock from the sawyer—I had the pleasure of seeing Capt. [George] Smith at the mouth of the yazoo, the Cavalry all well and will meet me tomorrow at Natchez, or cantonment washington—I sent on Major Car-rol two days since to the Natchez for letters and to meet the Cavalry—I have Just recd. a note from him covering a number of letters from my friends in Nashville and its vicinity amongst them was one from my friend Robert Butler, in which he states that you with our dear little son is in good health This letter was truly gratifying to me—as it was the first information I have recd from you since the recpt of your letter of the 10th. of Decbr[1] It is probable from Major Carrols letter that we shall be disembarked at the Natchez—this I shall know early on tomorrow[2]—I only prepare this letter for you to night, to send by tomorrows mail knowing that you are anxious to hear from me, and that I will not have time to write you after I reach Natchez tomorrow—I wrote you on my passage down cumberland, whether you have recd. them I cannot say[3]—having several letters to write to night, and a general order—I have only to add a renewal of my prayers to the Sovereign of the universe for his superintending care and protection of you and our dear little Andrew—

Say to Patsey that Doctor [William Edward] Butler is well, and getting quite *fat*—give my compliments to Colo Hays Mrs. Hays and the family and all enquiring friends, and accept for yourself an affectonate adieu—and kiss andrew for me—your affectionate Husband

Andrew Jackson

ALS, CSmH. Published in *Huntington Library Bulletin*, 3(1933): 111–12.
1. Carroll's note not found; Robert Butler's and Rachel Jackson's letters not found. Jackson was mistaken about the date he had last received a letter from Rachel, for on January 8 (see above), he acknowledged a letter and her miniature delivered by Dinwiddie.
2. On February 16 Jackson received Wilkinson's letter of January 22, ordering him to remain at Natchez.
3. Letters not found.

To James Wilkinson

Head quarters Natchez Feby 16 1813

Sir,

I Reached the vicinity of this city on last evening and this morning I received your several communications of the 6. & 22d. January.[1] I have been much impeded in my progress by the running of the Ice in the Ohio and Mississippi.

The second Regiment that was detained for the want of Boats, reached me on the evening of the 13. inst. The Cavalry will reach Cantonment Washington this evening. My Detachment when united, amounts to about two thousand and seventy, fourteen hundred of whom are Infantry. The amount of the Sick, (not having recd. a report from the 2d Regiment since its arrival) I cannot at present state.

So soon as the Cavalry reaches me, I will communicate to you the strength & Condition of my detachment, and will inclose you a copy of my marching orders. The Substance of which is to proceed to New orleans and there await the orders of Government.[2] But from the communications I have just received from you, will disembark my Infantry and await the orders of the Government here. In the meantime I will be happy to communicate with you on the public safety and defence of the lower country, and will move my Troops to any point best calculated for this object. My wish is to keep them employed in active service, as Indolence creates disquiet.

I have marched with the true spirit of a soldier to serve my country at any and every point where service can be rendered.

I will be happy to receive your Communications frequently.

With consideration I am yr. obt.

Andrew Jackson

LC, DLC; Copy, DNA-RG 107. Published in Bassett, 1:276–77.
1. See above.
2. For Jackson's orders, see above, Willie Blount to AJ, December 31, 1812.

From John Armstrong

War Department February 16th. 1813.

Sir,

Herewith inclosed you will receive a Duplicate of an Order addressed to you at New Orleans.[1] Should this reach you before you descend the Mississippi, you will have delivered over to the Commanding Officer at Fort Massac, all munitions and property belonging to the United States, which have been put into the possession of your Detachment.

Very Respectfully I am Sir yr most obt. Humble Servant.

John Armstrong

LS and LC, DNA-RG 107; LC and Copy, DLC. Published in Bassett, 1:277.
    1. For the enclosure, see above, Armstrong to AJ, February 6.

To James Wilkinson

Cantonment near Washington Feby 20. 1813.

Sir,

I had the honour to acknowledge your orders of the 6th. and 22d Jany. on the 16. instant. Yours of the 25 January reached me the same evening[1]

Before the receipt of yours of the 25, and agreable to your request and advice contained in that of the 6th. and 22d. Jany, I dropped my Boats to the landing, and ordered a disembarkation of the Troops on the morning of the 17th. instant.

From a conversation with Capt. Hughs and Colo Covington (from whom I have received every mark of attention and Politeness) I intended to have fixed my Encampment at the Cantonment built by the 2d. Regiment; but a view of the place and the necessity of keeping my Troops together for the purpose of discipline, determined me to pitch my Tents on the West of Washington on the land owned by Mr [Joseph] Perkins.[2]

This scite promises health and affords a supply of wood and the best water of the country, added to this an open field for the exercise & discipline of the Troops. So soon as they are encamped on this ground, I will have them mustered & inspected.

The Enclosed from No. 1. to 5 will give you the information required in yours of the 25 January and No. 6 will shew the strength and condition of the detachment under my command[3]

I have taken the precaution pointed out by you in yours of the 25 Jany. by leaving a sufficient Guard with the Boats under the command of a discreet subaltern Officer in the Bason at Natchez, finding impossible to have landed on the right Bank of the River from where they lay. Added to this the difficulty of crossing the Troops over to them on a sudden call to embark and descend the River determined me to keep them tied to the left Bank.

Your Views in requesting the detachment under my command to halt here perfectly meet my own, and will warrant me in the departure from the Order of his Excellency Gov. Blount, which directed me "to descend to New orleans and there await the orders of the President of the united states."[4]

It was understood in Nashville at the time I received orders to march, that you were at Fort Stoddart.[5] The notification and requisition therefore was made on the Contractor & quarter master through Gov. Claiborne as the surest and best channel to reach them.[6]

The Detachment under my command shall be kept in compleat readiness to move to any point at which an Enemy may appear at the shortest notice and to Co-operate with you in all measures efficiently to defend the lower Country. To this End, my eyes are turned to the south East.

I have the honor to be Yr. obt. sevt.

Andrew Jackson

P.S. Before my march from Nashville advices were received that Government had on the Road a quantity of fixed Ammunition for the use of this detachment

But I am sorry to say that it had not arrived, nor was there any information when it probably would be at that place. The Rumor of danger below, made our immediate departure necessary. We are entirely without ammunition and would be happy to be advised where a supply can be had.

Permit me further to add, that about half of our Cavalry are entirely without Swords, and that there is no possible chance of a supply in this Territory   A. J.

LC, DLC; Copies, LNHiC and DNA-RG 107. Published in Bassett, 1:277–78.
    1. See above.
    2. Perkins, a local farmer, was paid $250 for the use of his land and wood (AJ to Robert Andrews, March 23).
    3. Enclosures not found.
    4. See above, Blount to AJ, December 31, 1812.
    5. Fort Stoddert, located below the junction of the Alabama and Tombigbee rivers, forty miles north of Mobile.
    6. See above, AJ to Claiborne, January 5.

To William Berkeley Lewis

Head quarters near Washington M.T.
February 21st. 1813

Dear Sir

I approached the vicinity of Natchez late on the evening of the 15th. instant, and by express from major Carrol who I had sent a head to meet the cavalry, and forward me any communications from the Post office Natchez, I recd. two letters from Genl Wilkinson of the 6th and 22nd. January which induced me to put to shore about 2 miles above the town[1]—These communications were of the most friendly kind, advising me of the scarcity of forrage below, and the propriety of landing at Natchez for health of my troops and the most advantageous position from which to make a movement to any point that an enemy might shew a front—These reasons cogent in themselves, and perfectly meeting my views, with a belief that the would Justify, a deviation from the orders of the Governor which directed me to proceed to Neworleans—I determined to drop down to Natchez and disembark my troops; for this purpose on the morning of the 16th. I dropped down to the Natchez and tied to the shore where I recd. another letter from Genl Wilkingson of the 25 ulto.[2] reiterating his reasons in stronger terms and advising and requesting me to disembark my troops and encamp them at or in the neighbourhood of this place—which I accordingly did on the morning of the 17th. and marched them to the cantonment washington where I met the Cavalry, who had arived the evening of the 16th. in good health—finding the cantonment washington in a state of decay, the houses rotting down, and a collection of as much filth that with one weeks sun would create a plaige I have laid out an encampment on a beautifull plain about a mile west of washington and 4 miles from Natchez, to which place this day I should have removed my troops, was it not for the torrent of rain that has & is now falling—This place affords a plentifull supply of wood & good water and promises health to my troops—I experienced seven days detention by the running of the ice in the ohio & cumberland one day by the loss of Capt. [John] Wallaces[3] boat which went down in three [minutes] to her roof, but by the exertions of the officers, all the men were saved, and all the Baggage, a few musquetts, bayonets & Boxes were lost—we lost on our passage two men out of the second regiment, none out of the first—The Detachment are as healthy as we could expect, in fine spirits and under good subordination—and has improved more on their discipline for the time and opportunity than any troops ever did before—

I recd. your letter of the 8th. instant on the 16th.[4] and beg of you to accept my thanks for your attention to the arms returned, you will retain the soldier left in the hospital, for the purpose of keeping the arms clean advise me of his name and to what company he belongs, by the earliest opportunity—

I am not astonished that I should have enemies in my absence—and feel grateful for your friendship on this occasion—you can with Justice & propriety, give the report the direct contradiction—every officer of my detachment, who ever heard me speak a word upon the subject does know, that I always declared, that I marched with the true spirit of a soldier that I come to fight the battles of my country, and not to contend for rank but to harmonise—that if any dispute should arise between me and the Genl—the Publick service should not be interrupted thereby, if I had the power to controle it, but that the genl and myself would settle any dispute if any should arise without injury to the publick service or disturbance to the public—

I regret the death of Major Lewis—I fear his business is verry much unsettled—and that his family may be injured thereby—I shall be happy to hear from you often—direct to me at Natchez—and accept assurances of my warmest friendship and Esteem

Andrew Jackson

PS. you will see that paper prepared for a muster return has been converted into this letter in haste I am too busy in the act of preparing to move to coopy   A. J.

ALS copy, DLC. Extract published in Bassett, 1:278–79.
  1. See above.
  2. See also above.
  3. Wallace (d. 1816), a company commander in the 1st Regiment, Tennessee Volunteers, was from Rutherford County.
  4. See above.

To Rachel Jackson

Headquarters near Washington M. T.
February 22nd. 1813.

My Love

On my approach near Natchez, on the night of the 15th Instant I wrote you,[1] It was then uncertain whether I should disembark my troops at Natchez or proceed on to New-orleans—on the morning of the 16th. I took a small craft & went down to Natchez, where I recd. advices that determined me to disembark my troops and form an encampment near Natchez—on the morning of the 17th. I marched my troops to cantonment washington, where I formed a Junction with Colo. Coffee's Regiment, who had reached that place on the preceding evening, annd found them all in good health and spirits—I am forming an encampment on a beautifull plain, that affords a prospect of health a supply of wood and water about four miles from Natchez—how long I may remain at this point I cannot tell—This will entirely depend upon the appearence of an enemy—and the probable point of attack—any letters you may write me direct them to Natchez—should I leave the neighbourhood, before the reach me the will be forwarded after me—all my Detachment, are now with me, and health with a few exceptions prevades the whole—I am happy to have such orderly men—they are easily commanded improve in discipline—and if we should meet an enemy I have no doubt will support the honor of the state to which they belong—we have no news here of an enemy—But, my heart bleeds, for the disaster that has lately befel Genl Winchester in the north west—If true; what an ocean of blood, from the chocest veins of the western sons has been spilt—It appears that fate has destined our best heroes to perish in those deserts, or can these misfortunes arise, from want of Judgt. incaution, or is it from a fixed destiny of heaven—[2]

I regret exceedingly the fate of Genl Winchester—had he fallen bravely as he did fall, with victory on his side I should have rejoced—But fall even bravely in defeat always in an ungratefull world leaves stains and stings behind—Such brave and good men as him deserved a better fate— I am anxiously to hear from you & my sweet little Andrew, Capt Butlers letter[3] advised me you were both well—May heaven grant a continuation of that blessing on you both untill I return.

I would be glad to hear how my overseer conducts—whether he has come up to his contract & whether he has complied with his promise in his attention to you—Colo. Purdy and Mrs Purdy desires their compliments to you they will set out to Nashville in a few days—please say to Colo. Ward and Mr [Francis] Sanders,[4] that I will write them as soon as I can obtain sufficient information of the marketts—to Justify me—corn now selling at five bits pr. bushel good sifted meal, for from 75 cents to a dollars—but no contract can be made for a large quantity—But it is my oppinion that meal will be in May an excellent price—and also corn.

Make my compliments to Colo. Hays & family Capt Butler and Rachel, to Patsey and tell her William is in good health—and to all friends— tell Peggy[5] howde for me—and kiss Andrew, and believe me to be your affectionate husband—

Andrew Jackson

ALS, DLC. Published in Bassett, 1:280–81.
1. See above.
2. Winchester's army had been captured by a force of British and Indians at the River Raisin, Mich. Terr., on January 22.
3. Not found.
4. Sanders, former justice of the peace in Davidson County, was Jackson's neighbor.
5. Possibly William T. Lewis's daughter Margaret (1793–1816), who married William B. Lewis in August 1813.

From James Wilkinson

New Orleans Feby. 22d. 1813

Sir,

I had the satisfaction to receive yesterday by the Steam Boat, your letter of the 16th. inst.[1] and congratulate you & the corps of your command on your safe arrival at Natchez.

I have been left without information respecting your destination or Instructions, further than the communications from the war department to his Excellency Governor Blount, in the month of October last (which Col. Covington has been requested to submit to your examination) and the Governor's annunciation to myself of your intended departure from Nashville. But from the tenor of your letter, I perceive you are instructed "to proceed to this city & await the orders of Government."

It necessarily follows, that however singular the circumstance, we are to act independently of each other, in the department, which had been formally & officially assigned to my command, by the executive of the United States, anterior to my departure from the city of Washington.

Yet, Sir, the novelty of the case will not I trust, produce any injury to the public service, because I shall not pretend to exercise any authority, with which I am not explicitly invested, But I shall cordially cooperate with you, in whatever may be deemed necessary to the cause of our common country; in full confidence that I shall experience from you, the same spirit of harmonious concert.

It is highly important to the government of the United States, and, I do conceive, deeply interesting to [our] own characters, that we should be prepared to repel the attacks of the Enemy, at whatever point, and at every peril and hardship, to retrieve the character of our arms, which has been deeply tarnished by the events of the last campaign.

While the maritime superiority of the enemy puts it in his power, to land at Pensacola or Mobile, or to make a descent on the coast, at various points, between the latter place and the River Tesche, I think your position in the vicinity of Natchez preferable to any other, on the score of accommodation, Forage, Subsistance, Health & military merits, until the views of the Enemy may become manifest; because by keeping your corps on the alert, and carefully preserving your boats, by a Suitable guard, on the opposite Shore of the River, you will always be in readiness for a prompt movement, across the country to the Side of Mobile, or to descend the Mississipi to this quarter. These, Sir, and the impossibility in the present state of our magazines, to subsist either your men or horses below Natchez, are the chief motives which induced me to advise you to halt at that place.

I shall receive with much pleasure the copy of your marching orders and the report of the strength & condition of the corps of your command, which you have promised me, because it may be necessary for my Government; and should you think proper, I will cheerfully exchange with you, copies of all orders we may respectively receive from the general goverment.

I forbear to trespass on you further at this time, because you must be much occupied in providing for the accommodation, comfort & Health of the patriot soldiers Intrusted to your care; and would to god! it were in my power to contribute effectually to either, in a country without means & without resources.

I have the honor to be respectfully, Sir, Your obedt. Servt.

Ja: Wilkinson

LS and LC, DLC; Copy, DNA-RG 107. Published in Bassett, 1:281–82.
   1. See above.

To Rachel Jackson

Head quarters camp Jackson March the 1st. 1813.

My Love

The place from whence I now write, is the place named in my last to you that I was about to move my troops to—late last night from New-orleans I recd. your letter of the 8th. February[1] and Colo. Hays of the 9th.[2] I have no doubt but my presence at home would be agreable to all— and beneficial to our interest, but my love, if you can enjoy health, and calm your mind, and our little Andrew be spared to us, and I to return and find you in health I shall be content and thankfull for the blessing—I am sorry Sandy[3] has turned out such a rascal as Colo Hays advises me—I hope the overseer has done his duty, and amply punished him—Colo Hays has stated that Mr [Thomas] Watson will give five hundred dollars for him—I leave this entirely to yourself—it is a good price if the cash is paid in hand—but on the event of a sale there must be no credit unless there is a note payable in bank, with good endorsers—such as Mr. John Anderson[4] will advise is good—I think from the disposition of Sandy— that if five hundred dollars will be paid by Watson you had better sell him, and turn out one of the wenches under the overseer—inform the overseer tha[t he] must attend to his duty—and as to Mr Fields, I shall recollect his conduct—what may be my future destination as yet I am unadvised—or how long we may be detained here—from any advices as yet recd. there is verry little use for us in this quarter—I am happy to hear that Catharine has returned—I have not seen or heard from Mrs Cafferry since I have been here, I am told Mr Green is preparing to move his family to Cumberland—he has lost three of his children as I am informed—I write to Mrs. Cafferry to day, and has requested her to let Jackey come down and see me, if convenient,[5] say to Colo Hays I have but little time to write to my friends or I should have wrote him—forever busied with my troops, and their supplies I have little leisure—I have recd every mark of attention from the citizens of this country, the good order of my troops, and their perfect subordination has drew forth the praises of the citizens—from alarm for their persons and property, they find in us a perfect shield—

On the receipt of this letter I wish you to send for Mr F Sanders, and say to him from every advice and information recd. through the best channels, that kill dried meal will command a good price—that flower has been up to $18 but has lately taken a fall—If the present Number of troops should be kept up for any length of time every kind of supplies must bear a good price—That I have been trying to make an engagement for him and myself and Colo. Ward but as yet has failed—that If I can I shall write him immediately and I request that Mr Sanders may give Colo Ward the above information—Having an inspec[ti]on of my troops tomorrow—I have no time [to] write to any other of my friends to day

Major Haynes & Carroll, beg me to present their compliments to you—Say to Patsey her Doctor is with me in good health and if we should be detained long in this country William and myself intend sending for you—My Compliments to Colo Hays & family Capt Butler & Rachel—and all my female friends who has been good anough to send their compliments to me—give my love [to] Catharine, my respects to Peggy and kiss my little Andrew for me give my respects to Capt [John] Donelson and his family and accept from me the sincere wishes of an affectionate Husband

Andrew Jackson

P.S. I had the pleasure of spending a few day with Colo. Purdy and Mrs. Purdy the request their compliments to you—on the evening of the 25th. they set out for Nashville, got a short distance—and on friday proceeded on their Journey—I hope they will reach Nashville in 2[?] days, Mrs. Purdy and the Colo has promised to visit you shortly after their arival at Nashville—say to little Andrew I have sent him a kiss by *Martha*—god bless you farewell   A. J.

ALS, MH-H.
  1. See above.
  2. Not found.
  3. A slave.
  4. Anderson was the cashier of the Nashville Bank. In 1808 he had married Elizabeth Glasgow Martin Donelson, Stockley's widow.
  5. Letter not found.

From James Wilkinson

New Orleans March 1st. 1813

Sir

I am honored by your letter of the 20th Instant,[1] with its enclosures, for which be pleased to accept my thanks—Put faith in a Soldiers word when I tell you, that altho' the experience of many years convince me the wisest organisation of military bodies will admit but one head, I meet you with cordiality, on the ground of mutual concert & cooperation, as far as the obligations of duty & the orders of our Government may permit me.

Your orders clearly justify you in acknowledging no authority but that of the President of the United States; and it is equally clear that your halt at Natchez is warranted, by every consideration of regard to the patriotic band you command, and the virtuous cause you have volunteered to Serve, under circumstances which "try Men's Souls."

Were I authorised to approve, I Should Say that under Similar circumstances, I would have adopted the course you have pursued, in the disposition of your corps; for you estimate justly the importance of keeping it together, and too much praise cannot be bestowed on men, who, in the cause of their country, voluntarily exchange the comforts of domestic ease, for the frosty bed & a flimsy Canopy; But Sir, let me advise you to be regardful of your Health, for desease begets discontent, and a Sickly camp afflicts every feeling & enfeebles every faculty. I Speak from the experience of 1777 in Canada & at Tyconderoga, and from successive scenes, down to the late mortality on the lakes.

I would we could find action, for that will contribute to Health & insure content, But for this we must depend on the Enemy; & in the mean time, we must practice patience, the second virtue of a Soldier.

Col. Covington who is placed in charge of the national arsenal at Washington Cantonment, will receive by this mail & will communicate to you my Ideas, of the course which I conceive Should be pursued, for the accommodation of your Corps, & the avoidance of difficulties, in the settlements of public accounts, with which I have had heretofore much trouble.

Heading an Independent corps, It follows, necessarily, that you should possess power adequate to its rightful & necessary accommodation in all things; and therefore the most plain and, to me, the most acceptable course would be, that your separate staff under your own distinct orders, should provide whatever may appertain to the Quarter Masters & medical Departments [(]medicine & Hospital Stores are furnished by the D. Q. Genl.[)] while the Army contractor will necessarily be Subject to your orders. But Should you find any difficulty in the way of this proposition, Then let the permanent public agents provide & furnish, under your authority to your Staff, taking their accountable receipts to the Department of war.

While I feel a proper Solicitude for the correctness of my own conduct, & experience has taught me caution, I have no disposition to split Hairs or make difficulties; For the march of two Thousand Free men, a thousand miles in the dead of winter, for the public defense, is a novel scene, which must call forth the sympathies of every Patriot Bosom, and entitle the actors to an extraordinary indulgence.

I regret your Dragoons are not armed, because I have not the means to Supply the defect, for I assure you, we have not in all our Stores fifty Swords, altho' I have again & again written for five hundred—Cannot you convert those of that corps who are unarmed, into mounted Gunmen, until cavalry Equipments may arrive? I believe we have some musquets at Washington & altho' destined to another Service, you have but to confer with Col. Covington to obtain them—

With respect to fixt ammunition for your musquets, & Powder & lead for your Rifles, I am happy it is in my power to promise you an ample Supply, but you must have patience for the next passage of the Steam Boat, as it is the Safest & most expeditious mode by which it can be sent to you.

A few words more Sir, and I will terminate this trespass; The law under cover will account to you, for the attempts which have been made, to Inlist into the Regular army from the volunteer corps; I understand those attempts are offensive & have put a stop to them, as far as I dare, in the inclosed order.[2]

I conclude by beseeching you to suffer no want, accommodation or convenience, in my power to remedy or furnish; the character & the conduct or your corps, such as it comes to me, from all persons & all quarters, deserve every thing from their country, & as far as my means extend they shall not be disappointed.

With much consideration & respect, I am Sir, Your obedient Servant

Jas. Wilkinson

LS and LC, DLC; Copy, DNA-RG 107. Published in Bassett, 1:285–87.
    1. Wilkinson was referring to Jackson's letter of February 20 (above).
    2. Wilkinson probably enclosed a copy of the amendment to the act "for the more perfect organization of the Army of the United States," approved on January 20, 1813, and stipulating that "it shall be lawful for any person during the time he may be performing a tour of militia duty to enlist in the regular army of the United States" (2 *U.S. Statutes at Large* 791–92). On March 2, Wilkinson ordered that "the enlistment of volunteers into the Regular service is not to be attempted, without the consent of the commanding officers of those corps" (DLC).

To Robert Andrews

Head-quarters Camp Jackson March 3d 1813

Sir,

After perusing your note of this day's date[1] and reflecting on the novelty of the request, and that too coming from the asst. Depy qr. master Genl. of the united states Colo. [Bartholomew] Shaumburg,[2] who has been as well as yourself notified by me of date "Nashville Jany 5. 1813[3] That the Detachment under my command consisting of Fourteen Hundred Infantry and six hundred & seventy Cavalry and mounted Infantry destined for new orleans, would leave that place in the present week" and notifying him & you that the requisite supplies for this detachment be furnished without delay on their arrival makes it necessary & proper before I answer these *unusual & unmilitary interogatories* to call upon you for a copy of the deputy Quarter Master Generals instructions to you and also a copy of his letter to you on which your note is predicated,[4] and by and under what instructions you have been thus far furnishing supplies to .the Cavalry? Whether it has not been under my notification to Yourself here? or instructions from Colo. Shamburgh? on my notification to him. When this Information is given I will give your interrogatories a proper answer For your own satisfaction, which perhaps wants experience (not so with Colo. Shamburgh[)] I will barily observe, that I command ["]no officer, from a colonel down to a captain, who does not hold a commission signed by the President of the United States, and ordered into Service by competent authority"

If this had been doubted by Col. Shamburgh, he had sufficient time to inform himself after my notification.

There is one thing you may assure Colo. Shamburgh, that the Government wants no underwriters; and he must be either very ignorant, or think me so, to ask such a question.

Being ordered by the president of the United States into its service for the defence of the lower Mississippi, I expect supplies from the Quarter Masters for my Cavalry. When the Quarter Master refuses to furnish, I will adopt such means for the procurement of them as the necessity may require, until I can advise the secretary thereof.

I am Sir Respectfully yr. Hml. St.

Andrew Jackson

LS copy, DLC. Published in Bassett, 1:287–88. Andrews was a captain in the regular army and assistant deputy quartermaster at Cantonment Washington.

1. Not found.

2. Schaumburgh (d. 1835) was deputy quartermaster general of the 7th Military District, stationed at New Orleans.

3. See AJ to [Bartholomew Schaumburgh]; [Robert Andrews] and contractor, January 5.

4. Copies of Schaumburgh's letters to Andrews, January 21 and February 25, were sent to Jackson (DLC). He ordered Andrews to determine the standing of Jackson's cavalry under the law inasmuch as rations could be authorized only for legally constituted units.

To William Berkeley Lewis

Head quarters Camp Jackson March 4th. 1813

Dear Sir,

I had the pleasure of receiving a letter from my friend Mr [Charles] Cassedy of the 24th. of February,[1] which stated that a differrence was likley to arise between you and Col. Benton—This was an unexpected subject to me, untill yesterday I had the perusal of the Whig, that contained your adress to the publick[2]—The Journal, that appears to have gave rise to it I have never seen—nor did I hear of untill I saw your address[3]—I am truly sorry that this dispute has arisen or that any thing should have been stated in the public prints, that should have made it necessary for your address—as soon as I was advised of the dispute I saw Col. Benton, & had a conversation with him on the subject—and I do suppose, that from him nothing will appear in the papers that will make it necessary for you to make any further remarks, I do sincerely wish that the publick may not see or hear any thing more on the subject you know my oppion as to appeals to the publick and I hope you know that I hold your feelings & charector as dear as my own—and unless you are compelled in self defence—to again appear before the publick—my advice as a friend is that you remain silent—but let it be clearly understood that this advice is predicated on an idea, that nothing will appear from the other quarter that will make it necessary—Should I be disappointed in this, then Sir you will understand, that my advice ceases, as the ideas on which it is predicated—is disappointed[4]—The duties of my station keep, me constantly employed—Some dificulty, has likely to have arisen with the quarter master here from some instructions, he has recd. from Colo. Shamburgh Deputy Q Master General of this department, in due time I shall give you a detailed account of this Novel conduct of Colo. Shamburgh—I have obtained this day from the Deputy Asst. Q Master here, coopies of his instructions and have given the D.A. Q Master an answer to some impertenant Questions of Shamburgh,[5] that will make the old satelite of duplicity sc[ream] with rage—The Questions were whether I was ordered into service by competant authority—and whether I would become personally responsible for the supplies of the Cavalry &c &c—Such impertinence did not originate with this old German

Several communications of the most friendly and polite kind has passed from Genl. W. to me and from me to him, it appears from his letters to me that he has no instructions, with respect to me or my detachment—my orders were to descend to *Neworleans* and there await the *orders* of the

President—But from the Genl's advice and request, and the reasons given by him for my disembarking my troops here—the health of the place— the want of supplies below—the situation in case of a movement being necessary to any point on the approach of an enemy—were sufficient in my mind and I hope will be to the governor for my not proceeding directly to Neworleans

I am here without any advice orders or directions, as to my future operations—no enemy to face—or any thing to do—no medicine chest, or medicinal supply for the troops. I shall on tomorrow purchase out of my own funds and depend on goverment—for payment—my men cannot nor shall not die for the want of medical supply—I recd. a letter from Mr Moss[6]—from whom Capt. [James] Mcferren[7] got a Boat which was inspected and vallued by Colo. Bradley I enclose you Colo. Bradleys certificate[8] and have to request that you will pay the same—

I wish we were ordered to upper Canedy—there we could be of service—I have wrote on to the Secretary of war requesting to be moved on to that quarter[9]—My Detachment would move on to that quarter with alacrity—I have them under good subordination—and will have them in excellent discipline—no meneuvre [or opera]tion that the first regiment cannot perform and several companies of the Second regiment in fact they have all done much, but still a great deal more is to be done—but the Indefatigability of Carrol will do anything—he is I think the best Brigade Major in the armies of the united States—he ought and must be at the head of a regiment—you shall hear from me shortly, I have to set out on the grand rounds, and I must bid you an affectionate good night

Andrew Jackson

ALS, NN; Copy (fragment), DLC.

1. Cassedy (c1782–1858), later a writer and newspaper editor, served briefly as a secretary to John Overton; in the summer of 1814 Jackson employed him as secretary and clerk to the commission for the Creek cession. Letter not found.

2. See Lewis to the public, February 18, published in *Nashville Whig*, February 24.

3. Jackson was referring to Thomas Hart Benton's "Journal of a voyage from Nashville to Orleans, by the Tennessee Volunteers," published in the *Democratic Clarion*, February 9, 16; March 9. In the first instalment, Benton had alleged that Lewis was an incompetent quartermaster, having failed to have on hand the necessary supplies and boats for the Natchez expedition. Lewis responded by questioning Benton's motives and personal courage.

4. Before Jackson intervened in the Benton-Lewis dispute, "A Citizen" and William P. Anderson had published remarks on Lewis's letter (*Democratic Clarion*, March 2), and Lewis had again responded that "it was *Col. Benton* who attacked me; it is *Col. Benton* whom I shall notice and not any collateral publications" (*Democratic Clarion*, March 9). When Benton returned from Natchez in April, he challenged Lewis, but no evidence has been found that he and Lewis fought a duel (*Democratic Clarion*, May 4).

5. See Schaumburgh to Andrews, February 16, 25 (DLC). For Jackson's response to Andrews, upon seeing Schaumburgh's letters, see above and AJ to Andrews, March 4.

6. Moss not identified; letter not found.

7. McFerrin (1784–1840) commanded a cavalry company in the Natchez expedition and during the Creek War. He later entered the Methodist ministry.

8. Not found.

9. See AJ to John Armstrong, March 1.

To Rachel Jackson

Headquarters Camp Jackson
near Washington March 7th. 1813

My love

When I wrote you last mail[1] I was labouring under a distressing cough proceeding from a violent cold, which had fell upon my lungs, and had assumed inflamatory symptoms—a free use of the Lancet by William [Butler] relieved me, and I am nearly restored to my former heath—I should have then named it, but I knew it would have given you pain—

I am still without advices of our future destination—there is no enemy that I can hear of in this quarter—of course nothing for us to do here. The troops are healthy, and George [Washington] Martin[2] [doin]g verry well—and so is Stockley [Donelson] Hutchings—[3]

Mr. Abraham Green is now with me—he has lost both his daughters, and is preparing to move to Tennessee in a few weeks—your sister Caffery he tells me is in bad health anxious to get up to Tennessee, should I return direct to Tennessee will take her on with me—If I should not will if possible, aid her in getting up—certainly there can be but little family affection existing if one sister cannot be taken from the Jaws of sickness, and (of course before long if left where she is) the grave—I am so pressed with attention to the duties of my station that I have but little time to spend in the sweet converse of writing to my boosom friend—you must give my compliments to all my friends—& kiss & bless my sweet little andrew for me, Tell *patsey* & *Polly Coffee* that their lords are well & fat, god bless you goodnight

Andrew Jackson

P.S. Mr. Blackman sends his best wishes to you, so does Majors Haynes and Carroll—

ALS, DLC. Published in Bassett, 1:289.
1. See above, AJ to Rachel Jackson, March 1.
2. Martin (1792–1854), the son of John and Elizabeth Glasgow Martin, served as a major in Coffee's cavalry. In 1830, he married Severn Donelson's daughter, Lucinda Rucker, and later settled on a plantation in Mississippi.
3. Hutchings, Rachel Jackson's nephew, was a quartermaster sergeant in Coffee's cavalry regiment. He settled in Huntsville, Ala.

To James Wilkinson

Head quarters March 8th 1813.

Sir,

I had the pleasure of receiving your favor on yesterday, under date of the first instant.[1]

I am sensible of the correctness of your observation, contained in the first paragraph of it, and I am pleased with the frankness with which you speak of our respective commands.

As to the supplies from the quartermasters department, the usual and only mode of drawing them is clearly defined by the law creating that department. The Quarter master Genl. the deputy qr master Genl. and their assistant deputies, plainly shew that all supplies for an army must be drawn from them. The Regimental and Brigade Quarter masters attached to an army, are for the purpose of receiving, receipting for, and distributing such supplies as are wanted and directed by the commanding officer of the detachment. This is my understanding of the laws establishing this department.[2]

It has been the plan pursued by me in obtaining all supplies heretofore, and is the only one that has system, and can prevent confusion in the settlements of accounts. It has been the plan pursued by me since I have been in the limits of the department of Colo. Shaumburgh, and I intend to pursue this plan until the supplies are withheld from me, thro' the regular channels, and then I must adopt such irregular ways, as will ensure them until I can advise the Secretary at War.

I have directed my quarter masters to sign receipts in the usual form. Being ordered by the President of the united States, for the defence of the lower country, and advised that the officers of the proper departments would furnish all legal, and necessary supplies, I cannot feel authorised to direct my quarter masters to sign any other receipts than those in the usual form. In the meantime accept my thanks for your very polite and friendly tender [of] accommodations to my detachment as far as your power extends.

I am truly sorry that swords for part of my Cavalry cannot be obtained, and thank you for the offer of muskets in the place of them. Being taught at a tender age to know that a soldier without pride, never rendered beneficial services to his country, and a soldier without arms was like a Beau in a ball room without shoes, each being unprepared for action. I therefore took the precaution before I marched from Nashville to arm such of my Cavalry with good muskets who had not swords. There is no uniformity in the arms of the troops, part are composed of muskets and part of swords. My wish in asking for swords was to have uniformity in their arms, as it is very unpleasant to transfer men, from one Capt to another merely for the want of uniformity of equipment, particularly as they volunteered under the privilege of choosing their own officers.

I am happy that it in your power to furnish the requisite supplies, of ammunition for my detachment. It is important to have it, in case of any sudden emergency, that no delay be occasioned for the want of it. I have noted your order respecting enlistments, and read with attention the enclosed law. The order is a proper one, and may prevent young and inexperienced officers from running into error and danger. The act enclosed refers to detached militia under the act of congress of April 10th and has no bearing or relation, to the Volunteers who have entered themselves under the acts of Feby. 6th & July 6th 1812. These are as much enlisted as any troops of the united States and as I understand the law, are expresly forbidden by the rules and articles of war, to be enlisted into any other corps and the officer knowing them to be such is liable to all the pains expressed by that article.[3]

The late disasters in the Northwest, will occasion a want of Troops there, and if it be correct, that Congress have witheld from the President powers to take possession of the Floridas, part of the object of the Troops under my command will, I presume cease to exist. Should the safety of this lower Country permit and Goverment so order, I would with pleasure march to the lines of Canada, and there offer my feeble aid, to the arms of our Country and endeavor to wipe off the stain on our military character, occasioned by the recent disasters since the declartion of war.

You having command of this department, and whenever your judgement, may conclude that the safety and defence of the lower Mississippi does not require the aid of my detachment; at your signifying to me this fact, I will at your request and advice, withdraw my detachment and move to any point where Government may want active service performed.

I am happy here, but should be more so, if I could render Government any service for the beef which is eaten by my detachment.

I have the honor to be Very respectfully yr. Obt Servt.

Andrew Jackson

LC, DLC; Copy, DNA-RG 107. Published in Bassett, 1:289–90.
1. See above, Wilkinson to AJ, March 1.
2. The quartermaster's department was established on March 28, 1812 (2 *U.S. Statutes at Large* 696–99).
3. See above, Wilkinson to AJ, March 1.

To William Berkeley Lewis

Headquarters Camp Jackson
March 13th 1813

Dear Sir

By last mail I had the pleasure of receiving your two several letters of the 2nd. of March[1]—yours of the 22nd. which you name to me forwarded to Neworleans, I shall receive tomorrow,[2] as I have directed all my letters to be forwarded to me that has been sent on to that place, and which when recd. shall be carefully attended to as requested by you—

When I write Colo. Anderson I shall with pleasure name to him the Justice you have done him in your letter to me of the 2nd of this month— I have here barely to remark, that I was sorry to see made use of in your publication any remarks as it respected the supplies of provision at clarksville[3]—There are no men I have a greater Esteem for than those concerned in the contract at Nashville and I am free to confess, that I believe Mr Woods, confidently expected the supply wanted, and for which the differrent captains had due bills for at Clarksville, but the fact is that there was not half the quantity of flower engaged & that three miles distance from clarksville and the Pork not half packed or salted when we arived and not salt to secure it—by which means, we were detained a whole day and two nights and a great part of the provissions spoiled for the want of salt & being put up into whiskey barrels—and it is a fact that in several barrels were found seven hogs heads I mean sculls—this is in open violation of the laws on this head—on the subject of [Aizea] Hays I never recollect of hearing that he had joined the 2d. regiment, untill I was at Clarksville, Colo. Benton there I believed named some that he had intruded himself into Capt Gibbs company, and that as soon as he come up he would have him put out—this is all I knew or heard of Hays untill I saw your publication—he never was discharged by my order nor had he joined with my knowledge or consent, and when Colo Benton named the thing to me at Clarksville I did heartily disapprobate the act of Hays being permitted to be with the Volunteers— [4]

I have now to draw your attention to another subject—If Governor Blount is with you by applying to him for a sight of the correspondance between me and the assistant D Q. master of this Department you will find that my situation as it reguards supplies from this department is not the most pleasant—The fact is the sick must be taken care of—the sick of the Cavalry on their march, was obliged to be left on the road, they were to be supplied and to procure this Colo John Coffee was obliged to become bound to the individuals at whose houses they were left that there bills on him for the expense of the sick should be paid—The quarter master says this expence appertains to your department—and to meet this expence Colo. Coffee this day has drew two Bills on you one for one hundred dollars in favour of James Lauderdale, the other for two hundred dollars in favour of James Gallaspie[5]—These two bills it is supposed will bring the sick up, they are on their way and the Gentlemen in whose favour the Bills are drawn has advanced the cash—and you must honor and pay them—if theer should be any thing left over paying the expence of the sick it shall be faithfully accounted for if not anough to fully meet the expence you shall be duly notified—To be without funds medicine and a number sick is an unpleasant situation—we are here without any orders or advices, from any quarter, fed some times on the poorest beef on earth—and without an[y] necessity for us being here—But no discontent [pre]vails—perfect harmony—and I will stay here untill the goverment orders me to march to some point without murmur or complaint, if we were on the north west we could be of some service, here none—and we would with cheerfulness march tomorrow to Canady if goverment ordered us—The mode of supplying the army must be altered, or it never can act with expedition or effect—it will be always badly supplied and with bad provisions—When I receive yrs of the 22nd. I shall write you, I am busily engaged preparing my troops for the field—who progress in discipline faster than any troops I ever saw—¿has the fixed amunition ever reached Nashville? or where is it, ¿what shall my Detachment do for munitions of war and supplies of medicine—I am buying medicine here at my own risque—my men shall not die, If my credit or purse can prevent it—I am truly astonished that the governor has not wrote me—I have not recd a single line from, The Secratary of war, or member of Congress, and here I am with 2000 of the finest Troops in the world inactive and eating the Publick beef—without service when men are so much wanted to the north west—Our goverment must act with more energy activity, and system—or they are lost, and the Liberties of our country gone—disgrace will bring on general disgust—the expence will create a national debt and heavy taxes—and the inquiry will be made how all this expence and no service done—I can answer for one; I am sent where there is no enemy—nothing to do, and where there never existed in fact sufficient ground of alarm to have authorised us being sent here—but the voice of my [country] I have and will obay. It is my duty to oba[y, the] duty of the President to order—we have [had ?] funerals since we disembarked—

Give my Compliments to all friends [and] believe me to be sincerely your friend—

Andrew Jackso[n]

Photostat, Stanley F. Horn.
1. Only one of the letters of March 2 has been found.
2. Not found. According to his letter of [March 15], below, Jackson "put it to the flames."
3. In his letter to the public, February 18 (published in *Nashville Whig*, February 24), Lewis stated that since the contracts had been made before his appointment as assistant deputy quartermaster general, the failure of the Clarksville contractors should not be imputed to him.
4. According to Lewis, Hays had been arrested and dismissed from service by Benton and Anderson without a court martial for stealing a "game fowl" from Anderson. On May 4, following their return from Natchez, Jackson and Benton prepared an affidavit on the dismissal of the "noted gambler" Hays, which was published in the *Democratic Clarion*, May 25.
5. Lauderdale (d. 1814), a resident of Sumner County, and Gillespie (d. 1814), from Franklin County, both served in Coffee's brigade.

To John Armstrong

(Copy)   Camp of Volunteers near
                                          Washington, M.T. March 15, 1813
Sir,

By this days mail I recd. yr. letter bearing date of the 5th. Jany. war department 1813[1]—This was previous to yr. being in office at the head of that department which induces me to believe, that their must be a mistake in the date, otherwise it must be an unofficial act, as the official acct. of yr. taking possession of that office appears to be of date the 3rd. Feby. 1813.[2] Allways obedient to the orders of my superiors and the will of the government when made known through a proper organ, I shall in persuance of the above advice, immediately deliver over to the Q. Master of this department all public property in my hands that can be spared from the convenience and health of my troops on their return to Nashville—it being the place where they were rendexvouzed by the orders of the president of the United States, and to which place I shall march them, so soon as the necessary supplies can be had for that purpose.

If it is intended by yr. letter or order which runs thus "The causes for embodying and marching the corps under yr. command to New Orleans having ceased to exist, you'll on receipt of this letter consider it dismissed from public service and have delivered over to Majr. Genl. Wilkinson all articles of public property that have been put into its possession["]—If it was intended by this order that we should be dismissed eight hundred miles from home, deprived of arms, tents and supplies for the sick—of our arms and supplies for the well, it appears that these brave men, who certainly deserve better fate and return from their government was intended by this order to be sacrificed—Those that could escape from the insalubrious climate, are to be deprived of the necessary support and meet death by famine The remaining few to be deprived of their arms pass through the savage land, where our women children and defenceless citizens are daily murdered—Yet thro. that barbarous clime, must our band of citizen soldiers wander and fall a sacrafice to the Tomhawk and scalping knife of the wilderness our sick left naked in the open field and remain without supplies without nourishment or an earthly comfort— Was this the language of the act calling on the citizens to rally round the Government of their choice, which brought this band of heroes the best citizens and wealth of our country into the field, and whose attention to order discipline and harmony forbade ample services to their country— who tendered their services to march and support the Eagles of their country to the hights of Abraham on the North, or to the burning and unwholesome climate of the South—These men had no constitutional bounderies but that of their insulted Government, its rights privileges and its laws—Yet this order is given by a friend of the war measures, an old revolutionary officer—who knows the privations of a soldier who exercised his talents (not at a very prudent moment) in their behalf at the close of the last war This same hand! Yes, the same hand writes an order to consign to distruction a well organised detachment of near two thousand men, well disciplined for the time (I say none better) fit for the service, willing to march any where and that too Eight hundred miles from home—I annimated those brave men to take the field—I thank my God they are entittled to their Arms to defend them from the Indians scalping knife and believing as I do that it is such patriots as I have the honor to

command that our country and its liberties are to be saved and defended—
that a well organized militia is the bulwark of our Nation—I have no
hesitation in giving the lie to the modern doctrine that it is inefficient to
defend the liberties of our country, and that standing armies are necessary—in time of peace—I mean to commence my march to Nashville in a
few days at which place I expect the troops to be paid and the necessary
supplies furnished by the agents of Government while payment is making, after which I will dismiss them to their homes and their families—[3]

Andrew Jackson

LS copy and LC, DLC. Published in Bassett, 1:291–92.
1. Jackson was referring to Armstrong's order above of February 6, inadvertently dated
January 5 in the copies he first received.
2. Armstrong, appointed secretary of war on January 13, officially entered upon the duties of the office on February 5 instead of February 3.
3. According to Thomas Hart Benton, Jackson summoned him to his headquarters in
March 1813 to read the above letter. Benton recalled that he suggested softening the tone
but Jackson refused (*Addresses on the Presentation of the Sword of Gen. Andrew Jackson
to the Congress of the United States* [Washington, 1855], pp. 35–36).

To [Felix Grundy]

Camp Jackson Head quarters March 15th 1813

Sir.

By the new orleans mail of yesterday I recd the extraordinary order, of
the extraordinary date, of which the enclosed is a copy[1]—It speaks for it
self, & rests with the representatives of the state, to account to this detachment, how it has happened, that we were thus neglected & left to be
sacrificed, by the incumbent in the war department, if it had been in his
power. is this the way, the best patriots of the Land is to be treated—
Solicited, intreated, & urged by your eloquence, calculated to rouse every
patriotic feeling to rally around the standards of their country—marched
to an inhospitable clime supposed to be eight hundred miles from home—
dismissed—The sick stripped of every comfort or covering & the means
of getting back to their country and their friends—without money and
wi[t]hout means. the [w]hole detachment given [u]p as a prey to pestilence and famine and if they shoud escape that, to make destruction sure
they are ordered to surrender their arms, that they may fall an easy prey
to the scalping knife of the ruthless savage on their return—These questions will be asked of you as their representitive; of the President, and
this new incumbent who must have been drunk when he wrote it or so
proud of his appointment as to have lost all feelings of humanity & duty,
that he commenced by anticipation on the duties of his office a month
before he was really in office, such treatment as this [is] well calculated, to
bring about disgu[st,] which will never gain the object in view. It is time
for the people to recollect, that Sempronius in the Roman Senate cried

out that he was for war, when he was in the act of betraying his country. I fear it is the case now that many cry out "I am a republican," when they are endeavouring to disgust the citizens—trying to disgrace the constitutional *bulwark* of the nation. *The Militia*—This done the path is plain. The Militia not being competant to defend the country on a sudden war it is necessary that a [st]anding army in time of peace shoud be kept up to meet the sudden emergencies of war. this once done (and I have very little doubt of the intentions of some) the liberties of the country are gone forever. The late incumbent at the close of the revolutionary war has given a good specimen of what he woud do with a soldiary (I mean a mercenary soldiary) under his controll, but it is time for the people to awake from their slumber & false delusions. The gause covering is too thin to hide such flagrant acts. Hull surrenders an army & a whole Territory—a court martial calld his trial postpon'd to the end of the war and why and for what reason—Genl. [Alexander] Smith makes an attempt on Canady—fails:[2] all the blame is laid on the militia—a call is made on our state, t[he] Volunteers the best materials on earth march, against whom? there coud be nothing alleged, & who was certain to support their own reputation & that of their country & Return with credit—but this must not be permitted. they destroy all our plans. they woud reinstate the lost reputation of the militia. it is necessary that they be destroy'd & they are attempted to be dismissed 800 miles from home, without money, stripped by the order of this new incumbent of every necessary furnished by gov-[ern]ment & left to perish with hunger and disea[s]e—but I thank my God the law under which they were raised give them their arms until they choose to resign them—And as long as I have friends or credit, I will stick by them. I shall march them to Nashville or bury them with the honors of war. shoud I die I know they will bury me. And as soon as I arrive—the necessary enquiries of the intended sacrifice of the whole of this detachment will be made & the publick will be able to judge how far certain representatives & men in office are the friends or traitors to their country[3]—The history of all *Barbarous Europe* cannot furnish a parrallel. The bloody buoy does not contain a mo[re] damning transaction than the intention of this order[4] As I expect the representatives in Congress have secured directions from the proper department for the payment of this detachment and a fulfilment of the engagements with them under the law of Feby 6th & July 6th 1812, I shall say nothing on the subject expecting that the paymaster will be prepared to pay us off. This must be done before I discharge the Troops—and they have a right to expect you [to attend] to this business before you left Congress.

I am Sir in haste Your Obt. H. St.

Andrew Jackson

Copy with revisions in AJ's hand, MoSHi; Typescript, T. Published in *AHM*, 5(April 1900):134–36.
    1. For the orders of the secretary of war, see above, Armstrong to AJ, February 6.

2. Jackson was referring to Smyth's aborted efforts to invade Canada from upstate New York in November and December 1812.

3. Grundy was at this time a candidate for reelection to Congress. In response to the dismissal of the Tennessee Volunteers, he wrote on February 15 that "I cannot account for this proceeding. I know of no cause, which can justify the ordering them out, & withdrawing them so suddenly, I hope, the government has sufficient reasons for its conduct" (*Democratic Clarion*, March 2). Jackson apparently had not yet seen Grundy's public letter.

4. Jackson was referring to William Cobbett's 1796 tract, condemning the excesses of the French Revolution, *The Bloody Buoy, Thrown out as a Warning to the Political Pilots of America.*

To Rachel Jackson

Camp Jackson March 15th. 1813

My love

On last night by mail from Neworleans I recd advices from the war department that our services was not longer wanted, and I shall march with my detachment so soon as convayence for my sick can be had, and portage for my provisions—I hope to order the line of march in a few days, my duty my feelings, and Justice to those brave fellows who followed me at the call of their country, deserve more from their Goverment, than what they have recd They at least deserved, by the orders of their goverment, to have recd. every necessary comfort for the sick, convayences that would insure them a safe return to their family their country and their homes—This has not been the case, it is only by and through me, that these things can be [done] the sick shall be taken back as far as lif[e] lasts, and supplies shall be had—altho their Patriotism has been but illy rewarded by an ungratefull officer, (not Country) it is therefore my duty to act as a father to the sick and to the well and stay with them untill I march them into Nashville—I shall use industry, but that must be with caution not to founder my troops when they first set out—I recd yours by Stockley Hays last night, and one from my sweet andrew,[1] I am happy if life lasts that I shall shortly see you—I am sorry my overseer does not act with industry you may say to him I will soon be at home, and expect my farm and stock in good order—I have but little leisure—nor will I, untill I am ready to march, kiss my little andrew for me tell him his papa is coming home—give my compliments to all friends, and receve from me the tenderest Esteem of an affectionate Husband

Andrew Jackson

ALS, DLC. Published in Bassett, 1:296.
1. Probably Rachel Jackson to AJ, February 28; letter from Andrew Jackson, Jr., not found.

To William Berkeley Lewis

[March 15, 1813]

Dear Sir

On last evening I recd. advices from John armstrong *now* Secratary of war, stating that the causes that give rise to the organization of the corps under my command having ceased to exist[1]—our services is no longer required—so soon as I can get the proper transport for my sick, I shall take up the line of march for Nashville—I have to request that you will have a supply of provissions and forrage at Colberts ferry, against we arive—I have drew on the Contractor and quarter master for supplies to this Point and expect you to furnish supplies down Elk and the Tennessee sufficient for this detachment—to last to the line

I have recd. last night your letter of the 22[2] and after perusal, ha[ving] so many on hand put it to the flames [I d]o not think it necessary to write to Colo A[n]derson—when I see him I can assure him of the substance of your letter, and that you have done him every Justice[3]—I have enclosed to Governor Blount a certified coopy of armstrongs letter it bears date 5th. of January 1813, one month before he came into office, by applying to Governor Blount you will see A coopy,[4] and you can *Judge whether in all civilized urope, or the barberous climes* of *africa it has its fellow*—the supposition when the order was written that we were 800 miles from home—and our whole detachment sick and well deprived of every supply furnished by goverment even the Pack horses that might have removed the sick home &c &c, But I have not thought proper to yield all. I bring home my sick or perish in the at[tempt]—an enquiry will be made how this [busine]ss has been transacted when time will permit and how far our representative after his pompous call on the Patriotism of his constituents under the act of February & July 6th can Justify this neglect towards those brave fellows who has turned out to defend their country[5]—I feel too much I must change the subject—Supplies I am intitled to, and I will have, I have credit, no money but when all resources fails I have horses adieu my friend—

Andrew Jackson

ALS, TxGR.

1. See above, John Armstrong to AJ, February 6.
2. Not found.
3. In his rejoinder to Benton's journal in the *Nashville Whig* (February 24) and *Democratic Clarion* (February 23) Lewis questioned Benton's and William P. Anderson's conduct and methods of military discipline. On February 28, Anderson wrote Lewis asking if he intended in that publication "to detract from my character as an officer or gentleman." Lewis responded that he did not, that the publication "was intended to apply to Col. Benton *alone*" (see *Democratic Clarion*, March 2).
4. See AJ to Willie Blount, March 15.

5. Jackson apparently was under the impression that Felix Grundy had done nothing to dissuade the administration from dismissing the Tennessee Volunteers. In April, however, he learned that Grundy had interceded on behalf of the Tennessee troops (see below, Andrew Hynes to AJ, April 15).

From James Wilkinson

New-Orleans, March 16, 1813.

Sir;

I was yesterday honored by your letter of the 8th. inst.[1] and regret that the policy of Government should not permit the maturation of our association in arms; because I believe much public good would have grown out of it.

I am sorry any misunderstanding should have taken place with the Dep. Qr. master General; because he is a well intentioned and correct officer. His difficulty arose from the tenor of his instructions, and the obligations by which he is bound, to obey the commanding officer of the Department alone; who being placed in trust for the whole, is responsible for the whole, and must necessarily controul the whole. This is the broad rule of service, and it must govern, so long as power & responsbility are inseparable. I hope, however, no inconvenience has arisen from a diversity of opinion.

In consequence of the receipt, by yesterday's mail, of the enclosed copies of the Secretary of war's letters to you of the 6 & 16th. ultimo,[2] which I take the liberty to transmit you, I have considered it my duty to issue the Genl. Order which you will find under cover,[3] to prevent any difficulties or unnecessary delays with the paymaster or contractor, being convinced the Executive will justify every usual measure, which may be adopted for the accommodation & comfort of the patriotic citizens of Tennessee, on their return home. I beg leave to offer you and them, Sir, my best wishes for health, pleasant weather, an agreeable march, and a happy meeting with your friends & families.

I have the honor to be, with much consideration and respect, Sir, Yr. Obt. Servant,

Ja. Wilkinson.

LC, DLC; Copies, DNA-RG 107 and PHi. Published in Bassett, 1:296–97.
1. See above.
2. See above, John Armstrong to AJ, February 6 and 16.
3. See below.

ENCLOSURE: ORDER TO ROBERT ANDREWS

New Orleans, March 15, 1813.

G[eneral] O[rder]
P[arole] Jackson
C[ountersign] Tennessee

(Enclosed under cover, directed to Majr. Genl Jackson, near Washington, M.T.)

The President having been pleased to discharge from further service, the Patriotic intrepid Volunteers of Tennessee, encamped near Natchez, under the orders of Major Genl. Jackson; they are to be mustered up to the day of their discharge; and in addition to the pay due them, are to receive from the District paymaster the usual allowance for mileage in returning home, and the Contractor will furnish provisions for the same period.

The Asst Dep. Qr. Master Genl. is to receive and receipt for whatever public property, Genl. Jackson may order to be delivered to him, and will have the same put in order & well secured.

(Signed)   Ja. Wilkinson,
Majr Genl.

LC and AL fragment, DLC; Copies, DNA-RG 107 and PHi. Published in Bassett, 1:297.

To the Tennessee Volunteers

[March 16, 1813]

Fellow Soldiers

Long since the clouds of war hovered around your beloved country, its constituted authorities announced it in danger, and invited you to rally round the goverment of your choice for its support and defence—It was anough for such patriots as you, descended from the heroes of the revolution to know that the patrimony procured by the best blood of your fathers were endangered you rushed to the support of your country and volluntary enlisted yourselfs for its defence—and tendered your services to the President which was with expressions of gratitude which carried balm to each patriot boosom accepted off—your tender was on the broad basis of your countries will not confined within any constitutional limits, but the orders of your goverment war was declared, you stood panting for the call of your goverment, with eyes turned to the north the seat of war, ready to mingle your strenth with that of your distressed brethren in arms, to defend them from the ferocious Indian scalping knife and British Bayonets, your representative in congress with all his eloquence made known your patriotism to the goverment adressed you as part of his constituents, with the eloquence of a cicero (this your patriotism did not require) urged you enmass to enroll yourselves under the acts of congress in the support of a Just proper & necessary war and pledged himself for your patriotism—enrolled you had been and only awaited the call of your goverment—an army was basely surrendered, a Territory lost—Men were wanted—Still you were not called to the field—at length it was said that the inhospitable clime of the lower Mississippi was endangered by threatened invassion—The goverment called—There was no climes that could damp your ardor—The 10th. of Decem will be with pleasure recollected by every patriot boosom—you with the spirit of freemen whose rights were invaded bore without murmur the snowy blasts—you entered the camp with the ardor of good citizens you bore its privations like soldiers—The alacrity with which you entered on the duty of soldiers, foretold to your general, that you would soon be disciplined—his highest wishes were realized—with the attention, industry, and knowledge of tactics of Capt Carrol Brigade inspector added to your attention to duty, I knew in a short time you would fit to meet an enemy in the open plain and contend for the victory at the point of the Bayonet—in this your Genl. was not disappointed—your orders were given to descend the river Mississippi, you obayed it with alacrity and in every act has reallised the fondest wishes of your general and your Country—

your uniform good conduct, you attention to the rights of the citizens through which you have passed has secured to you the plaudits of the citizens of this country[1] and entitle you to the esteem and thanks of your general—he knows if you had met an enemy, from your pride your patriotism and attention to discipline you would have gained laurels for yourself, and honor for the country from which you come you are about to return to your country, and it remains for time to unfold whether you have been truly the agents of goverment, with that attention your patriotism entitled you to expect—and whether you have not been shamefully forgotten by your representative in congress—[2]

It becomes the duty of the Major Genl to make known to the detachment under his command that he has received advices, that "the causes for embodying and marching to this lower country the corps under his command has ceased to exist" and we are now to turn our faces to the north—and I must repeat again and again and never shall forget it that you have done much and met privations, with the firmness of soldiers—you have behaved with that order and propriety that becomes citizens soldiers to step forward in defence and vindication of their countries rights—having thus merrittedly established a reputation and obtained the praises of the good citizens with whom we have mingled and in whose neighbourhood we have encamped—it is necessary to support this reputation on our returning—and the general has full confidence, that in no instance will one of his officers or soldiers, infringe the right of the citizen or depart from his usual sobriety, should he be disappointed in this immediate punishment awaits the offender—when we turn our eyes to the west and behold our profused bleeding brethren that are wounded and then surrender to savage cruelty I well know your boosoms pants for retaliation and vengeance, Should our destination be to that point I have confidence you will do your duty—but to be prepared for action, we must not relax in our discipline—fellow citizens in arms—we have to pass a savage country—their rights must be respected and notwithstanding your humanity is shocked at the late unheard of brutality and murders of our brethern, still it becomes us untill we are ordered by goverment to withhold our hands from vengeance least we might strike the innocent and bring disgrace and guilt upon our heads—It is therefore ordered and commanded that neither the persons nor property of the indians be disturbed by any officer or soldier under my command whilst returning through their country—It is necessary for the safety of the detachment, that we march in good order, and that the whole detachment continue together untill we arive at Nashville—The order of march will be duly communicated through the Brigade inspector and all officers are forbidden to give any furloughs or permit any of the soldiary to leave the encampment for a longer time than four hours and then must be accompanied by a commissioned or non commissioned officer, as soon as the necessary supplies are recd from the contractors and quarter master of this department—the line of march will be taken up—The Major Genl, Having pledged himself that he never would abandon one of his men, and that he would act the part of a father to them—has to repeat that he will not leave one of the sick nor one of the detachment behind, that he has lead you here he will lead you back again to your country and your friends—The sick as far as he has the power and the means shall be made comfortable—they shall all be taken along not one shall be left unless those that die and in that event we will pay to him the last tribute of respect, they shall be buried with all the honors of war—should your general die he knows it is a respect you would pay to him; it is a debt due to the honest and brave soldier, it is due to every member of the detachment—it is a respect that shall be paid to each—The guards at their fires are permitted to sleep keeping one up at the fires untill otherwise ordered—

AD draft and LC, DLC; LC, AHAB.
1. See, for example, David Holmes to AJ, March 16.
2. For Jackson's comments to Felix Grundy on the dismissal of his troops, see above, March 15.

From James Wilkinson

New Orleans March 20th. 1813

Sir,

I had the honor a few minutes since to receive your letter of the 15th. Inst.[1] & hasten to answer it.

It is with unfeigned concern, I perceive the embarrassments under which you labour, because it is not in my power to alleviate them.

From the Tenor of the orders of the Secretary of war to you, under date of the 6th. & 16th. ultimo copies of which, I had the honor to transmit you on the 16th. Inst.,[2] you will perceive that no provision has been made, for marching back your corps to Tenessee, in array of arms, from the position where those orders might reach you, and under such circumstances, I could safely appeal to your candour for the admission, that were you even under my orders, I should not be warranted in proceeding further than I have done in my order of the 16th. Inst.[3] which I forwarded you in my last; indeed I have in that order exceeded the strict limits of my authority, but I am persuaded the occasion will justify me. I beg you to be assured of my disposition, to render you & the Gentlemen of your command, every facility & accommodation in my power; but I dare not incur the responsibility of the expense which must attend the march of the corps of your command back to Tenessee.

I have &c—

Sigd   Ja: Wilkinson.

Copy, PHi.
1. See AJ to Wilkinson, March 15.
2. See above.
3. See above.

To Rachel Jackson

Head quarters Camp Jackson March 21st. 1813

My Love

This will be handed you by my friend and aid de camp Major A. Haynes—to whom I refer you for news—I send him on to make arangement for the supply of my brave companions in arms, who have been lead on from love of country into the tented fields and by the agent of goverment attempted to be sacraficed, by being dismissed from service 800 miles from home, deprived of every particle of publick property, without pay or any means of transporting the sick—or supplies for the well, and this too as I believe with the base design to compel them from want to enlist into the regular Service of the united States. The law I think has better provided and these brave men deserve a better return—I led them into the field I will at all hazard and risque lead them out, I [will] bring on the sick, or be with them—it never shall be said if they have been abandoned by the agents of the goverment they have been abandoned by their general—I have made the necessary requisitions on the contractors and quartermaster, the dismissal (unoficial) by the Secratary of war notwithstanding in past they have been furnished, and I hope the will be fully, and I hope in a day or two to be able to take up the line of march—I shall remain with the troops untill I see them safe in their own country—paid, and discharged—I shall write you occasionally by the post as it passes me—and shall expect you with my little son to meet me in Nashville— tell him I will make a general of him—that he shall have a soldiers coat, and sword—you can say to the overseer I am returning and shall expect my farm in good order—give my love to Miss Kitty and all my friends, may god bless you adieu

Andrew Jackson

ALS, MH-H.

To John Armstrong

Headquarters near Washington
Mississippi Territory March 22. 1813

Sir,

my letter of the 15th. Inst.[1] informed you, that I had recd. yrs of the 5th. of Jany. 1813[2]—I have now the honor to inform you that I recd. under cover from Major Genl. Wilkinson of date March 8th.[3] your notification to him, without date, but post marked Feby. 8th 1813, which was as follows

> "Sir
> The militia force organized by Governor Blount under command of Genl. Jackson expedited to New orleans early in the last month is discharged from further service. The Genl. is required to have delivered over to yr. directions, such articles of public property as have been commited to them—

your notification to me received as above, and having no "Militia force organized" under my command places me in a delicate situation. I have the honor to command only an organized volunteer corps enrolled and tendered to the President of the United States under the act of Feby. 6th 1812 and whose services with my own were accepted and made known to me through Governor Blount, by the President under date war department July 11th. 1812[4]—and all the officers under my command down to a Capt have been commissioned by the President of the United States on the 21st. of Novr. 1812 in pursuance of his authority under the act of congress of July 6th. 1812—hence the words, in your notification to Genl. Wilkinson "*organized militia*" cannot be applied to the detachment under my command. But from your communications to Governor Blount, Majr. Genl. Wilkinson and your unofficial note to me of Jany. 5th. 1813—I infer, that the wishes of the government are, that the detachment under my command is to be discharged. I have therefore ordered their return to Nashville Tennessee. Their being no direction for the payment of the troops, or their supplies on their return home, by you directed, from a perusal of the law on the subject, I find I have been correct and anticipated the intention of the Government, in ordering supplies of provisions—and conveyence for the sick and their necessary baggage to Nashville, where they will be discharged. The law runs thus— "that whenever any officer or soldier shall be discharged from the service, he shall be allowed his pay and rations or an equivelent in mony for such term of time as shall be sufficient for him to travel from the place of his discharge to the place of his residence, computing at the rate of twenty miles to a day"[5]—There being no direction to pay the troops here; no compensation directed to be given to them in lieu of rations—I have ordered the contractor and quarter master, as you have been advised in mine of date, the 15th Inst. to furnish the necessary supplies for my detachment on their return to Nashville. I have been detained here since the 18th. Inst. by the agents of government, but in Justice to Mr [John] Brandt[6] I would observe, that every exertion has been used on his part to expedite our departure—I have however been notified that the necessary supplies will be ready against the 25th. Inst.—when I shall take up the line of March for Nashville, at which point or some other within the State of Tennessee, I hope they will be directed to be paid off, and the paymaster be furnished with funds for this purpose I have, a hope, (altho not ordered to a theatre of war) that my detachment merit as much from our Government, as the detached Militia from this Territory who are ordered to be paid, and discharged at Baton Rouge[7]—Your note of the 5th. of Jany. 1813 directs that two thousand well organized volunteers under the acts of congress of Feby the 6th. and July 6th. 1812 are to be dismissed at New Orleans without pay or a compensation for rations. Is this yr. impartial rule. and this reward to whom? men of the first character patriotism and wealth of the Union; who left their comfortable homes and families for the tented fields, to support the Eagles of their country at any point ordered by the constituted authority—

Andrew Jackson

LS, DNA-RG 107; ALS draft, LC, and Copy, DLC. Published in *National Intelligencer*, June 13, 1828; Bassett, 1: 297–98.
1. See above.
2. See above, Armstrong to AJ, February 6.
3. See Wilkinson to AJ, March 8.
4. See above, William Eustis to Willie Blount, July 11, 1812, enclosed in Blount to AJ, July 21, 1812.
5. Jackson was quoting from Section 22 of the act to raise an additional military force, signed into law on January 11, 1812 (2 *U.S. Statutes at Large* 671–74).
6. Brandt was an agent for the army contractors in Natchez.
7. A force of Mississippi Territory militia commanded by Ferdinand Leigh Claiborne.

To James Wilkinson

Camp Jackson, March 22, 1813.

Sir,

About two O'clock, P.M. this day, I received yr. letter of the 16th inst. with its enclosures;[1] and am truly sorry that the originals have not reached me. I still more regret to see so many blunders creep into the Secretary's communications. The paper stated by him to be a duplicate, altho' substantially the same, is not a copy; and further, the date of the original, of which he says he sends a duplicate, bears date "War Department, Jany. 5, 1813." The enclosed bears date "War Department, Feby 6, 1813."[2] The original is in his own hand writing; or every letter, word and figure a forgery. I cannot help smiling when I read the Secretary's note, a copy of which you send me, bearing date "War Department, Feby. 16, 1813," expressed as if wrote at a date to overtake me at Massac; when on the evening before its date, I had reached the vicinity of Natchez; and on the 4th of Jany. I had wrote him from Nashville,[3] advising him that in a few days I should march; and he was advised by the Governor, as he writes me,[4] that on the 7th. of January my troops did march. This gauze is too thin, too flimsy to hide the baseness of the act, even from my dull apprehension. But as I have not received from the Secretary the originals, of which your enclosures are copies, and he not having notified me, that we were to be paid off any where, the law allowing me so many days to return; and as I have sent on my Aid-de-Camp this morning, before the receipt of yours, to Nashville, to procure supplies to meet me at Tennessee, I shall commence the line of march on Thursday the 25th. inst. Should the contractor not feel himself justified in sending on provisions for my Infantry, or the qr. master, waggons for the transportation of my sick, I shall dismount the Cavalry; carry them on, and provide the means for their support out of my private funds. If that should fail, I thank my God, we have plenty of horses to feed my troops to the Tennessee, where I know my country will meet me with ample supplies.

These brave men, at the call of their country, voluntarily rallied 'round its insulted standard. They followed me into the field—I shall carefully march them back to their homes. It is for the agent of Government to account to the state of Tennessee, & the whole world, for their singular and unusual treatment to this detachment. The feelings of the whole state is alive and awakened. The administration must render a justifiable reason, why they have singled out this detachment, whose tendered service they so flatteringly accepted, as victims of their destruction; and why they have not been discharged in the usual way.

I tender you my thanks for the Genl. Order issued, a copy of which is enclosed,[5] for directing that to be done, which the law secures to be done some where. But as the secretary at war has given no directions to me on this head, I cannot now detain my march. I have notified the President, of date the 15th. instant, and forwarded it by last mail, enclosing him a copy of the singular order I had received.[6] (I am persuaded he never sanctioned it.) and stating to him that I would march my men to Nashville, and there await his orders for the discharge of my detachment. I know from advices received, our services will be wanted in the North West; and no act of the agents of Government, can withdraw our attachment from our Government, however we may be induced to despise the baseness of its agents.

These reasons will govern me in taking up the line of march on the 25th inst. supplies or not.

Accept a tender of thanks for your offered friendship to the Detachment I have the honor to command. I am with the highest consideration of respect, Yr Mo ob Sert.

Andrew Jackson

LC, DLC. Published in Bassett, 1:298–99.
1. See above.
2. For the two letters, see above, Armstrong to AJ, February 6 and 16.
3. See above, AJ to James Monroe, January 4.
4. Blount's letter not found.
5. See above, Order to Robert Andrews, March 15, enclosed in Wilkinson to AJ, March 16.
6. See AJ to James Madison, March 15.

To Ferdinand Leigh Claiborne

Camp Jackson March 25th. 1813

Dear Genl.

This will be handed you by my Nephew Thomas Hutchings,[1] who you and Colo [William C.] Mead had the goodness to furlough to see me, and for the friendly act, please to accept a tender of my thanks—I have detained him untill this morning awaiting your letter permitting me to have the power of liberating him—from not receiving any, I infer you have not been able to obtain the boon and this morning I send him back with his furlough enclosed—should he not reach you within the time specified in his furlough, please to forgive him, the fault was in me—

I march today, without supplies from the quartermaster they have been refused, he says by orders[2]—Strange to tell that this detachment has been ordered to be discharged, and no provisions made for the sick or supplies for the cavalry on their return, no directions by the Secratary of war for their payment &c &c &c. This will be long recollected by Tennessee and her sons—who at the call of the President voluntarily tendered their service, which was accepted by him ordered to a distant clime ordered to be *dismissed* the service in a way that would disgrace the barbarous climes

From the polite attention recd. from your lady[3] & yourself, a lasting gratitude is left on my mind and it will afford me great pleasure to have it in my power to return the kindness—present me to Colo Mead and his family and accept for yourself a tender of my high esteem and respect

Andrew Jackson

ALS, DLC. Claiborne (c1772–1815), brother of William C.C., had earlier served in the U.S. Army. At this time, he was brigadier general of the Mississippi volunteers.
1. Hutchings was the son of Thomas and Catherine Donelson Hutchings.
2. See Robert Andrews to AJ, March 23.
3. Magdalene Hutchens Claiborne, whom Claiborne married in 1802.

To the Adams County Superior Court from John Coffee and AJ

Camp Jackson, Mississippi Territory,
25th March, 1813.

Being informed by *General Jackson* that he was summoned as garnishee, to say what money or effects he had in his possession that properly belonged to *Aaron Burr*,[1] and at the same time being requested by the General, to make a statement of facts that had come to my knowledge respecting money matters between himself and Aaron Burr.

In compliance with which I do say, that some time in the year 1806 (to the best of my recollection) Aaron Burr was engaged in an expedition or enterprise down the Mississippi, and which he said he was authorised to do by government; and for the purpose of procuring provisions and boats for his contemplated plans, he the said Burr, did forward a sum of between three and four thousand dollars in Kentucky bank notes, to Gen. Jackson, with a request that he would procure for him, by purchase, the amount in boats and provisions. At the time Gen. Jackson received the sum alluded to, I was connected with him in mercantile business, at the Clover Bottom, Tennessee, and on the receipt thereof, the General shew me his instructions, and handed the money or notes over to me, with a request that I would transact the business, for Mr. Burr, and in behalf of the mercantile firm above alluded to, I did so; and made contracts for several boats for Mr. Burr; when report reached Tennessee, that his projects or plans, was not, nor would not, be countenanced by government. On hearing this rumour, by and with the advice of Gen. Jackson, I declined making contracts for Mr. Burr any further than had been done before that time; and still held in my possession a considerable part of the sum first remitted by Mr. Burr, to Gen. Jackson: Some time after that, when Mr. Burr came on to Tennessee, on his way down the river, he *stopped* at the Clover Bottom, near which place lay some of the boats that I had contracted for his use, and where he fitted himself out for his voyage down the river. The report of his acting in opposition to the wishes of government, prevented his procuring supplies of provision; and as such, he had not use for all the boats, that had been made for him—two I believe was the number he made use of for himself and those with him. The balance of the boats, the number I do not recollect, was left by Mr. Burr; and afterwards by virtue of his order in favour of Pattan Anderson, the boats or the proceeds thereof was handed or paid over to him, Mr. Anderson. When Mr. Burr was at the Clover Bottom, Gen. Jackson and myself made a settlement with him the said Burr, and after charging him with the boats and other articles furnished him for his voyage down the river, I returned him all the balance of his money, in the very same notes first sent on by him, and the accounts was then completely closed and paid on both sides as I understood it after closing the accounts, there were some few articles with which the firm of Jackson & Hutchings (and which I before said I was concerned in) furnished Mr. Burr that he left unpaid when he left the State, and which is yet unpaid, so far as ever come to my knowledge.[2] I recollect after Mr. Burr left the state, that Gen. Jackson as *endorser* for *him* had to pay five hundred dollars or thereabouts, for him the said Burr on some transaction that the General perhaps had before thought was *settled*, and for which I never knew of the General receiving *renumeration*[3]—Nor do I believe he has received payment therefor—I never knew of General Jackson having any other monied transactions with Mr. Burr, but those above stated, and on which I verily believe that Burr, is in his debt, at this time—the lapse of time have been very considerable, and the notice for this statement very short, and which is made without reference to any memorandums or dates, and as to the time I am not positive I am correct, but otherwise this statement is substantially correct, and fairly stated to the best of my knowledge and belief.[4]

JOHN COFFEE.

Personally appeared General Andrew Jackson who having been summoned as a garnishee in the above case to appear at a Superior Court to be holden at the Court house in and for the county aforesaid, on the second Monday in April next before the undersigned Clerk of the said court and a justice of the Peace in and for the county aforesaid, who being duly sworn saith that he is not indebted to the Defendant any thing and that he has not any effects of the Defendant in his hands, nor does he know of any effects or debts of the Defendant in the hands of any other person to the best of his knowledge and belief.

Sworn to and subscribed before me this 25th day of March, 1813.

AN'D. JACKSON
THEODORE STARK, J.P.

Text from Natchez *Ariel*, July 26, 1828. Original not found.

1. See White Turpin to AJ, March 22. For the origin of Jackson's involvement in the case, see above, Jonathan Thompson to AJ, July 3 and September 30, 1812.
2. For the transactions, see above, Account with Aaron Burr, October 4, 1806.
3. See above, John Wilkes to AJ, January 29, 1807.
4. Coffee's statement, like Jackson's, was made before Theodore Stark, justice of the peace and sometime clerk of the superior court.

From Rachel Jackson

Aprile the 5the 1813—

My Dear Husband

I received your affectionate Letter[1] By Major Hines and Mr Blackman I was very glad indeed to See them it was the greatest marke of your attention and regard to me I was happy to Here you wer in good health that I Should Shortely Bee blesst with my Deares Self once more with you In this Life never an other painfull Seperation—But I Saw a Letter you wrote Genl overton Wherein you Expresst a wish to go to the Northw Oh how hard it appeard and one to Colo Warde of the Same tennuee[2] how Can you wish Such a perilous tower but the Love of Country the thirst for Honour and patriotisem is your motive—After a feeble acknowledgment of the maney polite and friendly attentions I have received through your goodness by your Friends I Shall Never forget—I have a melencholy peice of news to relaite how shall I Express my Simpathy for our Dear friend Johney his Polley[3] is no more She Departad This Life Last wednesdays Evening the 31 of March Poor fellow was here on munday, previous to her Death he was on his waye to Doctor [John] Newnon[4] I Do not think he thought her Daingerous when he was here o blooming youth those arte not Exempt from the tyrent king of sorrors well may Those be valed by that Name I regret I Did not See her before her Exit Poor Dear J when he bid me Farwell I Saw he was much affected asked me Come up I promised him I would but it has raind almost Ever Since Creeks and river high No one to go with me I herd it Last Night I could Sleepe o what I feel for our unfortunate Friend I wish to See him, Shall I See you in twenty Days. O God Send Showers or Scorching wethering grass will not be more reviveing Gladly will I meete you when Ever you bid me our farm Looks well I Could write you all Day Long but Such a Pen I feare you never can read it pray my Dear write me on the way home—and may The Lord bless you health Safely restore you to my armes in mutuel Love is The prayers of your affectionate wife

Rachel Jackson

ALS, MB.
1. See above, March 21.
2. Neither letter found.
3. John Hutchings's wife, Mary Smith.
4. Newnan (c1770-c1826) was born in Salisbury, N.C., studied medicine in Philadelphia, and moved to Nashville in 1809.

To William Berkeley Lewis

Chickasaw Nation 13 miles South of the agency
April 9th 1813—9 oclock at night—

Dr Sir

I this moment recd. a letter by the Post rider from major [Andrew] Hay[n]es[1] who states you will do nothing or furnish no means for the convayence of the sick from the Tennessee to Nashville—This to me is unaccountable—and are these brave men who are at the call of their country, rallied around its standards for its defence, to be left a pray to the Vultures of the savage wilderness—is this the reward of a virtuous administration, to its patriotic sons—or is it, done by a wicked minister, to satiate the vengeance, of a combination of hypocritical Political Villains, who would sacrafice the best blood of our Country—to satiate the spleen of a Villain who their connection with in acts of wickedness they are afraid to offend—and will you lend a helping hand to aid the wicked machinations of an armstrong a W___n[2] &c. by witholding from us that which by law we are entitled to—I hope not where is the governor—will he too set silent & see his own citizens, that he organized, that met with his plaudits for their patriotism—thus surrendered as a pray to the wolf in an howling desert—The supplies I call for I am entitled to by law, the bills I have drew on you, does not amount to the amount of the due bills, of the asst D. q. master of the Mississippi Territory, these I expect to be accepted & paid—my sick I will have on regardless of the neglect of the agents of Government—I shall make a full and fair statement of facts, as it respects the treatment of the agents of government, and it would fill me with extreme pain and regret, to have to number you, with such a set of publick agents when I give publicity to the documents I hold in my possession, it will make every honest man possessing humanity shudder—I know your situation, and I hope you know, that I would be the last man on earth, that would request you to do an act inconsistant with your duty and the agents of government are bound to pay my requisitions—and I hope they will be furnished—I am as usual yr Sincere friend

Andrew Jackson

P.S. I have not rode 20 miles, the field & staff are and have been on foot and the sick mounted on their horses—without hospital stores or medicine for the sick only what I have procured through my own means—attempted to be dismissed, without pay, 800 miles from home—no provisions for the sick—they to be stripped of every particle of covering—and left a pray to faminine & pestilence But, the *Bloody Bouy* was arrested—The Tyranick stroke was attempted in open Violation of the law—they are entitled to pay & rations or a commutation in money in lieu of the

ration calculating one day for every 20 miles—as the money was not offered—and as I never recd a communication official from the war department untill I got into the chocktaw nation, I am entitled to the means of
taking me to where my men can be mustered paid and discharged this
Justice requires and I will have, and I will try whether the publick agents
or myself has the right of Judging   A. J—

Copy, DLC-Gist Blair Collection. Published in Bassett, 1:304–305.
    1. Not found.
    2. James Wilkinson. Jackson was particularly angered over attempts to recruit his volun-
teers into regular service (see AJ to [John Armstrong], April 24, below).

From Andrew Hynes

Nashville April 15. 1813.

Dear Genl.,

    I was extremely happy in seeing Mr. [Robert] Armstrong[1] to day, who
was the bearer of your Letter of the 9. inst.,[2] by which I have learned your
rapid advancement towards home. I congratulate you and all those with
you on the safety of yr. journey thus far. I hope no difficulties may intervene to prevent your & their speedy arrival and happy meeting with your
friends.

    There will be no chance of payment for the Troops, untill Capt. Kings-
ley gets his instructions from the war office. I transmitted his Letter to me
on that subject by the post Rider. Perhaps you have not recd it—I now
send you another copy.[3]

    I wrote a subscription Paper to raise money for the employment of Ten
waggons immediately after the asst. dep. qr. master said that he could not
act, and Mr. Lewis carried it round town and almost every body subscribed to it. There are near one hundred & fifty subscribers.[4] It will be a
small portion to each man to pay. Mr. Woods went out to Columbia &
sent them on with the provisions in them under the care of Mr. [William]
Compton.[5] I hope they have reached Tennessee River in proper time.

    Colo. Coffee has ordered his Calvalry to Rendesvous at Clover Bottom
on the 24. instant.

    I have seen Mr Grundy since my return—He regrets that there should
be any imputations of misconduct alledged to him about the discharge of
the Volunteers.[6] He asserts that their discharge was determined on by the
Cabinet and the order issued several days before he knew it—that application was immediately made to Mr. Monro by a note addressed to him
by Mr Grundy to know the causes of their recall. Mr. G. has permitted
me to take a copy of this note which I will submit to you when we meet.

    I hope you may be blessed with health—comfort & as little trouble as
is possible, untill you reach Home. Yr. friend

A. Hynes

ALS, DLC. Published in Bassett, 1:305–306.
    1. Armstrong (1792–1854) served in Jackson's artillery during the Creek War and as an aide during the New Orleans campaign. He supported Jackson's presidential candidacy and was rewarded with appointment as Nashville's postmaster in 1829.
    2. Not found.
    3. Hynes enclosed a copy of his letter from Alpha Kingsley (dated April 6, DLC), stating that the troops should be dismissed to await payment in their respective counties upon authorization by the war department.
    4. According to Lewis, subscriptions totaled nearly $600, a sum inadequate, however, to defray the entire transportation costs (Lewis to John Coffee, April 9, DLC, identified in Bassett, 1:305, as Lewis to Jackson). The subscription list has not been found.
    5. Compton (b. 1767), a Davidson County carpenter and joiner, served as an assistant to army contractor Joseph Woods.
    6. For Jackson's comments to Grundy on the discharge of the volunteers, see above, AJ to [Felix Grundy], March 15.

To [John Armstrong]

Nashville April 24th 1813.

Sir.

I have the honor to acknowledge the receipt of your letter of the 10th instant covering a copy of yours to me of the 22nd of March last[1] the original of which has not yet come to hand. This I exceedingly regret— the difficulties I experienced in procureing means of conveyance for my sick—forage for the cattle and horses that carried and drew them would have been much aleviated, and what was still equally desireable, the heart burnings occasioned by the apparent neglect of the Goverment towards this detachment, and impressions, that they were intended by that neglect to be reduced by want to enlist into the armies of the United States.[2] The number of officers of the regular army ordered up to my encampment for this purpose, all combined to embitter their minds, all of which would have been prevented by the receipt of your letter of the 22nd of March last. However the promulgation of your letters of the 10th of April and 22nd of March, received by last fridays mail will do away those impressions and convince them if they were for a short time neglected by the agents of Goverment they were not forgotten. I reached Columbia on the evening of the 19th instant and finding from advices which I received from Major Hynes, my aid de camp, (whom I had sent on to Nashville and there rejoined me) that there were no orders for payment.[3] On the 20th. I halted and discharged the second Regiment of Infantry and part of the first—On the 22d. I reached this place and discharged the residue of the first Regt. with the Guards, and on this day agreeably to my order the Regiment of Cavalry are to be mustered out of Service (at the clover bottom nine miles distant from this place) and discharged. On the discharge of the Infantry I obtained their pledge that if Goverment ordered and I gave the call they would rally again under the Eagles of their country and march to any point required. I shall on the discharge of the Cavalry hold them bound to rendezvous at any point that may be ordered. I have no doubt but the Infantry, should Goverment order, can be again brought speedily into the field. I could have marched them on to Malden[4] without a halt had I received your orders before they were discharged. I could have reached Malden, being well supplied, in thirty days, with sixteen hundred effective men, as well disciplined as any troops in the United States. This may not be credited—from the shortness of the time and a water voyage of 800 miles—but nevertheless it is true. Industry, with the capacity of my Major of Brigade has introduced this discipline into the detachment. We had taken the field raw and undisciplined with the intention to fight the Battles of our country and experience had taught me to know that without discipline, courage alone would not do. My own reputation, the reputation of the detachment and the benefit of the service required that discipline and subordination should be introduced, or disgrace and defeat would be the consequence—hence all our 'exertions and industry was bent to that object and we succeeded.

I am happy to find that the expence of the return march will be paid. I found some difficulty in procureing funds to meet the expence, but your order has relieved me,[5] and the Quarter Master of this Department has as far as he has had the funds applied them. You will find that oeconomy has been strictly attended to, and the expence of the Cavalry on their return march has not come up to the sum due from the Assistant Deputy Quarter Master of the Mississippi Territory, and Pr his due Bills for Forage, not issued to the Cavalry on returns made to him, which he refused to furnish in kind or pay for when I was about to march notwithstanding he had compleat returns, for the whole forage ration, and the Regimental Quarter Master of Cavalry[6] held his due Bills for the quantity not delivered.

I have the pleasure to inform you I have the whole of my detachment on except six sick men I was obliged to leave on the way and their attendants—Those have recovered and are on their way.

I am Sir with due respect yr most obdt Svt.

Andrew Jackson

Copy, PHi.
1. See Armstrong to AJ, April 10 and March 22.
2. For Wilkinson's comments on the U.S. Army recruiting efforts among Jackson's volunteers, see above, James Wilkinson to AJ, March 1.
3. See above, Andrew Hynes to AJ, April 15.
4. Fort Malden on the Canadian shore of the Detroit River.
5. In his letter of March 22, Armstrong promised that the troops would be paid on their return to Tennessee.
6. Neil B. Rose (1780–1838), later a merchant in Huntsville, Ala., served as quartermaster to the cavalry in both the Natchez expedition and the Creek War.

To John Armstrong

Nashville May 10th. 1813

Sir

This will be handed you by Colo Thos. H. Benton commandant of the 2nd Regt of Tennessee Volunteer Infantry—who having detained here since the 22nd ultimo for the determination of the President on the further service, of the Detachment of Volunteers under my command—from the delay of communications on this subject, a belief has arisen, that our services to the North west will not be called for by the President—Colo. Benton having abandoned a profitable profession for the tented fields, and having determined during the continuation of the war, to continue in the field of Mars if goverment will give him employ in her armies, goes on with this view to the city of washington—did I think any thing was necessary to be said on the fitness of Colo. Benton to command, it would be here added—his uniform good conduct, his industry and attention to the decipline & police of his Regiment speak more for his fitness than words—and a personal acquaintance with Colo. Benton will soon decide on the capacity of his mind relative tacticts and military operations—

I have recd advices from Natchez stating that the asst D. q. Master of that department, has refused to pay the waggoners employed by him to hall the sick and necessary baggage of my detachment to the Tennessee river[1]—and he further states as I am advised by letter from the waggoners,[2] *that he is thus instructed by Colo. Shamburgh not to pay them*—I have to ask that instructions be given for this expence to be paid, and that no other circumstance will be permitted to arise, farther to embitter the minds of the Detachment[3]—they took the field with the promptness—the have and do stand ready to obay the call of their goverment for the tendered north west service—they merit more attention than they have recd—their minds from the privations they have sufferred from the agents of goverment witholding from them their Just and necessary supplies are sufficiently disgusted—and if the agents of goverment are thus permitted to act with impunity the disgust will become so general in the west that the administration will loose that united support that it uniformly recd in this State—in this believe a candid man—

I refer you to Colo. Benton for information you will find him capable of giving it on every subject—I am sir with due consideration and respect—

Andrew Jackson

ALS, DNA-RG 107; ALS draft, DLC. Published in Bassett, 1:307.
1. Not found.
2. Not found.
3. The wagoners were paid. See AJ to [John Henderson], July 4.

From Thomas Hart Benton

Washington City, June 15th. 1813.

Dear Sir,

I have been three weeks in this city, and had intended to have written to you by each successive mail, but put it off from one day to another in hopes of getting a definitive and satisfactory answer on the subject of the transportation. You had already had so much vexation on that subject that I was unwilling to add to it by letting you know that there was any thing like delay or uncertainty to attend the payment of these accounts. A satisfactory answer I have now receved; but not until this very day (Tuesday 15th. June.)

Soon after my arrival here I presented your letter to the Sec. of War.[1] Two or three days afterwards I called upon him, to receve his answer, and give such information as he might require. He was particular in his inquiry whether the Dep. Q. M. General at New Orleans had refused the payment of the draughts which you had drawn in favor of the waggoners. I detailed to him the reasons which I had for knowing that, notwithstanding those draughts had not been presented to him, yet that Mr. Andrews in refusing to pay them was acting in conformity to instructions which he had receved from Col. Shambourg. The answer which he gave me was verbal; to wit; that the claims would have to be transmitted to this place, and to pass through the Accountants office. The delay, to say the least of it, that would have attended this mode, made it far from being satisfactory; and I determined to give the business a more serious turn. I then addressed to the Sec. a formal note,[2] stating my objections to the mode he had proposed, and suggesting another, which would keep clear of the accountants office, and come at once to the justice of the case. A copy of that note was enclosed. I took care to require his answer in writing. This note was delivered to the chief clerk of the War office[3] on the day of its date; and I called soon after for the answer. The clerk informed me that the Sec. had carried out my note to consider of it on the sunday following at his leisure; and now on this day, having called again at the war office, I secured from him the note of which I enclose you a copy,[4] so that at least this agent is ordered to pay.

Things go on but slowly here. The tax bills, tho reported, have not yet been taken up: but they will be passed I conceive by considerable majorities. The Senate have been sitting for three weeks with closed doors. It is very well known that they are engaged on the subject of Mr. Gallatins appointment. The scuffle is to get Gallatin out of the treasury; and to do that, a strong party in the Senate, perhaps the majority, require his resignation of Secretaryship before they confirm his nomination of ambassador.[5]

Hampton has passed on to the north; Wilkinson is ordered there also, but is very slow in going.[6] The third regiment from New Orleans is also ordered there. [William Richardson] Davie and [Aaron] Ogden have refused their appointments;[7] Dinsmoor is here; upon what business I do not exactly know, but expect that he is called to some account for his some of official conduct, perhaps touching the passports.

The President inquired after your health on terms of particular kindness. Your Volunteers are spoken of here in the most honorable terms. Those who were so friendly to us at Natchez have extended their good offices even here, and transmitted the best accounts of our conduct. I understand from some of the members that they intend to take advantage in the first suitable opening, and to press you for a Brigadier Generalship.

I have no prospect of immediate active service. The best prospect I see is to be sent back to recruit a new regiment; of which it is proposed that John Williams of Knoxville shall be Colonel; myself Lt. Col. Carroll Major, and Geor. West 2d. do.[8] I undertook to convince the Sec. of War that two regiments could be raised sooner than one. When I gave him all my reasons he said he thought so too; but there was but one regiment but what was appropriated to other states. By the present regulations two regiments make a brigade; two brigades make a division &c. so that, if two regiments had been allotted to our state, a General would have been appointed of course.

Lt. [James Allison] Dudley,[9] of the marines has arrived within this twenty four hours from Sackets harbour. I enquired of him about Gen. Winchester. He says that the General, with his officers are in Quebec; and that they are not permitted to return on their parole. What does this mean? Does the enemy dread the reprisals to which he knows he has subjected himself by the massacre of the wounded prisoners, and does he retain these officers as a security against what may happen?

I hope to leave here in three days, and to be at home the first week in July. Respects to Mrs. Jackson. With the greatest respect &c.

Thomas H. Benton.

ALS, DLC. Extract published in Bassett, 1:308–309.
  1. See above, AJ to John Armstrong, May 10.
  2. Possibly Benton to [John Armstrong], June 10 (fragment), DLC.
  3. Daniel Parker served as chief clerk of the war department until November 1814, when he was appointed adjutant and inspector general of the army.
  4. See John Armstrong to Benton, [June 15], enclosed in AJ to [John Henderson], July 4.
  5. President Madison had sent Gallatin's nomination as one of the commissioners to negotiate treaties of commerce with Russia and of peace and commerce with Great Britain to the Senate on May 29, three weeks after Gallatin's departure for Russia. The Senate rejected the nomination on the ground that the offices of commissioner and secretary of the treasury were incompatible. Gallatin's confirmation finally came on February 9, 1814, following Madison's nomination of George W. Campbell as secretary of the treasury and Gallatin's renomination as commissioner.
  6. Both Hampton and Wilkinson were assigned to the 9th Military District (Vermont

and parts of New York and Pennsylvania), Wilkinson as district commander, Hampton in command of the army on Lake Champlain.

7. Both had been nominated for major generalships.

8. On June 18, Williams and Benton were appointed colonel and lieutenant colonel respectively of the 39th Infantry. Carroll and West declined appointments.

9. Dudley (d. 1817), a South Carolinian, was appointed midshipman in the U.S. Navy in 1809 and acted as lieutenant for a time before confirmation of the rank in July 1813. He had recently been granted parole as a prisoner of war and released by the British at Kingston, Ontario, and so would have had information about Winchester and his men. There is no evidence that he served in the marines as Benton reported.

Thomas Hart Benton had left Nashville in May as Jackson's friend and trusted aide; he returned in July as Jackson's accuser and eventual enemy. With Jackson's blessing and recommendation, Benton had gone to Washington to settle the Natchez expedition accounts and seek a commission in the regular army. While there he heard a rumor that Jackson had written to the war department, assigning him particular blame for the Tennessee Volunteers' protest against serving under the command of James Wilkinson. Though angered by this report, Benton completed his mission and returned to Tennessee. He thereupon learned that Jackson had become involved in a duel between his brother, Jesse Benton (d.1843), and William Carroll, Jackson's brigade major. The Carroll-Benton quarrel had grown out of a previous dispute between Carroll and U.S. Army officer Littleton Johnston, whom Carroll had refused to fight. When Jesse Benton challenged, Carroll accepted, and the two dueled on June 14. Both were wounded, Benton embarrassingly so, having been hit in the buttocks while stooping to escape Carroll's fire.

Upon his return to Nashville, Thomas Hart Benton demanded an explanation of the duel from Jackson, who had served as Carroll's second. The two exchanged several accusatory letters in which they hinted at the need for a duel (see below), but neither challenged. This heated verbal posturing erupted into physical combat on September 4, when Jackson and Benton met in front of the City Hotel in Nashville. According to witnesses, Jackson charged Benton with a whip and demanded that he defend himself. Jesse Benton rushed to his brother's defense, firing a pistol shot which shattered Jackson's left shoulder, whereupon John Coffee, Stockley D. Hays, Eli Hammond, and Alexander Donelson joined the fray with pistols and knives (see Thomas Hart Benton to the Public, September 10, below). Bystanders finally separated the combatants. Jackson was then rushed to the Nashville Inn for medical attention, where, by some accounts, he lay for nearly three weeks recovering from the wound and a heavy loss of blood.

Jackson and Thomas Hart Benton remained enemies for another ten years. In 1823, while serving together in the United States Senate, they reconciled their differences and set the stage for their future political al-

liance. Jesse Benton, however, refused to make peace and campaigned against Jackson's bids for the presidency in 1824 and 1828. He moved to Texas in the early 1830s, participated in the revolution of 1836, and later settled on a plantation in Louisiana.

From Thomas Hart Benton

Nashville, July 9th. 1813.

Sir,

Shortly before the Tennessee Volunteers descended the Mississippi under your command it was proposed by Col. Coffee that we (the field officers) should remonstrate to the President against serving under the command of Wilkinson. Five or six of us were present. I objected to it; gave my reasons in detail, and was joined by all the officers present. The remonstrance was no further pressed by Col. Coffee.

About the same time in two conversations which I had with you I took the liberty of pointing out the unhappy effect it would have upon the public service and our own reputations if, after going into the department assigned to the command of Gen. Wilkinson, we should raise a question about submitting to his authority.

After recalling these things to your mind I have the honor to request that you will inform me whether you have caused it to be communicated to the war department that the Tennessee Volunteers would not fight under the orders of General Wilkinson?[1]

Respectfully, &c.

Thomas H. Benton.

ALS, DLC. Endorsed by AJ: "Note the remarks on the other side A. J."
1. For Jackson's comments on serving under Wilkinson see above, AJ to Willie Blount, November 11, 1812; to George Washington Campbell, [November 29, 1812]; and to William B. Lewis, February 21. Campbell probably broached this matter with the secretary of war (see above, pp. 343–45).

Memorandum re Thomas Hart Benton's Letter of July 9

Nashville July 13th. 1813

This letter recd. this moment from the hand of Ensign [Littleton] Johnston[1]—The first sentence I know nothing of, nor did I hear of a meeting of the officers on that subject, until it was over—as soon as I did, I made use of the observations, that Colo. Benton asscribes to himself in second sentence—no recollection of having but one conversation with Colo. Benton on that subject—recollects distinctly, that at all times Colo. Benton, spoke with the same disgust of Genl Wilkison as any of the officers, but all agreed with me, that it would be an impropper moment to re-monstrate on this subject, as it might be construed that our tender of service was a mere bombast; before this happened, I was informed thro [Go]vr Blount—that when my Tender thro him reached the President—an officer, high in office, after reading or hearing it read, said my tender was a tender on paper only—hence resulted the sentence in my letter to Grundy[2]—"that grating as it might be to my feelings, to be command[ed] by Wilkinson, that I had (Tendered my service) entered the service with the true spirit of a soldier, and determined to defend my country and obay any order from my superior["] (This is the substance of the letter to Grundy but not the letter)—and this a subterfuge—wrote no letters to the Secretary of war on this subject, wrote to Grundy & George W. Campbell[3] Colo Benton had a view of them and approbated their contents—he then acted as one of my aids—

enquired of Mr. Johnston where Colo Benton was—informed him to say to Colo. Benton that I should not answer his note untill I s[aw] him, requested him to say to Colo. Benton that I wanted to see him—Queries to be put to Colo. Benton, ¿for what purpose do you ask the information within ¿have you not been at the seat of the information required and did you not see the letter wrote to Grundy at the City, which was submitted to you before it was sent—did you not state to Grundy that I intended to oppose him at next election—and if you did, did you not know, that this was not the fact—and why did you make the statement &c. &c.

Andw Jackson

note, that before I heard any thing of a meeting of the officers on the subject of the within letter, that it had got to the ears of the Detachment, that we were ordered under the command of Genl Wilkinson—it raged like wild fire, and as Colo. Benton well know[s] ([if] he will speak the truth) that it took all my influence and the influence of the officers of the Detachment, to lay it to sleep—

ADS, DLC. Jackson's memorandum appears on the verso of Benton's letter of July 9, above.
1. See above. Johnston served in the 24th U.S. Infantry, 1812–15, and later settled as a merchant in Tuscumbia, Ala.
2. Not found.
3. See above, AJ to George Washington Campbell, [November 29, 1812].

To Felix Grundy

Hermitage July 15th. 1813

Sir

I am requested to make known to you the wishes of Doctor [James Loudon] Armstrong (of Jefferson) that through you the may be made known to the Secy. of war; he has a desire to enroll himself as one of the defenders of his country—finding that his voluntary services tendered and accepted of, under the act of February 6th. & July 6th. will not be farther required—he wishes to enter the regular service—he will accept of a majority or a captaincy under Colo. Williams—you personally know the Doctor I need say nothing of his merit. he is young robust & healthy he served as surgeon for the Regt. of Cavalry under my command and Demeaned himself well.[1] Mr John S Williamson will accept of a Lieutenancy or ensign in said Regt. he is personally known to you—he has served in the guards and has some knowledge of discipline—[2]

I have to ask the favour of you on recpt of this to send me a copy of a letter I wrote you before I descended the river with my detachment of Tennessee Volunteers—stating in substance the disquietude of the Detachment at the idea of being ordered under the command of Wilkinson—and stating to you the spirit with which as a soldier I took the field &c &c[3]—I have no recollection of writing you but one letter on this subject—I find I have but the copy of one to you on this subject, and that is endorsed by Colo. Benton—If this letter to you is in my handwriting, all I want is a copy—if not in my handwriting I wish you to keep a copy, and send me on the original, or enclose it to Major Hayns Nashville, with instructions to let me have the use of it—I wish you also, to say whether, you have ever recd. any others from me on that subject, since the month of october 1812. I have to ask of you also in answer to this to state whether Colo. Benton whilst at washington City since 10th day of May did state to you that I was to oppose you at next election for representative to Congress or not—These appear trivial requests, but from some hints this day given, the copy of my letter to you may be material—the other satisfactory to know—

I am respectfully yrs &c

Andrew Jackson

I am advised Major Carroll will not accept of a majority in the Regt. to be raised in this state—rumor says Major west will not—There may be room for Mr Alexander Donelson & Armstrong   A. J—

ALS copy, DLC.
1. Armstrong (1782–1868) of Rutherford County did not receive a U.S. Army appointment; he continued as surgeon in the Tennessee Volunteers until November 1813.
2. Williamson was appointed lieutenant in the 24th U.S. Infantry in August 1813, and served to the end of the war.
3. Letter not found.

From Andrew Hynes

Nashville July 16. 1813.

Dear General,

Your favour by your Boy of today is recd.; together with the enclosures[1] which are put into the Post Office.

With respect to the rumors that are in circulation of ill natured expressions of Colo. Benton toward you, I have but little knowledge. Yet I have heard thus much, that he, on his return from Washington was represented to be very wrothfull against you for your friendship to Majr. Carroll in the affair with his Brother Jesse.

I Probably should have heard more, had I been in the confidence of the Colo's Friends, but moving in the Sphere that I do, I have never come within the Circle of his Slander, nor would any of his minions dare retail it in my presence without being checked.

The Colo. has kept himself remarkably close since his return, he has scarcely been in town, and I have never had an oppy of a single word with him.

His august consequence is not calculated to procure him many real friends, altho' he may have some Sycophants who will be panders to his ambition.

I would extremely regret that the Colo. would be so far lost to himself and all sense of Honour & Gratitude as to forget that he is indebted to you for the consideration in which he is held in society.

I am unwilling to believe that any man could be so stamped with ingratitude as to turn traitor to his Patron and to be the Reviler of Him, who brought him out of obscurity into fame & consequence in the world.

Ingratitude has always been considered among all nations and in all countries the basest of crimes. Yet there can be no punishment for it, except the honest indignation of all good men. A man who is ungratefull, renounces all moral obligation, and is capable of committing every species of iniquity.

You I know can foresee that there are persons behind the curtain, who would be willing to make any body an instrument to act as a kind of *Autoumaton* to excite and promote disaffection toward you in order to keep themselves from danger.[2]

I would not take any notice of the Idle rumors that are floating in this Slanderous world. They can do no harm, when the source from which they originate is known, but will recoil on their authors.

Your standing in society is like the Rock in the Ocean. It may be assailed, but it cannot be moved. The swift winds of Slander may blow, and the rough billows of Detraction roll, yet you are stedfast & no impression is made. You can stand secure within yourself and look with contempt on [the p]etty rascality of designing men—

Majr. Carroll has been very ill, but is much better.

Colo. Purdy left town this evening for Jno Phillips's, where he intends remaining, untill he takes his final departure northwardly.[3]

Please to give my friendly respects to Mrs Jackson & family & am sincerely yrs

A Hynes

ALS, DLC. Extract published in Bassett, 1 : 309–10.
1. Neither Jackson's letter nor the enclosures have been found.
2. In later years Jackson claimed that Boyd and Nathaniel McNairy used Benton as a foil in their continuing battle with him (see AJ to John Coffee, January 21, 1832, THi; AJ to Amos Kendall, December 12, 1842, DLC).
3. Purdy was en route to his new assignment with Hampton's army on Lake Champlain. Philips was Mrs. Purdy's brother.

To Thomas Hart Benton

(a Copy)   July 19. 1813.

Sir,

When I first extended to you the arm of Friendship, I never expected to substitute the language of reproach instead of Friendship. But late rumors and information has reached me of some conduct, expressions & threats of yours as they relate to me of the basest kind. It is always due to Friendship—Justice & propriety that credit should not be given to reports—altho' coming thro' the most respectable channels, untill the person who is said to be the author is called upon for an avowal or disavowel of them.

I have therefore to call upon you to say whether you did not leave my house on the 10th of May in perfect Friendship with me carrying with you a Letter from me to the secretary of war to promote your welfare and your views?[1]

Have you not on your return and since spoken disrespectfully of me—and when chided by my Friend[2] who said he would write to me, Did you not say to him that you rode a good Horse—would soon be with me and give me personally the information of your conduct and language to save him the trouble? And have you given me any Such information since your return? Have you threatened to make a Publication against me since you left my House on the 10th of May? Has any act of my life towards you since I took you by the hand in Friendship and appointed you my aid de Camp been inconsistent with the strictest principles of Friendship? And if any, in what did it consist? and lastly have you or have you not threatened to challenge me[3]—I am Sir respectfully yours

Andrew Jackson

LS copy in Andrew Hynes's hand (with revisions by AJ), DLC. Published in Bassett, 1 : 310.
1. See above, AJ to John Armstrong, May 10.
2. Not identified.
3. The clause "and lastly . . . me" is in Jackson's hand.

From Thomas Hart Benton

Franklin, July 25th. 1813.

Sir,

Your letter of the 19th. instant[1] was delivered me this day. The following general statement is intended to cover the whole of your inquiries.

On my way to Washington city 10th. May, I passed your house, at your request, and received from you, unsolicited, a letter of introduction to the Secretary of War,[2] more honorable to me than my merits had deserved. That I was friendly to you at that time, and for more than a month afterwards, is evidenced by the fact, well known to you, that on monday the 14th. day of June, The day on which you superintended the shooting of my brother, I was in the war office in Washington city, exerting my very poor abilities according to your wishes on a subject which lay very near to your heart. If you want any other evidence of my disposition towards you at that time, you can get it by applying to the gentlemen in congress from this state.

On my return I heard of my brothers duel with Mr. Carrol, and of your agency in that affair. what I have since said on this subject may be reduced to three or four heads.

1. That it was very poor business in a man of your age and standing to be conducting a duel about nothing between young men who had no harm against each; and that you would have done yourself more honor by advising them to reserve their courage for the public enemy.

2. That it was mean in you to draw a challenge from my brother by carrying him a bullying note from Mr. C. dictated by yourself,[3] and which left him no alternative but a duel or disgrace.

3. That if you could not have prevented a duel you ought at least to have conducted it in the usual mode, and on terms equal to both parties.

4. That on the contrary you conducted it in a savage, unequal, unfair, and base manner.

Savage: Because the young men were made to fight at ten feet distance, contrary to your own mode, to what is usual among gentlemen;[4] and against the remonstrance of my brother.

Unequal: Because the parties were made to wheel; an evolution which Mr. C. perfectly understood, but which my brother knew nothing about, and against which he earnestly objected.

Unfair: Because you concealed the mode of fighting from my brother, put off the duel on a frivolous pretext from friday until monday; and in the mean time secretly practised Mr. C. to wheel and fire ten feet at a small saplin, until he could strike the center of it at every shot.

Base: Because you avowed yourself to be the friend of my brother while giving to his adversary all these advantages over him.

In consequence of all which my brother was drawn into a duel against his wishes, and fought under circumstances wherein the chances, according to Mr. Carrols calculation, and your own must have been the same, were *twenty to one against him*.

I know your answer to all this: "Mr. C. would have it so." To which I reply: From your known influence over Mr. C. you might have managed the affair as you pleased; if not, you were at least a free man, and might have quit him if you did not approve of his course.

To this effect, but in language much stronger, I have expressed myself when speaking of this matter.

You have been pleased to remind me of the services you have rendered me. I needed not the admonition. The same persons who carried you evil reports, might, if I am not mistaken, also have told you that I remembered the numerous acts of kindness you had done me, and regretted that I had not been able to make you any return. But because you had been my friend I could not sit, and smile assent upon your cowd. act, when I saw you doing what you could to break the heart of an aged and widowed mother,[5] and hurrying into his grave, a young man, a brother, whose life ought to have been preserved for the comfort of his family and the service of his country.

My subjects of complaint against you are limited to two: your conduct towards my brother; and the communication which it is *believed* that you made to the war office, and in which, as one of the Tennessee Volunteers, I was implicated in a charge of mutiny. If you did represent these troops, as unwilling to fight under Wilkinson, without making an exception in my favor, you have done me a serious injury, and took a liberty with my name which the best of friends should not take with each other. For it was known to you that notwithstanding my prejudicies against Gen. Wilkinson and the evil I had spoken of him, that yet I was satisfied of his right to command us; and as a military subaltern should render to him respect and obedience. That this point might be cleared up between us, I addressed you a note on the day after my arrival from Washington city:[6] a note which you have not condescended to answer, or to notice in any shape.

The balance of your interrogatories may be quickly answered:

I have not threatened to tell you my sentiments, except in the event of your calling upon me.

I have not threatened to make any publication against you, except in the case of my brother; and that idea I relinquished from a total repugnance to going into the newspapers.

I have not threatened to challenge you. On the contrary I have said that I would not do so; and I say so still. The same time the terror of your pistols is not to seal up my lips. What I believe to be true, I shall speak; and if for this I am called to account, it must ever be so. I shall neither seek, nor decline, a duel with you.

Respectfully, &c.

Thomas H. Benton.

ALS, DLC. Published in Bassett, 1:311–14.
1. See above.
2. See above, AJ to John Armstrong, May 10.
3. Carroll quoted his note of June 11 to Jesse Benton in his statement to Andrew Jackson Donelson, October 4, 1824. Carroll said that he, not Jackson, was the author (see Bassett, 1:311–12).

4. The Thomas J. Overton-John Dickinson duel, in which Jackson served as Overton's second, and the Andrew Jackson-Charles Dickinson duel were both fought at twenty-four feet.

5. Ann (Nancy) Gooch Benton (1758–1838) was widowed in 1791 and moved her family of eight children from North Carolina to Williamson County in 1800.

6. See above, Benton to AJ, July 9.

The aborted Natchez expedition and American reverses on the northern frontier tormented Jackson. State volunteer and militia forces, including his own from Tennessee, stood idle, while the federal government dawdled in its prosecution of the war effort. When he heard from George W. Campbell that Washington anticipated sending an expedition against the Creeks, Jackson wrote the letter below to Governor Blount, urging a strong and unified strike in the South. As Jackson anticipated, Blount forwarded the recommendations to the secretary of war, for whom Jackson undoubtedly intended them (see Blount to John Armstrong, August 1, DNA-RG 107).

To Willie Blount

Nashville July 31st. 1813.

Dear sir,

From a letter recd. from the Hon'ble G. W. Campbell last mail I am advised that Government has come to a determination to march an expedition against the Creeks; the writer further observes "that part of the troops will be from West Tennessee, under your command it is presumed, this will afford employ for your detachment should they still be disposed to be engaged in active service"—[1]

From the above it appears that I may have some part in the contemplated expedition, and from which I take the liberty of giving you my ideas on the subject—and first it is my duty to make known to you that the Volunteers composing my detachment in the late expedition down the Mississippi two thousand strong stand ready at the call of their country to march at a moment's warning—

There can be no doubt but the Creeks and lower Choctaws are excited to hostilities by the influence of the British; if so, there is no doubt but we will have to fight the combined powers of both—There is no instance within my recollection wherein an Indian Tribe or Nation has been invaded but they united their whole force against the Invaders Therefore in the calculation of the force to be employed by the U. S. against the Creeks and their Allies no calculation ought to be made on the division of the Nation—The force employed may either unite them or create divisions; if an incompetent force is employed against them, they will be united and on the first reverse of our army in that quarter we will not only have to fight the whole Creek Nation, but the greater part of the Choctaws—If a competent force is employed to insure success the Creek Nation will be divided to secure their Territory and their property—The scenes in the N. W. is an awful lesson on this subject to the Government, and to every beholder, and from which we ought to learn from experience that the true way to oeconomize is to employ sufficient force to insure success and crush all opposition in that quarter at one blow—The question therefore will occur what force will be competent to the object. Will the number pointed out by the Secy of War, say 1500 from Tennessee, and 1500 from Georgia, with the 3d. U. S. Regt., say 500 strong be a sufficient force to ensure success and crush the hostile Indians and their allies in that quarter? I answer in the negative—If it was intended to barely make an incursion thro' their Towns, burn their houses, destroy their crops and hastily to return, this force would be more than competent for a flying camp, but I understand the object of the expedition to be different, that is, to crush all hostility in that quarter, this then will require fortified places in the heart of the Creek Nation, and a military campaign—

It is a large calculation to say that three fourths of any military force will be any length of time fit for service: it will take one fourth to guard the baggage &c. &c., one half therefore of the force ordered into the field may be calculated on to be a disposable force, we can therefore count with certainty only a disposable force of 1750 men after a junction is formed in the Creek or Cherokee Country—I will hazard an opinion that no military man impressed with a belief that the Indians are excited to hostilities by the British, and knowing their contiguity to Pensacola, and the ease with which Britain can land a reinforcement and cooperate with the Indians will say, that the above force is competent to insure success— The experience of the N. W. armies forbid such a belief—and when any force that may be required can be had, I am of opinion that from three to five thousand from this state ought to be employed on this expedition, the latter perhaps the better calculation, these with the 3d. U. S. regt., and a Brigade from Georgia would be amply sufficient to drive the Indians and their Allies into the Ocean, and should the Spaniards give our Enemies an Assylum in Pensacola would be sufficient to take possession of that place, cut off all supplies from the straggling Indians and put an end to hostility in that quarter—

As soon as the expedition is determined on I shall do myself the pleasure of submitting some ideas on the details of the campaign; the field ordinance necessary; the proportion of Cavalry and mounted men to that of the Infantry; the point of concentration; the Scite for a Garrison & depot of provisions, Magazine stores &c &c.

At present I shall close these remarks by observing that four thousand men can be rendezvoused in my Division in twenty days from the pro-

mulgation of the order—My brave volunteers two thousand strong stand
ready for the call—I am sir, with due consideration and respect,

(Signed)   Andrew Jackson

Copy, DNA-RG 46. Published in *ASP, Indian Affairs*, 1:850.
 1. See Campbell to AJ, July 19.

To [Thomas Hart Benton]

Nashville August 4th. 1813

[Your lett]er of the 25th ultimo is now before me[1]—[surely m]y note of
of the 19th[2] is too obvious to require [explanation.] "It was due to friendship" which certainly [until late]ly existed between us. In our passage
[through a] transitory life, I have ever found that [unless our] paths are
smoothed by social intercourse [no frien]dship exists; and no rule has
been more [plain to] me than this; "never to place confidence [in derog]a-
tory reports as comeing from a man [to whom] the sacred hand of friendship has been [exte]nded, untill it is unequivocally ascertained from the
person himself.["] It is evident from my letter that I doubted with respect
to the correctness of these reports. You have fully explained yourself, no
doubt or dificulty, remains respecting the present disposition of your
mind; whether correctly founded is for yourself to determine, after a cool
and dispassionate review, after the explanation I shall make. This ecclair-
cissement *is due to myself*, the highest tribunal on earth in point of
honor, which I have ever considered as indispensable attendants on friendship—you are however not to understand that I consider friendship as
still existing; your language cannot be misunderstood; it is that of hostility in the extreme. This appears the more extraordinary as you had
never called on me, either personally, verbally, through a friend, or by
letter, for an explanation. You were a young man in the practice of the
law of reputed sprightliness of talents and attention; in this situation
about Eighteen months ago (the date not recollected) on Colo. Andersons resignation as my aid de camp, he recommended you warmly to my
notice as his successor. At this time an acqua[intance with] you was but
slight; but on the Co[l's. recommen]dation in which I had the greatest
co[nfidence you] was appointed my aid as Major [General, Tennessee]
militia. In the transaction of [the duties of] that office, of course an intimacy [developed.] the Volunteers being ordered to the L[ower country]
by the President, last fall you were [given command] of the second regiment, in the procur[ing of which] I used my best exertions—of the ex[pe-
dition to that] country I had the command—C[arroll at] Nashville was
appointed Brigade M[ajor of the] Detachment—He became a mem[ber
of my] family of course During the expedition; [from] Major Carrols ca-

pacity, his constant and un[re]mitted attention to his duty, and living in my family I had conceived a friendship for him—in the same manner I had for you brought about by your acting as my aid; and I hope it will not be imputed as a fault much less a crime that I had formed a good oppinion of another besides yourself—For both I entertained the most friendly disposition. This brings me to the time of your departure for the city of washington, and which is refferred to in my note. In your absence Major Carrol came to my house, stated to me, that he had been assailed in his reputation, and that he was about being oppressed, by accumulated insults, challenges, and injuries from different quarters. I then & still believe Major Carrol to be a man of worth and honor; and it is well to remark that at this time Major Carrol had received by another hand—beside your brother, and with his knowledge a challenge to fight the friend of Mr Johnston—It was well known Major Carrol had declined having any thing to do with or fighting Mr Johnston, for causes I know nothing of[. In no way wa]s it material with me, as the grounds [he opposed] to meeting Johnston (whatever they [were see]med to be lost sight of) in the interest [your brother] had taken in the affair. When I even[tually came] to act as the friend of Carrol, it was [yet un]certain with whom he (Major Carrol) [would have] to contend on the theatre of action. [When I ha]d recd. a note from Johnston by your [brother³ he ha]d no idea it would be with him he would have [to fight, no]t that I was able to Judge of this from [having no p]ersonal enmity against any of the par[ties c]oncerned your brother included, whom I scarc[e]ly knew—It was because I knew your brother was not the first person who bore an innimical note to Major Carrol, in the course of these transactions, It became, in the oppinion of Major Carrol indispensably necessary that he should answer your brothers note though pressed by honourable feelings by the note of the other individual, to whom allusion is made—He thought honor bound him to do so. I was the bearer of that note. In this stage I hoped to compromise the affair honourably for both It was not understood to be a challenge, nor do I believe any individual ought to view it in that light— your brother seemed to think it must be viewed as a challenge or containing such language as was intended to extract a challenge—I had received Major Carrols assurances, that it was not intended for either purpose—*I assured your brother it was not*, nor should it be considered in that light, and requested him to consult with some experienced and honourable friend—He mentioned an individual to whom I assured him his honor might be confided I sincerely wished a compromise honourable to both; th[at no perso]nal enmity against your brother [existed.]—In this particular affa[ir he was seen] as acting on mistaken grounds [as I have] noted, whether from impetuosity, [excitement,] from other causes, or both, it was u[rged no] further than I wished that he should [take a different] view of the subject. And to this end I us[ed my influence], but in vain— Whilst, however, my h[ope was for amic]able, and honourable accomo-

dation [but to] my astonishment, your broth[er challenged] Major Carrol. Was I Sir to aba[ndon him] in this situation? *because your br[other]*
thou[ght] proper to intrude himself into th[e] disputes of other men, in
which on princip[les] of honor he was not bound to take any part. Could
you or any man living expect I would abandon a friend at this criticle
moment let who would unexpectedly obtrude himself—[No]! It is believed not—suppose Carrol had a brother and you in his situation, would
you expect me to abandon you—If you would Sir I know myself inca-
pable of such an act!

It seems to you however, that the mode of fighti[ng] which took place
in the affair of your brother was peculiarly exceptionable, and has created such a lively sensibility as to cause you to lose sight of that decorum
of language, which gentlemen use, and is always expected from them in
any situation. you certainly might on cool reflection have known and had
reason to believe that there was no necessity to adopt the language employed in the 4th. division of your letter in order to obtain satisfaction
for the violation of honourable feelings—It is the charector of the man of
honor and particularly of the *soldier* not to quarrel & brawl and <*back
bite*> like the fish-woman—I defy the world to say that if an injury or
supposed injury had proceeded from my hand, that I was unwilling to
repair it—If in an error (as all men are fallable) on *friendly* explanation I
hasten to acknowledge it—but if driven by any of the wicked passions to
the alternative of acknowledging a falshood, doing a dishonourable act,
or appealing to the last resort of men of honor, I never did, nor never *will*
hesitate on the subject.

But in relation to the mode of fighting of which you so much complain,
it is well known I acted as the friend of Major Carrol—and this your
brother knew in every stage of this affair—When he challenged my friend
according to the universal laws of honor, *my friend* had the right to chuse
his mode, time, and place of fighting—nor is it true either in *fact* or
honourable presumption that my friend made this choice through my
agency— It is presumable he knew the manner of fighting for which he
was best qualified and would consequently make choice of it—It is the
first time I ever heard a challenger complain of the manner his adversary
had chosen to fight, or that he would not get round to meet his enemy—
The range of the ball, the fire of the pistols at the same time, Major Carrol being wounded—all shew he did get round, and I make no doubt
your brother has informed you how and in what manner. It is true they
stood back to back before the word was given, a mod[e] not unusual and
a precaution thought necessary to prevent firing before the word, as such
accidents had happened—As to the distance it is well known that it is as
various as the differrent qualifications of the persons challenged—When
I profess to be a mans friend I never abandon him on trifling occasions;
and much less in an affair of honour, when he thinks proper to persue his
own mode of fighting. Nay I should deem it my duty consecrated by the

hallowed dictates of friendship to offer my friend all the advice in my power for the preservation of his life consistant with the laws of honor and propriety. As it respects the particular affair under discussion had Major Carrol left the distance to me after having heard and understood the quallification[s] of the two persons opposed to each other, I should have recommended him to have fought at a short distance—It was reported & acknowledged that your brother was a first rate marksman at the distance of ten paces—Major Carrol is as remarkably defective—Hence, then the necessity of bringin[g] them to a short distance to place them on an equality with each other—to the extent of my influence it certainly became my duty to see that he, my friend should be on an equality with his antagonis[t.] In no other way could this be done except reducing the distance that marksmen usually select, to something like the same number of feet that they would choose in paces—Nothing was concealed from your brother that could with propriety have been made known to him. The whole transaction on our part was [. . .]

AL draft fragment, T. Published in Bassett, 1:314–15.
1. See above.
2. See also above.
3. Not found.

[. . .] From the Tennor hereof and [. . .] manner of your first communication of 9th. July,[4] you could not believe me so lost to feelings as to expect an answer, it was easy to collect from the letter that your feelings were innimical; and as the interrogatories were not prefaced by any reasons for putting them, it was natural for me to conclude you did not expect an answer to a letter couched in such language, but that you intended it for some other purpose. The aspect of things are changed by your letter under review. As a part of this explanation it may be with propriety given—you have not hazarded an assertion that I had written to the Secratary of war though lately from his office The letter to Mr. Grundy our delegate in congress you had a knowledge of before it [wa]s transmitted—As you are now on t[. . .] establishment and may be placed [under the] command of Genl Wilkinson, I hav[e no ob]jections to your obtaining as f[avorable] as standing with him, as you [can con]sistant with propriety so far a[s it relates to] me. In Justice to myself [I have given] you a particular view of the w[hole affair.]

I had [. . .] that those of whom we have [. . .] right and others wrong. Sensibility [in] its highest stages cannot stoop to view things in a cool and dispassionate manner. There will soon be time to enquire into the particulars of this affair, and for cool deliberate reflection, attended by feelings of honor, to resume its seat.

After this explanation it is expected you will do me the justice to believe that the harsh and indecorous expressions you have thought proper to adopt, were unmeritted, and that you will retract them. But should you believe that because *your brother* made this appearance in hostile array that all my connections [?] in life must instantly dissolve it would [. . .] certainly be [. . .] of which you will be convinced on the slightest reflection. Thus sir I have fully [and] frankly explained the circumstances of th[is affair] to you. If satisfactory I shall be gratified, [but if] otherwise; and you persist in the course [you se]emed to have taken, I am always ame[nable] to the process of honourable men—[. . .]t that your letter puts it out of my [power to] hold any further communication [with you], except you shall be convinced you [have done] me injustice and so state it [. . . .]—My friend Mr James Jackson [who will] hand you this is authorised to receive

AL fragment, DLC.
   4. See above.

[y]our answer if ballanced on one or [the o]ther of two grounds and no other viz that you are sensible of having done me injustice, or a demand of such satisfaction as one man of honor usually thinks he has a right to ask of another. This Sir I have a right to expect from the military commission which you now possess—This sir comports with the magnanimity of a soldier, if in Error to say or promptly to demand of me satisfaction for any injury you may think I have done you—
  I am yrs &c &c

Andrew Jackson

ALS fragment, T.

Affidavit of Felix Robertson

Nashville Augst. 5th. 1813.

Being called on by Genl. A. Jackson to state the substance of a conversation which took place in my presence on the morning of 14th June last between himself Mr. John M. Armstrong[1] & Mr. Jessee Benton—Relative to the affair which had recently taken place between Majr. Wm. Carroll & Jesse Benton—When I came up to Mr. Benton he was exclaiming against the proceedings, observing they were ungenerous &c Genl. Jackson asked him how he could talk in that manner & turning to Mr. Armstrong put the question to him, whether or not on his part every thing had been conducted in a fair & Gentlemanly manner, Mr Armstrong answered in the affirmative without hesitation Mr. Benton then replied that his observations alluded entirely to the shortness of the distance & the wheeling, which he had no doubt given his antagonist an advantage over him—[2]

Felix Robertson

ADS, DLC. Published in *Cincinnati Commercial*, February 9, 1880.
1. Armstrong, a resident of Williamson County, was a lieutenant in the 21st Regiment, Tennessee militia.
2. For other comments on the Benton-Carroll affair, see affidavits of William Quarles, July 21, and Lemuel Purnell Montgomery, [July-Aug]; and Thomas H. Fletcher to AJ, August 11.

To John M. Armstrong with Armstrong's Responses

Nashville August 9th. 1813—

Sir,

I have recd. yr. note of the 7 Inst. in answer to mine of the same date,[1] and finding that it does not meet the interrogatories, furnished you, I have to ask you to answer them directly, as of your own knowledge of the matter, and not as of the knowlege of any other person. I call on you as a man of honor & being the friend of Mr. Benton in an affair of honor between him and Majr. Carroll, and in which situation a candid statement agreeable to the existing facts is always required.[2]

1st. Had I any personal acquaintence with you untill you made yr. self known to me on Sunday the 13th. of June 1813 at Clayton Talbots tavern, Nashville.[3]

[John M. Armstrong] *I had not*

2—On yr. making yr. self known to me as the friend of Mr. J. Benton, did'nt we retire to a private room immediately—and there make a rough draft of the rules, and then you returned to yr. friend to consult him on the subject before they were signed by either of us—

[JMA] *I did*

3—When you returned and objected to the distance of ten feet, did'nt I say to you that this was Majr. Carrolls own distance, that he was advised that Mr Benton was a good marksman that he was not, and did not you & Mr. Benton acknowledge that Mr Benton was a good shot—did I not tell you that to bring them to an equality this distance was chosen that by every rule of Dueling Major Carrol had a right to name the distance

[JMA] *You did*

4th. did I not say to you the second time that you objected to the distance, that I would see Major Carrol on the subject & did I not return with his answer, that Justice to himself (not being a marksman) would not permit him to change the distance back to back and wheeling at the word—

[JMA] *you did*

5th. did I not on the mode of standing give you the following reasons, why it was proper & right that firing before the word had taken place and to prevent accidents they ought to stand back to back, as the least deviation from the rules by either, would place us under the disagreeably situation of shooting the individual who, deviated from them

[JMA] *you did*

6th. was not every indulgence given as to time and did you not yourself name the time of the parties meeting

[JMA] *every indulgence was given I named the time*

7th. did not Colonel Purdy drill Mr. J. Benton in the art of wheeling

[JMA] *not in my presence*

8th. when you came to the ground of meeting on the 14th. yourself without your friend, and seeing the delay was occationed by the want of a Pistol, did I not say to you as I had always before said to you every indulgence would be given

[JMA] *you did*

9th. after We were all upon the ground was not the rules explained and when Mr. J. Benton observed he did not perfectly understand how they were to wheel, did I not get up & shew them how they were to wheel, did I not explain to them that they were to wheel erect—the left foot never to leave the mark, and did not Major Carrol wheel erect as shewn by me—

[JMA] *Question 9th—asked by Gen Jackson the Rules were expland Mr Benton wishd [to] know how they were to wheel you Explained the manner of wheeling by wheeling erect twice or thrice in their presence but I did not under stand that the right of Stooping was prohibited as They fired*

10th. was ever there an intimation given that either party in wheeling, had a right to stoop or squat—but to explain the rule did I not get up from the Log where I was sitting and explain it by actual experiment and did not Major Carrol wheel agreeable to the example given by me

[JMA] *10th there never was; Bentons reason for taking that liberty was decided on By the person we applyd to for information*

Majr Carroll Whelled agreeable to your instructions

11th. was not the rules by which the parties were governed wrote in your own hand writing[4] and our names torn from them by mutual consent on the grounds—

[JMA] *they were*

12th. did you not obtain choice of stands & did you not give the word

[JMA] *I won everything that was decided by Lot*

13th. did you not on the ground declare in the presence of Doctor Robertson when I called upon you for that purpose—that every act of ours was consistant with honour bravery & liberality and agreeable to rule and have you not acknowledged this to myself every time we have conversed on the subject and have you not stated the same to many others on the day that the affair took place—

[JMA] *I did.*

14th. did not Mr. J Benton state to you, that I had stated to him that the note from Major Carrol was not a challenge, he said that it should not be so considered that he was not in my opinion in honor or in feeling bound to fight Mr. Johnsons battles having come forward after one challenge had been refused and as there was no personal dispute between him and

Major Carrol, as he was young, that he had better apply to some experienced honourable man for advice—that he named Colonel Purdy—I replyed he could not apply to a better and recommended him to Col. Purdy for advice, stating to take his time because all indulgence as to time should be given that was asked for—

[JMA] *Answer Question 14th—*

Mr Benton gave the last his consideration Returned an answer to Majr Carrols note which gives his reasons for considering the note as a challenge or rather as dictated in the spirit of hostility at full length—Both of which notes will answer for themselves[5]

15th. did not you and myself at your request thru Mr. [Washington L.] Hannum[6] meet on the same day at Mr. Hannums office and did not you there state to me that every thing was honourable and fairly done on our part, and did you not in company with me and Mr. Hannum walk to Weatherald & Yateman's store—and did not you there acknowledge in the presence of all, that the whole was honourably fairly & bravely done on our part

[JMA] *15th Question We met at Hannums office I then stated as I have done on all occasions since that you & the Majr as far As I had any thing to do with you & when in my presence conducted like Gentlemen & men of Honor J M Armstrong*

The above interogitories I wish you to answer in the affirmative or negative upon honour

I am Sir verry respectfully yr. mo. ob. serv.

Andrew Jackson

LS with ANS answers by Armstrong (printed above in italics), AL draft, DLC. Published in *Cincinnati Commercial*, February 9, 1880.
1. Neither letter found.
2. For an account of the Benton-Carroll duel, signed by Jackson and Armstrong and based upon Jackson's queries and Armstrong's responses in this letter, see Affidavit, August 23.
3. Talbot's Tavern was located on the courthouse square.
4. The rules have not been found.
5. Notes not found.
6. Hannum was a Nashville lawyer.

Thomas Hart Benton to the Public

FRANKLIN, TENNESSEE, SEPT. 10, 1813.

A difference which had been for some months brewing between General Jackson and myself, produced on Saturday the 4th inst. in the town of Nashville, the most outrageous affray ever witnessed in a civilized country. In communicating this affair to my friends and fellow citizens, I limit myself to the statement of a few leading facts, the truth of which I am ready to establish by judicial proofs.

1. That myself and my brother Jesse Benton arriving in Nashville on the morning of the affray, & knowing of Gen. Jackson's threats, went and took lodgings in a different house from the one in which he staid, on purpose to avoid him.[1]

2. That the general and some of his friends came to the house where we had put up, and commenced the attack by levelling a pistol at me, *when I had no weapon drawn*, and advancing upon me at a quick pace, *without giving me time to draw one.*

3. That seeing this my brother fired upon Gen. Jackson when he had got within eight or ten feet of me.

4. That four other pistols were fired in quick succession: one by Genl. Jackson at me: two by me at the General: and one by Col. Coffee at me. In the course of this firing Gen. Jackson was brought to the ground; but I received no hurt.

5. That daggers were then drawn. Col. Coffee and Mr. Alexander Donelson made at me, and gave me five slight wounds. Capt. [Eli] Hammond and Mr. Stokley Hays engaged my brother, who being still weak from the effect of a severe wound he had lately received in a duel, was not able to resist two men. They got him down; and while Captain Hammond beat him on the head to make him lay still, Mr. Hays attempted to stab him, and wounded him in both arms, as he lay on his back parrying the thrusts with his naked hands. From this situation a generous hearted citizen of Nashville, Mr. [Thomas E.?] Sumner,[2] relieved him. Before he came to the ground my brother clapped a pistol to the body of Mr. Hays to blow him through, but it missed fire

6. My own and my brothers pistols carried two balls each: for it was our intention, if driven to arms, to have no childs play. The pistols fired at me were so near that the blaze of the muzzle of one of them burnt the sleeve of my coat, and the other aimed at my head, at little more than arms length from it.

7. Capt. Carroll was to have taken part in the affray, but was absent by the permission of General Jackson, as he has since proved by the Generals certificate:[3] a certificate which reflects I know not whether less honor upon the General or upon the Captain.

8. That this attack was made upon me in the house where the judge of the district Mr. [Bennett] Searcy,[4] had his lodgings! So little are the laws and its ministers respected! Nor has the civil authority yet taken cognizance of this horrible outrage.

These facts are sufficient to fix the public opinion. For my own part I think it scandalous that such things should take place at any time, but particularly so at the present moment when the public service requires the aid of all its citizens. As for the name of *courage*, God forbid that I should ever attempt to gain it by becoming a bully. Those who know me, know full well that I would give a thousand times more for the reputation of [George] *Croghan* in defending his fort,[5] than I would for the reputations of all the duellists and gladiators that ever appeared upon the face of the earth.

THOMAS HART BENTON.
Lieutenant Colonel 39th Infantry.

Printed broadside, THi; Copy, DLC-Julia Alves Clore Papers; Copy, NcU. Published in Bassett, 1:317–18.
1. The Bentons lodged at the City Hotel; Jackson and his friends, at the Nashville Inn.
2. Sumner (1769?-1819) was the son of General Jethro Sumner of North Carolina.
3. Not found. Jackson's certificate may have referred to Carroll's upcoming marriage to Cecilia Bradford (September 9). Carroll responded to Benton's publication with one of his own (not found), whereupon Benton challenged Carroll. It has not been established, however, that they fought a duel (see Carroll to Benton and Benton to Carroll, September 16, DLC).
4. Searcy (1765–1818) had been commissioned circuit court judge on June 22. A native of North Carolina, he had accompanied Jackson and John McNairy on their move to Tennessee in 1788.
5. Croghan's fame rested on his valiant defense of Fort Stephenson in northern Ohio in August 1813, where with a small number of men and one cannon he held off a large force of British and Indians.

From James Robertson

Chickasaw agency Septr 16th 1813—

genl. Jakson.

from my hart I am sorry for your misfortune in as to your person. and as to the loos the publick will sustain for the want of your service in my opinion is incalculable. what a pitey it is that men who clame some sheare among the brave and honorable, that thay should forgit thare creator Colo Benton had past through Nashville two or three days before I left it and I understood had spoaking very rashley respecting you. my son the Dr.[1] Ither told me that he had heard you say or was told you should have said that you would not take aney notice of what he might say or write exsept personaly presant. this was very pleasing to me. my son expressed the same and said you had gained much creadit in takeing souch a Resulution. I had heard Jessee Benton while lying wounded, make maney unjest and imprudant expressions, but I had not the most distant Idia that the Colo would have gon on as I undersood he did. if thare conduct is such as is Represented—shorley they can not have maney frends. and from the manner I under[stand] Jessee attemted to assasinate you, he sartainly has forfited all clame to that of a gentelman. and ought not to be consided as such I under stand it is your left arm that is broak—if you should git able to write without deficalty which I hope you will plese to let me heare from you. I am so ounderfully uneasey to heare the plan of the camppain again[st] the creeks, and who co[mm]ands. I can not harber the smallest hopes that you will [be ab]le. Shorley by this time the trupes are in move[men]t if the goverment will not suffer those barbarans, to masacrce at thare wanton pleasure much longer. we consider our selves in a critacal situation heare. and as the Chickasaws have not had no anser to thare offer of service thay now apear much more indepent respecting the ware. and them as well as the choctaws have doubts wheather the u s will not put up with the conduct of the creeks and give piece if asked for.[2] I conclude with my best wishes for your Speedey Recovery, while I am your most Humbel Servant

Jas. Robertson

ALS, DLC. Published in Bassett, 1:319.
  1. Felix Robertson.
  2. In the late summer and early fall of 1813, there was concern that the Chickasaws and other Indian tribes might join with the Creeks, especially when, as Robertson pointed out, the federal government initially ignored their offer to fight against the Creeks (see also Robertson to AJ, August 13).

During the summer of 1813, clashes between the Creek Indians and settlers greatly increased on the southern frontier. In July, Peter McQueen, son of a Scots trader and a Tallassee woman, led three hundred warriors in a skirmish with a detachment of the Mississippi militia at Burnt Corn Creek. On August 30, over a thousand Creek warriors under William Weatherford attacked Fort Mims, located north of Mobile on the Alabama River, killing nearly four hundred settlers.

By mid-September, as alarm spread through Mississippi Territory, southern Tennessee, and western Georgia, the federal government once again ordered into service the volunteer and detached militias of the states and territories along the southern frontier. Upon notification from Governor Blount, Jackson immediately called out the Tennessee Volunteers who had accompanied him on the Natchez expedition.

To *the Tennessee Volunteers*

Order   Head Quarters Nashville Sept. 24th 1813—
Brave Tennesseans!

Your frontier is threatened with invasion by the savage foe! Already do they advance towards your frontier with their scalping knifes unsheathed, to butcher your wives, your children, and your helpless babes. Time is not to be lost. We must hasten to the frontier, or we will find it drenched in the blood of our fellow-citizens.

I am commanded by his Excellency Gov. Blount, to call into the field, at the shortest possible day, two thousand men of the Volunteer infantry and militia of my division.[1] The undersigned therefore orders, that the whole of his volunteer Infantry, that composed the detachment under his command in the late Expedition for the defence of the lower country, rendezvous at Fayetteville, Lincoln County, on Monday the 4th of October next, well equipped for active service—And the Brigadier-Generals commanding the 4th. 5th. 6th. 7th. and 9th. brigades, composing my division will respectively furnish from their brigades two hundred men well equipped for active service who will rendezvous on the said 4th day of October, at Fayetteville aforesaid—They will be taken from the first class for duty, unless furnished by voluntary tender of service.

The present crisis will try the patriotism of my division—Your Country relies on it. Your General has the utmost confidence that the full number will appear at the day and place well equipped and ready to meet the foe.

The health of your General is restored—he will command in person.

Brigadier General Isaac Roberts is ordered to take command of the Militia. The senior Colonels John K Winn and Thomas McCrory[2]—and the two senior first Majors,[3] and the two senior second Majors[4] are ordered for Duty.

The Volunteers will be commanded by their own officers.

The Captains of their respective companies when organized, will furnish each of them a Waggon and team to transport the baggage &c of their companies the expence of which will be paid by the assistant deputy quarter master.

Andrew Jackson
Majr Gen. 2d. Division. T.

LC, DLC; Copy, T. Published in *Democratic Clarion*, September 25; *Nashville Whig*, September 28.

1. See Willie Blount to AJ, September 24.

2. McCrory (1766–1819), a Williamson County farmer and land speculator, commanded the 2nd Regiment, Tennessee militia, until January 1814.

3. Samuel Taylor of the 1st Regiment and Anthony J. Turner of the 2nd Regiment.

4. Josephus H. Conn (d. 1820) was second major in the 1st Regiment, Tennessee militia. He represented Sumner County in the General Assembly, 1819. Charles Robertson Sevier (1778–1855), nephew of John Sevier, served as second major in the 2nd Regiment, Tennessee militia. He represented Overton County in the state legislature after the war and later settled in Madison County.

To the Adams County Superior Court

[September 25, 1813]

The representation of Andrew Jackson, who was summoned as garnishee at the suit of _____ Blennerhassett against Aaron Burr, depending in said court.

Your respondent states, that while at Camp Jackson, near Washington, in the Territory aforesaid, in the month of March last as commanding officer of a detachment of Volunteers from the State of Tennessee, ordered by the President of the United States, for the protection of the lower country, and a few days before the troops started on their return to Tennessee, he was summoned as a garnishee in the suit aforesaid, that his duty imperiously required his accompanying the volunteers to Tennessee, consequently he could not appear at the time to which he was summoned, but he made a statement on oath and left with his attorney to be presented to the court,[1] and did hope that statement would have discharged him, as it was thereby shown to the court, that he owed the defendant Aaron Burr nothing.

Your respondent now show to your hands by the annexed affidavit of William Eastin, that the said Aaron Burr is indebted to him the amount of five hundred dollars and upward, and which your respondent positively states is the fact.

But least these statements should not be satisfactory to the court— your respondent is willing to answer on oath under an order of court interrogatories to be filed by the Court or the plaintiff, and this he prays may be ordered by your honors, as it will be out of the power of your respondent to appear at the ensuing term of said court, in consequence of his being now under orders to command an expedition against the Creek Indians, and will march in five or six days.[2]

Your respondent further states to your hands that it is not in contempt of the authority of the court that he does not appear but the reason before stated.

ANDREW JACKSON.

Text from Natchez *Ariel*, July 26, 1828. Original not found.
  1. See above, AJ to the Adams County Superior Court, March 25.
  2. See Blount to AJ, September 24.

ENCLOSURE: AFFIDAVIT OF WILLIAM EASTIN

I do certify, that some time about the 10th of November, 1806, I purchased a bill of exchange from Aaron Burr, drawn by him on George M. Ogden of New York, at ninety days sight, for five hundred dollars, and said bill was sent on to New York and presented to said George M. Ogden for acceptance, which he refused, and the said bill was noted for protest, as I was informed, and at the expiration of the ninety days the said bill was returned to me protested for non-payment,[1] and Aaron Burr having left this country, I made application to the indorser, Andrew Jackson, for payment, and about the 1st day of April, 1807, he, the said Andrew Jackson, paid the amount of bill with charges and interest, amounting to five hundred and nineteen dollars. Given under my hand at Nashville, this 4th day of September, 1813.

WILLIAM EASTAN.

Text from Natchez *Ariel*, July 26, 1828. Original not found.
  1. See above, John Wilkes to AJ, January 29, 1807.

To John Coffee

for yourself   Hermitage Sept. 29th. 1813
Dr Colo.

On yesterday when I wrote you[1] I was so much interrupted, and pestered with company that I fear my letter was not verry intelligable hurried on all sides with starting my runners to endeavour out of the mass of contradictory rumors & information through so many contradictory channels, to acquire some correct information—added to the pain of my arm—all combined to confuse my ideas. In the midst of my letter the express arived with [George Strother] Gains letter covering one from Judge Tollman[2]—the former I had copied & enclosed to you—the latter contained the intelligence that the Creeks were collecting all their force and in conjunction with the Spaniards, intended to make an attack on Mobile, and great fears was entertained that, that post would be carried before relief could be afforded; you are in possession of the other rumor from the choctaw interpreter—that they creeks are moving with their families to cross the Mississippi at the chikasaw Bluffs—other rumors that they creeks are collecting all their force to attack Huntsville and the frontier of Tennessee[3]—These various rumours, are in my oppinion created by the British agents to amuse & distract us and draw our attention from their true point of attack—I am inclined to believe that they will never abandon their nation untill they are severely Drubed—and that they will concentrate their whole force at some point where they can be best supported by their allies the British and Spaniards—and it is highly probable that there whole force may be bent against Mobile—Correct information is all important before we make a movement with our whole force, you will therefore—on your march to Fort St. Stephens (to which point on the most mature reflection it is best for you with all the force that meets you at Huntsville you had better expeditiously proceed) if you should collect information that the creeks are about to make a movement with their families—you will take an advantageous situation at a point best calculated to intercept th[em] and advise me thereof by express, and by forced marches I will form a Junction with you with my Infantry leaving a sufficient escort to bring up the supplies—Should you find that they are not moving from the Nation with their families, but are contemplating an attack in conjunction with the Spaniards on Mobile—you will immediately notify me by express, and give me the information whether the force in that quarter is sufficient to check them with yours united, and whether from that point an attack upon the Nation would not be as favourable to success as from Dittos landing[4]—I shall exert all my Industry to save Mobile—leaving Genl Cockes Division to cooperate with the Georgians and enter the Nation by the way of coosa river—Keep me well advised from every point the creeks must be scurged—and if the other troops from east Tennessee moves with expedition and I can get supplies we can invelope them—they creeks cannot escape—If I enter the creek country down the coosa, I shall order you to Join me at some point where you can do it in safety

Should the 3rd. Regt. of U. S. Infantry be ordered to cooperate with me—and I am advised thereof, I shall order a Junction at some point in the heart of the Nation—for all this information I shall rely on you for—and act accordingly—I rode home from 4 oclock against dark last evening—from which I find I will be able to move on Sunday next without inconvenience say to your regt. I shall certainly be at Fayettville on the evening of the 6th. of october—prepared to enter the creek country as early as I can get supplies, and correct information where I can make the Blow—I have ordered Colo. [Robert] Hays to proceed direct to Huntsville to muster your mounted rifflemen[5]—whilst this is doing, you can have as many days provision as will carry you to St. Stephens with such supplies as you can get in the nation—May the gods protect you adieu—

Andrew Jackson

ALS, NjP. Published in *Cincinnati Commercial Gazette*, January 13, 1883.
1. See AJ to Coffee, September 28.
2. Gaines, the factor for the Choctaw nation, was headquartered at Fort St. Stephens, Miss. Terr., 1806–19. An extract of Gaines's letter to Willie Blount, September 17, is in DLC. Toulmin's letter has not been found.
3. On the latter rumor, see John Read to AJ, August 28.
4. Located ten miles south of Huntsville, Ala. (then Miss. Terr.), on the north bank of the Tennessee River.
5. On September 26 Hays had been appointed assistant inspector general.

From Willie Blount

In public service   Nashville Octr. 4th. 1813
Sir,

You will herewith receive a letter to Capt. [William] McClellan of the U. S. Army commanding at Fort Hampton requesting the loan of arms for the use of your detachment[1]—also my letter of this date to the Governor of Georgia, or the officers commanding the Troops in service from that State, destined to act against the hostile Creek Indians[2]—you will please transmit those letters according to address, keeping yourself a copy of each, & also cause a copy of the latter to be forwarded to Major Genl. Cocke, and also send to the Genl. a copy of this; & say to him, that he will please consider it as addressed to him for his government—This will save much time as I may not know where to address him—Upon your arrival at rendezvous you will without delay organize your detachment, and when ready march against the hostile Creeks, and act in conjunction with the forces relied upon for the expedition; or separately as

your knowledge of circumstances may teach the propriety of, first making the necessary arrangements for concert with Major Genl. Cocke, &
Col. [Return Jonathan] Meigs,[3] and as far as practicable with the detachment from Georgia, & conforming as nearly as will be proper with the
substance of my letter of this date above mentioned to the Governor of
Georgia or the commanding officers of the Troops in service from that
State—with best wishes for your welfare & success I am very respectfully, your Obt. Servant

Willie Blount

ALS, LC, and Copy, DLC; ALS copy, DNA-RG 107.
  1. McClellan (d. 1829), a native of Tennessee, served with the U.S. Army from 1808 to
1815. Blount's letter to McClellan, which Jackson forwarded, has not been found. Mc-
Clellan did, however, furnish Jackson the arms he had available (see McClellan to AJ, October 9).
  2. See Blount to David B. Mitchell, October 4, DLC. In his letter, Blount informed
Mitchell that Jackson and Cocke "are now in service of the Government, and that they,
each, command a detachment of two thousand five hundred men, ordered into service to act
seperately against the hostile Creek Indians, or in concert with the Troops ordered from the
State of Georgia by Government for the same purpose, together with such regular Troops as
may be ordered to co-operate with them, as a knowledge of circumstances may teach the
propriety of—"
  3. Meigs was agent to the Cherokees with headquarters at Hiwassee Garrison.

From John Strother

At Colo. Lowrys Octr. 5th. 1813—

Dear General
    I have been here three days in which time two runners arrived from
Wills town about 25 mile from Turkey town[1]—the best information of
the situation of the enemy is—that they are in force at three points the
lowest of which is at the hickory ground, where they built a fort[2]—the
last information States that the party destined to meet our Tennesseians
were about 3000—that they had got tired of waiting, and had moved up
their country with an intention of attacking the friendly Towns at Coweta—From the best information that our friends at Turkey town can get,
& on which, they appear to rely with confidence is, that the greatest force
of the Enemy is at the hickory ground—they state about four Thousand—the hickory ground is 150 mi. from Turkey town—a force is left
near it to watch the movement of our Tennesseians I think there is but
little doubt, but we will be gratified (if a gratification it may be) in meeting them, & I am induced to believe, in considerable force—
    I set out in the morning for Dick Browns, a half breed who is raising a
party to meet us at Turkey town[3]—I shall cross the Tennessee at what is
called the creek path or creek crossing—Brown lives about 30 or 40. mi.
from Turkey town, & about 25 or 30 mi. from Ditto's landing—This
Brown is a man that has long tryed to get a road cut from Ditto's landing

near Turkey town to Georgia, but could not obtain the consent of the
Creeks—from this circumstance—& his being friendly—I thought it advisable to see him & endeavour to get him & his party as pilotes from
Ditto's landing to the Turkey Town—Colo. Lowry advises me to make
this attempt & has wrote to Brown a Very friendly & pressing Letter on
the subject—I shall be at Browns on Thursday & as soon as arrangements can be made with him—will set out to meet you at Ditto's landing
or at such other place as you may be—

Colo. Lowry will set out on this day week his party rendezvous's at the
Turkey town—he states to me that he will want some arms—particularly
ammunition & provisions—of these two last articles he will barely have
a supply to take him to his place of rendezvous—on this subject I advised
him to write to Colo. Meigs, also informing him of his time of Departure,
& place of rendezvous—I have taken the liberty of writing to the Colo.
on the same subject, tho touched it with all the politeness, I was filled
with at the moment.

Colo. Lowry states that there is some company of our men ranging in
the mountains—who has given him notice to keep his young men at
home for fear they might fall in with them, & not be able to distinguish
them from Enemies—he also states—(& with much propriety) that in as
much as the Cherokees are going to war with us against the Creeks—that
the young men left, & the situation of the two settlements with the movement of the army—are a better security to our frontiers, than a thousand
rangers—that it is not possible for the hostile creeks to get across Tennessee river in force above Madison Cty. without being discovered by his
people—in which event the white's should have immediate information,
& that he knew it was his interest to keep a good lookout for the security
of his own women & children: then shrewdly remarked—that if the Citizens of Elk & Sequachee, wished to range for Creek Indians—let them
go on to the frontiers of his nation, there they might be found; but no
nearer—I wish a stop was put to these mountain raingers, I fear if continued that they may produce more serious evils, than it is possible to
effect good—In order that no misunderstanding could take place of mis-
taking our friends for our enemies—those that will be with, either on
Ditto's landing, or at some other point according to circumstances will
either have white plumes in their hair, or a deers tail. it will be well for
those men ordered on the South side of the river, if any before I get there,
to be notified of this mark of distinction—I shall wear one myself—

With a hope of meeting you soon as perfectly restored to health as the
nature of things will admit—I conclude with sentiments of Due respect
Yr. Mo. obt. Hble. Servant—

John Strother

Colo. wishes that 3 or 400 Deers tails could be procured for his men—As
they will be hard to get here—

ALS and LC, DLC.
1. Will's Town, located on Big Will's Creek in present-day DeKalb County, Ala., and Turkey Town, on the Coosa River in Cherokee County, were Cherokee villages.
2. The Hickory Ground was a major gathering place for hostile Creeks at the junction of the Coosa and Tallapoosa rivers, later the site of Fort Jackson.
3. Richard Brown, a Cherokee chief, furnished spies and guides in the war against the Creeks.

To John Coffee

Camp Blount.[1] 7th. Octr. 1813 9 Oclk at night

Sir

I arrived at this place, this evening, about 4 OClk, in good health & beter spirits. It is surely high gratification to learn that the Creeks are so attentive to my situation, as to save me the pain of traveling. I must not be outdone in politeness, & will therefore endeavour to meet them on the middle ground.

I lament that on my arrival here, I did not find either so many men as I had expected, or them so well equipped. This evil however I shall endeavour to remedy as speedily as practicable, and in a few days I hope to realise my wishes.

I cannot believe that the Creeks have, at this time, any serious intention of an attack upon our frontiers; & yet I would not have you entirely disregard the information you have received. But whether they have such an intention or not, it seems to me that a rapid movement, into their own country, will be the most effectual means of discomfiting their measures. So soon as I can organise a force sufficient for the undertaking, & procure the necessary supplies, I shall certainly commence it. Your Co-operation will then be indispensably necessary; & for that reason I wish you to occupy some eligible position in the quarter where you now are, until you receive further orders from me. In the meantime I wish you to receive, & to treat with great kindness all such spies from the Creek nation as may offer you any communication. Let them not be discharged until my arrival. We must have the truth; & whilst *that* shall be duly rewarded, false information must be severely punished.

I shall move from this place to Ditto's landing, but *when*, I really have it not in my power to inform you. I agree with you however entirely that the sooner I can be there the better.

By advises this moment received from Capt Strother (dated Lowry's 5th. Octr)[2] it appears that the enemy are in force at three points—the lower of which is at the Hickory ground, where they have erected a fort; & that *that* portion of them destined against us amount to about 3000. The whole force at Hickory ground is stated to be 4000, which is their principal reliance. Having become tired of waiting our approach, it is said they have commenced moving up their country with an intention of attacking the Friendly towns, at Coweta.

In order to make a distinction between our friends & our enemies it is arranged by Capt Strother with the Cherokees, that our friends shall wear white plumes in their hair, or Deer's tails.

Altho the letter from Strother would seem to confirm the reports which you have received, yet it has not altered my opinion as the course to be pursued.

Be good enough to send to me here, all such men as may apply to you to be received. I should prefer them as Infantry; but in some capacity or other I must have them. At any event let them come & see me.

You will appoint Majr. [Basil] Shaw[3] adjutant of the mounted Riflemen

Andrew Jackson
Major Genl

LS and Copy, DLC. Published in Bassett, 1:328–29.

1. Near Fayetteville, about eighty miles south of Nashville and thirty miles north of Huntsville.

2. See above.

3. Shaw, an early settler of Smith County, was Coffee's first adjutant on the Natchez expedition. He had returned home by March 1814.

To Rachel Jackson

Camp Blount Octobr 11th. 1813 6 oclock A. M—

My Dear

I recd your kind an affectionate letter of the 8th. instant, last night by Jame[1]—I write in haste and in the Bustle of a hasty movement, owing to an express recd. from Colo Coffee this morning one oclock[2]—I refer you to Colo Hays for the news of the camp—my health is good and my arm mending fast, the little place on my shoulder gives me more pain than my arm—both I hope will soon be well—

I enclose a note to Mr Nollyboy[3]—I have directed Colo. Hays & Mr John Hutchings, to dismiss him, allowing him to be present at the gathering of the corn, and the Division, thereof and of the cotton—I wish Fields employed, untill I return and the hands put under him and his sole controle, and kept constantly employed at gathering the crop untill it is in— Mr Nollyboy owes me three hundred & fifty pounds of good merchantable ginned cotton—to be paid out of his present crop, should he not have that amount when gathered then as much of his corn must be detained as will be sufficient at the markett price to make up the deficiency—you shall not be pestered with him any more—Tell our little Andrew that I will be soon at home and bring him some pretty—I send him by Colo. Hays a pretty that I have been presented with, which you must say to him he must not let fall or will break—

with my best prayers for your health believe me affectionately yours

Andrew Jackson

ALS, MH-H.
1. Letter not found. Jame was a Hermitage slave.
2. See John Coffee to AJ, October 6.
3. Nollyboy was overseer at the Hermitage for about a year and a half. Note not found.

To Rachel Jackson

Camp Coffee[1] October 13th. 1813

My Dear
I reached this Camp on yesterday—Colo. Hays no doubt advised you of my sudden departure from Camp Blount, we marched thirty miles in Eight hours & 20 minutes—and I am happy to say; that the alarm was unfounded and I do believe that what is called the friendly creeks are spies—I am in good health & my arm mending fast—I shall write you fully before I leave this, which will be some days—with sincere affection I am yrs

Andrew Jackson

Tell my sweet little Andrew that papa will soon be back—and say to all our friends that we are all well here—   A. J—

ALS, MH-H.
1. Near Huntsville.

To Rachel Jackson

Head quarters Camp Coffee Octobr 18th. 1813

My Love
By Mr [John] Nichols[1] returning to Nashville, this will be convayed; By Doctor [Bennett P.] Sanders[2] I learn & Colo. Hays letter[3] that you enjoy health with the young ladies and our dear little Andrew—Colo. Hays says to me he delivered him the pipe—and he was pleased with it— I hope Mr Nolly has removed and you will no longer be pestered with his neglect or impertinence—I enjoy Health and my arm still mending—I write you this in the Hurry of business preparing to move forward to-morrow at six oclock in the morning—my spies are just in, and all the horrid news of their advancing in great force are untrue—and I must advance to find them—all our friends here are well—Colo. Coffee left me with 700 men four days ago on command[4] I expect him tomorrow, and by him some news of the movement of the Creeks When I Halt at the next deposit for provisions I shall write you—I am sufficiently strong I think to penetrate—to pensacola—with fervent prays for your health our little Andrew and all friends believe me to be yr affectionate Husband

Andrew Jackson

ALS, MH-H.
1. Nichols (d. 1842) was a Nashville merchant.
2. Sanders (d. 1832), a physician, living at this time in Tennessee, later settled in Jefferson County, Miss.
3. Not found.
4. Jackson had ordered Coffee on reconnaissance to the headwaters of the Black Warrior River (AJ to Coffee, October 9).

From John Coffee

Indian lands 22nd. Oct. 1813 12 OClock

Genl. Jackson,

Agreably to your orders,[1] I proceeded, to cross the River at the upper end of the shoals, all my efforts failed to procure a pilot. I took with me one of [John] Meltons sons,[2] who said he knew not the road. he shewd me a path that had been reputed the Black Warriers path—I proceeded on it in its whole course about 10 degrees East of South, in the early part of the third days march I met [James] Russell[3] who said I was on the right way—at the distance of 80 miles, I crossed a river about 60 yards wide runing to the west, where there is a small deserted Indian Village, which Russell said was the Black Warriers town, being convinced it was not, I proceeded over the River, and at about two miles found a cross path leading nearly west, but not in late use, I turned on that path west, and at 13 miles distance come to a small Indian village. corn in the fields but no person to be found got about 100. bushels corn, burnt the houses, and proceeded eight miles further, come to the main Black Warrirs town[4] abandoned by the Inhabitants found some corn in the fields and some old corn in cribbs, fresh signs of One or two Indians, and no other signs—got in the whole about 300. bushels corn, burnt their town or counsel house and about 50 other buildings this town is supposed to be the principal one of the tribe and the lowest down the river. (I am certain its not the nearest to the Shoals) and seeing that the Indians had fled I deemed it not adviseable to go further in search of villages where no other spoils can be had than such as we have found, and having no pilot or even any one that ever had been in the country with me am uninformed if any more are in this quarter, having been two days out of rations the most of the men living on parched corn, I have determined to meet your army, the nearest possible—am now on a path that Russel went out and he says about 30 miles from Dick Browns. have sent on to you the bearer, and must beg that you will order provisions put in a State of readiness for my men when we come up with you[5]—have not heard of you since I left—suppose you will be in advance of Browns, if so will follow on, otherwise will meet you—

very respectfully your obt. Sevt.

Jno. Coffee C[ommander of] C[avalry]

LS and LC, DLC. Published in Bassett, 1:334–35.

1. See AJ to Coffee, October 9.

2. Melton (d. 1816), an Irishman and allegedly a pirate on the river, was married to a Cherokee (Anne Newport Royall, *Letters from Alabama, 1817–1822*. Reprint edition, University, Ala., 1969, pp. 134–38). It has not been determined which of his sons accompanied Coffee.

3. Some weeks earlier Jackson had sent Russell, not further identified, to scout Creek encampments (see AJ to Russell, October 9).

4. Located on the Black Warrior River, and possibly the site of present-day Tuscaloosa, Ala.

5. Coffee rejoined Jackson's army on October 24.

From Pathkiller

Turky Town October 22sd. 1813

Friend and Brother:

I have now to communicate to you the substance of a Talk I had yesterday with two of the hostile Creeks who were sent as messengers from the alabama warrior,[1] who says he had raised a large army with the seminolies to attack the Coweatahs,[2] that they were forced to do so by the Coweatahs, by Killing their people and stealing their horses and that they were Determined to take satisfaction for the Injury his people had received.

he informs me also that he had ordered out another army to be raised to take a revenge for the lives of his people who had been killed—some where not far from Elk river, and the weokee warrior[3] were ordered to head them—they messengers said that it was three nights ago &c. since this last army had crossed the coosee river and the would take the musle shoal path—that they crossed the river below the Ten Islands,[4] and on the return of the army, they Intended to attack old Chenibee[5] and I am advised to be causious how I acted.

they say they will act candid and give me this information to show they were sincere, and peaceable policy has been persued with them, as my situation required me to do so.

about fifteen or sixteen of my people have arrived to Join your army. more will arive today untill the all come, and some others of my people will join General [James] whites army,[6] who I understand arrived at the point of look out mountain (at Ross's)[7] five nights ago—and I expect he is on his way—

I have spys. out constantly, and send out two for Twenty four hours Tour, and the day before yesterday our spies returned and they only Discovered eleven fires about fifteen miles from this place. my son[8] was one of the spys. and from this account, I concluded they were not warring because women seen about the fires—I have sent two other spys out this morning, and they are Directed to view their camps again

I am your friend & Brother

[his]
Path **X** Killer
[mark]

PS; I Should be very Glad to hear from you the probable time I might Expect you and army here. am your friend   Path Killer.

Ch. Hicks[9]

LS and LC, DLC. Pathkiller (d. 1827) was principal chief of the Cherokee nation, 1811–27. From Turkey Town, Ala., he recruited and organized Cherokee warriors to serve under Jackson.

1. Probably Peter McQueen.
2. The Coweta tribe, friendly lower Creeks, sent warriors to serve with John Floyd's Georgia militia.
3. Probably Tustunnuggeeoochee.
4. On the Coosa River, fifty miles south of Fort Deposit; the site of Fort Strother, erected by Jackson just before the Battle of Talladega.
5. Chennabee was a chief of the friendly Creeks at Natchee Creek, near present-day Talladega, Ala. During the Creek War, he recruited warriors and provided information to the U.S. forces.
6. White was brigadier general in command of an advance detachment of 1,000 from Cocke's East Tennessee division.
7. Ross's Landing on the Tennessee River.
8. Not identified.
9. Hicks (d. 1827) was also a chief of the Cherokee Nation, more influential in the tribe than Pathkiller after the Creek War.

To Pathkiller

Camp on Thompson's Creek 23d Oct. 1813

Brother

I thank you for the information you have sent me[1] & will always be obli[ged] to you, for any information [t]hat may be of use to m[e.]

I approve your policy of sending your spies to examine the fires again, which they saw the other day. If they make any important discoveries, communicate them to me without delay. And let me recommend to you, constantly to keep out, as spies, some of your men, in whom you can most confide.

I shall leave this encampment tomorrow; & shall probably not pass by the Turkey-town, but take the nearest rout to the Ten-Islands. It will give me great pleasure, if I can fall in with that party of the hostile Creeks who were sent against our frontiers. I think it will be the last of their adventures.

It is time that *all* our enemies should feel the force of that power, which has indulged them so long, & which they have, so long, treated with insult

Respectfully

Andrew Jackson
Major general

Copies, CSmH, ICHi.
1. See above, Pathkiller to AJ, October 22.

To Thomas Flournoy

Camp Deposit[1] 24th. Oct. 1813

After having encountered every difficulty that can possibly arise from the want of Supplies, & from ruggedness of mountains, I have at length reached this place. Here I established a Depot for the reception of such supplies as may be sent me, either up or down the river; & shall leave a sufficient number of men to guard it.

Tomorrow I shall recommence my march by the nearest rout to the "Ten Islands" I understand the hostile Creeks are assembling in considerable numbers in the neighborhood of that place. It is probable I shall get in sight of them in a few days; & after having dispersed them, I shall move with as little delay as practicable, to the junction of the Coosa & Tallapoosa, at that point it is my present purpose, to establish a garrison & remain some time—

What I dread (when I shall arrive there) infinitely more than the fact of the enemy, is the want of supplies.[2] Can you, by any exertion, procure me supplies of bread stuff & have it forwarded up the river? No service you could render me would be so important, nor impose upon me so lasting and obligation. I shall calculate upon your doing everything in this respect, that possibly can be done.

The E. T. troops have not yet joined me; but I expect a junction to be formed with me in a few days by General White who commands the advance Division

I shall be happy at all times to hear from you

I have the honor &c

Andrew Jackson

LC, DLC. Flournoy (1775–1857), a lawyer of Augusta, Ga., who had held his commission as brigadier general since June 1812, succeeded James Wilkinson as commander of the 7th Military District, headquartered at New Orleans. Upon Flournoy's resignation in the spring of 1814, Jackson succeeded to the 7th District command.
1. Located on the south bank of the Tennessee River at the mouth of Thompson's Creek, in present-day Marshall County.
2. On the supply question, see for example AJ to William B. Lewis, to Willie Blount, and to Neil B. Rose, October 24.

To Willie Blount

Camp Wills 28th. Octr. 1813

Sir

Inclosed I send you a letter from the Govr. of Georgia, which was this evening handed me, by the express I forwarded to him from Huntsville.[1]

We are now within twenty miles of the "Ten Islands" & it is said, within sixteen of the enemy. Any force they may have so near us, I cannot believe to be very great; The number however is stated to be about a thousand.

We shall recommence our march in the morning—having been detained here today, for the purpose of procuring from the neighbouring Indians, some small supplies of corn—This acquisition, while it enables us to subsist for the present encourages our hopes for the future—

Indeed Sir we have been very wretchedly supplied. Scarcely two rations in succession have been regularly drawn. Yet we are not despondent, whilst we can procure an ear of corn a piece, or anything that will serve as a substitute for it we shall continue our exertions to accomplish the objects for which we were sent out—

The cheefullness with which my men submit to privations, & are ready to encounter danger, does honor to the government whose rights they are defending.

Every measure within my power, for procuring the requisite supplies, I have taken, & am continuing to take. East, West, North, & South have been applied to, with the most pressing solicitation. The Governor of Georgia in a letter, which my express delivered this evening informs me that a sufficiency can be had in his state, both for the men under my command & those under Genl. Cocke; but he does not signify that he is about to take any measures for the purpose of procuring them.

The Contractor (Mr. [Isaac] Brownlow)[2] who supplied the place of the Reads,[3] has spared no exertion, to fulfill his contract; but the inconveniences under which he labors, will I am fearful, render his efforts unavailing. Colo. [Leroy] Pope[4] of Huntsville is better prepared than any person of my acquaintance, for such an undertaking; & I yesterday learnt that he was willing to engage in it. I accordingly wrote to him[5] as the best precautionary measure in my power, making him the offer, on the condition that he would indemnify Brownlow, for the trouble he had been at, & recommending that he should be taken in as a partner If he accepts this offer, as no doubt he will, my apprehensions will be greatly diminished

Genl. White has not yet united with me, but I expect to see him in a few days. He is yet in the Cherokee nation, but I can not tell precisely where.

Old Chenubbee is now with me—having brought in as prisoners two of the hostile Creeks

I yesterday sent out Lieut. Col. [Robert Henry] Dyer[6] with two hundred of the Cavalry to attack a Town called, Littefutchee[7] about 20 miles distant. This morning about 4 O.Clock they returned bringing with them about thirty prisoners, men, women, & children—The Village they burnt. What is very agreeable they state they found in the fields near the Village, a considerable quantity of corn & in the Country round-about many beeves; but they brought in none.

LC, DLC. Copy extract, DNA-RG 107.
1. See David Brydie Mitchell to AJ, October 19; and AJ to Mitchell, October 10.
2. Brownlow (c1783–1831) was a resident of Lauderdale County, Ala.
3. Read, Mitchell & Company, headed by John Read, former clerk in the land office in Nashville who had settled in Huntsville in 1810 as a merchant. On the matter of furnishing supplies, see Read, Mitchell & Company to AJ, October 18.
4. Pope (1765–1844), one of the founders of Huntsville, was a justice of the earliest Madison County court and later a banker.
5. See AJ to Pope, October 28.
6. Dyer (c1774–1826), a Rutherford County farmer, was a colonel in Coffee's cavalry during the Natchez expedition and Creek War. He served in the state senate, 1815–17, and later lived in Madison and Dyer counties.
7. Littafuchee or Litafatci, south of Fort Deposit on Big Canoe Creek.

To Leroy Pope

[October 31, 1813]

Sir

Amonghst the prisoners sent to your charge 28 in number, I find their is a choctaw woman who many years ago was made a prisoner and a slave purchased by Cotala[1] whose village we have destroyed, and given to his negro fellow for a wife her & her three children are considered slaves, they will be held by us as such untill I can discover her family, in the choctaws and restored to them—This wench & her children will not be considered as prisoners for exchange or ransom

we have got a good supply of Beef, and hope you will furnish us with regular supplies of meal & meat hereafter—The irregularity of supplies has retarded my progress verry much, and I am anxious to reach the center of the creek country, and give them a final blow, and then strike at the root of the disseas pensacola—I am verry respectfully yr mo ob serv

Andrew Jackson

P S. Make my compliments acceptable to your lady & Miss Maria[2]— I think shortly I shall be able to send Miss Maria the princesses necklace
A.J

ALS copy, DLC. Published in Bassett, 1:339. Date from endorsement.
1. Bob Cotalla (Catawla) was a Creek chief. On October 31, he was captured by a raiding party (see AJ to Willie Blount and to Leroy Pope, November 1).
2. Judith Sale Pope (1770–1827) married Leroy Pope in Virginia before their removal to Mississippi Territory. Their daughter Maria (d. 1847) married Thomas G. Percy, a Madison County, Ala., planter.

To Rachel Jackson

Head quarters 10 Islands
Cosa river Novbr. 4th. 1813

My Dear

In the hurry of the moment I have but a moment to write you—I detached Genl John Coffee with part of his Brigade of Cavalry and mounted men to destroy the Creek Town Talus,hatchey,[1] he has executed this order in elegant stile leaving dead on the field one hundred & seventy six, and taking 80, prisoners, forty prisoners was left on the ground many of them wounded, others to take care of them—since writing the above Genl Coffee reports 180, found dead, and there is no doubt but 200 was killed[2]—I have here forty two added to the thirty two heretofore captured & sent on to Huntsville, in all 74—I have been and is still badly supplied with provisions, as soon as I can get a supply will proceed on to the heart of the creek nation—Mr Alexander and Jack Donelson[3] were both in the action are safe & behaved like what I could wish & expected, all friends safe, Capt Hammond had 5 of his men wounded—all behaved bravely and as I could wish—I send on a little Indian boy[4] for Andrew to Huntsville—with a request to Colo. Pope to take care of him untill he is sent on—all his family is destroyed—he is about the age of *Theodore*[5]—In haste your affectionate Husband

Andrew Jackson

ALS, MH-H.

1. See AJ to John Coffee, November 2.
2. Coffee's losses were five killed and forty-one wounded. The victory at Tallushatchee was the first major blow to the hostile Creeks in upper Mississippi Territory. For details of the battle, see Coffee to AJ, November 4.
3. John ("Jack") Donelson (1787–1840), brother of Alexander, was a lieutenant in Coffee's cavalry brigade and commanded a company of mounted infantry at the Battle of New Orleans. In 1823 he married Edward Butler's daughter, Eliza, and settled near Florence, Ala.
4. Lyncoya (c1813–28), a Creek infant orphaned at the Battle of Tallushatchee, reached the Hermitage in May 1814. He remained in the Jackson household until his death.
5. Theodore (c1813–14) was probably another Indian child at the Hermitage. Jackson and Rachel mentioned his death in their letters of March 4 and 21, 1814 (DLC).

From Leroy Pope

Huntsville Novr. 4th. 1813

Sir

I have recd. your letter dated at Camp Bradley 1st. inst pr. Lt. [Walker] Gannaway,[1] together with five prisoners. In consequence of a horrid massacre which took place night before last within 13 miles of this place[2] I have determined to send the whole of the prisoners this day under a strong guard to Nashville;[3] the reasons which have induced me to do this is, we have no place that I can secure the prisoners in our Jail is entirely insufficient. And another strong motive was, the relatives of the unfortunate victims are determined to come to this place & massacre the prisoners, & I was informed last night by two respectable persons of this Town that they were present when the persons massacred were buried & that upwards of twenty persons offered to assist the son of the man that was kill'd in taking the prisoners & murdering of them. And I sincerely wish I may be able to get them off before the threats are put into execution. Another reason has had great weight with me to send them from here is the consternation & alarm which the county is thrown into in consequence of the murder. A great portion of the Citizens of the County as well as the Town will be immediately called on to guard the frontiers this will leave us a very weak guard at this place

I hope Sir that this proceedure will meet with your approbation—The number of persons massacred were two men, two women, & one child

I am Sir &c

Leroy Pope

LC, DLC.
1. See AJ to Pope, November 1. Gannaway was first lieutenant in a cavalry company from Rutherford County.
2. On November 1 a group of Indians killed a family of five settlers on Limestone Creek west of Huntsville (see Thomas Austin to AJ, November 3).
3. Thirty-five prisoners, among them "an intelligent warrior, by the name of Bob" (probably Bob Cotalla), arrived in Nashville on November 9 (*Democratic Clarion*, November 16).

From John Lowry to AJ and John Strother

7th. November *1813* Turkey town

Dear frinds and Brothers—

I address you with these few lines to inform you I am well and all of my Men at presant and it is my eardant wosh these lines may find you and yours in the same. we came to this place on the 3d. of this Inst. and on the 4th. I started with my small company and went to the Creek villeges whare you have distroyed in order to do something but you was two fast for me—I found them compleatly distroyed when I got there. which I think was very well done for my company was small and of corse I should lost a grate many of my Men. but we got 20 Women and children and brought them to this place, but the grater parte of them is badly wounded. we have taken care of them drest there wounds, and gave them something to eate, and my pepeal woshes to keept them by your leave pervided you dont want them your self. if you want them we will give them oup— and also we found 3 horses and 2 sadd[l]es which we think belongs to your detachment, brown Gillden and 1 Black Gilden 1 rown mair with a balld face—1 of the saddles is remarkably good you can get them by applying to me—if there are yours, and also the prisinors if you want them. Sir, I wosh you to give me an anstoer as quick as posable, concerning those prisoners and horses and also I wosh you to write me how many Cherokees you have with you.[1] and whether you wosh me to come on to you or not. I will thank you for you advice—we have but a small company only about 400 but we shall be reinforstd. I think in a few days—I am Sir without deseption Yours—

Jno. Lowry

ALS and LC, DLC.
  1. For Jackson's response, see below.

To John Lowry

Camp near the ten Islands Novr. 7th 1813

Sir
    Yr. letter of the 7th dated at Turkey Town has this moment been handed me[1]
    The prisoners you found at Tallushatchee belong to the government of the U.S. & I have no power to let you retain them, until I learn the will of the President. In the meantime I shall direct them to be placed under the care of some of General White's surgeons: & after they are sufficiently recovered to be by him sent on to Huntsville, or some other place that shall be appointed, for safe keeping
    The horses & Saddles you found, are no doubt the property of some of the detachment who were ordered to Tallushatchee. We shall expect them to be restored to their owners, on your arrival here
    I am happy to learn that you have a force of 400 Cherokees, under your command. I wish you to bring them on as speedily as you can.[2]
    There are not more than twenty Cherokees with me.
    I am respectfully yours

Andw. Jackson

LC, DLC. Published in Bassett, 1:342.
  1. See above.
  2. By the time Lowry received Jackson's letter, John Cocke had ordered him to join the East Tennessee Volunteers (see Lowry to AJ, November 7).

From James White

Camp Turkey Town Nov. 7th. 1813

My dear Genl.
    I was on my march to meet you at the Ten Islands when I recd. a

positive order from Majr. Genl. Cocke to alter my rout & form a junction with him near the mouth of Chatuga, which I have done.[1] And am sorry so many disappointments have taken place, that our junction has not sooner been formed. I presume Genl. Cocke will in future confer with you he having taken the command

I am dear Genl &c

James White

LC, DLC. Published in Bassett, 1:342.
    1. Also on November 7, Jackson urged White to join him with supplies.

From Thomas Flournoy

Mount Vernon[1] 9th. Nov. 1813—

Sir,

I have the honor to acknowledge the receipt of yours of the 24th. last month, which came to my hands last night[2]—Before this, I presume, you must be at the junction of the Coosa & Tallapoosa.

I wish it were possible to Send you a supply of provisions immediately—but the distance up to that place, & the danger of sending up boats is so great, & withall, the force under my command in this quarter of the district is so small, that it is impossible for me to give you that timely support, which my wishes, & your necessity calls for.

I shall without delay adopt a plan which may have the effect of giving you relief, & aiding in crippling the enemy—

Genl. Claiborne, who commands the united States Volunteers on this frontier, will immediately take a position on the Alabama, at *Weatherford's* about 100 miles below the junction of the Coosa & Tallapoosa, to which place I shall immediately forward provisions—This is the highest place, I think he can penetrate to, with safety.

As your men are mounted, it will be much more practicable to make a forced march to that place, than it would be to send up to you, even if I were in sufficient force to venture it—

I deem it unfortunate that I can not cooperate more effectively with you, but the difficulties I have had to encounter, & the necessity, I am under of returning to Orleans, will prevent the high gratification I should feel in joining you in person, & contributing by every means in my power to your comfort & relief—

I pray you to corrispond more immediately with Genl. Claiborne, & with Lt. Colo. Russell 3rd Regt. Infty, who will also proceed with his Regiment, to the Alabama—but as he is under orders from the war department to corrispond with, & place himself under the command of the Georgia forces, I consider him independant of my controul—

I regret that you have not before now given me notice of your movements, & that you have not *now* mentioned your numbers—But Colo.

McKee (who is at Mobile with a number of Choctaw Indians, who will take the field against the Creeks, so soon as they can get ammunition) informs me that you are 5000 strong—

This force will enable you to put an end to the Creek War in a short time.

Wishing you the full possession, and enjoyment of that fame, and reputation, which your Conquest is calculated to inspire, I have the honor to be, yr. Brother Soldier

Tho. Flournoy

(Be pleased to write me frequently)

ALS and LC, DLC; ALS copy, Ms-Ar. Published in Bassett, 1:343–44.
1. Mount Vernon Cantonment, headquarters of General Ferdinand Leigh Claiborne during the Creek War, was located thirty miles north of Mobile.
2. See above, AJ to Flournoy, October 24.

To Rachel Jackson

Head quarters Fort Strother
10 Islands Novbr. 12th. 1813

My Dear

On last night I returned, from an excursion against the chosen warriors of the creeks from Ten Towns, who I was informed by express from Tulladego or Lessleys fort, had there collected first to destroy the friendly creeks forted there and next to give me battle[1]—This express reached me at 5 oclock on the evening of the 7th. at 12 oclock at night I marched with 2000 men, and on the night of the 8th. lay within 6 miles of the enemy—on the morning of the 9th. I attacked them at 8 oclock, the victory was compleat two hundred and ninty nine of their chosen warriors lay dead on the field, and as many more may be safly calculated to have been killed not found and will die of their wounds—had we had provissions, this stroke by following it up would have put and end to the war— Genl White had promised to Join me on the 7th at the 10 Islands,[2] not reaching me agreable to promise at 5 oclock I Started an express to him ordering him by a force march to reach my encampment, protect my sick, and those wounded on the 3rd in the battle of Taleshatchey, and leaving instructions for him to leave part of his army to aid in finishing the fort at this place and to follow me with my baggage to Tulladego[3]—on the night of the Eight when in 6 mile of the enemy and late in the night I recd. his answer dated on the 7th.[4] seven mile in the rear of where he was when he wrote me that on the 7th. he would Join me—you can easily Judge of my feelings, within 6 mile of the main force of the creeks in front, and my sick wounded and baggage twenty five miles in the rear, almost unprotected, and which by the retrograde of Genl White, might fall a sacrafice to the enemy—Still I was compelled to risque my baggage & all to whip the enemy in front I have no doubt, but this order by Genl Cocke to Genl White, was intended to cripple me, and defeat my intended opperations[5]—to shield himself from that censure that will fall upon him for his delay—there was no alternative left me—after whipping they creeks at Tulladego, but to burry our dead and return to this place with my wounded. we were out of provisions, and half starved for many days— and to highten my mortification when we returned here last evening had not one mouthfull to give the wounded or well; but that god that fed moses in the wilderness—in the night brought us a partial Supply—a small quantity of meat & meal was brought in by the contractor—we have been fed on parched corn half our time one third fasted, and about third had bread & beef—I hope for better times—we have lost some brave fellows, fifteen were killed on the field of battle and Eighty five wounded, two of whom are since dead the carnage of the enemy would have been much greater, I had formed a compleat circle round them, the creeks were about 1000 strong and when they approched the militia line it in part gave way, this occassioned me to dismount my reserve commanded by Colo. Dyer composed of Capt [David] Smiths [James] Tyrrells, Hammonds [William] Edwards and [Michael] Moltons companies[6] who met them like Bull dogs, and at two fires repulsed them killing 27 on the spot—had I had these men still on horseback in persuit, not one of the 1000 would have Escaped[7]—the Volunteers officers & men did their duty [a]nd the militia officers & men except as above stat[ed a]lso did theirs—as soon as the reserve checked them, [the] militia that had broke, rallyed and persued there was at no time of the action more than one half of my men engaged—and at every point my men beat them man for man, & when my reserve met them there was at least three indians for one white man—They reserve met them in Eight yards of where I was Standing & at two fires, drove the enemy—I have not time to write to Colo Hays shew him this letter—my mind for the want of provision is harassed—My feelings excoriated with the complaints of the men—I enjoy health—& may god bless you farewell

Andrew Jackson

ALS, OkTG.

1. Jackson's information probably came from Gideon Morgan, colonel commanding the Cherokee regiment serving with the East Tennessee volunteers (see Morgan to AJ, November 2).

2. See James White to AJ, November 5.

3. See AJ to White, November 7.

4. See above, White to AJ, November 7.

5. In his orders to White (November 6, DLC), Cocke wrote: "If we follow Genl. Jackson's army we must suffer for supplies—nor can we expect to gain a victory—Let us then take a direction in which we can share some of the dangers & glories of the field."

6. The captains were commanders of the following companies: Smith (1753–1835),

Robertson County cavalry; Terrill, Davidson County dragoons in Coffee's brigade; William Edwards, Jr., of Gallatin, mounted riflemen; Molton (d. 1817), mounted gunmen.

7. For another account of the Battle of Talladega, see AJ to Willie Blount, November 15.

From William Berkeley Lewis

Nashville Nov. 12th. 1813

Dear Genl.

Yours of the 4th Inst. (Ten Islands Coose) has been recd.[1] and strictly attended to. I have purchased and forwarded for the use of the army under your command, 3101 lbs. lead and 2222 lbs. powder: The powder, I am of opinion, you will find of the best quality. The medicine and hospital stores, as per bill handed by Mr. [Theodorick B.] Rice,[2] have been purchased and forwarded with the waggons transporting the ammunition. I found no difficulty in furnishing every article, except the butter, and instead of 100 lbs. I could only procure between 40 and 50 lbs. I have forwarded, as a complement, one cheese weighing 17 lbs., for your own private use.

Nothing could have been more gratifying to the people of this place than the inteligence of Genl. Coffee's victory over the Creeks.[3] Never was more wine drunk, or, tallow burnt on any occasion, than on that. I hope, indeed I have no doubt but you will accomplish the object of the expedition in the same stilish manner that you have commenced your opperations—The pets which you have sent his Excellency as a complement, arrived here on Tuesday evening last. They have been boarding with brother [Edward D.] Hobbs[4] ever since; what ultimate disposition will be made of them I know not, nor do I believe the Govr. knows how to dispose of them. I mean the creek Indian prisoners. No news from the north of any importance by the last mail. I suppose our troops in that quarter will winter in Montreal. The last time I heard from Mrs. Jackson she was well. Your friends are generally well.

Give my respects to all of my friends and acquaintances and believe me your friend

W. B. Lewis

ALS and LC, DLC.

1. See AJ to Lewis, November 4.

2. Rice rode express to Nashville for a time, then accepted a commission as lieutenant in the 7th U.S. Infantry, serving to the end of the war (Rice to AJ, November 17).

3. At Tallushatchee.

4. Hobbs was keeper of the Nashville jail.

From Robert Grierson

Hillabee 13th. Nov. 1813.

Hond. Sir,

Altho' perhaps unknown to your Excellency I beg leave as an old resi-denter, that has long resided in this place, and now suffering under a most grievous disease, the palsey, besides suffering all the outrages of these outrageous lawless band of Savages, who after committing all their out-ragous depredations on me and my family for five months past, on Satur-day fourteen days past, they consumed my house with every thing we possessed, and left me to the inclemency of the weather, without food or raiment for self or family; they this day wait on me begging me to offer to your Excellency terms of pacification with the United States—The glori-ous action you obtained the victory of, on Tuesday last, has such a good effect on their passions, as soon to wish to sue for peace: I beg leave to communicate to you such things, as needful, by this flag, which I send to you, humbly praying for your protection for myself and family, and Ne-groes; together with any other property we have left here; and humbly pray, that in your Clemency and mercy, that you will be graciously pleased to consider this my state of affliction, and afford me such aid & assis-tance, in order to procure my future preservation, as the nature of your Commission will admit you to advance—The Terms they advance to you are, that they the Hillabees from this day forever offer to lay down their arms, and to join in peace and amity with the United States of America, & ever to evade every hostile measure that may be offensive to the inter-est and peace of the said United States Government; together with any other proposition your Excellency may see cause to enjoin them to: Now as a person properly licensed from the United States agent here, I humbly pray, that if you see cause to admit them to a neutrality, as projected, you will be graciously pleased to cause them to give satisfaction for the mur-der of David Grierson on the 21st. April last, and Pinckney Hawkins, on the 12th. July, together with their families, with the exile of Walker Wil-liams & Alexander Grierson,[1] with their families, with a restitution of all other property, wilfully destroyed by the Hillabee & Fish Pond Indians—Whatever answer your Excellency may be pleased to confer on such sub-jects, from me, will be esteemed a favour of the highest importance at such a period as this, you may rely on me confidentially for every thing that is true: If your force is sufficient say 2000. and can march imme-diately to Saccapatae,[2] and there build a fort, you will be in the centre to act against all the hostile Indians, and will conquer them in two weeks, they are panic struck with Tuesdays defeat and now is the time to follow it up—they have no ammunition nor resources of any kind—The Oakfuskee, Newyork & Tallapoosa Tribes are out against the (friendly) Cow-etas[3] seven days.

I beg leave to forward this to you by my negro man (Pompey) and beg you to send him with the Indian safe back to me with such Answer as your Excellency may please to confer on,[4] and am to remain with high esteem, wishing God may protect you with your Army, and bless you with success to procure peace and safety to the injured Inhabitants of the land—

I, am hond. Sir Your Obt. Servant

Signed   Robt Grierson

Monday 15th. Nov. 1813.

Since closing my letter an Indian arrived here, & informs that the Georgia Army are on their march by the Suwanee[5] The Indians are evacuating their War Camps, and flying in every direction—200 invested my Plantation last night—for God sake come forward with your brave men and keep them running—

These from Hond sir your Obt. Servant

Signed   Robt Grierson

Copy, DNA-RG 107; LC and Copy, DLC. Published in *Democratic Clarion*, November 30. Grierson, a Scotsman married to an Indian, was a licensed trader with the Creeks. He lived at Hillabee, located about sixty miles southeast of Fort Strother.

1. David and Alexander Grierson were probably Robert's sons; Hawkins and Williams, probably settlers in the Hillabee area.

2. Possibly Sakapadai, at this time an abandoned Creek village about thirty-five miles south of Fort Strother.

3. The Cowetas lived on the west bank of the Chattahoochee River in present-day Russell County, Ala.

4. See AJ to [Grierson], November 17, below.

5. Floyd commanded the 1st Brigade, Georgia militia, 1813–15. Creek scouts had alerted the warring parties to Floyd's advance.

Within a month after they marched to the Creek country, Jackson and his Tennessee Volunteers had won signal victories over the Creeks at Tallushatchee and Talladega. But thereafter the campaign foundered until the early months of 1814.

As the documents below reveal, Jackson's problems, not unique to his command, were the result of severe supply shortages; mutiny and desertion, arising from disagreements over terms of enlistment as defined in a confusing series of federal and state laws; jealousies for honor and glory among some of the commanders; and the inability of the federal and state governments and field commanders to coordinate their efforts to bring the Creeks to terms. Jackson was forced to retreat to Fort Strother in De-

cember, there to await supplies and reinforcements before resuming the campaign.

To Willie Blount

Camp Strother Novr. 14th. 1813

Sir

It is with extreme pain I inform you that a turbulent & mutinous disposition has manifested itself in my Camp, from a quarter least expected.

Petition on petition has been handed from the officers of the different Brigade's containing statements of their privations & sufferings & requesting me to return into the settlements with my Division in order to give the men an opportunity to provide themselves with articles necessary for the campaign & to meet the provisions that was coming on.[1] In reply to their representation of grievances, I made a general order acknowledging to my Division that their sufferings were known & felt by me, & that every exertion had been made by me both to prevent & relieve them.[2] that a number of beeves had been seen in the neighbourhood & meal expected hourly from Fort Deposit where I was informed there were ample supplies, that there were several of the wounded whose deaths would be inevitable if moved & farther urged them not to cause the laurels they had so nobly & so bravely won to wither by a disgraceful return in the moment of victory—Limiting the time for departure to two days if provisions did not arrive; when we would all march & lay the blame at the door of those who merited it. Yesterday, as was expected, about forty five beeves were brought into camp. Still their murmurs were not silenced, but continued to increase until I was compelled to call a council of all the Field Officers & Capts. in my Division. To these officers I stated that information which could be relied on had been given me that there were at Fort Deposit between 50 & 60,000 weight of meal & 266 barrels of flour. that upwards of 100 hogs were on the way which would be here tomorrow or the day after at the farthest & after stating to them the impossibility of carrying on our baggage in consequence of having dispatched the waggons for meal & that we must either destroy or leave it—after conjuring them not move or leave their brave comrades who had fought & bled by their sides, after entreating them by their love of country & of glory not to abandon a campaign so gloriously begun without striking the finishing stroke & having the honor of its completion—I dismissed them with a request that the officers of each Brigade would hold a separate consultation & report their determination. Genls Roberts & Coffees Brigades first reported their resolution to stay by their baggage their wounded & their Genl. until it could be accurately ascertained whether supplies would arrive or not & if they did not in the course of three or four days that then they would return & meet it—Genl Coffee's Brigade also reported that the half or the whole of the cavalry would remain if the camp was deserted by the Infantry—notwithstanding the permission they had had for half of the men to go in to Huntsville & feed their horses which were perishing. Both of these Brigade have my warmest approbation & highest praise & merit the applause of gratitude of their Country for preferring privations & sufferings to disgrace—

Genl. Hall's Brigade then reported that after taking into consideration & weighing maturely all the circumstances they had determined by the vow of every officer in the Brigade with the exception of Genl. Hall himself to march back to meet the provisions at the same time recommending to me to permit the men to go to their homes & make preparations for the campaign & representing that if they were not permitted that the Soldiers would forcible desert—such a determination was not expected from those who had been trained & disciplined under my command—I did think they would have followed me through every danger & hardship without a murmur—they are the first to desert me. But the conduct of Genl. Hall is as usual, firm & humane, he says he will stay & die in the camp before he will move the wounded or destroy the baggage or sully the glory they have already acquired.

Copy, DLC. Published in Bassett, 1:345–46.
1. See, for example, the petitions of Andrew Patterson et al., November 12; Newton Cannon et al., [November 12]; Isaiah Renshaw et al., November 13; and William Martin and Henry L. Douglass, [November 14].
2. See Robert Searcy (AJ aide) to the Tennessee Volunteers, November 13.

To John Cocke

Head Quarters Camp Strother 16th. Novr. 1813

Sir

I have recd. your letter by Judge White;[1] & perfectly agree with you in opinion that it essential to the success of the campaign that the forces from Tennessee should act in concert, the reason why this has hitherto been prevented, notwithstanding my utmost exertions to effect it have been explained to me by the Judge: & a[l]tho. no man can be more disposed than myself, to admit the irresistable of those reasons, yet the consequences of them have proved excessively injurious to my plans—Had Genl. White been able to arrive at this encampment at the time I left it for Talledega & when I had a right to expect he would, I should not have returned hither; but should have been able in a few weeks, notwithstanding all privations & difficulties, to have broken down the Creek force & made them fully sensible that they have heretofore been indebted for their safety to our forbearance alone—But a retrogade motion is dangerous in an Army & becomes fatal when accompanied with hunger The force of this truth I was made to feel on my return to this encampment. Those men who had faced the enemy with so much bravery schrunk on their return from privations which they had previously submitted to with alacrity I was obliged to permit a majority of them to return to Fort Deposit for supplies but when their appetites are satiated & their sense of duty revived, as it will by the first cool view of the prospect before them they will return with cheerfulness to the standard of their country. In the meantime I shall with the forces here go on with the fortification I have begun, & continue to use every exertion for the attainment of the object of the expedition The contractors who have hitherto furnished me so poorly, continue to assure me of supplies & I shall continue to apply to every source where there can be any hope of obtaining them. I beg that you will add your own exertions to mine, & prepare to form a junction with me whenever you shall be advised. The want of punctuality in this respect is calculated to produce consequences of the most dangerous kind

Whatever supplies you may be able to obtain beyond what may be indispensibly necessary for the support of your own army you will be good enough to forward with all dispatch to Ft. Deposit

So soon as I shall find myself in a situation to move I will advise you of it by express; & shall then calculate on your speedy arrival & cooperation.

If you should be able to obtain a sufficiency of supplies & find yourself in a situation to move, previous to any further advices from me you will be good enough to inform me & I will afford you my most hearty cooperation

Andrew Jackson
Major Genl

LC, DLC. Extract published in Bassett, 1:353–54.
    1. See Cocke to AJ, November 14. Hugh Lawson White had gone to Alabama to visit his father, General James.

From Thomas Pinckney

Head Quarters Sixth District
Charleston 16th November 1813.

Sir,

The mail which arrived on Sunday last brought to me the President's order to take the direction of the expedition against the Creek Indians: I purpose in consequence thereof to set out for Millegeville as soon as I shall have made some indispensible arrangements here.

I am as yet unapprized of the directions given by Governor Mitchell to whom the Command of the expedition was originally confided by the President, nor am I accurately informed of the present positions or actual force of the Enemy or of our own detachments. Until I shall have received more correct intelligence, it would be improper to issue instructions a compliance wherewith might be rendered inexpedient by circumstances of which I am ignorant: I think it right however to communicate to you a general outline of the mode in which I am at present of opinion this Campaign should be conducted which is herewith inclosed:[1] but as more ample information may occasion an alteration in that opinion, you will please to act in conformity to it, only so far as your knowledge of the present circumstances may induce you to think it expedient.

You will please, Sir, by the return of the Messenger who conveys this, to inform me of your present position and intended movements, of your present supply and future prospect of provision & other necessaries, together with all the information concerning the Enemy which you may have obtained.[2]

You will also please to order the Officer acting as Adjutant General to the detachment under your command to make a return of the Troops of the State of Tennessee in the Service of the United States upon the expedition against the Creek Indians, to the Adjutant General of the 6th Military District at Milledgeville: and if you will please, Sir, to communicate to me your ideas of the best mode of conducting the operations of the Campaign[3] your suggestions will be received & attended to with all the respect due to your military rank & personal character

I have the honor to be very respectfully your most obt sevt.

Thomas Pinckney

LS and LS copy, DLC; LC, ScHi. Published in Bassett, 1:351–52.

1. See Thomas Pinckney to AJ and John Floyd, November 16.

2. In response to notification by Governor Blount that Pinckney commanded the Creek expedition (see Blount to AJ, November 20), Jackson informed Pinckney of his activities (see AJ to Pinckney, December 3, below).

3. Jackson responded on December 11, the day he received Pinckney's letter.

To [Robert Grierson]

Camp Strother Novr 17th 1813

I recd. your letter of the 13th & 15th. Inst.[1] proposing terms of peace for the hostile party in the Hillabies.

We took up arms in order to bring to a proper sense of duty those barbarians who had committed so many unprovoked depredations upon us, & we shall lay them down only when we are certain we have accomplished this object. I am taking means to enable me to effect this in a short time beyond the reach of doubt. Upon those who are friendly I neither wish nor intend to make war, but then they must furnish me indubitable proof of their sincerity. Let all those who were lately our enemies & who now wish to become our friends restore forthwith all the property & prisoners they may at any time have taken either from the whites or friendly Creeks—Let them deliver up all the Instigators of the present war let them meet me on my arrival with a flag & furnish my army with such provisions as they may have to spare—let them unite their forces with mine in prosecuting the war against those who still hold out & then they may expect my hand in friendship The terms upon which a final peace will be granted them will greatly depend upon their conduct in the meantime

I cannot say with absolute certainty when I shall be at your Towns; I am preparing supplies to enable me to carry a war of destruction through every part of the Creek nation that remains unfriendly & in a few days I calculate on commencing my march. I will shew them what kind of reliance is to be placed on these prophets & those who instigated them to this war. Long shall they remember Ft. Mims in bitterness & tears

I am &c

Andrew Jackson & &c

P.S. the indian you sent on with Pompey came no farther than Talledega

LC, DLC.
   1. See above.

To John Cocke

Camp Chennubee. Nov 18th. 1813.

Sir;

I am compelled by the embarrasments of my army, occasioned by the want of supplies, to set out last evening with all the forces that then remained with me (except 150 whom I left to compleat & defend Ft Strother in my absence) for Fort Deposit—Previous to my setting out, a flag arrived from the Hillabee's accompanied by a letter from Robt Grayson,[1] soliciting peace for the Indians of those towns, & offering to receive it upon any terms I might think proper to propose—They admit that the late engagement at Talledega had proved fatal to their hopes, & they believed it had brought the greater part of the nation to a proper sense of their duty—I stated to the Hillabees the terms on which we would cease to reckon them among our enemies Viz: that they should deliver up forthwith all the property & prisoners that they had taken from the whites or the friendly Creeks, that they should deliver up the murderers of our citizens & the instigators of the war—& that on our arrival in that Quarter they should unite their forces with ours in the prosecution of the war against those who still held out[2]—Believing that two thousand men in the center of the nation would speedily bring an termination, I must request that you will detach to Ft Strother 600 men at least with as little delay as possible, & with as full a supply as you can obtain—[3]

Be good enough to take measures for having purchased all the hogs &

cattle that can be furnished by the Cherokees—I say *all*, presuming they will not have more to spare than we will stand in need of—At this place (which is about 12 miles from Ft Strother) I met about 150 beeves & nine waggons of flour sent on by our Contractor—In consequence of this I shall order back to Ft Strother a greater part of who have been returning with me. I myself shall continue to Deposit & endeavor to provide against any future s[c]arcity—This I have not a doubt I shall be able to effect in a few days & then I shall return to Ft Strother with a force which when united with yours, will be fully sufficient for the accomplishment of our object—

I am exceedingly anxious to be in the center of the nation, but we must prepare the means beforehand of retaining our position afterwards. The supplies I met to day & the assurances of the contractors, have given me a confidence, which I was far from possessing a few days ago. Whatever supplies may be obtained in the Cherokee nation or in E. Tennessee for the benefit of the army under my command, I wish to be forwarded to Deposit or the mouth of Thomsons creek—

I shall be happy to see you with the detachment you may send to Ft Strother—I would not by any means pretend to regulate the number of men to compose the detachment—I have stated the number which I suppose would be necessary & sufficient—but you will exercise your own discretion on this subject

Yrs &c

Andrew Jackson
Major Genl.

LC, DLC. Extract published in Bassett, 1:354–55.
1. See above, Grierson to AJ, November 13, 15.
2. For Jackson's terms to the Hillabees, see above, AJ to [Grierson], November 17.
3. On November 17, Jackson had requested from Cocke 600 men as reinforcements, but Cocke's troops did not reach Fort Strother until December 12.

From William Carroll

Camp Strother Novr. 20th: 1813

Dear Genl.

We commencd work very early on the morning of the 18th. and almost compleated the picketing of our fort last night—we had no lazy man, our own safety mad[e u]s industrious—The men you sent back arrived last night—we have them encamped in good order—Some dificulty took place on their arrival about who should command—The two Generals command in conjunction.[1] I was persuaded of the right being in Hall by virtue of your order,[2] but he is a gentleman and would cede any thing for the benfit of the service—a private in Capt [James] Coles[3] company brot. in a scalp last evening—he killed the Indian some distance from this place I have Just interrogated him and have no doubt but he must have been a creek Spy—Our Spies report last evening that they saw where an Indian had been the evening before—he was no doubt a spy—we will have order in camp, till your return, those who are not on fatigue, shall be driled. I fear you will have some dificulty in getting back the troops— That no dificulty may take place, I beg leave to suggest the propriety of stating a time to them, when you think the campaign will terminate— You will please to o[bser]ve that the Militia were enrolled for 3 Mos. their time will expire about the first Jany. the object of the campaign can be compleated, in that, and an assurance from you that the whole of the troops will be discharged at that time, will quell the turbalent disposition that exists not only among the soldiers but officers—The officers of the volunteers know, that they were enrolled for a year on the 10th Decr. last, their time they presume, ends the 10th. this Decr.

We have done much; our actions will be recorded in the history of the American Republic—and I pray God, they may not be bloted by the desertion of those who once had the confidence of their country—I feel as great a disposition to serve my country as any man, but this campaign terminates my military career if one act of the army be calculated to tarnish the fame we have already purchased at the expence of some of our best citizens

My dear Genl., Militia becomes restive on lying at one place, have n[othi]ng t[o] do—would'nt it be best for the d[ispi]rited men to return (as soon as provisions can be attained), and pursue the campaign 2000 effective man, can do every thing you want done, a rapid push without baggage will soon put an end to creek hostility—That you may soon b[e] with us in good health is the Sincere wish of Sir, Yr. Servt. &c.

Wm. Carroll

ALS, DLC.
1. Carroll was referring to Generals Isaac Roberts and William Hall.
2. See AJ to William Hall, November 17.
3. Cole, a resident of White County, served in Roberts's brigade of Tennessee militia.

To Rachel Jackson

Dittos landing Novbr. 21st 1813

My Dear

I wrote you on yesterday by Mr [Jesse] Searcy[1] but to find out the certainty of supplies I have come on this far with Major [Robert] Searcy and Genl Coffee[2]—and since writing you on yesterday, I have determined to send on Colo. S. D Hays who is quarter master Genl to lay in farther supplies for my army

You may Judge of my hurry when you see in mine of yesterday that I overlooked that part of your letter[3] that related to the distresses of Mrs.

Cafferry, have a house put up for her on any part of the tract where she will be convenient to us and where you choose, or let her live in the house with us as you please, we can always raise a supply for her as well as ourselves, present her with my best wishes & compliments to Betsy Green, tell Andrew god bless him & his mother affectionately farewell

Andrew Jackson

ALS, MH-H.
1. Letter not found. Searcy (1785–1840) operated a store in Huntsville in partnership with John P. Hickman.
2. Jackson had ordered Searcy to Nashville to recruit more volunteers and Coffee northward to refit and obtain supplies for his brigade (see AJ to the Brigade of Volunteer Cavalry and Mounted Riflemen, November 21). Searcy (1768–1820), a lawyer, sometime merchant, and government official in Nashville, replaced Andrew Hynes as Jackson's aide on October 7, 1813.
3. Neither letter found.

From Willie Blount

Nashville Novr. 24th. 1813

Dear Sir,

I have just recd. your several letters by Major Searcy[1] all which shall be attended to as fully as in my power—I have forwarded copies to the War Dept. of Grierson's letters to you,[2] & a copy of yours to me of the 20th. Instant, for the information of the President; and for his determination respecting the term of service by the Volunteers; for his order for raising an equal number to supply their places if he orders their discharge, and for a supply of Blankets &c. The discharge of U. S. Troops, & the order for raising others for that service, solely belongs to him to determine on & to order—my authority does not extend to such cases—my confidence in the volunteers is so great, and the confidence of their countrymen in them is so great, and the object before them is so great, and the laurels before them so great, for it is to give peace to our country by their valor, that I do not believe that they would wish to be discharged before they reap those laurels—their privations have been great but I hope & believe they are now at an end—for their firmness & valor they have obtained the plaudits of their country—but former successes tho' considerable are not to be compared to those which are to be atchieved by their valor— were I to say that they ought to be discharged on the 10th. Decr., I have no power to order their discharge; neither have I any orders to call out an equal number of men—and without such an order to call them out to do so would be to treat men ill because their pay & supplies would be doubtful—I have said to the Secy. War that the orders of the Government would be attended to on these subjects—I can only say for myself that was I a volunteer under the act of Congress that I should consider myself bound to serve twelve months if called upon as such to serve, if under present circumstances I as a volunteer was in service I should feel myself in honor bound to await the order of Government for a discharge—This is my individual opinion: as an Executive officer of a State having no instructions from the President, & no right to controul men in the U. S. service I can give no binding opinion on the act of Congress in question; therefore I can only say what my private opinion is, as above expressed—I without further authority than I have to interfere would feel great delicacy in offering an opinion of the law which should affect others—I feel a peculiar pleasure in doing any thing I can to promote the public service at any time, but particularly when our brave Tennesseans are the actors in that description of service which is calculated to permanently secure the best interest of this fine section of the United States—we look to your Heroes for this important good to be effected—The Creek country & the Floridas added to ours would do it exactly—

Your answer to the Hillabees is very good,[3] but there is a propriety in annexing one or two other conditions to a peace with the Creeks, to wit, that we shall at any time in future be at liberty to navigate their rivers unmolested, to improve the beds of those rivers, build places of deposit for produce, Garrisons &c.; and open roads thro' their country and travel them without passports, just as we do thro' our own settlements—I am told that a Mr. Morgan[4] has gone out to your Camp to act as a sutler & if he has not he can get all the articles you suggested on your speaking to him about it—I am with respect & esteem, with the fullest confidence that harmony will prevail in your camp & that every good will be produced by your actions

 your friend

            Willie Blount

ALS, DLC. Published in Bassett, 1:359–60. Endorsed: "Came to hand 31st Decr. 1813 Teste E. Foster Secy." This is one of several letters misplaced by an express rider or a clerk in Hickman & Searcy's Store in Huntsville. In late December, Robert Searcy discovered the missing letters as he passed through Huntsville on his return to the army after spending several weeks in Nashville recruiting (Robert Searcy to AJ, December 27; AJ to Blount, January 2, 1814, DLC).

1. See AJ to Blount, November 20 and November 21.
2. See above, Robert Grierson to AJ, November 13, 15.
3. See above, AJ to [Robert Grierson], November 17.
4. Not identified.

Owing to slow communication between armies, the Hillabee Creeks, the first to sue for peace, became the unyielding, last-to-surrender foe. Two days after Robert Grierson notified Jackson of their willingness to surrender, James White's brigade destroyed Hillabee Town on Cocke's orders. The Hillabees responded with a determination to fight on.

Parton reported that Jackson expressed "grief and rage" over the inci-

dent (1:453), a judgment generally accepted by later scholars. But the evidence of the documents suggests that Jackson's concern was minimal. His reply to Cocke on December 2, although restrained in its praise, in no way condemned the attack. Nor can "grief and rage" be found in any of Jackson's other letters written at the time, and his report to Thomas Pinckney of December 3, below, ignored the incident.

From John Cocke

Ft Armstrong.[1] Nov. 27th. 1813

Dear Genl.

The d[et]achment ordered under Genl. White to the Hillibees has returned—On the 18th. Inst. they attacked the town at dawn—killed 64 warriors & took 256 prisoners, 29 of whom are warriors, the residue women & children—The prisoners I have sent to Highwassee Garrison—In this affair I did not loose one man either killed or wounded. I have one of the principal warriors among these prisoners by the name of Billy Scott.[2] he was slightly wounded at Lashley Fort—I am as yet unprovided with provisions—I am building boats to transport supplies down the river—Cattle are scar[c]e among the Cherokees—I dispair of geting a considerable number from them—I have men however in all directions in search for beef—they will return in eight or nine days—I shall then march for Ft Strother—Should you not hear from me again before the 6th of next month, you may rely on meeting me at the Fort by the 12th. with the force at least which you required—Should I be able to move sooner I will inform you by express

I am most respt. yrs

John Cocke
Major Genl.

LC, DLC. Published in Bassett, 1:361.
1. On the Coosa River in present-day Cherokee County, Ala.
2. Scott lived at Abihkutchee on Nauchee Creek southwest of Talledega. He still resided there in 1832.

From Thomas Pinckney

Head Quarters Milledgeville 29th November 1813.

Sir,

You will herewith receive a letter which I had the honor of addressing to you from Charleston[1] directed to the care of the late Governor Mitchell at this place, hoping that a communication of intelligence between you & the Commanding Officer of the Georgia Troops had been established; but finding on my arrival here that desirable measure has not been effected I now forward it by express.

I have received no intelligence or instruction from Government since I wrote that letter which has induced me to alter the opinion I then formed of the best mode of effectually subduing the Creek Nation, having at the same time in view what may possibly be the ulterior intention of our Government in this Expedition. temporary incursions of short duration which alone can take place when the Troops are to be supplied with provisions by waggons or pack horses may harrass and distress the Enemy, but will be far less efficatious than the establishment of good Posts in the heart of their country whence expeditions may be made in every direction with the certainty of an adequate supply of provisions and a retreat to a place of security in case of misfortune; add to this that if the Indians accept the invitation said to be given to them by the Spaniards, to take refuge with them, we should not be able to pursue them unless we have Depots of provisions whence the Army can be supplied.

These considerations have induced me after obtaining the best information to be had at this place to send my Aide de Camp Lt. [William E.] Morris[2] to the places whereat our transportation by Land from the fertile settlements of Georgia & Tennessee to the head of boat navigation on the waters of the Chatahouchie and Alabama Rivers may be effected; directing him to proceed to Col. R. J. Meigs at Highwassee who it is presumed can furnish accurate information of the practicability and best mode of effecting the objects in contemplation: He will thence forward to you this Dispatch together with such further information as he may obtain on this subject and is authorised, if he shall find it necessary, to proceed to have a personal communication with you. if he should not, you will please to send your answer to this dispatch by the express; wherein you will please to communicate all necessary information concerning your situation & prospects: the Adjutant General of the District writes to the Officer acting as such with you for the necessary returns which you will please to forward at the same time.

By our last accounts Genl. Floyd commanding the Georgia Troops had reached Coweta on the Chatahouchie, where he is directed to establish a Post, and whereat we are endeavoring to collect a Depot of Provisions.

Genl. [David] Adams[3] who commands a Body of Five hundred mounted Infantry of Georgia, will proceed from the Oakmulgee on an expediton against the Oakfuskee Towns near the burnt Village on the Eighth or Ninth of this month; the distance about ninety miles; if this information should reach you in time it would be desireable that you should send a detachment to operate in the same quarter at the same time.

Genl. Floyd who is within about sixty miles of the same point, will be instructed to make a simultaneous attack from his present position.

If you have any late intelligence from or concerning Genl. Flournoy, Genl. Claiborne or the Officer commanding any Troops which may be destined for this expedition from the 7th military District, you will oblige me by communicating it.

I have the honor to be very respectfully Sir your most Obedient Servant

Thomas Pinckney

LS, DLC; LC, ScHi; Copy, DNA-RG 107. Published in Bassett, 1:363–64.
1. See above, Pinckney to AJ, November 16.
2. Morris, a South Carolinian, was commissioned a lieutenant in the 18th U.S. Infantry in 1812 and discharged as a captain in 1815.
3. Adams (1766–1834), a native of the Waxhaw district of South Carolina and a veteran of the Revolution, was major general of the Georgia militia. He served for twenty-five years in the Georgia legislature, occasionally as speaker of the house.

To Gideon Blackburn

Ft Strother. 3d. Decr. 1813

Revd. Sir

Your letter of the 20th. ultimo has just been handed me by Mr. Johnston.[1] I thank you for it; I thank you most sincerely. It arrived at a moment when my spirits needed such a support as it afforded.

I left Tennessee with the bravest army, I believed, that any general ever commanded. I have seen them in battle; & my opinion of their bravery is not changed. But their fortitude—upon this too I relyed, but it has been too severly [tes]ted. You know not the privations we have suffered, nor do I like to describe them. Perhaps I was wrong in belie[ving that] nothing but death could conquer the spirits of brave men. I am *sure* I was, for my men, I know, *are* brave. Yet privations have rendered them discontented: that is enough. The Campaign must nevertheless be prosecuted; & brought to a successful termination. New volunteers must be raised to accomplish what the old ones so auspiciously began. Gladly would I have saved these men from themselves, & secured them the harvest which they themselves had sown. But if they *will* abandon it to others, & it must even be so.

You have said, if I needed your assistance you would cheerfully afford it. I do need it in a high degree. [The influence you possess over the minds of men is great & well founded; &] can never be better applied than in summoning Volunteers to the defence of their Country—its liberty & its religion. While we fight the savage who goes to war, only that he may gather scalps, & who feels malignity only because he delights in blood, we are (through him) contending against a foe of more inveterate character, & deeper designs—who would demolish a fabrick cemented by the blood of our fathers & endeared to us by all the happiness we enjoy. So far as *my* exertions can contribute to it, the purposes both of the savage & his instigator shall be defeated; & so far as *yours* can, I know they will be employed. I have said enough. I want Volunteers; & I want them immediately. You will endeavour to raise them, & will put yourself at their h[ead,] if that should not occassion you too great a sacrafice. By the 15th of this month at farthest I shall recross the Coosa, & recommence my operations. A few weeks will then put a termination to the war if I receive the support I expect. I have made arrangements to provide against any future scarcity, & in doing this I have overcome the only enemy whose presence need be feared. The instigation of their Allies may again bring the Creeks into the field, but can never make them forget Tallushatchee or Telladega.

Genl Cocke is still in the Cherokee nation, but promises to form a junction with me on the 12th.

I shall write to Major [Abram Poindexter] Maury requesting his influence in raising Volunteers.[2] You will see him soon, & will, I trust, unite your efforts. I should be happy to see you both at the preliminary treaty with the Creeks; & at the "laying-out" of a town at the junction of the Coosa & Tallapoosa.

I am most respectfully yr. obt. sert.

Andrew Jackson

P.S. It is rumoured that the Georgians have had an engagement with the Creeks, in which the latter proved successful.[3] This information was given me by Jim Fife.[4]

The Genl. wishes you to address the citizens of Williamson on the day of meeting. I have sent orders to the commanders of regts to meet at your place on Monday. A little exertion and we will be able to accomplish the object we set out for. I took the liberty to open your letter having seen it before sealed, and to get some information I had forgotten—In haste your friend   Wm. Carroll

LS with ANS by William Carroll, Mrs. Dorothy C. Elder; LC, DLC. Published in Bassett, 1:365–66. Bracketed portions (except for given names) from LC. Blackburn was a Presbyterian clergyman and missionary to the Tennessee Indians.
    1. See Blackburn to AJ, November 20. Johnston has not been identified.
    2. Maury, Sr. (1766–1825), a native of Virginia, was one of the founders of the town of Franklin in Williamson County.
    3. On November 29, John Floyd's Georgia militia attacked a large force of Creeks at Autosse Creek, burning two villages and killing nearly two hundred Indians. With Floyd wounded in the battle and supplies exhausted, the Georgia militia was forced to retreat to its base on the Chattahoochee River.
    4. James Fife was a friendly Creek whose village was located a few miles east of Talladega. In addition to supplying Jackson with intelligence, he organized friendly Creek warriors, two hundred of whom aided Jackson at the Battle of Emuckfau, January 1814.

To Thomas Pinckney

Fort Strother 3d. Decr. 1813

Sir

The Govr. of Tennessee has just transmitted a letter from the War Department stating that you had been ordered to take the direction of the expedition against the hostile Creeks & urging me to communicate with you relative to the measures to be pursued.[1]

I had calculated on forming a junction with the forces from Georgia at the confluence of the Coosa & Tallapoosa & on the 10th. of Octr. wrote to the Govr. of that State signifying my wishes & expectations. By return of my express the Govr. advised me that the detachment from that State consisting of one Brigade under the command of Brigadier General Floyd, was then on its march into the Creek Nation.[2] That the advance had reached the Agency, & that he would immediately forward a Copy of my letters to Genl. Floyd in order to produce concert in our movements. Since then I have recd. no intelligence from that quarter.[3]

On the 2d. Ulto. having arrived within a few miles of the Ten Islands on the Coosa, I detached Brigr. Genl. John Coffee with 900. of the Cavalry & mounted riflemen to destroy Tallushatchee which was situated a few miles on the South of that river & where I understood a considerable force of the enemy to be embodied On the morning of the 3d. this order was executed. The Town was burnt—One hundred & eighty six of the enemy slain & eighty taken prisoners. Our loss was five killed & forty wounded one of whom has since died

On the morning of the 9th. we had a more General engagement. Having learned on the evening of the 7th. that the enemy had assembled in great force about 30 miles below me for the purpose of destroying Talladega (a fort of the friendly party) & then of attacking my army, I set out immediately to the relief of that place with 1200 Infantry & 800 Cavalry; & on the evening of the 8th. arrived within six miles of them. Having recommenced my march, very early on the ensuing morning we came up to the Enemy, (whom we found encamped within a quarter of a mile of the Fort) by half an hour by sun. The engagement commenced, & in a short time terminated in their entire defeat. two hundred and ninety nine of the enemy were found dead on the ground & it is since well ascertained that this falls far short of the number really killed

Our loss was 15 killed & 87. wounded, three of whom have since died.

The number of the enemy engaged is not known; but judging from their fires, the space of ground the occupied—& their own representations it must have exceeded a thousand

The Creek war could now have been terminated in a few weeks had I not been compelled by the want of supplies & for the protection of my rear to return to my late encampment at the Ten Islands. Compelled by the emergency I had set out to Talladega with only one day's rations (which indeed was all we had) under an assurance that the Troops from E. T. would arrive in a few hours after my departure for the protection of the sick wounded & baggage I had left behind. In the course of the following night, however, I learned that they had entirely changed, their course & would not arrive at the Ten Islands at all.

On our return to the Ten Islands on the 11th. where we expected to find a plentiful supply of provisions we found those whom we had left there, as destitute as ourselves—This produced very disagreeable embarrassments, which I have ever since been endeavoring to remove By the 15th. Inst. I hope I shall have provided means which will enable me, to recommence the campaign with vigour & success—

The East Tennessee Troops have not yet joined me & are still in the Cherokee nation. I am assured by Genl. Cocke, however that he will form a junction with me at this place on the 12th. inst; & it is then our purpose to move forward to the confluence of the Coosa & Tallapoosa where we shall establish a Garrison & where it is believed the Creek war can be terminated in a short time & without much difficulty.

If this plan shall be approved I shall be happy in your cooperation with the forces from Georgia, and, at all events, in being advised of your situation—intended movements, & ultimate purpose.

I have the honour to be with great respect yr. obt st.

Andrew Jackson

LC, DLC; Copy, DNA-RG 107. Published in Bassett, 1:366–67. According to the DNA Copy, Jackson addressed his letter to "Majr Genl Thomas Pinckney Commanding the Georgia Army."

1. On November 20 Blount had forwarded to Jackson a copy of Daniel Parker's letter of November 7, informing Blount that "the President has ordered Major-General Pinckney to take direction of the Expedition against the hostile Indians."

2. See AJ to David Brydie Mitchell, October 10; and Mitchell to AJ, October 19.

3. It was not until December 18 that Floyd wrote Jackson.

From William Martin

Ft Strother 4th Decr 1813

Sir

Painful as it may be & certainly is to me it nevertheless becomes my duty to disclose to you a disposition which prevails the regiment which I command and by which I fear you will on the tenth day of this month lose that portion of your present force. This will be a serious misfortune as it will go far to frustrate for the present the further operations of the campaign which is every way important to prosecute with vigor. But it is unavoidable. On that day they will claim their discharge as a matter of right so they contend and beyond that day they cannot by coertion be kept as I believe. They further contend that [they] thought themselves finally discharged on the 20th of April last,[1] and never understood to the contrary until your order of the   day of September last appeared ordering them to rendezvous at Fayetteville on the 4th October.[2] When for the first time they were informed that they owed further service pursuant to their former tender the discharge which you had given to the contrary notwithstanding. Thus situated there was a considerable disinclination to obey that order. On which the officers generally as I am advised and I know myself in particular gave it as an unequivocal opinion that their service would terminate on the said 10th. day of December. This was done from a conviction of the correctness of the opinion and further to stimulate the men to turn out on which they were generally prevailed on to join the Army agreeably to your orders. this having been the fact they have steadily kept their eye on that day as the time of their release. It having contemplated twelve months from the time they rendezvoused at Nashville and were regularly mustered into the service of the United States pursuant to the proper Authority. They therefore look to their General who holds their confidence for an honorable discharge on that day. and that he will also see that justice is every way done. They request that their peculiar situations requires them to leave their General at a time when their services are important to the common cause. Their apology for this step is that when the order of march was received they were taken at surprise not expecting again to be called on, and further more the time allowed for preparation was so short, it being by many not more than one or two days, that there were many who were poor, had not time to make arra[n]gements for their families or provide themselves cloathing necessary for a Winter Campaign Nay they were assured they would not be Kept in service beyond the said 10th day of Decr. and if they do not get home soon there are many of them who will be literally ruined. This Sir is a concise representation of the state of things in this Regiment. But should you construe the law in question otherwise than has been mentioned it will be placing the officers in general and myself in particular in a delicate situation for all or nearly so having conceived that from the law they could not be kept in service longer than the day mentioned and having avowed that opinion repeatedly and publicly before they joined the army and having had no reason to change that opinion have never attempted to conceal it. This has been the case with myself and all those with whom I have conversed on the subject say that it was the case with them also. In fact this was one of our strongest arguments to get the men out. It has been insinuated by some that the General has said that they the men should not be discharged before next summer, but this they will not believe until they receive it from himself which they believe they never will. It is with me Sir to Know much of what is passing in the regt. being always in my place and never asleep on my post. It is needless to hint at the consequence (which beyond this place) will result from a disorderly movement from hence.

From a sense of duty I owe you sir, myself, & the Regiment I have the honor to command, I take the liberty with much deference to make to you this representation. It would be desirable for those men who have served with honor, to be honorably discharged, and that they should return to their families & friends without even the semblance of disgrace, and it is believed that it is with their General whom they love, to place them in that situation. They say, and with truth, that with him they have suffered—have fought & have conquered, they feel a pride of having fought under his Command. They have received him as an affectionate father, while they have honored revered & obeyed him; but having devoted [a] considerable portion of their time to the service of their Country, by which their domestic concerns are much deranged: they wish to return & attend to their own affairs—Above all things they wish to part with their General with that cordiality, with which they have servd. together. A different state of things would blunt the agreeable recollection of their former services together, and would be by them considered as one of their greatest misfortunes. This is the language and those are the feelings, of these noble hearted soldiers.

I am aware of the difficulties with which you have had, and still have to contend, & for myself can only say that my public aid has been on your side.

Two advantages may be derived from discharging the men at the time mentioned, *Vizt.* the most of them would give up their arms for an equivalent, and furthermore it is believed that many of the young men will re-engage—

with due respect & high consideration I am your sincere friend

Wm. Martin

LC, DLC. Published in *National Banner and Nashville Whig*, July 25, 1828; Bassett, 1: 368–70. Endorsed by clerk: "(not hon[ore]d, till the 6th.—[)]."
    1. After the Natchez expedition.
    2. See above, AJ to the Tennessee Volunteers, September 24.

To John Cocke

Ft Strother mong of 6 Decr 1813

Sir

I have received your letters of the 3d & 5th Inst.[1] & am equally surprised & concerned to hear your supplies continue deficient. In the name of God what is [Barclay] McGee doing & what has he been about?[2] Every letter I recive from the governor assures me I am to receive plentiful supplies from him, & takes for granted, that they have hitherto been regularly furnished: Considering the generous loan he obtained for this purpose, & the facility of procuring bread-stuff in E. Tennessee & transporting it by water to Ft Deposit it is wholly unaccountable that not a pound of it has ever arrived there.

It is my wish that you arrive here by the 12th. Inst with 1500 men. This will leave a sufficient number to protect the fort you have erected.

It is believed the enemy are assembling on the Cahawba to my right; but this fact will be better ascertained by the time of yr. arrival here.

The number of effective men now with me is abt. 900. The Cavalry & mounted gunmen who have been ordered into the Settlements to recruit

their horses, will return by the 12th. Int The latter will be prepared for, &
require, a vigorous & speedy prosecution of the campaign

I shall have beef & pork sufficient, I think, for our armies; & I have
forty waggons in requisition for the transportation of bread-stuff. I have
also ordered the purchase of 200 pack horses for the purpose of facilitat-
ing the conveyance.

My contractors are directed to furnish with all practicable dispatch,
thirty days rations at Fort Strother—forty days at Talladega, & forty
days at the junction of the Coosa & Tallapoosa.

I nevertheless expect & through you beg leave to require, Barckly
McGee to furnish at Ft Deposit in twenty days, all the bread-stuff he can
procure.

I have lately learned the Georgia Troops in conjunction with the Cowetas have had an engagement with the enemy in which the former were
unsuccessful. This, if it be correct would form an additional reason for
our forces being speedily united; & for a speedy movement afterwards—
The battle was fought 75 miles from Talladega.

I have the honr. &c

> Andrew Jackson
> Majr. Genl.

LC, DLC. Extract published in Bassett, 1:374.
1. See Cocke to AJ, December 3 and 5.
2. On September 24, McGhee (1760–1819), a Blount County merchant and land speculator, had received a contract to supply Tennessee troops on the Creek campaign.

To William Martin

Ft Strother 6th. Decr. 1813

Sir

I have received by the hands of Majr. West yr. letter of this eveng;[1] &
having perused it with great attention I shall give it a deliberate answer.

I know not what disagreeable scenes are to be produced on the 10th.
Inst; but whatever they may be as I shall have the consciousness that they
are not chargeable to any conduct of mine, I trust I shall not be driven by
them, from the performance of *my* duty.

It will be well however, for those who claim to be discharged from further service on that day & who are about to hazard their honour & their
lives upon the correctness of their pretensions, to examine beforehand,
with great caution & deliberation, the grounds of their claims. Are they
founded upon any false assurances of mine, or upon any deception which
I have practised upon them? Was not the act of congress under which
they are engaged, directed by my general order, to be read & expounded
to them before they enrolled themselves? That order will testify; & so
will the recollection, of every general officer in my division. It is not then

pretended that those who claim now to be discharged, were not legally & fairly enrolled under the act of Congress of the 6th. February 1813 [1812]. Have they performed the service required of them by that act, & which they then solemnly undertook to perform? That act required of them one year's service out of two, to be computed for the time of their being rendezvoused, unless they should be sooner discharged. Have they performed one year's service?[2] This cannot be seriously pretended. Have they then been discharged? And here it is proper to ask, who has the power to discharge them; & surely, but one answer will be given—"The president alone, in the recess of Congress, through his organ the Secy at War.["] Has the president then ever exercised this power with which he is thus exclusively invested. He has not; & so far from it, that organ through whom, on such occassions, he speaks, has told us, that he did not believe he could exercise it, until they had performed that term of service, for which they had pledged themselves to their government. How then has the opinion obtained currency that the Tennessee Volunteers have once been discharged? To account for so extraordinary a belief, it may be necessary to take a review of past circumstances. More than 12 months have elapsed since we were called upon to avenge the injured rights of our country. We obeyed the Call. On the 10th. of Decr. 1812—a day ever memorable in the annals of patriotism, we rendezvoused at Nashville. In the midst of hardships, which none but those to whom liberty is dear can bear without a murmur, we descended the Mississippi— It was believed our services were wanted in the prosecution of that just war in which our Country was engaged; & we were prepared to render them. But tho, we were disappointed in our expectations, we established for Tennessee a name which will long do her honour. At length we received a letter from the Secretary at War, dated I think, the 16th March 1812 (I write from memory) dismissing us from service.[3] I say *dismissing us*; but we were not *discharged*. You will recollect the circumstances of wretchedness in which this order was calculated to place us. We were deprived by it of every description of public property—no provision was made for the payment of our troops, or their subsistance on their return march. Against the opinion of many I hazarded a disobediance of that order which was so manifestly unjust, & contrary to law. I marched my men to Columbia (Ten) where it was thought advisable to dismiss (not discharge) your regiment. And surely it cannot be forgotten by any officer or soldier of that Regiment, what a sacred pledge they all gave, before they were dismissed, or had obtained my "Certificate" (which is now so strangely attempted to be construed a "discharge"), to obey the call of their goverment if it should resummon them into service! But for that *pledge*, that certificate had never been given. Neither can it be forgotten, I dare hope, for what purpose that certificate was given. It was to entitle those brave men, who with so much readiness, had obeyed the call of their country, to certain extra emoluments specified in the 7th. section of the act under which they had engaged themselves, & which they were to enjoy, if not recalled into service, for the balance of their term, by the order of government.

A copy of that section I send you, & need not therefore be particular upon its contents.[4] Is it true then that my solicitude for the interests of the Volunteers, is to become the pretext under which they would disgrace a name rendered illustrious through the land? Is the "*certificate*" by which I would have secured them emoluments—which they would, but for that, have been unintitled to, the "*discharges*" under which they are about to become mutineers? Surely it cannot be. Where then, I would ask again are the grounds upon which these men claim to be discharged? Have they performed the term of service required of them by the act of Congress under which they enrolled themselves? They have not. Have they been discharged by any competent authority? They have not. Have I any power to discharge them unless authorized by my Government, or until the arrival of that time at which the *Law* discharges them? I have not. Even if I were weak or wicked enough to attempt the exercise of a power which I do not possess can any one believe that the soldier would be thereby exonerated, from the obligation which he has voluntarily taken upon himself to his government? Does any one think so lightly of my head or of my heart as to believe I would attempt it? Indeed he is mistaken. I know my duties; & it shall be seen that I will perform them. If I were to arrogate a power which is not given me by the laws or the constituted authorities in discharging my men before their term of service is expired, I should become a traitor to the great concern which has been intrusted to my management & the soldier who had been deceived by a false hope of liberation, would be still liable to redeem the pledge he had made to his government. I should disgrace myself, without benefiting them. It would be the most pleasing act of my life to save from that infamy which awaits them, if they attempt to carry their present purpose into execution, those brave men who have done so much for their country, & who by that country have been so much honoured. The very moment the power is given me of discharging them, I will exercise it. It would pain me exceedingly that any other sentiment should ever be felt towards them, by their fellow citizens, than that of gratitude & approbation; & as I have always endeavoured, so I shall continue to endeavour to secure them this great blessing. My feelings towards them are indeed those of a father to his children: But a father never deceives his children: Neither have I ever deceived them, nor will I deceive them now. On all occassions I have sought to promote their interest & even to gratify their wishes where that could be done with propriety. When they had been so strangely dismissed in the Country below, "without food, & without raiment" I applied to the proper authorities & obtained a discharge of their arrearages & a compensation for their return expenses. Believing that they had been improperly treated, I even solicited the government to discharge them from the obligation they had entered into—So anxious was I to gratify their wishes, & secure them the extra emoluments which those are entitled to, who have been honourably discharged. You know the answer of the Secy. at war—that neither he, nor the president, as he believed, had then the power to discharge us

I have written to the governor of Tennessee even for *permission* to discharge the volunteers: his answer is hourly expected, & the moment it arrives, whatever may be its nature, it shall be publickly announced.[5] If *he* will even signify to me (and I have asked his opinion in such a way that he will not be able to refuse it) that *I* am authorised to discharge them, I will obey it as a command. I have even gone farther. I have sent to raise volunteers, on my own responsibility to complete the object of the campaign which has been so happily begun, & thus far, so fortunately prosecuted. The moment they arrive—and I am assured that fired by the name we have acquired, they will hasten in crowds at the first intimation that we need their services—I will permit them to substitute the places of those who are discontented here & the latter to return to their homes, with all the honour which under such circumstances, they can carry along with them. I who have always been so jealous of the fame of the volunteers, will not, even in the moment in which they have forgotten themselves, become their traducer. But I still cherish the hope that the evil has been magnified, & will be dissipated by the exercise of reflection. I cling to the belief, as I would to the last hold on life, that when the hour of trial comes the "Volunteers of Tennessee"—a name ever dear to fame, will not disgrace themselves, & a country which they have honoured, by abandoning its standard as mutineers & deserters. But should I be disappointed, & compelled to resign this "last, best hope," one thing I will not resign—my duty. Mutiny & desertion *shall* be put down, so long as I retain the power of quelling them; & when deprived of this, I shall in the last extremity, be still found in the discharge of my duty

I can only deplore the situation of those officers who undertook to assure their men that their term of service wd. expire on the 10th. Inst—but surely this is not understood as sufficient to vacate or affect the contract which those men had previously entered into with their government, or as furnishing any good reason for me to exercise a power which I do not possess. I presume too, they merely expressed their opinion, as men, upon the construction of an act which however indiscreet, they had a right to do, without giving any assurance, as officers, which they had no authority to give.

I have said that the moment the volunteers have performed the service required of them by the act of Congress under which they engaged themselves, or it is signified to me by any competent authority, even the gov. of Tennessee, or Genl Pinckney who is now appointed to the command, that they may be sooner discharged, that moment I will pronounce their discharge. I have only the power of *pronouncing* a discharge; not of *giving* it in any case; a distinction which I could wish all the volunteers would bear in mind. I have even gone farther & said that when the new Volunteers arrive (& it will not be long before they do) so as to enable me to prosecute the campaign, those of the present corps who are disaffected, will be permitted to resign their places to them, & return to their homes— leaving their guns with the quarter master, for which they will receive ten dollars each. Farther than this I cannot go, & farther than this I ought not to be expected to go.

I am very respectfully yr. obt st

Andrew Jackson
Majr. Genl.

LC and ALS draft (dated December 4), DLC. Published in *National Banner and Nashville Whig*, July 22, 1828. ALS draft published in Bassett, 1:370–73.
1. See above, Martin to AJ, December 4.
2. The February 6 law stipulated "that any company, battalion, regiment, brigade or division, thus offering itself for service . . . shall be bound to continue in service for the term of twelve months after they shall have arrived at the place of rendezvous, unless sooner discharged. . . ." (2 *U.S. Statutes at Large* 676).
3. See above, Armstrong to AJ, February 6; and Wilkinson to AJ, March 16.
4. Section 7 of the act entitled the volunteers to keep their government-issued arms if they had been in actual service for at least a month (2 *U.S. Statutes at Large* 677).
5. See AJ to Blount, November 22. Blount's reply, November 24 (above) did not reach Jackson until December 31.

From William Martin

Ft. Strother 8th Decr. 1813

Sir,

Your letter of the 6th Inst. was handed me yesterday by Majr. [Archibald] Potter[1]—the contents of which resolve themselves into but few points—to which I beg leave to make such remarks as may occur. In doing this, I wish it to be understood, that I consider this as a case, different from the ordinary concerns of an army. It has been a maxim with me, & ought *to be*, with every Soldier, to obey, without hesitation, the commands of his superior officers But on a question, which involves, the legal, and constitutional rights of the Soldier, he has a right to speak in his own defence

The main question, at issue, between the Genl. and his Regt. is, whether, by the acts of Feb'y & July 1812, this Regt. is entitled to an honorable discharge on the 10th Decr. 1813, together with all the emoluments provided for by law—or whether, it is not. You say it is not: and as it is my misfortune to be of a different opinion; it becomes my duty, to assign my reasons for that opinion; and to contend for a principal which involves much interest, & which I think correct. I wish again to call your attention to the act of Congress of the 6th of Febr. 1812 which I have not access to;

but which I am confident I recollect substantially. That act after prescrib-
ing the mode of tender, acceptance &c. provides "that if they (the volunteers) should be called into actual service, they shall be bound to continue
in service, twelve months, after they shall have arrived at the place of rendezvous; unless sooner discharged.["] It is admitted by all that these volunteers, were called into actual service and rendezvoused on the 10th of
Decr. 1812. It follows, then, as a necessary consequence, that, unless
"sooner discharged,["] the term of service, for which they engaged, will
expire on the tenth of Decr. 1813. Much stress has been laid on the word
discharge And who has the power to give, or order such discharge? You
say the president alone, in the recess of Congress through the secretary at
war. Be it so. Here it may be necessary to take a view of some transactions which took place after the rendezvous at Nashville. After descending the Mississippi, you received an order from the Secr. at War; directing
you, on the recpt. of that order, (for certain reasons) to dismiss the detachment, then under your command, from *further service.* I feel confident that the words "further service" were mentioned.[2] But, for good &
sufficient causes, you did not literally obey that order; but marched the
men to Columbia the section of Country from which they were taken.
For this you recd. the plaudits of your Country. There you gave, or ordered, each man a formal discharge, in the following words (to wit) "I
certify that A. B enrolled himself a volunteer, under the acts of Congress
of Febr. 6th 1812 & July 6th 1812, and that he has served as such under
my command, on a tour to the Natchez Country from the 10th Decr.
1812 to the 20 of Apl. 1813 & is hereby discharged signed A. Jackson M.
Genl." I say formal, because the discharge was not only so in point of
words; but the men were previously, in due form, as I conceived, mustered out of service—and this was, by the whole detachment, at that time
considered a compleat and final discharge—Even yourself, Sir, I did then
believe, thought it so. If any scruples, on that head, had remained, your
own declarations, on that day, were sufficient to remove them—which
were, to some of the officers (as I am advised) that the discharges were
complete—& by which, as they understood you, the men could not again
be called into service. From all of which I say, the Officers & Soldiers,
had a right to suppose themselves absolved from the obligation which
they had laid themselves under, by their tender of Service—Hence they
returned to their homes under this impression, either selling or carrying
their arms with them, without any injunctions not to part with them
    But it seems from your letter, that you understood it to have been "dis-
missed"—not "dischargd." Which is the expression in the instrument?
The sentence in yr. letter is "I marched my men to Columbia when it was
thought adviseable to dismiss (not discharge[)] yr. Regt.—And surely it
cannot be forgotten by any officer, or soldier, of that Regt. what a sacred
pledge, they all gave before they were dismissed, or had obtained my cer-

tificate (which is now so strangely attempted to be construed a discharge) to obey the call of their Govt., if it should resummon them into service—but for that pledge the certificate had never been given."

Now, Sir, the expression is "discharge" (not "dismiss") as will appear on the face of the instrument itself. That this should have been forgotten is, to me, matter of surprise—and I am still surprised that I should have so completely forgotten the solemn pledge made by the Regt. which you speak of, & on which your certificate (as you term it but which I call a discharge) was given. However there is one thing I well remember (to wit) That after the men were mustered out of Service and the Column was marched into Columbia, they formed and fired the parting Salute—& then formed into a solid column, when your farewell order was read: The Officers were then told (I think by Majr. Carroll) to display the column & the officers commanding Companies, to apply to him for the discharges of their respective Companies—deliver them to the men & disperse—On which the 1st Regt. did display; & marched off—Colo. Benton then called the attention of the 2nd Regt. and read an answer to your farewell address,[3] expressive of the high sense they (the officers & Soldiers) felt of your merits, their respect for your person, & their confidence in you as their leader &c. &c. This was unanimously agreed to—and this is the only pledge of which I have any Knowledge. And I believe every officer in the Regt. is prepared to say, that *it* was the *only* one given—& *this* after all the arrangements for discharging were made; & which pledge, *I did believe* you knew nothing of untill it was over. Nay—some of the officers Say, that at the time it was made they had the discharges for their men, in their pockets. How, then, this could be the condition, on which the discharges, or certificates were given, is, to me, a mystery. so much for the discharge in question.

I now beg leave to state some of the reasons which gave rise to a different opinion (to wit) That they owed further Service, & that, that service would be compleated on the 10th of Decr. 1813. It *may* & I presume, *will*, on calling your recollection to the subject, be remembered, that, when the committee, which met at Nashville, in Sepr. last for the purpose of taking into consideration, the then state of things, a sub-committee was appointed to wait on you, to obtain you opinion on some particular points—In the course of conversation a campaign against the Creek Indians was talked of; and that the volunteers late under your command, were named as a desirable force—On which a question arose on the legality of calling them again into service—(they having thought themselves discharged)—On which you stated the opinion of the Secry. at war on that subject & produced his answer to your enquiry (through Mr. Campbell)[4] touching that point (viz) That neither he, nor the president as he conceived had the power to discharge them untill the time, for which they were engaged, had expired. They then wd. be entitled to a stand of arms and all the emoluments provided for by law. It was then observed by a member of the committee that if we were not discharged, we were, as matter of course, still in service—You replied certainly—It was then observed by the same member, that, if in service, we must be in pay—you replied, To be sure (or words tantamount to that) and you further added that you would hold on the Secry. for the pay during the whole time. I do not rest this on my own recollection only—but it is supported by the recollection of some officers of high rank and character now in the army. This opinion coming from our Genl. (whose opinion with us was all but, orthodoxy) it was dissemenated among the volunteers with great industry—which could lead to no other conclusion, than, that the term of service would expire on the sd. 10th Decr. 1813 This conclusion was enforced (after giving up the idea of having been discharged) from a review of the law of Febr. 6th. 1812; and also by referring to the muster rolls made out at Nashville which, emphatically state in seperate columns, the time when enlisted, say 10th Decr. 1812—the time engaged or enlisted for—say—untill the 10th Decr. 1813. This appears of record in several Company Books now in Camp; & was used as an argument to get the men out, & to prove to them that they could not be kept in service longer than the 10th of Decr. Now if all this was not sufficient to authorise the officers to give their assurances to their men without compromitting their honor, or betraying a deplorable weakness—I *know not* what would: especially at a time when this description of force was considered important to ensure success in the contemplated campaign

But on the other hand, if they have from any unauthorised assurances, betrayed the men into a false belief & by which they are brought into a perilous situation, their cause is deplorable indeed; & certainly ought to render them unworthy of future confidence. But they do conscientiously believe, they were every way authorised to make these assurances without which the men would not have been got out: & that in any event they are blameless

However, let this business terminate as it may I trust I never shall have cause to surrender that high respect I have always entertained for your person, your character as a gentleman, & your great military talents— And in this correspondence, if any expression has escaped me, not every way respectful I assure you it is not intended

I am very respectfully yr. obt. sevt.

Wm Martin

LS matched fragments, ICHi and WHi. Published in *National Banner and Nashville Whig,* July 22, 1828.

1. See above. Potter served as deputy quartermaster general on Jackson's staff from September 1813 to February 1814.

2. In his orders to James Wilkinson, February 8, Armstrong had used the phrase "further service" in referring to Jackson's troops (see above, AJ to Armstrong, March 22), but no instance has been found in which Jackson used it in addressing his volunteers.

3. Neither Jackson's address nor Benton's reply has been found.

4. Campbell's letter not found. For Jackson's efforts to deal with the term-of-service issue at that time, see AJ to the Tennessee Volunteers, October 8.

To Rachel Jackson

Head quarters Fort Deposit Decbr. 9th. 1813

My love

I am still here, waiting for supplies and the Junction of Genl Coke, and the coming up of my Cavalry,[1] in a few days I hope to be able to move forward, with a competant force to put a speedy end to the war—but from *report if true* we will have to fight again—*if report is true* the Georgia army are defeated—I have no doubt but they have had a battle and the advance has been compelled to retreat—This may give those who the other day we beat and who were suing for peace on any terms, confidence and they may & report says are concentrating their forces to give us battle—I am sorry to say that my Volunteer infantry, in whom I had so much confidence, and in whom our country had so much and who had acquired a Charector for themselves and a reputation for their country are about to disgrace themselves by a mutinuous disposition in the face of an enemy, but the officers are more to blame than they men—and hereafter when Some cry out Boisterously at home that he is a patriot he will be met in the teeth with their shameful abandonment of the camp in the face of the enemy

my arm is mending—Kiss Andrew for me give my compliments to all friends and accept for yourself my warmest affection—

Andrew Jackson

ALS, CSmH. Published in *Huntington Library Bulletin*, 3(1933):112–13.
1. On November 21, Jackson detached Coffee's cavalry brigade to the Huntsville area for equipment and new volunteers. But because of Coffee's illness and the loss of men who claimed their terms of service had expired, Coffee rejoined Jackson with only remnants of the unit early in January 1814.

To John Cocke

Fort Strother Decr. 12th. 1813

Sir

It becomes my duty to inform you that Major General Thomas Pinkney of the United States army is authorised by the President to take command of all the troops ordered out against the hostile creeks. And being called on by him for a return of the strength and condition of all the Troops on duty from the State of Tennessee, also of the medical and hospital stores on hand together with such addition as will be necessary to constitute a supply for three months; of all the provision on hand in the commissaries; and stores in the Quarter Masters Department; I have therefore to request that you will forthwith cause a return to be made to me of the number of troops composing your Division now in actual service and what part of your Division are in the field under the order of the Governor pursuant to the order of the Secretary of war calling on you for fifteen hundred detached militia; and if any others for what time engaged and how many; you will also cause your Hospital Surgeon (if you have) if not your regimental Surgeons to make retur[n]s of the amount of Hospital and medical stores and what addition will be necessary to constitute a supply for three months. You will also cause your Quarter Master to make report of the stores on hand in his department. Having learnt that you were on your march to this place, I have detained the express from Genl. Pinkney in order to give him every information required I hope therefore you will cause reports to be made without delay as herein required.[1] I am most respectfully yours &c.

Andrew Jackson
Major Genl.

P.S. The express will set out early tomorrow I cannot detain him longer than 10 oclock A. M.

LC, DLC. Published in Bassett, 1: 388–89.
1. On December 13, Cocke reported to Jackson that the three regiments of General White's brigade comprised 1,605 men and that their terms of service would expire on December 23 and about January 1 and 14.

To Willie Blount

Ft Strother Decbr 12th. 1813

Dr Sir

Circumstances of the most unpleasant kind, and the delay in the return of Major Searcy, by whom I expected your answer, either ordering me to discharge the Volunteer infantry commanded by Genl Hall, or giving me firm authority to dismiss or discharge them—has induced me on the most deliberate reflection to permit them to return to Nashville, for your, or the orders of the Government of the united States—The discontent that has prevailed amonghst them—the Mutiny that shew itself on the 9th. instn which was only put down by the determined appearencee of the corps of artilery—the determination displayed by Capt Gordons Company of Spies, and the whole body of the Militia[1]—the information recd. from Genl Hall (always true to his duty) who advised me that they officers and men were determined not to advance or cross Cosa river has determined me to save them, & the State from disgrace, to take this Step—I hope therefore you may feel your self authorised to discharge them, and to order the muster master to muster them out of service. from the rules and articles of war I have no power to discharge them; being the commander of the Dept Genl Pinckney alone has this power, if any person, except the President or congress, For the lords sake, exercise the power, and discharge them, or they, the first military affections of my heart, are disgraced and myself and country, must partake of it.

will you have the goodness to send me a copy of your order to Genl Cocke, for bringing into the field, his quota of men—and your exposition of the order, as it respects the term of service[2]—as to the 1500, ordered by the Secratary of War, there can be no doubt—They are & must be in service for 6 months—the residue under the late law for the campaign—From the order of Genl Pinckney,[3] I have to give him a report of the strength & condition of the whole troops in service from Tennessee, their time of service is necessary to know in making out this report, and your exposition of the law will govern me, as it respects their service. I have to request your speedy answer to this letter least mutiny, which I will put down, may rear its head again in my camp—Genl Cocke has Just Joined me with (as he verbally states) 1450 men Genl White & the Judge is with me and on this morning I had not one pound of bread stuff—This evening 34 Barrells reached me down the Cosa from fort armstrong—I have a supply of Beef & Pork, and I will forward, and depend on Genl Pinckney furnishing bread stuff, at the Junction of the Cosa & Talaposa—for I have lost all confidence in McGee & the other contractors for supplies of breadstuffs—I must forward & will at all hazards, commence crossing Cosa on the 14th. *it is now high*, and on the 16th. make a movement—I order up Genl Coffee on tomorrow & on the 18th. or 19th. expect to meet the enemy, and if the god of war wills it—give them such a stroke as will put an end to the war—I know their positions—and before any more discharges can take place, or Cosa fevers lessen my numbers, I will hazard every thing—to put down the rising opposition of the Cosas, from the report of the late Victory by them over the Georgia army. with due respect &c &c &c—

AL draft, DLC.
1. Late on December 9 Jackson ordered the 1st Brigade to the parade ground where they were met with assembled militia units to disarm them and two artillery pieces. According to Martin, William Hall, and others, Jackson threatened to fire upon any man who attempted to leave (William Martin, *Self Vindication of Colonel William Martin . . .*, Nashville, 1829, pp. 14–15). On December 13 he again addressed the brigade (see below) and ordered Hall to conduct them to Tennessee to await a decision from Governor Blount.
2. See Blount to John Cocke, September 25, enclosed in Blount to AJ, December 22. Blount made no reference to the term of service in his letter to Cocke.
3. See above, Thomas Pinckney to AJ, November 16.

From Thomas Pinckney

Head Quarters Sixth & Seventh Districts
Milledgeville 12th December 1813.

Sir,
I had the honor of receiving last night your Letter of the 3rd of this

month.[1] You have I hope before this time received my dispatches sent from hence by Express on the first of this month, which will have informed you of the plan on which I proposed to conduct the Campaign,[2] and I am happy to find that it coincides so generally with your ideas on the subject. Nothing need be added therefore concerning your operations except to recommend that you insure a supply of provisions by water conveyance. I am happy to find by information from the Express that boats were building on the Coosa, and provisions collecting to load them: as this measure will I trust in future secure you from the embarrasments to which you have been subject for want of that indispensible article.

General Floyd who commands the Troops of the State of Georgia in the service of the United States on this expedition marched from the Post established at Coweta with 950 of his Men and some friendly Indians on the 20th of the last month, and on the morning of the 29th attacked a body of the Enemy collected at Autosee on the Talipoosa about 60 miles from Coweta; whom he defeated, & returned immediately to Coweta. I inclose a Copy of his official report of the action for your information. I am sorry to add that I fear General Floyds wound will disable him from resuming the command of the Georgia Troops during the remainder of the Campaign. Instructions have been given to the Commanding officer of these Troops to establish an intermediate post between Coweta and the Talipoosa whence the operations of the Georgia Troops may be advantageously carried on against the Settlements on that river; and another post will be established on the River as soon as circumstances will admit; whereby a chain of posts will be established distant from thirty to forty miles of each other from Fort Hawkins to the Fork of the Coosa & Talipoosa. If you should succeed in establishing the water conveyance for your Provisions you will not require so complete a chain, but I would recommend that a few posts should be established on your line of communication as places of security for your sick & wounded, and to be furnished with depots of provisions from your boats, (or collected if practicable in the Country) to which access may be had, when the boats may not be so accessible; a considerable supply of meat may with advantage follow the army on the hoof.

If our plans succeed I hope the Tennessee and Georgia Troops may form a junction near the confluence of the Rivers before Christmas.

It was part of my plan that the 3rd Regt. of U. S. Infantry should in conjunction with such Troops as could be spared from the Mississippi Territory have assailed the Enemy from below, and marching up the Alabama have formed a junction at the same place; but since I have arrived here I understand the 3rd Regiment has been sent to New-orleans by orders direct from the Department of War.

I find by the address on the outside of your letter that you mistake me for an officer of the State of Georgia;[3] and it being necessary that this misapprehension should not exist; I have to inform you that I have the honor of bearing the Commission of Major General in the Army of the United States, that I have during the present war been intrusted with the Command of the 6th Military District; and that for the purpose of directing the expedition against the Creek Indians the 7th military District has been added to my command by order of the President of the United States, whereby all the Troops in the service of the United States acting on this expedition are placed at my disposal.

I have the honor to be with great respect Your most obedient Servant

Thomas Pinckney

P.S. I send herewith the duplicate of my last letter to you which was intrusted to the Care of a friendly Indian, but may not have reached you.[4]

I take the liberty of forwarding by your Express a dispatch for Genl. Flournoy, if you have the means of conveying it safely in a direct course to the place of its destination you will oblige me by so doing, if not please to send it in the circuitous route by mail.

ALS, DLC; LC, ScHi; Copy, DNA-RG 107. Addressed: "General Jackson Commdg. the Troops of the State of Tennessee in this Service of the U. S. on the Expedition against the Creek Indians."
1. See above.
2. See above, Pinckney to AJ, November 16 and 29.
3. See above, AJ to Pinckney, December 3.
4. Probably Pinckney to AJ, December 2.

To the 1st Brigade, Tennessee Volunteer Infantry

Ft Strother. 13th. Decr 1813

On the 10th. of December 1812 you assembled at the call of your country. As if to test at once the sincerity of your professions of patriotism, & your ability to indure fatigue you were immediately visited with the most inclement weather. Destitute of the ordinary comforts of a camp you bore your situation without a murmur. Breaking your way through sheets of ice, you descended the river to the point where you were ordered to halt. There, contrary as much to the expectation of your General, as of yourselves you were ordered to be dismissed from the service in which you were engaged. This order yr. General was bound to obey. He saw men, who he believed deserved better of their Country—many hundred miles from their homes—in a strange land, without friends—without funds—destitute of everything necessary for a comfortable return. Your General was not long in determining on the course he should pursue. He resolved at all hazards that his fate should remain identified with yours until your own country was reached. The means for marching you back were procured—every difficulty was surmounted, & as soon as the point from which you had first embarked was reached, the order for your dismissal was carried into effect. The promptness of your assembling—the regularity of your conduct, & attention to your duties—the determination manifested on every occasion to carry into effect the will of the Government, placed you in the front ranks of patriots. You not only distinguished yourselves; but through you, Tennessee stood distinguished among her sister states. The government was taught to believe that the honour of the nation would never be tarnished when entrusted to the holy keeping of the brave Volunteers of Tennessee.

In the progress of that war which the eternal enemies of our Independence has caused to be waged we have found that without cause on our part, a portion of the Creek nation is added to the number of our enemies. This miserable & contemptible enemy was to be subdued: by what force. As was to be expected, the first glance of the eye of administration fell upon the brave volunteers of Tennessee. You were again summoned to the field of honour. In full possession of your former spirit that summons was again cheerfully obeyed. Before your enemy thought you in motion you were at Tallushatchee—at Talladega. The thunder of your arms was the signal to your enemy, that the slaughter of your countrymen would certainly be avenged You fought—you conquered; barely enough of the enemy escaped to recount to their savage associates your deeds of valour. You returned to this place loaded with laurels—oppressed with the applauses of your country.

What shall I next say? Can it be, that such brave men are about to become the tarnishers of their own fame, & the destroyers of a name which does even their country honour? Yes, it is a lamentable truth, too well known to your Genl. that cheerfulness has been exchanged for complaints. Instead of those expressions of hilarity & life which once gladdened his heart, he hears now only the murmurings of discontent. Men who a little while ago, were offering up prayers for permission to chastise the Creeks, & to teach them how much they had hitherto been indebted to our forbearance, are now, that a finishing can be put to their former wishes & their late atchievements, become anxious to be discharged. The heart of your General has been pierced. The first object of his military affection, & the first glory of his life was the Volunteers of Tennessee. That very name calls back to his heart a thousand endearing recollections, which he can never forget. Yet these men—these Volunteers of Tennessee have become MUTINEERS! Your General has been compelled to suppress the feelings of a father. He has been compelled by that subordination which he is bound to see observed, & which is, so essentially necessary to the support of every army, to check the disorder which would have destroyed you. You have not been permitted to disgrace yourselves & your country. Tranquility has been restored in your camp; & your General is about to restore contentment there also. This can only be done, by permitting all those to retire whose dissatisfaction proceeds from causes over which he has no controul. This permission he is about to give. Your country will (can) now dispense with your services, if you can surrender that fame which you have so nobly earned. Yes fellow Soldiers, you who were once so brave, & to whom honour was once so dear; you shall be permitted to return to your homes if you desire it. But with what language, when you arrive there will you address your families & your friends? Will you tell them that you abandoned your General & y[our] late associates in arms, within fifty miles of an assemblage of a savage enemy, that as much delights in sheding the blood of the innocent female & her sleeping babe as that of the warrior contending in battle? Lamentable, disgraceful tale! If your dispositions are really changed, if you fear an enemy whom you so lately conquered, if your characters have been radically mistaken both by myself & by the world, this day will prove it. I now put it to yourselves—determine upon the part you shall act, uninfluenced by any thing but your own judgments & your own hearts. All who prefer an inglorious retirement, in this time of need I will immediately order to Nashville, to be there discharged at such time & in such manner as the Governor or the President may think proper to direct. All who choose to remain, & unite with their General in the further prosecution of the campaign, will thereby furnish a proof that they have been greatly traduced; & that altho dissatisfaction & cowardice may have reached the hearts of some, they never reached theirs. To all such the General pledges his assurance that former irregularities will not be attributed to them. They shall be immediately organised into a corps under officers of their own chusing; & in a little time it is confidently believed, they will be able to add fresher & more durable colour to the laurels they have already won.

Andrew Jackson
Major General

Copy in John Reid's hand, NjMoHP; LC, DLC. Published in *Nashville Whig*, January 11, 1814. The publication of this letter and others concerning the "mutiny" of the troops was in response to criticism leveled against Jackson by the discharged troops after they had returned to Nashville.

To Thomas Pinckney

(Copy)   Ft Strother 13th Decr. 1813 at night—
Sir,

I have detained your Express, in order to obtain from Genl Cocke a report of the strength & Condition of his division. You will find, from his letter to me of this date,[1] which I herewith send you, that his Men's term of service will expire in a few days; and I have learnt since my dispatch to you was closed, that they are resolved to return home the moment that time arrives. They are a fine set of men, but quite in a State of insubordination.

As soon as I was apprised of Genl. Cocke's appearance I ordered Genl. Coffee on with all the supplies of breadstuff that could be procured,[2] if the quantity should be sufficient to justify it: determining immediately to take up the line of march for the junction of the two Rivers, & in my way to destroy a number of the Enemy who had collected at the Fish traps on the Coosa.[3] The moment I was advised that the term of service of the greater part of Genl. Cocke's men would expire on the 23rd Inst: & of the balance on the 1st Jany. and that they were resolved to prosecute the Campaign no further, when those periods should arrive, it became necessary that I should countermand my order to Genl. Coffee and direct him to halt & await my further order, where his horses can be foraged.[4] My Volunteer Brigade having marched for Nashville, the strength of Genl Coffee's mounted men added to that of the Militia commanded by Genl Roberts is not sufficient to protect Fort Deposit, afford a Convoy to the Provisions, maintain this place, & enable us to advance to the junction of the two rivers, there erect a garrison & protect it; keep open the communication with this place, & afford sufficient Convoys to the transports of provision. To advance far into the Enemy's Country with Troops whose term of service is nearly expired, & who are ripe for mutiny would be risking too much. I have written to the Governor of Tennessee for other Troops to be enrolled for the Campaign.[5] I did believe that fifteen hundred of Genl. Cocke's men were in the field for six months, as they were raised under the requisition of the Secretary of War to prosecute the Campaign against the Creek Nation. How it has happened otherwise, remains to be explained by the Governor & the General.

It is not difficult to be foreseen that an expedition which could after the battle at Talladega, have been brought to so speedy & successful a termination, is about to be procrastinated until the expense of it will exceed the value of the Country to be conquered, & until Great Britain & the Spaniards can furnish such succour to their Savage Allies as will make the prosecution of it in the Spring, as bloody as expensive. Now is the time to crush the Enemy; & the moment I can by the utmost exertion of my powers, obtain a force sufficient for the purpose, that force shall be thus applied—

My situation for several weeks past has been exceedingly unpleasant—discontented Troops—scarcity of Provisions and an Enemy before me whom I could not advance to conquer. Rest assured I have left no means in my power unassayed to bring the Campaign to a speedy & prosperous termination; & tho' I have not been able to obtain complete success, I have endeavoured to deserve it.

From my late exposure to the inclemency of the weather—the wound of my arm & the want of rest, my health is a little impaired; & I must refer you for any further information to Mr Cooper[6] who has been with me several days, & has been no inattentive observer.

I shall be happy to receive your Commands and to execute them.

I have the honor to be with great respect Your Obt Sevt—

(signed)   Andrew Jackson

Copy, DNA-RG 107; ALS draft, DLC.
1. See Cocke to AJ, December 13.
2. See AJ to Coffee, December 12.
3. The Fish Traps was a dam erected on the Coosa, about sixty miles below Fort Strother.
4. See AJ to Coffee, December 13.
5. See below, AJ to Blount, December 13.
6. Cooper, otherwise unidentified, was the express rider who had delivered Pinckney's letters to Jackson.

To Rachel Jackson

Head quarters Fort Strother Decbr 14th 1813

My love
I have recd. your verry affectionate letter of the 3rd instant,[1] and by Capt Allen[2] who has come out to see his three sons (and certainly a father never was blest with three better) has promised to hand you this Pressed with mutiny and sedition of the Volunteer infantry—To surpress it, having been compelled to arange my artilery, against them, whom I once loved like a father loves his children—was a scene—that created feelings better to be Judged of than expressed—a once conquered foe in front, rallying to give us battle, and a Whole Brigade, whose patriotism was once the boast of their Genl and their country, abandoning the service and declaring they never would advance across Cosa again, and to their own eternal disgrace, and that of their country, turning their backs on an enemy fifty miles in advance—when all was wanted was a force to advance to destroy them—has been scenes that has given me much pain and trouble and is for their country to pronounce praise or censure on— one thing is certain, that notwithstanding the officers attempted to lay the blame on the soldiary—the result proved that the officers, and not the soldiers were at the root of the discontent, and when they were put to the Test but one commissioned officer turned out, to support the Eagles of their country and prosecute the campaign—That was old Capt [Thomas] Williamson and for this act of patriotism he was huted at by Colo. Bradly—Capt Allen can tell the ballance—I observe the rascallity of Nollyboy—Mr [Samuel] Scott and [James] witworth[3] can prove the contract and his acknowledgement of the debt, I called upon them as witnesses, and if he has a sufficient quantity of cotton in my ginn to discharge the debt of 350 lb of good merchantable gind Cotton, it must be detained, if he has not let him have a credit for what good cotton he has, have him warrented, and Mr Saml Scott and Mr Whiworth summoned as a witnesses, have a Judgt for the ballance, and as he has proved such a scoundrel, let him have no indulgence I have not recd your verry acceptable presents—they will come on in good time I would to god, I had a

place I could bring you to, I would certainly send for you and my little Andrew, and if Genl Pinckney under whose command I am will, direct me to take a stand at any stationary point—for any specified time I will send for you—My heart is with you, my duty compels me to remain in the field whether we will have men anough to progress with the campaing I cannot say—for I fear the boasted patriotism of the State was a mere buble, that expires, on the approach of an enemy—and if I am compelled to abandon the campaign for the want of men—such scenes will be acted on our frontier, that nothing can parralel unless the scenes of the north west and this too after the enemy has been beaten and conquered—and nothing remained but a sufficient force and supply to advance—we have now a prospect of ample supplies of provision, and no troops to eat it—What may be the result time alone can determine my old friend Allen waits this letter if I had time I have many things to say to you—It may not be long before I can either send for you or see you at home But you know my motto, I know you approve of it—that is death before dishonor Kiss my little andrew and give my best wishes to all my friends and enquiring acquaintance—I shall write you by Colo. Hays if he comes up—May heaven bless & protect you is the nightly prayer of your affectionate Husband—

Andrew Jackson

ALS, DLC. Published in Bassett, 1:391–92.
1. Not found.
2. Not identified.
3. Scott and Whitworth were Davidson County farmers.

To Willie Blount

Fort Strother Headquarters Decbr. 15th. 1813—

Dr. Sir

My several letters, by three differrent expresses will have advised you of my situation, occasioned by the mutinous disposition of the Volunteers,[1] and altho quelled by force and fear, still being advised by Genl Hall of their determination both officers and men not to cross the river cosa, if ordered, and having ordered Genl Cocke to Join me with fifteen hundred men, expecting he had this number in the field under the requisition of the secratary of war made thro you whose time of service could not expire sooner than six months—having heard that the hostile creeks had concentrated their forces at the big fishtrap on the Cosa, and hearing that Genl Cocke was near me I had determined to order my troops to cross cosa on the 14th. instant, and had by express ordered Genl Coffee to form a Junction with me on the South East Side of the Cosa on the 16th.[2] To prevent the Volunteers from disgrace and save the efusion of blood, I had an address prepared & read to them on the morning of the

13th.[3] in which I announ[c]ed to them the causes that had determined me to give all those permission to return to Nashville that had a wish to abandon the service and turn their backs on an advancing enemy &c &c &c—I had a hope that many still possessed a spirit of bravery and a thirst for Glory and military fame—but Judge of my surprise when not one but Capt Williamson, was found in the rank of further service, I Issued the order they are marching to Nashville to seek a discharge from you or the Goverment of the united States—Still determined to march with Genl Whites Brigade 1450 strong and Genl Coffees Brigade I commenced preparations for the march when I was advised, that there was not a man in service under the requistion of the Secretary of war, that there terms expired on the 23 & 29th and the 14th. of January,[4] and that they were determined to go home the moment there times were out, and one regt. had swore that if they were marched and in front of the Indians and had their guns up with their fingers on the trickers and their times that moment expire they would take down their guns and not fire, but march directly home—I called on Genl Cocke agreable to the order of Genl Pinckney for a report, and found the time of service as stated before—disappointed in my expectations of their time of service, I appealed to the officers to know if their men would agree to march forward destroy the Indians and remain with me to keep the ground thus obtained, the answer was they wanted to fight and they were willing to advance untill their times was expired but they then must & would go home, that they were lightly cloathed, and came out only for three months—They have my order to return tomorrow except the regt. commanded by Colo. [William] Lillard[5] whose time does not expire untill the 14th. of next month—Thus has my whole hopes of advancing and again chastising the indians, vanished ¿how has this happened? no men in the field from east Tennessee for longer than three months when you by your order had ordered the 1500 detached militia agreably to the order of the Secratary of war from the first division—that there times are expired and shortly expiring, The secratary thinks we have a large force in the field, and no force ordered, to fill up the vacancy that will happen by the discharge of the east Tennessee Militia—and in the mean time Genl Pinckney ordering me to advance—under an expectation that I have sufficient force not only to advance and maintain my ground but to spare from the Troops of the state a sufficient number to fill the requisition, lately ordered and subject to the call of Genl Floronoy—every officer of Tennessee must exert himself to save the state from disgrace, and prevent our frontier from destruction—This can only be done by furnishing me with sufficient force to keep my ground and advance to the Junction of the cosa & Tallaposa where I may unite with the Georgia troops—I have said for the purpose of an immediate movement, I had ordered Genl Coffee up, I have ordered him to keep his horses forraging and ready to Join me at a moment—you must my Dr Governor exert your power, if you discharge the Volunteers you must order a draft to fill their places, if that number is not filled by Voluntary enlistment—if you do not discharge them—and if you do not think there times up you must order them back—we must have men to carry on the campaign—we must have the Volunteers or others in their room speedily or all will be lost, and the boasted patriotism of the State tarnished forever—If I had two thousand men of a disposable force, with sufficient guards for the forts and transportation of Provisions I could in two months carry the eagles of our country any where—I am advised, that Genl Coffees Brigade, has taken the infection of The Tennessee Volunteers—I have no doubt but they will take every pains to corrupt all the troops they can Colo. Bradley was through the whole Tennessee Troops, trying to sow sedition amonghst them this I have from the best authority—such men ought to be punished, but if you think their time of service not yet expired, send them back let me have Colo. Williams with his regt.[6] and I will pledge myself to make them yet as good troops as they ever were, and once they were as good as any—let me repeat again men I must have—to retrograde from my present position is disgrace to the whole state—and without men I cannot keep my post—retrograde I never will without the orders of Genl Pinckney, and I hope I am not left here with a few brave fellows to Perish—but perish we will before we retrograde in disgrace ourselves as others has done—Chenebee & [Alexander L.] Lashly,[7] my two faithfull creeks has this evening come to me, with information that the creeks are advancing to destroy their Fort, and then come up and attack my camp—I have no doubt but they are collecting in considerable force, and I will at all hazard, save these friendly creeks if I can—and I depend on you and the patriotts of west Tennessee to support me and give me the means of carrying on the campaign with Vigor—

I have ordered Genl Cocke (after consulting with him) to return to his Division and with all possible dispatch bring into the field the 1500 men ordered by the Secratary of war thro you of the Detached Militia into the field[8] and I have a hope that a number of Colo [John] Browns men will return as Volunteers for the campaign[9]—I have directed Genl Cocke to have an eye to our supplies, and prevent hereafter that want, that has occasioned the obstruction of our enterprise, and ruinous to the objects of our campaign—McGee's conduct has been such that he ought to be scurged, and I fear that my wants has risen in part from other causes, these causes, if they have existed I hope will hereafter not exist, there is plenty of bread stuff in Holston and plenty can be procured at ten dollars a barrel for flower and a dollar pr bushel for corn meal delivered at Rosses or Fort Deposit—if supplies is not got at this price it is the neglect of the contractors for which they ought to be punished—I have to repeat that men and supplies we must have or the campaingn will terminate ingloriously to Tennessee—I want your Speedy answer on all the points in this letter[10]—it is after 12 oclock at night my taper dim no time to copy—and I must bid you good night—but before I lie down I must beg of you to take some energetic means to send men into the field—this you can do by ordering a draft—

Andrew Jackson

ALS, NjMoHP.
1. See, for example, AJ to Blount, December 12 (above) and 13.
2. See AJ to Coffee, December 12.
3. See above, AJ to the 1st Brigade, Tennessee Volunteer Infantry, December 13.
4. See Cocke to AJ, December 13.
5. See AJ to the East Tennessee Volunteers, December 15. Lillard (1744–1830) served in the Tennessee General Assembly. During the Creek War he commanded the 2nd Regiment of East Tennessee Volunteers.
6. By the fall of 1813, John Williams had completed the organization of the 39th U.S. Infantry, and Jackson greatly desired the services of those regulars to bolster his depleted army (see AJ to Blount, November 29). Because of conflicting orders from Pinckney and Flournoy, however, Williams did not join Jackson until February 6, 1814.
7. Leslie (sometimes Lashley), was owner of the blockhouse at Talladega (Lashley's Fort). His father, Alexander F., was half Creek and Alexander McGillivray's chief assistant.
8. See AJ to Cocke, December 15, below.
9. Brown (1779–1843) of Roane County commanded a regiment of East Tennessee volunteers. When his unit's term of enlistment ended in late December, he returned to East Tennessee and recruited a new regiment.
10. For Blount's response, see Blount to AJ, December 22, below.

To John Cocke

Head Quarters, 15th Dec. 1813

Sir;

Finding from the report made to me by you of the 13th Inst.,[1] that there is not now of your Division, here under the requisition of the Secretary of War, made thro' his Excellency Gov. Blount on your Division for fifteen hundred men; & the term of service of Genl. Whites Brige. (who alone of your Division are here) terminate on the 23rd & 29 Inst. except Col. Lillards Regt. whose term of service expires on the 14th Janry

The campaign must not terminate untill its object is compleatly effected. The character of the state is at stake, and it requires every exertion of the brave Tennesseans to support it—It can only be done by furnishing a competent number of troops, agreeably to the requisition of the Secretary of War made on you thro' the Govr., and then to make up the Quota of one thousand men to appeal to the patriotism of your Division, & bring into the field, by voluntary enlistments to be commanded by their own officers one thousand men for the campaign—You will therefore forthwith return to Fort Armstrong, make arraingments for keeping up that post as a place of Deposit; & order your Quarter Master to transport the provision to this place as they arrive, in boats;

You will then proceed to your Division by the way of Ross's, make arraingments with the Contractor of East Tennessee for a compleat supply of bread stuffs agreeably to former requisition's; and you will direct your

Quarter Master to have the same transported to Fort Armstrong & Fort Deposit without delay: and you will make arraingments for any farther supply for any numbers of men you may bring into the field for six months: & in case you have any doubts that the contractor will fail again in his supply, you will please have a sufficient supply brought & sent on, that the fatal consequences that have ensued to the campaign for want of supplies, thro' the shear neglect of McGee may not again be experienced—You will without delay, by draft or voluntary enlistments for six months or the campaign, furnish the full quota of the requisition of the Secretary of war thro' the Govr., on you for fifteen hundred detatched Militia: and as soon as raised send the same thither by detatchments of Battalions of Regts.

You know my situation—You are apprised of the expectations of the Commander in Chief Genl. Pinckney. You know the expectations of government, that we have 5000 troops in the field, when we have but about 400 effectives, whose services can be calculated on for more than one month. Expedition therefore is necessary or our posts will be abandoned; & if ever they are, the aid expected by government from Tennessee will be lost, & with it the reputation of the State. I have sent on to my Division to endeavor to raise by voluntary enlistments a sufficient number of men to fill up the vacancy that is made in my ranks, by the retrograde of my volunteers. Should I fail in this attempt I have requested the Govr. to issue his order for a draft. No exertions on my part will be wanting to push the campaign to an honorable issue & in you I have the greatest confidence. I must repeat again, that our bread stuff must principally come from East Tennessee, & you must have an eye that a compleat & ample supply be had, that no want may be experienced in future.

I have signifyed to the officers of your Division that all volunteers enrolled for the campaign under their own officers, will be accepted, to make up the Quota from this state, as well in your Division as mine: one fifth mounted gunmen or Cavalry will be admissable—The Militia, under the order of the Secretary of war, must be infantry. Finding that from the shortness of the term of service of Genl. Whites Brige. that I cannot move forward as I expected & fully calculated on: & as the brave Soldiers composed his Brige. were only enrolled for three months & prepared for that time, may again wish to return to the support of their country's Eagle, & to consummate a campaign so fortunately begun: that they may reach their families as early as possible, you will please order Genl. White, with Cols. Browns & [Samuel] Wears Regts[2] to take up the line of march, so soon as waggons & a sufficient supply of rations can be furnished them. You will please inform them the waggons will be ready tomorrow some time in the day; & that their return rout will be left to the direction of Genl. White, who will direct it, in such manner as in his judgement, will be most to their ease & convenience. You will please have procured by your Quarter Master or some active agent, & transported to Fort Armstrong & this place, as early as possible, all the corn that can be procured in the Cherokee country, near the navigable streams that empty in the Coosa. This will be all important to the existence of your horses & what cannot be done without

Most &c &c yours

Andrew Jackson
Major Genl.

LC, DLC; AL draft, ICHi. Published in Bassett, 1:393–95.
  1. See Cocke to AJ, December 13.
  2. Wear (1753–1817), from Sevier County, commanded the 1st Regiment, East Tennessee Volunteers.

To John Armstrong

Ft Strother. at the Ten Islands on Coosa
16th. Decr. 1813.

Sir

The Volunteers who enrolled themselves under the acts of Congress of the 6th. February & 6th. July 1812, & who composed a part of my forces in the expedition against the hostile Creeks, believing their term of service to have expired on the 10th. Inst, have refused to prosecute the Campaign any farther. Not considering myself empowered to discharge them, I have permitted them to be marched to Nashville—there to await any orders which the governor, or you might think proper to give them.

I have learnt since the arrival of Majr. Genl. Cocke who formed a junction with me on the 12th. Inst that the term of service of the greater part of the forces under his command will expire in a few days, & of the whole, in a few weeks. I had supposed that fifteen hundred of his men had been raised under the order of the governour, founded upon the requisition of the president. This not being the case, I have thought proper, this morning, to order Maj. Genl. Cocke back to his district to raise the fifteen hundred men according to that requisition, & whose term of service when thus raised, will, I apprehend, be six months.[1] I permit him to march back & discharge that portion of his troops whose term of service is within a few days of expiring. That part of them whose engagements are not quite so nearly at an end will remain, to aid me in retaining possession of the posts which I have established, & in keeping open the communication between them.

The want of supplies alone has prevented me from terminating the Creek war, before this time. That, with want of cooperation from the East Tennessee troops, at a moment when their cooperation was indespensably necessary, compelled me to retrogade to this place, after the battle of Telladega; & it continues to prevent me from recommencing operations. All that my utmost exertions could effect has been accomplished; & yet I have not at this time a sufficiency of breadstuff to justify another movement, even if I had troops to authorise it. All the difficulties & delays of the Campaign are to be ascribed, primarily, to the negligence of the contractors. Had they furnished us with supplies, no discontent would have arisen among my men; nor would they once have thought of the expiration of their term of service until they had accomplished the objects of the expedition; or rather those objects had been accomplished before that term, according to their own, estimation, had expired. I shall not, however, cease my exertions to provide both men & supplies to enable me to prosecute the campaign to a successful termination. Its importance to our country is too great, & the progress of it has been too fortunate to abandon it now.

After the battle at Telladega I was compelled to send my cavalry & mounted gunmen to Madison to recruit their horses. They will return, when I shall be justifyed, by the approach of supplies, to order them on.

I have sent to West Tennessee to have other troops raised by voluntary enlistment, to aid in terminating the campaign; & they are expected to arrive by the 25th. Inst.[2] By that time, it is hoped, there will be a sufficiency of supplies to justify another movement.

I received on the 11th. Inst a letter of instructions from Maj. Genl. Pinckney who wrote from Milledgeville; & advised him by the return of his express, of my situation.[3]

Chenubby & Lashly (from Lashly's fort, at Telladega) two friendly & faithful Creeks arrived here this evening, & advised me that the advance of the Georgia army, aided by the Cowetas, in a late engagement with the enemy were compelled to retreat—that the hostile Creeks are assembled about sixty miles below me in great force—that they are about to advance & destroy their fort, & afterwards to attack me. Should this information prove correct I will try my feeble force, once more to save those friendly Creeks, & defeat the enemy again on the heights of Telladega. Had I one regiment of Regulars added to those few heroes who will die with me or accomplish the objects of the expedition, I am well convinced I could, in two months, reach the walls of Pensacola. That is the source of the war; & thence it derives its support. Chenubby & Lashly inform me that the Spaniards at Pensacola have furnished one town with large supplies of powder & lead; & that they have invited the other town to receive their supplies. Delenda est Carthago; or we shall never have peace with the Indians

The 39th Regiment would be of great service in defending the garrisons erected, & in keeping open the communications between them, if you should think proper to order them to aid in the prosecution of the campaign.

In haste I have the honor to be &c

Andrew Jackson

LS, DNA-RG 107; ALS copy, LC, and Copy, DLC; Copy, DNA-RG 233. Published in Bassett, 1:396–97.
1. See above.
2. For a report on those efforts, see William Carroll to AJ, December 15.
3. See above, Pinckney to AJ, November 29; see also AJ to Pinckney, December 11.

To Rachel Jackson

Head quarters Fort Strother Debr. 19th. 1813

My Dear—

I have the pleasure to acknowledge the recpt. of your verry acceptable supplies by Colo. Hays—for a few days we have had ample supplies of bread & meat—and had it not have been for the disgracefull retrograde of the Volunteers, ere this you would have heard of our advance, again to have met the savage foe, and put an end to the campaign—but the scenes of sedition and mutiny has been such, throughout, the whole body of Volunteers both infantry and Cavalry together with the mounted men, that it is impossible for me to say, whether I shall have any force or what, from the whole boasted patriotism of the Volunteers—or mounted patriotts—The Phisic of the indians prophets must have curiously worked upon them to occasion those men, once so brave, once so patriotic to conduct so strangely and so disgracefully to themselves and country

The time of the greater part of the militia from East Tennessee has expired and they are gone home one regt. alone remains, and whose time will expire on the 14th. of next month—My own militia has taken the home mania, and every man expects to be marching home on the 4th. of next month—and here am I within sixty five or seventy five miles of the whole hostile strength of the creek nation, no force that I can count on to march forward to chastise them—And no information from Govr Blount whether any force is to be sent me to enable me to carry on the campaign—Should it stop here I feel for the Scenes that will be transacted on our frontier—The creeks, conquered and beaten, on a retrograde of our forces, will give them new vigor, and full confidence in their prophets and we will have to fight them on our frontier. I am here and by the orders of Genl Pinckney, compelled to remain, and expected to advance untill I form a Junction with the Georgia troops and I expect to be left from the present prospects to be left with my brave artillery company and the spies to defend the posts and prosecute the war—But fear not my better self— The guardian angles will protect us, and support us, under every trial danger and dificulty, so long as we are engaged in so riteous a cause—I refer you to Colo Hays for further news, of my situation and my views, My brave friend Genl Coffee is verry ill in Huntsville if he should not be able to come on I loose my best prop—

I have Directed Major [William] White[1] to carry to you, the little Lyncoya—he is the only branch of his family left—and the others when offerred to them to take care of would have nothing to do with him but wanted him to be killed—Quals my interpreter[2] Took him up carried him on his back and brought him to me—charity and christianity says he ought to be taken care of and I send to my little Andrew, and I hope will adopt him as one of our family Kiss my little son and receive my blessing, and present me affectionately to all my friends—yr affectionate Husband

Andrew Jackson

ALS, MoSW. Published in Bassett, 1:400–401.
    1. White (1781–1833) was judge advocate for Jackson's division.
    2. Probably James Quarles, who had been trading with the Creeks as early as 1796.

To William Berkeley Lewis

Head quarters Fort Strother Decbr. 19th. 1813

Dr. Sir

The Blanketts has not reached this place as yet Whenever they come up, I will send you the order to cover the number sent on, and the quarter masters recpt for the Same—I fear before they reach me I Shall have no men to buy, or wear them—and my Camp will be deserted without any means taken by the Governor fill their vacancy, by draft, I have wrote by several expresses, in due time to have reached him and his answer have been to hand before the 10th. instant, had [h]is answer been such as I am now told it is the Tennessee Volunteer Infantry would have been still here doing there duty as good soldiers or receiving examplarory punishment for disobedience

The East Tennessee Troop it appears was only brought into the field for three months, and not one under the requisition of the secratary of war all home & marching home but one regt. whose time will be up the 14th. proximo, and behold the militia from my Division has caught the disease, and home the must be on the 4th. next months—I have said to them—that they are in for the campaign or under the act of Congress but I shall be governed by the oppinion of the governor[1]—Thus a campaign so necessary for the safety and protection of the frontiers, so far as Tennessee has to take a part in it is likely to be shamefully abandoned, and the reputation of the State eternally disgraced, and no eficient act as I can learn to prevent it. ¿What is the Governor about? is his feelings ready to submit to such a disgracefull scene, after our boasted patriotism, and fervent wishes to be permitted to carry war and destruction into the hands of the creek nation, and after the fortunate entrance made into it, contrary to the underhand endeavours to prevent me from opperating from the want of supplies, which I expected from Genl Cocke *and his command* to *Genl White* (which I *enclose to the governor and will explain all* and every matter and thing as it respects the cooperation and supplies promised by

Genl Cocke, all which is noted and in due time will be attended, to[)]—for the Lords Sake arouse the Governor from his Lethergy—bring to his view the disgraceful precipice, on which the credit of the State Stands and he will exert himself—let the militia under the requisition of the President, as adopted under the late law of the State be drafted for six months, and Sent on to fill up the disgraceful retrograde of the Volunteers—or let him preremtory, order the Vollunteers to return if he believes he has not the power to discharge them—and let him Issue a general order, directing all disserters to be apprehended, and transferred to the regular army there to Serve the ballance of their time, let him do this and explain at what time Genl Roberts Brigade Service ends, and should it end on the 4th. proximo say to him unless at that Period our cooperation or aid from Tennessee as promised & expected by the President of the united States, and by Genl Pinckney the commander chief, is to end and our State eternaly disgraced, that he must exert himself fulfill his powers and order a requisition to be up against the day, that Those in service expires, this is the conduct of the Georgians—and altho Genl Floyds Brigade time of service has expired having served 6 months, Till the express informs me, that the Governor o[f] Georgia[2] has the relief is at hand and wi[ll] reach him before the first requisition is discharged—this is proper and right—and I hope the governor will exert himself, and save our State from everlasting disgrace—I have ordered Genl Cocke back to fill up the requisition of the secratary of war made thro Governor of the State,[3] had this been done at first regardless of the disgracefull retrograde of the T. V. V. Infantry I should been moving on and soon put an end to the Creek War—My respects to your lady Mrs. Lewis and all the family & receive my thanks for the cheese & Butter &c and believe me respectfully yrs &c &c &c

                                                                    Andrew Jackson

ALS, THi.
    1. Jackson's second brigade was composed of militia, enrolled under a resolution of the Tennessee legislature the preceding September. Commanded by Isaac Roberts, they had volunteered to serve for a three-months' tour of duty as prescribed by state law. Jackson, however, maintained that they were to serve for six months, the maximum fixed by the federal law governing militia called into service of the United States. On January 4, the militia bolted camp and left for home, asserting that their terms were over, a view confirmed by Secretary of War Armstrong (see Armstrong to Blount, January 3, 1814, DLC).
    2. Peter Early, inaugurated governor on November 5, served to November 9, 1815.
    3. See above, AJ to John Cocke, December 15.

To John Coffee

                                        Headquarters Fort Strother Debr. 22nd. 1813
Dr. Genl
    I have the pleasure to acknowledge the recpt of your letter of the 18th. Instant[1]—and with sincere regret I learn your indisposition, at this mo-

ment when your service was all important. But indisposition—and health are not within our control, and ought not to be subjects of inquietude, altho your present indisposition—fills me with regret, when I find your Brigades patriotism is as much indisposed, as you are in body, which in all probability would have been prevented had your health been such as you could have been at their head—their disgrace prevented, and also examplanary punishment to many—Can it be true what I hear! that the Voluntary defenders of their countries rights has been the first to Violate the laws of the Territory that they were called upon to protect—insult their citizens and their laws, and instead of repelling and subduing lawless mobs, were the first to become riotters themselves—I have to request a report of every individual both officer and men that were engaged in overawing the Goeler of Huntsville, and compelling him to liberate the prisoners—and also a full report of every officer and man of your Brigade, who have deserted the service without a discharge, that I may take the most efficent means in my power to have them arrested and punished agreable to law—I have the pleasure to inform you that I have Just recd. a letter from Governor Blount, a copy of which with my order of this date I have sent you,[2] and directed to be delivered to Major Shaw, at Fort Deposit there to be read to your Brigade by him. Should you not be there which I do not expect—and which will be forwarded by him to you. It will give the Volunteers & detached militia his Ideas of the law & their time of service, and I hope produce the former quietude and harmony, that has existed in our camp again to prevade it—and that no ideas will prevail but the chastise of the creeks, and cheerfull services, untill honourably discharged. I have to repeat again that you will urge the contractors to send up ample supplies of breadstuff, on the pack horses, and in all waggons that can be had, and that you will order up your Brigade with it—Deerskins can be got in abundance, three skins will make three bags that will pack a horse, two side bags, and one on the Top, they are better than any other kind of bags, the hair will keep the meal dry, and they will last the campaign—I have ordered back the quartermaster general, to have them brought up with the asst D. adjutant General Major [Joseph] Antony[3] with powers to purchase in case they contractors has not a sufficient supply on hand—A movement I must make, supplies I must have to make the movement, and with supplies you must order up your Brigade—you will find from the Governors letter the prospect of provisions on the allabama and ample supply of corn which is reallised by express recd from Genl Flouronoy & Genl Claibourne—could we get on we would soon reach the promised land that flows with milk and honey—use your utmost with the contractors and hurry on supplies—wishing you a speedy restoration to your health, and Junction with me, I am Dr Genl yr mo ob. Serv.

Andrew Jackson
Major Genl

ALS, DLC. Published in Bassett, 1:404–405.
1. See Coffee to AJ, December 18.
2. See Blount to AJ, December 7; order not found.
3. Anthony, commissioned a lieutenant in the 24th U.S. Infantry in March 1812, had resigned in August 1813 after serving at the Battle of Lower Sandusky in Ohio. He accepted appointment as Jackson's assistant adjutant general and served until March 1814, when he resigned to return to his home in Huntsville.

From Willie Blount

Nashville Decr. 22d. 1813.

Dear Sir,

I have recd. yours of the 12th. & 13th. Instant[1] and had previously written to you by Express two or three times on several of the heads mentioned—I much regret the situation of Affairs at your Camp occasioned by circumstances which neither you nor I could controul with our best exertions—

The U. S. volunteers from your Army have not yet arrived here—on their arrival I will endeavor to act for the best in some provisional or conditional way as I have no authority or instructions from Government about their discharge—it appears to me to be too great a responsability for me to take to discharge them absolutely—I cannot yet say what can be done respecting their return; however, from your request, & from my own feelings, I will do all I can to serve them, and to serve the public—I respect them as brave men, & for their services which have been important—I want them to get their pay—and hope that the President who alone can order their discharge will order that they shall be paid.

I send you a copy of the Secy. War's letter to me of the 13th. July last,[2] and of his chief clerk, Mr. D. Parker's letter of subsequent date to Col. Meigs,[3] under which two letters, I acted in calling out the 1500 men, as you will see by a copy of my orders to Major Genl. John Cocke,[4] now at your request sent to you—I also send the copy of my letter to the Secy War of the 10th. Instant,[5] on the subject of instructions relative to the term of service of the Troops generally now with you and Genl. Cocke, and if to be discharged, enquiring when, by whose order, and how their places are to be supplied, which will shew you & those with you that I have been endeavoring to get the necessary information respecting the term of service of the forces with you, and that I had written before respecting the volunteers—It is the clearest exposition that I can give of his instructions, or of the law of this State of the 24th. Septr. last—I send you copies of the Acts of our Assembly respecting the 3500 men, and exempting them from process whilst in service[6]—copies of all which I think you had best send to Genl. Pinckney—You will see by all those letters &c. &c., that I could not when calling out the men into service, know how long they were expected to serve, & that I have no instructions about their discharge—The Executive of a State cannot without orders from Government discharge U. S. Troops—I may surely expect an answer to my letters which I will make known to you when recd.—all Troops in the service of the U. S. must of course expect the President's order for their discharge—I have sent a copy of all the orders which I issued to you, and to Genl. Cocke, on to the War Dept. for the information of Government, long since—I do most earnestly wish that all the Troops that have been in service, or that now are on this campaign may be paid: their services have been very important; they have done much; but if the Government should not think with them about the term of service I should regret it & the consequences to them may be serious, and they, to be sure on that head, had better continue a short time longer in service, than the time they consider to be a tour, than to jeopardize their pay; I say this as their friend—I wrote Genl. Roberts the other day to this effect in reply to a good letter from him on the subject of the term of service—it is in the power of the Troops alone, at this time, to obviate all difficulties on this head by waiting the instructions of the President in reply to my letter of the 10th. Instant, which I should have written sooner, if their wishes had been made known to me—advise them to think of this in due time—I know your feelings—don't fret—the Genl. Government will restore all things—they have much to do—[7]

I recd. a letter the other day from Mr. Morris Genl. Pinckney's aid informing me of the necessity of his appointing an A.D.Q. Master to attend the Troops, and that he should be advised by you as to the man he should appoint—Surely he ought to have been advised by the Secy War, if the appointment is to affect Mr. Lewis; that W. B. Lewis was appointed last winter by the President; and my orders to you shew that he is acting as such now—I have mentioned this to Mr. Lewis—He will write you—Surely he ought to be continued, as no other man can settle his accounts—if there is to be no A.D.Q. Master here, supplies in that Dept. can not be from time to time forwarded from this; which is mentioned, that you may guard against such evils—would it not be well for you to write to Genl. Pinckney about the propriety of appointing Mr. Lewis, either to stay here and act, or appoint him to attend the Troops? but if he goes on with them, there should be one here, and one in Et. Tenn. also; his recommendation of the necessity for one in each Division, as well as for one to be with the Army, would induce their appointments[8]—the peculiar local situation of the State would shew the necessity—I am, your friend

Willie Blount

ALS, DLC; Copy, DNA-RG 107; Extract, THi. Extract published in Bassett, 1:405–406.
1. See AJ to Blount, December 12 (above) and 13.
2. Armstrong to Blount, July 13, DLC.
3. Daniel Parker to Return Jonathan Meigs, August 16, DLC.
4. Blount to Cocke, September 25, DLC.
5. Blount to Armstrong, December 10, DLC.
6. *Laws of Tennessee*, 10th General Assembly, Ch. 2.

7. On January 3, 1814, Armstrong replied to Blount's letter of December 10, agreeing to accept the 1st Brigade Volunteers' interpretation of their one-year service and the militia's contention that they were entitled to discharge after three months, noting that his decision in both cases was an exception to the law (DLC).

8. Blount misinterpreted Pinckney's plan to appoint an assistant deputy quartermaster for the East Tennessee troops as an effort to replace Lewis. Jackson, who had received a copy of Morris's letter to Blount (see Morris to AJ, December 12), understood Pinckney's purpose and appointed James Baxter to oversee supplies for the 1st Division from headquarters at Fort Armstrong (see AJ to Pinckney, December 27).

From William Carroll

Huntsville Decr. 23rd. 1813

Dear Genl.,

On my arrival at this place I found that there was no provisions at Camp Strother I therefore thought it prudent to remain 'till I recd. orders from you—

The roads are uncommonly bad—The volunteers have not all arrived, it is therefore out of my power to say how many we will have—I hazard an opinion that we will have 600 nearly all well equiped—

I hope you will do me the Justice to believe that every thing in the power of man has been done by me, but when oposed by influential characters of the country without even the approbation of the Govr. I fell far short of what I could have Wished—Dr. [John] Shelby[1] who has done much for the common cause, tells me that he had innumerable dificulties to surmount, the minds of the people are compleatly poisoned by a set of designing characters and the return of some of the volunteers—

I have discovered since my arrival in this place that mutiny and discord reigns among the cavalry and mounted men; they have distroyed much forage have come on to Dittos landing and are determined to start home to morrow, this confusion originated with Officers of high rank and is supported by more than you would immagine—You need not expect to have any more of *their* services—I have understood that an Officer dare not speak to them—An idea has suggested itself to me, which I beg leave to mention It is said the indians are embodying at the hickory ground— Suppose you give an order immediately for us to form a Junction with you at headquarters that we proceed and defeat the indians at that place after which you will discharge those irritable men I mean the mounted men and cavalry—they will go home—You cant stop them, I however will address them to morrow and indeavour to get them to remain 'till I receive your answer—The men I have brot on are mounted, they together with the cavalry & mounted men, can carry as much provisions and corn, as will accomplish the above object—I have understood that Genl. Pinckneys orders to you are to hold all the ground You take, a good plan could it be effected. I know the consequince of a retrigade movement— But would'nt it be better to fight the indians at the hickory ground while you have men; and fall back if necessary to your present position—than to remain where you are—the men to go home and nothing be effected—You cant form an idea of the restless disposition of the mounted men & cavalry. Genl. Coffee has been sick, & no opportunity has been lost to injure him—The men I have brought with me are anxious for the fight and I pray God you would order us as above. I know, and time and experience will prove it, that it is the last good West Tennessee will do. I wish I was mistaken—but when I have the honor of seeing you—I will tell you more than you could wish to believe—You have a copy of the order I issued,[2] some officers obayed it, some did not—numbers of men collected for the purpose of coming on, but were stopt by the base insinuations of designing men—Genl. Roberts done the cause an injury by stating, that I had not authority from you to act and that even if I had, you could not give it legally—Whether I have acted agreeably to your wish or not, it was as I thought best and such as I thought would meet your approbation—I have deviated in no respect from your order except in getting mounted men—on that you were silent—and had I issued an order for footmen, I could not have marched fifty men to your relief—and you know that they are much the best for indian warfare—they can make quick excurtions and carry their own provisions—no baggage waggons are necessary—While I wait your answer I will be engaged in mustering the men into service and having their horses valued—I will issue and order this night for camp police, disaffected volunteers shall not approach us—I beg your answer to the foregoing as well as the following—will the men after having been formed into a regt be under the command of Genl. Coffee? I will not elect field officers 'till I hear from you—will they be elected by the platoon officers? The men at least some of them want me to command them—Can you permit me to disc[h]arge the duties of Colo. of the line and Inspector Genl.?[3] I dont want it but am willing to do any thing for the Genl. good? will the three companies of Madison troops[4] be organized with the Tennessee troops. They wont make more than a large regt.? I can prepare twelve days provisions—and come on against any time you please to order—

Majr. Searcy is very sick at this place—he came out with me, and took ill on the way—I will remain at this place till I hear your answer to the foregoing and such orders as you may please to give—regulating the new troops as much as possible—If it is in my power to detain the volunteers and mounted men till I hear from you, I will do so—I do hope you will take one fight out of them before you go home—I will want some arms, I understand you have detained some—on that please advise me—I had to give an order for the impressment of arms—Thought it proper that the man who would not fight should at least furnish a gun if he had it—You can have no confidence in Colo. [John] Stump[5]—on my arrival at Nashville I gave him an order to raise volunteers—he notified me that he had 40 ready to march—he did not attend the day appointed—I sent him an order to report himself without delay or I would make known his conduct at Headquarters The truth then came out, he had'nt a man—many more acted in a similar way—I will make you an accurate return the moment I have it in my power

I conclude, in hast, your sincere friend

Wm. Carroll

I have Just discovered that the officers commanding the new volunteer corps have enrolled them for only Sixty days now you will perceive that I did'not authorize a thing of the kind—but so it is and Cant be helped Good God I wish you knew every thing they can be activly employed during that time—I dont know what you will make of the Govrs. order about the discharge of the volunteers.[6] I think I would send them home and discharge them   Wm. Carroll

ALS, DLC.
1. Shelby (1786–1859; University of Pennsylvania) opened a medical practice in Nashville about 1810. He served as Jackson's hospital surgeon until losing an eye in battle in early 1814. After the war he continued to practice in Nashville and promoted Jackson's political fortunes.
2. Not found.
3. For Jackson's response, see AJ to Carroll, December 27, below.
4. Volunteers raised in Madison County, Ala., and mustered into service at Huntsville.
5. Stump (1776–1848), Frederick's son and Nashville merchant of the firm Stump & Cox, was commissioned lieutenant colonel commandant of the 20th Regiment, Tennessee militia, in 1811. He was court martialed for cowardice after the Battle of Enotochopco in January 1814.
6. See Blount to AJ, December 15.

From Thomas Pinckney

Head Quarters Sixth & Seventh Districts—
Fort Hawkins[1] 24th December 1813—

Sir,

Mr Cooper brought to me at Milledgeville on Wednesday last your dispatches of the 11th. 12th. & 13th. of this month.[2] The enclosed Copies of Letters the originals whereof I dispatched to Knoxville by the last Mail will shew you the measures I immediately adopted in consequence of the information contained in your last.[3] Be assured, Sir, I sympathize sincerely in the mortification you must have suffered in finding the progress of your career so suddenly checked by the want of provision and by short enlistments. I however hope that an enterprize wherein the zeal & bravery of the Tennessee Troops has been already signalized by two complete victories will still afford you fresh laurels, and that as you have observed, so you will finally obtain complete success.

Until your re-inforcements shall arrive, if you find your present force, aided by such of the Cherokees as you can rely upon, will be adequate to effect temporary expeditions against such of the Enemy's Towns or

Settlements as are within striking distance you will please to do so. You will find your Soldiers always best satisfied when employed; and unless you harrass the Enemy they will be tempted to plague you. If they should have judgment and enterprize enough to throw themselves in your Convoys of Provisions between Forts Deposit & Strother or between the Look out Mountain & Fort Armstrong they would do you incalculable injury.

The great extent of this land carriage made me at first prefer the transportation by land of about ten miles, afforded by the approach of the Highwassee to Conosauga Creek: which I hope my Aide de Camp Lt. Morris (who has not yet returned) with the aid of Governor Blount may put in operation. If you should find difficulties in the way of your transportation on the Coosa below Talladega, You will be obliged to adopt the more tedious and less efficacious method of erecting a chain of posts on your way to the Fork.

Inclosed you have a seperate Letter authorizing you to draw on the Department of War for money to pay for supplies when the Contractors fail to furnish them.[4] I think it probable the Knoxvile Banks will furnish money upon such drafts. I have no cash or I would send you a part of my stock for this purpose.

Genl. Floyd commanding the Georgia Troops very properly opened your letter addressed to me brought by the friendly Indian, and by his return informed you of his situation.[5] He is directed to advance a Post in Front of Coweta and his next movement will be on the Tallipoosa near the Fork.

I fear your re-inforcements and provisions will not arrive in time for you to meet him there; but such operations as you can with safety carry on against the Enemy nearest to you may occasion a diversion in his favor.

I have written to desire Genl. Flournoy to send from Fort Stoddart a Convoy of Provisions up the Alabama to the Fork as soon as he can procure it and can send a Detachment strong enough to fight its way up—but I know not when he will be able to effect it.

Genl Floyd will accompany this by a Letter informing you of his present situation & intention.[6]

I have the honor to be very respectfully Sir Your Most Obedient Servant.

Thomas Pinckney

LS and Copy, DLC; LC, ScHi. Extract published in Bassett, 1:408–409.
1. On the Ocmulgee River in Georgia, opposite Macon.
2. See AJ to Pinckney, December 11 and 13 (above). Letter of December 12 not found.
3. See Pinckney to Blount and to John Williams, and Francis K. Huger to Williams, December 23, DLC.
4. See Pinckney to AJ, December 23.
5. See AJ to Pinckney, December 8, and John Floyd to AJ, December 18.
6. Floyd's letter has not been found.

To Willie Blount

Head quarters Fort Strother
December 26th. at Night 10 oclock

Dear Sir

I am wearied with dating letters at this place—every exertion that was within my power has been made, to progress with the campaign and save the State from disgrace—still insurmountable difficulties present themselfs, and it appears, that I am to be left alone struggling to obtain the object—I have advised you, of the failure of General Cocke to bring into the field, the fifteen hundred men agreable to requisition of the Secratary of war that was so anxiously sought for by him to fill from his division—I have transmitted you his letters promising supplies of breadstuffs, which was never forwarded, I have advised you of my order to him to return and pass by the way of Fort armstrong and there make arangements, for transporting, from thence to this place a sufficient supply of bread stuff, and to go from there to Rosses, and see that the contractor had a sufficient supply there, and direct his quarter master to have it immediately transported to Fort armstrong, and in case there was not sufficient supplies delivered at Rosses by the contractor agreable to his requisition forthwith to order the quarter master to purchase at any price to fill the requisition—The enclosed letters from Colo. [William] Snodgrass will shew you how far the regulations of the general has afforded supplies here—The finishing of the Fort in the heart of the Cherokee nation, appears to be a primary object instead of supplies for this army[1]—I have enclosed you heretofore his order to Genl White,[2] that occasioned the general to retrograde and not form a Junction with me and which occasioned my retrograde from Tulladega, after the battle *that* has proved fatal to my arangements—I enclose you a note I sent to Colo Lillard of this day with his answer which will shew you with what intentions and expectations the Junction was formed with me, by the east Tennessee troops[3]— was it not for the declarations of Colo Lillard personally, added to the expressions of his Regt. I could not believe, that the general would have made such a promise to men whose service was much needed as the one contained in Colo. Lillards note, without notifying me thereof—I enclose them however for your perusal, and a further evidence of the boasted patriotism of the State, when danger approaches—

I have just recd a letter from Colo. Carroll, from Huntsville advising me that he has about six hundred mounted men, whose officers say they have Volunteered their service for sixty days,[4] I have no authority to accept of the service of men for so short a term nor do I know of any law that would authorize it—I gave Colo. Carroll orders to raise on my own responsibility one thousand footmen for six months or during the campaign—I have wrote to Colo Carroll,[5] if they will on the responsibility, of the government for payment, without any responsibility on me, come on and serve Sixty days to bring them on, but explain to them, that they are not in the field by my orders or on my responsibility—I am ordered by Genl Pinckney to advance and fortify and retain the ground I take possession of,[6] men for sixty days service answers but little purpose in such a campaign as contemplated by the goverment—the Goverment intends to conquer the Creek nation and hold possession of it—The President has predicated his orders to Genl Pinckney on the reliance that the state of Tennessee has 5000 troops in the field; when in fact she has not one thousand that she can calculate on—I cannot think it possible that you will hesitate under existing circumstances, to order a draft to fill up the Deficiency, occasioned by the ommission of General Cocke and the desertion of the Volunteers—when we view the conduct of the Governors [Return Jonathan] Meigs and [Isaac] Shelby,[7] to aid Harrison with men, and how gratefull the general Goverment has been to them for their patriotism— will it be sufferred to be said and recorded in history, that the Governor of Tennessee will permit a campaign so prosperously begun, defeated and with it the reputation of the State for patriotism damd forever, for the want of his exertions, and the fear of taking a little responsibility on himself—I cannot, I will not believe it—is the freeman of the State so lost to every feeling of true americans, lost to every feeling of the soldier and the patriot to shrink from the contest, with a savage tribe that has murdered our *fathers* our *wives* and our *sleeping babes*—If this is the case, which I fear it is, then Sir your powers is looked up to cure the evil, and to save the state and the citizens (who are devoid of noble feelings) from eternal disgrace, by immediately ordering a draft under the requisition of the late law of the State[8]—and the requisition of the Secratary of war—I say under the law of the State—for inasmuch as the campaign is not finished contemplated by that act—and as the number of thirty five hundred men is not in the field, it is your duty to require, not only to have the requistion of the Secratary of war, but the requisition of the law of the State filled, and the campaign carried on with that vigor contemplated by the late law—here Sir, permit me to be plain, is a greater responsibility upon you; in not ordering, than to order, here is a positive law that requires you to act untill the thing contemplated by the law is completly carried into effect, and particularly so as the general goverment has sanctioned the act of the State and believes and has a right so to do, that five thousand men are in the field for the campaign or for six months—The men having been once in the field and having retrograded, does not do away your powers under the law—or your obligations to the state and the general govment—in having the campaign continued to the full extent now contemplated by the general goverment—where does the Governor of Georgia obtain his power from—the same as yours, from a requisition of the Secratary of war for fifteen hundred men and a law of the State—The time of the first class have expired—The Governor of Georgia has ordered a draft, as I am informed by Mr. Cooper—express from Genl. Pinckney and are now marching [some] thirty five hundred men up to relieve those that have served six months under Genl Floyd—and will it be permitted to be said that the governor of the once patriotic State of Tennessee, at such an important crisis as the present, when the creeks are more than half conquered, a British force on the coast ready to aid and supply them—and reanimate their sinking spirits—I repeat will it be permitted to be recorded in the page of history that the governor of Tennessee hesitated one moment on the subject of exercising his power to carry into effect the grand object of the State and the general goverment in bringing the campaign to a speedy happy conclusion by ordering a draft for such number of men as will fill the deficiency of the quota of this state—but now absent from the service—I *hope not*—delay will not do, the campaign must not be delayed—every exertion must be made to put down the creeks and meet the British at the walls of Pensacola—There is the Point to put a speedy end to the war—and I hope your exertions will not be wanting, to enable me agreable to Genl Pinckneys orders, there to meet the eternal enemies of our peace put an end to the war, and give peace to our southern and western frontiers—These sentiments grow out of your letter to Colo. Carrol which this evening reached me from Colo. Carrol[9]—in which you say you have no power to order men out—and I have given you mine with the frankness of a friend, in the present disagreable situation of our country—I believe you have the power, I believe every patriot, will Justify your exercising of it, and the publick good requires you should promptly exercise it—I wish you to give me a speedy answer that I may know my true situation and advise Genl Pinckney what he may rely on—Genl Pinckney having requested that I should name some fit person to act as asst. D. q master for East Tennessee—I have named Mr [James] Baxter, who sets out tomorrow morning to take a peep into the causes why I have got no supplies from East Tennessee of breadstuff with the necessary instructions to purchase[10]—I will try if I can not to punish McGees pockett for his conduct—let me hear from you by [the next] express, my situation is a critical one, and the frontier of your State will be in an equal critical situation, if I am compelled to retrograde, with a British army to supply and aid the creeks—a posponement will not do, it will have the same evills of a retrograde and attended with equal expense to the goverment, the expense is more than half incurred, if you will from the whole State give me Twenty five hundred men—I will hazard with my life and reputation a full completion of the campaign with that number if spedily furnished and supplied—

I am sir respectfully, yr mo. ob. serv.

Andrew Jackson

ALS copy, DLC. Published in Bassett, 1:409–11.

1. See Snodgrass to AJ, December 21 and 24. Snodgrass (1760–1849), a Revolutionary War veteran, had represented Sullivan County in the state House of Representatives. He commanded a regiment of East Tennessee volunteers during the Creek War. Jackson assumed that Snodgrass had been ordered to construct boats for transporting supplies across the Coosa River, but Snodgrass reported that his men were being used to construct Fort Armstrong. Jackson asked Cocke for an explanation and ordered Snodgrass to shift his efforts to boat construction (AJ to Cocke and to Snodgrass, December 24).

2. See Cocke to James White, November 6, DLC, and above, p. 449n (extract quoted).

3. See AJ to William Lillard and Lillard to AJ, December 26. Jackson asked Lillard to canvass his regiment on their willingness to march immediately toward a junction with Floyd's forces. Lillard's refusal on behalf of the men was prompt and definite, based on Cocke's promise that they would be marched back to Fort Armstrong immediately and discharged January 14.

4. See above, Carroll to AJ, December 23.

5. See below. The letter to Carroll is dated December 27 but may have been drafted the evening of December 26.

6. See Pinckney to AJ, December 2.

7. Governors of Ohio and Kentucky respectively. Meigs was the son of Cherokee agent Return Jonathan Meigs.

8. Jackson was referring to the act passed September 24, authorizing the governor to march 3,500 militiamen of Tennessee against the Creeks (*Laws of Tennessee*, 10th General Assembly, Ch. 1).

9. See Blount to Carroll, December 7, DLC.

10. See AJ to Baxter, December 27.

To William Carroll

Head Quarters Ft. Strother. Decr. 27th. 1813

Dr Sir

I recd. last night late your letter of the 23d. Inst datd Huntsville,[1] & am sorry to hear that such confusion reigns among the volunteer Cavalry and mounted gun men, & such shamful & disgraceful waste of the scanty supplies that have been collected for the army—this must be done with the same view there as the contractors hogs & horses were killed here—to produce a scarcity & form some excuse for their disgraceful desertion of the service of their country, when the enemy were embodied in front; and before they received a discharge from the competent authority to give it.

It fills me with regret, that those volunteers who you have brought into the field, should be enrolled for two months only—I know of no law that will authorise their being accepted of, or under which they can be paid—I was willing to hazard, under existing circumstances every responsibility, to get as many men into the field as would be sufficient in number to be substituted for, and in the stead of the volunteer infantry, not expecting, from the written pledge of the officers of both volunteer cavalry and mounted gun-men, that there would be a discontent or murmur in continuing the campaign. When I first heard of their desertion, and mutinous disposition, and received your letter, that you were bringing on all mounted gun-men—believing that they were engaged for the campaign, or six months, agreeably to my order to you,[2] I was content, and willing still to hazard the responsibility myself. Men for sixty days, under present circumstances, and the orders of General Pinckney, will answer the government but little purpose—but still I will be grateful for their services, & they are entitled to & receive my thanks for their patriotism— You must frankly explain them their situation, endeavor to have their term of service changed agreeably to my order; I then will become responsible for their pay & cheerful acceptance by the government—otherwise you will explain to them, that for their services for 60 days they must depend on the liberality of the government & not upon any responsibility on me, still stating as frankly that no influence on my part will be wanting to procure them justice & full compensation for their services, or in other words say to them that I have no power to order or accept the services of men for 60 days, that there is no law authorizing such a term of service that it must be for 6 months or during the campaign, & that my order to you was predicated upon that term of service—Under the above explanation, I shall freely & thankfully accept of their service & shortly lead them on to battle, with a sanguine hope of victory—I have duly weighed your observations on the subject of ordering up the mounted men & volunteers, with those that have come on with you—A number of points present themselves on the subject when considered—first will they obey the order & march with the supplies of beef & pork on hand, (for we have no bread here)—we have beef & pork on hand from the contractors report yesterday for forty days rations for 2000 men 2d. will their force, with what can be spared from Genl. Roberts Brige. be a sufficient force to make the intended movement. I know not your numbers & therefore cannot form an opinion (about 500 may be calculated from that Brige.[)]—if it is I authorize the order to be given—there is no dependence to be placed on the Regt from E. T., that when ordered they will march—I tried that on yesterday, anxious to be moving forward, & often hearing them say they wanted to fight before they returned home—and to have one fight out of them, I addressed Col Lillard a note upon the subject, intending to order you up immediately by forced marches, if the consent was given—They answered in the negative, that Genl Cocke had promised them that they should be marched home in 15 days after they left Ft Armstrong & they ment to go home &c &c &c[3]—I am anxious to move forward—the whole force on Tallapoosee & Coosee are now on the west side of the Tallapoosee & the East side of the Coosee & with sufficient force a fatal blow could be struck—With 1500 men, exclusive of 500 that may be counted on here I would hazard every thing, nay even with 1200—recollect, situated as I am it would not do to hazard a defeat—& if Genl Coffee & you can ascertain that the mounted men & cavalry, that will march under these circumstances, fairly understanding the supplies, let the order be issued to bring them up speedily, by Genl

Coffee—The new raised troops brought on by you are entitled to be commanded by officers of their own choice—the field officers to be chosen by the Platoon officers—& you will direct them thus to be organized—The Madison troops will be left to their own choice, whether to remain as a separate Regt or Battalion or join the other—the whole if constituting a Brige. will be commanded by Genl. Coffee if his health permits to be in the field—if yr force will in yr opinion & Genl. Coffees be sufficient to authorise a movement agreeably to the within ideas, & he will agree to march, I inclose an order to Genl. Coffee to march them up immediately,[4] be pleased to shew this letter to Genl Coffee—

> Andrew Jackson
> Major Genl.

I have not time to look into the rules & articles of war to determine the point in yr letter, but should you be the choice of the officers of the Regt. the thing can be easily adjusted   A. J.

Copy, DLC.
1. See above.
2. See AJ to Carroll, December 3.
3. See AJ to William Lillard, and Lillard to AJ, December 26.
4. See AJ to Coffee, December 27.

To John Floyd

(Copy)   Fort Strother Ten Islands 27th Decr 1813
Sir,

On the 23rd Inst: I received dispatches from Genl. Pinckney; among which was an account of your fortunate engagement with the Enemy at Autossee on the 29th ultimo.[1] I offer you my sincere congratulations on the success of that affair; and at the same time that I do so, I must be permitted to lament that there has been so little concert in the operations of the Georgia, and Tennessee Troops.

When the Campaign was opened, I did all I could to establish a perfect harmony in their movements. Believing that irregular, & temporary incursions into the Enemy's Country would be far from producing those Effects, for which the War was undertaken.

In this endeavor however I was very unfortunate. when I had approached nearly to the heart of the Enemy's Country, I found myself standing alone, unsupported by the Georgia Troops, or those from E. Tennessee; and what was worse, unsupported by the contractors. But it was then too late to make new arrangements. I fought the Enemy & obtained two signal victories over them. Had I then received either co-operation I expected from the E. Tennessee Troops, or, supplies, the Creek War before this had been ended—But I received neither, and for the worst of both, was compelled to retrograde from Talladega to this point. Since then I have had a thousand difficulties to contend against which need not be mentioned. A greater part of my Men, unwilling to submit to further privation, and believing their term of service to have expired, have gone home; many of those who remain, operated upon by the same causes threaten soon to return. Thus situated I found it necessary to send back to Tennessee to raise a new Corps of Volunteers upon my own responsibility; and I understand a thousand are now on their way to join me. They are all mounted men; & I have sent an Express to meet them, with orders that they shall remain in Madison County, where their horses can be fed, until supplies shall have been furnished to enable me to make another movement from this point.

Those supplies I expect in a few days; not with great confidence it is true; because I have been too often disappointed by the Contractor already, to form such an Expectation; but with some degree of hope, in speaking of supplies, I now allude particularly to bread stuff, and forage for our horses: but whether they be furnished or not, it is my present purpose to assemble all my forces, and commence another movement from here about the 6th of next month, for the junction of the Coosa & Talipoosa.

Our provisions of meat will I believe justify such a measure, and the situation of our affairs renders it necessary. If I am correctly informed (and I have omited no means to procure the most correct information) the principal force of the Enemy is now on the West of the Talipoosa, on this River at the "fish Traps" and near the hickory grounds They have been led into false notions by the delays which I have been made to experience, and ought to be soon undeceived.

Whenever I recommence another movement from this point, I will advise you of it by express, & then I shall desire and expect co-operation from the Troops now under your command; permit me to say, I lament very sincerely the wound you have received, and to express a hope that it may not disable you from continuing in the present Campaign.

If any occurrence should make it necessary that I should be advised of the situation & intended movements of the Georgia Army, I hope it will be immediately communicated by Express.

I am very respectfully Yr Obt. Servt.

(signed)　Andrew Jackson

Major Genl. T.V. Service U.S.

Copy, DNA-RG 107; LC, DLC.
1. See above, Pinckney to AJ, December 12.

To John Cocke

Head quarters Fort Strother Decr. 28th. 1813.

Sir

you will receive herewith enclosed, a complaint lodged by the path killer,[1] against part of your Division on their return march from this place—If the statement, should be correct, it is a reflection on the State, as well as on the Regt. Brigade or Division to whom they belong, and ought to meet with speedy and ample punishment—If any thing could have been proved against old Rattcliff, of any Treason, or hostility against the united States, then and in that case he was amenable to the laws of the united States, and ought to have been arrested and tried by such tribunal as had competant Jurisdiction of the offence—But that a sett of men should without any authority rob a man who is claimed as a member of the Cherokee nation, who is now friendly and engaged with us in a war against the hostile creeks, is such an outrage, to the rules of war—the laws of nations and of civil Society, and well calculated to sower the minds of the whole nation against the united States—and is such as ought to meet with the frowns of every good citizen, and the agents be promptly prosecuted and punished as robers—I have to request on the receipt of this you will cause old Rattcliff to be liberated, his property returned, and the offenders arrested and punished.[2] I have wrote to governor Blount upon this subject and Colo. Jonathan J. Meigs,[3] whose duty it is as well as ours, to have Justice done in all such cases, and the offenders punished—for the credit of the Troops from your Division it is that the guilty should be apprehended and punished, that the reputation of the honest part of your Division, may not be Tarnished by the acts of the dishonest—Is it not cruel that the *whooping boy*,[4] who fought bravely at Talushatchey and got wounded at the Battle of Talladega—should be plundered, by the east Tennessee troops, whilst confined with his wounds—what will the general goverment think of the State, if such things is permitted to go unpunished—It is as much Theft as tho the property, was stolen from one of our own citizens, and the laws of the united States provide amply for the punishment—Strict inquiry ought to be made whether any commissioned officers were present, or had any knowledge of this atrocious act, and if so they ought to be immediately arrested, and tried by a court martial, and afterwards transferred to the civil authority—I have just learnt by Doctor Vandyke that it was Colo. Wears Regt. that has committed the above fellonies—and I have the fullest confidence in your exertion to have this business well prosecuted and by that means have the stain that it has inflicted on the reputation of our State thereby washed out and blotted forever—for I hope and trust it is the last of the kind that will ever be recorded, and I have to repeat again, that it is best, that all officers should be arrested and tried by a court martial—it is stated that Colo Wear was privy to it, if so, have him arrested, if he is innocent, it is due to him than an investigation should be had, that his character may not be under the stigma that it now labours under—May it be done away—Before I close this letter I must name again to you, that we have not one pound of bread stuff and information from Fort armstrong states there is none at that place—It appears that there is some enchantment, wrought, by the Indian prophets on our contractors, that will lead to our Starvation but to counteract this *phisic*—as I advised you in mine of yesterday,[5] I have at the request of the commander in chief of this army Genl Pinckney appointed Major James Baxter Asst. D. quarter Master and sent him to overlook the contractors, with full powers to buy in case he has not an ample supplies agreable to your and Genl Pinckney requisitions—I now know in a few days we will have ample supplies—I wish you on the recpt of this forthwith to inform me by express—in what forwardness the fifteen hundred troops, under the requisition of the President is in and at what time they will be in the field—existing circumstances requires promptness in execution—The Indians are in our front and a British force Just arived at Pensacola

I have the honor to be verry respectfully yr mo. ob. serv.

Andrew Jackson
Major—

ALS draft, DLC. Published in Bassett, 1:414–16.

1. See Pathkiller to AJ, December 28.

2. Ratcliff, a wealthy half-Cherokee, was arrested by East Tennessee cavalry on suspicion of collaborating with the hostile Creeks. Several slaves and horses belonging to him and other Cherokees were confiscated. For the resolution of the Ratcliff case, see Rufus Morgan to AJ, January 11; Hugh Lawson White to AJ, January 14; Cocke to AJ, January 16, and AJ to Cocke, January 31; AJ to Morgan, February 1, 1814 (DLC).

3. Neither letter found. Jackson meant Return Jonathan Meigs, the Cherokee agent.

4. Not further identified. According to Pathkiller, the cavalry took eight of Whooping Boy's horses.

5. See AJ to Cocke, December 27.

To John Coffee

Head quarters Fort Strother
Decbr 29th. 10 oclock at night 1813

I had the pleasure of receiving by last nights express yours of the 27th. instant[1] and thank you for pushing on the express, but it really brought nothing but lengthy milk and cider recommendations of retrograding by the governor assertions of good wishes to the cause I am engaged in, and regret of want of power to aid me by men untill instructed by the Secratary of war[2]—I have give him a good natured tickler by Lt [Joel] Parish,[3] by the express that goes on with this, I give him a godgen,[4] that will make him look and see his own situation and that of the consequences of a failure or delay of the campaign—I have pointed out his duty and his power in strong language not to be mistaken—I have give him the orders of the goverment to me their expectations of the force in the field from Tennessee, their disappointment in not finding it in the field when a Spanish force is before pensacola—and have asked him what answer he can make to the goverment on not having 1500 in the field under the requisition of the secratary of war from the Eastern section of the state under his order—and why he has not called on his officer, for an answer why he has not brought them into the field—and lastly painted in high colours, the pledge we have made of protection to the friendly indians their situation if I retrograde—with a British force at pensacola, the Choctaws wavering, my orders to advance—and the situation of the georgia army in case I retreat—and wind up with shewing his responsibility with his certain damnation if the campaign fails & him sitting with his arms folded and waiting for orders from the Secratary of war—I think it will arouse him from his lethargy & make him act—

I hope my answer to the address of the mounted gunmen & cavalry reached you before they seperated and that it was read to them—I also hope you have had it published in the Huntsville gazett and then send it on to Nashville for publication[5]—let the world see how Colo. [John] Alcorn[6] will look in the future with his sacred pledge signed with his own hand—& exciting and encouraging desertion & mutiny—if they go let them go and as Capt David Smith writes to me "they will be met with the curses of their country both in front and rear."[7]

I wrote you the other day, by express and refered you to Colo Carrols letter for further information,[8] I hope he has made my powers known to those brave men that has come on with him, a soldier never ought to be deceved he never ought to do service for which he will not be paid. of their pay I have no doubt, but as their term of service does not bring them within any law or order, the power of directing payment rests not with me and I do not wish them to be deceved—

In the name of god what is the contractors quarter masters, and adjutant Antony about[9]—Where is the pack horses, and waggons I sent the quarter master to purchase and send on with meal—we have not one pound of bread stuff nor have we had for two days.

Can it be possable that the contractors has employed the publick horses to carry there meal from the mills to Fort Deposit—I hope not—you will please see to that—they are bound to furnish the transportation to the south bank of the Tennessee the U.S. afterwards—I am anxious to make a movement before the Holston Regt[10] leaves me, their time is up on the 14 of January—I have sent Baxter up to Fort Armstrong and Rosses, with instructions to purchase supplies at any price and to have them pushed forward to us—he will do his duty and I feel confident will discover the combination that has starved us, founded on the intention of destroying our operations—all things will be right I hope shortly as soon as my letter get on to the war office—should any supplies come down the river I will advise you, and as soon as breadstuff and the portage can be procured with you, to Justify a movement and your force added to the force here, is 2000, move up without further orders, should the supplies not come in a few days we will loose the Holston troops which is Eight hundred strong, few of them will march forward without coertion, and when they have but a few days to serve coertion would be improper—in a few days we could reach the hickory ground and one blow will finish the war on Cosa and Tallaposa—I learn that Genl Adams is some where on the head of Tallaposa, but what he has done as yet I have not heard—

accept of my congratulations on your returning health—I hope you will be able to command through the campaign—your name is verry highly spoken off in the Presidents message[11]—This will be a killing stroke to your envious enemies and is as highly gratifying to me—I wish if I can to make a bold stroke, and form a Junction with the Georgia troops, and conjointly form a Junction with Claibourne—scouring the country [o]n both banks of the allabama—I have a party [of] two hundred and fifty out now on the Cahaba [and h]ope they may bring me some hair—

with sentiments of Esteem I am yours respectfully

Andrew Jackson

P.S. I wish this express pushed on to Nashville

ALS, DLC. Published in Bassett, 1:420–22.
1. See above.
2. See Blount to AJ, December 26.
3. Parrish, Jr. (d. 1834), of Williamson County, commanded a company at the Battle of Horseshoe Bend. For the "tickler," see above, AJ to Blount, December 26.
4. Jackson possibly meant "goading" (see AJ to Blount, December 29).
5. See AJ to Coffee, December 25, published in *Nashville Whig*, January 25, 1814.
6. Allcorn (1769–1829), from Wilson County, was lieutenant colonel on the Natchez expedition. He commanded a regiment of volunteer cavalry in the Creek War until December 1813.
7. See Smith to AJ, December 23.
8. See AJ to Coffee, December 27.
9. Jackson had dispatched Anthony to Huntsville to expedite the forwarding of supplies to the army.
10. William Lillard's regiment from East Tennessee.
11. In his annual message to Congress, delivered December 7, President Madison mentioned Coffee's name in commending the victory at Tallushatchee (*Annals of Congress*, 13th Cong., 2nd sess., p. 540).

To Rachel Jackson

Head quarters Fort Strother
Decbr 29th. 1813. ½ past 11 oclock at night

My love

After twenty four hours of labour in preparing dispatches for Major Genl Pinckney, the Secratary of war and Governor Blount, during which time Major Read my aid, and myself has not Slept one hour, before I lie down—(as the express is to Start at day light) I take up my pen to Say to you that I am well, my arm mending I hope I will be able to wear my coat Sleeve on it Soon—I have been much pestered and vexed with the shamefull retrograde of the Volunteers and mounted gunmen—and with the still more shamefull indolence of the contractors, in not supplying us with provisions—I have been anxious to advance and meet the wishes of the commander in chief by putting a Speedy end to the war and return to you again, but our supplies will not Justify a movement as yet—at present we have not one pound of meal but plenty of good beef and pork—with this I tried if I could prevail on the Troops to advance but the Holston Regt. except two fine companies commanded by Capts. [William] Hamilton and [George] argenbright refused[1]—five days we could have cleared the cosa and Talleposa, and opened communication with Genl Floyd who commands the Georgia Troops—But they did not come to fight—altho it was there complaint that they had come for that purpose and was sorry they could not have one fight that induced me to make the proposition with the supply of Beef & pork on hand—I found it would not do and I am fearfull when I get supplies up, which I am making every exertion to do I shall have no men to fight with The shamefull desertion from their posts of the Volunteer Infantry—The Violated Pledge of the cavalry & mounted infantry under their own proper signatures, and the apathy displayed in the interior of the state by the fireside Patriotts will sink the reputation of our State—and I weep for its fall—and with it the reputation of the once brave and patriotic Volunteers—who a few privations, sunk from the highest elevation of patriots—to mere, wining, complaining, sedioners and mutineers—to keep whom from open acts of mutiny I have been compelled to point my cannon against, with a lighted match to destroy them—This was a grating moment of my life—I felt the pangs of an affectionate parent, compelled from duty, to chastise his child—to prevent him from destruction & disgrace and it being his duty he shrunk not from it—even when he knew death might ensue—This was a painfull moment, but it is still more painfull, to hear of their disorderly, and disgracefull conduct on their return—had I have been with them this should not have happened—what a contrast between their present return and there return last spring Then they return cloathed with a good reputation, praised by all, ¿what now—retreating from the field, leaving a half conquered enemy behind them within 65 miles in force, their conduct rude and disorderly—There abandonment of the service may destroy the campaign and leave our frontier again exposed to the Tomhawk of the ruthless savage—and now the return disgraced—hated and cursed by all—for there shamefull and disgracefull retrograde—no doubt you will hear of my situation being a critical and hazardous one—be not uneasy—that god that protects you at home, protects me here, and if I have trials, and Perils, he has fortified me with fortitude to do my duty under every circumstance—reguardless of consequences, and when I return, I return like a true patriot, without a tarnish on my reputation—

I must ask you to say to fields to have as much land cleared as he can, take care of my stock, and see that you are comfortable—if Mr Trigg of Gallatine comes for Truxton, on his shewing you my letter[2] and in making his election as to the choce of Terms on paper you will deliver him Truxton and Dinwodie if he wants Dun, for the Season—If Mr Trigg does not call for him capt David Smith was saying that he would take [hi]m & thought he could do well with him—do my love for the best—

Please write me how my little andrew [is] and whether, his little Indian Lyncoya was taken to him by Major Whyte[3] of Gallatine—if he has got him how & what he thinks of him—Keep Lyncoya in the house—he is a Savage [but one] that fortune has thrown in my h[ands when] his own female matrons wanted to k[ill him] because the whole race & family of his [blood] was destroyed—I therefore want him well taken care of, he may have been given to me for some Valuable purpose—in fact when I reflect that he as to his relations is so much like myself I feel an unusual sympathy for him—tell my dear little andrew to treat him well—and kiss andrew for me, and with love to all friends accept the blessing of your affectionate husband

Andrew Jackson

P.S. two days since I sent you my famous pipe taken from the famous Bob Catala by Mr Parish—keep it for my sake

ALS, CSmH. Published in *Huntington Library Bulletin*, 3(1933):113–15.
    1. Hamilton (d. 1814) of Grainger County and Argenbright of Hawkins County were the only two company commanders in Lillard's 2nd Regiment who accepted Jackson's invitation to join him for an immediate march to attack the Creeks (see Hamilton and Argenbright to AJ, December 17). Hamilton was killed at the Battle of Enotochopco, January 24, 1814.
    2. Letter not found.
    3. William White.

From John Coffee

Huntsville 29th. Decr. 1813

Sir,

On the 26th Instant, I met your Order at Tennessee River, to my Cavalry Regt. wherein you gave your assent to their quiting the service on their own responsibility, &c.—the order together with the Govrs. letter to you, was read to them immediately;[1] when the Regt. generally (such as had not deserted the service before) availed themselves of the priviledges therein given—some few of the officers who had endeavoured to do their duty, has been permitted by me, to raise new companies and bring them on to join your army at a short day—but none have been prevailed on to stay except a few individuals, not sufficient to form a company, and some few officers, who are determined not to leave the service, some few of the men have joined the new Tennessee troops under Col Carroll, but very few, I think that Captains Molton, Kavanaugh, and [Robert] Jetton,[2] will very soon return with companies and join you—On the night of the 27th. Inst. I recd. your reply, (at this place) to the address of the Rifle Regt. demanding their discharge from further Service,[3] prior to that, they had recrossed the river and had encamped four miles north of this place, determined to go home at all events, but had been prevailed on by some of the officers to halt there untill they could hear from you, yesterday morning had them drawn up in solid Column, and read to them, their written pledges to you, (and which I knew not of before I recd them enclosed) and your reply thereto,[4] which was followed by an animated address from the Revd. Parson Blackburn, but all to no effect, they were much confused, some of the men denied authorising the pledge being made, while others who could not deny, said that as you did not give them an immediate written answer, they did not consider themselves bound thereby, and some few, honestly confessed they had acted imprudently, in that state of minds, the whole broke off, and went home, with like exceptions to that of the Cavalry Regt.—thus the Brigade has abandoned the Service, with the exception of Captain [Louis] Winstons Company of Madison County men[5] (who it is also believed will desert the service) and Captain Hammonds Company of Rangers, who has reported all ready to march but 6 or 8. who have deserted—there has been mustered into Service One Battalion of Madison County mounted men, that has been reported to me, but not their precise numbers, supposed to be about 240. One company I have ordered into the contractors service in packing meal and guarding it for the use of the army, the balance are a part in camp and some on furlough, to return to camp tomorrow when they will subject to my orders, the remaining part of this Battalion after deducting the company in the pack service, will not exceed from 160 to 180 men add to them Captain Hammonds company say 50, will make from 210 to 230 men exclusive of Captain Winstons Company if they come out—there will be some of the Spie companies, perhaps but I have no regular report of them. The Tennessee troops, I have nothing to do with further than to feed their horses. I ordered my quartermaster, and forage master[6] to furnish them in forage seeing they had no provisions made in that way. I have but little knowledge of them. I presume Col Carrol will give you a full account by this express, presume the whole amount of mounted men here to be about 850, whole term of service is 60 days. I shall proceed to have the procedings relative to the Rifle Regt. published, but cannot do it, untill you send me the address demanding a discharge; I did not keep a copy and none exist but the one in your possession, will you send it to me with such other and further advice as you may please on that Subject[7]—I can say nothing to you on the Subject of the contractors further than I have heretofore said to you I had concluded to start what few men are here under my directions, with the second load of packs, but on reflection will wait your Orders further on this Subject. I would be exceedingly glad to make a move towards you, and will the very moment you signify it to me. Several applications of officers who are left without commands are made to me, on the subject of their continuing in the service. I have advised all to stay, will it be better for Captains to return and raise companies of mounted men and come on with them, than to continue themselves now alone in service I would be glad of your advice on that subject, and any other in this unhappy moment of our army—

I am Dr. Genl. very respectfully your Obedent Servt.

Jno. Coffee

ALS, DLC.
1. See AJ to Coffee, December 24, enclosing Blount to AJ, December 15.
2. Jetton (1781–1840), a tavern owner in Murfreesboro, commanded a company of volunteer cavalry during the Natchez expedition and in the Creek War. He was a colonel of volunteers in the Seminole War, 1817–18, and later served in the state legislature.
3. See AJ to Coffee, December 25.
4. See Newton Cannon, et al. to AJ, [November 12], and AJ to Brigade of Volunteer Cavalry and Mounted Riflemen, November 21.
5. Winston was appointed register of the land office west of Pearl River in 1820.
6. Neil B. Rose and Joshua Haskell.
7. The address of the rifle regiment to Coffee, signed by John Harpole and twenty-one other officers, requested discharge on December 28 upon expiration of their three-month enlistment. Along with Jackson's reply of December 25, the address was published in the *Nashville Whig*, January 25, 1814.

To Thomas Pinckney

Head Quarters. Ft. Strother Decr. 31st. 1813.

Sir:

I advised you on the 27th Inst. of my situation, prospects & intentions[1]—Having since recd. from Govr. Blount two letters[2] answering certain enquiries which I had put to him, & recommending to me a course of conduct neither corresponding with my wishes, my sense of duty—nor my ideas of correct policy—I feel myself bound to transmit you copies thereof, together with the act of Assembly under which the troops were called into service[3]—To return into the settlements & wholly abandon, for a time the campaign, can only be justifyd. in my belief by the last extremities—Great as the difficulties are by which I am surrounded & they are greater than when I wrote you last, I cannot consider such an extremity as having yet arrived—should such a measure be adopted I am fearful that but little reliance need afterwards be placed on the aid of Tennessee in conquering the Creeks—Under this view, I am determined to retain my position until I am ordered to abandon them, or until I can really retain them no longer—I have said my situation was even less favorable than when I wrote you last: it is so in this, the 200 militia whom I advised you were coming on with Genl. Roberts, after having gotten within two miles of this place, have turned about, & are gone home, without my ever geting even sight of them—Genl. Roberts reported to me in writing on the morning of the 29th.[4] that in obediance to my order he had brought 191 men, to fill up the deficiency of his Brige.—Upon which I ordered him to parade them before the fort at 9 O'Clock on the next day: & the result was nevertheless that which I have mentioned: Added to this we are now wholly without corn—corn meal or flour: & I am not advised when any will arrive—

Gloomy as the prospect is, I have not abandoned the idea of advancing forward in a short time—Nothing, I find but the entire want of the means of moving can under some circumstances, justify the keeping militia long stationary—This want I may continue to experience, but nothing less shall prevent me from attempting at least, the execution of the purposes which I have heretofore expresed; & even in that event, I will not, if It can possibly be retained, abandon the present post until I receive positive instructions to do so.

I have ordered Genl. Roberts in pursuit of those new troops lately brought on by him & who after having been regularly mustered into service, so shamefully deserted on the 28th Inst. with instructions to use all the means & the power he possesses or can command to have them arrested & brought to head Quarters without delay, under a strong guard: & in the event of his not being able to command a force, by calling to his aid any of the U.S. troops within the State of Tennessee, sufficient to guard them safely to Head Quarters to have them safely confined in some secure jail, & make report thereof to me immediately—It has become indispensibly necessary that the most energetic measures should be adopted in regard to these citizen soldiers: & shall be happy to rec. yr. advice & instructions as to the proper manner of dealing with them in cases of such delinquency—A very feeble hope can be entertained that the rules & articles of war, will be properly enforced by any Court Martial that can be had here.

4 o clock P.M. I have just recd. a letter from Govr. Blount, a copy of which I send you,[5] stating, that altho he did not consider himself authorised to grant a discharge to the Militia or to say decisively, how long they were bound to remain in the field, yet that it was his opinion when they were called out it was only for a term of three months, & recommending that at the expiration of that period they should be discharged or dismissed until the Presidents will be known—The contents of this letter I have been requested by him to make known to them, which I shall accordingly do this evening: & the consequences then are not difficult to be foreseen—They will almost to a man abandon the service on the 4th. Jany. & altho I conceive I have no power to discharge or dismiss them, I shall not under such circumstances, attempt to oppose their return by force—They will quit the service at their own risk, & not unapprised of the probable consequences—Owing to this unfortunate occurrence I shall be compelled for the defense of this place which I am still determined to maintain so long as I can possibly maintain it, to order up immediately the new raised forces whom I advised were stationed in Madison—As I have just learned, I am likely to soon to receive more plentiful supplies, than I have hitherto been furnished with, if when those troops arrive, I should consider them sufficient for the purpose, I will advance & dislodge a body of the enemy who are assembled about 60 miles below us—even if it should be necessary to return immediately afterwards, to this point—As to this movement however I can now give you no such assurance as will justify you in making any confident calculations upon it—Indeed I am by no means certain that the new raised volunteers will not be seized with the spirit of discontent, with which they will be so industriously attempted to be inspired by those who are returning, & never arrive here: Should even that be the case, I still hope & believe I shall be able with a few companies who will remain, to keep my position until further & effectual provision can be made for the prosecution of the Campaign. I have the honor &c.

Andrew Jackson
Major Genl.

LC, DLC; Copy, DNA-RG 107.
    1. See AJ to Pinckney, December 27.
    2. See Blount to AJ, December 22 (two letters, one above).
    3. The "act to repel the invasion of Tennessee by the Creek Indians, and to afford relief to the citizens of Mississippi Territory," passed on October 8 (*Laws of Tennessee*, 10th General Assembly, Ch. 1).
    4. See Roberts to AJ, December 28.
    5. See Blount to AJ, December 26.

Calendar, 1804–1813

1804

Jan 4   Authorization by AJ for the registration of deed from Thomas Masten to Jenkin Whiteside. DS, THi.

Jan 7   To John Coffee with enclosure.   3

Jan 8   From William Dickson. ALS, DLC. Bassett, 1:81. Discusses congressional investigation of federal judges Samuel Chase and Richard Peters and impeachment of John Pickering.

Jan 11   From Henry Dearborn. LS, NjP; LC, DNA-RG 107. Orders AJ to sell all but one of the boats built for the war department in 1803.

Jan 11   Receipt to William Nevels from Jesse Dawson (for AJ) for cotton. ADS copy, DLC.

Jan 13   To Henry Dearborn.   4

Jan 14   From John Rhea. ALS, DLC. Describes a congressional bill regulating the sale of lands for non-payment of the direct tax.

Jan 17   Receipt by Richard Waugh (for John Smith T) for merchandise received from Jackson & Hutchings. ADS, THer.

Jan 20   Account of David Campbell with the Gallatin store of Jackson & Hutchings. AD copy, DLC.

Jan 22   To [Henry Dearborn]. ALS, MHi. Discusses boat-building for the war department.

Jan 25   To Thomas Watson. ALS draft, DLC. Bassett, 1:81–82. Discusses the dissolution of their partnership and a discrepancy in the cotton account at Watson's gin.

Jan 26   Decision in *Andrew Jackson & Co. v. Thomas Mitchel*. Copy, CPQS Minutes, Vol. D:197, TNDa.

Jan 30   Receipt from Mark Mitchell for original copy of agreement between Mitchell and James McNare. AD in AJ's hand, signed by Mitchell, DLC.

Feb 6   To Rachel Jackson. ANS, THer. Instructs her to pay $45 to Edmond Melvin for his work on the war department boats.

Feb 10   Account of costs for building war department boats. AD, THi.

Feb 10   Promissory note for $111 from John Coffee & Co. to Jackson & Hutchings. ADS, DLC.

Feb 17   Abstract of war department warrant for payment of $3,566 to Thomas & John Clifford on AJ's account. AD, DNA-RG 59.

Feb 18   Memorandum of the sale of boats built for the war department. ADS, DLC.

Feb 22   From John Gordon. ALS, DLC. Discusses the building of ferry boats on the Duck and Tennessee rivers.

Feb 22–23   Promissory notes for $102.86½ from James McKinsey to Jackson

& Hutchings (DS, Sumner County Records, T); for $62.72¾ from John True to Jackson & Hutchings (DS, DLC); Feb 23, for $228 from Jackson & Hutchings to Isham F. and John Davis (ADS in AJ's hand, ICHi).

March 8   To Henry Dearborn. Abstract, DNA-RG 107. Discusses sale of the war department boats and the building of ferry boats.

March 11   To James Stephenson. ALS copy, DLC. Encloses a power of attorney (not found) and asks Stephenson to help secure title to a lot in Martinsburg, Pa., for AJ's wards, the children of Edward Butler.

March 13   Certification of AJ's attendance at March Term of Washington District Superior Court. ADS, Treasury Records, T.

March 15   Promissory note for $2.77½ from Sampson Powell to Jackson & Hutchings. DS, DLC.

March 31   Receipt from Elisha Fisher & Co. for $62.74 on account of Jackson, Watson & Co. ADS, DLC.

April 5   To Henry Dearborn. Abstract, DNA-RG 107. Advises of $140 draft in favor of Gilbert C. Russell for ferry boats.

April 5   Certification of the registration of deed for Samuel Houston. AD signed by AJ, THi.

April 12   Promissory note for $4.04 from Micajah Axim to Jackson & Hutchings. DS, DLC.

April 15   To Francis Preston. Printed, *New York Genealogical and Biographical Record*, 23(1892):154. Asks Preston to cancel his order for iron goods unless it can be shipped before May 20.

April 17   Receipt from Joseph Morton for $5.00. ADS, DLC.

April 19   License for operation of a retail store in Davidson County under firm name Andrew Jackson & Co. ADS, DLC.

April 22   Receipt to Edward Jones from Mary Donelson. AD in AJ's hand, signed by Mary Donelson, TNJ.

April 23   From John Coffee. ALS, DLC. Discusses business affairs of Andrew Jackson & Co.; lists goods to be purchased in Philadelphia.

April 23   Account of Jackson & Hutchings with Robert R. Smith for merchandise. AD, DLC.

April 23   Receipt for payment of account to Thomas Deaderick for hardware and jewelry. AD, DLC.

April 24   Account with Thos. & S. Prother for board and lodging of horse. Copy, Invoice book, THer. Runs to April 25.

April 28   Certification of account with the war department for $440.54 for expenses and compensation in procuring twenty-nine boats for the Louisiana expedition. LC, DNA-RG 217.

April   Certification of AJ's attendance at the Hamilton District Superior Court. ADS, Treasury Records, T.

[cApril]   Memorandum of goods purchased from Philadelphia merchants. AD, DLC.

May 3   *To John Coffee.*   21

May 4   Accounts of Jackson & Hutchings with merchants in Philadelphia and New Orleans. AD, THer. Run to July 23, 1806.

May 4   Invoice book, Jackson & Hutchings, for goods bought from Philadelphia and Pittsburgh merchants. AD, THer. Runs to July 23, 1805.

May 7   Memorandum of account of Jackson, Watson & Co. with Samuel Meeker. AD, DLC. Runs to March 26, 1805.

May 8–12   Bills of lading of goods shipped from Philadelphia to Pittsburgh, May 8, by Hayes Irwin (DS, DLC); May 11, by Benjamin Hoover (DS, DLC. Bassett, 1:92–93); May 11, by Jacob Grace and Adam Miller (DS, DLC); May 12, by George Gibson (DS, DLC).

May 13   *To John Coffee.*   22

May 14   Promissory note for $206.09 from Jackson & Hutchings to John Morrell & Son. Copy, DLC.

May 24   From William Stothart. ALS, DLC. Summarizes William P. Anderson's letter discussing militia election and the marriages of Willie Blount and Jesse Wharton, which reached Philadelphia after AJ left; encloses letter from Rachel Jackson (not found).

May 26   Memorandum from Charles S. Carson. AD, DLC. Bassett, 1:95. Asks AJ to take charge of merchandise awaiting shipment from Pittsburgh.

May 28   *Account with Thomas Gassaway Watkins.*   24

June 19   Deed, lot in Gallatin from James Trousdale to AJ and John Hutchings for $75. Copy, Deed Book 3(1800–1805):468, TGSum.

June 21   *To John Coffee.*   24

[cJune 21]   Memorandum of instructions regarding shipment of Jackson & Hutchings's merchandise (probably enclosed with AJ to John Coffee, June 21). AD, THi.

June 25   Promissory note for $28.90 from John Rice to Jackson & Hutchings. AD in AJ's hand, signed by Rice, DLC.

[June 27]   From Thomas & John Clifford. ALS fragment, DLC. Announces that the Clifford firm will receive accounts due to the recently dissolved Elisha Fisher & Co.

June 29   Inventory of merchandise on hand. AD, DLC.

[cJuly 1]   Memorandum of expenses incurred in shipping goods from Philadelphia to Nashville. AD, DLC. Bassett, 1:94–95 (dated Spring 1804).

July 4   To Henry Dearborn. Abstract, DNA-RG 107. Encloses Lieutenant William Simmons's receipt for two ferry boats delivered at Kentucky River.

July 4   Memorandum of payments made by William Stothart to merchants on the accounts of Jackson, Watson & Co. AD, DLC. Runs to November 10.

July 6   Deed, 640 acres (Grant No. 206 from North Carolina to Lewis Roberts [Robards]) to Edward Ward for $10,000. DS, DLC.

July 9   Account book, Hunter's Hill store. AD, THer. Runs to April 5, 1805.

July 11   Receipt from William Newell for $62.10 on Stothart & Bell's account. AD in AJ's hand, signed by Newell, T.

July 14   From Nathan Davidson. ALS, DLC. Bassett, 1:96–98. Replies to AJ's accusation that he mismanaged the sale of Jackson & Hutchings's cotton in New Orleans.

July 14   Account with Charles V. Lorumier for painting and wallpapering. ADS, DLC.

[July 14]   From Charles V. Lorumier. ANS, THi. Requests AJ to pay $25.48 on his account with John Coffee & Co.

July 15   From Isaac Roberts. ALS, DLC. Complains about delay in the issuing of his commission as general of the 5th Brigade.

July 15   From William Stothart.   25

July 16   Account of Jackson & Hutchings with James & Washington Jackson. AD endorsed by AJ, DLC. Runs to September 25, 1807.

July 16   List of payments made by James Jackson on the account of Andrew Jackson & Co. with Meeker, Denman & Co. AD extract, Mrs. Uhland O. Redd.

July 16   Memorandum of payments made to John Jackson, Philadelphia. AD endorsed by AJ, DLC. Runs to May 1805.

July 17   To Thomas Masten. ALS copy, DLC. Bassett, 1:98–99 (extract). Urges Masten to settle his land dispute with AJ and Thomas Hutchings.

July 18   Day book, Lebanon store. AD, THer. Runs to January 5, 1805.

July 19   Abstract of war department warrant for $140 paid to William Claggett on AJ's account. AD, DNA-RG 59.

July 20   From George Gillespie, addressed to "Gen. Daniel Jackson, Davidson." ALS, DLC. Discusses the collection of an execution.

July 20   From John Overton. AL fragment, DLC. Discusses business with John Smith T at Southwest Point.

July 22   From William Stothart. ALS, DLC. Advises that he has received advance payment on cotton shipped by Boggs & Davidson to Liverpool which he has applied to AJ's accounts with Philadelphia merchants.

July 23   Registration of Stock Mark.   27

July 23, 24   Record of receipt of AJ's resignation as superior court judge. Printed, Tennessee, *Senate Journal*, p. 10; *House Journal*, p. 11 (5th General Assembly, 2nd sess.).

July 24   To Thomas & John Clifford.   27

July 25   From Robert Weakley. ALS, DLC. Submits returns from the contested election of Isaac Roberts as brigadier general of militia and his own resignation as colonel; discusses legislative deliberations.

July 25   Decision in *AJ* v. *James Jamerson*. Copy, CPQS Minutes, Vol. D:298–99, TNDa.

July 28   From Willie Blount. ALS fragment, ICHi. Introduces John Strother and his nephew, John Gray Blount, Jr.

July 28   Agreement with James Crawford. ADS, DLC. Agrees to convey a tract of land in Robertson County.

July 30   From John Smith T.   29

July 31   To Boggs & Davidson from Jackson & Hutchings.   30

July 31   Invoice of goods sent from Hunter's Hill to the Tennessee cantonment store. Copy, Invoice book, THer.

[cJuly]   Memorandum of a note to Stothart & Bell. AN, DLC.

[cAug 1]   From Thomas Butler. ALS fragment, DLC. Discusses a letter of protest to Thomas Jefferson concerning charges lodged against him by James Wilkinson.

[Aug 3]   To T[homas] J[efferson].   33

Aug 4   From Thomas Butler. ALS, DLC. Bassett, 1:104. Discusses AJ's letter asking Jefferson to consider Butler's case.

Aug 10   From Francis Graves. ALS, DLC. Inquires about AJ's proposed shipment of goods to Natchez.

Aug 16   From Robert Weakley. ALS, DLC. Asks AJ to issue a writ to fill the colonelcy left vacant by Weakley's resignation.

Aug 17   From Robert Weakley. ALS, DLC. Encloses tally of votes (not found) for general of 5th Brigade.

Aug 20   Promissory note for $113.50 from Nathaniel Hays to William Donelson, assumed by AJ. ADS, DLC.

Aug 23   From Thomas Butler. ALS, DLC. Bassett, 1:105. Requests advice on whether to proceed to New Orleans as ordered or to await Jefferson's reply to his appeal.

Aug 23   Deed, 425 acres of the Hermitage property from Nathaniel Hays for $3,400. ADS, DLC; Copy, Deed Book F(1796–1805):241, TNDa.

Aug 25   To Thomas Butler.   36
Aug 25   To Nathan Davidson.   37

Aug 30   From Richard C. Napier (enclosure: tally of votes). ALS, DLC. Transmits returns for election of general of the 6th Brigade.

Aug 31   Promissory note for $100 from William London and Maclin Cross to Jeremiah Grizzard, endorsed to Jackson & Hutchings. DS, DLC.

Aug   Account with Deaderick & Sittler for making a still. AD, DLC.

Sept 1   Contract with Henry Gowyer for services as overseer. DS, DLC.

Sept 15   To John Sevier. ADS, THi. Certifies the election of Thomas Johnson as general of the 6th Brigade.

Sept 15   To John Sevier (enclosure: duplicate certification of Isaac Roberts's election as general of the 5th Brigade). LS, THi. Requests that Sevier issue commission.

Sept 18   From William Preston Anderson. ALS, DLC. Mentions horse purchase that he was unable to conclude for AJ.

Sept 19   Inventory of the estate of Samuel Donelson. DS with ms insertions by AJ, Sumner County Records, T.

Sept 19   Record of posting of $10,000 bond as executor of Samuel Donelson's estate. Copy, Executors' Bonds and Letters, July 1796-August 1816, p. 118, TGSum.

Sept 21   From Patton Anderson. ALS, DLC. Discusses horse purchases and racing.

Sept 21   From John Hutchings. ALS, DLC. Discusses horses and horseracing.

[Sept 21]   Decision in *Jackson & Hutchings* v. *Thomas Barrott* (with case file, T). Copy, CPQS Minute Book V(1804–1805):481, TGSum.

[Sept 21]   Decision in *Jackson & Hutchings* v. *John C. Henderson* (with case file). Copy, CPQS Minute Book V(1804–1805):471, TGSum.

[Sept 21]   Decision in *Jackson & Hutchings* v. *James McKinsey* (with case file). Copy, CPQS Minute Book V(1804–1805):469, TGSum.

Sept 24   From Oliver Johnson. ALS, DLC. Asks AJ to settle account for lead purchased by Jackson, Watson & Co.

[Sept 26]   Advertisement for Runaway Slave.   40

Sept   Account with Thomas Taylor for labor on property improvements. ADS, DLC.

Sept   Day book, Hunter's Hill store. AD, THer. Runs to April 7, 1805.

Oct 2   From John Coffee. ALS, DLC. Discusses shipment of iron and other goods and encloses a letter from Kentucky (not found).

Oct 3   From Ebenezer Rees. ALS fragment, DLC. Discusses a promissory note of AJ's.

[Oct 3]   Scire facias to AJ in *John C. Henderson* v. *AJ, administrator of the Samuel Donelson estate* (with case file). AD, Sumner County Records, T.

Oct 7   Receipt for taxes to AJ as guardian of Edward Butler's minors. AD in AJ's hand, signed by administrators of the estate, DLC.

Oct 10   From Thomas K. Harris. ALS, DLC. Bassett, 1:109–10. Asks AJ to be his second in a duel.

Oct 14   Bill of sale for a horse from Joseph Erwin. ADS, DLC.

Oct 15   From Thomas Butler. ALS, DLC. *PMHB*, 17(1893):502. Reports on his arrival in New Orleans and the yellow fever epidemic there.

Oct 15   From James Smith & Son to Jackson & Hutchings. ALS, DLC. Requests payment of account.

Oct 15   Promissory note to John Sevier from AJ and Howell Tatum for cotton gin tax. DS, DLC.

Oct 18   From Joseph Erwin. ALS fragment, ICHi. Agrees to reclaim an unsatisfactory horse sold to AJ.

Oct 19   From Peter Brawner. ALS, DLC. Describes his difficulties in transporting a load of goods from Pittsburgh; asks AJ's custom at his tanyard.

Oct 20   From Gilbert Christian Russell. ALS, DLC. Asks AJ to recommend him to the secretary of war for a captaincy in the U.S. Army.

Oct 21   From Thomas Butler.   41

Oct 22   From John Armstrong (enclosure: account with Francis Preston for iron goods, 1804). ALS, THer. Responds to AJ's request for a statement of his account with Preston.

Oct 22   From Samuel Meeker. ALS, THi. Announces that William P. Meeker will be his agent in Tennessee.

Oct 22   Account with John Jordan, Jr. ADS, DLC.

[Oct 24]   Decision in *Jackson & Hutchings* v. *John Gordon* (appealed). Copy, CPQS Minutes, Vol. D:366–67, TNDa.

[Oct]   Announcement of public sale of Samuel Donelson's chattels, by AJ as estate administrator. ADS draft, Ledger of Gallatin and Lebanon stores, 1802–1803, THer.

Nov 1   Promissory note to AJ as administrator of Samuel Donelson's estate. AD draft in AJ's hand, DLC.

Nov 1   Receipt of sales of the estate of Samuel Donelson. Copy endorsed in AJ's hand, Sumner County Records, T.

Nov 5   From Thomas Butler. ALS, DLC. *Cincinnati Commercial*, Jan 9, 1882. Complains of lack of mail from Washington and Tennessee; mentions yellow fever epidemic in New Orleans.

Nov 8   From William Tharp. ALS, DLC. Solicits AJ's help in securing appointment as factor at the Tellico trading station.

Nov 9   From James Irwin. Copy, Invoice book, THer. Discusses his plans to leave Nashville for the store at the Tennessee River cantonment.

Nov 10   From William Stothart to Jackson & Hutchings. ALS, THi. Reports payments made on AJ's behalf to a Philadelphia merchant.

Nov 18   Receipt from Richard Mitchell to Robert Hays for a bay horse. AD in AJ's hand, signed by Mitchell, DLC.

Nov 20   From Thomas Butler.   42

Nov 23   To Thomas & John Clifford from Jackson & Hutchings. ALS in AJ's hand, PHi. Discusses plans for settling account with the Clifford firm.

Nov 23   Account of AJ and Jackson & Hutchings with James & Washington Jackson. AD, DLC. Runs to October 31, 1805.

Nov 24   To Henry Dearborn. Abstract, DNA-RG 107. Recommends Robert Purdy for major's commission, James Desha for captain's.

Nov 24   To Henry Dearborn. Abstract, DNA-RG 107. Recommends Dr. Thomas Vandyke and Hinchey Pettway to succeed Hooker as factor at Tellico.

Dec 6   From George Washington Campbell.   43

Dec 13   From Henry Dearborn. LC, DNA-RG 107. Explains why Purdy and Desha cannot be appointed to the grades they desire in the U.S. Army.

Dec 14   From Thomas & John Clifford. ALS, PHi. Announces that George Poyzer will call on AJ to collect the firm's accounts.

Dec 17   From Thomas Butler. ALS, DLC. *PMHB*, 17(1893):504. Reports lack of progress on his appeals to Washington.

Dec 17   Decision in *John C. Henderson* v. *AJ* (assault; appealed). Copy, CPQS Minute Book V(1804–1805):497, TGSum.

Dec 18   From Francis Preston. ALS, DLC. Requests payment for an order of iron goods.

Dec 18   Deed, lot in Gallatin from Shadrach Nye et al., commissioners for Sumner County, to AJ and John Hutchings for $45. Copy, Deed Book 4(1806–10):74, TGSum.

Dec 20   Promissory note for $15 to Elias McFaddin by Jacob Dickinson for Andrew Jackson & Co. ADS, DLC.

Dec 21   From Seth Lewis. ALS, DLC. Acknowledges receipt of John Hutchings's deposition and discusses cotton prices in Natchez.

Dec 22   From William Dickson. ALS, DLC. Discusses a militiaman's claim for compensation and the Thomas Butler case.

Dec 24   From Thomas Butler. ALS, DLC. *Cincinnati Commercial*, Jan 9, 1882. Asks AJ to intervene with Jefferson to secure a speedy trial for Butler.

Dec 31   From Thomas Butler.   44

[cDec]   To Thomas Jefferson from AJ et al.   45

[cDec]   Remonstrance to the U.S. Congress, protesting arrest of Thomas Butler. AD in William P. Anderson's hand, signed by AJ et al., DNA-RG 46; Copy, DLC, Thomas Jefferson Papers.

[cDec]   From Samuel Meeker. ALS fragment, DLC. Discusses sale of AJ's cotton in New Orleans.

1804   Tax list for AJ's landholdings in Wilson County. AD, CPQS Minutes, 1803–1807, p. 87, TLWil.

[1804–1806]   Memorandum on report that the runaway slave George is at a gunsmith's near the mouth of Wabash River. AD, DLC.

[c1804]   Memorandum of accounts with various merchants. AD, DLC.

[c1804]   Memorandum of settlement of accounts, Jackson, Watson & Co. AD in AJ's hand, ICHi.

[c1804]   Proposal to Edward Ward. ADS copy in AJ's hand, DLC. AJ and John Hutchings, executors of Thomas Hutchings's estate, offer for sale the land occupied by Hutchings's widow.

[1804–1807]   Rachel Jackson to Edward Roberts. ANS, William C. Cook. Orders goods from store.

1805

Jan 6   To Francis Preston. ALS, NIC. Discusses order of iron goods.

Jan 8   From John Morrell & Son to Jackson & Hutchings. ALS, DLC. Requests payment of accounts.

Jan 17   From George Washington Campbell. ALS, DLC. Reports on the deliberations of Congress.

Jan 18   From Thomas Norris Clark. ALS, DLC. States that John Smith T has started down the river with four slaves.

Jan 23   To Francis Preston. ALS, KHi. Transmits $1,000 in partial payment for iron goods.

Jan 25   From James Irwin.   47

Jan 25   From James Lyon (enclosure: proposal for a line of barges on the Ohio and Mississippi rivers). ALS, DLC. Solicits AJ's influence with the Tennessee legislature to secure incorporation of a barge company.

Jan 28   From Thomas Butler. ALS, DLC. *PMHB*, 17(1893):505–506. Reports lack of progress in securing information from Washington about his impending court martial.

Jan 31   From William P. Meeker. ALS, DLC. Solicits cotton to complete a load he is ready to ship from the mouth of the Cumberland.

[Jan 31]   From Bickham & Reese to Jackson, Watson & Co. ALS fragment, DLC. Discusses settlement of account.

Feb 1   Promissory note for $29.58 from Edmond Jacobs to Jackson & Hutchings. AD in AJ's hand, signed by Jacobs, DLC.

Feb 4   Power of attorney from AJ and John Hutchings to John Coffee to settle debt due from John Smith T. ADS, DLC.

Feb 8   Deed, 640 acres in Wilson County from AJ and John Hutchings, executors of Thomas Hutchings, to Edward Douglass for $1. Copy, Deed Book B(1805–1807):189, TLWil.

Feb 9   From James Irwin.   48

Feb 11   Memorandum of agreement to sell cotton to John Instone. ADS, DLC.

Feb 12   Receipt from John M. Garrard, Jr., for $215.84 in part payment for two slaves, Orange and Priss. AD in AJ's hand, signed by Garrard, DLC.

Feb 16   From Patton Anderson. ALS, DLC. Asks AJ to send him $30 for fodder and corn.

Feb 16   Accounts of AJ, William P. Anderson, and John Hutchings with John Hoggatt for lumber. AD, ICHi. Run to June 17, 1806, and include an entry of grits for Colonel Burr.

Feb 17   To James Winchester. ALS, THi. Discusses negotiations for Winchester's purchase of AJ's store in Gallatin.

Feb 18   From Thomas Butler.   50

Feb 20   From Thomas Terry Davis.   51

Feb 22   From John Morrell & Son to Jackson & Hutchings. ALS, DLC. Acknowledges receipt of a payment on the firm's account.

Feb 22   Promissory note for $29.98¾ from James Crabtree to Andrew Jackson & Co. DS, DLC.

Feb 24   Memorandum of $370 payment on account by John Smith T. AD, DLC.

Feb 24   Promissory note for $4,848 to Jackson & Hutchings from John Smith T. DS in John Coffee's hand, signed by Smith T, MoStgA.

Feb 25   Bill of sale from John Orr to Jackson & Hutchings for a slave, Nancy. DS, DLC.

Feb 28   From William Hickman. ALS, DLC. Writes from Ste. Genevieve District, La. Terr., that he has discovered a lead mine in which AJ might be interested.

March 3   To Thomas & John Clifford. ALS, PHi. Discusses his order of goods from Philadelphia.

March 4   From Thomas Butler.   51

March 7   From Washington Jackson. ALS, DLC. Discusses business affairs of AJ with Washington's brothers, James and John.

March 11   From John Coffee. ALS, DLC. Urges AJ to meet with John Smith T in Haysborough.

March 15   Agreement of AJ, John Hutchings, and William P. Anderson, partners in the lease of Clover Bottom Turf. DS, THi.

March 17   Subpoena to William Wright to appear as witness before the Sumner County court in *Edward Williams* v. *William Edwards*. ADS, endorsed by AJ, Sumner County Records, T.

March 18   Bond for Mary Donelson in suit against Elisha Prewitt and John Watt Crunk. Printed form with ms insertions, signed by AJ, TxHU.

March 25   To Thomas & John Clifford from Jackson & Hutchings. ALS, PHi. Discusses the recent order for goods and their accounts.

March 25   From Felix Robertson.   53

March 27   Accounts of AJ and Andrew Jackson & Co. with James Jackson. AD, Mrs. Uhland O. Redd. Runs to July 2.

March 29   From John Jackson. ALS, DLC. Discusses his handling of AJ's business affairs in Philadelphia.

March 30   Records in *AJ* v. *Rosegill Wells* (ejectment). Copies, Superior Court Documents, TKL.

March   Memorandum of cotton delivered to Jackson & Hutchings by William Hall for Charles M. Hall. ADS, DLC.

April 8   From John H. Smith & Co. ALS, DLC. Transmits invoice of goods.

April 8   Agreement between Jackson & Hutchings and James F. Moore & Co. for the purchase of 1,000 bushels of salt. ADS, DLC.

April 9   Account book, Clover Bottom store. AD, THer. Runs to July 10.

April 12   Day book, Clover Bottom store. AD, THer. Runs to November 24.

April 17   From Thomas Butler.   55

April 18   From William Charles Cole Claiborne. Abstract, Carnegie Book Shop, catalog no. 180 (1953). Discusses Butler's impending court martial.

April 19   Deed, 640 acres in Wilson County to Anthony Foster for $1,000. Printed form with ms insertions, signed by AJ, DLC.

April 30   From Winchester & Cage. ALS, DLC. Explains delay in arrival of a keelboat for AJ.

April 30   Statement of John H. Smith & Co. of weight deficiency of cotton delivered by AJ. ADS, THi.

May 1   Account with John Thomas for carpentry. AD, ICHi. Runs to June 3.

May 1   Order of John M. Garrard, Jr., to John Winston to pay $10 to Edward Roberts. ADS with AJ endorsement, DLC.

May 7   To Edward Ward. Printed extract, American Art Association catalog, April 8, 1926, Item 250. Presses Ward to pay the balance owed for the Hunter's Hill property.

May 10   From Samuel Meeker. ALS, DLC. Bassett, 1:112–13. Regrets that AJ has already sold his cotton; solicits the settlement of the Jackson, Watson & Co. account.

May 11   Memorandum of Agreement with John Verell for the Purchase of Truxton.   57

May 13   From James O'Hara. ALS, DLC. Discusses efforts to settle Edward Butler's estate in Pennsylvania.

May 21   Receipt for $146.87½ to John Smith T from Jackson & Hutchings. ADS in AJ's hand, MoStgA.

[May 21]   From Thomas Butler. ALS matched fragments, DLC, ICHi. States that no date has yet been set for his court martial.

May 22   Decision in *John Lawrence* v. *Francis Hall, AJ, and Francis R. Nash.* Copy, MDSC Minutes, 1803–1805, pp. 433–35, TNDa.

[May 24]   Decision in *Jackson & Hutchings* v. *John Gordon* (appealed). Copy, MDSC Minutes, 1803–1805, pp. 481–83, TNDa.

May 25   List of owners of mares put to Truxton. AD, ICHi. Runs to December 10.

May 27   From Thomas Butler. ALS, DLC. *Cincinnati Commercial*, Jan 9, 1882. Reports on arrangements for his court martial.

May 28   Decision in *AJ, guardian for the heirs of Samuel Hays* v. *George Augustus Sugg.* Copy, MDSC Equity Minute Book, 1803–1806, pp. 343–47, TNDa.

June 2   From John Campbell. ALS, ICHi. Offers to negotiate for purchase of the store on the Tennessee River.

[June 2]   From Aaron Burr.   59

June 3   From John Williamson. ALS, DLC. Solicits AJ's custom for Meeker, Williamson & Patton and annexes prices current for New Orleans.

June 9   From Thomas Butler. ALS, DLC. *PMHB*, 17(1893):507. Discusses difficulty of securing information about his court martial.

June 10   To Edward Ward.   59

June 10   From Edward Ward. ALS fragment, ICHi. Discusses the settlement of his indebtedness to AJ.

June 14   From John Jackson to Jackson & Hutchings. ALS, DLC. Discusses purchasing goods and settling accounts for AJ in Philadelphia.

June 15   From James Smith, Jr., & Son. ALS, DLC. Acknowledges receipt of a draft on the war department, applied to AJ's account.

[June 17]   Decision in *John C. Henderson* v. *AJ, administrator of the Samuel*

Donelson estate (with case file, T). Copy, CPQS Minute Book V(1804–1805): 545–46, TGSum.

June 18   *To John Jackson.*   61

June 20   Record of action in *Jackson & Hutchings* v. *James Orr* (dismissed by AJ). Copy, CPQS Minute Book V(1804–1805): 547, TGSum.

June 22   To the Public. Printed, *Tennessee Gazette*, July 3. Testifies to the good character of Edward Sanders.

June 22   From James Winchester. ALS, DLC. Encloses a list of specifications for barrel staves.

June 27   To William Preston Anderson. ANS, NN. Asks Anderson to borrow $100 from any Nashville merchant.

[cJuly 1]   Toasts for Independence Day Celebration.   63

July 2   From John M. Garrard, Jr. ALS, DLC. Bassett, 1: 116. Writes from Paris, Ky., concerning horseracing.

July 4   Toast at the Independence Day celebration, Nashville: "The rising greatness of the West—may it never be impeded by the jealousy of the East." Printed, *Tennessee Gazette*, July 17.

July 8   From Thomas Butler. ALS, DLC. *PMHB*, 17(1893): 507–508. Reports on progress of his court martial.

July 8–9   Promissory notes for $1,280 from Jackson & Hutchings to James F. Moore & Co. (ADS, DLC); July 9, for $27.11½ from Thomas Clark to Jackson & Hutchings (DS, DLC).

July 10   Account of Jackson & Hutchings with James & Washington Jackson. AD, DLC. Runs to February 27, 1806.

July 10   Memorandum of freight for William Tait brought from the mouth of the Cumberland River by Eli Hammond. AD, DLC.

July 15   From Thomas Butler.   65

July 18   From George Washington Campbell. ALS, DLC. Introduces his brother Collier and discusses the failure of negotiations with the Cherokees.

July 27   From Samuel Meeker. ALS, DLC. Bassett, 1: 116–17. Discusses an adjustment on a shipment of damaged blankets and complains of John Jackson's handling of AJ's interests in Philadelphia.

[cJuly 28]   Memorandum of Duel between Thomas Jefferson Overton and John Dickinson.   67

July 29   From Meeker, Williamson & Patton to Jackson & Hutchings. ALS, DLC. Reports on the cotton market in New Orleans and Liverpool.

July 29   Account of Simpson Harris with Jackson & Hutchings. AD, THi. Runs to October 16, 1806.

Aug 1   From Thomas Jefferson Overton.   69

Aug 3   From Meeker, Williamson & Patton to Jackson & Hutchings. Printed form with ANS by John Williamson, DLC. Lists prices current in New Orleans and informs AJ of their agent in Natchez.

Aug 5   To George Washington Campbell. ALS, NjP. Bassett, 1: 189–90 (dated Aug 5, 1808). Discusses his efforts to buy Duck River land from Norton Pryor.

Aug 5   Account of William Sample with Jackson & Hutchings. AD, Sumner County Records, T.

Aug 6   From John Childress, Jr. ALS, DLC. Discusses his statement (not found) on the Overton-Dickinson duel.

Aug 10   To James Jackson. ALS copy, DLC. Discusses his effort to buy Duck River land from Norton Pryor.

Aug 10   From Duncan & Jackson to Jackson & Hutchings. ALS, DLC. Replies to Hutchings's request for information about barrel stave prices in New Orleans.

Aug 11   From Waller Taylor. ALS, DLC. Solicits AJ's help in securing a commission in the U.S. Army.

Aug 12   Toast to Thomas Butler delivered at a dinner for Aaron Burr. Printed, *Tennessee Gazette*, Aug 21.

Aug 18   From George Bickham, Jr. to Jackson & Hutchings. ALS, DLC. Requests payment on the firm's account with Bickham & Reese.

Aug 23   From James Winchester to Jackson & Hutchings. ANS, THer. Orders nails.

Aug 26   From Thomas Butler.   70

Aug 26   From Thomas Butler. ALS, DLC. Instructs AJ on the disposition of his mother-in-law's estate.

Aug 31   Record of county tax enumeration, showing two free white males and nine taxable slaves. AD, Davidson County Tax List, T.

Sept 2   Account of Elizabeth Whitson with Jackson & Hutchings. AD, DLC.

Sept 7   From James Swanson. Printed extract, American Art Association catalog, April 8, 1926, Item 347. Certifies damage to two blankets in a shipment.

Sept 7   Memorandum of gold weighed by Washington Jackson for AJ. ADS endorsed by AJ, TNJ.

Sept 8   From James Overton. ALS, DLC. Regrets that pressing business prevents his accepting AJ's invitation to meet an unidentified visitor.

Sept 9   From John Conrad & Co. to Jackson & Hutchings. ALS, DLC. Acknowledges receipt of Aaron Burr's draft on William M. Biddle, placed to the credit of Jackson & Hutchings.

Sept 9   From John Williamson (enclosure: prices current in New Orleans). ALS, DLC. Reports the death of Thomas Butler.

[cSept 10]   To Bickham & Reese. ALS copy, DLC. Bassett, 1:110–11 (dated 1805?). Discusses account with Jackson, Watson & Co.

Sept 21   From James Jackson. ALS, DLC. Reports on mercantile and land business being handled for AJ.

Sept 23   To Thomas Jefferson.   72

Sept 23   Promissory note for $43.39½ from AJ as administrator of Samuel Donelson's estate to Eli Hammond. ADS, DLC.

Sept 24   Deposition of John Caffery regarding Robert Hays as surety for Stockley Donelson. AD in AJ's hand, signed by Caffery, DLC.

Oct 1   Decision in *Governor* v. *Robert Searcy, AJ, and William Dickson* (debt). Copy, HDSC Minutes, 1793–1807, p. 307, TKL.

Oct 4   Promissory note for $4.75 from Samuel Thompson to Jackson & Hutchings. ADS, DLC.

Oct 14   From James Irwin. ALS, DLC. Informs AJ of his intention to leave the store at the cantonment on the Tennessee River.

Oct 15   Memorandum of William Crenshaw's agreement to build two boats for Jackson & Hutchings. DS, DLC.

Oct 15   Statement of the account of Joseph Cole with AJ and John Hutchings as executors of Thomas Hutchings's estate. AD, THi.

Oct 22   Record of AJ's bond and oath as cotton inspector. Copy, CPQS Minutes, Vol. E:132, TNDa. Bassett, 1:190 (dated October 1808).

Oct   License permitting Jackson & Co. to operate an ordinary. Printed extract, American Art Association catalog, April 8, 1926, Item 347.

Nov 2   From Robert Butler (enclosure: order of James Wilkinson, Sept 20). ALS, DLC. Transmits a copy of the court's verdict in his father's court martial.

Nov 7   From John Williamson to Jackson & Hutchings (enclosure: New Orleans prices current). ALS, DLC. Discusses cotton market in New Orleans and England.

Nov 9   From Barclay, Salkeld & Co. to Jackson & Hutchings. Printed form with AN, DLC. Reports on commodities market in Liverpool and progress of the war against France.

Nov 12   Record of the supplementary apportionment of John Donelson's estate among his heirs, including Rachel Jackson. Copy, Wills and Inventories, 3(1805–11):82–83, TNDa.

Nov 19   Memorandum of a bet on the Truxton-Ploughboy race between William Terrell Lewis and William Lytle. ADS in AJ's hand, also signed by Lewis and Lytle, DLC.

Nov 25   Day book, Clover Bottom store. AD, THer. Runs to May 20, 1806.

Nov 26   Promissory note for $16.02 from AJ to ?. Printed extract, American Art Association catalog, April 8, 1926, Item 347.

Nov 29   From Bickham & Reese to Jackson & Hutchings. ALS, DLC. Requests payment of account.

Nov 29   From John Sevier. LS, DLC; ALS draft, T. Requests returns of the 2nd Division.

Nov 29   Account of John Verell at Clover Bottom for board for self, Thomas Jordan, and horses. AD, DLC.

Nov 30   From Daniel Sayre. ALS, DLC. Reports news of a runaway slave at Baton Rouge.

Dec 2   From James O'Hara to Jackson & Hutchings. ALS, THer. Bills the firm for glassware purchased at his Pittsburgh factory.

Dec 13   Receipt for $48.75 from Nathaniel Toland. ADS, THi.

[Dec 16]   Answer of AJ to David Shelby in *David Shelby* v. *AJ, administrator of the Samuel Donelson estate.* ADS by Thomas Stuart, also signed by AJ, Sumner County Records, T.

Dec 16   Decision in *Shelby* v. *AJ* (covenant). Copy, CPQS Minutes, September 1805-December 1808, pp. 28–29, TGSum.

Dec 20   Receipt from Bennett H. Henderson for final payment by the estate of Samuel Donelson, AJ administrator. DS, DLC.

Dec 21   From Thomas Johnson. ALS, DLC. Transmits partial return for the 6th Brigade (not found).

Dec 24   Receipt from T. Bradley for payment on account of the estate of Samuel Donelson, AJ administrator. DS, DLC.

Dec 30   To John Sevier. LS and ALS draft, DLC. Transmits returns of the 2nd Division (not found).

Dec 30   Agreement between AJ, Samuel Pryor, John Hutchings, Patton Anderson, William P. Anderson, and John Verell re winnings of three horse races. AD, signed by AJ, Pryor, P. Anderson, and Verell, DLC. Bassett, 6 : 425–26.

[Dec 30]   Bill of sale from Andrew Steele to Jackson & Hutchings for a slave, Fan. DS, DLC. Bassett, 1 : 120.

[1805]   From Tilman Dixon. ALS, DLC. Bassett, 1 : 120. Attempts to resolve difficulty over land AJ won from Dixon and transferred to John Verell.

[1805]   Memorandum of winnings and expenses of Truxton race. AD in AJ's hand, DLC.

[c1805]   To James Jackson. ANS, TNJ. Memoranda concerning his account.

[c1805]   Memorandum of agreement between AJ and William Edwards re construction of a mill. AD, DLC.

1806

Jan 1   To James Winchester, Isaac Roberts, and Thomas Johnson. LS copy, DLC. Informs them that he has appointed Robert Purdy his second aide de camp.

Jan 2   To Isaac Roberts. ALS copy, DLC. Bassett, 1 : 121. Presses Roberts to send his overdue brigade return.

Jan 2   To John Sevier. ALS copy, DLC. Explains delay in forwarding division returns.

Jan 3   From Isaac Roberts. ALS, DLC. Justifies his delay in sending militia returns.

Jan 3   From Thomas Swann.   78

Jan 4   From John Strother. ALS, DLC. Inquires about a land transaction.

[Jan 4]   Affidavit of Joseph Erwin re Forfeit in the Truxton-Ploughboy Race. 79

Jan 5   From Joseph Anderson. ALS, DLC. Reports the ratification of cession treaties with several Indian tribes; discusses resurveying of his and Norton Pryor's land on Duck River.

Jan 6   To John Sevier. ALS draft, DLC. Bassett, 1 : 121. Reports the readiness of the 2nd Division for action and encloses division return (not found).

Jan 6   From Robert Purdy (enclosures: militia returns). ALS (misdated 1805), DLC. Forwards reports from 4th, 5th, and 6th brigades.

Jan 7   To Thomas Swann.   79

Jan 9   From Sanderson & White. ALS, DLC. Predicts decline of cotton prices in New Orleans and Liverpool; annexes prices current in New Orleans.

Jan 10   From Percival Butler. ALS, DLC. Writes concerning a suit over a land transaction.

Jan 10   From Charles Henry Dickinson.   81

Jan 12   From Thomas Swann.   82

Jan 13   From Joseph Anderson. ALS, DLC. Discusses Senate action on Cherokee treaties and encloses messages of the president.

Jan 17   From John McNairy. ALS, DLC. Discusses court judgments re a land transaction.

Jan 17   From Nathaniel A. McNairy. ALS, DLC. Asks AJ to contact him.

Jan 24   Temperance pledge by AJ and John Verell. AD, THi. Bassett, 1 : 122.

Jan 27   Promissory note for $11.78 from Reuben Noels to Jackson & Hutchings. ADS, DLC.

Jan 27   Deed, 2,240 acres on Duck River from Samuel Jackson to AJ, William P. Anderson, John Childress, and Samuel Pryor for $2,240. Copy, Deed Book A(1810–16):33, TWHu.

Jan 27   Decision in *Tennessee* v. *AJ* (assault and battery). Copy, CPQS Minutes, Vol. E:208, TNDa. AJ found guilty of assault and battery upon Timothy Baird and fined.

Jan 28   Decision in *AJ* v. *Charles J. Love* (debt). Copy, CPQS Minutes, Vol. E:238, TNDa.

Jan 29   Bill of sale from John Verell for the slave Dinwiddie. ADS, DLC.

Jan 30   Record of action in *AJ and John Hutchings* v. *William Sawyers* (debt). Copy, CPQS Minutes, Vol. E:223, TNDa.

Jan 31   Affidavit of Robert Purdy on Nathaniel McNairy's involvement in the AJ-Swann quarrel (enclosed in AJ to Eastin, Feb 10). ADS, T. *Impartial Review*, Feb 15; Bassett, 1:132.

Feb 1   *From James Robertson.*   83

Feb 1   Statement of Thomas Swann re quarrel with AJ. Printed, *Impartial Review*, Feb 1; Bassett, 1:122–26.

Feb 1   Affidavit of Thomas Augustine Claiborne on the AJ-Swann quarrel (enclosed in AJ to Eastin, Feb 10). ADS, T. *Impartial Review*, Feb 15; Bassett, 1:133–34.

Feb 1   Decision in *AJ* v. *Betsey Harding and John Cockrill* (debt). Copy, CPQS Minutes, Vol. E:235, TNDa.

[cFeb 1]   Affidavit of John Baird on the AJ-Swann quarrel (enclosed in AJ to Eastin, Feb 10). ADS, T. *Impartial Review*, Feb 15; Bassett, 1:132.

Feb 3   From Robert Butler (enclosed in AJ to Eastin, Feb 10). ALS, T. *Impartial Review*, Feb 15; Bassett, 1:133. Encloses affidavit on the AJ-Swann quarrel.

Feb 3   Statement of account, John Overton with Jackson & Hutchings for goods bought at the Clover Bottom store. AD, THi.

Feb 3   Affidavit of Robert Hays on the AJ-Swann quarrel (enclosed in AJ to Eastin, Feb 10). DS, T. *Impartial Review*, Feb 15; Bassett, 1:133.

Feb 5   Affidavit of John Coffee (enclosed in AJ to Eastin, Feb 10). ADS, T. *Impartial Review*, Feb 15; Bassett, 1:129–32.

Feb 5   Affidavit of John Hutchings on the AJ-Swann quarrel (enclosed in AJ to Eastin, Feb 10). DS, T. *Impartial Review*, Feb 15; Bassett, 1:128.

Feb 7   To Thomas Eastin. Printed, *Impartial Review*, Feb 8; Bassett, 1:127. Explains that his reply to Swann's statement of February 1 will be postponed for a week, owing to delay in securing William P. Anderson's affidavit.

Feb 8   From William Preston Anderson (enclosed in AJ to Eastin, Feb 10). ALS, T. *Impartial Review*, Feb 15; Bassett, 1:134–35. Summarizes his knowledge of the events relating to payment of the forfeit in the Truxton-Ploughboy race.

Feb 8   Affidavit of Charles S. Carson on the payment of the forfeit in the Truxton-Ploughboy race (enclosed in AJ to Eastin, Feb 10). ADS, T. *Impartial Review*, Feb 15; Bassett, 1:135.

Feb 8   Affidavit of Robert Purdy on Thomas Swann (enclosed in AJ to Eastin, Feb 10). ADS, T. *Impartial Review*, Feb 15; Bassett, 1:135.

Feb 10   *To Thomas Eastin.*   84
Feb 11   Deed, 367 acres on Stone's River to Severn Donelson for $200. Copy,
         Deed Book B(1804–1808):118, TMRu.
Feb 13   Statement of John Erwin, giving full text of Charles Dickinson to AJ,
         Jan 10, 1806. Printed, *Impartial Review*, Feb 22; Bassett, 1:139–40.
Feb 15   Nathaniel McNairy to Thomas Eastin. Printed, *Impartial Review*, Feb
         22; Bassett, 1:140. Chides AJ for cowardice, citing his attacks on Swann
         and Sevier and his firing a pistol at "*a man that has none, and driv[ing]
         him off to Kentucky. . . .*"
Feb 18   Order to William Bradford from Benjamin Rawlings to pay Jackson &
         Hutchings $481.09. Copy, DLC.
Feb 19   From James F. Moore. ALS, DLC. Presses AJ for payment of his account.
Feb 19   From Daniel Smith. ALS, DLC. Reports congressional action on foreign
         affairs; thanks AJ for his help to Smith's widowed daughter.
Feb 21   Nathaniel McNairy to Thomas Eastin. Printed, *Impartial Review*,
         Feb 22. Offers affidavits of witnesses to his fight with John Coffee, growing
         out of AJ-Swann quarrel.
Feb 22   Notice by Corbin Lee that Joseph Erwin, now absent from Nashville,
         left him $1,000 to bet on Ploughboy in the April 3 race. Printed, *Impartial
         Review*, Feb 22 and March 1.
Feb 26   From Thomas & John Clifford to Jackson & Hutchings. ALS, DLC. In-
         troduces Ebenezer Clark, who will collect accounts for the firm.
Feb 27   From Meeker, Williamson & Patton to Jackson & Hutchings. ALS,
         DLC. Bassett, 1:140–41. Discusses prices for barrel staves in New Or-
         leans and prospects for the cotton market.
Feb 28   Notice by Thomas Swann that civil authorities have prohibited his re-
         plying to AJ's recent article. Printed, *Impartial Review*, March 1; Bassett,
         1:138.
March 1   Announcement of Race between Truxton and Ploughboy.   90
March 4   From Thomas Overton. ANS, DLC. Requests delivery of whiskey.
March 5   To James Crawford. ALS, DLC. Arranges to pay for a horse bought
         from Crawford.
March 6   Robert Purdy to Thomas Eastin. Printed, *Impartial Review*, March 8.
         Describes the duel between John Coffee and Nathaniel McNairy, March 1.
March 8   Robert Purdy to Thomas Eastin. Printed, *Impartial Review*, March 15.
         Gives additional information on Coffee-McNairy duel.
March 8   John Brahan to John Overton.   90
March 9   From James Sanders. ALS, DLC. Writes respecting Samuel Donelson's
         children being returned to AJ for a visit.
March 17   From Samuel Jackson. ALS, DLC. Discusses notes to be used as stake
         for a horserace.
[March 17]   Decision in *Jackson & Hutchings* v. *Robert Trousdale* (appealed;
         with case file, T). Copy, CPQS Minutes, Sept 1805-Dec 1808, pp. 66–67,
         TGSum.
March 18   To Robert Whyte. ALS, NjMoHP. Requests information on a lawsuit
         pending in Williamson County court.
March 21   Memorandum of payments to be made by James & Washington
         Jackson for AJ from proceeds of £1000 bond on Edward Ward. AD, DLC.
March 22   Announcement by AJ and George Poyzer, opening subscriptions for

the Ohio Canal Co. Printed, *Impartial Review* and *Tennessee Gazette*, March 22.

March 24   From Joseph Anderson. ALS, DLC. Offers to sell some Duck River lands.

March 24   From Aaron Burr.   91

March 24   Memorandum of goods for Jackson & Hutchings from Washington Jackson. Copy, THer.

March 26   From Meeker, Williamson & Patton to Jackson & Hutchings. ALS, DLC. Reports arrival of barrel staves and lists prices current in New Orleans.

March 28   Account of Shippey Allen Puckett with AJ for goods. ADS, DLC.

March   Decision in *Edward Williams* (for the use of AJ and John Hutchings) v. *William Edwards.* Copy, Sumner County Records, T.

[cMarch]   Decision in *AJ* v. *Ellis Maddox.* Copy, CPQS Minutes, Vol. E:319, TNDa.

[March, April]   To Cuthbert Banks. Printed extract, *Quarterly Publication of the Historical and Philosophical Society of Ohio,* 12(1917):85. States that "Mr. Burr would eventually prove to be the saviour of this Western country."

April 3   From Meeker, Williamson & Patton to Jackson & Hutchings. ALS, DLC. Reports on sale of barrel staves and the loss of a boat belonging to Jackson & Hutchings.

April 4   Receipt for $700 to John Smith T from Edward Roberts (for Jackson & Hutchings). ADS, MoStgA.

April 5   From Aaron Burr.   93

April 7   To John Hutchings.   93

April 8   Advertisement of Truxton's stud season. Printed, *Tennessee Gazette,* May 3.

April 8   Agreement between William Preston Anderson and John Coffee re transfer of Anderson's interest in the Clover Bottom Turf. AD in AJ's hand, signed by Anderson and Coffee, THi.

April 12   From Daniel Smith. ALS, DLC. Reports on deliberations of Congress and thanks AJ for helping Smith's daughter with settlement of her husband's estate.

[cApril 15]   To Francis May. ALS, DLC. Asks May to pursue a land transaction with Archibald Roane.

April 16   From John Hutchings. ALS, DLC. Bassett, 1:141 (extract). Reports on Jackson & Hutchings's business in New Orleans.

April 16   Statement of account with Thomas E. Waggaman for cloth and a comb. ADS, DLC.

April 21   From Archibald Roane. ALS, DLC. Discusses land transaction.

April 24   From John Hutchings.   95

April 25   Receipt to John Boyd for $171.40 re costs and damages in *John C. Henderson* v. *AJ, administrator of the Samuel Donelson estate* (with case file). ADS, Sumner County Records, T.

May 1   Deed, 640 acres on Duck River to Charles Harryman for $600. Copy, Deed Book A(1804–1808):23, TMRu.

[May 3]   To Benjamin J. Bradford. Printed, *Tennesseee Gazette,* May 3. Defends reputation of Truxton against attack by Simeon Buford.

May 7   From William Preston Anderson. ALS, DLC. Reports on his investigation of the "report concerning Capt. Pryor and his Lady."

May 8   Cargo manifest of goods shipped by Meeker, Williamson & Patton to Jackson & Hutchings aboard the barge *Relief*. Printed form with ms insertions, DNA-RG 36.

[May 12]   Scire facias to AJ, re settlement of estate of Stockley Donelson, in *William Terrell Lewis* v. *Stockley Donelson*. ADS, East Tennessee Supreme Court Records, T.

May 13   Receipt from Eli Hammond for payment by AJ as executor of Samuel Donelson's estate. ADS, DLC.

May 19   From Mark Mitchell. ALS, DLC. Instructs AJ re the horses he is sending for breeding and racing.

May 20   Thomas Swann to Thomas Eastin. Printed, *Impartial Review*, May 24. Transmits letters from men in Virginia and Nashville testifying to his character as a gentleman.

May 23   From John Hutchings. ALS, DLC. Bassett, 1:145–46. Reports that he has sold the cotton and laments that the firm faces another unprofitable year.

May 25   Patton Anderson's statement in reply to Thomas Swann's article of May 20. ALS, THer. *Impartial Review*, May 31.

May 29   From John Williamson. ALS, ICHi. Reports that Hutchings has left New Orleans.

May 29   Deed, 1,280 acres (sheriff's sale of David Allison's property) on Obed River from Reuben Cage and John Overton for $80. ADS, Deed Book A(1806–1809):200, TLOv.

June 13   From William Preston Anderson. Printed, *Cincinnati Commercial*, Jan 8, 1880. Warns AJ not to become embroiled with Dickinson's friends.

June 14   Memorandum of the transfer of Samuel Donelson lands from John Boyd to AJ. AD in AJ's hand, signed by Boyd, Sumner County Records, T.

[June 14]   Memorandum of damages and costs in *John C. Henderson* v. *AJ, administrator of the Samuel Donelson estate* (with case file). AD, Sumner County Records, T.

[cJune 14]   To John Coffee. ALS, THi. Asks Coffee to pursue business on behalf of Samuel Donelson's heirs.

June 19   From Washington Jackson. ALS, DLC. Bassett, 1:146–47. Comments on AJ's duel and discusses mercantile business.

June 21   Statement of Joseph Erwin on the duel. Printed, *Impartial Review*, June 21; Bassett, 1:147–49.

June 24   From John Hoggatt (enclosed in AJ to Eastin, June 28). ALS, T. *Tennessee Gazette*, June 28. Reports a conversation between Joseph Erwin and Charles Dickinson in December 1805 concerning prospect of a duel with AJ.

June 25 Deposition of George Ridley (enclosed in AJ to Eastin, June 28). ADS, T. *Tennessee Gazette*, June 28. Testifies that Corbin Lee, a friend of Dickinson's present at the duel, told him that Jackson "behaved himself with a great deal of honor upon that occasion. . . ."

June 28 To Thomas Eastin (enclosures: affidavits of Hanson Catlet, Thomas Overton, George Ridley, John Hoggatt, and Charles S. Carson and Joseph Erwin's statement, Jan 4). Printed, *Tennessee Gazette*, June 28. Replies to Joseph Erwin's accusations of irregularities in the Dickinson duel.

June 29 From James Winchester (enclosures: muster rolls). ALS, DLC. Transmits return of the 4th Brigade.

June 30   From William Harrison.   105

[cJune]   To Thomas Eastin.   106

[June Term] Bill of complaint in *Jackson & Hutchings* v. *John Smith T* (debt). ADS by George Bullitt, MoStgA.

[June-July] To Samuel Pryor. Printed extract, "An Account of some of the Bloody Deeds of General Jackson," 1828. Writes regarding duel, "I reserved my fire, and when I did shoot, you may be assured I left the damned rascal weltering in his blood."

July 3 Corbin Lee to Thomas Eastin. Printed, *Impartial Review*, July 5. States that AJ had fought the duel "agreeably to the stipulations."

July 4 From John Coffee. ALS, DLC. Writes concerning financial affairs of Jackson & Co. and the quarrel between Thomas Claiborne and Thomas G. Watkins.

July 4 Decision in *Jackson & Hutchings* v. *Michael Osbrooks* (with case file). ADS, Sumner County Records, T.

July 8 Decision in *AJ and John Hutchings* v. *Edward Radford*. Copy, CPQS Minutes, A(1804–1808):179, TMRu.

July 9 Memorandum of a conversation with Ethelred Williams concerning Roberts Hays's settlement of a judgment against Stockley Donelson. ADS, DLC.

July 10 Thomas Augustine Claiborne to Benjamin J. Bradford and Samuel Miller. Printed, *Tennessee Gazette Extra*, July 12. Encloses AJ to Thomas G. Watkins, [cJune 15], and discusses Watkins's attack upon Claiborne.

July 17 Deed, 150 acres on Wartrace fork of Duck River to Timothy O'Neal for $150. Copy, Deed Book E(1804–1808):392, TMRu.

July 18–20 Promissory notes from Jonathan Pumfrey to Jackson & Hutchings, totaling $135.61. DS, DLC.

July 19 From John Inskeepe. ALS, DLC. Thanks AJ for inspecting his Duck River lands and mentions that he intends to send settlers.

July 19 Thomas Gassaway Watkins to the public. Printed, *Tennessee Gazette Extra*, July 19. Gives his version of the quarrel with AJ and Claiborne.

[July 20] From George Michael Deaderick. ALS, THi. Asks AJ to inform Coffee of his wish to settle a lawsuit by mediation.

[July 20] To John Coffee. ALS, THi. Transmits Deaderick's letter of [July 20].

July 21 Deed, one undivided quarter-interest in 2,240 acres on Duck River to John Dickinson. DS, Deed Book A(1810–16):35, TWHu.

July 25   From David Shelby. ALS, DLC. Explains his inability to meet AJ's request for money.

July 26   Thomas Augustine Claiborne to Benjamin J. Bradford and Samuel Miller. Printed, *Tennessee Gazette Extra*, July 26. Continues discussion of the dispute with Watkins.

July 27   Deed, 1,540 acres (portion of Allison lands purchased by AJ, July 13, 1802) to Alexander Ewing and John Gannaway. Copy, Deed Book E(1804–1808):363, TMRu.

July 29   To Bickham & Reese from Jackson & Hutchings. ALS in AJ's hand, DLC. Complains of unsatisfactory handling of their firm's account.

July 29   Deed, 320 acres in Rutherford County to John Shelby for $900. Copy, Deed Book A(1808–1809):63, TSBe.

July 31   From Rachel Jackson to Jackson & Hutchings. Copy, ICHi. Requests that Dinwiddie be given one dollar in merchandise, charged to AJ.

[July]   Decision in *Jackson & Hutchings* v. *John Gordon* (debt). Copy, CPQS Minutes, Vol. F:6, TNDa.

Aug 6   From Elizabeth Glasgow Donelson. ALS, DLC. Asks AJ's help in clearing a land title.

Aug 9   Thomas Gassaway Watkins to the public. Printed, *Tennessee Gazette Extra*, Aug 9. Continues his defense against Claiborne's charge.

Aug 12   Promissory note for $30 from Jackson & Hutchings to Leven Donelson. DS, DLC.

Aug 19   Agreement between Cage & Black and AJ and James S. Rawlings re renting of house, lot, and stables in Gallatin to AJ and Rawlings. Copy, DLC.

Aug 22   From Benjamin J. Bradford. ALS, T. Replies to AJ's request for information on the circumstances leading to the appearance of the *Tennessee Gazette* in mourning edition.

Aug 22   Simeon Buford to "United Sportsmen." Printed, *Tennessee Gazette*, Aug 30. Challenges AJ to run Truxton against his horse, The President.

Aug 23   To Robert Whyte. ALS, T. Engages Whyte as attorney in a legal matter.

Aug 23   *From Randal McGavock.*   107

Aug 23   From Winchester & Cage. ALS, DLC. Sends instructions for putting a mare to Truxton.

Aug 25   From Donelson Caffery. ALS, T. Encloses a memorandum of his conversation with Thomas G. Watkins concerning the mourning-border issues of the newspapers.

Aug 29   Receipt to Jackson & Hutchings for $400 payment on account with John Morrell & Son. ADS, DLC.

Sept 5–25   Decision in *Jackson & Hutchings* v. *Robert Barnett* (debt; with case file, THi). Copy, CPQS Minutes, 1803–1807, p. 252, TLWil.

Sept 10   Order to Edward Roberts at the Clover Bottom store to let Mrs. Castleman have six plates. ADS by Robert Butler for Rachel Jackson, NN.

Sept 12   *From John Overton.*   108

Sept 23   Decision in *Jackson & Hutchings* v. *John Hattum*. Copy, CPQS Minutes, 1803–1807, p. 254, TLWil.

Sept 24   Decision in *Jackson & Hutchings* v. *William Brown* (debt). Copy, CPQS Minutes, 1803–1807, p. 260, TLWil.

Sept 25   *To [William Preston Anderson].*   110

Sept 25 Docket entry for *Jackson & Hutchings* v. *Francis Anderson*. Copy, CPQS Execution Docket, 1806–22, p. 23, TLWil.

Sept 25 Docket entry for *Jackson & Hutchings* v. *Richard Anderson*. Copy, CPQS Execution Docket, 1806–22, p. 22, TLWil.

Sept 27 Toast at dinner for Aaron Burr: "Millions for defence, not a cent for tribute." Printed, *Tennessee Gazette*, Oct 4.

Sept Day book, Clover Bottom store. AD, THer. Runs to August 1808.

Sept Decision in *AJ and John Hutchings, executors of Thomas Hutchings*, v. *Joseph Cole* (with case file). AD, THi.

[Sept] Decision in *Jackson & Hutchings* v. *Joseph Cole* (with case file). AD, THi.

[Sept-Dec] Docket entries for *Jackson & Hutchings* v. *Thomas Seawell*. CPQS Execution Docket, 1806–22, pp. 24, 30, TLWil.

Oct [5] To "AB and Lady" from J[ackson] and H[utchings]. ADS, THi. Invite them to a ball at James Rawlings's on October 17.

Oct 20 Accounts of AJ and Jackson & Hutchings with James Jackson. AD, Mrs. Uhland O. Redd. Run to December 25.

Oct 20 Bond for Nathaniel W. Williams, clerk and master in equity for Winchester District. AD, signed by Williams, AJ, William Walton, Samuel Hogg, and John Williams, T.

Oct 21 Rachel Jackson to Edward Roberts. Printed extract, Anderson Galleries catalog, Nov 1935, p. 194. Requests that he give $3 worth of goods to Mrs. Matthew Payne.

Oct 25 Promissory note for $18.75 from Joel Bolton to Jackson & Hutchings. ADS, DLC.

Oct 27 From Joseph Anderson (enclosed in Anderson to AJ, Jan 28, 1807). ALS copy, DLC. Discusses a land transaction.

Oct 28 Bill of sale from James Stewart to Jackson & Hutchings for a slave, Steven. DS, DLC. Bassett, 1:151–52.

Oct Term Inventory of the estate of Thomas Hutchings, submitted to the Davidson County Court by AJ and John Hutchings, executors. Copy, Wills and Inventories, 3(1805–11):135, TNDa.

Nov 1 Decision in *Jackson & Hutchings* v. *Foster Sayers* (debt). Copy, MDSC Equity Minute Book, 1805–1807, pp. 207–209, TNDa.

Nov 3 To William Hankins from Jackson & Hutchings. ALS in AJ's hand, DLC. Requests Hankins to pay $25 to Isaac Pearce.

Nov 6 Memorandum of agreement between Jackson & Hutchings and Samuel Pryor. Copy, Middle Tennessee Supreme Court Records, T.

Nov 8 Deed, 640 acres on Duck River from Joseph Anderson "for and in Consideration of his proportional part of the Expences of prosecuting a Sute in equity in the District Court of West Tennessee." Copy, Deed Book A(1808–1809):364, TSBe.

Nov 10 Deed, 100 acres on the Cumberland River to Francis Sanders for $1,000. Copy, Deed Book G(1805–1809):490, TNDa.

1807

March 17, 1807). Denounces Dearborn's letter of December 19, 1806; discusses the Burr conspiracy.

Jan 21–27   Receipts to Henry Flowers, Jan 21; Ezekiel Clampet, Jan 22; Hardy Flowers, Jan 23; Richard Tate, Jan 24; Hardy Flowers, Jan 26; John J. Winston, Jan 27, from Wright Willis (for AJ) for cotton. ADS, DLC.

Jan 27   Remonstrance of Thomas Cavitt et al. to the court of equity for a division of the land of the estate of Thomas Hutchings; AJ and John and Catherine Hutchings, executors. Copy, DLC.

Jan 28   From Joseph Anderson (enclosure: Joseph Anderson to AJ, Oct 27, 1806). ALS, DLC. Expresses the hope that AJ has received deed.

Jan 29   From John Wilkes.   150

Jan 31   Account of Jackson & Hutchings with James & Washington Jackson. AD, DLC. Runs to January 28, 1808.

Jan 31   Summary of account with James & Washington Jackson. AD, DLC.

Jan 31   Receipts to Patrick McElyea and Henry Thompson from Wright Willis (for AJ) for cotton. ADS, DLC.

Jan   Account of AJ and Jackson & Hutchings with James & Washington Jackson. AD, Mrs. Uhland O. Redd. Runs through February.

Jan   Supplementary inventory of the estate of Thomas Hutchings, filed by AJ and John Hutchings, executors. Copy, Wills and Inventories, 3(1805–11):146, TNDa.

Jan   Decision in *AJ* v. *Samuel Jackson* (debt; appealed). Copy, CPQS Minutes, Vol. F:84–85, TNDa.

Feb 2–5   Receipts to Arthur Owen, Feb 2; Spencer Glasscock, Feb 3; Henry Cowgill, Feb 5, from Wright Willis (for AJ) for cotton. ADS, DLC.

Feb 6   From George Washington Campbell.   151

Feb 7   Receipts to John McCulloch for cotton. ADS, DLC.

Feb 9   From Jenkin Whiteside. ALS, DLC. Discusses the settlement of a judgment involving Robert Hays and Ethelred Williams.

Feb 9   Promissory note to Jackson & Hutchings from Thomas Edwards for 1,000 pounds of cotton. AD in AJ's hand, signed by Edwards, DLC.

Feb 9–10   Receipts to John Robertson, Feb 9, and Joseph Newcom, Feb 10, from Wright Willis (for AJ) for cotton. ADS, DLC.

Feb 11   To Daniel Smith.   154

Feb 13   From Samuel Dorsey Jackson. ALS, DLC. Bassett, 1:172. Agrees to deliver "the Negro woman" and to settle account.

Feb 14   Receipts to John Castleman, Arthur Owen, and Zachariah Tate for cotton. ADS, DLC.

Feb 15   From Samuel Dorsey Jackson. ALS fragment, DLC. Discusses the settlement of a "gaming Debt."

Feb 16   Receipts to John Archer and Joseph Canton from Wright Willis (for AJ) for cotton. ADS, DLC.

Feb 17   From George Wilson. LS, DLC. Sends forms and instructions for state militia returns.

Feb 18   Deed, 457 acres in Wilson County to Andrew Hays for $457. Copy, Deed Book D(1809–12):505, TLWil.

Feb 21   From Waller Taylor. ALS, DLC. Asks AJ's assistance in selling lottery tickets for the university at Vincennes, Ind. Terr.

Feb 21–27   Receipts to Henry Castleman, Feb 21; Flowers McGregor, Feb 26;

Matthew Payne, Feb 27, from Wright Willis (for AJ) for cotton. ADS, DLC.

March 1   From George Poyzer. ALS, DLC. Offers to take cotton from AJ.

March 2   Receipt to Leven Donelson from Jackson & Hutchings for seed cotton. ADS, DLC.

March 3   From Frederick Stump. ALS, DLC. Asks for the renewal of his military commission and offers to raise a company of light infantry.

March 5   From Samuel Pryor. ALS, DLC. Instructs AJ to look after his interest at the races since he will not be able to attend.

March 5   Receipt to Joseph Lantern for ginned cotton. ADS, DLC.

March 7   Bill of sale at sheriff's auction of fifteen slaves belonging to Robert Hays to AJ. Copy, Wills and Inventories, 3 : 179, TNDa.

March 8–11   Receipts to Eli Hammond, March 8 (Abstract, American Art Association catalog, April 8, 1926, Item 254), and John Castleman, March 11 (ADS, DLC), for cotton.

March 12   Advertisement of stud season for Truxton. Printed, *Tennessee Gazette*, March 28.

March 17   To Henry Dearborn.   155

March 18   From John Gannaway, Jr. ALS, ICHi. Sends payment of $1,000.

March 18   Memoranda of land entries made by John Coffee for AJ. ADS, THi. Run to October 1, 1810.

March 20   Memorandum of receipt, John McNairy to James Robertson. AD, DLC.

March 21   From John Coffee. ALS, PHi. Forwards memorandum of AJ's account with D. Robertson.

March 21   From Thomas Jefferson. LS, DLC; LS, DNA-RG 107. *Tennessee Gazette*, April 18; Bassett, 1 : 178. Sends copy of the act on the acceptance of volunteers and instructs him on action to be taken.

March 24   From William Ballard. ALS, DLC. Requests payment of tuition for John Samuel and Andrew Jackson, children of Samuel Donelson.

March 24   From Thomas Sumter. ALS, NjP. Introduces Anthony Butler of South Carolina.

March 25   Memoranda of accounts of Robert Goodloe and William Hall with Jackson & Hutchings. AD, DLC.

March 26   From Samuel Hughes. ALS, ICHi. Discusses exchange of land.

March 27   From William Charles Cole Claiborne.   159

March 30   Receipt to John Winston for ginned cotton. ADS, DLC.

[March]   Decision in *Joseph McKain* v. *AJ, administrator of the Samuel Donelson estate*. Copy, CPQS Minutes, Sept 1805-Dec 1808, pp. 145–56, TGSum.

April 1   To John Coffee. ALS, DLC. Asks Coffee to pay a "Scholling" bill.

April 3   Promissory note for $165 from Robert Simpson. ADS, DLC.

April 6   Receipt from John Dickson for registering land grants in Rutherford County. ADS, DLC.

April 8   To [Matthew Paine] from Jackson & Hutchings. ANS in AJ's hand, DLC. Asks that James Crawford be sold twenty-four bushels of corn on credit.

April 10   To the 2nd Division. Printed, *Tennessee Gazette* and *Impartial Re-*

view, April 18. Asks regimental officers to recruit volunteer companies and submit returns.

April 10   From John Morrell & Son. ALS, DLC. Asks for payment of accounts.

April 11   Promissory note to John Boyd, sheriff of Davidson County, for $78.88, costs and fee for the sale of Robert Hays's slaves and land. ADS, DLC.

April 15   Decision in *AJ* v. *Archibald Roane* (enquiry). Copy, Knox County CPQS Minutes, Vol. 11:49, TKL.

April 17   From Duncan & Jackson to Jackson & Hutchings. ALS, DLC. Request attention to their account.

April 18   From Adam Clement. ALS, DLC. Asks AJ's attention to a Duck River land claim.

April 24   To Henry Dearborn. Abstract, DNA-RG 107. Advises that he has made a draft for $45 on the department of war.

April 25   Memorandum of Jacob Dickerson's account with Jackson & Hutchings. AD in Coffee's hand, THi.

April 29   To Meeker, Williamson & Patton from Jackson & Hutchings. ALS copy in AJ's hand, DLC. Bassett, 1:180–81. Asks for an explanation of their account.

April   Decision in *AJ, administrator of the Samuel Donelson estate* v. *Benjamin Seawell*. Copy, CPQS Minutes, Vol. F:118, TNDa.

April   Decision in *Jackson & Hutchings* v. *William London* (debt). Copy, CPQS Minutes, Vol. F:124–25, TNDa.

April   Inventory of the sale of the estate of Thomas Hutchings (AJ and John Hutchings, executors), including purchases from the estate by AJ. Copy, Wills and Inventories, 3(1805–11):165, TNDa.

May 1   Decision in *AJ* v. *Richard C. Napier*. Copy, CPQS Minutes, Vol. F:137, TNDa.

May 6   Memorandum of account of Jackson & Hutchings with Joshua Kelley. ADS, DLC.

May 11   From Isaac Roberts. ALS, DLC. Reports on the volunteers of the 5th Brigade.

May 11   Conveyance of fifteen slaves from AJ to Severn Donelson, in trust for Jane Hays. Copy, Wills and Inventories, 3(1805–11):179, TNDa.

May 11   Deed, 640 acres in Rutherford County to Jeremiah Whiteworth and Benjamin Hooper for $1,200. Copy, Deed Book E:404, TMRu.

May 15   From John Sevier. Printed form (circular); DLC. Sends copy of congressional military act and urges the raising of volunteers.

May 16   Promissory note for $120 from John Coffee to Enoch Enochs, taken up by AJ. AD, THi.

[May]   Memoranda of legal arguments to be submitted in *Robert Hays* v. *Ethelred Williams*. AD fragment, DLC.

June 1   Report on the state of the volunteers, 2nd Division. ADS, DLC.

June 4   Account of Jackson & Hutchings with Duncan & Jackson of New Orleans (enclosed in Duncan & Jackson to Jackson & Hutchings, July 9). ADS, DLC.

June 15   Statement of account with Henry McFall for carriage repairs (enclosed in Henry McFall to AJ, April 15, 1808). ADS, DLC.

[June 16]   To [William Preston Anderson].   167

[cJune 20]   From Thomas Monteagle Bayly. AL, DLC. Asks AJ to write him at Chillicothe, Ohio, and upon his return to Accomack County, Va.

June 23   From John Morrell & Son to Jackson & Hutchings. ALS, DLC. Sends statement of account.

June 25   Testimony before the Grand Jury in the Case of Aaron Burr.   168

June 27   To Thomas Monteagle Bayly.   169

June   Decision in *Jackson & Hutchings* v. *Francis Comperry* (debt). Copy, CPQS Minutes, Sept 1805-Dec 1808, p. 211, TGSum.

July 2   To Andrew Hamilton.   170

July 9   From Duncan & Jackson to Jackson & Hutchings (enclosure: account, June 4). ALS, DLC. Reports on their sale of cotton and staves in New Orleans.

July 9   Decision in *Jackson & Hutchings* v. *John Glover.* CPQS Minutes, 1 (1796–1807):457, TSRob.

July 10   From William P. Tebbs.   171

July 16   From James Winchester. ALS, DLC. Reports on the recruitment of volunteers, 4th Brigade.

[July 17]   Decision in *Jackson & Hutchings* v. *William Johnston* (debt). Copy, CPQS Minutes, 1(1800–12):287, TFWi.

July 22   Certificate of non-ownership of certain tracts of land sold to David Allison. DS, Deed Book A(1806–1809):198, TLOv.

July 29   Motion to appoint a corresponding committee on U.S.-British affairs. Printed, *Impartial Review,* July 30; *Mississippi Messenger,* Aug 25.

July 29   Decision in *George Bickham and Jacob Reese* v. *AJ and John Hutchings.* Copy, CPQS Minutes, Vol. F:158, TNDa.

July 29   Decision in *James Boggs and Nathan Davidson* v. *AJ, Thomas Watson, and John Hutchings.* Copy, CPQS Minutes, Vol. F:158, TNDa.

July 29   Decision in *Samuel Denman and William P. Meeker* v. *AJ, Thomas Watson, and John Hutchings.* Copy, CPQS Minutes, Vol. F:157, TNDa.

[July]   Decision in *AJ and John Hutchings* v. *Samuel Jackson* (appealed). Copy, CPQS Minutes, Vol. F:158–59, TNDa.

July-Oct   Decisions in *John Campbell* v. *AJ and John Hutchings, executors of Thomas Hutchings* (appealed). Copies, CPQS Minutes, Vol. F:166–69, TNDa.

Aug 1   To Henry Dearborn (enclosure: report on volunteers, June 1). ALS copy, Charles J. Bednar. Sends report.

Aug 1   Decision in *Jackson & Hutchings* v. *Anthony Winston.* Copy, CPQS Minutes, Vol. F:160, TNDa.

[Aug 1]   To Andrew Hamilton. AL (signature removed), ViU. Writes that in light of Hamilton and Tebbs's letters, he no longer holds them responsible for the rumor that he greeted Wilkinson in Richmond.

Aug 19   Statement of account of John Husbands and AJ with Samuel Pryor. AD, DLC.

Aug 26   Receipt from William Baker for $50 for carriage repairs. AD, DLC.

Aug 27   Receipt from Samuel Pryor acknowledging transferal of goods at Clover Bottom. AD in AJ's hand, signed by Pryor, Middle Tennessee Supreme Court Records, T.

[cSept 1]   Promissory note of August 21, from John Coffee to John Sparks, taken in by AJ. ADS, THi.

[Sept 15]   Memorandum of note paid John McNairy, Robert Hays et al. AD, DLC.

Sept 29   Deed, 580 acres on Red River to Benjamin Powell for $850. Copy, Deed Book G(1808–1809): 10, TSRob.

Sept 30   From Thomas Moors. ALS, DLC. Discusses conveyance of land.

Sept   Decision in *Jackson & Hutchings* v. *James McKain* (debt). Copy, CPQS Minutes, Sept 1805-Dec 1808, pp. 270–71, TGSum.

Sept   Execution docket for *Jackson & Hutchings* v. *John Hallum, Jr.* Copy, CPQS Execution Docket, 1806–22, p. 39, TLWil.

Sept   Statement re abatement of Edward Bondurant in *State* v. *Bondurant*, addressed to AJ. Copy fragment, THer.

Oct 6   Deed, 1,000 acres in White County to Matt Martin from AJ and John Hutchings. Abstract, Sotheby Parke Bernet catalog, Sale No. 4998 (January 26, 1983), Item 79.

Oct 17   Deed, 640 acres on Stone's River from John Boyd for $40. ADS, DLC.

[Oct 17]   Statement of costs in *Ethelred Williams* v. *Robert Hays*, addressed to AJ (enclosed in John Sommerville to AJ, Nov 17). AD, DLC.

Oct 27   Decision in *AJ and John Hutchings* v. *Thomas Harney* (debt). Copy, CPQS Minutes, Vol. F:196, TNDa.

Nov 2   From Basil Shaw (enclosure: muster rolls). ALS, DLC. Reports on regiments, 4th Brigade.

Nov 5   From Charles Blalock. ALS, THer. Resigns as major, 17th Regiment.

Nov [9]   Court Minutes in State v. Andrew Jackson.   173

[Nov?] 14   From William Preston Anderson. ALS fragment, THer. Transmits his order for the election of a militia officer.

Nov 17   From John Sommerville (enclosure: statement of costs, *Williams* v. *Hays*, Oct 17). ALS, DLC. Asks AJ's help in paying a debt.

Nov 19   From Joseph Neely to Jackson & Hutchings[?]. Copy, Sumner County Records, T. Informs them that he intends to take oath of insolvency.

Nov 23   From William Tait. ALS, DLC. Discusses the sale of cotton in New Orleans.

Nov 28   To Daniel Smith.   174

Nov   Decision in *Jackson & Hutchings* v. *Joseph Neely* (debt; with partial case file, T). Copy, CPQS Minutes, Sept 1805-Dec 1808, p. 215, TGSum.

[Nov-Dec]   From John McNairy. ALS, DLC. Discusses shipment of cotton to New Orleans.

Dec 1   Account with John Donelson. AD, Mrs. John Donelson VI.

Dec 3   From William Charles Cole Claiborne.   177

Dec 5   Memorandum of merchandise furnished Tennessee cantonment store since December 5, 1803. AD, DLC.

Dec 7   To Robert Hays.   178

Dec 9   From Pierce Butler. ALS, DLC. Discusses the sale of Butler property near Carlisle, Pa.

Dec 14   From John Stokely. ALS, DLC. Inquires about his land near Nashville and discusses briefly relations with Great Britain.
Dec 15   Receipt to Thomas Williamson from Wright Willis (for AJ) for cotton. ADS, DLC.
Dec 16   Account of Jackson & Hutchings with John Morrell & Son. ADS, DLC.
Dec 17   From Francis Preston.   179
Dec 17   Account with Will Lytle. ADS, DLC. Runs to June [1], 1811.
Dec 17   Receipt for $68.37, judgment in *Jackson & Hutchings* v. *James Mc-Kain*. ADS in John Hutchings's hand, Sumner County Records, T.
Dec 31   Account with Samuel Pryor for "keeping the Bibb mare." AD, DLC.
[Dec 31]   Account with racing company for boarding the "Bibb Filly." AD, DLC.

1808

Jan 3   Receipts from William Ballard for tuition of Jacob T. Blount, John Samuel and Andrew Jackson Donelson. ADS, DLC.
Jan 6   Account with Samuel Pryor. AD, THer. Runs to October 14.
Jan 8   Memorandum of settlement of account of Jackson & Hutchings with Samuel Pryor. AD, DLC.
Jan 8   Receipt for settlement of the private accounts of AJ, John Hutchings, and John Coffee at store and tavern. AD, DLC.
Jan 8   Receipt to Samuel Pryor from Jackson & Hutchings for payment on store purchase. ADS, Middle Tennessee Supreme Court Records, T.
Jan 12   From Joseph Anderson.   180
Jan 15   From George Michael Deaderick. ALS, DLC. Discusses AJ's account and the impact that a war with England or France might have on the cotton market.
Jan 20   To John McNairy.   182
Jan 21   To whom it may concern. Printed, *Impartial Review*, Feb 11. States that he will claim lands granted by North Carolina to Martin Armstrong and Stockley Donelson and purchased earlier.
Jan 22   From John McNairy. ALS, DLC. Writes that he will answer AJ's letter on January 23.
Jan 23   From John McNairy.   184
Jan 24   Decision in *AJ, John Hutchings, and John Coffee* v. *Samuel Pryor* (attachment). Copy, CPQS Minutes, Vol. F:212, TNDa.
Jan 27   From Daniel Smith.   185
Jan 29   Decision in *AJ and John Hutchings* v. *Samuel Pryor*. Copy, CPQS Minutes, Vol. F:236, TNDa.
[Jan]   Statement of settlement made with AJ and John Hutchings, executors of the Thomas Hutchings estate. Copy, Wills and Inventories, 3(1805–11): 206–207, TNDa.
Feb 5   To Robert Hays. Printed extract, *The Collector*, Feb 1949, Item 290. Reports that he has received an answer on Hays's business from McNairy.
Feb 6   Deed, 640 acres on Stone's River to Richard H. Jones for $1,600. Copy, Deed Book G(1805–1809):339, TNDa.
Feb 8   From John McClellan. ALS, DLC. Asks AJ to examine some deeds.

Feb 13 To Thomas Stuart. ALS, DLC. Sends his letter to McNairy for Stuart's perusal.

Feb 15 Affidavit of Robert Purdy re Rachel Hays. ADS, DLC.

Feb 26 From Edward Thursby to Jackson & Hutchings. ALS, DLC. Sends copy of account.

March 1 Advertisement of stud season for Truxton. Printed, *Impartial Review*, March 3; *Democratic Clarion*, March 14.

March 3 From George Gordon. ALS, THi. Discusses the Armstrong and Donelson grants purchased by AJ.

March 4 From James Jackson. ALS, DLC. Discusses a horserace.

March 5 Account of Jackson & Hutchings with James & Washington Jackson. AD, DLC. Runs to June 14, 1809.

March 10 To Samuel Jackson. ALS copy (fragment), DLC. Discusses the circulation of a "scandalous report" about Rachel Hays.

March 10 Promissory note for $100 to William Donelson. AD signature removed, DLC.

March 12 Affidavit of [John?] Boyd re Rachel Hays. ADS, DLC.

March 13 Deed, 860 acres in Bedford County from Alexander Ewing for $1. Copy, Deed Book B(1809–11):359, TSBe.

March 13 Decision in *Richard Cavitt et al.* v. *AJ and Catherine Hutchings et al., executors and devisees of Thomas Hutchings.* Copy, HDSC Minutes, 1(1793–1808):270–72, TKL.

March 18 From James Jackson. ALS, DLC. Discusses horses and a "frolick."

March 18 From John Overton to AJ or John Coffee. ALS, THi. Discusses a land warrant.

March 20–22 Affidavits of Shadrach Nye, March 20 (ADS, DLC); George Blakemore, March 22 (ADS in AJ's hand, signed by Blakemore, DLC); Benjamin Rawlings, March 22 (ADS in AJ's hand, signed by Rawlings, DLC); Robert Williamson, March 22 (ADS, DLC), re Rachel Hays.

April 10 From James Jackson. ALS, DLC. Sends memorandum of account (not found).

April 12 Account with James & Washington Jackson. AD, MoSHi. Runs to February 1, 1809.

April 15 From Henry McFall (enclosure: statement of account). ADS, DLC. Urges AJ to pay bill.

April 19 Memorandum of account of John Smith T with Jackson & Hutchings. AD, DLC.

April 20 To John Sevier. Copies, DLC and DNA-RG 107. Bassett, 1:187–88. Encloses a statement of William Meadows regarding Creek attack and reports on his response.

April 24 Subpoena to Rachel Jackson to appear as defendant in *Joel Lewis* v. *William Terrell Lewis et al.* Copy, Middle Tennessee Supreme Court Records, T.

April 25   From Sampson Williams.   195
April 25   Account with John Caldwell for tuition of John Samuel and Andrew
Jackson Donelson. AD, DLC.
April 28   Account of AJ, guardian of Elizabeth Wilkinson, with the estate of
Jesse Wilkinson. Copy, Wills and Inventories, 3(1805–11):223–24,
TNDa.
May 7   From Thomas Johnson. ALS, PHi. Reports on the scouting expedition of
Thomas Swann.
May 9   Receipt from John Griffin for payment of Rutherford County land taxes.
ADS, DLC.
May 9   Subpoena to Rachel Jackson to appear as defendant in *Lewis* v. *Lewis et
al.* Copy, Middle Tennessee Supreme Court Records, T.
May 13   From Thomas Johnson. ALS, PHi. Reports that the war department
has refused to reimburse him for expenses incurred in "defeating the
machinations of Aaron Burr & his associates" in January 1807.
May 14   To Thomas Jefferson.   196
May 15   Receipt to AJ, administrator of the Samuel Donelson estate, from John
Bosley. AD in AJ's hand, signed by Bosley, DLC.
May 16   To Eli Hammond. ALS, DLC. Asks Hammond to pay a debt.
May 18   Grant of 224 acres in Rutherford County from Tennessee. Copy, Book
GGB:107, Land Grant Records, T.
May 18   Answer to charges in *John McNairy* v. *John Caffery and AJ.* Copy,
MDSC Minutes, 1807–1809, pp. 294–97, TNDa.
May 21   Statement of AJ's account with Thomas Kirkman. AD, DLC. Runs to
December 5, 1809.
May 21   Grants of land in Rutherford (320 acres and 457 acres) and White
(1,000 acres) counties from Tennessee. Copies, Books GGA:189, 171,
GGB:108, Land Grant Records, T.
June 16   Decision in *William Douglass* v. *AJ and John Hutchings* (appealed;
final decision rendered April 1, 1816). Copy, CPQS Minutes, Sept 1805-
Dec 1808, pp. 390–91, TGSum.
June 18   Scire facias to AJ and John Hutchings, in *Jackson & Hutchings* v. *John
Lafferty.* Copy, CPQS Record Book, 1808–1809, p. 8, TGSum.
June 21   Promissory note for $78.82¼ from John Mitchel to Jackson & Hutch-
ings. ADS, Sumner County Records, T.
[June-Nov?]   From Robert Purdy. ALS fragment, ICHi. Discusses intruders on
the Cherokee lands and inquires after the Hays family and Robert Butler.
July 9   Deed, 215 acres in Bedford County to William Waite for $215. Copy,
Deed Book B(1809–11):440, TSBe.
July 12   Deed, 345½ acres in Davidson County from AJ and John and Catherine
Hutchings, executors of Thomas Hutchings, to John H. Camp for $3,456.
Typed copy, DNA-RG 153.
July 13   From George Bullitt to Jackson & Hutchings.   198
July 19   Deeds, 175 acres in Bedford County to Nathaniel Hays for $200; 200
acres, to Joseph Cook for $200; 263 acres, to Michael Gleaves for $263.
Printed forms with ms insertions by AJ, DLC. Copies, Deed Book B(1809–
11):16, 282, TSBe.
July 20   Grants of land in Rutherford (110 acres; 70 acres; 30 acres; 20 acres)

and Bedford (640 acres) counties from Tennessee. Copies, Book GGA:172, 173, 174, 175, 176, Land Grant Records, T.

July 22　Decision in *AJ* v. *Samuel Jackson* (covenant; appealed). Copy, CPQS Minutes, Vol. F:315–1[8], TNDa.

July 28　From Christopher Bullard. ALS, THi. Discusses land claim on Elk River.

July 28　Decision in *Jackson & Hutchings* v. *Gabriel Enochs* (debt). Copy, CPQS Minutes, Vol. F:341, TNDa.

July　Report and order of court directing AJ et al. to engage in road work in the Hermitage area. Copy, DLC.

Aug 6　To George Bullitt from Jackson & Hutchings.　　　　　　　198

Aug 13　Receipt for loan of $390 from John Donelson to Jackson & Hutchings. ADS, DLC.

Aug 13　Deed, 640 acres in Wilson County from Anthony Foster. ADS, DLC.

[Sept 15]　Decision in *Jackson & Hutchings* v. *Redmond Dillon Barry*. Copy, CPQS Record Book, 1808–1809, p. 52, TGSum.

Sept 16　Decision in *AJ and John Hutchings* v. *Benjamin Rawlings* (covenant; appealed). Copies, CPQS Record Book, 1808–1809, pp. 59–60; CPQS Minutes, Sept 1805-Dec 1808, pp. 431–33, TGSum.

Sept 17　Statement of account with Samuel Goode. AD, DLC.

Sept 21　Scire facias to AJ and John Hutchings, re payment of a debt, in *AJ and John Hutchings* v. *James Odam*. Copy, CPQS Record Book, 1808–1809, p. 60, TGSum.

Sept 21　Scire facias to AJ and John Hutchings, re payment of debt, in *AJ and John Hutchings* v. *Micajah Viverett*. Copy, CPQS Record Book 1808–1809, p. 69, TGSum.

Sept 22　Record of dismissal (by plaintiffs) in *AJ and John Hutchings* v. *Lazarus Cotton*. Copy, CPQS Record Rook, 1808–1809, p. 74, TGSum.

Sept 22　Action in *AJ and John Hutchings* v. *John A. Cathey* (debt). Copy, CPQS Record Book, 1808–1809, p. 73, TGSum.

Sept 23　From John Caffery. ALS, DLC. Reports a shortage of funds and asks if his deposition might be taken in Mississippi.

Sept 23　Receipt to Samuel Pryor for payment, to be credited to the judgment of Jackson & Hutchings. ADS, DLC.

Sept 28　From Joseph Hamilton Daveiss. ALS, DLC. Informs AJ of his intention to practice law in Nashville.

Sept 30　Statement of account of Nathaniel [Hays] with Jackson & Hutchings. ADS fragment, THer.

Oct 4　From John Peacock. ALS, ICHi. Discusses a debt.

Oct 6　From John Wesley Hunt. ALS fragment, DLC. *Cincinnati Commercial*, Jan 8, 1881. States that Henry Clay will be attorney in the Garrard case.

Oct 9　From James B. Risque. ALS, DLC. Reports that he paid Francis Preston $800.

Oct 10　From Alexander E. Outlaw. ALS, ICHi. States that he will appear before the Nashville court; discusses horseracing.

Oct 12　Account with James & Washington Jackson. AD, Mrs. Uhland O. Redd. Runs to September 16, 1809.

Oct 15　From David Campbell. ALS, ICHi. Discusses his illness and a land claim.

Oct 17   Grant of 100 acres in Bedford County from Tennessee. Copy, Book GGA:373, Land Grant Records, T.

Oct 24   Memorandum of court costs due to Sheriff Michael C. Dunn. ADS, ICHi.

Oct 24   Receipt for Fifty Shares of Bank Stock.   200

Oct 27   To Henry Clay from Jackson & Hutchings.   200

Oct   From Ephraim Davidson. ALS, DLC. Sends mares for stud service with Truxton.

Nov 1   From John Brahan. ALS, DLC. Discusses settlement of a debt and remarks on the lack of "party spirit" among the Cherokees.

Nov 5   From Thomas Harney. ALS, DLC. Comments on his negotiations with Samuel Pryor.

Nov 5   Memorandum of settlement of account with Samuel Pryor. AD in AJ's hand, signed by Pryor, WHi.

Nov 5   Statement of the account between Jackson & Hutchings and Pryor in *Samuel Pryor* v. *Jackson & Hutchings*. ADS copy, Middle Tennessee Supreme Court Records, T.

Nov 6   From Stockley Donelson Hays.   201

Nov 9   Account with James & Washington Jackson. AD, DLC. Runs to February 15, 1809.

Nov 16   Documents re *Pryor* v. *Jackson & Hutchings*: Bill of complaint (ADS); injunction to Jackson & Hutchings (ADS copy); record of action in the case, running to November 1, 1809 (Copy). Middle Tennessee Supreme Court Records, T.

Nov 18   Receipt from A. White and Joseph H. Carson for payment on Francis Campbell's account. ADS, DLC.

Nov 22   Receipt from John Hall for Clover Bottom Turf subscription. ADS, DLC.

Nov 26   Subpoena to AJ to answer Samuel Pryor's complaint. Copy, Middle Tennessee Supreme Court Records, T.

Nov 28   Answer to Pryor's bill of complaint in *Pryor* v. *Jackson & Hutchings*. ADS, Middle Tennessee Supreme Court Records, T.

Nov 29   Answer of AJ and Rachel Jackson to complaint in *Lewis* v. *Lewis et al.* ADS, Middle Tennessee Supreme Court Records, T.

Nov   Draft by Joseph Cook for $6.50. ADS, DLC.

Nov   Decision in *John C. Henderson* v. *AJ* (assault and battery, on appeal). Copy, MDSC Record Book D(1806–1809):285–87, TNDa.

[Nov]   From John Coffee. ALS fragment, DLC. Discusses land surveys.

[Nov]   Memorandum of AJ's debts with Philadelphia merchants. AD, DLC. Bassett, 1:190–91.

Dec 3   Deed, 250 acres in Knox County to Robert Holt. Copy, Deed Book N1:278, TKKn.

Dec 5   Account of Hinchey Pettway with Jackson & Hutchings. ADS by John Coffee for Jackson & Hutchings, THi.

Dec 17   Scire facias to AJ and John Hutchings, in *AJ and John Hutchings* v. *John Crawley*. Copy, CPQS Record Book, 1808–1809, p. 111, TGSum.

Dec 19   From James Cage. ALS, DLC. Discusses accounts.

[Dec 19]   To the Public. Printed, *Democratic Clarion*, Jan 3, 1809. Issues call for delegation from each county of West Tennessee to meet in Nashville on January 16 to discuss "business of importance."

Dec 19   *To the Brigadier Generals of the 2nd Division.*   203

Dec 22   From William Edward Butler. ALS matched fragments, DLC and ICHi. Discusses family and friends.

Dec 24   To John Coffee. ALS, THi. Reports that he will not be able to meet Coffee as scheduled. ·

[1808]   From [William Preston Anderson]. AL fragment, DLC. Discusses financial affairs.

[1808]   Receipt from Benjamin Bradford for land taxes. ADS, THi.

[1808]   Record of AJ lands in Bedford, Davidson, Franklin, and Rutherford counties to be returned for taxation. AD by John Coffee, THi.

[c1808]   Memorandum of accounts between John Coffee, John Drake, and William P. Anderson, including entries for surveys of land for AJ and Jackson & Hutchings. ADS, THi.

[1808–28]   From William Edward Butler. ALS fragment, ICHi. Sends respects to Mrs. Jackson.

1809

Jan 2   From Anthony Foster. ALS, ICHi. Discusses a land transaction.

Jan 4   From William Martin. ALS, DLC. Bassett, 1:192 (extract). Discusses an evaluation of slaves.

Jan 12   *From John Sevier.*   205

Jan 15   From Lemuel Hutchings. ALS, DLC. Discusses horse-breeding debts.

[Jan 16]   *Resolutions of 2nd Division Officers.*   208

[Jan 16]   *Address to Citizens of Nashville.*   210

Jan 16   Resolutions (drafted by AJ, James Winchester, Robert Weakley, Jenkin Whiteside, and Felix Grundy) adopted by meeting of citizens of West Tennessee in support of the administration in Washington. Printed, *Democratic Clarion*, Jan 24.

Jan 19   Receipt from David Killogh for cotton. AD in AJ's hand, signed by Killogh, DLC.

Jan 23   From John Peacock. ALS, DLC. Explains delay in paying account.

Jan 28   *From Stockley Donelson Hays.*   211

Jan 29   From ? AL fragment, DLC. Discusses Robert Hays's affairs.

[Feb 20]   Order to 2nd Division directing preparedness. ADS draft, DLC. Bassett, 1:195.

Feb 21   From John Coffee. ALS, THi. Asks AJ to close contract with Thomas E. Waggaman.

Feb 23   Advertisement for stud season of Truxton. Printed, *Impartial Review*, March 16. Bassett, 1:113–14.

March 4   From James Winchester. ALS, DLC. Discusses organization of his brigade.

March 4   Agreement with Robert Butler for the transfer of one undivided half of the Paines Mill tract to Butler. ADS by Butler, signed also by AJ, DLC.

March 5   *From George Michael Deaderick.*   211

March 10   Receipt from James & Washington Jackson for a draft on Abner Barker by AJ, guardian of Lydia and William Butler. AD in AJ's hand, signed by James and Washington Jackson, DLC.

March 11   Bond to Thomas E. Waggaman to transfer 224 acres in Bedford County. DS, THi.

March 15   To James Winchester.   214

March 17   To John Coffee. ALS, THi. Reports execution of the deed to Waggaman.

March 20   Deed, 224 acres in Bedford County to Thomas E. Waggaman for $672. Copy, Deed Book A(1810–11):355, TFLi.

March 20   Memorandum of agreement by John Castleman to transfer land to AJ. AD in AJ's hand, signed by Castleman, Mike Collier.

March 22   Grants of land in Franklin (640 acres) and Rutherford (320 acres) counties. Copies, Book GGB:76, 77, Land Grant Records, T.

March 25   From James O'Hara (enclosure: account). ALS, ICHi. Discusses debt of Edward Butler estate.

March 25   Decision in *AJ and John Hutchings* v. *Thomas Blakemore* (debt). Copy, CPQS Minutes, Dec 1808-April 1812, pp. 49–50, TGSum.

March 26   From James Sanders.   215

March 31   From T. L. Ferguson. ALS, DLC. Acknowledges receipt of an order for goods.

March   Record of action (ejectment) in *Jackson & Hutchings* v. *Joseph Johnson.* Copy, CPQS Execution Docket, 1806–22, p. 65, TLWil.

April 25   Receipt for taxes, Franklin County. ADS, THi.

May 4   Deed, lot in Lebanon from AJ and John Hutchings to James S. Rawlings for $200. Copy, Deed Book D(1809–12):98, TLWil.

May 7   Account of payments made by James & Washington Jackson for AJ. ADS, DLC. Runs to March 15, 1810.

May 14   Deed, 230 acres in Bedford County to Enoch Enochs for $345. Copy, Deed Book A(1808–1809):343, TSBe.

May 15   Deed, undivided half of a 640-acre tract in Wilson County from AJ and John Hutchings to Edward Douglass for $1. ADS, Stanley F. Horn; Copy, Deed Book H(1819–21):163, TLWil.

May 15   Deed, 640 acres in Bedford County to Matt Martin for $1,280. Copy, Deed Book A(1808–1809):330, TSBe.

May 15   Deed, 1,000 acres along Elk River from AJ and John Hutchings to William Finch for $1,500. Copy, Deed Book A(1808–10):43, TWFr.

May 18   Decision in *AJ* v. *Samuel Jackson* (debt; on appeal). Copy, MDSC Record Book D(1806–1809):348–50, TNDa.

May 20   Report re account of Jackson & Hutchings with Samuel Pryor. Copy, Middle Tennessee Supreme Court Records, Order Book A(1810–13):220, T.

May 26   From Thomas Swann.   215

June 1   Decision in *John McNairy* v. *John Caffery and AJ.* Copy, MDSC Equity Minute Book, 1807–1809, pp. 286–303, TNDa.

June 2   Receipt for the payment of account with King, Carson & King. ADS, DLC.

June 5   From John Cocke. ALS, THi. *Cincinnati Commercial*, Jan 8, 1881. Reports on arrangements for a duel between L. L. Henderson and Henry L. Sheffey (fought on June 23).

[June 7]   From Nathaniel Hays. ALS, DLC. Asks AJ to make out deed to Joseph Taylor.

June 15   Deed, 640 acres in Bedford County to Matt Martin for $1,000. Copy, Deed Book A(1808–1809):328, TSBe.

June 15   Deed, 640 acres in Bedford County from John Donelson for $1,000. Copy, Deed Book A(1808–1809):326, TSBe.

June 17   From Stockley Donelson Hays. ALS, DLC. Discusses efforts to collect certain Jackson debts in Kentucky.

June 17   Grants of land in Rutherford County (368 acres; 640 acres). Copies, Book GGB:241, 242, Land Grant Records, T.

June 21   From William Lyon. ALS matched fragments, DLC and ICHi. Discusses land dispute involving AJ in Rhea County.

July 8   Deed, 175 acres in Bedford County to Joseph Taylor for $200. Copy, Deed Book B(1809–11):114, TSBe.

July 22   From Anna Moore. AL, DLC. Inquires about land which her deceased husband had with Samuel Donelson.

July 22   Deed, 320 acres in Bedford County to John Peacock for $175. Copy, Deed Book F(1815–17):187, TSBe.

Aug 9   Deed, 640 acres in Wilson County to Samuel Crawford for $640. Copy, Deed Book E(1812–16):64, TLWil.

Aug 15   Grant of 320 acres in Bedford County. Copy, Book GGB:554, Land Grant Records, T.

Aug 20   From James Winchester. AL fragment, DLC. Sends annual militia returns (not found).

Aug 29   Agreement between Thomas York, Jonathan York, Samuel Montgomery, and AJ re lease of land on Duck River. ADS, DLC.

[cSept 13]   Resolutions (drafted by James Robertson, AJ, John Childress, Jr., Felix Grundy, and Thomas Stuart) adopted by meeting of citizens of Nashville denouncing British officials and policy and expressing their support for the American stance. Printed, *Democratic Clarion*, Sept 15.

Oct 3   Receipt from James Marshall for the transfer of papers in the Samuel Donelson file. AD in AJ's hand, signed by Marshall, DLC.

Oct 7   Agreement between William P. Anderson, William B. Vinson, Robert Bell, and AJ re Edward Butler's estate. Copy, Wills, Inventories, and Bonds, 1(1796–1812):319–20, TSRob.

Oct 9   Receipt for the payment of the proceeds of the estate of Edward Butler to Eliza E. Butler. Copy, Wills, Inventories, and Bonds, 1(1796–1812):322, TSRob.

Oct 14   Account with Ward & Panton. ADS, DLC. Runs to June 29, 1812.

Oct 17   Decision in *David Knox* v. *AJ* (debt). Copy, CPQS Minutes, Vol. G:13, TNDa.

Oct 17   Decision in *George Bickham and Jacob Reese* v. *AJ* (debt). Copy, CPQS Minutes, Vol. G:13, TNDa.

Oct 20   Decision in *AJ* v. *Joseph Erwin*. Copy, CPQS Minutes, Vol. F:507, TNDa.

Nov 8   From James B. Risque. ALS fragment, DLC. Discusses business matters.

Nov 18   *James W. Camp to William Purnell.*   224
Nov 19   *From William Purnell.*   225
Nov 22   From James Jackson. Printed extract, *The Collector*, June 1951, p. 130.
          Asks AJ's plans for a spring horserace.
Nov 30   To George Washington Campbell. ALS, OFH. *Southern Historical So-
          ciety Papers*, 9(1881): 40. Asks Campbell to represent a Mr. Powell in the
          federal court.
Dec 8   Receipt from N. Wilson & Co. for $4.00 for earrings. ADS, DLC.
Dec 14   Receipt for the payment of $270.50 to Thomas and Jonathan York for
          improvements on land on Duck River. AD in AJ's hand, signed by Thomas
          and Jonathan York, DLC.
Dec 20   *From Washington Jackson.*   225
Dec 28   *From Willie Blount.*   226
1809   From Charles McClung. ALS fragment, DLC. Discusses business and land
          dealings.
[1809]   From Robert Purdy. ALS fragment, DLC. Discusses military affairs.
[1809]   From Robert Purdy. Abstract, *The Collector*, Omnibus Supplement No.
          2(1963): 12. "Asks assistance in refuting printed attack by 'Russell.'"

1810

[cJan 2] Memorandum of accounts. AD, DLC.
Jan 10   *From William Oliver Allen.*   228
Jan 10   From Willie Blount. ALS fragment, DLC. Discusses secret proceedings
          in Tennessee legislature.
Jan 10   Action in *AJ* v. *Francis Nash* (attachment). Copy, Trial and Appearance
          Docket, 1808—10, p. 68, TMRu.
Jan 15   Decision in *AJ and John Hutchings* v. *Samuel Pryor, William Terrell
          Lewis, and Charles M. Hall* (appealed). Copy, CPQS Minutes, Vol. G: 108,
          TNDa.
Jan 17   From Sampson Williams. ALS, DLC. Asks AJ's plans for the horses at
          Dixon Springs.
Jan 24   From Joseph Atkins, Sr. ALS, DLC. Discusses a land warrant.
Jan 26   *From Jenkin Whiteside.*   230
Feb 2   Deposition of Leven Donelson re land transaction between Alexander
          Donelson and Abraham Sublett. AD in AJ's hand, signed by Leven Donel-
          son, Case file of *Alexander Donelson* v. *Abraham Sublett*, Circuit Court
          Case #6219, KyCTa.
Feb 10   *To [Jenkin Whiteside].*   230
Feb 10   *To Jenkin Whiteside.*   233
[cFeb 10] *To John Randolph.*   234
[Feb 15] *To Willie Blount.*   236
Feb 15—16 Account with James & Washington Jackson. ADS, DLC.
Feb 17   From John Williams. ALS, DLC. Offers advice on a land claim.
[Feb 20] From Robert Purdy. ALS fragment, ICHi. Reports the arrest of
          Thomas J. Vandyke; writes of his "fear [that] the day of *grace is passed*"
          when AJ and Rachel will have a son of their own.
March 5   Authorization for John W. Clay to hire a groom for Truxton. AD sig-
          nature removed, DLC.

March 11   From [Jenkin Whiteside]. AL fragment, DLC. Informs AJ that Madison appointed Obadiah Jones judge in Mississippi Territory.

March 13   Deed, 640 acres in Franklin County to Alexander Ewing for $1,280. Copy, Deed Book A(1808–10):60, TWFr.

March 15   From Willie Blount.   238

March 26   From John Hutchings. AL fragment, DLC. Reports on efforts to collect debts in Mississippi Territory.

March   Petition to the judges of the Second Circuit Court of Tennessee. Copy, TDRh. Requests a correction in the survey of a land grant.

April 3   Deed, 100 acres in Bedford County to John Scivally for $250. Copy, Deed Book A(1810–11):96, TFLi.

April 11   Deed, 25 acres in Davidson County from William Ward for $500. ADS, DLC; Copy, Deed Book I(1811–13):44, TNDa.

April 14   Decision in *Jackson & Hutchings* v. *Richard Orton and James B. Thompson* (with case file). Copy, CPQS Minutes, 1(1800–12):483, TFWi.

April 20   From Robert Purdy. ALS fragment, DLC. Discusses a court case and comments on Wilkinson.

April 21   To William Edwards. ALS, THi. States that he will take depositions on behalf of Edward Williams in Warren County, Miss. Terr., on May 13.

May 1   From Bennett Smith.   240

May 3   To Francis Preston.   243

May 10   Memorandum of Nashville Turf accounts. AD, DLC.

May 14   From John Coffee.   245

May 15   To Joseph Hamilton Daveiss. ALS, KyLoF. Introduces Robert King, who seeks to locate stolen slaves.

May 16   Letter of credit for $200 to James & Washington Jackson from Washington Jackson for AJ. ADS, DLC.

May 20   From Donelson Caffery.   246

May 23   From John Hutchings. ALS, DLC. Again reports on efforts to collect debts.

May 24   From Robert Purdy.   247

May 26   Account with the Nashville Bank. AD, THer. Runs to September 20, 1815.

May 31   From Lemuel Hutchings. ALS, DLC. Reports on disputed accounts with Cage & Black.

June 3   From Wade Hampton.   248

June 4   Receipt from George Michael Deaderick for payment of second installment on Nashville Bank shares. ADS, DLC.

June 6   Receipt for the 1806 rent of Clover Bottom. AD in AJ's hand, signed by James Buchanan, DLC.

June 6   To James Priestly and Felix Grundy. Microcopy, Colonial Dames Film, TNJ. Authorizes payment of $125 to Thomas Stuart.

June 6   Promissory note for $95.50 to Thomas Stuart. AD signature removed, DLC.

June 10   From Donelson Caffery.   249

June 10   From James S. Rawlings. ALS, DLC. Reports that he and Moses Fisk want AJ and Randal McGavock to arbitrate their business dispute.

June 13   Bill of sale from Felix Grundy for the slave Sucke for $400. ADS, DLC.

June 16   Promissory note to Jenkin Whiteside. ADS, DLC.

June 16   Bill of sale from Felix Grundy for the slave Silvay, Sucke's daughter, for $200. ADS, DLC.

June 18   To Cuthbert Banks. ALS, OkChicW. Introduces Duncan Robertson, who seeks information on Henry Clay's progress in the Garrard suit.

[cJuly 1]   From William Preston Anderson. ALS, DLC. Reports the pending election of general of the 7th Brigade; mentions the Jacksons' suffering "dear little baby."

July 2   Order to field officers of the 7th Brigade to meet and elect a general. ADS draft, DLC.

July 3   From Sampson Williams. ALS, DLC. Asks for clarification of brigade orders.

July 16   From Samuel Armistead. ALS, DLC. Asks AJ to take proper steps to see that his bond is paid.

July 18   Statement of indebtedness to John Dickinson. DS, DLC.

July 19   Record of action in *Jackson & Hutchings* v. *Obadiah M. Benge*. Copy, CPQS Execution Docket, 1810–13, p. 1, TMRu.

July 20   From Donelson Caffery.   250

July 20   From Robert Purdy. ALS, DLC. Discusses military developments and orders from Wade Hampton for a court of inquiry for Gilbert C. Russell.

Aug 3   From James Jackson. ALS, DLC. Sends a slave to take care of horse.

Aug 15   From Donelson Caffery. ALS, DLC. Discusses family, a land grant, and the situation in West Florida.

Aug 18   From Wilson Cage. ALS, DLC. Discusses a promissory note.

Aug 18   Promissory note for $717.50 to Henry Thomson. AD signature removed, DLC.

Aug 18   Original bill of complaint in *John Overton* v. *AJ and the heirs and devisees of David Allison*. Copy, Middle Tennessee Supreme Court Records, T.

Aug 26   From James Hart. ALS, DLC. Discusses business affairs.

Aug 30   To Doctor Potter. ALS, DLC. Asks him to pay a stud fee to Harmon Hays.

Sept 10   From Isabella Vinson.   251

Sept 10   Decision in *AJ* v. *Samuel Jackson* (covenant). Copy, CC Minutes, March 1810-Sept 1812, p. 19, TNDa.

Sept 12   Decision in *Samuel Jackson* v. *AJ and John Hutchings*. Copy, CC Minutes, March 1810-Sept 1812, p. 81, TNDa.

Sept 20   Promissory note for $9.36½ from George Goodman. ADS, DLC.

Sept 20   Deed, 200 acres in Bedford County to Samuel Gibson for $400. Deed Book C(1810–12):341, TSBe.

Sept 22   Decision in *John McNairy* v. *AJ, James Jackson, and Thomas Shackelford*. Copy, CC Minutes, March 1810-Sept 1812, p. 134–35, TNDa.

Sept 26   From Walter Hampden Overton.   252

Oct 8   From Thomas Overton. Typed copy, DLC. Introduces a Mr. Owen of North Carolina.

Oct 23   From James Hart. ALS, DLC. Asks AJ to pay debt.

Oct 24   From Daniel Sayre. ALS, DLC. Thanks AJ for courtesies extended him during his recent visit to Nashville.

Oct 25   Receipt for payment of $1 from Matthew Payne. AD in AJ's hand, signed by Payne, DLC.

Feb 13   Receipt to Edmond Cooper for cotton. ADS, DLC.

[cFeb 15]   Certification by AJ et al. to the quality and performance of the stud horse, Royalist. Printed, *Democratic Clarion*, March 15.

Feb 16   Receipt from John Griffin for Rutherford County land taxes, 1809 and 1810. DS, THi.

Feb 18   From Joseph H. Hawkins. ALS, DLC. Discusses the Garrard litigation.

Feb 26   From Willie Blount. 259

March 1   Receipt for promissory note of $150 to McKiernan & Stout. ADS, DLC.

March 5   Memorandum asking dismissal of a complaint against him by John M. Garrard. Abstract, *ABPC*, (1966–67):1153.

March 11   Memorandum of proceedings in *AJ and John Hutchings* v. *Samuel Pryor, William Terrell Lewis, and Charles M. Hall.* Copy, CC Minutes, March 1810-Sept 1812, p. 156, TNDa.

March 15   Deed, 100 acres in Davidson County from Andrew Hays et al. for bond given by Samuel Hays to John Castleman. ADS in AJ's hand, DLC; Copy, Deed Book Y(1835–36):497, TNDa.

March 18   Deed, land in Davidson County to Stockley Donelson Hays, trustee for Jane Hays, for $900. Copy, Deed Book K(1813–15):441, TNDa.

March 19   From Felix Grundy. ALS, DLC. Discusses a debt.

March 20   Bill of complaint in *AJ* v. *William Bush.* Copy, CC Minutes, March 1810-Sept 1812, p. 191, TNDa.

March 26   Deed, lot in Gallatin to Daniel Cherry for $130. DS, Sumner County Records, T; Copy, Deed Book 6(1811–14):263, TGSum.

March   Tax receipt for lots and store in Gallatin. ADS, Sumner County Tax Books, 1802–11, T.

April 23   Promissory note for $92.37½ to Jesse Jackson for blacksmith work. ADS, DLC.

April 24   Account with Addison Carrick for cloth. ADS, DLC.

May 8   From William Carroll, Joshua Paxton, and Wilkins Tannehill (enclosed in AJ to William Eustis, May 10). DS, DNA-RG 107. Request muskets for their newly-organized infantry volunteer corps.

May 10   To William Eustis. 260

May 18   Memorandum re Purchase of Slaves from Richard Apperson and Cotton and Tobacco from Bennett Smith. 262

May 18   Promissory notes for $4,000 from Horace Green to Richard Apperson, endorsed by Coleman and Jackson, paid by AJ on November 20 (DS, DLC); for $4,000 to Richard Apperson, paid by AJ on May 6, 1812 (AD, endorsed by AJ and Joseph Coleman, DLC).

May 22   Promissory note for $100 from AJ and Joseph Coleman to Wetherald & Yeatman. DS, DLC.

May 24   Receipt from James H. Gamble for $11.50. ADS, DLC.

May 25   From Branch H. Anderson. ALS, DLC. Discusses settlement of his account for the construction of Robert Hays's house.

May 28   From Robert Purdy. 263

May 29   From William Eustis. LC, DNA-RG 107. Promises to supply muskets for company of volunteers.

May 30   Account with Wetherald & Yeatman for general merchandise. ADS, DLC.

June 4   From [Walter Hampden Overton]. AL fragment, DLC. Reports that he
commands post at Natchitoches, La., and describes topography and people
of Red River country.

June 9   From Joseph H. Hawkins. ALS, DLC. Discusses Garrard litigation.

June 26   From Thomas Augustine Claiborne.   264

June 26   Deed, 200 acres in Davidson County from Michael C. Dunn, sheriff,
for $2,000. Copy, Deed Book I(1811–13):162, TNDa.

June 26   Deed, 226½ acres in Davidson County to James Priestley for $3,000.
Copy, Deed Book I(1811–13):163, TNDa.

July 3   Check to Jenkin Whiteside for $50. DS, DLC.

July 3   Notification of possession of a 640-acre tract on Stone's River, owned by
Richard Jones. ADS, DLC.

July 13   From Stephen Cantrell. ALS, DLC. Sends statement for salt and sugar;
asks about cotton.

July 17   Check to Cumberland College for $1,031.75. DS, DLC.

July 24   Checks to William Eastin for $300 (DS, DLC); to self for $125 (DS,
DLC).

Aug 5   To George Washington Campbell. ALS, DLC. Bassett, 1:206. Discusses
breeding of Campbell's mare.

Aug 8   From William Carroll. ALS, DLC. Suggests that he and AJ combine their
cotton to sell.

Aug 21   From John Hartwell Marable. ALS, DLC. Discusses sale of cotton.

Sept 7   From Thomas G. Bradford. ALS, DLC. Thanks AJ for recommending his
publication, *The Military Instructor.*

Sept 12   Account of Rachel Jackson with Thomas Childress. ADS, DLC.

Sept 19   From James Winchester. ALS, PHi. Responds to AJ's letter (not found)
urging him to become a candidate for Congress.

Sept 20   Bill of complaint in *AJ v. William Bush.* Copy, CC Minutes, March
1810-Sept 1812, p. 295, TNDa.

Sept 28   From Anthony Butler.   265

Oct 2   Check to J. Childress for $369.28. DS, DLC.

Oct 9   From Alexander Donelson.   266

Oct 9   Check to self for $20. DS, DLC.

Oct 12   From Anthony Butler.   267

Oct 16   Check to ? for $1,350. DS, DLC.

Oct 16   Decision in *William Douglass* v. *AJ and John Hutchings* (on appeal).
Copy, CC Minutes, 1810–15, pp. 109–10, TGSum.

Oct 19   From David Campbell. ALS, DLC. Discusses a land title and horses.

Oct 23   From Donelson Caffery.   268

Oct 23   Checks to Joseph Coleman for $613.39 (DS, DLC); to self for $60 (DS,
DLC).

Oct 29   From Anthony Butler. ALS, DLC. Bassett, 1:207 (dated Oct 28). Discusses horseracing in Kentucky.

Nov 4   Deed, 320 acres in Montgomery County from Samuel Mitchell for $200.
AD in AJ's hand, signed by Mitchell, DLC.

Nov 16   From William Preston Anderson. ALS, DLC. Sends material (not found)
for newspaper publication.

Nov 19   From P. Harrison. ALS, DLC. Discusses horse business.

April 17   From Willie Blount. ALS, DLC. Issues general orders concerning organization and preparations of the militia.

April 18   From Willie Blount. Printed, *Democratic Clarion*, April 28; *Knoxville Gazette*, May 18. Authorizes AJ to investigate report that Indian intruders have settled near Chickasaw Bluffs.

April 22   From Thomas Johnson. AL fragment, DLC. Reports the stationing of men in Stewart County to protect the frontier.

April 23   To Willie Blount (enclosure: certificate of Thomas Washington's election as general of the 9th Brigade). ALS copy, NjP. Reports readiness of troops to protect frontier.

April 23   Certification of Thomas Washington's election as general of the 9th Brigade (enclosed in AJ to Blount, April 23). ADS, T; ADS draft, NjP.

[April 23]   From James Winchester. ALS, DLC. Resigns commission in the Tennessee militia to accept post in the regular army.

[April 23]   To James Winchester. LC fragment, THer. Accepts his resignation.

April 24   To the field officers, 4th Brigade. ADS, NjP. *Democratic Clarion*, April 28. Orders them to meet in Gallatin to elect a general.

[April 24]   To the brigade commanders, 2nd Division. Printed, *Democratic Clarion*, April 28; *Knoxville Gazette*, May 18. Transmits Blount's orders of April 17.

May 1   To John Strother.   297

May 2   From Thomas Johnson. ALS, DLC. States that the intruders on Sandy River are reported to be Muscogee Indians and transmits copy of his orders to the brigade for protection of the frontier.

May 4   Deed, 640 acres in Wilson County from James Crawford for $720. Copy, Deed Book E(1812–16):65, TLWil.

May 8   Bill from Benjamin Foy for securing and keeping AJ's runaway slave Jesse. ADS, DLC.

May 9   To Willie Blount. Printed extract, *Knoxville Gazette*, May 25. Reports that troops have been ordered from Fort Hampton to overtake a group of Creek Indians.

May 9   From William Oliver Allen. ALS, DLC. In light of a recent military appointment, asks for letters of introduction to James Winchester and W.C.C. Claiborne.

May 27   From Thomas Johnson.   298
May 28   From Kinchen T. Wilkinson.   299

May 31   From John Crafford. ALS, DLC. Reports on his patrol west of Tennessee River.

June 4   To Willie Blount.   300

June 4   From Willie Blount (enclosure: Blount to David Mason, June 4). ALS and ALS copy, DLC. States that he has ordered David Mason's company of rangers to patrol the West Tennessee frontier.

June 5   To Willie Blount.   301
June 5   To George Colbert.   302

June 5   From Felix Grundy. ALS, DLC. Reports that the House of Representatives and the Senate have been meeting in secret session.

[June 5]   To the 2nd Division. AD draft (fragment), DLC. Orders preparedness.

June 6   From William Preston Anderson. Printed, *Democratic Clarion*, June 16. Resigns as aide.

June 7   To William Preston Anderson. Printed, *Democratic Clarion*, June 16. Accepts resignation.

June 8   From Thomas Johnson (enclosed in AJ to Thomas G. Bradford, June 10). ALS, THi. *Democratic Clarion*, June 10. Reports attempts to apprehend Indians responsible for Duck River massacre.

[June 10]   To Thomas G. Bradford (enclosure: Thomas Johnson to AJ, June 8). ALS, THi. *Democratic Clarion*, June 10. Sends Johnson's letter for publication.

[cJune 10]   From Benjamin Bradford. ALS, DLC. Reports on volunteers for the 47th Regiment.

June 11   From David Mason. ALS, DLC. Asks about military regulations applicable to his company of rangers.

June 12   From Willie Blount.   303

June 12   From Willie Blount. ALS, DLC. Instructs AJ to send emissary to Newport, Ky., for guns offered by the federal government, acknowledges AJ's letters of June 8, 9 (not found), and discusses rumor of murders committed by Cherokees.

June 14   From Willie Blount. ALS, DLC. Expresses support for a Creek campaign but disclaims power to authorize an offensive; reveals that murder report was a hoax.

June 15   From John Murrey. ALS, DLC. Volunteers his services for a Creek offensive.

June 15   Certification of William Hall's election as general of the 4th Brigade. ADS, T; ADS copy, DLC.

[cJune 15]   From Benjamin Bradford. ALS, DLC. Encloses for publication returns of the 47th Regiment (not found).

June 16   From John Williams. ALS, DLC. Discusses militia organization.

June 17   To Willie Blount.   305

June 17   From Willie Blount. Printed, *Knoxville Gazette*, June 29; *Democratic Clarion*, June 30. Discusses the secretary of war's response to the enrollment and acceptance of volunteers.

June 17   Partial return of volunteers from the 2nd Division (enclosed in Willie Blount to William Eustis, June 25). Copy, DNA-RG 107.

June 18   From Willie Blount (enclosures: Blount to David Mason, June 4; Blount to Benjamin Hawkins, June 8). ALS, DLC. Reports the acceptance of Mason's company of rangers into U.S. service and discusses his efforts to recover Martha Crawley from the Creeks.

June 18   From Richard Winn. ALS, NjP. Announces that war has been declared against Great Britain.

June 19   To the 2nd Division. Printed, *Democratic Clarion*, June 23. Orders the detachment of 1,400 men from the 2nd Division into separate units of cavalry, artillery, and infantry.

June 19   From Joshua Cox. ALS fragment, DLC. Offers services against the Creeks.

June 22   From Thomas McCrory to AJ or Thomas Washington. ALS, DLC. Transmits returns from the 21st Regiment.

June 23   From Willie Blount. ALS, DLC. Bassett, 1:229 (extract). Discusses arrangements for financing the procurement of arms in Kentucky.

July 24   From Willie Blount. ALS, DLC. Introduces a Mr. Skillern, who brings commissions to officers in Eli Hammond's ranger company.

July 24   Decision in *AJ* v. *William Bush* (equity). Copies, DLC and Middle Tennessee Supreme Court Records, Order Book A(1810–13):180–83, T.

[July 24]   Account with William Blount, steersman on the boat conveying arms to Nashville. AD, DLC. Runs to August 4.

July 27   From Thomas Johnson. ALS, DLC. Discusses muster rolls and the desire to organize a company of rangers in Hickman County.

July 27   From Samuel H. Williams. ALS, DLC. Reports on organization of his Maury County regiment.

July 29   Decision in *Samuel Pryor* v. *Jackson & Hutchings* (with case file). Copy, Middle Tennessee Supreme Court Records, Order Book A(1810–13):206–20, T.

July 31   To the Tennessee Volunteers.   317

July   Decision in *John Overton* v. *AJ and the heirs of David Allison* (with partial case file). Copies, Middle Tennessee Supreme Court Records, Order Book A(1810–13):269–74, T.

Aug 1   From Benjamin Bradford (enclosures: muster rolls). ALS, DLC. Submits muster rolls of 47th Regiment and comments on shortage of munitions.

Aug 3   Deed, David Allison's Tennessee lands from Alexander Allison et al. for $500 and satisfaction of Allison's debts. Copies, Middle Tennessee Supreme Court Records, T; Deed Book I(1811–13):396, TNDa; and Deed Book 6:288–91, TDSt.

Aug 5   Check to William Preston Anderson for $2,214.62. DS by Anderson (for AJ), DLC.

Aug 7   From Willie Blount (enclosure: Blount to William Eustis, Aug 6). ALS, DLC. Recommends three men as colonels of the volunteers.

Aug 7   From Benjamin Bradford. ALS, DLC. Asks for clarification of the term of service for volunteers.

Aug 10   To Isaac Roberts. ALS fragment, TU. Orders Roberts to be more punctual in making militia returns.

Aug 10   Account of Edward G. W. Butler (AJ's ward) with John H. Smith. AD endorsed by AJ, DLC. Runs to January 4, 1813.

Aug 13   To Bird Smith. ALS copy, DLC. Bassett, 1:232–33. Chastises Smith for failure to submit volunteer returns.

Aug 17   From Cave Johnson et al. Printed, *Democratic Clarion*, Aug 25. Volunteer services of Cumberland College students.

[Aug 17]   To Cave Johnson et al. Printed, *Democratic Clarion*, Aug 25. Accepts tender of service.

Aug 18   From Wilson Yandell. ALS, DLC. Reveals the scheming for political power and favors of an officer raising volunteers.

Aug 21   From John Doak. ALS, DLC. Offers services as lieutenant colonel commandant of volunteers from the 4th Brigade.

Aug 22   To Willie Blount. ALS draft, DLC. Discusses arms delivered by Hammond and Hammond's expense account.

Aug 22   From Robert Henry Dyer. ALS, DLC. Promises to send muster roll of his company within a few days.

Aug 22   From James Jackson. ALS, DLC. States that the assignment of rights from an Allison heir has arrived.

Aug 24   From John Coffee (enclosure: muster roll). ALS, DLC. Submits roll of volunteer cavalry and returns from Thomas Washington's 9th Brigade (not found).

Aug 25   To John Williams.   318

Aug 25   To John Knibb Wynne. ALS copy, THi. Bassett, 1:233. Orders Wynne to prepare for command of a detached regiment in the division.

Aug 25   Inspection return, detachment from 2nd Division (enclosed in AJ to John Williams, Aug 25). AD draft, DLC.

Aug 29   From David Humphreys. ALS, DLC. Offers services as a volunteer.

Aug 31   From Thomas Johnson (enclosure: record of court martial of Lt. Col. Jesse Denson). ALS, DLC. Discusses Denson court martial and reports on a Creek encampment.

[Aug]   From Alpha Kingsley. Printed extract, *Democratic Clarion*, Aug 25; *Knoxville Gazette*, Aug 31. Reports on Creek Indians' preparation for war near Fort Hampton.

Sept 1   From James Terrill (enclosure: muster roll). ALS, DLC. Discusses plans to raise more volunteers and inquires about uniform for cavalry.

[cSept 1]   Memorandum of account with racing company. ADS, James S. Copley Library, La Jolla, Calif. Bassett, 1:245–46. Runs to November 6.

Sept 8   To Willie Blount.   319

Sept 8   To the 2nd Division.   320

Sept 8   To Bird Smith. ALS, DLC. Orders Smith to forward his brigade muster rolls.

Sept 10   To Thomas Claiborne. ALS draft, DLC. Bassett, 1:234. Urges careful attention to legislation affecting volunteers now being considered by the General Assembly.

Sept 13   From Isaac Roberts. ALS, THer. Encloses muster rolls from Lincoln County regiment (not found).

Sept 15   To John Coffee. ALS, T. Bassett, 6:427–28. States his opposition to the choice of field officers by election and criticizes the secretary of war.

Sept 15   From Robert Henry Dyer. ALS, DLC. Discusses enrollment of volunteers in the cavalry.

Sept 26   Certificate of John Gordon regarding the Silas Dinsmoor affair (enclosed in AJ to George Washington Campbell, Oct 15). ADS endorsed by AJ, DNA-RG 107. Bassett, 1:234–35.

Sept 28   From David Smith. ALS, ICHi. Recommends Anthony Butler to command AJ's cavalry and discusses war on the Canadian border.

Sept 30   From Jonathan Thompson.   322

Sept   Record of action in *AJ, administrator*, v. *Francis Hall*. Copy, CPQS Execution Docket, 1806–22, p. 113, TLWil.

[Sept]   Remonstrance of Robert Hays requesting compensation for property lost on treaty mission in 1789. AD draft in AJ's hand, DLC; Copy fragment, TNJ. *Jackson*, 1:86–87 (abstract, dated cApril 1796).

Oct 4   To Robert Sprigg. ALS, DLC. Discusses payment of account with Benjamin Foy for apprehension of runaway slave Jesse.

Oct 6   From Brice Martin (enclosure: certificate of election for officers, Sept 30). ALS, DLC. Discusses organization of his mounted infantry company.

Oct 8   From Thomas G. Bradford. ALS, DNA-RG 107. *National Intelligencer,*

April 9, 1828; Bassett, 1:235–36. Certifies that note published in *Democratic Clarion*, Sept 26, was written by Silas Dinsmoor.

Oct 8   Authorization to Eli Hammond to draw on the treasurer of West Tennessee for expenses in procuring arms in Kentucky. AD in AJ's hand, signed by Hammond, DLC.

Oct 15   To George Washington Campbell.   334

Oct 23   Account with James Porter for dry goods. ADS, DLC. Runs to October 4, 1813.

Nov 3   From Robert Sprigg. ALS, DLC. Discusses settlement of bill for runaway slave Jesse.

Nov 8   From William W. Cooke. ALS, DLC. Offers his service as an aide.

Nov 10   To Willie Blount (enclosure: militia returns, 2nd Division). LC, DLC. Submits muster rolls and inspection returns.

Nov 11   To Willie Blount.   336
Nov 11   From Willie Blount.   338

Nov 11   To the detached militia. Printed, *Democratic Clarion*, Nov 17; *Nashville Whig*, Nov 18. Orders units to be prepared for muster into service.

Nov 11   To William Hall (enclosures: Willie Blount to AJ and AJ to the detached militia and volunteer companies, Nov 11). ALS copy and LC, DLC. Orders Hall to muster his regiment in Nashville on November 21.

Nov 12   To Robert West Alston.   340
[Nov 14]   To the Tennessee Volunteers.   340

Nov 16   From Hugh Lawson White. ALS, DLC. Asks AJ to settle his account re lottery tickets for East Tennessee College.

Nov 16   Public notice requesting boats for upcoming campaign to New Orleans. Printed, *Democratic Clarion*, Nov 17; *Nashville Whig*, Nov 18.

Nov 18   Account with Arenton Sowell for blacksmithing. AD with receipt for payment in AJ's hand, DLC. Runs to July 16, 1813.

Nov 18   Bill to AJ from John H. Smith for Edward G. W. Butler's clothing and school supplies. AD, DLC. Runs to July 14, 1813.

Nov 21   To William Berkeley Lewis. DS, InU-Li. Orders Lewis to furnish fuel and quarters.

Nov 21   From George W. Gibbs. ALS, DLC. Tenders service of a company of volunteers.

Nov 21   Receipt for payment of courier. ADS, DLC.

Nov 22   From Anthony Butler. ALS, DLC. Explains why he was unable to attend the muster in Nashville on November 21; offers his services to AJ.

Nov 23   From Willie Blount. ALS, LC, and Copy, DLC; Copy, DNA-RG 107. Bassett, 1:243. Orders AJ to have his volunteers rendezvous on December 10 in Nashville.

[Nov 24]   To the Tennessee Volunteers.   342

Nov 25   To Cantrell & Read. ALS copy, DLC. Orders Cantrell & Read to furnish rations for troops by December 10.

Nov 27   To Willie Blount. ALS, William Dearborn. Asks Blount to order Assistant Deputy Quartermaster Lewis to procure additional camp equipment.

[Nov 29]   To George Washington Campbell.   343

[Nov]   To Robert Henderson. LC, DLC. Invites Henderson to serve as chaplain on expedition to New Orleans.

Dec 4   To Robert Hays. Photocopy, William C. Cook. Orders Hays to muster volunteers into service at Nashville on December 10.

Dec 8   Receipt from Obadiah Jackson, administrator of the Jesse Jackson estate, for blacksmithing. AD in AJ's hand, signed by Obadiah Jackson, DLC.

Dec 9   To William Carroll. ALS and Copy, DLC. Orders preparation of ground for rendezvous of troops in Nashville on December 10.

Dec 10   Military accounts for AJ's pay (runs to Feb 9, 1813); for pay and clothing of three servants (runs to April 13, 1813); for subsistence (runs to April 27, 1813). Printed forms with ms insertions, DNA-RG 94.

Dec 10   Provision return for two soldiers in 2nd Regiment, Tennessee Volunteers. ADS endorsed by AJ, InU-Li.

Dec 11   To Gideon Blackburn. ALS, Dorothy C. Elder. Asks Blackburn to serve as staff chaplain.

Dec 11   To John Reid. LS and LC, DLC. Bassett, 1:246. Appoints Reid second aide.

[Dec 11]   From John Reid. LC, DLC. Bassett, 1:246–47. Accepts appointment.

Dec 12   Order directing consolidation of incomplete companies into brigade in preparation for defense of the "lower country." LC, DLC.

Dec 12   Deed, 320 acres in Franklin County to John Overton for $1. Copies, THi, and Deed Book J(1815–26):11, TWFr.

Dec 13   To Willie Blount. ALS and LC, DLC. Discusses appointment and pay of staff officers.

Dec 13   To John Coffee. LC, DLC. Orders election of the lieutenant colonel in Coffee's cavalry regiment.

Dec 13   Order informing troops of the organization of the army. LC, DLC. Bassett, 1:247–50.

[Dec 13]   From Willie Blount. ALS and LC, DLC. Agrees with AJ on appointment and pay of staff officers.

Dec 14   To William Carroll. LC and Copy, DLC. Prescribes arming and equipping of troops.

Dec 14   Account with Raworth & Biddle for mounting sword. ADS, DLC. Bassett, 1:251. Runs to December 29.

Dec 15   To William Carroll. LC, DLC. Directs noncommissioned officers to serve as privates on guard duty and subalterns to act as noncommissioned officers for training purposes.

Dec 15   From Willie Blount. LC, DLC. States that he cannot issue letters of appointment for subaltern officers until complete returns are made.

Dec 17   To headquarters guard. LC, DLC. Orders arrangements for funeral of William Rickard.

Dec 17   From Willie Blount. ALS, LC, and Copies, DLC; LC, AHAB. *Nashville Whig*, Dec 23. Praises troops rendezvoused in Nashville for their willingness to defend the "lower country."

Dec 17   From George Poyzer. ALS, ICHi. Requests that John Allen be exempted from service.

Dec 18   To the Tennessee Volunteers. DS, LC, and Copy, DLC; LC, AHAB. Prescribes camp discipline.

Dec 18   Account with John Garner for repairing sword and jewelry. ADS, DLC.

Dec 19   To John Coffee. LC and Copies, DLC; LC, AHAB. Orders appraisal of horses in his cavalry regiment.

Dec 20   To Cantrell & Read. ALS draft and LC, DLC. Reports on complaints of quality and quantity of supplies.

Dec 20   To William Carroll. LS and LC, DLC. Orders articles of war read to troops.

Dec 20   To William Carroll. LS, LC, and Copy, DLC; LC, AHAB. Orders reply to Governor Blount read to troops.

Dec 21   To Willie Blount. LC and Copies, DLC; LC, AHAB. *Nashville Whig*, Dec 23; Bassett, 1:250–51. Acknowledges Blount's address of December 17.

Dec 21   To Travis C. Nash and Henry M. Newlin. LC, DLC. Orders transfer of their companies to 1st Regiment.

Dec 23   To Alpha Kingsley.   345

Dec 23   Deed, 658 acres in Bedford County to Rice Coffee for $2,000. Copy, Deed Book E(1814–15):494, TSBe.

Dec 24   To 1st and 2nd Regiments. ADS draft and LC, DLC. Announces appointment of Andrew Hynes as aide to replace Thomas Hart Benton.

Dec 24   To Alpha Kingsley. ALS and LC, DLC. Offers Kingsley two clerks to speed payment of troops.

Dec 24   From Willie Blount. ALS, DLC. States that he will attend the parade on December 25 if time permits.

Dec 24   From Alpha Kingsley. ALS and LC, DLC. Accepts AJ's offer of two clerks.

Dec 27   To the Troops. LS draft with revisions in AJ's hand, DLC. Discusses payment of troops.

Dec 27   From Willie Blount. ALS, DLC. Discusses letters of appointment for officers and arrangements for provisioning troops.

Dec 27   From Willie Blount. ALS, DLC. Discusses legal requirements for terms of service of volunteers.

[cDec 27]   Memorandum re commander of the Tennessee Volunteers. Copy, DLC.

Dec 28   To Thomas Hart Benton and William Hall. AD in AJ's hand, signed by Andrew Hynes, and LC, DLC. Orders payment of troops in their regiments.

Dec 30   To Thomas Hart Benton. AD in AJ's hand, signed by Andrew Hynes, and LC, DLC. Orders arrest of a deserter.

Dec 30   To William Hall. LC, DLC. Orders arrest of deserters.

Dec 30   From John Reid.   346
Dec 30   To John Reid.   347

Dec 30   Promissory note for $1,650 to James Jackson and John H. Smith. DS, DLC.

Dec 30   Receipt from Alpha Kingsley for a deserter from the U.S. Army who had enlisted in AJ's army. ADS, ICHi.

Dec 31   To Cantrell & Read. LC, DLC. Asks when provisions for troops will be loaded onto keelboats.

Dec 31   To the Tennessee Volunteers.   348
Dec 31   From Willie Blount.   349

Dec 31   From Willie Blount. ALS and LC, DLC. Transmits letters of appointment for staff and company officers (not found).

Dec 31 From Willie Blount. ALS and LC, DLC. States that appointment of aides will be made without distinction between first and second.

Dec 31 From Cantrell & Read. LC, DLC. Report that they will start issuing rations on January 1.

Dec 31 Order convening court martial proceedings. LC, DLC.

[Dec 31] From William Berkeley Lewis. LC, DLC. Discusses equipment and supplies.

[Dec 31] From John Reid. AL copy fragment, DLC. Apologizes for the tone of his letter of December 30.

Dec Memorandum of accounts. AD, DLC. Runs to October 1814.

[Dec] From Nathaniel Carroll. ALS fragment, ICHi. Discusses appointments on AJ's staff.

1813

Jan 1 To John Coffee. LC and Copy, DLC. Directs him to capture deserters.

Jan 1 To Travis C. Nash. LC, DLC. Orders temporary release of Samuel McLaughlin from the hospital.

Jan 1 From Willie Blount. ALS, DLC. Expresses doubt that he has authority to appoint a judge advocate.

Jan 1 From William Carroll. ALS fragment, ICHi. Asks to borrow AJ's epaulets.

Jan 1 Receipt to William Berkeley Lewis for $54.80 for payment of express riders. ADS copy, TU.

[Jan 1] To John Coffee. ALS, DLC. Discusses potential shortage of forage if some of Coffee's cavalry are not converted to infantry.

Jan 2 To Thomas Hart Benton. LC, DLC. Orders capture of deserters.

Jan 2 From Willie Blount. ALS and LC, DLC. Discusses assignment of musicians and the transfer of volunteers to regular service.

Jan 2 Order approving sentence of court martial of Samuel Goode. LC, DLC.

Jan 3 To Willie Blount. ALS and LC, DLC. Discusses assignment of musicians and transfer of volunteers to regular service.

Jan 3 From Willie Blount. ALS and LC, DLC. Urges the importance of reporting sources and valuations of military supplies and equipment.

Jan 4 To Thomas Hart Benton. LC, DLC. Orders convening of court martial to try Andrew Dorton.

Jan 4 To Willie Blount. AL draft, LC, and Copy, DLC; Copies, DNA-RG 107. Bassett, 1:254–55. States that as soon as troops are paid, he and his troops will start for New Orleans.

Jan 4 *To James Monroe.*   351

Jan 5 To [Robert Andrews] and contractor, Natchez (enclosed in AJ to David Holmes, Jan 5). LS copy, DLC; Copies, PHi, TxU. Asks Andrews to have the requisite supplies on hand when the troops reach Natchez.

Jan 5 *To William Charles Cole Claiborne.*   352

Jan 5 To David Holmes. Copy, PHi. Announces his forthcoming departure for New Orleans and asks Holmes also to forward copies of letters to the contractor and assistant deputy quartermaster in Natchez.

Jan 5 To Washington Jackson. LC, DLC. Asks Jackson to deliver copies of letters to contractor and assistant deputy quartermaster in Natchez.

Jan 5   To William Berkeley Lewis. LS, InHi; ALS draft, LNHiC; LC, DLC. Discusses arrangements for provisions and equipment.

Jan 5   To [Benjamin Morgan] (enclosed in AJ to W.C.C. Claiborne, Jan 5). LC, DLC. Orders supplies ready for troops when they arrive in New Orleans.

Jan 5   To Bartholomew Schaumburgh (enclosed in AJ to W.C.C. Claiborne, Jan 5). Copy, PHi. Asks him to have necessary supplies for the troops when they reach New Orleans.

Jan 5   From Clement Nash Read. ALS, DLC. States that John F. Read, surgeon's mate in 2nd Regiment, will soon report for duty.

Jan 5   From John Reid. AL copy, DLC. Resigns as aide because of poor health.

Jan 6   To James Henderson. AD draft and LC, DLC. Directs him to obtain supply of tents.

Jan 6   To William Smith. LC, DLC. Orders Hambleton Reaves's discharge for health reasons.

Jan 6   To the Volunteer Brigade, ADS draft and LC, DLC. Bassett, 1:255–56. Orders troops to prepare to embark on expedition.

Jan 6   From James Wilkinson.   353

Jan 7   To Edward Bradley. ADS draft, William C. Cook; LC, signed by Andrew Hynes, DLC. Orders delivery of supplies to Nashville.

Jan 7   To Edward Bradley and David Samuel Deaderick. LC, DLC. Appoints Bradley and Deaderick as president and judge advocate respectively of a court martial.

Jan 7   To Cantrell & Read. LC, DLC. Orders rations for cavalry.

Jan 7   To William Carroll. LC, DLC. Orders appointment of two officer replacements on court martial.

Jan 7   To John Coffee. ADS draft; ADS and LC, signed by Andrew Hynes, DLC. Orders Coffee to march his cavalry to Washington, Miss. Terr., to await AJ's arrival at Natchez.

Jan 7   To George W. Gibbs. ALS, THer; LC, DLC. Orders Gibbs to discharge an underage recruit.

Jan 7   To James Henderson. LC, DLC. Assigns Henderson to the cavalry detachment.

Jan 7   To Thomas Hart Benton. AD draft in AJ's hand, signed by Hynes, and LC, DLC; ADS by Hynes, ICHi. Orders dissolution of court martial.

Jan 8   To Rachel Jackson.   353

Jan 8   To John Reid. ALS, DLC. *Cincinnati Commercial Gazette*, Jan 13, 1883. Accepts Reid's resignation.

Jan 9   To Willie Blount. ALS, LC, and Copy, DLC. States that final preparations are made for the southern expedition.

Jan 9   To John Casey. LC, DLC. Orders his transfer from cavalry to infantry.

Jan 9   To William Berkeley Lewis. ADS, InHi; LC, DLC. Orders issuance of ammunition.

Jan 9   From Thomas Hart Benton.   355

Jan 9   From Willie Blount. ALS, DLC. Advises on dealing with troops.

Jan 9   Receipt to William Berkeley Lewis for arms and ammunition. DS with ANS, DLC.

Jan 9   Agreement between AJ, James Jackson, and Jenkin Whiteside re Allison lands. Copy, Middle Tennessee Supreme Court Records, T.

Feb 16   To the 2nd Division Infantry. LC, DLC. Orders decorum upon disembarking in Natchez.

Feb 19   To Alexander McKain. LC, DLC. Informs McKain that he is under arrest.

Feb 20   Order convening court martial of Alexander McKain. LC, DLC.

Feb 21   To Willie Blount. ALS copy, DLC. Bassett, 1:279–80. Reports that he has set up camp near Washington Cantonment.

Feb 21   From Daniel Rawlings. ALS, DLC. Discusses medical services available for AJ's troops.

Feb 22   From Donelson Caffery. ALS, DLC. Discusses business concerns.

Feb 22   From David Holmes. LC, DNA-RG 59; Copy, Ms-Ar. Discusses loaning tents to AJ's troops.

Feb 25   To Thomas Hart Benton. LC, DLC. Discusses court martial of Benjamin Hewitt.

Feb 25   To Edward Bradley. LC, DLC. Orders Bradley to inspect pork believed to be spoiled.

Feb 25   Receipt from Neil B. Rose for tents for cavalry regiment. ADS, DLC.

Feb 26   To the army contractor. LC, DLC. Accuses him of issuing bad meat and demands wholesome rations.

Feb 27   From Thomas Hart Benton. ADS, DLC. Reports arrest of James Terrill for neglect of duty.

Feb 28   From Rachel Jackson. ALS fragment, DLC. Bassett, 1:283 (extract). Discusses family concerns.

March 1   To John Armstrong. LS, DNA-RG 107; LC, DLC. Bassett, 1:283–85. Reports movement of army to Natchez.

March 1   To James Wilkinson. LC, DLC. Bassett, 1:285. Acknowledges Wilkinson's letter of February 22 and requests that his army be allowed to remain in Natchez.

March 1   Approval of sentence in court martial of Benjamin Hewitt. LC, DLC.

March 2   From William Berkeley Lewis. ALS, DLC. Expresses hope that AJ received the private letter addressed to New Orleans.

March 3   Promissory note for $1,365 to James Jackson by John H. Smith (for AJ). ADS, DLC.

March 4   To Robert Andrews. LC, DLC. Bassett, 1:288. Chastises him for failing to keep an appointment.

March 4   To [Robert Andrews]. LC, DLC. Discusses authority to draw supplies.

March 4   To John Coffee. LC, AHAB. Orders Coffee to detain John Lawrence and James Johnston until their courts martial.

March 15   To James Wilkinson. LC and Copy, DLC; Copy, PHi. Bassett, 1:294–95. Agrees to surrender public property before march to Tennessee.

March 15   From William Charles Cole Claiborne. Printed, Dunbar Rowland, ed., *Official Letter Books of W.C.C. Claiborne, 1801–1816,* 8 vols. (Jackson, Miss., 1917), 6:213–14. Expresses displeasure at dismissal of AJ's troops.

March 15   From James Robertson. ALS, DLC. Expresses hope that before their discharge AJ's troops will conduct a campaign to "Humble the Creeks."

[March 15]   To William Berkeley Lewis.   388

March 16   To David Holmes. LS, TNJ; LC and ALS copy, DLC. Thanks Holmes for his attention to the needs of AJ's troops.

March 16   From David Holmes. LC, DLC; LC, DNA-RG 59; AL draft, Ms-Ar. Acknowledges AJ's letter and commends his troops for their conduct.

March 16   From James Wilkinson with enclosure.   389

[March 16]   To the Tennessee Volunteers.   390

March 19   To John Brandt. LC, DLC. Inquires about provisions for troops on march to Tennessee.

March 19   From John Brandt. LC, DLC. Reports that he is assembling necessary provisions for the march.

March 20   To John Coffee. LC, DLC; LC, AHAB. Orders Coffee to mount a patrol of dragoons.

March 20   To John Coffee. LC and AD fragment, DLC; LC, AHAB. Orders Coffee to make arrangements for provisioning cavalry.

March 20   From James Wilkinson.   392

March 21   To John Anderson. ALS copy and LC, DLC. Discusses payment of troops.

March 21   To Andrew Hynes. ADS copy and LC, DLC. Orders Hynes to proceed to Nashville and make preparations for payment of the troops at their discharge.

March 21   To Rachel Jackson.   393

March 21   To Alpha Kingsley. ALS copy, THi; LC, DLC. Discusses the dismissal of his troops by the secretary of war and requests that Kingsley prepare to pay them.

March 21   To Alpha Kingsley. DS, MGrS; DS and LC, signed by Andrew Hynes, DLC. Asks Kingsley to prepare to pay troops.

March 21   To William Berkeley Lewis. LS, OClWHi. Discusses payment and provisioning of troops upon their arrival in Nashville.

March 22   To John Armstrong.   394

March 22   To John Brandt. LC, DLC. Discusses preparations for march to Tennessee.

March 22   To James Wilkinson.   396

March 22   From John Armstrong (enclosed in Armstrong to AJ, April 10). AL draft, PHi; LC fragment, DNA-RG 107; Copy, DLC. *Democratic Clarion,* April 27; Bassett, 1:300. Recognizes services performed by AJ's troops and promises to pay them on their return to Tennessee.

March 22   From White Turpin. Printed, Natchez *Ariel,* July 26, 1828. Summons AJ as garnishee in *Blennerhassett* v. *Burr,* to appear in Superior Court, Adams County, Miss. Terr., in April.

March 23   To Robert Andrews. LC, DLC. Bassett, 1:300–301. Orders him to provide supplies for the Volunteers' return to Tennessee.

March 23   To Robert Andrews. Printed extract, Kenneth W. Rendell, Catalog 100. Orders payment of $250 to Joseph Perkins for use of his land and wood.

March 23   From Robert Andrews. LC, DLC. Bassett, 1:301. States that he cannot provide requested supplies or transportation for AJ's cavalry after their move.

March 24   To Robert Andrews. ALS copy and LC, DLC. Bassett, 1:302–303. Urges settlement of accounts with cavalry.

March 24   From Robert Andrews. LC, DLC. States that he cannot comply with AJ's request to settle accounts with cavalry.

March 24   To Robert Andrews. ALS copy and LC, DLC. Bassett, 1:302. Again orders Andrews to settle accounts with cavalry and to provide forage for them.

March 24   To John Coffee. LC, DLC. Bassett, 1:301–302. Orders Coffee to procure provisions in Natchez.

March 24   To the regimental quartermasters. ADS copy, DLC. Orders return of tents to Robert Andrews.

March 25   To Robert Andrews (enclosed in Andrews to John Armstrong, Dec 14). DS, DNA-RG 107. Asks for settlement of $206.92 account.

March 26   From John Coffee. ALS, MB. Discusses march of the cavalry and difficulties in obtaining supplies.

March 28   To Samuel Goode. ADS, OkTG. Directs Goode to bring detachment of sick troops from Greenville, Miss. Terr., to Nashville.

March 28   From John Coffee. ALS, OMC. Reports gathering of supplies on return march of cavalry to Tennessee.

March 30   To John Armstrong. LS, DNA-RG 107; LC, DLC. Bassett, 1:303. Reports on march to Nashville.

March 30   Account with Ward & Taylor for foodstuff. ADS, DLC. Runs to May 5.

March 31   Promissory note for $1,000 to John Childress from John H. Smith (for AJ). ADS, DLC.

March   Decision (on appeal) in *AJ and John Hutchings* v. *Benjamin Rawlings.* Copy, CC Minutes, 1810–15, pp. 203–29 passim, TGSum.

April 3   To the Tennessee Volunteers. Copy, MeHi. Prescribes conduct during march to Tennessee.

April 4   From John Coffee. ALS, DLC. Discusses march of cavalry to Tennessee.

April 5   From John Coffee. ALS, DLC. Again reports on the progress of his regiment.

April 7   Order to pay John Braberton for use of horses and wagons. Copy, William Dearborn.

April 8   To John Armstrong. LS, DNA-RG 107. Bassett, 1:303. Reports on march to Tennessee and expresses willingness to command his men elsewhere if needed.

April 10   From John Armstrong (enclosure: Armstrong to AJ, March 22). LC, DNA-RG 107; LC, PHi; Copy, DLC. *Democratic Clarion*, April 27; Bassett, 1:305. Again explains reasons for discharge of AJ's troops.

April 11   From John Coffee. ALS, DLC. Discusses arrival of cavalry at Franklin and mustering out of troops.

April 14   To [David Holmes]. ALS, InU-Li. Discusses return of remaining tents loaned to the Volunteers.

April 15   From Andrew Hynes.   402

April 18   From ? AL fragment, DLC. Discusses settlement of account re a team of oxen.

April 19   From John Coffee. ALS, DLC. Discusses rendezvous of cavalry at Clover Bottom on April 24.

April 20   Discharge of "AB." Printed, *National Banner*, July 22, 1828.

April 21   To John Armstrong. Abstract, DNA-RG 107. Acknowledges letters of March 22 and April 10, which "will do away many disagreeable impressions."

April 22   From William Grainger Blount. Printed, *Democratic Clarion*, April 27; *Nashville Whig*, April 28. Presents AJ with stand of colors made by "female friends of East Tennessee."

April 22   To William Grainger Blount. Printed, *Democratic Clarion*, April 27; *Nashville Whig*, April 28. Accepts stand of colors.

April 23   Account with Cantrell & Read for general merchandise. AD, DLC. Runs to May 31.

April 24   To [John Armstrong].   403

April 24   To David Holmes. ALS copy, DLC. Bassett, 1:306–307. Discusses return to Tennessee and payment of discharged troops.

April 24   To the Tennessee Volunteers. Printed, *Democratic Clarion*, April 27; *Nashville Whig*, April 28. Thanks them for their service and announces war department agreement to pay them.

April 25   From Alpha Kingsley. ALS, DLC. States that he will pay the volunteers as soon as funds are available.

April 26   Bill for tuition of Edward G. W. Butler. AD, DLC.

April 27   From Willie Blount. ALS, DLC. Discusses arrangements to supply and pay troops.

[April 27]   To William Berkeley Lewis. ADS, TNJ. Orders him to pay the military account of Charles Baker.

April 29   From William Carroll. ALS, DLC. Asks AJ's aid in securing appointment as adjutant general.

May 4   Affidavit of AJ concerning dismissal of "the noted gambler [Aizea] Hays" from Gibbs's company (enclosure: deposition of Thomas Hart Benton). Typed copy, DLC. *Democratic Clarion*, May 25.

May 6   To William Berkeley Lewis. ADS, William Dearborn. Orders Lewis to pay Thomas Hart Benton.

May 8   Decision (on appeal) in *John Campbell* v. *AJ and John Hutchings, executors of Thomas Hutchings*. Copy, CC Record Book B:349–53, TNDa.

May 10   To John Armstrong.   405

May 10   From Samuel Butler. ALS, DLC. Complains that Robert Andrews has not paid him.

May 11   From John Jouett. ALS, DLC. Discusses a proposed horserace.

May 19   To Samuel Carswell. ALS, PHC. Discusses cotton and tobacco consigned to Gray & Taylor from Coleman, Green & Jackson.

May 19   Promissory note for $754 to John H. Smith. DS, DLC.

May 22   Notice to present claims against the estate of William Terrell Lewis (AJ,
Thomas Crutcher, and Alfred Balch, executors). Printed, *Democratic
Clarion*, June 1.

May 23   From Anthony Butler. ALS, DLC. Discusses the Kentucky militia's
activities.

May 25   From Robert Andrews. AL fragment, DLC. Discusses problems in payment of accounts for wagoners.

May 26   Power of attorney from AJ, Thomas Crutcher, and Alfred Balch, executors of the estate of William Terrell Lewis, to William Berkeley Lewis.
Copy, Deed Book E(1816–31):166, TDRh.

June 2   Promissory note for $1,000 to John Childress. DS, DLC.

June 5   Deed, undivided half of 428 acres in Wilson County from Thomas
Bradley, sheriff. Copy, Deed Book E(1812–16):175, TLWil.

June 13   From John H. Smith. ALS, DLC. Sends fabric and discusses mail.

June 15   From Thomas Hart Benton.   406

June 15   From John Henderson. ALS, DLC. Encloses a protested draft (not
found) on Robert Andrews.

June 18, 22   From John Freeman Schermerhorn. ALS, DLC. Discusses deliberations of Congress and progress of the war in northern theatre.

June 21   From John Armstrong. LC, DNA-RG 107; LC, PHi; Copy, DLC. Discusses payment for transportation of AJ's army.

June 22   Receipt from John Waugh for payment for room and board of Edward
G. W. Butler. AD in AJ's hand, signed by Waugh, DLC.

June 23   Promissory note for $1,000 to John H. Smith. DS, DLC.

June 25   From George Washington Campbell. Typed copy, DLC. Reports on
army reorganization and on progress of war in northern theatre.

July 4   To Robert Andrews. ALS draft, DLC. Informs Andrews that Armstrong
has ordered payment of wagoners.

July 4   To [John Henderson] (enclosure: John Armstrong to Thomas Hart Benton, June 15). ALS copy, DLC. States that Armstrong has authorized payment of AJ's wagoners.

July 7   Check to bills payable for $1,365. DS, DLC.

July 8   To Samuel Carswell. Printed, *Nashville Republican*, Aug 8, 1828. States
that he was merely a security for purchase of cotton in 1811 by Coleman,
Green & Jackson.

July 9   From Thomas Hart Benton.   409

July 12   To Robert Andrews. ALS draft, DLC. Samuel Gordon Heiskell, *Andrew
Jackson and Early Tennessee History*, 2nd ed. (Nashville, 1921), 3:139.
Encloses copy of John Armstrong's letter to Andrews (not found) ordering
payment of accounts for transportation.

July 13   Memorandum re Thomas Hart Benton's Letter of July 9.   409

July 13   Check to Michael C. Dunn for $29.25. DS, DLC.

July 15   To Felix Grundy.   410

July 15   From William Preston Anderson. ALS, ICHi. Discusses problems surrounding the campaign in northern Ohio.

July 16   From Andrew Hynes.   411

July 19   *To Thomas Hart Benton.*   413
July 19   From George Washington Campbell. ALS, InU-Li. Discusses raising of a regiment of Tennessee Volunteers and prospect of AJ's leading a campaign against the Creeks.
July 20   To the Tennessee Volunteers. Printed, *Democratic Clarion* and *Nashville Whig*, July 27. Reports recent uprising of Creek Indians and urges preparation for service.
July 20   Receipt for tuition at grammar school of Cumberland College for Edward G. W. Butler. ADS, ICHi; Copy, DLC.
[July 20]   From Robert Andrews. ALS matched fragments, DLC and ICHi. Discusses supplies and settlement of accounts for Natchez campaign.
July 21   Check to bills payable for $755. DS, DLC.
July 21   Promissory note for $754 to James Jackson. DS, DLC.
July 21   Affidavit of William Quarles. ADS, ICHi. States that he has heard Benton praise Jackson for returning the Volunteers to Tennessee.
July 21   Deed relinquishing AJ's interest in a 5,000-acre tract (purchased from Allison's heirs) to John Overton for $1. Copy, Deed Book E(1814–15):95, TSBe.
July 22   Check to Elihu S. Hall for $25.29. DS, DLC.
July 25   *From Thomas Hart Benton.*   413
July 26   From Felix Grundy. ALS, DLC. Discusses deliberations of Congress.
July 26   Advertisement for sale of part of William Terrell Lewis's estate, AJ, Thomas Crutcher, and Alfred Balch, executors. Printed, *Democratic Clarion*, Aug 3.
July 28   From Robert Butler. ALS, DLC. Discusses military developments near Fort Meigs, Ohio.
July 30   From John McNairy. ALS, DLC. Asks AJ's opinion on court case involving John Gordon and William Preston Anderson.
July 31   *To Willie Blount.*   416
July 31   From Robert Butler. ALS, DLC. Describes British-Indian attack on Fort Meigs.
[July-Aug]   Affidavit of Lemuel Purnell Montgomery. ADS, ICHi. On Jackson's request, reports a conversation with a Mr. Williams re Thomas Hart Benton's statements about Jackson's role in the Jesse Benton-William Carroll duel.
Aug 4   *To [Thomas Hart Benton].*   418
Aug 4   Promissory note for $1,000 to John Childress. DS, DLC.
Aug 5   *Affidavit of Felix Robertson.*   422
Aug 6   Check to William Johnston for $20. ADS, DLC.
Aug 6   Check to Edward Ward for $150. ADS, DLC.
[Aug 8]   From William Carroll. ALS, DLC. Reports that he is ill in Franklin.
Aug 9   *To John M. Armstrong with Armstrong's Responses.*   423
Aug 10   Account of Edward G. W. Butler with John H. Smith. AD, DLC. Runs to September 7, 1814.
Aug 10   Checks to Jordan Bass for $100, John Waugh for $11, and J. Woods for $31. DS, DLC.
Aug 10   Receipts from Jordan Bass for payment of debt due from the Samuel Donelson estate. (AD in AJ's hand, signed by Bass, DLC); from John Waugh for payment of board for Edward G. W. Butler (AD in AJ's hand, signed by Waugh, DLC).

Aug 11   From Thomas H. Fletcher. AL copy, DLC. *Cincinnati Commercial*, Feb 9, 1880. Discusses John M. Armstrong's role in Jesse Benton-William Carroll duel.

Aug 13   From James Robertson. ALS, DLC. Requests muskets and six rangers to help maintain control at Chickasaw agency.

Aug 14   From Willie Blount. ALS, DLC. Bassett, 1:315–17. Orders AJ to prepare his militia division for possible invasion of the Creek Nation.

Aug 14   Account with James Condon for tailoring. DS, DLC. Bassett, 2:14. Runs to May 7, 1814.

Aug 15   From William B. Shields. ALS fragment, DLC. Discusses AJ's role in the Blennerhassett-Burr trial in Adams County, Miss. Terr.

Aug 18   From Robert Butler. ALS, DLC. Reports on fighting around Fort Meigs.

[Aug 20]   To the brigade commanders of the 2nd Division. Printed, *Nashville Whig*, Aug 24. Orders preparations for war with the Creeks.

Aug 23   From George Walker. ALS, DLC. Discusses military affairs and his family.

Aug 23   Affidavit concerning the Jesse Benton-William Carroll duel. DS by AJ and John M. Armstrong, DLC. *Cincinnati Commercial*, Jan 8, 1880.

Aug 24   Check to self for $10. DS, DLC.

Aug 25   Promissory note for $1,000 to John H. Smith. DS, DLC.

Aug 28   From [Andrew Hynes]. AL fragment, DLC. Discusses progress of the war.

Aug 28   From John V. McKinney. ALS, DLC. Offers service of a company of volunteers from Fayetteville.

Aug 28   From John Read. ALS, DNA-RG 107. Discusses movements and activities of Creek Indians.

Aug 29   From John Brahan. ALS, DNA-RG 107. Reports that a large body of Creek warriors is ready to attack and urges AJ to march troops south.

Aug   Decision in *AJ, Thomas Crutcher, and Alfred Balch, executors of William Terrell Lewis,* v. *John Maclin and John Newnan* (injunction). Copy, Middle Tennessee Supreme Court Records, Order Book B(1813–15):83–89, T.

Sept 1   From Andrew Hynes. ALS matched fragments, DLC and ICHi. States that he is leaving on a business trip to Pittsburgh.

Sept 2   From Ezekiel Polk. ALS, DLC. Reports on dissatisfaction among Maury County volunteers over their company commander.

Sept 4   Checks to Dulce May for $30 (DS, DLC); to self for $20 (DS, DLC).

Sept 4   Account with Kirkman & Erwin. AD, DLC. Runs to January 11, 1814.

Sept 5   Deposition of James W. Sittler concerning AJ-Thomas Hart Benton quarrel. ADS, DLC. Bassett, 1:317.

Sept 6   From William Carroll. ALS, ICHi. Discusses collection of material for publication (not found) relating to Benton controversy.

Sept 8   From James Long. ALS, DLC. Proposes raising a company of volunteers to patrol in Hickman County.

Sept 9   From Andrew Hynes. ALS, DLC. Reports that Kentucky Governor Isaac Shelby has organized a volunteer army.

Sept 10   From William McReynolds. ALS, DLC. Offers Warren County volunteers for service.

Sept 14   To the Tennessee Volunteers. Printed, *Nashville Whig*, Sept 14; *Frank-*

lin Advocate, Sept 15. Urges volunteers to rally at Fort St. Stephens in response to Fort Mims massacre.

Sept 14   Check to self for $30. DS, DLC.

Sept 16   From James Robertson.   427

Sept 17   From David Smith. ALS, DLC. Regrets AJ's clash with the Bentons and discusses raising a company of mounted infantry.

Sept 19   To John Coffee. LC, DLC. *Nashville Whig*, Sept 21; Bassett, 1:319–20. Orders Coffee to muster his cavalry brigade at Camp Good Exchange in preparation for campaign against Creeks.

Sept 22   From Hugh Lawson White. ALS fragment, DLC. Discusses jailing of a runaway slave of William Butler's and preparations in the Knoxville area for Creek campaign.

Sept 22   Promissory note for $754 to James Jackson. DS, DLC.

Sept 23   From William Martin. ALS, DLC. Discusses attitude in Smith County toward the Creek campaign and recommends services of a Revolutionary War veteran.

Sept 24   From Willie Blount. ALS, LC, and Copies, DLC; ALS copy, DNA-RG 107. *Nashville Whig*, Sept 28. Orders AJ to muster 2,000 volunteers into service at Fayetteville.

Sept 24   From Willie Blount. ALS copy, DNA-RG 107; LC, DLC. Bassett, 1: 320–21. Orders AJ to muster into service John Coffee's cavalry regiment.

Sept 24   To the Tennessee Volunteers.   428

Sept 25   To John Coffee. DS and LC, DLC. Bassett, 1:321. Orders Coffee to march detachments to Huntsville and to spread rumor that AJ's army will eventually march to Mobile.

Sept 25   To Vance Greer. LC, DLC. Orders provisioning of troops in Fayetteville.

Sept 25   To William Berkeley Lewis. LS, TNJ; LC, DLC. Orders Lewis to have ammunition and supplies ready for army at Fayetteville.

Sept 25   To William Berkeley Lewis. LC, DLC. Orders Lewis to employ John Cockerill to repair arms.

Sept 25   To John Reid. LC, DLC. Orders Reid to report to headquarters.

Sept 25   From Brice Martin. ALS and LC, DLC. Asks for clarification of rules for mustering volunteers.

Sept 25   To the Adams County Superior Court with enclosure.   429

Sept 26   To John Coffee (enclosure: AJ to Coffee, [Sept 26]). LS, ALS draft, ALS copy, and LC, DLC. Bassett, 1:323. Encloses Coffee's marching orders and asks for information on locations of Creek forces.

Sept 26   To David Holmes. LS, William Dearborn; ALS copy, DLC. Bassett, 1:322–23. Discusses response in Tennessee to the Creek attacks.

Sept 26   To Benjamin Taylor. Copy, DLC. Urges immediate attention to troop supplies.

Sept 26   To the Volunteer cavalry regiment. DS and LC, DLC. Orders maintenance of strict discipline in forthcoming campaign.

Sept 26   From Joseph Dickson Smith. ALS, DLC. Requests endorsement for an appointment as captain in U.S. Army.

Sept 26   Certificates for subsistence accounts and payment of salary as major general. Printed forms with ms insertions, DNA-RG 94. Run to May 25, 1814.

Sept 26   Military account for clothing allowance for six servants. ADS, DLC. Runs to May 25, 1814.

[Sept 26]   To John Coffee (enclosed in AJ to Coffee, Sept 26). LC, DLC. Bassett, 1:321. Orders Coffee to march his cavalry to Huntsville and then to Fort St. Stephens to await further orders.

Sept 27   To William Berkeley Lewis. LC, DLC. Orders Lewis to supply each cavalry company with two axes.

Sept 27   To William Berkeley Lewis. LC, DLC. Orders Lewis to provide a tent for Dr. James Loudon Armstrong.

Sept 27   To James Russell. LS, DLC. Requests Russell to report for assignment on a secret reconnaissance.

[Sept 27]   To John Coffee. ALS, DLC. Bassett, 1:323–24. Orders Coffee to send scouting patrols into Creek territory.

Sept 28   To John Coffee. ALS, DLC. Bassett, 1:324–25. Discusses Russell's spying mission and orders Coffee to proceed to Fort St. Stephens when Madison County frontier is deemed safe.

Sept 28   To John Coffee. Copy, DLC. Directs Coffee to order contractor at Huntsville to have supply of provisions for AJ's troops.

Sept 28   To David Samuel Deaderick. LC, DLC; Copy, ICHi. Orders Deaderick to organize artillery at Fort Hampton.

Sept 28   To John Strother. LS, CLCM. Orders Strother on a scouting mission to determine strength of Creek war party and of friendly Cherokees.

Sept 28   From Pleasant Moorman Miller. ALS matched fragments, DLC and ICHi. Reports on court judgments in Roane County.

Sept 29   To John Coffee.   431

Sept 30   From Return Jonathan Meigs. LC, DLC. Bassett, 1:325 (extract). Discusses arrangements for raising a unit of Cherokees to fight Creeks.

[Sept]   To George Cunningham. ADS, DLC. Appoints him interim secretary.

[cSept]   From John W. Overton. ALS fragment, ICHi. Offers to raise cavalry companies.

Oct 1   From Vance Greer. ALS, DLC. Discusses problems in supplying troops.

Oct 2   To John Reid. Printed extract, *Cincinnati Commercial Gazette*, Jan 13, 1883. Discusses arrangements for his departure for Fayetteville.

Oct 2   From John Cocke. LC, DLC. Bassett, 1:325–26. Discusses supply and troop movements.

Oct 3   From James Davis. ALS and LC, DLC. Resigns as paymaster of 2nd Regiment, Tennessee Volunteers.

Oct 3   From Peter Perkins. LC, DLC. Reports posting of Coffee's cavalry to secure the area near Huntsville.

Oct 3   From Tustunnugalocko (Big Warrior). Printed extract, *ABPC* (1938–39):314. Complains of want of provisions for his tribe.

Oct 4   From Willie Blount.   432

Oct 4   From John Coffee. ALS and LC, DLC. Bassett, 1:326 (extract). Reports on scouting activities into Creek country and on supplies.

Oct 4   From John Coffee. ALS and LC, DLC. Reports that large numbers of volunteers are gathering in Huntsville and discusses appointment of an adjutant.

Oct 4   From James Henderson. ALS, DLC. Asks for an infantry command.

Oct 4   Account with E. and G. Hewlett, saddlers. ADS, DLC. Bassett, 2:12 (extract). Runs to June 25, 1814.

Oct 4   Check to John the Barber for $35. DS, DLC.

Oct 4   Receipt from John Waugh for payment of board for Edward G. W. Butler. ADS, DLC.

Oct 4   Receipt to William Berkeley Lewis for $2,000 in contingent funds for campaign against Creeks. AD signature removed, DLC.

Oct 5   From David Holmes. ALS and LC, DLC; LC, DNA-RG 59. Bassett, 1:326–27 (extract). Thanks AJ for the response of his volunteers to the Creek threat and discusses arrangements for coordinating with Ferdinand Leigh Claiborne's army.

Oct 5   *From John Strother.*   433

Oct 6   From James W. Campbell. ALS and LC, DLC. Discusses recruitment difficulties.

Oct 6   From John Coffee. ALS and LC, DLC. Warns AJ of an impending Creek attack and asks for instructions.

Oct 6   From John Coffee. ALS, DLC. Discusses possible invasion of Creek towns on Coosa River.

Oct 6   From David Samuel Deaderick. ALS and LC, DLC. Reports on artillery battery at Fort Hampton.

Oct 6   From John H. Martin. ALS, DLC. Introduces Alexander Montgomery.

Oct 6   From Peter Perkins. ALS, ICHi; LC, DLC. Reports the disbanding of some volunteers.

Oct 6   From Charles Simpson. ALS and LC, DLC. Resigns commission as surgeon's mate.

Oct 6   From James White. LC, DLC. Bassett, 1:327–28. Reports his brigade's arrival at Hiwassee Garrison.

Oct 6   Promissory note for $1,000 to James Jackson. DS, DLC.

Oct 7   *To John Coffee.*   435

Oct 7   To the Tennessee Volunteers. ADS by Reid, T; AD copy by Reid, LC, and Copy, DLC; Copy, WHi. Parton, 1:426 (extract). Urges troops to seek revenge against Creeks while maintaining strict discipline.

Oct 7   From John Brahan. ALS and LC, DLC. Encloses letter to William B. Lewis (not found) discussing availability of specie to meet drafts on the government.

Oct 7   From Joshua B. Hopson. ALS, DLC. Resigns as surgeon's mate.

Oct 7   From Robert Searcy. ALS and LC, DLC. Encloses letter from Coffee (not found) and reports a deficiency in the number of volunteers.

Oct 8   To William Russell. ALS copy, DLC. Orders him to Franklin County to raise volunteers.

Oct 8   To the Tennessee Volunteers. AD draft and LC, DLC; Copies, DLC, ICHi, WHi. Warns that terms of service have not expired and that those who leave the army under that pretense will be considered deserters.

Oct 8   From Henry Crabb. ALS, DLC. Discusses raising volunteers in Franklin County.

Oct 9   To John Coffee. ALS, DLC. Bassett, 1:329. Discusses provisions and scouting patrols into Creek territory.

Oct 9   To John Coffee. LC, DLC. Orders cavalry patrol into Creek territory.

Oct 9   To James Russell. LC, DLC. Orders him to determine strength of Indian forces.

Oct 9   From William McClellan. LC, DLC. Discusses arrangements for obtaining arms and organizing a battery of artillery at Fort Hampton.

Oct 9   From John Strother. ALS and LC, DLC. Bassett, 1:329–30 (extract). Discusses organizing Cherokee warriors to fight Creeks and describes topography of Creek territory.

Oct 9   Receipt from James Russell for payment of services as scout on a cavalry patrol. ADS, DLC.

Oct 10   To [James] Bradley and William A. Alexander. LC, DLC. Orders appraisal of wagons and teams.

Oct 10   To John Cocke. AL draft and LC, DLC. Bassett, 1:331–32. Informs Cocke of military movements and urges him to rendezvous at Turkey Town.

Oct 10   To David Brydie Mitchell (enclosure: Willie Blount to AJ and John Cocke, Oct 4). LS, G-Ar; AL draft, DLC; Copy, DNA-RG 107. *National Intelligencer*, Nov 24; Bassett, 1:331 (extract, addressed to Peter Early). Discusses movement into Creek territory.

Oct 10   From Robert Butler. ALS, DLC. Discusses the Battle of the Thames.

Oct 10   From David Samuel Deaderick. ALS, DLC. Discusses transfer of small arms and artillery from Fort Hampton to Huntsville.

Oct 10   Receipts from Joshua Jones and George Cunningham for payment as express riders. DS, DLC.

Oct 11   To Robert Allen. Typed copy, DLC. Orders Allen to report to John Coffee.

Oct 11   To Rachel Jackson.   436

[Oct 11]   To Willie Blount. ALS copy, DLC. Discusses lack of weapons and proposed movements against Creeks.

Oct 12   From William Grainger Blount. ALS and LC, DLC. Reports Governor Blount's illness and the capture of British fleet on Lake Ontario.

Oct 13   To Rachel Jackson.   437

Oct 13   To Read, Mitchell & Company. LC, DLC. Inquires about supplies.

Oct 13   From William McClellan. ALS, DLC. Reports that he cannot transfer a drummer to AJ and discusses movements of the Creeks.

Oct 13   From James White. LC, DLC. Reports that about 1,300 men have gathered at Hiwassee Garrison and discusses route he proposes to take to join AJ.

[Oct 13]   To Willie Blount. AL draft, DLC. Bassett, 1:332–33. Announces his arrival at Camp Coffee and discusses supply and arms problems.

Oct 14   To Willie Blount. Copy, DLC. Reports the detachment of Coffee's cavalry for protection of Fort Hampton.

Oct 14   From George W. Gibbs. ALS and LC, DLC. Resigns as a company commander to serve in the state legislature.

Oct 14   From William McClellan. ALS, ICHi; LC, DLC. Reports that the five men AJ sent to Fort Hampton have joined the regular army.

Oct 15   From Willie Blount. ALS and LC, DLC. Acknowledges AJ's letter of October 11 and promises aid.

Oct 15–17   Orders convening and approving courts martial proceedings against

Allen Moore (LC, THi. *AHM*, 6[1901]:251, 253); Anthony Metcalf (LC, THi; LC, DLC. *AHM*, 6[1901]:254–56).

Oct 16   From Isaac Roberts. ALS, PHi. Reports arrest of Anthony Metcalf.

Oct 17   To David Holmes. ALS, Ms-Ar. Bassett, 6:428–29. Reports that he plans to move into Creek territory and asks about reinforcements.

Oct 18   To Rachel Jackson.   437

Oct 18   To William McClellan. ALS copy, DLC. Objects to McClellan's enlisting volunteers into regular service.

Oct 18   From Willie Blount. ALS, DLC. Bassett, 1:332–33 (extract). Discusses activities of the British, Spanish, and Creeks near Pensacola, reinforcements for AJ, and military activities along Canadian border.

Oct 18   From Read, Mitchell & Company. ALS and LC, DLC. Bassett, 1:333–34. Discusses problems of supplying flour.

Oct 18   From James Roulston. ALS, DLC. Bassett, 1:333. Reports on unrest within his company.

Oct 19   To Isaac Brownlow. Copy, DLC. Discusses transportation arrangements for beef, meal, and supplies.

Oct 19   To Chief Chennabee. Copy, DLC. Bassett, 1:334. Urges Chennabee to hold out if attacked and promises to protect him.

Oct 19   From David Brydie Mitchell. LC and AL fragment, DLC. *National Intelligencer*, Nov 24. Reports on movements of Gen. John Floyd's Georgia militia and expresses hope that Floyd will communicate with AJ.

Oct 19   From Peter Perkins. LC, DLC. Reports his arrival at Camp Coffee and requests further orders.

Oct 20   To Willie Blount. Copy, DLC; extract, DNA-RG 107. Reports on his movements and discusses supply problems.

Oct 20   To William Berkeley Lewis. ALS, DLC. Complains of contractors' failure to furnish supplies.

Oct 20   To Peter Perkins. Copy, DLC. Discusses supply problems.

Oct 20   From Isaac Brownlow. ALS, DLC. Discusses transporting of foodstuff from Ditto's Landing.

Oct 20   From Thomas Casey. ALS, DLC. Advises AJ to build a supply fort in Creek territory and comments on use of friendly Cherokees in upcoming campaign.

Oct 21   From Willie Blount. ALS and LC, DLC. Expresses hope that AJ's troops are all armed and discusses reports of naval action.

Oct 22   From John Coffee.   438

Oct 22   From Pathkiller.   439

Oct 23   To John Cocke and James White. LC, DLC; Photocopy, OkTG. Reports his movements and complains about delay of supplies from East Tennessee.

Oct 23   To Pathkiller.   440

Oct 23   To Leroy Pope et al. (enclosed in Pope to John Armstrong, March 7, 1814). LC, DLC; Copy, DNA-RG 107. Bassett, 1:335–36. Asks assistance in relieving the shortage of provisions.

Oct 23   From Pathkiller. ALS and LC, DLC. Discusses scouting reports from Creek territory.

Oct 23   To Pathkiller and Charles Hicks. LC, DLC; Copy, MiU-Hi. Urges them to continue furnishing information; asks their help in securing supplies.

Oct 24 To Willie Blount. LC, DLC. Bassett, 1:336–37. States that he will march against Creeks despite supply problems.

Oct 24 To Thomas Flournoy.   441

Oct 24 To William Berkeley Lewis. ALS, DLC. Bassett, 1:336. Reports arrival at Fort Deposit; discusses shortage of supplies.

Oct 24 To John McKee. LC, DLC. Reports Coffee's raid on Creek villages and problems of supplies.

Oct 24 To Neil B. Rose. LC, DLC. Orders acquisition and transporting of supplies.

Oct 24 To the Tennessee Volunteers. LC and Copy, DLC; Copy, WHi. Bassett, 1:337–38. Urges troops to avenge wrongs committed by Creeks, to remain vigilant, and to maintain strict discipline.

Oct 24 Order approving sentences in courts martial of John L. Bartlett, James Bates, John Bradley, and William Clifton. LC, THi.

Oct 25 From Neil B. Rose. ALS and LC, DLC. Discusses supply and transportation problems.

Oct 26 From Robert Hays. ALS, DLC. Reports his arrival with a company of infantry at Ditto's Landing.

Oct 27 From James Lyon. ALS, DLC. Offers to transport artillery from Mobile for an attack on Pensacola.

Oct 27 From Peter Perkins. LC, DLC. Reports on orders from Gov. David Holmes and on an ambush at Colbert's Landing.

Oct 27 From Neil B. Rose. ALS and LC, DLC. Reports delivery of meal at Ditto's Landing.

Oct 27 Promissory note for $1,000 to James Jackson. DS, DLC.

Oct 27 Order convening courts martial of William Parker and James Sanders. LC, THi.

[Oct 27] Report of Alsander J. Acklen at Fort Deposit. AD fragment, DLC.

Oct 28 To Willie Blount.   442

Oct 28 To Isaac Brownlow. LC, DLC. William Cobbett, *Life of Andrew Jackson, President of the United States of America*, Reprint ed. (New York, 1837), pp. 49–50 (extract). Informs him that supply contract will be turned over to Leroy Pope and John Brahan.

Oct 28 To Leroy Pope. LC, DLC; Copy, DNA-RG 107. Asks Pope to accept contract for supplying AJ's army.

Oct 29 To George Branden. LC, DLC; Copy, THer. Orders Branden to deliver Indian prisoners to Leroy Pope.

Oct 29 To William Berkeley Lewis. Printed extract, Parke Bernet Catalog, May 22, 1956, p. 39. Complains that Read & Co. have failed to furnish his division with rations.

Oct 29 To Peter Perkins. LC, DLC. Reports sending twenty-nine Indian prisoners to Huntsville.

Oct 29 To Leroy Pope. LC, DLC. States that he is sending Indian prisoners.

Oct 29 From John Coffee. ADS, DLC. Reports organization of a mounted infantry regiment.

Oct 29 From Pathkiller. ALS, DLC. Asks AJ for weapons and relays reports from spies.

Oct 29 Order approving sentence in courts martial of Samuel Alexander, Pleasant Hawkins, and Samuel Prime. LC, DLC.

Oct 30   To John Coffee. DS and ADS copy, DLC. Appoints Coffee commander of newly formed cavalry brigade and promotes him to rank of brigadier general.

Oct 30   From James Allison. ALS, DLC. Discusses an account for the care of a sick officer.

Oct 30   From Pathkiller. ALS, DLC. States that he expects arrival of James White's brigade and relays spy reports.

Oct 30   From George West, Robert Branch, and Alsander J. Acklen. ALS, DLC. Complain that their commanding officer is not placing sufficient guard around their camp.

Oct 30   Order pardoning William Parker and James Saunderson, soldiers court martialed for sleeping while on guard. LC, DLC.

Oct 31   To John Cocke and James White. LC, DLC; ALS copy, OkTG. Complains of delay in arrival of White's brigade and supplies from East Tennessee.

Oct 31   From James Lyon. ALS, DLC. Repeats offer to transport artillery to the Alabama River.

[Oct 31]   To Rachel Jackson. Printed extract, Rosenbach Company, *History of America in Documents*, Pt. 2 (New York and Philadelphia, 1950), p. 80. Discusses attack on Littafuchee.

[Oct 31]   To Leroy Pope.   443

[Oct]   To John Ross. Printed extract, *The Collector*, 32(1919):36. Mentions impending campaign against Creeks.

[Oct]   From [Peter Perkins]. AL fragment, DLC. Discusses troop movements.

[Oct-Dec]   From ? AL fragment, DLC. Discusses military organization.

Nov 1   To Willie Blount. LC, DLC. Bassett, 1:339−40. Discusses efforts to obtain supplies and the capture of four Creeks.

Nov 1   To Leroy Pope. LC, DLC. Bassett, 1:340 (extract). Informs Pope he is sending Creek Chief Cotalla and other captured Indians.

Nov 1   From James White. LC, DLC; Photocopy, OkTG. Promises to join AJ as soon as supplies allow.

Nov 2   To John Coffee. ADS draft, CSmH; AD signed by John Reid, DLC. Bassett, 1:340. Orders Coffee to destroy Creek village of Tallushatchee.

Nov 2   To Pathkiller. Copy, DLC. States that he has no extra weapons to distribute and expresses hope that Pathkiller can supply 400 warriors.

Nov 2   From Robert Hays. ALS, DLC. Discusses family affairs at the Hermitage and in Nashville.

Nov 2   From William Martin. ALS, DLC. Offers services for detached duty.

Nov 2   From Gideon Morgan. LC and AL fragment, DLC. Reports on location of Creek war parties and on organizing Cherokees to fight with AJ's army.

Nov 2   From Leroy Pope. LC, DLC. Acknowledges arrival of Indian prisoners and discusses supplies.

[Nov 2]   From John Coffee. ALS, DLC. Bassett, 1:340−41. Discusses difficulties in crossing Coosa River en route to Tallushatchee.

Nov 3   From Thomas Austin. ALS, DLC. Reports that Indians murdered seven settlers near Huntsville.

Nov 3   From Willie Blount to AJ and John Cocke (enclosure: James Monroe to Blount, Oct 19). ALS and Copy, DLC; ALS copy, DNA-RG 107. Discusses supplies and progress of the campaign against the Creeks.

Nov 7   To James White. LC, DLC; Photocopy, OkTG. Urges White to join him with supplies.

Nov 7   From James White.   446

Nov 7   Order appointing Howell Tatum commander at Fort Strother in AJ's absence. ADS, DLC. Bassett, 1:343.

Nov 8   From [Peter Perkins]. AL fragment, DLC. Discusses a massacre by Creeks and the use of Cherokees as allies.

Nov 8   From Ward & Taylor. ALS and LC, DLC. Discusses arrangements to supply AJ's army.

Nov 8   From [James Mitchell]. AL fragment, DLC. Discusses supplies.

Nov 9   From Willie Blount (enclosure: James Robertson to Blount, Nov 5). ALS, DLC. Congratulates AJ on Coffee's victory at Tallushatchee and discusses problems of supply and Indian affairs.

Nov 9   From Thomas Flournoy.   447

Nov 9   From Leroy Pope. LC, DLC. Discusses supplies.

Nov 10   From James Ditto. ALS, DLC. Offers to open a new ferry operation at Ditto's Landing.

Nov 11   To Willie Blount (enclosed in Blount to John Armstrong, Nov 22). LC, DLC; Extract, DNA-RG 107. *Democratic Clarion*, Nov 23 (extract). Reports victory at Talladega.

Nov 12   To Rachel Jackson.   448

Nov 12   To Leroy Pope. LC, DLC. Arthur St. Clair Colyar, *Life and Times of Andrew Jackson: Soldier-Statesman-President*, 2 vols. (Nashville, 1904), 1:131 (extract). Reports victory at Talladega and begs for more supplies.

Nov 12   From Willie Blount to AJ and John Cocke. ALS, DLC. Discusses legal complications of accepting additional volunteers and acknowledges receipt of Creek prisoners.

Nov 12   From Willie Blount. ALS, DLC. Reports that he has informed the war department of supply problem.

Nov 12   From Ferdinand Leigh Claiborne. ALS and LC, DLC; LC, Ms-Ar. Discusses movement of his army to Tombigbee River.

Nov 12   From William Berkeley Lewis.   450

Nov 12   From Andrew Patterson et al. ALS and LC, DLC. Request permission to return home for fresh horses and new equipment.

Nov 12   From Jesse Searcy. Typed copy, DLC. Congratulates AJ on recent victories.

[Nov 12]   To Willie Blount. Printed, *Nashville Whig*, Nov 24. Reports that he is sending a banner captured from Creeks.

[Nov 12]   From Newton Cannon et al. ALS and LC, DLC. *Nashville Whig*, Jan 11, 1814; Bassett, 1:374–75. Request that cavalry and mounted riflemen be allowed to return home for horses and winter clothing.

Nov 13, 15   From Robert Grierson.   451

Nov 13   From Isaiah Renshaw et al. ALS and LC, DLC. Urge discharge of their men if rations are not immediately available.

Nov 13   Order allowing certain wounded soldiers to return home. ADS, DNA-RG 94.

Nov 13   Order approving sentence of court martial of John Paine. LC, THi.

Nov 13   Robert Searcy, aide, to the Tennessee Volunteer Brigade platoon officers. LC, DLC. Bassett, 1:344–45. Promises officers that if supplies do not arrive in two days, the army will march back to Fort Deposit, taking with them the sick and wounded.

Nov 14 *To Willie Blount.* 453

Nov 14 To James Terrill. DS, A-Ar; LC, DLC. Orders procurement of hospital stores.

Nov 14 From John Cocke. LC, DLC. Bassett, 1:346. Reports that he has sent a detachment of cavalry to destroy Hillabee towns.

Nov 14 Order approving sentence of court martial of John Allcorn. LC, THi.

[Nov 14] To the Tennessee Volunteers. AD draft, DLC. Denies that he ordered troops to report for short terms of duty lightly clothed.

[Nov 14] From William Martin and Henry L. Douglass. ALS and LC, DLC. Bassett, 1:346–47. Discusses lack of provisions and warns that officers of the 1st Brigade will be unable to prevent a "forcible & tumultuous desertion of the Camp."

Nov 15 To William A. Alexander (enclosed in brigade order of Henry L. Douglass, Nov 15). Copies, DNA-RG 94 and WHi. Orders Alexander to issue a pork ration to his regiment.

Nov 15 To Willie Blount. LC, DLC. *Democratic Clarion* and *Nashville Whig*, Nov 30; Bassett, 1:348–50. Gives a detailed report of the Battle of Talladega.

Nov 15 To Willie Blount, LC, DLC. *Democratic Clarion*, Nov 30 (extract); Bassett, 1:350–51. Reports on James White's failure to join him and on the critical situation of his army.

Nov 15 To David Samuel Deaderick. LC, DLC. Orders Deaderick to guard supply wagons.

Nov 15 To the 1st Regiment, Tennessee Volunteers. LC, DLC; Copy, WHi. Orders regiment to escort supply wagons from Fort Deposit.

Nov 15 To William Hall. LC, DLC. Gives instructions for drawing rations from supply wagons.

Nov 15 To William Hall. LC, DLC. Orders delivery of provisions to troops.

Nov 15 From John Brahan (enclosure: Return Jonathan Meigs to Louis Winston and Brahan, Oct 30). ALS, DLC. Discusses Meigs's endorsement of Cherokee Chief Richard Brown and reports that he is forwarding supplies of meat.

Nov 15 From William Pillow et al. ALS and LC, DLC. Bassett, 1:347–48. Regret AJ's questioning of their devotion to duty and pledge to remain in service for a short time.

[Nov 15] From William Martin et al. Printed, *Nashville Whig*, Jan 11, 1814. Urge AJ to allow them to return home for rest and resupply.

Nov 16 *To John Cocke.* 454

Nov 16 To Leroy Pope. LC, DLC. John Stilwell Jenkins, *Life and Public Service of Gen. Andrew Jackson . . . ,* Reprint ed. (Philadelphia, 1880), p. 78. Urges Pope to provide supplies.

Nov 16 *From Thomas Pinckney.* 455

Nov 16 From Thomas Pinckney to AJ and John Floyd. LS and LS copy, DLC; LS copy, DNA-RG 107. Bassett, 1:352–53 (extract). Discusses detailed plans for mounting final coordinated campaign against the Creeks.

Nov 16   From Neil B. Rose. ALS, DLC. Bassett, 1:354. Promises to expedite supply shipments from Huntsville.

Nov 17   To John Cocke. LC, DLC. Reports that Hillabee Creeks are suing for peace and requests 600 men to reinforce his army.

Nov 17   To [Robert Grierson].   456

Nov 17   To William Hall. DS, THi. Places Hall in command at Fort Strother.

Nov 17   From Willie Blount. ALS and LC, DLC. Bassett, 1:350–51 (extract). Congratulates AJ for victories at Tallushatchee and Talladega, discusses arrangements for supplies, and comments on the failure of James White's brigade to join AJ's army.

Nov 17   From James Hardin. ALS, DLC. Congratulates AJ on victories and promises to recruit volunteers.

Nov 17   From William R. Hess. ALS, DLC. Discusses corn shipment from Huntsville.

Nov 17   From Theodorick B. Rice. ALS, DLC. Encloses a bill for express service.

Nov 17   From James Terrill. ALS, DLC. Discusses shipment of hospital stores from Huntsville.

Nov 18   To John Cocke.   457

Nov 18   From [Peter Perkins]. AL fragment, DLC. Discusses efforts with Huntsville contractors.

Nov 19   From Willie Blount. ALS, DLC. Acknowledges receipt of enemy battle flags.

Nov 19   From Willie Blount (enclosure: resolution of the Tennessee General Assembly, Nov 19). ALS, DLC. Congratulates AJ and his men on their victories.

Nov 20   To John Armstrong. LS, DNA-RG 107; Copy, DLC. Bassett, 1:355–57. Reports victories over Creeks and discusses supply problems.

Nov 20   To Willie Blount (enclosed in Blount to John Armstrong, Nov 24). Copy, DNA-RG 107. Reports on the Hillabee Creeks' disposition for peace and discusses troop morale.

Nov 20   To Leroy Pope and John Brahan. LC, DLC. Directs forwarding of supplies to Fort Strother.

Nov 20   From Gideon Blackburn. ALS and LC, DLC. Bassett, 1:357 (extract). Offers to recruit troops.

Nov 20   From Willie Blount (enclosures: Daniel Parker to Blount, Oct 30 and Nov 7). ALS and LC, DLC. Discusses the importance of a coordinated campaign against the Creeks.

Nov 20   From William Carroll.   458

Nov 20   From John Cocke. LC, DLC. Promises to forward 600 men to Fort Strother when supplies arrive.

Nov 20   Decision in *AJ, Thomas Crutcher, and Alfred Balch, executors of William T. Lewis,* v. *David Woods* (debt). Typed copy, Giles County Court Minute Book, p. 16, T.

Nov 21   To Willie Blount. Printed extract, *Democratic Clarion*, Nov 30. Discusses supply problems.

Nov 21   To the Brigade of Volunteer Cavalry and Mounted Riflemen. LC and Copy, DLC. *Nashville Whig*, Jan 11, 1814. Orders brigade to refit themselves and rejoin the army on December 8.

Nov 29   From Thomas Pinckney.   462
Nov 29   Order directing arrest and detention of deserters. ADS draft, DLC.
Democratic Clarion and *Nashville Whig*, Dec 7.
[Nov-Dec]   Memorandum of officers available for duty in William Martin's 1st
Regiment. AD, endorsed by AJ, DLC.
Dec 2   To John Cocke. LC, DLC. Bassett, 1:364 (extract). Expresses pleasure
that Cocke's army will join him on December 12.
Dec 2   To the Tennessee Volunteers. ADS and LC, DLC. Congratulates them for
their recent victories.
Dec 2   From David Love. ALS, DLC. Claims the rank and command of first ma-
jor in 2nd Regiment, Tennessee Volunteers.
Dec 2   From Thomas Pinckney. ALS, DLC; LC, ScHi. Bassett, 1:364–65. Dis-
cusses the use of signals for Cherokee runners and problems of supply.
Dec 2   From James Ridley. ALS, ICHi. Requests a furlough or discharge.
Dec 2   Orders convening and dissolving court martial of Gregory Empsey. LC,
THi.
Dec 2   Order convening courts martial of William Caruthers, John Cunning-
ham, Isaac Lamb, John Spinks, and Thomas Stanford. LC, THi.
[Dec 2]   Order approving sentences in courts martial of Jesse Barnes, John Camp-
bell, Thomas Loyd, Britain Hicks, James Smith, Henry Ellison, and James
Marlow. LC, THi.
Dec 3   To Gideon Blackburn.   464
Dec 3   From Edward Bradley. ALS and LC, DLC. Requests a court martial to
clear his record.
Dec 3   To Edward Bradley. LC, DLC. Promises to meet Bradley's request as soon
as arrangements can be made.
Dec 3   To William Carroll. LC, DLC. Orders Carroll to return to Tennessee to
recruit.
Dec 3   To Abram Poindexter Maury. LS, NjP. Bassett, 6:429. Asks Maury to
recruit new volunteers.
Dec 3   To Thomas Pinckney.   465
Dec 3   From John Cocke. LC, DLC. Bassett, 1:368. States that he is unable to
join AJ owing to lack of supplies.
Dec 4   From Edward Bradley. ALS, ALS copy, and LC, DLC; Copy, NN. Apolo-
gizes for tone of note of November 15 (not found).
Dec 4   From William Martin.   467
Dec 5   To Edward Bradley. LC, DLC. Releases Bradley from arrest.
Dec 5   To John Coffee. ALS, DLC. Bassett, 1:373. Orders Coffee to join him by
December 13.
Dec 5   From Samuel Owen. LC, DLC. Resigns as assistant surgeon of 2nd
Regiment.
Dec 5   To Samuel Owen. LC, DLC. Accepts resignation.
Dec 5   To Charles Perkins. LC, DLC. Appoints Perkins surgeon's mate in 2nd
Regiment.
Dec 5   From Ferdinand Leigh Claiborne. ALS, DLC. Bassett, 1:373–74, 425.
Reports on British naval activities off the Gulf coast.
Dec 5   From John Cocke. LC, DLC. Asks, in view of supply shortage, how many
men he should send to rendezvous.
Dec 5   From [Leroy Pope]. AL fragment, DLC. Discusses supplies.

Dec 6   Order approving sentences in courts martial of Micajah Hail, Burwell Anderson, John Reeves, William Ferrel, and Thomas Johnson. LC, THi.

Dec 7   From Willie Blount. ALS and LC, DLC. States that he has no authority to discharge the militia.

Dec 7   Order convening courts martial and approving sentences of Allan Howard, Joseph McCraw, and James Edmundson. LC, THi.

Dec 8   From David Humphreys. ALS and LC, DLC. Requests court martial of Joseph Anthony.

Dec 8   To David Humphreys. LC, DLC. Requests explanation of Humphreys's complaint against Anthony.

Dec 8   From David Humphreys. LC, DLC. Discusses charges against Anthony.

Dec 8   To David Humphreys. LC, DLC. Rejects Humphreys's court martial request.

Dec 8   From Brice Martin et al. LC, DLC. Advance reasons why the regiment should be discharged.

Dec 8   To Brice Martin et al. ALS and LC, DLC. Bassett, 1:376–77. Rejects their request to be discharged.

Dec 8   To William Martin. LC, DLC. Asks Martin to inform his regiment of AJ's views on their discharge.

Dec [8] From William Martin. ALS, THi; LC, DLC. *National Banner*, July 22, 1828. Asks for a copy of a pledge of service that AJ claims Martin's regiment made.

Dec 8   To William Martin. LC, DLC. *National Banner*, July 22, 1828; Bassett, 1:375. Replies to Martin's query that he has no written pledge of the volunteers' future service; refuses their request for honorable discharge.

Dec 8   To Thomas Pinckney. LC, DLC. States that he will rendezvous with John Cocke's division on December 12 and resume the campaign when sufficient supplies arrive.

Dec 8   To Leroy Pope & John Brahan. ALS copy, DLC. Bassett, 1:377–78. Reports urgent need of supplies.

Dec 8   To John Strother and [George] West. LC, DLC. Orders valuation of horses in John Gordon's company of spies.

[Dec 8] To James W. Sittler. ALS, Ia-HA; LC, DLC. Asks if he has made any changes in staff positions.

Dec 8   From Andrew Hynes. ALS, DLC. Offers to serve as AJ's private secretary.

Dec 8   From James W. Sittler. LC, DLC. Replies that he has made no staff changes.

Dec 8   Promissory note for $1,000 to James Jackson. DS, DLC.

Dec 9   To the army contractors. LC, DLC. Forbids issuance of provisions to troops without specific orders.

Dec 9   To John Coffee. ALS, DLC. Bassett, 1:378–79. Warns Coffee of threatened mutiny and orders him to arrest any deserters he intercepts.

Dec 9   To the 1st Brigade, Tennessee Volunteers. LC, DLC; Copy, WHi. William Cobbett, *Life of Andrew Jackson, President of the United States of America*, Reprint ed. (New York, 1837), p. 82. Forbids mutiny and orders parade of 1st Brigade.

Dec 13 To the 1st Brigade, Tennessee Volunteers. DS, THi; LC, DLC; Copy, WHi. Bassett, 1:392–93. Orders troops to march to Nashville for the governor's decision on discharge.

Dec 13 To William Hall. LS, MiD. Discusses arrangements for collecting arms from men being released.

Dec 13 To Stockley Donelson Hays. LC, DLC. Orders Hays to oversee issuance of rations.

Dec 13 From John Cocke. LC, DLC; Copy, DNA-RG 107. Reports troop strength and expiration date of enlistments.

Dec 13 To Thomas Pinckney.   484

Dec 13 To Bayliss E. Prince. LC, DLC; Copy, WHi. Transfers Prince and his company from a volunteer regiment to the militia.

Dec 14 To John Cocke. LC, DLC. Orders Cocke to hold Cherokee volunteers in readiness for further orders.

Dec 14 To Rachel Jackson.   486

Dec 14 To William Berkeley Lewis. LS, THi; LC, DLC. Orders Lewis to pay volunteers for equipment turned over to government.

Dec 14 To William Reynolds. LC, DLC. Orders him to give William Hall a receipt for arms and equipment.

Dec 14 From Gilbert D. Taylor. ALS, DLC. Discusses sickness among officers and a dispute over command at Fort Strother.

Dec 15 To Alsander J. Acklen. LC, DLC. Orders Acklen to report to Fort Strother.

Dec 15 To Willie Blount.   487

Dec 15 To Dr. Bostick. LC, DLC. Orders him to take charge of Fort Deposit hospital.

Dec 15 To John Cocke.   490

Dec 15 To the East Tennessee Volunteers. Copy, DLC. Bassett, 6:429–30. Urges them to continue campaign against Creeks.

Dec 15 To Leroy Pope and John Brahan. LC, DLC. Orders them to deposit rations at Fort Strother and Lashley's Fort.

Dec 15 From Willie Blount. ALS and LC, DLC. Bassett, 1:393. Contends that AJ should discharge volunteers and states that he is not certain of discharge date for militia.

Dec 15 From William Carroll. ALS, DLC. Discusses recruiting efforts in Nashville.

Dec 15 From Bird Smith. ALS, DLC. Reports that he is sending deserters and new draftees from McMinnville.

Dec 16 To John Armstrong.   492

Dec 16 To John Coffee. LS, DLC. Summarizes communications from John Cocke, Thomas Pinckney, and others.

Dec 16 To Joseph Gordon, Joseph Johnston, and Moses L. Peck. LC, DLC. Grants furloughs.

Dec 16 From William Carroll. ALS, DLC. Reports on recruitment efforts in Nashville and recommends William Hall to command new unit.

Dec 16 From Robert B. Harney et al. LS and LC, DLC. Request furlough for the Tennessee artillery company.

Dec 16 From Peter Perkins. ALS fragment and LC, DLC. Bassett, 1:395 (extract). Discusses recruitment in Huntsville.

Dec 17   To Robert B. Harney et al. LC, DLC. Denies request for furlough.

Dec 17   To William Lillard. LC, DLC. Orders Lillard to return his boat guards to their posts.

Dec 17   To Thomas Williamson. LC, DLC. Orders Williamson to return to Nashville on recruiting duty.

Dec 17   From William Carroll. ALS, DLC. Encloses extracts of letters from John Bowyer, Ferdinand Leigh Claiborne, and John McKee.

Dec 17   From John Coffee. ALS and LC, DLC. Reports that he will march the cavalry from Huntsville; discusses activities of the Choctaws and Chickasaws.

Dec 17   From John Coffee. ALS, DLC. Reports that because of illness he will not accompany the cavalry.

Dec 17   From William Hamilton and George Argenbright. ALS, DLC. Bassett, 1:397. Offer services of volunteers from the East Tennessee division.

Dec 18   To Willie Blount. LC, DLC. Bassett, 1:342–43 (extract). Discusses difficulties created by the expiration of enlistments of Cocke's men.

Dec 18   To Ferdinand Leigh Claiborne. LC, DLC. Reports that the embarrassments of his campaign were due to lack of supplies and men.

Dec 18   To John Coffee. LS and LC, DLC. Bassett, 1:397–98. Orders Coffee to join the main army as soon as supplies permit.

Dec 18   To William Hamilton and George Argenbright. LC, DLC. Accepts their volunteers' tender of service.

Dec 18   To William Berkeley Lewis. ADS, TNJ. Orders payment to Peter Perkins.

Dec 18   To Gideon Morgan. LC, DLC. Orders him to bring forward his unit of Cherokees.

Dec 18   To Peter Perkins. LC, DLC. Orders Perkins to send sick soldiers home and deserters to jail.

Dec 18   To Leroy Pope and John Brahan. LC, DLC. Orders delivery of breadstuff.

Dec 18   To Louis Winston. LC, DLC. Orders Winston to bring his men on from Huntsville.

Dec 18   From John Coffee. ALS and LC, DLC. Bassett, 1:398 (extract). Warns that his men's terms of enlistment will soon end.

Dec 18   From John Floyd. ALS, DLC. Bassett, 1:398–400. Reports movements of the Georgia militia.

Dec 18   From Louis Winston. ALS, DLC. Promises to bring his men to Fort Strother.

Dec 19   To George Smith. LC, DLC. Discusses problems of the Creek campaign.

Dec 19   To John Knibb Wynne. ADS and LC, DLC. Orders Wynne to appoint an officer to supervise forwarding of supplies from Fort Deposit.

Dec 19   From Alsander J. Acklen. ALS and LC, DLC. Reports that illness precludes taking up assigned duty.

Dec 19   From John Allcorn. ALS and LC, DLC. Warns that terms of enlistment for his cavalry regiment will soon expire.

[Dec 19]   To James White's Brigade. DS, LC, and Copy, DLC. Urges reenlistment.

Dec 20   To John Allcorn. LC, DLC. States that he has no authority to release Allcorn's regiment.

Dec 20   To Joseph Anthony. LC, DLC. Directs Anthony to Fort Deposit.

Dec 20   To Joseph Anthony. LC, DLC. Orders Anthony to report strength of William Hall's brigade at Fort Deposit.

Dec 20   From John Coffee. ALS, DLC. Bassett, 1:401–402. Reports that William Carroll has enlisted 1,000 men for mounted infantry service.

Dec 21   To John Cocke. LC and ALS draft, DLC. Urges Cocke to have as many men and supplies in the field as possible.

Dec 21   To John Coffee. LC, DLC. Orders Coffee to read Willie Blount's letter of December 7 to his brigade.

Dec 21   To William Hall. LS, THi; LC, DLC. Bassett, 1:403–404. Orders Hall to return his brigade to headquarters in response to the governor's opinion that their terms have not expired.

Dec 21   To Stockley Donelson Hays. LC, DLC. Orders Hays to expedite supplies from Huntsville.

Dec 21   From Stockley Donelson Hays. ALS, DLC. Discusses supply problems.

Dec 21   From William Snodgrass. LC, DLC. Reports that supplies are at Fort Armstrong but manpower shortage makes delivery impossible.

Dec 22   To John Coffee.   496

Dec 22   To John Gordon, Robert Evans, and William Mitchell. LC, DLC. Orders their spy companies to Fort Strother.

Dec 22   To John Gregory. LC, DLC. Orders Gregory to expedite supply shipments from Fort Armstrong.

Dec 22   To James Mitchell. LC, DLC. Orders Mitchell to East Tennessee for supplies.

Dec 22   To James W. Sittler. LC, DLC; Copy, MH-H. Orders reading of Governor Blount's letter concerning terms of enlistment to militia brigade.

Dec 22   From Willie Blount. ALS, DLC; AL extract, THi; Copy, DNA-RG 107. Bassett, 1:405–406 (extract). States that he has no authority to discharge volunteers and discusses the appointment of an assistant deputy quartermaster.

Dec 22   From Willie Blount.   498

Dec 22   From John Coffee (enclosure: John Harpole et al. to Coffee, Dec 21). ALS, DLC. Bassett, 1:405. Reports impending discharge of John Allcorn's regiment.

[Dec 22]   From Robert Jetton. LC, DLC. Reports death of Wilson Kerr.

Dec 22   Order directing funeral for Wilson Kerr. LC, DLC.

Dec 23   To William Carroll. LC, DLC. Bassett, 1:407–408 (extract). Congratulates Carroll for raising volunteers and stresses necessity of obtaining supplies in Nashville.

Dec 23   To John Coffee. ALS and LC, DLC. Bassett, 1:406–407. Grants permission for John Allcorn's regiment to return to Nashville and emphasizes necessity of remounting campaign.

Dec 23   From William Carroll.   500

Dec 23   From John Coffee. ALS, DLC. Reports that John Allcorn's regiment, now at Ditto's Landing, will not likely return to duty.

Dec 23   From John Coffee. ALS, DLC. Requests a sutler's permit for Nelson Patteson.

Dec 23   From William Berkeley Lewis. ALS, DLC. Discusses questions raised by Thomas Pinckney on appointment of an assistant deputy quartermaster.

Dec 23   From William Berkeley Lewis. ALS, DLC. Discusses payment of an express rider.

Dec 23   From Nelson Patteson. ALS, ICHi. Requests sutler's permit.

Dec 23   From Thomas Pinckney. ALS and ALS copy, DLC; LC, ScHi; Copy, DNA-RG 107. Authorizes AJ to purchase supplies if contractors fail to furnish.

Dec 23   From John Shelby. ALS, DLC. Requests permission to remain in Huntsville to care for the sick.

Dec 23   From David Smith. ALS, DLC. Reports on recruiting mission to Nashville.

Dec 24   To John Cocke. LC, DLC. Bassett, 1:408 (extract). Discusses efforts to secure supplies from Fort Armstrong.

Dec 24   To John Coffee and the Volunteer cavalry (enclosure: Willie Blount to AJ, Dec 15). LS, DLC. Forwards copy of Governor Blount's letter and orders it read to the troops.

Dec 24   To William Hall and Hall's Volunteer infantry (enclosure: Willie Blount to AJ, Dec 15). LS, THi; LS copy, DLC. Forwards Blount's letter for their information.

Dec 24   To William Snodgrass. ALS, NjP; LC, DLC. Orders Snodgrass to abandon work on Fort Armstrong and construct boats for transporting supplies.

Dec 24   To Thomas John Vandyke. ADS, MnHi; LC, DLC. Assigns him as surgeon to William Lillard's regiment.

Dec 24   From William Lillard, Anthony J. Turner, and Thomas Fearn. LC, DLC. Report on condition of provisions received from John McGee.

Dec 24   From John McKee. ALS, M. Clinton McGee. Reports on an engagement between Choctaws and Creeks.

Dec 24   From James Mitchell. ALS, ICHi. Discusses procurement of supplies.

Dec 24   From Thomas Pinckney.   502

Dec 24   From William J. Smith. ALS, DLC. Discusses volunteers' demands for discharge.

Dec 24   From William Snodgrass. LC, DLC. Reports that supplies are not available at Fort Armstrong.

Dec 25   To John Coffee. LS, DLC. *Nashville Whig*, Jan 25, 1814. Refutes claim of officers in John Allcorn's regiment concerning their discharge and asks that related correspondence be published in the newspapers.

Dec 26   To Willie Blount.   504

Dec 26   To Josephus H. Conn. LC, DLC. Orders Conn to lead a raiding party on the Black Warrior and Cahaba rivers.

Dec 26   To the deputy quartermaster general. LC, DLC. Orders completion of construction at Fort Strother.

Dec 26   To William Lillard. LC, DLC. Asks if Lillard's men are ready to march against Creeks.

Dec 26   To John Knibb Wynne and William Lillard. DS, T; LC, DLC. Orders Wynne and Lillard to furnish men for a reconnaissance patrol to the Cahaba.

Dec 26   From William Barker et al. LC, DLC. Reassert their willingness to march where ordered during their three-month term of service.

Dec 26   From Willie Blount. ALS, DLC. Repeats his contention that volunteers can be discharged only on authority of the president; states his personal view that three months was the term of enlistment.

Dec 26   From William Lillard. ALS and LC, DLC. Bassett, 1:411–12. Rejects Jackson's request to march against Creeks and insists that his regiment be discharged on January 14, 1814.

Dec 27   To James Baxter. LC, DLC. Appoints Baxter assistant deputy quartermaster and orders him to oversee shipment of supplies from Ross's Landing.

Dec 27   *To William Carroll.*   507

Dec 27   To John Cocke. LC, DLC. Reminds Cocke that he is required to furnish 1,500 men and supplies.

Dec 27   To John Coffee (enclosure: order to Coffee, Dec 27). ALS and LC, DLC. Bassett, 1:412–13. Notifies Coffee that he has accepted the offer of Carroll's volunteers for two-month service with understanding that they might not be paid.

Dec 27   To John Coffee (enclosed in AJ to Coffee, Dec 27). ADS and LC, DLC. Orders Coffee to march his new volunteers to Fort Strother.

Dec 27   *To John Floyd.*   509

Dec 27   To Thomas Pinckney. LC, DLC; Copy, DNA-RG 107. Discusses problems of supplies and enlistments.

Dec 27   From Joseph Anthony. ALS, DLC. Discusses supplies.

Dec 27   From John Coffee. ALS, DLC. Reports his arrival at Ditto's Landing; discusses attitude of troops.

Dec 27   From Stockley Donelson Hays. ALS, DLC. Reports on his efforts to expedite supplies.

Dec 27   From William Berkeley Lewis. ALS, DLC. Reports his conversation with Governor Blount on the importance of keeping 5,000 Tennesseans in service.

Dec 27   From Robert Searcy. ALS, DLC. Sends several letters that had been accidentally mislaid.

Dec 28   *To John Cocke.*   511

Dec 28   To Isaac Roberts. LC, DLC; Copy, DNA-RG 153. Requests written report of strength of his brigade.

Dec 28   To James W. Sittler. Copy, DNA-RG 153. Orders Sittler to march new volunteers to join Isaac Roberts's brigade.

Dec 28   From Joseph Anthony. ALS, DLC. Discusses supplies.

Dec 28   From John Armstrong. LS and Copies, DLC; LC, PHi; LC, DNA-RG 107. Bassett, 1:413. Praises AJ and his troops for their successes.

Dec 28   From John Brown. ALS, DLC. Requests compensation for livestock and equipment confiscated by East Tennessee volunteers.

Dec 28   From John Coffee. ALS and ALS draft, DLC. Bassett, 1:413–14. Reports that a large part of his brigade has left for home.

Dec 28   From William Hall. ALS, DLC; Copy, THi. Argues that the governor has authorized the return of his men to Nashville; reports that no men responded to AJ's directive to remain in the field.

Dec 28   From William R. Hess. ALS, DLC. Reports on progress of supply shipments.

Dec 28   From Pathkiller. LS, DLC. Demands return of slaves and horses taken from Cherokees and friendly Creeks by East Tennessee troops.

Dec 28   From Isaac Roberts. LC, DLC; Copy, DNA-RG 153. Reports strength of new volunteer unit.

Dec 29   To Willie Blount. LC, DLC. Bassett, 1:416–20. Chastises Blount for his indecision and urges him to raise more volunteers.

Dec 29   To John Coffee.   512

Dec 29   To [Richard?] Copeland. Copy, DLC. Denies permission for leave of absence.

Dec 29   To Rachel Jackson.   515

Dec 29   To Isaac Roberts. LC, DLC. Orders Roberts to parade his new volunteers.

Dec 29   To Recruits, 2nd Brigade, Tennessee Volunteers. LC, DLC; Copy, DNA-RG 153. Bassett, 1:422–23. Accepts their services and attempts to clarify the terms of their enlistment.

Dec 29   To Recruits, 2nd Brigade, Tennessee Volunteers. LC, DLC; Copy, DNA-RG 153. Reassures volunteers that he will not keep them beyond their three-month term of service.

Dec 29   From John Allcorn and Newton Cannon. ALS, DLC. Discuss ration returns.

Dec 29   From William Carroll. ALS, DLC. Reports that Robert Searcy, in recruiting new volunteers, authorized sixty-day enlistments.

Dec 29   From John Coffee.   517

Dec 29   From Stockley Donelson Hays. ALS, DLC. Reports that he is forwarding a supply of flour and corn meal to Fort Strother.

Dec 29   From Stockley Donelson Hays. ALS, DLC. Endorses AJ's opinion on terms of enlistments and discusses supply efforts.

Dec 29   From John Shelby. ALS, DLC. Reports that he has remained at Camp Comfort to attend the sick.

Dec 29   Order for arrest and court martial of Lieutenant Hartsill. LC, DLC.

Dec 29   Promissory note for $1,000 to James Jackson. DS, DLC.

Dec 30   From John Coffee. ALS, DLC. Reports on Gideon Blackburn's attempts to arouse patriotism of troops.

Dec 30   From Clement Nash Read. ALS, DLC. Requests a furlough or discharge from duties as surgeon's mate.

Dec 30   From James Reid. ALS, DLC. Discusses provisioning of AJ's army and asks permission to return home to recruit.

Dec 30   From Isaac Roberts. LC, DLC. Bassett, 1:402–403. Reports failure to retain new volunteers.

Dec 30   From John Shelby. ALS, DLC. Discusses availability of surgeons.

Dec 30, 31   To John Armstrong. LS, DNA-RG 107; LC, DLC; Copy, DNA-RG 233; Extract, T. Bassett, 1:423–28. Discusses problems of the campaign and urges Armstrong to grant Governor Blount authority to raise more volunteers.

Dec 31   To John Coffee. ALS, DLC. Bassett, 1:428–31. Defends his view of enlistment terms.

Dec 31   To Thomas Pinckney.   518

Dec 31   To Isaac Roberts. AL draft, NN; LC, DLC. Orders Roberts to arrest and detain new volunteers who have deserted.

Index

Page-entry numbers between 521 and 605 refer to the Calendar. Numbers set in boldface indicate identifications of persons. The symbol * indicates biographical information in the *Dictionary of American Biography*; the symbol †, in the *Biographical Directory of the American Congress*.

Donnell, Robert,* 252
Dorton, Andrew, 574
Doublehead, 47, **48**, 49, 247
Douglass, Edward, **46**, 528, 556
Douglass, Henry L., 594
Douglass, William, 552, 563
Dragon (horse), 189, 257
Drake, John, 555
Dudley, James Allison, 407, **408**
Duels and Quarrels: of William O. Allen,
229; Patton Anderson-Magnesses,
254–55; Jesse Benton-William Car-
roll, 408, 412, 419–25; Aaron Burr-
Alexander Hamilton, 26, 83; Henry
Clay-Humphrey Marshall, 211; John
Coffee-William Maclin, 14–15; John
Coffee-Nathaniel McNairy, 89, 90–
91; Micajah G. Lewis-Robert Ster-
rey, 50–51, 54; William B. Lewis-
Thomas H. Benton, 377, 378, 381–83,
388; Thomas J. Overton-John Dickin-
son, 66–70, 416; Thomas J. Overton-
Nathaniel McNairy, 66, 87, 89; George
Poindexter-Abijah Hunt, 264–65;
John Randolph-James Wilkinson, 181;
James Robertson's opposition to, 83–
84, 91; *see also* Andrew Jackson,
Duels and Quarrels
Dunbaugh, Joseph, 121
Duncan, Stephen, 264, **265**
Duncan & Jackson, 532, 547, 548
Dunn, Michael C., 554, 563, 565, 582
Dunwoody, *see* Dinwiddie
Dyer, Robert Henry, 442, **443**, 449, 569,
570

Early, Peter,* † 496, 506–507, 588
Earthquakes, 281, 282, 298
Eastin, Rachel Donelson (Mrs. William),
26
Eastin, Thomas, **84**, 535, 536, 538, 539;
as messenger, 347; on AJ's implication
in Burr affair, 145; newspaper of, 83;
letters to, 84, 101, 106; letter from
Charles Dickinson, 97
Eastin, William, **26**, 114, 252, 256, 309,
430, 543, 561, 563
Eaton, John Henry,* † 95
Eaton, William,* 150, 167
Edmiston, David, 174
Edmundson, James, 598
Edwards, Ninian,* † 338, 542
Edwards, Thomas, 545
Edwards, William, 529, 534, 537, 559
Edwards, William, Jr., 449, **450**

Elijah (slave), 561
Elliott, Daniel D., 226
Ellis, Matthew, **165**
Ellison, Henry, 597
Elliston, Joseph Thorp, 354, **355**
Empsey, Gregory, 597
Enochs, Enoch, 542, 547, 556
Enochs, Gabriel, 553
Eppes, John Wayles,* † 19
Eppes, Mary Jefferson (Mrs. John
Wayles), 18, **19**
Erwin, Andrew, **62**; and anti-Jackson
campaign in 1828, 110, 128, 262, 293;
as purchaser of Norton Pryor lands,
296, 297
Erwin, Jane, *see* Dickinson, Jane (Mrs.
Charles Henry)
Erwin, John, 97, **98**, 536
Erwin, Joseph, 526, 536, 538, 539, 557;
accused of goading Dickinson into
duel, 106; and Truxton-Ploughboy
race, **77**, 78, 79, 81, 85; as owner of
Ploughboy, 57, 90; on trip to Mary-
land, 96
Erwin & Patton, 565
Eustis, William,* † 562, 564, 565, 568,
569; and AJ's quarrel with Dinsmoor,
334–36; nominations for army commissions, 285; orders to Blount re Volunteer services, 315, 316, 338, 339,
359; service as secretary of war, 261;
silence on Martha Crawley capture
criticized, 316; letter from to Silas
Dinsmoor, 296; letter to, 260
Evans, Robert, 602
Evans, John B. & Co., 82
Ewing, Alexander, 540, 551, 559
Ewing, Andrew, 95
Ewing, Finis, 596

Fan (slave), 534
Faulkner, John, 95, **96**
Fearn, Thomas, 603
Felicity (brig), 31
Ferguson, T. L., 556
Ferrel, William, 598
Fields, John, **273**, 354, 373, 387, 516;
Rachel settles accounts with, 362; re-
employed as overseer, 436
Fife, James, **465**
Finch, William, 556
Fish Traps, located, 486
Fisher, Elisha, 10, **12**, 26
Fisher, Elisha & Co, 27, 522, 523
Fishing Ford, located, 294

The Papers of Andrew Jackson is set in Sabon type, which has been selected for its clean legibility and balanced character fit in the smaller point sizes. The text type is ten point with one point of line spacing. The italic display is also Sabon.

The book was designed by Jim Billingsley, composed on the Linotron 202 Phototypesetter by G&S Typesetters, Inc., Austin, Texas, printed by offset lithography at Thomson-Shore, Inc., Dexter, Michigan, and bound by John H. Dekker & Sons, Grand Rapids, Michigan. The text paper on which the book is printed is S. D. Warren's Olde Style wove, which adheres to the specifications of the National Historical Publications and Records Commission for archival permanence.

THE UNIVERSITY OF TENNESSEE PRESS